Advertising
and Public Relations Law

Advertising
and Public Relations Law

Roy L. Moore
University of Kentucky

Ronald T. Farrar
University of South Carolina

Erik L. Collins
University of South Carolina

1998

LAWRENCE ERLBAUM ASSOCIATES, PUBLISHERS
Mahwah, New Jersey   London

Lawrence Erlbaum Associates, Inc., Publishers
10 Industrial Avenue
Mahwah, New Jersey 07430

Library of Congress Cataloging-in-Publication-Data

Moore, Roy L.
Advertising and public relations law / by Roy L. Moore, Ronald Farrar,
Erik Collins.
    p. cm.
    Includes bibliographical references and index.
    ISBN 0-8058-1679-8 (cloth : alk. paper)
    1. Advertising laws—United States. 2. Public relations and
law—United States. I. Farrar, Ronald. II. Collins, Erik. III. Title.
    KF1614.M66 1997
    343.73'082–dc21   96-39933
                                            CIP

Books published by Lawrence Erlbaum Associates are printed on
acid-free paper, and their bindings are chosen for strength and
durability.

Printed in the United States of America
10   9   8   7   6   5   4   3   2   1

*This book is dedicated to Pam and Derek,
to Gayla and to Carmen*

Contents

Preface

In the early days of the 20th century, the original curriculum of the world's first school of journalism included a required course in communication law. The class dealt with libel and, to a substantial degree, with postal regulations. That made sense at the time; 85% of all journalism graduates went to work for community newspapers, and an understanding of law affecting mail was important.

Much about journalism is different now, and with the changes has come the recognition that the field is much broader. Today's graduates, especially advertising and public relations specialists, are assuming positions throughout the media.

Journalists and advertising and public relations practitioners need to acquire many of the same skills, including the ability to write and edit well and to engage in critical thinking. They also need to learn a great deal about public opinion and human behavior, and their professionalism and ethical values should be uniformly high. As was the case with those pioneering journalism students nearly a century ago, today's journalism and mass communication students must be aware of the laws and jurisprudence affecting their chosen fields.

But many of the specific issues and concerns of advertising and public relations executives are different from those of editors and reporters. This volume, designed to serve both the student and the practitioner, was written to address these issues and concerns.

Although there are some excellent general media law texts available, none has been developed to the extent this one has, to reflect the distinctive needs of advertising and public relations professionals.

Some of the specific differences you will notice are (a) two entire chapters devoted to the commercial speech doctrine, including its history and development; (b) separate chapters on public interest speech, on professional advertising and promotion, on product liability, and trademarks, patents and trade secrets; (c) extensive discussions of how federal agencies beyond the Federal Trade Commission regulate advertising and promotion and of product disparagement; (d) three chapters focusing on privacy rights and concerns; and (e) an appendix with model release forms, professional codes of ethics, a diagram of the United States court system, a copy of the United States Constitution, and copyright and trademark registration forms. Our concluding chapter deals with traditional journalistic concerns such as privilege, free-press-versus-fair-trial issues, and access.

Lawyers sometimes characterize seemingly conflicting court interpretations of law as "distinctions without a difference." We believe you will find this volume, in comparison with others on the topic, is a distinction *with* a difference. We hope that students and practitioners alike will find our text interesting, enjoyable, and most of all, highly informative.

We would be remiss if we did not thank those individuals who provided assistance in the production of this book: Bradley T. Farrar, Bradley Huebner, and Dorothy Smith for their research and to the folks at Lawrence Erlbaum Associates—Linda Bathgate, Sara Scudder, Anne Monaghan and Joe Petrowski—for their support and encouragement at various stages of the book.

—*Roy L. Moore*
—*Ronald T. Farrar*
—*Erik L. Collins*

I

THE COMMERCIAL SPEECH DOCTRINE

Introduction

Those picking up a 500-plus-page book filled with examples and discussions of laws regulating speech by advertising and public relations practitioners could be pardoned for being somewhat puzzled. After all, the language of the First Amendment to the federal constitution clearly mandates that "Congress [and by extension any lesser unit of government] shall make no law ... abridging freedom of speech or of the press. ..."[1] How can there be laws regulating any speech, let alone advertising or public relations, in the face of the constitution's emphatic statement that there can be "no law?" This puzzle requires us to begin with a brief overview of the First Amendment and how it is interpreted before we turn our attention to the principal subject matter of this book.

DEVELOPMENT OF FIRST AMENDMENT JURISPRUDENCE

Courts faced with cases challenging the constitutionality of laws and regulations affecting speech and press have developed a body of mass media law by weighing and balancing the interests of those supporting freedom of expression against those favoring competing interests. The dilemma faced by the courts in such situations today is that it is almost impossible to believe that those who created the First Amendment to the federal constitution more than 200 years ago meant to protect speech that is, for example, treasonous or criminally threatening, despite the emphatic "no law" language of the amendment. Yet judges and justices cannot simply ignore the First Amendment because they disapprove of the speech in question. Therefore, they have been forced to develop a logical, rational, and defensible method of interpretation. To understand how they have accomplished this, we need to take a brief look at how judges interpret law and how historians interpret history.

Role play the part of judge for a moment—not a supreme court justice, but a judge in a low-level court in which the cases usually involve petty crimes and minor disagreements. The next case on the docket is *City v. Jones*. Testifying for the city is the arresting officer who reports that the defendant was apprehended at 10 a.m. Saturday and charged with operating a motorized, self-propelled vehicle within a city park. A municipal ordinance makes such operation illegal for all persons, regardless of circumstances or status. The ordinance specifies that *all* persons so doing shall be sentenced to (a) no more than 30 and no fewer than 10 days in the city jail, and (b) a fine of no more than $100 and no less than $30. Because the defendant, Jones, is pleading guilty, this seems like an open-and-shut case.

Before you pass judgment, however, it seems only fair to hear what the defendant has to say. Unfortunately, Mr. Jones apparently is no place to be seen. When you ask the arresting officer, "Where's Jones?", the policeman gestures for you to lean forward and look over the front of your large, desk-like bench. On so doing, you discover that "Mr. Jones" is a curly headed, 7 year old clutching a giant toy truck on which a child can sit and ride by winding up a big key on the toy truck's top.

You are the judge. Now what do you do? You cannot very well issue a fine and throw the kid in the slammer, but you also are not free to ignore the law that clearly says it applies to *all* persons regardless of circumstances or status. This admittedly is a rather exaggerated example of a real dilemma that daily confronts those who must interpret the law and apply it to a set of facts. We know what the law says. The question is, what does the law mean? This is exactly what judges face when asked to interpret the First Amendment.

Let's go back to the courtroom, where everyone is awaiting your decision. If you thought about looking at the precedents set by other judges who have looked at this municipal ordinance in the past, you are on the right track. Judges do look to prior decisions and the rationales employed by the judges in those cases. But they do not stop there. They also look at the literal language of the law or regulation, and may take the additional step of doing research to find records of the debate and discussion surrounding its adoption by those who passed it in the first place. Judges often find this legislative history a helpful guide in interpreting and applying the language of the law to the unique set of facts in the case before them. As it happens in this case, the minutes taken at the city council meeting when the ordinance was passed reveal that the purpose of the municipal ordinance was to block off the streets going through city parks to prevent cars, trucks and buses from running over joggers, bike riders and rollerbladers (and children riding toy trucks) using the paved surfaces in city parks on weekends. With this knowledge, you as judge have a logical and justifiable reason to dismiss the charges against the boy (and perhaps admonish the arresting officer to be a little less zealous in enforcing this particular ordinance).

This same method of interpreting law can be applied to the First Amendment. A judge asked to decide a case concerning the constitutionality of a law regulating speech could gather evidence to assist in determining what the First Amendment *means* (we know what it *says*) and apply it to the facts of the present case by searching the records of the debates and discussions engaged in by the First Amendment framers in 1791.

Strange as it seems, however, such a search would produce little information. The actual discussions were conducted behind closed doors, and it appears the delegates were in enough agreement that the First Amendment should include the words "no law ... abridging speech or of the press" that they did not bother to make a record of what they meant by those words.

What can those who must interpret law do if the normal body of evidence for determining the meaning of the First Amendment is unavailable? Judges, lawyers, and other legal scholars have turned to the next-best evidence—the historical context of the writing of the First Amendment. This means that those seeking to interpret the First Amendment rely both on their general knowledge about the events in revolutionary America in the late 1700s and their interpretations of the historical evidence found in diaries, letters, essays, and state constitutional provisions written by the framers of the First Amendment.

The outcome of this historical detective work, combined with judicial precedents and evolving judicial philosophies over a 200-year span, has produced the conclusion, now generally accepted by the courts and legal scholars, that the framers of the First Amendment did not intend to protect all speech equally. This conclusion has led courts to differentiate categories or levels of speech that receive differing levels of constitutional protection. This protection can range from full First Amendment protection for speech involving issues of public interest, to no First Amendment protection for speech judged to be pornographic or criminal. Courts also have concluded that they have some constitutionally permitted leeway to differentiate among degrees and methods of abridgment. For example, although laws and regulations restricting the content of the speech in question generally invite judicial skepticism, courts may more readily permit limits either on where or how speech is permitted.

Categorizing speech into various subclasses with differing levels of First Amendment protection and allowing greater latitude for some methods of governmental regulation of speech play extremely important roles in determining the constitutionality of government attempts to regulate advertising and public relations speech. This is discussed in the remaining chapters of this book.

THE FIRST AMENDMENT IN THE 19TH CENTURY

If it is impossible (short of travel back in time) to know conclusively what kinds of speech the framers of the First Amendment meant to protect in the words "no law," it also is true that the weight of historical evidence points inescapably to the conclusion that the framers of the First Amendment meant, at the very least, to protect what Justice William Brennan once called "uninhibited, robust, and wide-open" public debate.[2] Often referred to as "political"[3] speech, such discussion of public issues was considered to be absolutely vital to the development and growth of American democracy. Thus, courts and legal scholars generally refer to speech dealing with public issues as being at the heart or a core value of protected First Amendment speech.

Perhaps somewhat surprisingly, however, the development of the doctrine that public-issue speech is central to the meaning of the First Amendment is a 20th-century concept. Between the ratification of the First Amendment in the 1790s and the first major court decisions involving challenges to laws regulating speech in the early 1900s, there was no significant litigation testing the constitutional limits of government to regulate speech. The reasons the 19th century (termed by one commentator as the "forgotten years" of media law[4]) saw few speech-related court cases are rooted in history and the new nation's "frontier mentality."

Think of America and Americans in the 19th century. Chances are the stereotypical view is of a bunch of self-reliant adventurers bent on carving out a livelihood by either taming the wilderness or building empires in business and commerce. Although American history is not quite that simple, one should not underestimate the effects of "rugged individualism" and the fear of centralized big government, that help form our national character. A century and a half ago, Americans readily discussed politics and were far from shy to express their views about controversial issues, but rarely were laws passed to limit debate or control ideas. Also, although individuals differed—sometimes violently—those differences were not fueled by ideologies like socialism or communism, or any other "isms" identified with or supported by foreign governments.

A third reason for the paucity of First Amendment court decisions was that those who disagreed with their neighbors for political or religious reasons (e.g., the believers in the teachings of the Church of Jesus Christ of Latter-Day Saints, often referred to as Mormons), who encountered hostility or attempts to regulate their speech, often just packed up and left, and there was lots of empty, wide-open space for them to settle. Another major factor in minimizing First Amendment jurisprudence during this time was an 1833 decision[5] by the Supreme Court of the United States that held that the provisions of the "Bill of Rights" in the federal constitution applied only to actions by the federal government, and thus did not apply to state laws and regulations. Considering all these reasons, the initially surprising lack of litigation involving the First Amendment during the 19th century becomes more understandable.

By the beginning of the 20th century, however, many of these factors were changing. With the closing of the frontier in the early 1890s,[6] fewer expanses of desirable land for community sites meant that those who shared other than mainstream ideologies or religious practices could no longer band together to form isolated communities of their own. The composition of the incoming tide of immigrants changed, bringing to American shores people from eastern and southern Europe; long-time inhabitants regarded these people as having exotic and perhaps threatening customs, traditions, and ideologies. By 1914, with storm clouds of war looming over Europe, conflicts over which side, if any, America should support in the upcoming conflict sharply divided Americans whose ancestors had settled the country many years before from those of more recent arrival.

This divided support for an American war effort was a major contributing factor to the passage of the Espionage Act of 1917.[7] The statute made it a federal crime to aid and comfort the enemy, and included provisions that, in certain circumstances, punished speaking out against the war effort as well. When those opposed to aspects of the war effort spoke out anyway, the stage was set for the first series of court cases where the central issue was to determine how much protection the First Amendment provided.

THE DEVELOPMENT OF MODERN FIRST AMENDMENT INTERPRETATION

Schenck v. U.S.[8] and *Abrams v. U.S.*[9] were the first two such cases. Both cases involved groups opposed to wartime activities. Schenck and his small band of socialists made their disapproval known by publishing a pamphlet that urged young men selected for the draft to refuse to report for induction. Abrams and his communist friends were concerned that bullets made to fight Germans might instead be used to kill Russian communists engaged in a civil war after the overthrow of the czar in 1917. Abrams helped publish pamphlets urging Americans working in munitions factories to strike. Although it is extremely doubtful that either Schenck or Abrams would have been successful in attracting many converts to his cause or in creating any real damage to the American war effort, federal authorities at the time took such matters seriously, and therefore arrested and convicted both men of conspiracy to violate the Espionage Act and other crimes.

On appeal of their convictions to the Supreme Court of the United States, both Schenck and Abrams cited the First Amendment as grounds for overturning the lower court decisions, arguing that Congress could not constitutionally pass a law that punished mere speech in such a fashion. The Court upheld the convictions in both instances and, in the process, began the development of so-called "speech tests" to be applied in such cases.

Although there was strong historical and precedential evidence supporting the government's claim that the authors of the First Amendment had meant only to prevent governmental censorship, and not punishment of dangerous or disagreeable speech after the fact, Justice Oliver Wendell Holmes' opinion in *Schenck* adopted the alternative position that the speech in question was undoubtedly protected from governmental interference in normal times and circumstances. However, he approved of the conviction of Schenck because, as he said, "When a nation is at war many things that might be said in time of peace are such a hindrance to its effort that their utterance will not be endured so long as men fight and that no Court could regard them as protected by any constitutional right."[10] For Justice Holmes, "The question in every case is whether the words used are used in such circumstances and are of such a nature as to create a clear and present danger that they will bring about the substantive evils that Congress has a right to prevent."[11] Schenck sent his antiwar pamphlets to young men about to be drafted into the armed services, which, said Holmes, was sufficient evidence that he intended his act to hinder the war effort.

In *Abrams*, however, Holmes dissented. He conceded that the outcome of Abrams' actions might impede the war effort against Germany (although even this was highly doubtful), but that the government could not convict Abrams of espionage because his purpose was to aid his comrades in Russia, and thus he lacked the specific intent to aid the enemy required by the wording of the Espionage Act. Justice Holmes used his dissenting opinion as well to present his famous analogy of a free marketplace of ideas, which he likened to the economic "laissez-faire" free marketplace of goods and services. According to Holmes, the antidote to Abrams' "bad" speech was not restricting speech through governmental regulation or subsequent punishment, but encouraging more "good" speech by those with counterveiling messages.

When the war ended in Europe, federal laws regulating speech involving political issues fell into disuse, but a new and potentially more dangerous threat to the free discussion of public issues was growing. The years between 1920 and 1940 were marked by the growth of labor unions—and to some degree influenced by socialist and communist ideologies—as workers organized to improve working conditions, hours, and benefits. These efforts were bitterly opposed by the captains of industry and their friends in state legislatures and statehouses, particularly when labor resorted to the ultimate weapon of a strike.

This era of industrial warfare frightened many in power with the specter of organized workers (dominated by "evil" forces) bent on destroying the democratic capitalist system by less than peaceful means if necessary. State lawmakers responded to these fears with the passage of criminal syndicalism or criminal anarchy statutes. Eventually 21 states adopted such laws, which were aimed at punishing those who spoke out in favor of the duty, propriety, or necessity of overturning lawful governments by force or violence.[12]

Historically, such state laws would have raised no federal First Amendment issues, but all this changed in 1925, when the Supreme Court of the United States decided the case of *Gitlow v. New York*.[13] Gitlow had been convicted of criminal anarchy for printing material urging labor unrest; the highest appeals court in New York had upheld the conviction, deciding that it did not violate the state constitution's protection of speech. Despite the odds and a century-old history of precedent against the success of such an appeal, Gitlow petitioned the U.S. Supreme Court to hear his case, and the Court surprised many observers by agreeing to do so.

Unfortunately for Gitlow, the Court agreed with the state court and upheld his conviction. Fortunately for free speech advocates, the Court also found that the due process clause of the 14th Amendment to the federal constitution gave jurisdiction to federal courts to review state court decisions that arguably infringe upon free speech rights.

Beginning with *Gitlow* in 1925, the Court reviewed a dozen or so speech-regulation cases emanating from state courts during the next decade. It usually upheld the convictions of speakers, but also created a series of precedents and contained dissenting opinions, usually by Justices Holmes and Brandeis, filled with ideas, historical analyses, and philosophical points for future arguments in favor of a limited ability for government at any level to regulate speech.

In one of the most important cases of the era, *Near v. Minnesota*,[14] the Court tackled the case of an alternative newspaper editor who had so outraged authorities in Minneapolis/St. Paul that he was denied the right to continue to publish any newspaper in the state on the basis that to do so would constitute a public nuisance. Rightfully seeing this as a prior restraint of speech about important public issues, the Court struck down the state regulation. In so doing, the Court affirmed that the most dangerous threats to free speech—and therefore those most disfavored by the First Amendment—are prior restraints, not only like the public nuisance law in *Near*, but also court orders, censorship boards, taxation policies, licensing schemes, limiting access to the means of production, and other government actions aimed at preventing speech from entering the marketplace of ideas.

The Court reaffirmed this position in the so-called "Pentagon Papers Case"[15] in the early 1970s, when the federal government asked the courts for injunctions to stop publication of classified defense documents by the *New York Times* and the *Washington Post*. The Court, in a 6–3 decision, noted that "any system of prior restraints of expression comes to the court bearing heavy presumption against its constitutionality,"[16] and that the government had not met that heavy burden. Therefore, the Court struck down a lower court order prohibiting the *Times* from continuing to publish the papers.

The number of state attempts to regulate protected speech declined in the mid-1930s, as the country concentrated on pulling itself out of the Great Depression. With little sympathy for either Germany or Japan in World War II, and with the Soviet Union as an ally, there was virtually no public speech favoring fascism and no organized popular resistance to fighting the war to engender the prosecution of speech-related activities at either the federal or state level. This hiatus came to an abrupt end, however, with the heating up of the so-called "cold war" in the mid to late 1940s. With the scare of a Moscow-inspired, sinister communist penetration into all aspects of American life, by the early 1950s, federal prosecutors and legislative investigating committees investigated a spate of espionage-related speech cases.

Two of the more famous of these cases were *Dennis v. U.S.*[17] and *Yates v. U.S.*[18] The Court in *Dennis*, the nadir of First Amendment protection for political speech, upheld a conviction apparently based solely on membership in the communist party. The Court noted that the defendant's participation in a "highly organized conspiracy"[19] ready for violence when "the time had come for action"[20] was enough of a threat to warrant criminal sanctions. The Court appeared to feel that simply by being a communist, Dennis was advocating treasonous activity. By 1957 and the *Yates* decision, however, cooler judgment prevailed, and the Court returned to the rationale that a showing of actual advocacy of illegal activity was necessary before the government could punish mere speech.

This trend toward greater protection of civil rights and fundamental personal liberties, including freedom of speech, begun in the late 1950s, accelerated in the 1960s. By 1969, the Court had evolved its thinking about the extent of protection for public interest speech to the degree that, in *Brandenburg v. Ohio*,[21] it struck down the conviction of a Ku Klux Klan member who spoke out in favor of racial violence, holding unconstitutional an Ohio statute with wording almost identical to that found in similar statutes in other states upheld by the Court in the 1920s and 1930s. Although the trend has slowed somewhat during the 1990s, it is still nonetheless true today that the government at both the federal and state levels will have a difficult job defending a law or regulation that either prohibits or punishes protected speech.

THE TESTS, CONSTITUTIONAL AND OTHERWISE, FOR PROTECTED SPEECH

If a legislature or regulatory agency wishes to regulate most everyday activities and the governmental action is challenged in court as unconstitutional, the government usually will prevail if it can demonstrate a well-drafted law or regulation designed to accomplish a reasonable governmental purpose. Sometimes referred to as a "rationality test," this historic court-made rule places the burden on those challenging the governmental action to demonstrate a lack of rational basis for the law or regulation—a difficult burden for the challenger to meet.[22]

Challenging the regulation of protected speech, however, automatically differentiates such a case from the norm. The first major exception to treating speech cases differently was Justice Holmes' "clear and present danger test"[23] in *Schenck*. Although the test's exact wording has been altered over the years, a modern-day court might still require the government to meet that test when the government, citing immediate catastrophe as the rationale for regulation, seeks an immediate cessation or punishment of political speech.

Even if the governmental interest in regulating speech is substantial, it is not automatic that the government will win a case involving regulation of protected speech. A court still must weigh and balance the government's interests against the other side's speech interests. How to do this represents another example of conflicting judicial philosophies and theories. Envision the statue of Justice holding a set of scales. One school of judicial thought suggests that, in speech cases, a court first should pile extra weight on the speech side of the scale and then look to the government to pile enough weight on its side to overcome the handicap created in favor of the speech interests. This approach, sometimes referred to as giving speech a "preferred position,"[24] suggests that a court require the government to meet an extra "heavy burden"[25] when it wants to regulate normally protected speech. This "definitional balancing"[26] permits the formulation of rules that can be uniformly applied from case to case. For example, such a test is often interpreted to mean that, when the government wishes to regulate an individual's fundamental constitutional right to speak and the government's action is challenged in court on constitutional grounds, the court will treat the law or regulation as presumptively unconstitutional.

Borrowing from 14th Amendment equal protection cases,[27] those who feel this approach best protects speech, yet accommodates important competing interests, suggest that only if the government can demonstrate a compelling need for its actions will the opposing speech interests be subject to the possibility of regulation. Such an approach is often used by the Court to protect so-called "fundamental liberties."[28] The Court has spent four decades developing an appropriate test to preserve constitutional values when a legislature or agency wishes to regulate "those functions essential to effective democracy."[29] Although the Court has never set out a definitive list of these "functions," clearly the right to freedom of speech and press is among them.

This so-called "compelling state interest test" has proven to be a major bulwark in the defense of individual liberties. The test places a heavy burden on the governmental body wishing to regulate, requiring that it must demonstrate (a) an overriding necessity for its actions, (b) that the law or regulation actually advances the governmental interest, (c) that it is "narrowly tailored" to accomplish the limited purpose the government may be permitted, and (d) that it is the least restrictive (of speech) means available to the government for accomplishing its ends.[30]

This unbalanced approach to deciding speech cases is by no means the only approach a court might follow, however. Many jurists and legal scholars argue that the correct approach for a court to take is to first determine if both the governmental and speech interests are substantial, and, if so, to adjudicate the actual case before the court by simply balancing the interests of both parties and arriving at a decision based on which has the greater weight on its side. For example, as Justice Harlan noted in his opinion in *Barenblatt v. United States*,[31] "Where First Amendment rights are asserted to bar governmental interrogation, resolution of the issue always involves a balancing by the courts of the competing private and public interests at stake in the particular circumstances."[32]

Courts have not been uniform in electing to follow either this "ad hoc balancing"[33] approach or the preferred position approach discussed earlier. This has created some confusion for those trying to predict the outcomes of cases, as well as those who believe First Amendment law should develop in a neat and orderly manner.

CONTENT-BASED REGULATION
OF "LESSER PROTECTED" SPEECH

As discussed previously, the development of First Amendment law during the
last eight decades of the 20th century has focused on the attempts to regulate
"political speech." Today it is generally agreed that, in most circumstances, a
legislature or agency wishing to regulate this constitutionally protected speech
faces a heavy burden of convincing a court that there is a compelling need for
the government's actions. What about attempts to regulate speech that does
not easily fit under the political speech rubric? Unfortunately for free speech
advocates, courts have proven less vigilant in striking down attempts to regulate this lesser protected speech.

As noted earlier, because of confusion about what the framers of the First
Amendment actually meant when they wrote "no law," courts historically have
differentiated among different kinds of speech by the degree of constitutional
protection afforded each. This differentiation is critical to understanding the
reasons underlying the degree of constitutionally permissible regulation of
advertising, public relations, and other forms of commercial speech (this is
discussed in more detail in chapter 2, this volume). Suffice it to say that courts
have consistently held that "purely" commercial speech does not receive the
same level of protection as speech about public issues.

Similarly, courts have held that lessened First Amendment protection holds
for over-the-air broadcast speech. The logic employed by the courts for so
holding is slightly different, however. Initially unregulated, radio broadcasters
went to Congress in the 1920s seeking help because broadcasters were imping-
ing on each other's radio frequencies. What they got was the Radio Act of
1927.[34] This was soon supplanted by the more comprehensive Communications
Act of 1934,[35] that also created the Federal Communications Commission (FCC)
to regulate use of frequencies and technical specifications, and to police the
content of broadcasts to ensure broadcasters operated in the public interest,
convenience and necessity.

Eventually, broadcasters challenged the FCC and the law as unconstitutionally infringing on their protected speech rights. In the combined *NBC v. U.S.*
and *CBS v. U.S.*[36] case in 1943, the Supreme Court of the United States upheld
the constitutionality of the act. It decided that Congress could set content
restrictions on broadcasters to police the use of the airwaves, which the government labeled a *scarce public resource*. The underlying legal premise was that
the authors of the First Amendment could not have anticipated over-the-air
broadcast speech, and that the government therefore was entitled to more
leeway in regulating such speech. The continuing need for such laws and
regulations, given today's plethora of media and communication channels, is
one of the major areas of potential free speech litigation facing lawmakers and
communicators in the next century.

Unlike commercial and broadcast speech, which are protected to some
degree from governmental regulation, courts have held that pornographic and

criminal (threatening, extorting, fraudulent, or perjurious) speech are totally without First Amendment protection. Although an extensive discussion of this court-sanctioned form of content restriction is beyond the scope of this book, readers should understand that, almost always, the issue in cases challenging government restrictions of this kind of speech is a definitional one (e.g., is the speech pornographic?).

The Court has spent decades wrestling with the definitional problems involved in pornography cases. The wording of the current test is from *Miller v. California*[37]—a case decided by the Court in 1973 involving a conviction under state law of a man accused of mailing sexually explicit advertisements for books and films. Upholding the conviction, the Court said that for a work to be defined as *legally pornographic*, the average person, applying contemporary community standards, must find that the work, taken as a whole, appeals to prurient interest in sex. In addition, the material must describe specifically defined content in a patently offensive manner, and the work, taken as a whole, must lack serious literary, artistic, political, or scientific value.[38]

NONCONTENT-BASED SPEECH REGULATIONS

The First Amendment clearly places barriers in the government's attempts to restrain or punish speech based on its content. However, other speech-related laws and regulations, although infringing on a speaker's ability to get his or her message across, may not raise the same degree of First Amendment concern for the courts.

One example is regulation based on "time, place, and manner." The criteria for such regulations are that they (a) advance a reasonable governmental interest, (b) be content neutral, (c) be reasonable, and (d) not be used to ban or make practically impossible the speaker's ability to disseminate his or her message by alternative means. Challenges to time, place, and manner regulations often occur when authorities try to regulate such speech activities as door-to-door solicitations, parades, demonstrations on public property, and so forth. Recently, courts have been faced with a series of cases involving billboards and newsracks resulting from municipalities attempting to limit the number and placement of signs and newsracks on city streets for safety or aesthetic reasons. Many of these cases involve advertising or commercial speech, and are discussed later.

Other types of cases raising noncontent-based speech issues involve efforts to gain access to government information, avoid disclosing the source of information to governmental agencies, or being required by law to publish information. Whether seeking to gain or avoid giving information, those so doing typically claim the right of free speech as the basis for their actions. Government representatives counter that it is reasonable to interpret the First Amendment as giving greater leeway to laws and regulations of such speech-related activities because they are not content based. Courts dealing with such claims have reacted inconsistently, sometimes recognizing First Amendment claims and sometimes giving them short shrift. These issues are discussed in subsequent chapters.

Finally, a noncontent-based rationale employed by those who wish to regulate speech is frequently raised in cases involving expressive conduct rather than pure speech. Some of the more recent controversial decisions have concerned flag burning, nude dancing, spray painting "hate speech" messages, and picketing abortion clinics. Those wishing to engage in such actions have argued that their activities are protected by the First Amendment from governmental censure or punishment because of the message inherent in their actions. Government representatives counter that conduct is different from speech, and can therefore legally be more controlled.

This so-called "speech–action dichotomy" has created conflicting rulings from courts grappling with the issues that such cases raise. The deciding issue has often been an ad hoc evaluation of the "importance" of the expression versus the strength of the competing governmental interest. Thus, the Court has held that flag burning[39] is expressive conduct that is protected because of its political nature, and that nude dancing is expressive conduct not protected because the message conveyed is of such a minor artistic nature that the government can ban or control it simply on public policy grounds.[40]

IMPORTANCE OF FREE SPEECH

As this introductory chapter concludes, it may occur to the reader that many people have gone to a lot of trouble to theorize, legislate, argue, and fight for the right of the individual to speak free of unwarranted governmental restraint or censure. The logical question that follows is: Why is free speech so important that many believe almost all other interests are subservient to it?

One of the reasons we might ask that question is that we have always lived in a society where free speech is protected. We take it for granted that we have the right to speak or write about almost anything we please without first getting it cleared by the official government censor or fearing the heavy tread of the stormtrooper's boot outside our door. However, the founders of this nation knew what it was like to fear both the censor and the police. Therefore, they were adamant in their belief that only in a society where people were free to criticize government and official conduct and to speak out on important public issues could a democratic form of government flourish.

This has led scholars like Melvin Nimmer to the conclusion that the chief function of unfettered speech is the "enlightenment function."[41] Nimmer quotes Justice Brandeis, one of the Court's generally acknowledged great 20th-century champions of freedom of speech and press, to the effect that, "freedom to think as you will and to speak as you think are means indispensable to the discovery and spread of political truth. . . ."[42] But Nimmer argues that focusing solely on political truth is too limiting: "The search for all forms of 'truth,' which is to say the search for all aspects of knowledge and the formulation of enlightened opinion on all subjects is dependent upon open channels of communication. Unless one is exposed to all the data on a given subject it is not possible to make an informed judgment as to which 'facts' and which views deserve to be accepted."[43]

Free speech is important to our society beyond its critical role in governance. In a country not controlled by an ideology or dogma, free speech is seen as crucial, both as a means to continually examine the status quo and as the mechanism to introduce new ideas and concepts into society as a leavening agent of change. The 17th-century philosopher John Milton was one of the first to publicly argue that the best path to truth is through uncensored exchange of ideas. Two centuries later, John Stuart Mill urged the correlative idea that even speech proved to be false is important and needs protection because it forces us to reexamine old ideas, rather than just assume them to be true.[44]

Critical to the enlightenment function of free speech is that the system for arriving at the outcome should be equally unrestricted. As Nimmer points out, "Absolute certainty on any issue of fact or opinion is beyond human capability. All determinations of 'truth' are necessarily tentative, subject to modifying or contradictory 'truths' which may later emerge."[45] However, if information that could lead to "contradictory truths" is limited or prohibited, the system becomes stagnant. Justice Oliver Wendell Holmes, Jr. likened this process to the free marketplace of goods and services in his famous dissenting view in *Abrams*.

Writing with a touch of irony, Justice Holmes first noted that, "Persecution for the expression of opinions seems to me perfectly logical. If you have no doubt of your premises or your power and want a certain result with all your heart you naturally express your wishes in law and sweep away all opposition." However, Justice Holmes was quick to point out that,

> when men have realized that time has upset many fighting faiths, they may come to believe even more than they believe the very foundations of their own conduct that the ultimate good desired is better reached by free trade in ideas—that the best test of truth is the power of the thought to get itself accepted in the competition of the market and that truth is the only ground upon which their wishes can be carried out. That at any rate is the theory of our Constitution. It is an experiment, as all life is an experiment.[46]

The authors of this text would not be surprised to find that those reading the passage from Justice Holmes' dissent would strongly affirm his views as their own. Yet when given specific examples of the kinds of ideas and opinions such a free marketplace of ideas would permit, a sizable number might not be as quick to agree, either because they may believe that a consensus idea arrived at in the marketplace may be wrong, or that a minority viewpoint may be incorrect, obnoxious, or dangerous, and therefore legitimately can and should be suppressed.

Nimmer, among others, responded to the criticism that truth will not always be the result of free marketplace forces by pointing out that such criticism "misses the point."[47] He noted that, "Justice Holmes did not state that truth is to be found in the power of the thought to get itself accepted in the competition of the market. He said rather that this constitutes 'the best test' of truth." As Nimmer said, "What is the alternative? It can only be acceptance of an idea by some individual or group narrower than that of the public at large. Thus the alternative to competition in the market must be some form of elitism. It seems hardly necessary to enlarge on the dangers of that path."[48]

Justice Holmes was responding to the second criticism of uninhibited free speech—the possibility that a minority view is "bad" or "false." Rather than governmental suppression, his solution was almost always the introduction of more speech. As Justice Brandeis noted, concurring in the decision in *Whitney v. California*,[49] "the fitting remedy for evil counsels is good ones. . . . If there be time to expose through discussion the falsehood and fallacies, to avert the evil by the process of education, the remedy to be applied is more speech, not enforced silence." The reason is obvious for those who believe in free speech. That which the majority believes "bad" or "false" today, if allowed to be tested in the marketplace of ideas, may prove to be the opposite. As Nimmer concludes, "It is only through the process of testing by hearing more speech from others that a reliable judgment can be made as to the worth of the objectionable speech. This is the very essence of the enlightenment function"[50] of free speech.

Those who do not believe that the best test of truth is in the marketplace of ideas, those who wish to limit or prohibit speech rather than encourage more speech when they encounter ideas and opinions they consider dangerous or odious, almost always wish to regulate or legislate for the best of motives. Perhaps they see people doing "unacceptable" things they wish to discourage by discouraging speech that promotes the behavior. Alternatively, those who wish to regulate speech may do so in the name of the afflicted or the weak. Unfortunately, these arguments are often raised in support of restricting or restraining advertising and public relations speech. This issue is discussed in greater detail later.

Although the enlightenment function may be the primary rationale for free speech recognized by most scholars, it is not the only one. One of the better known alternative (if complementary) functions was advanced by Vincent Blasi, who suggested that the primary value of free speech is to serve as a "checking function"[51] on the affairs of state. Free speech in this concept serves not so much as a means to test the truth of a multiplicity of views and opinions, but as a counterbalance to the power of government by ensuring that abuses of that power are restrained and exposed when they occur.

Alexander Meiklejohn proposed yet another slightly different argument. In this viewpoint, freedom of speech is important because it allows intelligent choices by the electorate in a self-governing democracy.[52] Meiklejohn's ideas have been instrumental in formulating the concept that the First Amendment's primary purpose is to protect "political speech" from government regulation. "Its purpose is to give to every voting member of the body politic the fullest possible participation in the understanding of those problems with which the citizens of a self-governing society must deal."[53]

Even commentators who dispute the value of free speech as essential to democratic government or an enlightened society do not dispute that there are individual and societal benefits to free speech. Both as a way to vent frustration, rage, or anger and as a means for self-expression, speech is an outlet for emotions that otherwise might lead to destructive acts or be repressed at psychological costs to the individual.

CONCLUSION

This introductory chapter gives the reader a brief overview of the development of First Amendment jurisprudence and an understanding of the major rationales for protection of speech and for governmental attempts to breech that protection. Many of the issues and ideas discussed—including the categorization of different kinds of speech afforded different levels of First Amendment protection, court-created tests for laws and regulations of speech, and noncontent-based restrictions on speech and expression—affect the regulation of advertising and public relations speech, which is discussed throughout the remainder of this book.

2

The Development of
Commercial Speech Doctrine

Advertising and public relations practitioners share many concerns about laws regulating the communication functions of both fields. However, there are distinct differences between the two as well. This chapter focuses on the development of the constitutional protections afforded speech that the courts have described as purely "commercial speech."

Clearly, most advertising of goods and services falls directly within the definition of pure commercial speech. Less clear is whether marketing/public relations efforts (e.g., a press release announcing a new product) by for-profit organizations come within the definition of pure commercial speech. Advertising and public relations speech not directly focused on a for-profit organization's goods or services (e.g., an advertisement in the local newspaper publicly thanking employees for community service efforts) is in an even more ambiguous position vis-à-vis its relation to pure commercial speech. Advertising and public relations speech advancing a social issue or discussing important public problems, and almost all speech by not-for-profit organizations, may not be classified as commercial speech at all, even if paid for. The major issues involving the status and degree of free speech protection for advertising and public relations efforts not clearly definable as pure commercial speech are discussed in subsequent chapters.

THE BEGINNINGS OF COMMERCIAL SPEECH
REGULATION

If you walk down the streets of colonial Williamsburg, Virginia, or Old Sturbridge Village in Massachusetts, or you read one of the newspapers these reconstructed communities of the late 18th and early 19th centuries produce, you might be struck by how little advertising there is compared with the neon street signs and commercial-filled mass media of a modern metropolis. This lack of advertising is no historic oversite.

In the days before the advent of regional or national mass distribution of goods by manufacturers, most of the items purchased by the residents of a community were produced by local craftspeople (with the exception of a few relatively expensive items shipped by sea from England). All that was necessary to inform a merchant's target market was a window display, small painted sign, or, in larger communities, a classified-sized advertisement in the local weekly or monthly newspaper. By the end of the 19th century, however, first the railroads and then the mail-order business had changed all that. Railroads made it possible for local stores to sell mass-produced goods shipped from sites perhaps hundreds of miles away. The mail-order catalog business meant that you need not depend only on your local tradesperson to make or purchase what you wanted.

Mass producers of items, such as soap, cereal, or wearing apparel, at first were forced to depend only on local merchants to push their products. Soon, however, smart manufacturers saw the need for their own marketing and advertising campaigns to spur demand for particular brands and to build brand loyalty. Thus, by the end of the 19th century, techniques of mass marketing and advertising were beginning to catch up with the techniques for the mass production and distribution of goods, particularly the use of display advertising in rapidly expanding mass-circulation newspapers and magazines.

Until the development of advertising via the mass media, few manufacturers, retailers, or consumers worried about the quality or truthfulness of commercial speech. Strange as it may seem in modern times, accustomed as we are to consumer watchdog groups and governmental regulatory agencies, most people in the 19th century followed the old maxim of "caveat emptor" (let the buyer beware). Consumers depended on their proximity to the makers and sellers of goods to ensure quality control of the items they purchased. If the clientele found the merchant's goods or services wanting, they were sure to mention it the next time they saw the merchant in the street or stopped by the shop. Much of the commercial speech of the time communicated simple information such as store hours or featured items. Most people saw little advertising or product publicity of any kind, as it would be defined today, and what little they did see generally was dismissed by all but the most gullible as inherently unbelievable, particularly because of the extravagant claims made for the benefits to be gained by selecting the touted products or services.

By the turn of the century, however, with mass media advertising and publicity becoming key determinants in purchasing behavior, both manufacturers and consumers began to be more concerned with the truthfulness of the factual claims for products and services. These concerns led to the adoption of so-called "printers ink" statutes at the state level (*Printer's Ink* magazine, a trade publication, had proposed a model statute in 1911). These statutes (discussed in more detail in later chapters) typically subjected those making false claims in their commercial speech to criminal prosecution, with a conviction punishable by a fine.

The Federal Trade Commission (FTC) was created by statute in 1914. Its mandate was to ensure a level playing field in the competitive arena by preventing, among other things, "deceptive acts or practices."[1] Eventually this included regulatory overview of commercial speech to ensure truthful, nondeceptive claims. The Food and Drug Administration (FDA) and the Bureau of Alcohol, Tobacco, and Firearms (BATF) were created in the 1930s to oversee specialized products like medicines, health care and beauty aides, and controlled substances, including claims and other information manufacturers could put on container labels for these products. These governmental efforts to control commercial speech paralleled the development of self-regulatory schemes by various trade associations, such as the Associated Advertising Clubs of America. However, these self-regulatory efforts depended largely on the use of moral suasion, rather than penalizing offenders (these regulatory efforts are discussed in more detail in later chapters).

From the beginning of the 20th century until World War II, these and other federal and state efforts to regulate commercial speech continued to grow, albeit in piecemeal fashion. Somewhat surprisingly, however, despite this nearly half century of regulatory efforts, it was not until 1942 that a major First Amendment challenge was made to all attempts by government to regulate commercial speech. It took an eccentric individual entrepreneur to see the issue all the way through to the Supreme Court of the United States.

THE COMMERCIAL SPEECH "DOCTRINE"

The stage was set for the Court's initial foray into examining the constitutionality of commercial speech regulation by its decision in the 1939 case of *Schneider v. State (Town of Irvington)*.[2] Clara Schneider was a Jehovah's Witness who was arrested for failing to obtain a permit before proselytizing her religious views door to door. The Court overturned her conviction on First Amendment speech and religion grounds, but, in so doing, was careful to note that "We are not to be taken as holding that *commercial* soliciting and canvassing may not be subjected to such regulation. . . ."[3] The Court seemed to suggest that, rather than control commercial speech by a content-neutral, time-place-and-manner regulation, the community could legitimately discriminate against the speech based on the content of the message—the rationale being that, under the First Amendment, commercial speech did not have the same degree of protection as other speech.

This apparent willingness by the Court to distinguish between regulation of commercial speech and other kinds of speech was borne out 3 years later in *Valentine v. Chrestensen*,[4] the first instance where the Court decided the First Amendment issues in the case solely on the basis that the content of the speech in question was purely commercial speech.

F. J. Chrestensen was a small-time entrepreneur/showman who hit on the idea of rescuing a decommissioned U.S. Navy submarine from the scrap heap by purchasing it and charging a small admission to tour the ship. After finally gaining permission from New York State officials to tie up at a pier in the East River (New York City officials had refused his initial request to use a city pier), Chrestensen was faced with the problem of how to attract visitors to his exhibition.

In New York City, it was virtually impossible for a small business to use conventional advertising to attract business. Because of scarcity and economies of scale, generally only large corporations or other organizations can either afford or need to reach the hundreds of thousands of readers, listeners, and viewers the city's mass media serve. A small businessman like Chrestensen might have been able to afford a small advertisement or two to publicize his submarine tours. But unless he could spend thousands of advertising dollars to get his message across on a grand scale, his commercial message was bound to be lost in the clutter of the other commercial messages vying for consumers' attention.

Having no large advertising budget at his disposal, Chrestensen turned instead to another traditional big-city publicity technique—handbills. Determining this to be a cheap (if less effective) means of reaching potential customers, Chrestensen created and had printed handbills that he distributed to passersby on the city's streets. Unfortunately for Chrestensen, this was in violation of the New York City Sanitary Code, which said, in part, "No person shall ... distribute ... any handbill, circular ... or other advertising matter whatsoever in or upon any street or public place. ..."[5] The city ordinance made an exception, however, for "the lawful distribution of anything other than commercial and business advertising matter."[6]

The governmental interests were straightforward—protecting pedestrians from being accosted and perhaps impeded by street solicitors, and preventing litter on city streets caused by the likelihood that those taking the handbills or other advertising matter would throw them on the pavement, rather than disposing of them in waste containers. The counterveiling interest of Chrestensen was equally clear—the freedom to advertise his submarine tour using a handbill containing legal, accurate, and truthful speech.

After a number of unpleasant encounters with the police, Chrestensen, rather than face the continuing risk of arrest, chose instead to reprint his handbill with the commercial message (minus any mention of a tour fee) on one side and, as the Court noted, "a protest against the action of the City Dock Department in refusing the respondent wharfage facilities at a city pier"[7] on the other. The police, seeing this as an effort by Chrestensen to get around the law by turning his commercial speech into a political protest (which the ordinance specifically exempted from regulation), again refused him permission to distribute his reprinted handbill, although they conceded that distributing a circular with just the protest message would be legal under the city code.

At this point, Chrestensen turned to the federal courts, seeking a restraining order to stop the police from interfering with the distribution of his handbills.

The district court found that the city ordinance indeed went too far and granted a permanent injunction against police enforcement of the disputed regulation. The second circuit federal appeals court agreed, upholding the lower court's order in a divided opinion.

The Supreme Court of the United States disagreed. The question, said the Court, is "whether the application of the ordinance to [Mr. Chrestensen's] activity was, in the circumstances, an unconstitutional abridgement of the freedom of the press and of speech."[8] While noting that previous decisions had "unequivocally held that the streets are proper places for the exercise of the freedom of communicating information and disseminating opinion and that . . . states and municipalities . . . may not unduly burden or proscribe its employment in these public thoroughfares . . . [W]e are equally clear that the Constitution imposes no such restraint on government as respects purely commercial advertising."[9]

This clear rejection of "purely commercial advertising" as a category of speech protected by the constitution created what eventually became known as the "commercial speech doctrine."[10] The Court did not return to evaluating the First Amendment status of pure commercial speech until more than 3 decades later, with its decision in *Pittsburgh Press Co. v. Pittsburgh Commission on Human Relations.*[11]

Pittsburgh Press is a complex case for a variety of reasons, not the least of which is that it requires the reader to think of by-gone times, when newspapers routinely ran classified advertising for employment under "Help Wanted—Male" and "Help Wanted—Female" columns. Typically, ads under the "Male" heading were for lawyers, doctors, and other professionals, whereas ads under the "Female" heading were for public school teachers, nurses, and office workers. The clear implication was that if you were female, you need not apply for jobs in the well-paid professions or for managerial positions in industry.

The general public gave little thought to such gender-based discrimination until challenged by civil rights laws passed by Congress in the late 1960s. These federal statutes inspired state and local ordinances prohibiting sexual bias in the workplace, including the Human Relations Ordinance legislated by the city of Pittsburgh. The regulation prohibited hiring based on the job seeker's gender, and made it unlawful "For any person whether or not an employer, employment agency or labor organization, to aid . . . in the doing of any act declared to be an unlawful employment practice by this ordinance . . . ," including publishing or circulating "any notice or advertisement relating to 'employment' or membership which indicates any discrimination because of . . . sex."[12]

In October 1969, the National Organization for Women (NOW) filed a complaint with the Pittsburgh Commission on Human Relations, charging that the *Pittsburgh Press* was in noncompliance with the ordinance. The Commission agreed and issued a cease-and-desist order instructing the newspaper to discontinue using the gender-based classification scheme. The newspaper's arguments that it was simply following the requests of advertisers, and that the ordinance violated its right to determine the layout and content of its advertising pages, were specifically rejected. The *Pittsburgh Press* appealed the Commission's order to the local court of common pleas, which upheld the order. On appeal, the Pennsylvania Commonwealth Court modified the order slightly, but basically left it intact. The Pennsylvania Supreme Court refused to review the case, and the newspaper appealed to the Supreme Court of the United States.

Conceding that protection of speech and press was paramount to a democracy, the Court nonetheless found that the city ordinance was not a significant infringement of the newspaper's economic well-being. Based on *Valentine*, the Court also found that the advertisements in question were "classic examples of commercial speech."[13] The newspaper argued that, unlike *Valentine*, the commercial speech distinction was inapplicable in this case because the issue was the regulation of the editorial judgment of a newspaper, rather than the control of commercial content or the actions of an advertiser. The Court rejected this argument, finding that decisions about placement of an advertisement failed to "lift the newspaper's actions from the category of commercial speech."[14]

The Court also rejected the newspaper's final argument that a distinction between commercial speech and other kinds of speech was inappropriate and should be abandoned. Saying this argument would best be left until a later day, the Court noted that the discriminatory advertising policy and contents of the advertisements in contention were "not only commercial activity but illegal commercial activity under the Ordinance."[15] The Court concluded that, "Any First Amendment interest which might be served by advertising an ordinary commercial proposal and which might arguably outweigh the governmental interest supporting the regulation is altogether absent when the commercial activity itself is illegal and the restriction on advertising is incidental to a valid limitation on economic activity."[16]

At first reading, the decision in *Pittsburgh Press* appeared to be a simple reaffirmation of the Court's commercial speech exception to the First Amendment. However, a more thorough analysis provided hope that the Court's blanket denial of constitutional protection for purely commercial speech was not as absolute as it seemed. Rather than simply refusing to hear the case or dismissing the newspaper's First Amendment arguments out of hand, the Court was careful to base its decision on the notion that the commercial speech in question was for an illegal purpose, and that the government's interests in regulation therefore outweighed the newspaper's speech interests. This opened the door ever so slightly to the idea that courts should scrutinize more carefully any governmental attempts to ban or in other ways regulate commercial speech for legal products or services.

This wedge in opening the way for at least some constitutional protection for commercial speech, and the unusual circumstances of the next important commercial speech case, *Bigelow v. Virginia*,[17] combined to create the first major breakthrough in the drive to place commercial speech within the ambit of the First Amendment.

The Court's decision in *Bigelow* emanated from a case involving an advertisement for an abortion referral service. Bigelow, the director and managing editor of his self-described "underground weekly newspaper,"[18] *The Virginia Weekly*, published a display advertisement that read as follows:

UNWANTED PREGNANCY
LET US HELP YOU
Abortions are now legal in New York.
There are no residency requirements.
FOR IMMEDIATE PLACEMENT
ACCREDITED
HOSPITALS AND CLINICS AT LOW
COST
Contact
WOMEN'S PAVILION
515 Madison Avenue
New York, N.Y. 10022
or call any time
(212) 371-6670 or (212) 371-6650
AVAILABLE 7 DAYS A WEEK
STRICTLY CONFIDENTIAL.
We will make all arrangements for you and help you
with information and counseling.[19]

All of the information in the advertisement was true, including the legality of regulated abortions, in New York State. Unfortunately for Bigelow, abortions were illegal at this time in his home state of Virginia, as, according to a Virginia statute, were efforts by "any person by publication, lecture, advertisement, or by the sale or circulation of any publication, or in any other manner, [to] encourage or prompt the procuring of abortion or miscarriage...."[20] The statute made such efforts a misdemeanor.

Bigelow was convicted of violating the statute, and was fined $500 ($350 of which was forgiven if he promised not to run similar advertisements in the future). The Virginia Supreme Court upheld his conviction, specifically rejecting his First Amendment-based claim that the statute was unconstitutional. The Virginia Supreme Court found that the speech in question was a "commercial advertisement," and therefore it could "constitutionally [be] prohibited by the state ... [when] the advertising relates to the medical-health field."[21]

On appeal, the Supreme Court of the United States vacated Bigelow's conviction and returned the case to Virginia for further consideration, without deciding on the merits of his First Amendment claims. It did so because the case of *Roe v. Wade*,[22] in which the Court—on a federal constitution-based, individual-privacy theory—limited a state's ability to regulate abortions. *Roe v. Wade* was decided soon after Bigelow's request for the Court to hear his case. On remand, the Virginia Supreme Court reaffirmed its earlier opinion, upholding Bigelow's conviction on the basis that *Roe v. Wade* had not "mentioned the subject of abortion advertising."[23] Bigelow again appealed to the Supreme Court of the United States, and the Court again reversed his conviction, this time on First Amendment grounds.

The Court began its opinion by noting that reliance on *Valentine* for the proposition that purely commercial speech is unprotected by the First Amendment is misplaced. "The fact that [*Valentine*] had the effect of banning a particular handbill does not mean that [it] is authority for the proposition that all statutes regulating commercial advertising are immune from constitutional challenge."[24] The Court said that, although the classified advertisements in the *Pittsburgh Press* were purely commercial speech, even they "would have received some degree of First Amendment protection if the commercial proposal had been legal."[25] The Court found that the advertisement in question

> did more than simply propose a commercial transaction. It contained factual material of clear "public interest." Viewed in its entirety, the advertisement conveyed information of potential interest and value to a diverse audience—not only to readers possibly in need of the services offered, but also to those with a general curiosity about, or genuine interest in, the subject matter or the law of another State and its development, and to readers seeking reform in Virginia.[26]

It seems reasonable to believe that underlying the Court's decision in *Bigelow* was concern that Virginia's regulation of commercial speech for an abortion-referral service was a none-too-subtle attempt to regulate a woman's constitutional right to seek an abortion. Support for this view comes from the language of the decision, including a disclaimer by the Court that, "We do not decide in this case the precise extent to which the First Amendment permits regulation of advertising that is related to activities the State may legitimately regulate or even prohibit."[27] Later in the opinion, the Court again noted that, "We need not decide here the extent to which constitutional protection is afforded commercial advertising under all circumstances and in the face of all kinds of regulation."[28]

However, the Court did find that, "To the extent that commercial activity is subject to regulation, the relationship of speech to that activity may be one factor among others, to be considered in weighing the First Amendment interest against the governmental interest alleged. Advertising is not thereby stripped of all First Amendment protection."[29] From now on, said the Court, "a court may not escape the task of assessing the First Amendment interest at stake and weighing it against the public interest allegedly served by the [governmental] regulation,"[30] particularly if the commercial speech is not deceptive or fraudulent and it is related to a legal product or service.

Although *Bigelow* represented a significant step forward in overcoming the Court's 30-year acquiescence to governmental regulation of purely commercial speech, the decision failed to address a number of major issues. Although after *Bigelow*, courts were required to balance speech interests against governmental regulatory interests, there was little discussion by the Court about how that balancing was to take place or how much weight should be assigned to either speech or governmental interests. (Remember that in other, earlier cases, the Court placed a "heavy burden" on those who wish to regulate fully protected speech.) Nor was there discussion of the range of activities the Court had in mind when it noted that, "the State may legitimately regulate or even prohibit"[31] advertising for some activities.

The Court also did not define the terms *deceptive* and *fraudulent*, or the legality of a state limiting nondeceptive, legal advertising in its media of an activity or product illegal in another state (e.g., a New York statute banning advertising of an illegal abortion-referral service in Virginia). Finally, the Court did not indicate what the result might have been if Virginia's regulation had been aimed at an advertiser rather than at the newspaper, or if potential consumers of the advertised service or product had any independent First Amendment rights to receive the information contained in the disputed advertising.

It was this last issue that formed the basis for the Court's decision in *Virginia State Board of Pharmacy v. Virginia Citizens Consumer Council, Inc.,*[32] the high-water mark in the development of First Amendment protection for purely commercial speech. The Virginia State Board of Pharmacy is the agency empowered by the state to license and regulate pharmacists and the practice of pharmacy in Virginia. The Board had ruled that advertising the price of prescription drugs was inherently "unprofessional conduct,"[33] and that such conduct could subject the pharmacist who violated this rule to sanctions, including license revocation. The Board's regulations were questioned not by advertisers or the media, but by a consumer group representing potential purchasers of prescription medicines. The council challenged the Board's anti-advertising rules on the somewhat novel thesis that consumers, who would benefit from information about prescription drug prices, had a First Amendment right to receive such information.

A three-judge district court weighed the state's stated interests in preventing abuse and deception in the practice of pharmacy against the speech-related arguments advanced by the plaintiff that price information could significantly reduce the costs of prescription medicines to consumers. Noting evidence that prices charged for the same drugs could vary as much as 600% from pharmacy to pharmacy, the court found that the consumer group's arguments carried greater weight, and thus struck down the anti-advertising regulation on First Amendment grounds. The Virginia State Board of Pharmacy appealed to the Supreme Court of the United States, arguing that Virginia's ban on advertising was a legitimate regulation of purely commercial speech.

The Court characterized the basic issue in the case as

> whether there is a First Amendment exception for "commercial speech. . . ." Our pharmacist does not wish to editorialize on any subject, cultural, philosophical, or political. He does not wish to report any particularly newsworthy fact, or to make generalized observations even about commercial matters. The "idea" he wishes to communicate is simply this: "I will sell you the X prescription drug at

the Y price." Our question then is whether this communication is wholly outside the protection of the First Amendment.[34]

The Court held that the answer was "no."

The Court stressed four factors favoring disseminating commercial information about the price of prescription drugs over the governmental regulatory interests in banning such information. First, the economic motivation behind the speech did not serve to disqualify it automatically from First Amendment protection. Second, a "consumer's interest in the free flow of commercial information . . . may be as keen, if not keener by far, than his interest in the day's most urgent political debate."[35] This was especially true in this case because the poor and elderly represented by the plaintiff tend to spend a disproportionate amount of income on prescription drugs, yet have little ability to comparison shop. The Court also found that striking down the ban on this form of commercial speech served to underly the more general interest society has "in the free flow of commercial information."[36] Information of general public interest, like advertisements discussing the benefits of environmentally friendly products, would likely be protected from such governmental regulation, and the Court said it could find little reason for not affording prescription drug advertising similar status. Finally, acknowledging that the American economic system is based on free enterprise, the Court concluded that the system, "no matter how tasteless and excessive it sometimes may seem is nonetheless [dependent on] dissemination of information as to who is producing and selling what product, for what reason, and at what price."[37] For it to work, said the Court, the system requires that "decisions, in the aggregate, be intelligent and well informed. To this end, the free flow of commercial information is indispensable."[38]

The Court accepted Virginia's arguments that prescription drug advertising could weaken the professionalism of licensed pharmacists, but rejected banning advertising as a legitimate means for the state to accomplish its ends, noting the existence of many other regulations controlling the licensing and practices of the profession. Most such regulations would be permissible, said the Court, but adopting the one that relies "in large measure on the advantages of [keeping the public] in ignorance"[39] is not among them. "It is precisely this kind of choice, between the dangers of suppressing information, and the dangers of its misuse if it is freely available, that the First Amendment makes for us."[40]

In striking down the ban on prescription drug advertising, the Court added that it was not affording fully protected, First Amendment status to purely commercial speech. Legitimate "time-place-and-manner" regulations would still be legal, said the Court, as would regulations restricting false, misleading, or deceptive commercial speech. In an extensive footnote, the Court stated that, because of the "hardiness" of commercial speech, and because the truth of the statements in such speech "may be more easily verifiable by its disseminator than, let us say, news reporting or political commentary,"[41] government could be granted greater leeway under the First Amendment to regulate purely commercial speech.

Since advertising is the sine qua non of commercial profits, there is little likelihood of its being chilled by proper regulation and foregone entirely. Attributes such as these, the greater objectivity and hardiness of commercial speech, may make it less necessary to tolerate inaccurate statement for fear of silencing the speaker. They may also make it appropriate to require that a commercial message appear in such a form or include such additional information, warnings and disclaimers as are necessary to prevent its being deceptive. They may also make inapplicable the prohibition against prior restraints.[42]

The Court concluded that none of these rationales for lawful regulation of purely commercial speech was applicable in this case. "What is at issue [here] is whether a State may completely suppress the dissemination of concededly truthful information about entirely lawful activity, fearful of that information's effect upon its disseminators and its recipients. . . . [W]e conclude that the answer . . . is in the negative."[43]

Despite the Court's reluctance to grant full First Amendment protection to pure commercial speech, the Court's change of focus in *Virginia State Board of Pharmacy* from protecting the rights of the speaker to protecting the needs and rights of the audience to receive information gave hope to commercial speech advocates that the commercial speech exception to the First Amendment was dead. With the possible exceptions of speech that touted an illegal product or activity, or of commercial claims that could mislead or deceive the potential consumer, such a consumer-based approach meant that government would be hard pressed to deny readers and viewers the information they needed to make informed choices when deciding how to conduct their personal commercial transactions. Unfortunately, the euphoria generated by *Virginia State Board of Pharmacy* was almost immediately tempered by the reasoning of the Court in *Bates et al. v. State Bar of Arizona*[44] just 1 year later.

John Bates and Van O'Steen, both attorneys practicing law in Phoenix, Arizona, formed a partnership to run a legal clinic to provide low-cost legal services for persons of moderate income. It became apparent almost immediately that they would need to advertise to build a client base. As part of this advertising, the partners decided they should include information about the fees charged for standard services, such as uncontested divorces and simple personal bankruptcies. Advertising was expressly forbidden, however, by the rules covering the practice of law in Arizona administered by the state bar association. When the two attorneys placed an advertisement in the *Arizona Republic*, the state bar president filed a complaint that eventually resulted in both Bates and O'Steen being suspended from the practice of law for 1 week. Both appealed their suspensions to the Arizona Supreme Court, arguing that the sanctions by the bar violated both antitrust and free speech laws. The Arizona court upheld the suspensions, and Bates and O'Steen appealed to the Supreme Court of the United States.

The Supreme Court of the United States dismissed contentions that the state bar rule violated federal antitrust provisions, but found merit in the attorneys' First Amendment arguments. First citing *Virginia State Board of Pharmacy* for the proposition that commercial speech was at least somewhat protected by the First Amendment, the Court then turned its attention to the state's arguments that lawyer advertising was an exception to this rule or, in the alternative, that the particular advertising by Bates and O'Steen was inherently false and deceptive.

Ordinarily, said the Court, there is no need for a finding that a specific speaker's rights have been violated before a court should strike down a law or regulation that suppresses speech as an infringement of the First Amendment. This, said the Court, "reflects the conclusion that the possible harm to society from allowing unprotected speech to go unpunished is outweighed by the possibility that protected speech will be muted."[45] In a case involving purely commercial speech, however, the Court noted that this overbreadth doctrine does not apply because there are " 'commonsense differences' between commercial speech and other varieties [of speech]."[46]

One such difference, said the Court, is that because

advertising is linked to commercial well-being, it seems unlikely that such speech is particularly susceptible to being crushed by overbroad regulations. Moreover, concerns for uncertainty in determining the scope of protection are reduced; the advertiser seeks to disseminate information about a product or service that he provides, and presumably he can determine more readily than others whether his speech is truthful and protected.[47]

The Court characterized the principal issue in Bates as "a narrow one"— whether "lawyers . . . may constitutionally advertise the prices at which certain routine services will be performed."[48] The state had argued that because the costs for legal services could only be determined on a case-by-case basis, advertising fixed prices was false and deceptive. The Court disagreed, holding that the state's total ban on lawyer advertising via the mass media (including advertising the price of standard services) was not permitted under the First Amendment, but also noting that pure commercial speech could still be regulated in ways that fully protected speech could not. For example, the Court explicitly stated that false, deceptive, or misleading commercial speech could be restrained, as could commercial speech about illegal products or transactions. Additionally, the Court noted that time-place-and-manner regulations could apply to commercial speech, and that "the special problems of advertising on the electronic broadcast media . . . [could] warrant special considerations."[49]

The focus of the Court in Bates—on "whether lawyers [i.e., the commercial speaker] . . . may constitutionally advertise"[50]—clearly indicated that the Court was no longer judging the constitutionality of laws regulating commercial speech by evaluating how much such laws infringe on the rights of the audience to receive commercial information. The Court could have characterized the issue in Bates as whether consumers of legal services have a right to information about the prices of standard legal services, but chose not to do so. Although the Court indulged in some discussion of the need for informed decision making on the part of potential clients, *Bates* signaled the beginning of a continuing retreat from the *Virginia State Board of Pharmacy* audience- centered focus and a return to evaluating regulation of purely commercial speech by balancing the rights of the speaker—and not the receiver—against the interests of the government.

Bates was the first in a series of commercial speech cases involving lawyers and other professionals. Schooled in a legal tradition that regarded advertising or other solicitation by lawyers as inherently unethical, these cases proved troublesome for a number of justices, and undoubtedly hindered an orderly development of First Amendment protection for commercial speech. For example, the two cases immediately following *Bates*—*Ohralik v. Ohio State Bar Association*[51] and *In re Primus*,[52]—involved similar facts, but produced opposite results.

Albert Ohralik, a practicing attorney in Ohio, ran afoul of the state bar association's rules against soliciting clients. Ohralik learned that two young women had been injured in a traffic mishap, and approached the family of one of the women with whom he had a slight acquaintance to offer advice about the legal implications of the woman's conduct and the possibility of bringing suit. He then made contact with both young women personally and urged them to retain his services. Both eventually refused his offer and complained about his actions to the grievance committee of the county bar. The case was referred to the state bar association, which eventually filed charges against Ohralik with the disciplinary commission of the Ohio Supreme Court. Ohralik argued that he was not guilty of ethical infractions, and that his activities were protected by the First and Fourteenth Amendments. The court rejected Ohralik's arguments and suspended him from the practice of law indefinitely.

Edna Primus was a civil liberties lawyer associated with the Carolina Community Law Firm and an officer in the South Carolina branch of the American Civil Liberties Union (ACLU). Primus was invited to discuss legal matters with a group of women whom county authorities had coerced into being sterilized as a condition of receiving public medical assistance. One of the women later indicated she might bring a suit against the local physician who had performed the medical procedure, and Primus wrote her a letter advising her of the ACLU's offer to provide legal assistance. Primus' letter eventually found its way to the grievance board of the South Carolina Supreme Court, which entered a public reprimand against her.

Both Ohralik and Primus took their complaints about the sanctions imposed on them to the Supreme Court of the United States and their cases were consolidated on appeal. In *Ohralik*, Justice Powell's majority opinion upheld the Ohio court's suspension of the plaintiff on the basis that commercial speech was entitled to only "a limited measure of protection"[53] under the First Amendment, and that Ohralik's solicitation of clients constituted commercial speech. Governmental regulation "impermissible in the realm of noncommercial expression,"[54] said Justice Powell, would be permissible if the speech contained commercial information. "While entitled to some constitutional protection, [Ohralik's] conduct is subject to regulation in furtherance of important State interests."[55]

In *Primus*, however, Justice Powell, writing for a six-member majority, rejected the South Carolina Supreme Court's censoring of Primus, holding that the attorney's speech offering legal assistance on behalf of the ACLU was not commercial speech, and therefore was entitled to full First Amendment protection. To the dismay of Justices Rehnquist and Marshall, the Court characterized Primus' solicitation letter as "political expression" and, said Justice Powell, "a State must regulate [such speech] with significantly greater precision."[56] He agreed, however, that the government would have been entitled to greater constitutional leeway in regulating Primus' message if it had been more commercial in nature.

Central Hudson Gas & Electric Corp.— The Court Creates a Test

The conflicting results of *Ohralik* and *Primus* were representative of the mixed signals sent by the Court to lower federal and state courts trying to determine how much First Amendment protection purely commercial speech should receive. In *Central Hudson Gas & Electric Corp. v. Public Service Commission*,[57] the Court attempted to resolve the confusion caused by the Court's nearly 4-decade-long, zigzag path through the world of commercial speech regulation by setting out a four-part test for judging the constitutionality of laws governing commercial speech.

The challenged regulations in *Central Hudson* banned advertising that promoted the use of electricity. Originally, the regulations had been promulgated by the state agency in charge of regulating utilities as a temporary response to an energy crisis in the early 1970s. The Public Service Commission extended the advertising ban after the immediate crisis had passed, however, as a general conservation measure. The Commission admitted that prohibiting advertising was not a perfect remedy because it restricted electric power utilities from encouraging the most efficient uses of electric power, and because the ban did not apply to alternative energy sources like oil or coal. Nonetheless, the Commission continued its ban because it feared that allowing advertising would send "misleading signals"[58] to consumers that conservation of electric power was no longer an important energy conservation goal. Central Hudson Gas & Electric challenged the Commission's ban in state court, but its arguments that the ban violated the corporation's First Amendment rights received little sympathy. Central Hudson then appealed to the Supreme Court of the United States.

Citing *Virginia State Board of Pharmacy*, Justice Powell, writing for the majority, reiterated that commercial speech is protected by the First Amendment from unwarranted governmental regulation, but also noted the Court's decisions recognizing differences in constitutional protection between commercial speech and other kinds of speech. Therefore, he said, protection for commercial speech "turns on the nature both of the expression and of the governmental interests served by its regulation."[59]

According to Justice Powell, "In commercial speech cases . . . a four-part analysis has developed. At the outset, we must determine whether the expression is protected by the First Amendment."[60] As examples of nonprotected speech, Justice Powell noted that there was little constitutional value in commercial speech that promotes illegal activities or products, or that contains statements that are false or tend to mislead or deceive. If the speech in question falls into one of these categories, it fails the first part of the four-part test, and the government may regulate it as it sees fit. However, if the commercial speech the government intends to regulate does not fall into any of these categories, it is protected by the First Amendment, and, said Justice Powell, "the government's power is more circumscribed."[61] Before regulating constitutionally protected commercial speech, the government must first show that such regulation serves a "substantial" governmental purpose and, in addition, that the actual manner in which the government proposes to regulate the speech directly aids the government in achieving its substantial purpose.[62] Finally, said the Court, the regulation must be "narrowly tailored" to ensure that the regulation "is not more extensive than is necessary to further the [substantial governmental purpose]."[63]

Applying its four-part test to the facts of *Central Hudson*, the Court first found that the constitution protected the company's commercial speech because there was nothing illegal, false, or deceptive about the commercial information the utility company was attempting to convey. Turning to the arguments of the state regulatory commission, the Court agreed that the state's interests in conserving natural resources and encouraging nonwasteful consumption of electric power were "substantial" governmental interests. The Court also accepted the Commission's arguments that the method chosen—regulating the utility's commercial speech—helped the state to realize its substantial interest in discouraging wasteful consumption of electric power. The Court based its holding on the premise that "there is an immediate connection between advertising and demand for electricity."[64]

However, the Court found that the actions by the state utility commission could not pass the fourth part of the test because the challenged regulations were overly broad. "The Commission's order," said the Court, "reaches all promotional advertising, regardless of the impact of the touted service on overall energy use."[65] The Court, noting that the utility company had argued that it would have informed consumers how to be more energy conscious if it were not for the advertising ban, held that "[T]o the extent that the Commission's order suppresses speech that in no way impairs the State's interest in energy conservation, [that] order violates the First and Fourteenth Amendments. . . ."[66] Justice Powell pointed out, however, that instead of a complete prohibition, the Court might accept alternative methods of regulating the utility company's commercial speech, like restricting the format or limiting or requiring additional content.

Although the four-part *Central Hudson* test gained the approval of a majority of the Court as a cogent summation of the evolution of constitutional protection for purely commercial speech, several justices remained skeptical. Some felt that providing any constitutional protection for commercial speech extended the protective umbrella of the First Amendment to speech the authors of the First Amendment never meant to include. Others feared that such protection for commercial speech could water down protection for more important kinds of speech.

Chief among these critics was Justice (now Chief Justice) Rehnquist. He expressed some of his sharpest criticisms in his dissenting opinion in *Metromedia, Inc. v. San Diego*,[67] the first major commercial speech case to reach the Court after *Central Hudson*. *Metromedia* involved a challenge to the city of San Diego's municipal ordinance banning billboards and other outdoor advertising signs "to eliminate hazards to pedestrians and motorists"[68] and for general aesthetic reasons. A billboard company challenged the ordinance, arguing that the ordinance's exceptions for on-premise advertising of commercial names and/or services offered and for off-premise signs of a religious, historical, or public service nature were not sufficient to protect the commercial billboard company's free speech interests.

The Court struck down the city ordinance, but the justices strenuously disagreed among themselves about how to apply the *Central Hudson* four-part test (Justice Rehnquist characterized the Court's collective opinions as "a virtual Tower of Babel").[69] Justice White and three other justices agreed that the city's regulatory scheme had passed the *Central Hudson* test for legally regulating commercial speech, but they nonetheless disallowed the ordinance on the grounds that permitting on-premise advertising of commercial messages but disallowing noncommercial messages unconstitutionally discriminated against noncommercial speech. Justices Blackmun and Brennan agreed that the ordinance should be struck down, but on the grounds that it did not pass any part of the *Central Hudson* test. Neither justice felt that the ban on outdoor advertising could be justified on aesthetic grounds. Even assuming a relationship between outdoor advertising and problems with traffic safety, neither justice believed the ban could be justified as either advancing an important governmental interest or being narrowly tailored to adequately address the city's traffic safety concerns. Chief Justice Burger and Justices Stevens and Rehnquist dissented in separate opinions, but each would have upheld the ordinance, agreeing that both the city's reasons for regulation and the means to accomplish its ends met the requirements of the *Central Hudson* test.

Similar internal divisions within the Court were evident in a series of subsequent commercial speech cases raising constitutional questions, in which shifting coalitions of justices alternately upheld and struck down government attempts to regulate commercial speech. The Court upheld a limited right for lawyers and other professionals to solicit business via media advertising in *Zauderer v. Office of Disciplinary Counsel*.[70] The case involved an advertising message that offered legal assistance to individuals who had suffered injury from use of a specific product on a straight contingency-fee basis. The Ohio Supreme Court had held that such advertising violated a rule against soliciting clients, but the Court's majority disagreed, noting that the speech was truthful and nondeceptive, and that, unlike *Ohralik*, it was not a solicitation of a specific client by an in-person appeal. However, the Court did agree with the state that the lessened protection for commercial speech would permit the state to require disclosing the percentage of any money recovered that the client would have to pay to his or her lawyer, although such a requirement to publish information or risk legal sanction would probably violate the First Amendment if the speech were not commercial in nature.

In *City Council v. Taxpayers for Vincent*,[71] the Court upheld a ban on signs even though the ban did not differentiate between commercial and noncommercial speech. Justices Brennan, Marshall, and Blackmun dissented on the grounds that the majority had granted too much deference to the city's aesthetics arguments, and had not carefully evaluated the competing speech interests. Justice Brennan would have required the city to at least demonstrate that it was engaged in a major, multimethod campaign to eradicate visual pollution, and that banning signs was a necessary step in this campaign, before he would give serious consideration to allowing the government to abridge speech interests.

Zauderer and *Taxpayers*, together with *Capital Cities Cable, Inc. v. Crisp*,[72] involving state regulation of alcoholic beverage advertising, and *Lowe v. SEC*,[73] concerning federal regulation of periodic investment publications—two cases in which constitutional issues were discussed, but did not form the basis of the decisions—indicated that the Court's *Central Hudson* test had not ended the confusion over the constitutional status of commercial speech, in part because the test lent itself to a degree of case-by-case interpretation perhaps unanticipated at the time of the *Central Hudson* decision.

Posadas De Puerto Rico—The Court Changes Direction Once Again

The elasticity of the *Central Hudson* test was best illustrated by the Court's decision in *Posadas de Puerto Rico Associates v. Tourism Company of Puerto Rico*.[74] The Puerto Rican legislature had passed a statute legalizing casino gambling to encourage economic development of the island, but the statute specified that casinos would not "be permitted to advertise or otherwise offer their facilities to the public of Puerto Rico."[75] A later modification of the statute permitted advertising in "newspapers, magazines, radio, television or other publicity media outside Puerto Rico,"[76] although such media might find their way into the hands of island residents. Posadas de Puerto Rico Associates, a corporation operating the Condado Plaza Hotel and Casino, was fined and threatened with suspension of its gambling license for violating the advertising provisions of the statute by the Tourism Company of Puerto Rico, the agency delegated power by the commonwealth to regulate casinos. The corporation paid the fine under protest, and asked the courts of Puerto Rico to judge the constitutionality of the statute. Although the courts eventually agreed that the statute had been interpreted too broadly (apparently even imprinting the name of the casino on matchbook covers had been prohibited), the statute's prohibition of advertising in the mass media of Puerto Rico was upheld.

Justice Rehnquist, writing for a five-person majority, applied the *Central Hudson* test, but in a manner that seemed to diminish the commercial speech protection provided in that case. "The ... commercial speech at issue here," said the Court, "... concerns a lawful activity and is not misleading or fraudulent, at least in the abstract. We must therefore proceed to the three remaining steps [of the test]. . . . The first of these . . . involves an assessment of the strength of the government's interest in restricting the speech."[77] The Court, without requiring the commonwealth to produce evidence justifying its conclusions, held that Puerto Rico had satisfied the second part of the *Central Hudson* four-part test, accepting the commonwealth's arguments that "casino gambling . . . would produce serious harmful effects on the health, safety and welfare of the Puerto Rican citizens, such as the disruption of moral and cultural patterns, the increase in local crime . . . and the infiltration of organized crime."[78] The Court added, "We have no difficulty in concluding that the Puerto Rico Legislature's interest . . . [in the] welfare of its citizens constitutes a 'substantial' governmental interest."[79]

The Court characterized Parts 3 and 4 of the *Central Hudson* test as requiring "a consideration of the 'fit' between the legislature's ends and means chosen to accomplish those ends."[80] Again without analysis, the Court accepted the commonwealth's "belief" that the "advertising of casino gambling aimed at the residents of Puerto Rico would serve to increase the demand for the product advertised. We think that the legislature's belief is a reasonable one, and the fact that appellant has chosen to litigate this case all the way to this Court indicates that appellant shares the legislature's view."[81] Part 4 of the *Central Hudson* test proved no more of an obstacle. "We also think it clear beyond peradventure that the challenged statute and regulations satisfy the fourth and last step . . . namely, whether the restrictions on commercial speech are no more extensive than necessary to serve the government's interest,"[82] the majority said.

The Court disagreed with the casino owners that the First Amendment required the government to accomplish its purpose by encouraging speech to discourage gambling, rather than banning speech advertising its availability. "We think it is up to the legislature to decide whether or not such a 'counter-speech' policy would be as effective in reducing the demand for casino gambling as a restriction of advertising."[83] In perhaps the most ominous part of the opinion for commercial speech advocates, Justice Rehnquist also rejected the arguments that the First Amendment prohibited the total ban of speech about a legal product or service that was not false, illegal, or deceptive.

Unlike other commercial speech cases that involved bans of commercial speech struck down on First Amendment grounds, the commercial speech in *Posadas* was not about a constitutionally protected activity like abortion or birth control. "In our view," said Justice Rehnquist, "appellant has the argument backwards. . . . [I]t is precisely because the government could have enacted a wholesale prohibition of the underlying conduct that it is permissible for the government to take the less intrusive step of allowing the conduct, but reducing the demand through restrictions on advertising."[84] The Court added that, "It would be . . . a strange constitutional doctrine which would concede to the legislature the authority to totally ban a product or activity but deny to the legislature the authority to forbid the stimulation of demand for the product or activity through advertising on behalf of those who would profit from such increased demand."[85]

Although the full effects of *Posadas* have yet to be felt on the development of constitutional protection of commercial speech, a number of commentators predict the case may have a severe negative impact, particularly for commercial speech about controversial products like alcohol, cigarettes, and pesticides. Others who disagree or wish to negate the possible effects of *Posadas* argue that the decision should be limited to the context of the case and its unique circumstances involving casino gambling in a commonwealth.

THE CURRENT STATUS OF THE COMMERCIAL SPEECH EXCEPTION

Since *Posadas*, the Court has continued to apply and further amplify the four-part *Central Hudson* test in a series of "pure" commercial speech cases. Unfortunately, the Court has lurched forward and backward, first finding increased First Amendment protection for commercial speech, then retreating from that position. The sum total of these cases has left the so-called "commercial speech exception" to the First Amendment intact, and has done little to clarify the exact parameters and permissible extent of governmental regulation of commercial speech.

The first of these post-*Posadas* cases, *Shapero v. Kentucky Bar Association*,[86] upheld the right of lawyers and other professionals to employ advertising by direct mail to reach potential consumers known to require specific assistance. Shapero wanted to mail promotional material to homeowners listed as facing possible foreclosure on their mortgages, urging them to avail themselves of his legal expertise in preventing such actions. Fearing that his method or message might get him in trouble, Shapero sought an advisory opinion about the ethics of such advertising from the Kentucky Bar Association. The bar association, and eventually the Kentucky Supreme Court, agreed that there was nothing misleading or false about Shapero's commercial information, but nonetheless held his direct mail method to be an ethical violation on the basis that it directly solicited potential clients.

Although *Posadas* would appear to have established that the government could rather easily constitutionally ban truthful and nondeceptive speech about any activity or product it could otherwise regulate, the Court in *Shapero* held that the Kentucky Bar Association's ethics rule against direct mail advertising violated the First Amendment. Writing for a six-person majority, Justice Brennan, who dissented in *Posadas*, applied the four-part *Central Hudson* test to the plaintiff's direct mail solicitation, but did so in a way that paid much less deference to the state's reasons for regulating the plaintiff's commercial speech than had the Court in *Posadas*. Therefore, the outcome provided hope to those who wished to treat *Posadas* as an aberration in the development of constitutional protection for commercial speech.

Justice Brennan compared Shapero's letter to the media advertisement in *Zauderer* and found no First Amendment difference between the two. The Kentucky Supreme Court focused on Shapero's use of letters directed toward specific individuals as differentiating his speech from Zauderer's, but the Court dismissed this concern. Shapero could have either advertised an identical message in the mass media or blanketed the target market by a mass mailing, said the Court, and either method would have reached individuals who might need the services Shapero offered to provide. The Court concluded that "the First Amendment does not permit a ban on certain speech merely because it is more efficient; the State may not constitutionally ban a particular letter on the theory that to mail it only to those whom it would most interest is somehow inherently 'objectionable.' "[87]

In *Board of Trustees of State University of New York v. Fox*,[88] however, the Court again took a significant step back from granting increased First Amendment protection for commercial speech. The case involved a Tupperware party in a college dorm room that ran afoul of a State University of New York (SUNY) policy against commercial solicitation in residence halls. A federal appeals court in the second circuit decided that the state's interests in maintaining an educational atmosphere in its residence halls (as well as safety considerations) met the "substantiality" requirement of Part 2 of the *Central Hudson* test. However, the court criticized the means chosen to achieve these interests, and faulted the university for not choosing a method that was the least restrictive of the student plaintiffs' speech interests.

The Supreme Court of the United States disagreed with this latter decision. Focusing on Part 4 of the *Central Hudson* test, the Court noted that "[W]hile we have insisted that the free flow of commercial information is valuable enough to justify imposing on would-be regulators the costs of distinguishing . . . the harmless from the harmful, we have not gone so far as to impose upon them the burden of demonstrating that . . . the manner of restriction is absolutely the least severe that will achieve the desired end."[89] The Court added, "What our decisions require is a 'fit' between the legislature's ends and the means chosen to accomplish those ends."[90]

This change in Part 4 of the *Central Hudson* test was seen by many commentators as a significant diminution of First Amendment protection for commercial speech. Although demanding more than the government simply show a rational reason for its regulation, the Court clarified that if the government can demonstrate that it has evaluated its options for regulation carefully, and presents evidence that it has adopted an option that is a reasonable means of accomplishing its legitimate ends, the Court will not require that the remedy chosen be the one least restrictive of speech.

The Court appeared to reverse direction yet again with its decision in *Peel v. Attorney Registration and Disciplinary Commission of Illinois*.[91] Peel, an Illinois attorney, wanted to highlight his certification by the National Board of Trial Advocacy (NBTA) on his letterhead and other promotional material. The NBTA is *not* an Illinois bar-recognized organization, and the Illinois Supreme Court ruled that including such information, although admittedly truthful, would be an ethical violation because potential clients might be deceived into believing that Peel was unusually qualified to practice.

Justice Stevens, writing for a four-person plurality, gave short shrift to the state's concerns about deception, noting that he saw little chance that consumers were so unsophisticated that they would be unable to evaluate the weight that should be accorded certification by the NBTA. He concluded that the state's total ban on such truthful information did not meet the heavy burden placed on the government when it wished to regulate in such a manner.[92]

Justice Marshall concurred in the outcome on the basis that Illinois could have chosen a less restrictive method of achieving its legitimate interest. Short of a total prohibition, said Justice Marshall, the state "could require a lawyer . . . to provide additional information . . . [or] require a disclaimer stating that [the organization was] not affiliated with, or sanctioned by the State or Federal Government."[93] Justice White dissented, arguing that the state was only required to be reasonable in its choice of remedies. Justices O'Connor and Scalia and Chief Justice Rehnquist dissented on the basis that Peel's letterhead at least had the potential to deceive, and therefore greater deference should have been given to the state's regulatory efforts.

Coming immediately after *SUNY*, free commercial speech advocates took some comfort in *Peel*, which was seen as a small step in the direction of greater constitutional protection for commercial speech. However, Justice Stevens' six-member majority opinion in the next major commercial speech case, *Cincinnati v. Discovery Network*,[94] was hailed as a major step forward, and one that appeared to breathe new life back into the fourth prong of the *Central Hudson* test.

Discovery Network Inc., a provider of "educational, recreational, and social programs to individuals,"[95] published a magazine publicizing its programs that was circulated nine times per year via street newsracks. Similarly, Harmon Publishing Co., a real estate business, promoted its property listings by distributing free publications in newsracks depicting and describing homes for sale. Both companies had sought and received permission to locate their newsracks at approximately 40 sites in the Cincinnati area, but this permission was rescinded by the city council in an attempt to beautify the downtown streets, as well as to make them safer for pedestrians and drivers. As applied, however, the removal order affected only the newsracks of Discovery and Harmon, and not those of news publications. The council justified this discrimination on the theory that the non-news publications constituted "commercial handbills," and therefore legally could be regulated much more stringently than news publications.

Discovery Network and Harmon challenged the enforcement of the ordinance, claiming First Amendment violations along with due process concerns. City officials, although conceding that application of the ordinance to newspapers and news magazines would raise First Amendment problems, countered that the plaintiffs' speech was commercial in nature, and that the city had greater license to regulate their speech because of the reduced First Amendment protection accorded commercial speech.

The federal trial court disagreed. Although accepting the argument that the speech in question was commercial in nature, the district court, applying the four-part *Central Hudson* test, found that the city had not passed Part 4 of the *Central Hudson* test because it had failed to demonstrate a reasonable fit between its desire for beauty and safety and its actions in banning the approximately 60 newsracks owned by the plaintiffs. This lack of fit was especially noticeable, said the court, because the city had left in place the 1,500–2,000 street racks used by newspapers and news magazines.

On appeal, the sixth circuit characterized the only issue as, "does Cincinnati's ordinance . . . prescribe a 'reasonable fit' between the ends asserted and the means chosen to advance them?"[96] The court found that it did not. Noting that the city was not concerned with the harm caused by the content of the publications, but rather the "harms caused by the manner of delivering that speech,"[97] the appeals court agreed with the trial court that banning distribution of the publications by means of newsracks was impermissible. Such actions, said the court, are not a "reasonable fit" between the city's interests and the "wide range of options open to the city to control the perceived ill effects of newsracks,"[98] including bolting the newsracks to the sidewalk, establishing color and design standards for the racks, and limiting the number of permits granted by employing a lottery-type system.

The Supreme Court of the United States accepted the city's appeal, observing that the "importance of the court of appeals decision, together with the dramatic growth in the use of newsracks throughout the country, prompted our grant of certiorari. . . ."[99] Writing for a six-person majority (Justice Blackman added a concurring opinion as well), Justice Stevens agreed with the sixth circuit's interpretation of the fourth prong of the *Central Hudson* test, holding that "It was the city's burden to establish a 'reasonable fit' between its legitimate interests . . . and the means chosen to serve those interests."[100] The Court concluded, "There is ample support in the record . . . that the city did not [meet the burden] we require."[101]

Because, said the Court, "the city failed to address its recently developed concern about newsracks by regulating their size, shape, appearance, or number . . . it has not [as required by *SUNY*] 'carefully calculated' the costs and benefits associated with the burden on speech imposed by its prohibition."[102] The Court briefly dismissed the city's contention that it could ban the specific street racks of the non-news-oriented companies on the theory that commercial speech is less protected by the First Amendment.

> [T]he city contends that the fact that assertedly more valuable publications are allowed to use newsracks does not undermine its judgement that its aesthetic and safety interests are stronger than the interest in allowing commercial speakers to have similar access to the reading public. We cannot agree. In our view, the city's argument attaches more importance to the distinction between commercial and noncommercial speech than our cases warrant and seriously underestimates the value of commercial speech.[103]

The majority opinion traced the development of the commercial speech exception, beginning with *Valentine*, to demonstrate that the city had erred in believing that merely because the publications in question contained a high ratio of advertising to text they should be exempted from normal constitutional protection. First, observing that "[S]ome ordinary newspapers try to maintain a ratio of 70 percent advertising to 30 percent editorial content,"[104] Justice Stevens pointed out that the Court's reasoning in earlier cases required the city to more strictly scrutinize the contents of the publications, noting that some of the material in question "is not what we have described as 'core' commercial speech."[105] The Court concluded that, "The regulation is not a permissible regulation of commercial speech, for on this record it is clear that the interests that Cincinnati has asserted are unrelated to any distinction between 'commercial handbills' and 'newspapers.' "[106]

The Court gave similar short shrift to the city's arguments that its ban was nothing more that a legitimate time-place-and-manner regulation. "[B]ecause the ban is predicated on the content of the publications distributed by the subject newsracks, it is not a valid . . . restriction of protected speech."[107] The Court concluded that, "Cincinnati's categorical ban on the distribution, via newsrack, of 'commercial handbills' cannot be squared with the dictates of the First Amendment."[108]

Chief Justice Rehnquist dissented, joined by Justices White and Thomas. The Chief Justice would have upheld the city's actions on the premises that the precedent-setting cases involving commercial speech clearly hold that commercial speech does not enjoy the same degree of constitutional protection as other categories of speech, and that the method chosen by the city of Cincinnati to accomplish its goals was reasonable—all that was required by the fourth prong of *Central Hudson*. The Chief Justice was especially critical of the majority's evaluation of the city's purposes for limiting newsracks distributing commercial messages because "there can be no question that Cincinnati's prohibition against respondents' newsracks 'directly advances' its safety and esthetic interests. . . ."[109] According to the Chief Justice, the majority's assertion that the city, if it had " 'carefully calculated' the costs and benefits associated with the burden on speech imposed by its prohibition,"[110] would have discovered alternative measures to accomplish its ends "rests on the discredited notion that the availability of 'less restrictive means' . . . renders [the city's] regulations of commercial speech unconstitutional."[111]

As to the underlying issue of the constitutional status of commercial speech regulations, the Chief Justice disagreed that the city had been mistaken in believing that it could burden commercial speech to a greater degree than fully protected speech. "Based on the different levels of protection we have accorded commercial and noncommercial speech, we have previously said that localities may not favor commercial over noncommercial speech. . . . [B]efore today, we have never even suggested that the converse holds true. . . ."[112]

Just when commercial speech advocates were celebrating the apparent resuscitation of the fourth part of the *Central Hudson* test by the Court's holding in *Discovery Network,* however, the Court handed down its opinion in *U.S. v. Edge Broadcasting Company*[113]—a case that, at the very least, made any celebration somewhat premature.

Edge Broadcasting Corporation is the license holder and operator of WMYK-FM, a radio station broadcasting from Elizabeth City, North Carolina. According to survey research, more than 90% of its listeners live over the border in the Hampton Roads, Virginia, metropolitan area. The North Carolina station's legal problems arose when station management decided to boost advertising revenues by running commercials for the Virginia state lottery. Virginia had instituted its lottery in 1988, and had publicized it via a statewide, multimillion-dollar advertising campaign designed to increase participation, a portion of which was spent in the Hampton Roads area. Unfortunately for Edge Broadcasting, WMYK was shut out from cashing in on this lucrative source of revenue. A North Carolina statute made it a misdemeanor to participate in or advertise a lottery. What complicated matters even more was a federal statute (Sections 1304 and 1307 of 18 U.S.C.) that specifically banned broadcasters like Edge Broadcasting from advertising lotteries in neighboring states if the state in which the station is licensed does not have a lottery. To avoid potentially unpleasant legal consequences, Edge Broadcasting sought to obtain a declaratory judgment in federal district court in the eastern district of Virginia that would hold the federal statute to be in violation of the broadcaster's First and Fourteenth Amendment rights.

The district court's opinion began by noting that the regulation of lotteries and lottery advertising by Congress was constitutionally permitted. The court also agreed with the government that Congress had the right to regulate over-the-air broadcasts in ways it could not constitutionally regulate other media, and that such regulation explicitly extended to disseminating information about lotteries.

The court then turned to the application of the challenged statutes to the facts in *Edge,* beginning with an examination of the applicability of the statutes to noncommercial speech. Observing that because "content-based restrictions on noncommercial speech meet First Amendment standards 'only in the most extraordinary circumstances,' " the court said that, "this Court's task with respect to section 1304's application to noncommercial speech is rendered considerably easier by the government's statement ... that [it] would not oppose a decree limiting application ... to the realm of commercial speech."[114] The court expressly added, however, that the statutes in question "should not be read to prohibit [the station broadcasting] noncommercial information about lotteries."[115]

The issue was not as clear for commercial information. The court had little trouble deciding that the statutes, in the proper circumstances, could apply to commercial speech, reading the long list of cases, beginning with *Valentine*, that plainly established commercial speech to be a lesser protected form of speech. "Nonetheless," the court continued, commercial speech "has been afforded significant First Amendment safeguards...."[116] Chief among these, said the court, was the *Central Hudson* four-part test, which the court then applied to the government's interpretation of the regulation as applied to *Edge Broadcasting*.

The court had little trouble deciding that the lottery commercials were protected by the First Amendment because Virginia had "lawfully created" its lottery program, and the information contained in the advertisements was neither false nor deceptive. The court, in turn, found that the government's overall interest in regulating commercial speech about lotteries was legitimately in "furtherance of fundamental interests of federalism enabling non-lottery states to discourage gambling."[117] The court gave short shrift to Edge's arguments that North Carolina's reasons for regulating gambling were outdated. As long as the state's ban on gambling was maintained, the court reasoned, "the federal government's interest in protecting the desires of non-lottery states ... to limit lottery participation must still be termed 'substantial.' "[118]

However, the district court found that both sections of the federal antilottery advertising statute ran afoul of the third prong of the *Central Hudson* test. The court found that the requirement that the challenged regulation directly advance an important governmental interest was not met by the statute's provisions because they were "ineffectual means of reducing lottery participation by North Carolina residents ... because the ... residents within the area of the [station's] signal receive most of their radio, newspaper and television communications from Virginia-based media."[119] Conversely, because so little of the station's listening audience resided in North Carolina, and because this audience was "exposed to significant lottery advertising on television" and print media emanating from Virginia, "sections 1304 and 1307 [of the federal statute], at most, have only a remote impact on Virginia lottery sales among North Carolina residents. . . ."[120]

Although the court faulted the statute for not meeting the "advance-an-important-governmental-interest" language of the third prong of the *Central Hudson* test, it found no problem with the method the government chose to achieve its purpose. In contrast to the trial court's handling of the ban on commercial newsracks in *Discovery Network*, the trial court in *Edge* ruled that the government had satisfied the fourth part of the *Central Hudson* test, simply noting in passing that "the statutory scheme [banning the lottery advertising completely] put in place by sections 1304 and 1307 is not unreasonable. . . ."[121]

On appeal, the Fourth Circuit U.S. Court of Appeals upheld the trial court in a brief, unpublished opinion. The government then petitioned the Supreme Court of the United States for a writ of certiorari, which was granted. Despite the government's urging to the contrary, the Court rejected the argument that regulation of gambling and commercial speech advocating or publicizing gambling were vice-related activities, and thus inherently within the power of government to control in any manner it chose. Instead, the Court elected to treat *Edge* as a normal commercial speech case requiring application of the four-part *Central Hudson* test.

Writing for the majority, Justice White noted that, although for much of its long history "purely commercial advertising was not considered to implicate the constitutional protection of the First Amendment,"[122] beginning with *Virginia State Board of Pharmacy*, such speech was somewhat protected. "Our decisions, however," continued the Court, "have recognized the 'commonsense' distinction between speech proposing a commercial transaction . . . and other varieties of speech."[123] Applying the *Central Hudson* test, the Court found that, for a lawful activity (in Virginia), Edge Broadcasting's speech was truthful and nondeceptive. They conversely found that the government had a substantial interest "in supporting the policy of nonlottery States, as well as not interfering with the policy of States that permit lotteries."[124]

However, the Court disagreed with the lower courts that the government had been unable to meet the third part of the *Central Hudson* test. Characterizing the lower court holdings as failing to "fully appreciate"[125] the government's interests, the Court observed that,

> this question cannot be answered by limiting the inquiry to whether the government interest is directly advanced as applied to a single person or entity. Even if there were no advancement as applied in that manner . . . there would remain the matter of the regulation's general application to others. . . . This is not to say that the validity of the statute's application to Edge is an irrelevant inquiry, but that issue properly should be dealt with under the fourth factor of the *Central Hudson* test.[126]

There is "no doubt," said the Court, "that . . . Congress might have continued to ban all radio or television lottery advertisements. . . . This it did not do. Neither did it permit stations such as Edge, located in a nonlottery State, to carry lottery ads if their signals reached into a State that sponsors lotteries; similarly, it did not forbid stations in a lottery State such as Virginia from carrying lottery ads if their signals reached into an adjoining state. . . ." The Court held that, "Congress surely knew that stations in one State could often be heard in another but expressly prevented each and every North Carolina station, including Edge, from carrying lottery ads. . . . This congressional policy of balancing the interests of lottery and nonlottery States is the substantial governmental interest that satisfies *Central Hudson*. . . ."[127]

Having concluded that the lower courts had incorrectly held that the government had not satisfied the third part of the *Central Hudson* test, however, did not end the case. "Left unresolved," said the Court, ". . . is the validity of applying the statutory restriction to Edge, an issue that we now address under the fourth *Central Hudson* factor."[128] The Court noted that this factor, "whether the regulation is more extensive than is necessary to serve the governmental interest," was modified in *SUNY* to only "require a fit between the restriction and the government interest that is not necessarily perfect, but reasonable. This was also the approach in *Posadas*."[129]

It was not the approach of the majority in *Discovery Network*, however, decided only 3 months prior to *Edge*. Somewhat oddly, the Court in *Edge* never mentioned *Discovery Network*. In the prior case, the Court recognized a First Amendment mandate placing a burden on the government to "carefully calculate" the costs of its regulatory actions or run the risk of "underestimating the value of commercial speech."[130] The language of the majority opinion in *Edge* seems quite the opposite. "We have no doubt," said the Court, "that the fit in this case was a reasonable one. Allowing [Edge Broadcasting] to carry lottery ads reaching over 90 percent of its listeners, all in Virginia, would surely enhance its revenues. But just as surely, because Edge's signals with lottery ads would be heard in the nine counties in North Carolina that its broadcasts reached, this would be in derogation of the substantial federal interest in supporting North Carolina's law. . . ."[131] According to the Court, the deciding factor should be the relationship the regulation "bears to the general problem of accommodating the policies of both lottery and nonlottery states."[132] The Court concluded that as long as the government could demonstrate that it had chosen a reasonable means to accomplish its ends, the burden of demonstrating the requirements for the fourth part of the *Central Hudson* test had been met, even if a careful calculation might demonstrate that alternative means were also feasible.

Justice Stevens, in dissent, was vehemently opposed to the majority's affirmation of the ban on the acceptance of lottery advertising by Edge Broadcasting. "Three months ago," he said, "this Court [in *Discovery Network*] reaffirmed that the proponents of a restriction on commercial speech bear the burden of demonstrating a 'reasonable fit' between the legislatures' goals and the means chosen to effectuate those goals."[133] To Justice Stevens, "suppressing truthful advertising regarding a neighboring State's lottery, an activity which is, of course, perfectly legal, is a patently unconstitutional means of effectuating the Government's asserted interest in protecting the policies of nonlottery States."[134] The government, concluded Justice Stevens, "has selected the most intrusive, and dangerous, form of regulation possible—a ban on truthful information regarding a lawful activity imposed for the purpose of manipulating, through ignorance, the consumer choices of some of its citizens. Unless justified by a truly substantial governmental interest, this extreme and extremely paternalistic, measure, surely cannot withstand scrutiny under the First Amendment."[135]

The direction the Court will take in determining the extent of constitutional protection remains to be seen. Cases such as *Edge* and *Posadas* involve attempts by government to regulate "vicelike" activities like gambling. They may prove to be the exception to a developing trend, typified by the Court's decision in *Discovery Network*, to afford full First Amendment protection for truthful and nondeceptive commercial speech about lawful products and services, absent some overriding governmental interest. Or *Edge* and *Posadas* may be predictors of the Court's continuing denial of full First Amendment protection for commercial speech, except in situations when the subject of the commercial speech is a constitutionally protected product or service like the abortion clinic advertising in *Bigelow*, or when the government has arbitrarily banned truthful and nondeceptive commercial speech without seriously investigating less restrictive means of accomplishing its ends.

The Court's most recent foray into regulation of commercial speech unfortunately could be seen as a continuation of either trend. In *44 Liquormart, Inc., v. Rhode Island*,[136] the Court faced a challenge to Rhode Island's complete ban on the advertisement of retail liquor prices except at the place of sale. Rejecting the state's argument that regulation of commercial speech about alcoholic beverages was granted special dispensation from constitutional protection because of the historic federal regulation of alcohol culminating in Prohibition, the Court found that Rhode Island had not met the heavy burden necessary to completely ban price advertising. However, the justices were widely split as to the rationale for arriving at this decision, ranging from Justice Thomas who apparently would never permit laws banning truthful, legal, and nondeceptive speech enacted solely for the purpose of manipulating consumer choices in the marketplace to Justices O'Connor, Souter, Breyer, and the Chief Justice who apparently believed that Rhode Island's total ban could not survive even a reasonable fit test under the fourth prong of *Central Hudson*.

Whether the Court will choose to go down the path of increasing protection of pure commercial speech or alternatively will follow a course of permitting regulation unless the Court finds the government's efforts to be too extreme even in terms of the First Amendment's limited protection of commercial speech (such as complete prohibition of content or means of distribution) is an open question.

Justices agreeing with opinions sympathetic to governmental attempts to regulate pure commercial speech, as well as justices antagonistic to such efforts, have recently retired from the Court, and their replacements have yet to stake out clear positions on these issues. Although it seems clear that the Court will continue to permit regulation of pure commercial speech to a degree deemed unacceptable for more fully protected speech, determining the kinds of acceptable regulations and the circumstances in which they will be permitted will have to wait for a later day.

CONCLUSION: WHAT'S SO DIFFERENT ABOUT COMMERCIAL SPEECH?

As we have seen, at times the Supreme Court of the United States has appeared to sympathize with those who wish to regulate commercial speech, at other times with those who desire it to be protected from such regulation. As this chapter concludes, perhaps we need to address a basic question. What is there about this kind of speech that has produced this ambivalence?

Legal commentators Alex Kozinski and Stuart Banner[137] offer some interesting answers. The first is that pure commercial speech is not pure (i.e., it is motivated by monetary desire). Whether it is advertisers, advertising agencies, other corporate speakers, or the media that carry the commercial messages, all have a profit-making motive for speaking. A second reason is the content of the speech. Much commercial speech is admittedly hyperbolic in nature, designed to influence and persuade the target market by appealing to psychological variables, rather than providing straightforward information about the attributes of a product or service. These two reasons lead many critics of such speech to the conclusion that such speech is valueless, and therefore not deserving of First Amendment protection.

Professors Ronald Collins and David Skover,[138] for example, suggest that the statement that pure commercial speech contains no value is an objective statement of fact. As Kosinski and Banner pointed out, these critics of commercial speech make arguments like, "people may think they prefer TV commercials to [the Greek tragedy] *The Iliad*, but if they think harder they'll realize their original preference was wrong."[139]

Additionally, critics of commercial speech may argue that commercial speech is less deserving of First Amendment protection than other forms of speech because of characteristics inherent in the speech itself. For example, in *Virginia State Board of Pharmacy*, the Supreme Court of the United States cited "common sense" differences between commercial and noncommercial speech as reasons for different levels of First Amendment protection. The Court noted that commercial speech is "verifiable," and therefore held to a higher standard than other forms of speech. Additionally, the Court found that commercial speech is a "more durable" type of speech because the speech is profit motivated, and not as easily chilled by regulations as other forms of speech. In theory, each of these rationales for commercial speech regulation could be subject to verification. Even if true, it does not necessarily follow that they require a lesser degree of First Amendment protection. However, courts have almost universally accepted these rationales without question because they have made the judgment that commercial speech should be a form of lesser protected speech.

As Kozinski and Banner pointed out, however, there is no obvious inherent distinction between commercial and noncommercial speech in the wording of the First Amendment. In fact, the term *commercial speech* was not employed by the Court until the *Pittsburgh Press* case in 1973. The two commentators speculated that the reasons courts used the terms *advertising* and *soliciting* prior to this case are significant. "In *Valentine* [the first major case], . . . the Court wasn't facing a case about commercial speech; it was facing a case about advertising [a kind of business]."[140] They concluded that, "In 1942 . . . [*Valentine*] was easy not because the Court thought of commercial speech as a category of speech deserving no protection, but because the Court didn't treat the case as involving speech at all."[141]

Because courts have given their consent to the possibility of greater regulation of pure commercial speech than other kinds of expression does not mean that either regulators or legislators need to or should pass such regulations and laws. Unfortunately for commercial speech advocates, they often have strong political motivation for doing so. Pure commercial speech may be the means by which consumers learn about the products and services they want and need, but most are ambivalent about the value of this speech, especially as compared with speech about important public issues. There are many activists in political, environmental, or social organizations who go beyond mere ambivalence to argue that commercial speech is, at best, inconsequential and, at worst, evil in the sense that it promotes unwanted behavior, products, or services harmful to the individual or environment. Not uncommonly, those who are active in promoting such causes believe strongly in them to the degree that, to quote Justice Holmes, they fall into the category of those who see regulation of "expression of opinions . . . [as] perfectly logical. If you have no doubt of your premises or your power and want a certain result with all your heart you naturally express your wishes in law and sweep away all opposition."[142] With the bulk of the voting public indifferent, and with only groups of economically self-interested advertisers and media to represent the other side, legislators and regulators often can be persuaded that regulating or banning commercial speech is a cheap, politically expedient, and easy way to tackle social ills.

3

Public Interest Information as Commercial Speech

Chapter 2 traced the somewhat erratic course the Supreme Court of the United States has followed to create and implement those tests that speakers, government regulators, and lower courts should employ to gauge the degree of constitutional protection afforded "pure" commercial speech. While protecting noncommercial speech about public issues from regulation in all but truly unusual situations, the Court has often treated pure commercial speech as a First Amendment second-class citizen. In most circumstances, the Court has disallowed regulation (a) only when the governmental interest asserted as the basis for regulation is insubstantial, or (b) there are other means less restrictive of speech that reasonably enable the government to achieve its ends.

In so doing, however, the Court has held unequivocally that the mere fact that speakers have paid for the space or time to publish their speech does not automatically define such speech as commercial speech for First Amendment purposes. This differentiation between paid-for speech and true commercial speech has created a series of commercial speech-related issues that are the focus of this chapter. These are: (a) What degree of constitutional protection should be accorded paid-for speech that deals with matters of general public interest? (b) How should courts define paid-for speech that contains a mixture of commercial and noncommercial messages, or that may be commercial speech in disguise? (c) Are there categories of commercial speech that merit more or less constitutional protection than other kinds of commercial speech? (d) How does the second-class status of commercial speech interact with other legal concepts like defamation or privacy? (e) Are there special problems when the commercial speech involves political advertisements?

Although the answers to these commercial speech-related questions obviously are significant to those in advertising, they are equally, if not more, important to public relations practitioners, particularly because the Court has never dealt specifically with the constitutional status or definition of public relations speech. Public relations professionals should remember that many First Amendment-based protections of speech are premised on the rationale that the speech in question deserves protection because it is speech about important public issues. Although the public relations speech of most for-profit corporations is important to the speaker, it is by no means clear that courts and legislators will also treat such speech as important to the general public, and therefore beyond the scope of laws and regulations that limit or in other ways regulate advertising and other commercial speech.

PAID-FOR SPEECH ABOUT MATTERS OF PUBLIC INTEREST BY NOT-FOR-PROFIT ORGANIZATIONS

In *Valentine v. Chrestensen*,[1] the Court's initial foray into determining the constitutional limits on the regulation of commercial speech, the Court made no attempt to define the terms it used in determining New York City's legal right to ban handbills advertising tours of Chrestensen's submarine. Chrestensen's disputed handbills did not contain any mention of an admission fee, but city authorities and the Court treated them as "commercial and business advertising matter"[2] forbidden by a municipal ordinance. The Court said that, although citizens may use city streets to disseminate opinion, "We are equally clear that the Constitution imposes no such restraint on government as respects purely commercial advertising."[3]

In noting that New York City officials would have much less latitude in regulating the distribution of handbills that only contained information or opinion, and that Chrestensen could not avoid regulation simply by adding a discussion of public issues if his speech remained basically commercial in nature, the Court's opinion foreshadowed two issues that continue to haunt commercial speech cases: (a) the constitutional status of speech that takes the form of commercial speech, but is not related to commercial activity; and (b) the differences, if any, in the protection of that speech, depending on the nature of the speaker.

Nearly 2 decades passed before the Court again made a major pronouncement about the constitutionality of governmental regulations of commercial speech. It did so in its discussion of a variety of issues in *New York Times v. Sullivan*,[4] a 1964 case that made a major impact on libel law and the civil rights movement. In *Sullivan*, the Court carved out an important exception for what today are often called "advertorials," as well as for other forms of paid-for speech used by not-for-profit organizations to discuss matters of public interest.

The backdrop of the case was the desegregation efforts led by Dr. Martin Luther King, Jr., in southern states in the late 1950s and 1960s. On March 29, 1960, *The New York Times* carried a full-page advertisement entitled "Heed Their Rising Voices" that detailed what the advertisement called "the wave of terror" directed against the civil rights activities of King and other activists. Included as examples were charges that students at Alabama State College in Montgomery had been harassed by police and other state authorities, and that Dr. King had been threatened and arrested on trumped-up charges. The advertising copy, signed by 64 prominent Americans, included a request for funds to help carry on the work of King and his followers.

The plaintiff in the libel suit was L. B. Sullivan, a Montgomery city commissioner whose duties included supervising the police department. Claiming that the statements in the advertisement about police misconduct libeled him, Sullivan brought suit against a number of African-American clergymen who had purchased the advertisement and against *The New York Times* for publishing it. An Alabama jury eventually awarded Sullivan $500,000—a verdict that eventually was appealed all the way to the Supreme Court of the United States.

All parties and the Court recognized that the fact the alleged libelous statements appeared in an advertisement was an important factor in the case. The newspaper received $4,800 for running the advertisement that had been purchased by a New York advertising agency. The manager of the department that determined acceptability of advertising material for the *Times* conceded that his department had made no effort to check the information in the advertisement against news stories carried in the newspaper, or in other ways verify the statements contained in the advertisement, arguing that the purchasers of the space were reputable and that he had no reason to doubt their representations of the events that had occurred in Montgomery.

Relying on the wording of the Court's opinion in *Valentine*, Sullivan's attorney argued that the Court lacked jurisdiction to hear the newspaper's appeal because there were no First Amendment issues present in the case. This argument was advanced on the premise that *Valentine* had determined that commercial advertisements had no special constitutional protection, and that the speech in question was admittedly in the form of a full-page advertisement.

The Court disagreed. Those relying on *Valentine*, said the Court, for the proposition that "the constitutional guarantees of freedom of speech and of the press are inapplicable here . . . because the allegedly libelous statements were published as part of a paid, 'commercial' advertisement"[5] were guilty of misinterpreting the Court's intent. According to the Court, the crucial distinction was that its earlier holding was based on the conclusion that, unlike the speech in the Sullivan case, the speech in *Valentine* was "purely commercial advertising."

The Court said in *Sullivan*, "The publication . . . was not a 'commercial' advertisement in the sense in which the word was used in [*Valentine*]. It communicated information, expressed opinion, recited grievances, protested claimed abuses, and sought financial support on behalf of a movement whose existence and objectives are matters of the highest public interest and concern."[6]

Saying that failure to provide First Amendment protection would discourage others from buying or running what the opinion called "editorial advertisements,"[7] the Court noted that this result "might shut off an important outlet for the promulgation of information and ideas by persons who do not themselves have access to publishing facilities—who wish to exercise their freedom of speech even though they are not members of the press."[8] The Court concluded that, "To avoid placing such a handicap upon the freedoms of expression, we hold that if the allegedly libelous statements would otherwise be constitutionally protected from the present judgment, they do not forfeit that protection because they were published in the form of a paid advertisement."[9]

Definitional problems may occur whenever courts make distinctions in levels of protection for either classes of speakers or speech itself. Such problems occasionally have surfaced involving organizations fraudulently claiming to be not-for-profit or charitable in nature. However, since *Sullivan*, there has been no serious challenge to its holding that generally protects "commercial" speech on matters of public interest by truly not-for-profit organizations, except in unusual circumstances.

PAID-FOR SPEECH ABOUT MATTERS OF PUBLIC INTEREST BY FOR-PROFIT ORGANIZATIONS

Roughly a decade after *New York Times v. Sullivan*, the Court returned to the subject of paid-for speech used to addresses public issues in *First National Bank of Boston v. Bellotti*.[10] This time, however, it was in the context of a case involving the government's efforts to regulate such speech by a *for*-profit corporation.

At issue was an attempt by the state of Massachusetts to enforce its statute limiting corporate expenditures "for the purpose of influencing the vote on referendum proposals. . . ."[11] The statute prohibited banks, telephone companies, public utilities, and most business corporations and their officers from spending money "for the purpose of . . . influencing or affecting the vote on any question submitted to the voters, other than one materially affecting any of the property, business or assets of the corporation."[12] Another provision of the statute specified that no questions "submitted to the voters solely concerning the taxation of the income, property or transactions of individuals shall be deemed materially to affect the property, business, or assets of the corporation."[13]

First National Bank and other corporations challenged the statute as violating free speech after a state constitutional amendment was proposed authorizing the state to institute a graduated personal income tax. The corporations desired to purchase advertising space and time to express their opposition to such a tax, but were informed by the state's attorney general, Francis X. Bellotti, that he would enforce the state's statutory prohibitions against such advertisements if the corporations persisted in their efforts to state their views via media advertising.

Because the penalties provided in the statute were severe (a fine of up to $50,000 for a corporation and/or a fine of up to $10,000 or imprisonment of up to 1 year or both for an officer or director of the corporation), First National Bank and its corporate allies sought a declaratory judgment to test the statute's constitutionality.

The state's highest court held the statute to be a valid limitation on the speech interests of the plaintiffs, finding that the First Amendment rights of a corporation could constitutionally be "limited to issues that materially affect its business, property or assets."[14] It characterized the issue as whether a corporation's First Amendment rights were coextensive with those of individuals, and found as a matter of law that they were not. The state court noted that the statute forbid neither speeches on the topic by corporate executives nor statements to the press, internal newsletters, bulletins to stockholders, or other typical corporate public relations activities as long as they did not involve contributions or "expenditure of corporate funds."[15]

On appeal, the Supreme Court of the United States made short work of the state's arguments. Refusing to frame the issue as the nature and extent of corporate First Amendment rights, the Court instead said, "The proper question ... is not whether corporations 'have' First Amendment rights and, if so, whether they are co-extensive with those of natural persons. Instead, the question must be whether [the statute] abridges expression that the First Amendment was meant to protect. We hold that it does."[16]

The Court rejected arguments that allowing for-profit corporations to spend corporate assets to campaign against such referenda or to speak out on public issues would overwhelm the marketplace of ideas by drowning out other voices. There was no evidence of such a threat, said the Court, and there were other less drastic measures a state might take to alert its citizens about potential abuses of the marketplace of ideas such as requiring advertisements placed by corporations to carry information identifying the source of the commercial speech. In short, said the Court, when a for-profit corporation wishes to use advertising or other forms of paid-for speech to discuss matters of general public interest not connected with its commercial activities, such speech should receive the same degree of constitutional protection as speech from other sources.

Four years after *Bellotti*, the Court, in *Consolidated Edison Co. of New York, Inc., v. Public Service Commission of New York*,[17] reversed a lower court decision that had upheld a commission policy banning discussion of public issues by the utility company in brochures and flyers included with monthly customer billings. The commission's policy was based on the nature of the utility as a state-regulated monopoly and the alleged privacy interests of ratepayers (characterized as a "captive audience"[18]) who would not want to receive such information and commentary.

The Court disagreed. Citing *Bellotti*, Justice Powell reiterated that, "the inherent worth of the speech in terms of its capacity for informing the public does not depend on the identity of its source."[19] Despite what Justice Blackmun in dissent called a "free ride"[20] for the utility's propaganda at ratepayer expense, the majority held that such a total ban "strikes at the heart of the freedom to speak."[21] Amplifying its dislike of government arguments for differing levels of protection for speech based on the nature of the speaker, first articulated in *Bellotti*, the Court noted that, "the First Amendment's hostility to content-based regulation [dependent on the speaker] extends not only to restrictions on particular viewpoints, but also to prohibition of public discussion of an entire topic."[22] The Court also dismissed the public service commission's arguments involving the privacy interests of ratepayers, noting that any harm could be avoided "simply by transferring the bill from envelope to waste basket."[23]

The general euphoria that free speech champions derived from the holdings in *Bellotti* and *Consolidated Edison* was dampened, however, by the opinion of the Court in *Austin v. Michigan Chamber of Commerce*,[24] a 1990 decision that appears to shine a caution light on the Court's willingness to require the government to surmount a rigorous First Amendment challenge to governmental regulations in such cases. In *Austin*, the Court upheld governmental restrictions on a corporation's political speech for reasons similar to those struck down in *Bellotti* because, said the Court, the government had satisfied the Court's definition of a compelling governmental interest.

Section 54(1) of the Michigan Campaign Act expressly prohibits corporations from contributing directly "to the nomination or election of a candidate."[25] The act defines such contributions as "a payment, donation, loan, pledge, or promise of payment of money or anything of ascertainable monetary value ...,"[26] although it allows corporations to spend money for such purposes if the money is kept segregated in a separate fund.

The Michigan Chamber of Commerce is a corporation established to encourage economic development and improve the state's business climate. Although not normally engaged in direct political support of candidates, the Chamber desired to buy advertising space in a local newspaper to support a candidate in a special election to fill a vacancy in the state legislature. The Chamber considered its candidate to be more probusiness than his opponent. Fearing that the campaign act would prohibit such activity, the Chamber sought a declaratory judgment in federal district court that would strike down the statute on First Amendment grounds.

Although the district court upheld the act as a legitimate limitation on corporate activity (the state statute was modeled, in part, on a similar federal statute), on appeal, the Sixth U.S. Circuit Court of Appeals ruled that the Michigan campaign finance act could not, for First Amendment reasons, apply to the Chamber because it was not a traditional corporation, and was formed expressly to spread economic and political messages. The federal appeals court also found no compelling interest that would justify infringing the speech interests of the Chamber. On appeal, the Supreme Court of the United States disagreed.

Although it was appropriate for the court of appeals to apply the compelling state interest test to this case, said the majority, the lower court had erred in not recognizing that the state had met this requirement. The Court held that Michigan obviously was concerned with "the corrosive and distorting effects of immense aggregations of wealth that [were] accumulated with the help of the corporate form and that have little or no correlation to the public's support for the corporation's political ideas."[27]

The Court conceded that the desire to support candidates for public office via advertising is speech that "constitute(s) 'political expression at the core of our electoral process and of the First Amendment freedoms,' " and that "The mere fact that the Chamber is a corporation does not remove its speech from the ambit of the First Amendment."[28]

However, said the Court, "the unique state-conferred corporate structure that facilitates the amassing of large treasuries warrants the limit in independent expenditures. Corporate wealth," continued the Court, "can unfairly influence elections when it is deployed in the form of independent expenditures. . . . We therefore hold that the State has articulated a sufficiently compelling rationale to support its restriction on independent expenditures. . . ."[29]

The Court also rejected the argument that the Chamber was a not-for-profit corporation, and therefore not subject to the statute. Citing earlier cases as precedent, the Court noted that the Chamber failed to meet the three criteria distinguishing not-for-profit corporations in terms of the campaign expenditure statute. "The first characteristic," said the Court, "[is] that the organization '[is] formed for the express purpose of promoting political ideas and cannot engage in business activities.' [T]he second feature [is] the absence of 'shareholders or other persons affiliated so as to have a claim on its assets or earnings.' The final characteristic [is] the organization's independence from the influence of business corporations."[30] The Court concluded that, "the Chamber does not possess the features that would compel the State to exempt it from restriction on independent political expenditures."[31]

In dissent, Justice Kennedy noted that in a situation involving the regulation of advertising constituting "a paradigm of political speech,"[32] the Court clearly "adopts a rule that allows Michigan to stifle the voices of some of the most respected groups in public life on subjects central to the integrity of our democratic system. . . ."[33] Those who thought that the First Amendment exists to protect all points of view in candidate elections will be disillusioned by the Court's opinion today because that protection is given only to a preferred class of nonprofit corporate speakers: small, single-issue nonprofit corporations that pass the Court's own vague test for determining who are the favored participants in the electoral process.[34] Justice Kennedy characterized the majority as demonstrating "hostility to the corporate form used by the speaker in this case,"[35] concluding that Michigan's "wholesale ban on corporate political speech"[36] could not be squared with the First Amendment.

The holding in *Austin* casts a pall over the continuing viability of what appeared to be almost absolute First Amendment protection recognized by the Court in *Bellotti*. Nonetheless, it seems safe to say that paid-for speech by not-for-profit organizations and paid-for speech by for-profit corporations—at least where there exists no close nexus between the speech and the for-profit corporation's commercial activities—will be free from regulation if that speech discusses matters of general public interest and there is not a governmental interest of great importance.

Admittedly, corporate and other organizational paid-for speech on matters of public interest usually is of little concern to most advertising professionals who make their fortunes promoting the goods and services a corporation sells for profit. For public relations professionals, however, the continuing viability of full First Amendment protection for such speech is particularly important because it provides protection for an important weapon in the arsenal of public relations techniques for communicating organizational messages to important publics.

PAID-FOR SPEECH ABOUT MATTERS
OF ECONOMIC INTEREST TO NOT-FOR-PROFIT
AND FOR-PROFIT ORGANIZATIONS:
IS IT COMMERCIAL OR NONCOMMERCIAL SPEECH?

It seems clear that, in most instances, the Court will treat speech by both not-for-profit and profit-making organizations as deserving of full First Amendment protection when that speech addresses important matters of public policy unrelated to the economic interests of the organizations. This includes speech appearing in time or space purchased by organizations to disseminate their views. It is by no means as clear, however, how the Court, lower courts, or federal or state regulatory agencies will (or should) treat speech that, although not directly urging the purchase of goods or services, is nonetheless arguably commercial in nature, and also more or less closely related to the speaker's economic interests.

This issue is particularly important to advertising and public relations professionals because those who advocate limitations on the speech of for-profit corporations may continue to press for greater regulation of such corporate speech on public policy grounds. If a corporation's speech is classified as commercial speech, there are a variety of legally acceptable means for regulating such speech that would be impermissible if the speech were fully protected under the First Amendment.

As discussed in chapter 1, prior restraint in the form of bans or limitations is the least preferred remedy that courts and regulators may employ. However, there are other remedies, arguably less restrictive of speech, that have found favor with the Court and lower courts. In *Central Hudson*, Justice Powell, while decrying the complete ban on the utility company's advertising, suggested that other regulations on the "format and content"[37] of the advertisements might be acceptable. For instance, citing *Banzhaf v. FCC*,[38] Justice Powell noted that requiring the advertising to include "information about the relative efficiency and expense of offered service, both under current conditions and for the foreseeable future"[39] would be preferable to the remedy sought by the state's public service commission.

As calls for regulation of corporate paid-for speech have increased over the past two decades, critics of such speech have also suggested such measures as limiting appeals to racial or ethnic groups (tobacco and liquor advertising), requiring commercial speakers to include additional information representing other points of view (such as warning labels), and restricting the design or graphic components of commercial speech presentations by banning cartoon characters or pictures of users of the product or service (so-called "tombstone ads"). Alternatively, regulation of paid-for speech might take the form of requirements, like those of the FTC, that the speaker bear the burden of demonstrating that the speech, if challenged, is neither false nor illegal nor deceptive. Additionally, such regulatory bodies have legally required speakers to back up factual claims with scientific data or results of rigorously conducted public opinion polls.

If speech designated as commercial speech continues to be accorded only second-class constitutional protection by the Supreme Court of the United States, it seems essential for the Court to draw a "bright line" that unambiguously provides a clear demarcation between speech defined as commercial and noncommercial (or, perhaps more to the point, speech that is fully protected and speech that is not). Despite numerous opportunities, the Court has failed to do so. What is worse, the Court appears to waiver in its handling of definitional issues related to commercial speech, depending on the nature and the facts of the case it is deciding.

For example, what is the First Amendment status of a cigarette company advertisement questioning the validity of antismoking research claims, a press release by an automobile manufacturer touting the virtues of its new models, a magazine or brochure containing some information of general interest but obviously intended to promote the publisher's instructional programs, or a brewing company that prominently affixes its logo design on the side of a NASCAR racer? All of these examples are taken from real-life cases (some of which are discussed later), producing results that are confusing and often appear to be in direct conflict with each other.

The Court's failure to clearly define commercial speech has left regulators and lower courts to wrestle with definitional issues as best they can. Not surprisingly, the results have been mixed at best, with decisions and policies that are ambiguous and at times contradictory, and with many issues yet to be satisfactorily resolved.

It is difficult (and perhaps overly simplistic) to attempt to categorize the many changing and, at times, overlapping opinions and discussions by the members of the Court who have wrestled with the problem of whether speech the government wants to regulate should be defined as commercial speech. Nonetheless, an analysis of the Court's cases in which this question has been raised leads to the conclusion that the Court generally follows one of two distinct definitions that have emerged for determining if speech is within the ambit of the commercial speech exception to the First Amendment.

The formulation of commercial speech preferred by partisans of unrestricted speech is the narrow definition mentioned in the Court's first modern-day "purely commercial speech" case—*Pittsburgh Press*.[40] Reacting to the split in rationales and outcomes in the *Valentine* and *Sullivan* decisions, the Court attempted to position the gender-based, help wanted ads at issue in *Pittsburgh Press* as more like those prohibited in *Valentine*. Characterizing the ads as "classic examples of commercial speech,"[41] the Court noted that the "critical feature" of the speech in question was that it "did no more than propose a commercial transaction."[42] The Court subsequently picked up this language in its decision in *Virginia State Board of Pharmacy*[43]—the case that stands as the high-water mark in the Court's meandering course toward ultimately establishing the level of First Amendment protection afforded commercial speech.

Before defining *commercial speech*, however, the Court in *Virginia State Board of Pharmacy* attempted to distinguish some examples of speech it did not consider to be commercial speech. According to Justice Blackmun, writing for the majority, it would be improper to characterize all speech that is published in paid-for space or time as commercial speech, citing the civil rights-related advertisement in *Sullivan*. Neither, said the Court, is speech automatically classified as commercial just because it appears in a medium that has a profit-making motive, citing cases involving bookstores and movies.

Also, the Court noted that speech soliciting financial contributions is not automatically commercial in nature even if paid for, again citing *Sullivan*. Finally, neither speech about subjects related to commerce, such as arguments for or against free trade, nor paid-for speech that simply communicates facts automatically makes the speech commercial speech. The Court cited, among others, the abortion clinic advertisements in *Bigelow*[44] as an example.

Having discussed examples of what it did *not* consider commercial speech, the Court characterized the issue in *Virginia State Board of Pharmacy* as "whether speech which does 'no more than propose a commercial transaction' [citing *Pittsburgh Press*] . . . is so removed from any 'exposition of ideas' . . . and from 'truth, science, morality, and arts in general, in the diffusion of liberal sentiments on the administration of Government' . . . that it lacks all protection."[45] As discussed in chapter 2, the Court then answered this question by holding it did not.

A number of justices (e.g., Stevens and Blackmun) hostile to regulating commercial speech have consistently used the narrow "commercial transaction" definition in subsequent opinions. Employing this definition, the Court in *SUNY*[46] (discussed in chap. 2) noted that, although speech involved in soliciting sales of Tupperware in college dormitories was commercial speech, it would be overly broad to encompass all "paid" speech within the definition of *commercial speech*. Expanding the definition beyond speech that "does no more than propose a commercial transaction,"[47] said the Court, would impermissibly define *commercial speech* as occurring in situations such as when payment is made for services like tutoring students, providing counseling sessions, and offering advice on medical or legal matters.

Similarly, in *Discovery Network, Inc.*,[48] Justice Stevens, writing for the Court, in part rejected the city's contention that it could regulate the placement and number of newsracks on city streets because of the difficulty in determining the differences between regular newspapers that are sold for profit and contain commercial messages and the commercial publications the city sought to control. Although not the deciding factor in the case, it is clear that at least some members of the majority in *Discovery Network, Inc.* rejected the city's reliance on language that first surfaced in *Bates*[49]—and was used again by the Court in the cases of *Friedman v. Rogers*[50] and *Central Hudson*[51]—that the correct method for determining if the speech in question is commercial speech is to evaluate the "economic motivation" for the speech, rather than requiring the speech to contain elements of actual commercial transactions.

This alternative definition, "economic motivation" rather than "speech proposing a commercial transaction," however, has found favor with a number of justices. For example, in *Dun & Bradstreet, Inc. v. Greenmoss Builders, Inc.*,[52] a credit reporting agency being sued for defamation argued it should receive First Amendment protection for its alleged defamatory statements (other constitutional issues involved in defamation commercial speech cases are discussed elsewhere in this chapter). The Court held that such reliance was improper, in part because the credit report that falsely accused the plaintiff of bankruptcy was like commercial speech in that it was "solely motivated by the desire for profit, which, we have noted is a force less likely to be deterred than others."[53] The dissent vigorously challenged this formulation, arguing that *economic motivation* was too broad a term, and that the "do no more than propose a commercial transaction"[54] language of *Pittsburgh Press* should be employed when defining commercial speech.

Perhaps the most notable use of the "economic motivation language," however, appears in the majority decision in *Bolger v. Youngs Drug Products Corp.*,[55] a case in which the classification of the speech in question was one of the key issues confronting the Court. In *Bolger*, the Court followed the lead of Justice Powell's majority opinion in *Central Hudson*. In that case, the majority held that promotional advertising by the electric utility corporation was commercial speech, defined as "expression related solely to the economic interests of the speaker and its audience."[56]

In *Central Hudson*, Justice Powell expressly rejected the contentions of Justice Stevens, who filed an opinion concurring in the judgment that the Court's use of "economic interests" as the basis for defining commercial speech would sweep more speech than was constitutionally permissible under the commercial speech umbrella. Judging the utility company's speech to *not* be commercial speech "would grant broad constitutional protection to any advertising that links a product to a current public debate. But many, if not most, products may be tied to public concerns. . . ."[57] Justice Powell, noting that in *Consolidated Edison* the Court provided utility companies with constitutional protection for their discussions of public issues, concluded, "There is no reason for providing similar constitutional protection when such statements are made only in the context of commercial transactions."[58]

Bolger involved an alleged violation of a federal postal regulation prohibiting the mailing of "[a]ny unsolicited advertisement of matter . . . designed, adapted, or intended for preventing conception. . . ."[59] Postal officials' interpretation of the statute excluded from this ban any "unsolicited advertisements in which the mailer has no commercial interest."[60] Youngs Drug Products Corp. manufactured a variety of contraceptive devices typically marketed through wholesalers, who in turn would sell the products to pharmacists for eventual sales to the public. To stimulate demand, Youngs employed a number of marketing tactics, including sending unsolicited direct mail publications to the general public. Among these items were a multipage flyer promoting the company's entire inventory of products, circulars devoted only to marketing prophylactics, and what the company characterized as "informational pamphlets" about the virtues of using prophylactics, especially those manufactured by Youngs.

When complaints reached postal authorities from customers concerned about receiving Youngs' direct marketing materials, the postal service warned Youngs that continuing to mail such materials would violate the antimailing statute. Because violating the statute could include both criminal and civil penalties, the company sought relief in the federal courts in the form of a declaratory judgment that threats to apply the statute's provisions would interfere with Youngs' First Amendment rights. The lower court held that all three direct mail publications were examples of commercial speech, but also held that the government's arguments for banning the mailing of the publications were insufficient to withstand a First Amendment challenge based on the *Central Hudson* four-part test.

The Supreme Court of the United States agreed that the government had not been able to satisfy the *Central Hudson* four-part test, but also agreed (over Justice Stevens' objections) that all three types of marketing materials mailed by Youngs were examples of commercial speech. Noting that the Court had long recognized the " 'common-sense' distinction"[61] between commercial and noncommercial speech, and that the Court had also determined that commercial speech was only entitled to limited First Amendment protection compared with fully protected speech, Justice Marshall characterized the Court's first task in *Bolger* as "first determin[ing] the proper classification of the mailings at issue here. Appellee contends that his proposed mailings constitute 'fully protected' speech. . . . Appellants argue . . . that the proposed mailings are all commercial speech."[62] The job of the Court, said Marshall, is to make sure "that speech deserving of greater constitutional protection is not inadvertently suppressed."[63]

The Court found that, although most of the mailings in question "fall within the core notion of commercial speech—'speech which does no more than propose a commercial transaction,' "[64] the company's publications containing general information about the merits of prophylactics posed "a closer question."[65] In attempting to answer this close question, the Court began by observing that just because the publication was admittedly a direct mail advertisement did not automatically classify it as commercial speech [citing *Sullivan*]. Neither did the fact that the publications referred to the products manufactured by Youngs. In addition, the Court noted that economic motivation by itself would normally not be a sufficient determinant of the status of the publication [citing *Bigelow*].

But, the Court continued, "the combination of all these characteristics . . . provides strong support for the . . . conclusion that the informational pamphlets are properly characterized as commercial speech. The mailings constitute commercial speech notwithstanding . . . that they contain discussions of important issues. . . ."[66] The Court added, "We have made clear that advertising which 'links a product to a current public debate' is not thereby entitled to the constitutional protection afforded noncommercial speech. A company has . . . protections available to its direct comments on public issues, so there is no reason for providing similar constitutional protection when such statements are made in the context of commercial [speech]."[67]

In a footnote to his opinion, Justice Marshall pointed out, however, that his three-part analysis was not meant to be a generalized test like the Court's four-prong *Central Hudson* test. The Court, said Marshall, does not "mean to suggest that each of the characteristics present in this case must necessarily be present in order for speech to be commercial. For example, we express no opinion as to whether reference to any particular product or service is a necessary element of commercial speech."[68]

Not surprisingly, lower courts and government agencies trying to interpret and apply the Court's varying definitions of *commercial speech* have produced a decidedly mixed bag of decisions and policy statements. A number of courts have rejected government attempts to regulate speech based on their judgments that the speech in question did not fall within the narrow "commercial transaction" definition of commercial speech. For example, in *In re Pan Am Corp. v. Delta Air Lines, Inc.*,[69] a federal district court rejected a request by a corporation in a bankruptcy proceeding that Standard & Poor, a corporate credit analyzing and reporting agency, produce subpoenaed documents the corporation claimed it needed to establish its claims. The court based its decision, in part, on its characterization of Standard & Poor's analysis as fully protected speech under the First Amendment because the activities of, and information produced by, the agency were more analogous to a journalistic, rather than a business, function. Pan Am argued that Standard & Poor should produce the material requested because the "market driven nature of the speech, and its objectively verifiable content"[70] should have categorized the speech as commercial speech, and therefore "made heightened First Amendment protection unnecessary."[71]

Similarly, in *New York Public Interest Research Group v. Insurance Information Institute*,[72] the court dismissed the plaintiff's complaint on the basis that the speech in question was not commercial, and therefore was fully protected. The plaintiff had filed suit under New York general business laws governing false and deceptive advertising, claiming that ads—paid for by an organization representing insurance companies that alleged a crisis in health care was being exacerbated by excessive malpractice lawsuits against physicians (insured by the insurance companies sponsoring the advertising)—were misleading. In rejecting the suit, the court noted, "The dividing line is . . . clear. If, within a common sense reading, an advertisement is obviously intended to promote sales, it is commercial speech. If a public message or discussion is incorporated, it is still commercial speech. If, however, the advertisement is a direct comment on a public issue, unrelated to proposing any particular commercial transaction, it is protected."[73]

In *New York City v. American School Publications*,[74] a New York court[75] rejected claims that the defendant's magazine was commercial speech, despite arguments by the plaintiff that much of the content of and motivation for publishing the magazine were intended to market the defendant's school course offerings. The court based its decision on the rationale that it was the content of the speech, rather than the intent of the speaker, that should rule in a definitional argument. Citing *Pittsburgh Press*, the court noted that the defendant's speech should be fully protected if it "communicates information, expresses opinion, recites grievances, protests claimed abuses or solicits financial support on behalf of a movement whose existence and objective are matters of public concern. . . ."[76]

Other courts have upheld government regulations based on a more expansive definition of commercial speech. In a decision that would appear to be a direct contradiction to the opinion in *American School*, a federal appeals court in Georgia, in *In re Domestic Air Transportation Antitrust Litigation*,[77] upheld an order issued in an antitrust dispute that required an airline's inflight magazine to carry notice of the antitrust suit against the airlines, reasoning that the publication was designed to further the company's economic interests, although most of the publication carried articles of general interest and there was little content that actually promoted the company. In *Abramson v. Gonzalez*,[78] the court recognized a definition of commercial speech broad enough to sanction a governmental regulation disallowing the use of the term *psychologist* by those lacking sufficient professional credentials, noting that the regulation was permissible because the speech related "solely to the economic interests of the speaker."[79]

In a 1977 case that helped starkly frame the continuing disagreement over the proper definition of *commercial speech*, a federal appeals court (in *National Commission on Egg Nutrition v. FTC*)[80] held that an advertisement claiming "there is no scientific evidence that eating eggs increases the risk of . . . heart disease"[81] fit within the definition of commercial speech, and thus was subject to government regulations involving potentially false or misleading advertising claims. According to the court, despite the language of the U.S. Supreme Court in *Pittsburgh Press* and *Virginia State Board of Pharmacy*, the definition of commercial speech "was not intended to be narrowly limited to the mere proposal of a commercial transaction but extend[s] to false claims as to the harmlessness of the advertiser's product asserted for the purpose of persuading members of the reading public to buy the product."[82] The case was not accepted for review by the Supreme Court of the United States.

The example that most clearly demonstrates the contrasting rationales for defining commercial speech, however, was not a fully adjudicated court case. R. J. Reynolds Tobacco Company, a major cigarette manufacturer, ran a series of advertisements reporting on the results of a federally funded study of health risk factors called "MR FIT." According to the tobacco company, the results of the study, which tracked long-term health records of a large sample of regular citizens, demonstrated that there was no evidence of the high correlation between smoking and various diseases claimed by antismoking forces. As the advertisement said, "We at R. J. Reynolds do not claim this study proves that smoking doesn't cause heart disease ... [only] ... that the controversy over smoking and health remains an open one."[83]

Although the advertising copy contained no mention of a specific brand or any hint of a sales pitch, the FTC claimed jurisdiction over the advertisements on the basis that their real purpose was to induce people to continue smoking cigarettes, and therefore constituted commercial speech that was false or misleading. However, an administrative law judge threw out the complaint, holding that the advertisements[84] were not commercial speech, but editorial statements published as advertisements. In rejecting the FTC's position, the judge found that deciding in favor of the FTC would make it virtually impossible for "any business firm ... [to] ever be able to publish an opinion in a newspaper or magazine ad on a controversial public issue which concerns one of its products without losing the full protection of the First Amendment and subjecting the firm and the ad to the Commission's jurisdiction."[85]

The FTC then overruled the administrative law judge (FTC procedures are discussed more fully in a later chapter) on the basis that he had mishandled the classification of the advertisements as noncommercial speech.[86] Acknowledging that the FTC would lack jurisdiction to regulate the advertising if the speech were not commercial speech, the FTC concluded that the U.S. Supreme Court had not set forth a definitive test of that term. Therefore, said the FTC, it would be necessary in each individual case to evaluate the factors to be considered (as found in the decisions by the Court and lower courts) in relation to the facts of the case.

According to the FTC, among the factors to be considered were whether: (a) the speech was published in paid-for time or space, (b) there was an economic motivation behind the speech, (c) the speech was designed to market or promote a product or service, and (d) the copy mentioned a particular product or service. Applying this formulation of the attributes of commercial speech to the advertisements by R. J. Reynolds, the agency concluded that the administrative law judge's decision was too hasty in that it failed to sufficiently take these factors into account. "A message that addresses health concerns that may be faced by purchasers or potential purchasers of the speaker's product," said the FTC, "may constitute commercial speech."[87] At this point, R. J. Reynolds decided to throw in the towel, and signed a consent decree that did not admit any violation, but contained an agreement not to misrepresent the data from the "MR FIT" study in future advertising.

From an advertising or public relations point of view, if the Court continues to hold that commercial speech is entitled to only limited First Amendment protection, the narrow definition of commercial speech as speech that "does no more than propose a commercial transaction" is by far preferable. Unfortunately, the continuing viability of this formulation of the term as the definition employed by courts, legislatures, and regulatory agencies is suspect.

The reasons for pessimism are simple: The Court's "commercial transaction" language has proven both unclear and inadequate. Perhaps this is because the Court, beginning in *Pittsburgh Press*, meant to use the term only as a "classic example" or as "the core meaning" of commercial speech, rather than as the final comprehensive definition. It also is unfortunately true (at least from the point of view of clarity and consistency in the law) that even those on the Court who defend this definition have not uniformly employed the "commercial transaction" definition in subsequent commercial speech cases.

The strongest reason for concern, however, is that the "commercial transaction" language just does not work. For example, it is simply too much to believe that (a) marketing press releases announcing and touting the virtues of a company's new product, (b) direct mail pieces that are "instructional" in nature but clearly require the purchase of a product for the instruction to be effective, (c) billboards depicting only a red bulldog with no other words or images (advertising Red Dog Beer), (d) broadcast advertisements featuring various physical feats of daring followed by the slogan "Just Do It" (a Nike commercial), or (e) letterhead stationery of physicians or attorneys claiming special skills will not be treated by courts and government regulatory agencies alike as commercial speech, despite the absence of any language proposing a commercial transaction. These examples are only a few of the myriad ways that profit-making organizations communicate in furtherance of their economic interests.

Of course, although of academic interest, all this might be moot if no one were motivated to seek regulation of broadly defined corporate speech. Unfortunately for free speech advocates, this is far from the case. Social engineers, governmental regulators, special interest representatives, and a whole host of others who believe that the public needs protecting from its own freely made choices are often dismayed to find that, despite information campaigns and logical arguments to the contrary, some people simply persist in doing what others feel is bad for them. Whether it is smoking cigarettes, not wearing seat belts, or eating high-fat foods, there seem to be the recalcitrant few who will not fall in line with the prevailing winds from Vichy.

Other critics of corporate speech argue that for-profit corporations, particularly if big, are inherently dangerous unless kept in check, and that restrictions on corporate speech are one of the few means of reining them in. Still others represent or claim to represent those—like children and the mentally and physically impaired—characterized as inherently unable to make informed choices about corporate activities.

Some social activists are content to limit their efforts to moral persuasion. Others, recognizing it would be difficult or perhaps impossible to regulate or ban the underlying corporate activity or product (e.g., prohibition), have adopted the tactic of lobbying for governmentally imposed limits on speech by the offending corporation. Such efforts often seem to be a sirenlike call for legislators and regulators who, by passing legislation or creating regulations, can claim credit for attacking important social problems without spending any tax dollars or adding to government bureaucracy.

However, expansive efforts to regulate corporate speech may founder on First Amendment shoals unless that speech falls under the rubric of commercial speech, as noted earlier, a lesser protected speech category. Therefore, those who want to regulate will be doing their level best to say that most or all corporate speech activity should be classified as commercial speech. This clearly includes advertising, but also such marketing "speech activities" as billboards, ballpark signage, race-car sponsorship, and a host of other promotional efforts. It seems inevitable that such efforts to sweep corporate speech into a regulatory framework will include marketing-oriented public relations corporate speech.

The question then becomes: How successful will these efforts be? It seems reasonable to predict that courts and regulators, seeking the defining term for characterizing commercial speech, will be inclined to adopt the more inclusive "economic motive," rather than the alternative "propose a commercial transaction." It is difficult to believe that those seeking to define and regulate such speech will not adopt the definition that those doing the speaking have long recognized and, increasingly, are making a cornerstone of their marketing efforts through increased sales promotions and other similar nonadvertising techniques.

If this prediction becomes a reality, joining all or significant parts of a corporation's public relations functions with advertising, and locating them within the framework of an integrated marketing communications department, becomes more problematic because of the tacit (if not overt) admission by the corporation that, by so doing, its public relations speech is speech made directly for economic motives.

This issue is already a potentially troubling one for those corporate public relations departments that now, within their corporate structure, ultimately report to the marketing side of the corporation. However, most of these can legitimately argue that this is a structural, and not a functional, relationship. Such arguments will be much more difficult to make, however, if function follows form.

Does this mean that all corporate speech will be subject to a commercial speech analysis? Those who want to regulate will certainly try to make that case, but it seems unlikely to be a winning one for speech about public issues as far removed from a corporation's business interests as First National Bank's anti-personal income tax stance. In such situations, *Bellotti* probably is still good law.

The pro-regulation argument will be much more powerful for corporate speech that touches even remotely on the interests of the corporation. The experience of R. J. Reynolds with the FTC may be just the first hint of the potential application of crippling commercial speech regulations and restrictions to corporate speech in all its varying forms—from paid advertising to in-house publications, speeches, or legislative testimony.

It would appear that the safest strategy for advertising and public relations professionals is to plan for a future in which any communication activities by a for-profit company that are reasonably related to the company's products or services (other than the news media or other mass communication companies) will likely be defined as commercial speech. If this proves true, advertising and public relations professionals should be prepared for their commercial communications to meet the *Central Hudson* test if challenged by a state or federal statute, and to survive the scrutiny of the various federal and state agencies regulating their commercial enterprises.

DEFAMATION AND COMMERCIAL SPEECH: CONSTITUTIONAL ISSUES

Although a later chapter contains a more thorough analysis of commercial defamation-related issues, this chapter briefly discusses the constitutional issues involving defamation and commercial speech because no better illustration of the problems caused by the failure of the Court to provide a precise definition of commercial speech exists than in the differences in outcomes that could occur in a lawsuit alleging defamation of character. Whether the defamatory statements are classified as commercial or noncommercial speech could mean the difference between winning or losing a suit potentially involving millions of dollars in damages.

A court action involving a claim of harm to reputation typically arises in response to a false statement of fact about the plaintiff, published or disseminated in other ways to a third party by the defendant, causing harm to reputation. Such cases are examples of state law-based, civil tort suits to permit recovery of monetary damages for harm to persons or personal property (see chap. 8 for a more thorough analysis of commercial defamation-related issues and other communication torts).

Until *Sullivan* in 1964, federal constitutional issues played almost no role in the resolution of such suits. However, in *Sullivan*, the Court was faced with a complex case involving political speech, civil rights, and editorial advertising that the Court felt demanded a First Amendment rule protecting false and defamatory speech directed against public officials in their official capacity. This rule was later extended to public figures in *Curtis Publishing Co. v. Butts*[88] and *A.P. v. Walker,*[89] and eventually to private plaintiffs as well in *Gertz v. Welch.*[90]

Although the levels of constitutional protection differ, the underlying rationale for First Amendment protection of false and defamatory speech is the same: a commitment to encouraging "wide open discussion of public issues"[91] that could be chilled by overly stringent defamation laws. The Court has recognized that different categories of plaintiffs and defendants are entitled to varying degrees of constitutional protection, depending on the extent of their voluntary actions and the degree to which they are in the public spotlight and thereby invite comment and criticism by the public.

Prior to *Sullivan*, state laws generally favored the plaintiff's cause in a defamation suit, holding the defendant to a strict standard for imposing liability. The holdings in *Sullivan* and *Butts* turned the tables almost 180 degrees, making it impossible for the plaintiff to win, at least if the plaintiff is a public person, unless the plaintiff could show *actual malice*—defined as whether the defendant either knew the defamatory statements the defendant made were false or the defendant entertained serious doubts about the truth of the statements before publishing them. *Gertz* extended this logic to private plaintiffs suing media defendants in matters of public interest, although only requiring that private plaintiffs in such situations prove that the defendant acted at least negligently.

Most corporations are extremely concerned about maintaining and protecting their standing and good name within their business or professional communities. Therefore, they not only have reputations to defend, but often are quick to do so. Corporations and other legally recognized organizations also can be guilty of issuing defamatory statements about individuals (e.g., a statement about reasons for employee termination) or other organizations (e.g., statements impugning the motives or activities of a competitor). Therefore, it is not unusual to find defamation suits involving corporations and other organizations as either plaintiffs or defendants. It is in such situations that the two competing First Amendment issues intersect, perhaps violently.

The potential conflict is straightforward. Normally, if the plaintiff in a defamation suit is a public person, the defendant can count on constitutional protection for the speech in question, unless the defendant knew the harmful speech was false or published with reckless disregard for the truth. If the plaintiff in such a suit is private, the defendant knows that the plaintiff will have to prove that the defendant was at least negligent. But what if the defamatory speech is also defined as commercial speech? Courts have decided that false or deceptive commercial speech merits no protection under the First Amendment, and that even truthful, nondeceptive commercial speech is deserving of less protection than other kinds of speech. Should the defendant in a defamation-by-commercial-speech case benefit from the constitutional protections erected by the Court to the same degree as other defendants, or are these First Amendment protections lost because the defamatory speech is commercial and therefore less protected?

The Court has obliquely recognized this conundrum, but has never directly addressed it. In *Bates*, the Court cited *Virginia State Board of Pharmacy* for the proposition that commercial speech should be differentiated from other speech in the context of advertising by attorneys and other professionals. "Since advertising is linked to commercial well being, it seems unlikely that such speech is particularly susceptible to being crushed by overbroad regulation. . . . [P]resumably [the advertiser] can determine more readily than others whether his speech is truthful and protected."[92] Similar sentiments surfaced in a footnote in *Central Hudson*. In *Greenmoss Builders*, the Court was faced with the appeal of a Vermont case involving a false credit report harming the business reputation of a corporation. Although the Court was badly fragmented in its ruling, one of the rationales advanced by some members of the Court for denying First Amendment protection to the defendant's speech was that the speech in question did not address matters of general interest or concern. This was true, said the Court, in part because the credit reports were economically motivated, and therefore less like constitutionally protected commercial speech.

In *U.S. Healthcare Inc. v. Blue Cross of Greater Philadelphia*,[93] the federal court of appeals for the 3rd Circuit directly addressed the "defamation-in-the-context-of-commercial-speech" issue. The case arose out of the entry of U.S. Healthcare into the health insurance market, which had been dominated by the insurance programs provided by Blue Cross. The cornerstone of the new type of insurance plan was the concept of the health maintenance organization (HMO) that provided savings in the costs of medical insurance, but required the participants in such plans to forego the freedom to choose their own health care providers. The HMO programs became so popular that Blue Cross decided to mount an "aggressive and provocative"[94] marketing campaign to convince both potential consumers and former customers that the more traditional insurance plans offered by Blue Cross were preferable.

As part of this campaign, Blue Cross sponsored advertisements in newspapers, broadcast stations, and direct mail circulars touting the benefits of its insurance plans, "in particular, Personal Choice [a Blue Cross preferred provider system] ... at the expense of HMO products."[95] The Blue Cross-sponsored advertisements, which did not mention U.S. Healthcare, consisted of informational comparative advertising claims (e.g., "I don't like those HMO health plans. You get one doctor. No choice of hospitals.")[96] and claims designed to appeal to the emotions (e.g., an obviously saddened woman lamenting that "The hospital my HMO sent me to just wasn't enough. It's my fault.")[97] In a countermove, U.S. Healthcare rolled out its own "responsive advertising campaign" to "counteract the Blue Cross/Blue Shield message."[98] Like the Blue Cross advertisements, the campaign consisted of informational and emotional messages, although, unlike its competition, a number of U.S. Healthcare's advertisements directly challenged Blue Cross and its Personal Choice plan by name.

However, not content to simply duel in the media, U.S. Healthcare also filed a lawsuit charging, among other things, that the Blue Cross-sponsored advertisements had defamed U.S. Healthcare's products and its standing in the community. Blue Cross responded with countersuits alleging similar claims. Trying to sort out the various claims and counterclaims, the jury in the federal district court trial[99] eventually rejected all of the claims by Blue Cross, but was unable to reach agreement on the claims by U.S. Healthcare. Before a new trial could begin, Blue Cross asked the court to rule that the First Amendment required a dismissal of U.S. Healthcare's claims because the plaintiff should be classified as a public person in the eyes of the law, and the issues raised in the advertisements and counteradvertisements were matters of general public interest and concern.

According to Blue Cross, because the Supreme Court of the United States had established that public persons defamed in a matter of public concern must show, by clear and convincing evidence, that the defendant knew the defamatory statements were false or was reckless about the truth of the statements, and because U.S. Healthcare could not meet this constitutionally imposed burden, the trial court should enter a judgment in favor of Blue Cross without the need for another trial. The district court agreed that the constitutional standards did apply, and thus granted the defendant's motion.

The court of appeals divided the advertisements into four categories, two of which, said the court, could give rise to a cause of action for defamation (the other advertisements created other, nondefamation claims). Because the appeals court agreed with the trial court that at least some of the speech in the competing comparative advertisements could be defamatory, it also agreed that determining whether full First Amendment protections applied to the advertisements was essential in determining the outcome of the case. The court disagreed with the lower court, however, that the constitutional protections should apply, holding that the commercial speech in question was not entitled to the "heightened protection under the First Amendment"[100] merited by fully protected speech.

In reviewing the line of Supreme Court of the United States decisions involving defamation beginning with *Sullivan*, the appeals court found that principal factors underlying their balancing of speech versus reputational interests were the status of the plaintiff and the classification of the speech. Focusing on the latter of these two criteria, the appeals court noted that the Supreme Court of the United States had established that commercial speech, although accorded some constitutional protection, nonetheless received "protection somewhat less extensive than that afforded 'noncommercial speech.'"[101] Therefore, noted the court, if the speech in question was truly commercial in nature, the First Amendment protections extended to other kinds of false and defamatory speech need not apply.

This was so, said the court, because allowing states greater latitude in regulating defamatory commercial speech would not inhibit such speech because the speaker, driven by economic considerations, would not be "deterred by proper regulation."[102] The court found that intolerance of false and defamatory statements of fact was justifiably higher in a situation in which commercial speakers were "uniquely qualified to evaluate the truthfulness of their speech"[103] because of their familiarity with the goods and services they provide, as well as the marketplace. On a more theoretical note, the court added that "requir[ing] a parity of constitutional protection for commercial and noncommercial speech alike could invite dilution, simply be a leveling process, of the force of the amendment's guarantee with respect to the latter kind of speech."[104]

The question that remained was whether any of the defamatory speech by either of the two health care insurers should be defined as commercial speech. Taking its definition from *Bolger*, the third circuit answered this question affirmatively, finding that the speech was in commercial form, was economically motivated, and referred to specific products or services. In addition, because of the large financial interests involved on both sides, the court observed that "it would have to be a cold day before these corporations would be chilled from speaking about the comparative merits of their products."[105]

Also, the court noted that a significant number of the advertisements had little or no true informational content, but rather were emotional appeals designed to discourage participation in the competitor's programs.

Finally, the court rejected the arguments advanced by Blue Cross—that its advertisements were part of an ongoing public controversy about health care systems, and therefore deserving of heightened First Amendment protection—quoting *Central Hudson* for the proposition that a corporation would be fully protected in discussing these issues in noncommercial speech, and therefore there was "[little] reason for providing similar constitutional protection when such statements are made only in the context of commercial transactions."[106]

The Supreme Court of the United States refused to accept the case on appeal, making *U.S. Healthcare* the only important decision on the issue of the constitutional protections accorded defamatory commercial speech to date. Although the circuit court's rationale has been criticized (and the issue may still be decided differently by the Court), the decision stands as a warning sign for advertising and public relations practitioners that their speech may not be afforded heightened First Amendment protection when sued for defamation, particularly when that speech involves criticism of the commercial products or practices of the competition.

Although there are no major cases raising similar constitutional issues involving other communication-related torts, like invasion of privacy or intentional infliction of emotional distress, there is no reason on the face of it to assume that courts would accord heightened First Amendment protection for commercial speech in cases raising such claims.

CONSTITUTIONAL PROTECTIONS OF CONTROVERSIAL COMMERCIAL SPEECH: THE "VIRTUE"/"VICE" DISTINCTION

Although the Supreme Court of the United States has never explicitly based a decision on these grounds, a number of commentators have noted that the Court seems to have created exemptions to the tests for government regulations involving otherwise normally protected commercial speech if that speech either involves constitutionally protected (or "virtuous") products or services, like contraceptives and abortion clinics, or "vice-like" activities, like gambling or alcoholic beverages.

Justice Marshall (in *Bolger*) noted that a "different conclusion" by the Court in treating the speech as commercial speech "[o]f course . . . may be appropriate in a case where the [speech] advertises an activity itself protected by the First Amendment."[107] Conversely, those attempting to distinguish cases like *Posadas* and *Edge Broadcasting Co.* have pointed out that both cases involve gambling, an activity long controlled, if not prohibited, by both state and federal laws. A similar question could be asked about whether the FTC in *In re R.J. Reynolds* would have taken the position that the corporation's speech was commercial speech if the case had not involved comments about smoking and health by a tobacco company.

It is possible that if the Court officially adopts the position that speech about such activities and products is an exception to the normal rules governing regular commercial speech (however it is defined), the Court would sanction either greater or lesser regulation of such speech than accorded other similar kinds of commercial speech. Alternatively, the Court might hold that such activities or products automatically create or deny a compelling reason for governmental regulation. For example, when Philip Morris Companies Incorporated sponsored a multistate tour of one of the original copies of the Declaration of Independence, critics of the company's cigarette products argued that the warning labels applied to cigarette packs and inserted in cigarette advertisements should be required in the company's advertisements about sponsorship of the tour. Following the rationale that regulations of speech related to cigarettes should be given more leeway because smoking is a "vice-like" activity, a court might sanction such a requirement for the advertisements placed by the cigarette company, although not on another kind of corporate speaker, based solely on its product. Whether this "virtue"/"vice" distinction will become the basis for distinctions in the level of protection for truthful and nondeceptive commercial speech remains to be seen.

REGULATION OF PAID-FOR POLITICAL SPEECH: CONSTITUTIONAL CONSIDERATIONS

To bring this chapter full circle, we need to return to *New York Times v. Sullivan* and *Bellotti* to examine the issues related to attempted government regulation of political speech. Both cases stand for the proposition that corporations and other organizations are free to spend money to publicize their views about issues of general public interest, including advocating the speaker's desired outcome of public referenda. Although corporate wealth would have the potential to make a substantial impact on the total amount of information available in the marketplace, said the Court in *Bellotti*, "the fact that advocacy may persuade the electorate is hardly a reason to suppress it. . . ."[108]

The vast majority of decisions in cases with fact patterns resembling *Bellotti* have been decided in favor of the paid-for speech interests. For example, in *C & C Plywood v. Hanson*,[109] a federal appeals court, citing *Bellotti*, struck down a Montana statute that proscribed corporate financial contributions in support of ballot issues. In *Let's Help Florida v. McCray*,[110] a federal appeals court[111] similarly held unconstitutional a Florida law limiting corporate contributions "to any political committee in support of, or in opposition to, an issue to be voted on in a statewide election."[112]

However, advertising and public relations professionals involved in political campaign advertising should note that the rules may change considerably when financial contributions—including paying for political advertising and other forms of communication—are made to assist *candidates* for public office. For example, the Federal Elections Campaign Act[113] regulates the amount individuals and organizations may contribute directly to candidates for federal office, and it creates rigorous disclosure and reporting requirements for those making such contributions. Many states have passed similar statutes to regulate campaigns at the state level.[114]

The constitutionality of the federal act was challenged in *Buckley v. Valeo.*[115] The Supreme Court of the United States ruled that restricting contributions to candidates was constitutional, although it struck down the provisions of the act limiting the amounts candidates could spend and the total spent on behalf of a candidate by groups or organizations working independently of the candidate. In *FEC v. National Conservative Political Action Committee,*[116] the Court invalidated limits on contributions by some kinds of independent political action committees (PACs)—a method many corporations have employed to channel financial contributions in support of issues and candidates they favor.

Despite these decisions restricting the scope of laws regulating campaign contributions, however, public relations and advertising professionals involved in political activities, representing candidates, parties, or those who wish to support them, should make it their business to familiarize themselves with both federal and state regulations covering such campaign contributions.

II

GOVERMENTAL REGULATION OF ADVERTISING AND COMMERCIAL SPEECH

4

The Federal Trade Commission

Later chapters discuss federal and state laws that allow competitors and consumers to initiate lawsuits against commercial speakers when their speech is alleged to be false, deceptive, or harmful. However, these laws are only some of the weapons available to those who wish to police commercial speech. Congress and state legislatures also have created numerous governmental regulatory agencies that have the power to make and enforce rules governing commercial enterprises and their business practices. Although a veritable alphabet soup of such federal and state agencies has been given jurisdiction over specific categories of commercial speech, the agency perhaps most involved on a comprehensive, day-to-day basis is the Federal Trade Commission (FTC). This agency, established at the beginning of the century, was originally given power to regulate unfair trade practices. Eventually, Congress expanded its role to investigate and remedy a variety of abuses, including false or deceptive commercial speech.

THE HISTORY OF THE FTC AND ITS JURISDICTION
OVER COMMERCIAL SPEECH

The origins of the FTC have their roots in the growth of monopolistic practices in industries like petroleum production, meat packing, and cigarette and steel manufacturing, beginning in the early 1880s. Even in this, the heyday of laissez-faire, free-market economic policy, cries soon were heard urging the federal government to combat these practices, which, it was feared, could result in a few powerful interests gaining control over the free marketplace of goods and services by artificially setting prices and using great concentrations of wealth to stifle competition.

The federal government's initial attempt to curb these abuses by the trusts and cartels was the passage of the Sherman Antitrust Act of 1890.[1] Although an important first step, the law proved ineffective in combating the major ills associated with economic monopolies. Continuing abuses led to demands that the federal government enact further legislation and set up a mechanism for ensuring that its provisions were followed. Congress responded to these demands with the passage of the Federal Trade Commission Act in 1914.[2]

Reflecting its purpose, the Act was directed toward business and industry, not toward consumers. It specified that, "Unfair methods of competition in commerce are hereby declared unlawful."[3] The Act further created the FTC, consisting of five commissioners and support staff, to oversee the enforcement of the Act by promulgating rules and regulations ultimately enforceable by civil lawsuits in federal courts.

A major modification of the Act, with direct significance to those engaged in commercial speech, occurred when Congress passed the Wheeler-Lea Amendment in 1938.[4] The addition of the words *Unfair or deceptive acts or practices in commerce* for the first time focused the attention of the FTC on issues of direct concern to consumers. This wording provided the basis for the FTC's jurisdiction over those who engage in "unfair or deceptive" practices by means of commercial speech. Thus, the Wheeler-Lea Amendment gave the FTC the authority to take direct action or bring civil suits in federal court against those attempting to deceive the public about the nature or quality of their own products, those maligning their competitors, and those engaged in unfair competitive practices.

THE FTC TODAY

The basic structure of the FTC remains the same as originally established by the 1914 Act. There are five commissions, each appointed by the president with the advice and consent of the Senate. No more than three members of the FTC may be from the same political party. Each commissioner is appointed to a 7-year term, and may be reappointed to additional terms. To ensure both continuity and a minimum of partisanship, FTC member terms are staggered to avoid a complete turnover in personnel at any one time. The president appoints one member to chair the FTC.

Originally staffed by a small number of employees absorbed from other government agencies when first formed, today the FTC has an expanded staff that encompasses numerous offices and bureaus, including public information, general counsel, administrative law judges, and compliance and litigation divisions. Of particular significance to commercial speech interests is the Bureau of Consumer Protection that contains within it the National Advertising Division. This department is responsible for investigating and enforcing laws and FTC regulations in cases of alleged deceptive or unfair commercial speech. The FTC also maintains 11 regional offices across the country to spot and deal with problems at the local level.

The FTC provides guidance to commercial speakers through a variety of communications and publications, including industry guides, informal responses to inquiries, and detailed advisory opinions issued when a commercial speaker wishes to determine in advance if proposed commercial messages meet FTC standards. FTC guidelines and publications can be obtained on written request to the FTC, and should be sought in advance by commercial speakers who have questions or doubts about the legality of their proposed commercial messages.

Cases typically arise when the FTC receives requests from consumers, competitors, or Congress to investigate an alleged violation of law or FTC regulations. Commissioners or their staff also may note possible violations on their own initiative. In either instance, the FTC staff members (usually from the Bureau of Consumer Protection) determine whether more formal procedures seem merited. If the investigators' conclusion is affirmative, the FTC typically sends an informal request for more information to the party under investigation. Should this request be ignored, or if the staff believes the information provided is nonresponsive or inadequate to meet the request, the investigators usually seek authority from the FTC for a more formal investigation.

Congress has granted the FTC sweeping subpoena power to obtain data and other relevant information from parties under investigation. The courts have held that the FTC may use its power to demand information before launching lawsuits or other more formal judical proceedings, even if there is only mere suspicion that a party may be in violation of the law. After the staff investigation is completed, a formal report is forwarded to the FTC suggesting what next steps need to be taken, if any. Should the conclusion be drawn that a legitimate complaint exists, the FTC may then authorize formal enforcement proceedings.

Normally the resolution of such complaints is made through use of a consent order, whereby the offending party, often without admitting any violation of the law, agrees to stop the actions challenged by the FTC. Typically the wording of such a consent order is open to negotiation with the FTC so as to avoid damaging publicity. If no agreement is reached, however, the FTC has broad authority to seek other remedies to enforce its orders. These and other possible actions by the FTC are discussed in more detail later in this chapter.

A dispute between the FTC and a party under investigation that cannot be settled by negotiation often results in a hearing before an FTC Administrative Law Judge (ALJ), who adjudicates the issue. Either the FTC staff or the other party may appeal the ALJ's ruling to the full FTC. Even if the decision is not appealed, however, the FTC on its own may elect to overrule its ALJ. The FTC's final ruling can be challenged in the federal courts of appeal and, if accepted, ultimately to the U.S. Supreme Court.

THE FTC'S REGULATION OF FALSE AND DECEPTIVE COMMERCIAL SPEECH

Until the 1970s, few gave much thought to the constitutionality of the FTC's regulations covering commercial speech, especially after the Supreme Court of the United States' decision in *Valentine*[5] that purely commercial speech merited no First Amendment protection. However, with the development of limited constitutional protection for such speech (beginning with *Pittsburgh Press*),[6] critics of the FTC began to question both its jurisdiction and its rulings on First Amendment grounds.

These issues were resolved in the FTC's favor by the Court's opinion in *Virginia State Board of Pharmacy*.[7] Justice Blackmun, while according commercial speech shelter under the umbrella of the First Amendment, also noted that "we . . . do not hold that it can never be regulated in any way."[8] Categories of commercial speech specifically mentioned as candidates for regulation included *untruthful speech*, which the Court defined as "false or misleading."[9] "Obviously," the Court added, "much commercial speech is not provably false, or even wholly false, but only deceptive or misleading. We foresee no obstacle to a State's dealing effectively with this problem."[10]

Although *Virginia State Board of Pharmacy* did not end challenges to the FTC's rulings on First Amendment grounds in lower courts, the Court has refused to grant a writ of certiorari to hear such a case. The Court has repeatedly reiterated its support for the constitutionality of the FTC's power to regulate commercial speech in a number of decisions, including *Young v. American Mini Theatres, Inc.*,[11] in which the Court observed that the FTC's "power . . . to restrain misleading, as well as false, statements in labels and advertisements has long been recognized."[12]

At the heart of the FTC's activities involving commercial speech are its attempts to eliminate speech considered "deceptive or misleading." Section 5 of the Federal Trade Commission Act 15 U.S.C. @ 45 (the FTC's basic enabling legislation) provides that the FTC shall be empowered to prevent "unfair or deceptive acts or practices in or affecting commerce."[13] Included in such "acts or practices" are what Section 12 of the Act calls "[disseminating] or . . . causing to be disseminated . . . any false advertisement"[14] involving the wide range of products and services covered in the act. By *false advertisement*, the Act means:

> an advertisement . . . which is misleading in a material respect; and in determining whether an advertisement is misleading, there shall be taken into account (among other things) not only representations made or suggested by statement, word, design, device, sound, or any combination thereof, but also the extent to which the advertisement fails to reveal facts material in the light of such representations or material with respect to consequences which may result from the use of the commodity to which the advertisement relates under the conditions prescribed in said advertisement, or under such conditions as are customary or usual.[15]

Although the language of the statute refers to *advertising*, the FTC's jurisdiction presumably extends to all forms of communication, including brochures, direct mail publications, press releases, and so forth if used for publicity or marketing purposes. Other similar causes of action have followed this logic as well. For example, in *Levitt Corporation v. Levitt*,[16] a federal court of appeals in the second circuit[17] upheld a lower court's injunctive order prohibiting the defendant from issuing press releases and other materials in a trademark infringement claim. Similarly, in *Smith-Victor Corporation v. Sylvania Electric Products, Inc.*,[18] a federal district court[19] found the defendant guilty of a Lanham Act product disparagement violation, in which the offending speech was disseminated by both advertisements and press releases.

It is important to note that, under the statute's definition, the determination of whether commercial speech is *false* is based on the perception, or possible perception, of the speech by the receiver of the message. This means the offending commercial speech is not limited to factual claims actually demonstrated to be untrue in important details. The FTC's definition of *false* is much broader. It includes statements or other commercial speech content, including pictures, graphic depictions, or sound, that in content or context reasonably might deceive the receiver of the message.

Normally, it will not avail a speaker to argue that technically there is no false statement in the advertisement or other communication if the reader or hearer could reasonably interpret the message in such a fashion as to receive a false impression or in other ways be deceived by the message. It is also important to note that the "reasonableness" requirement applies to the belief that a commercial speech claim makes a promise of performance, and not to whether it is reasonable to believe the claim.

This broad definition includes sins of omission as well. Therefore, it is equally unavailing for the commercial speaker to avoid liability for false and deceptive speech by including only statements that are true, and that the receiver interprets correctly if there is any significant information left out of the original message that, if included, would change the receiver's evaluation of the claim by casting it in a negative or different light. For example, in *Chrysler Corp v. FTC*,[20] the FTC found that advertisements comparing Chrysler automobiles to its competitors and claiming superior gas mileage for Chrysler products equipped with six-cylinder engines were deceptive because they failed to note that the same models with eight-cylinder engines were less fuel-efficient than similar models by other manufacturers.

The FTC has developed working definitions of *unfair* and *deceptive* commercial speech that have varied over time and with the political and economic philosophies of FTC members since the law was first enacted. The difficulty in defining an *unfair* act or practice in terms of commercial speech that would withstand a First Amendment challenge has severely limited the applicability of this concept in commercial speech situations. However, the FTC has vigorously applied its power in situations involving deceptive commercial speech.

The FTC's current definition of a *deceptive* act or practice was established in a policy statement in 1983.[21] Subsequently upheld by the FTC in *In re Cliffdale Assocs., Inc.*,[22] the statement defines such practices as: (a) a representation, practice, or omission likely to mislead consumers; (b) a message that consumers are interpreting reasonably under the circumstances; and (c) a material representation that could influence a consumer's decision with respect to the purchase of a product.[23]

The definition of a *material claim*, says the FTC, is a statement or omission of a statement that is "likely to affect a consumer's choice of or conduct regarding a product or service."[24] Such statements or omissions "pertain to the central characteristics of the products or services being marketed, such as their perform-ance, quality, cost or purpose."[25] The FTC is concerned with the probability that the average consumer might be likely to rely on a claim to the consumer's possible detriment. Therefore, the FTC may take action even if there is no proof that a consumer actually has so relied and suffered actual harm.

Representations involving material claims can be either express or implied. Express verbal claims, such as "Contains No Alcohol" or "Swiss-Made Watch," that prove false almost certainly are judged by the FTC to be deceptive. Similarly, visual messages are held to be deceptive if they expressly promise more than the product or service can deliver. Perhaps the most notable instance of visual deception eventually led to the case of *FTC v. Colgate-Palmolive*.[26] Colgate-Palmolive, makers of Rapid Shave, produced a commercial that made it appear the shaving cream was so good at softening beards for easy shaves that it could literally soften sandpaper. To demonstrate this softening power, however, the company used a Plexiglas panel covered with sand to simulate the process, rather than actual sandpaper, which, the company said, did not show up well on television. The FTC and the courts held that employing such procedures or techniques was deceptive because they could lead a consumer to believe he or she actually was witnessing product performance, despite that, given a little time to soak, Rapid Shave really could soften sandpaper as claimed.

Implied deceptive commercial speech claims usually involve a combination of true statements or visual representations that could cause deception because of the implications the listener takes away from the overall message. For example, one advertising technique that the FTC has determined has the tend-ency to deceive is to describe characteristics or properties of a product that, although true, have little to do with the product's actual intended use. For example, assume that, to demonstrate the superiority of a specific brand of paper towels, an advertising campaign has been designed featuring a single sheet of the product that has been dunked in water supporting the weight of an apple while two sheets of the competition's brand disintegrate under a similar weight. The FTC might find that such a demonstration makes deceptive claims if the advertising claims focus on the greater absorbency of the towels because there is no evidence that its product is superior to its competition when it came to actually absorbing liquids—the logical (and misleading) interpreta-tion the FTC might feel the average consumer would take away from the advertisement.[27]

Although the FTC has provided no specific guidelines for what evidence is necessary to prove how those receiving the information interpret such "repre-sentations," it has held (in *In re International Harvester Co.*[28]) that some omissions of fact are acceptable as long as the omitted facts concern "a subject upon which the seller has simply said nothing, in circumstances that do not give any particular meaning to his silence."[29] What the FTC called "pure omissions" were not actionable because they were not omissions that "presumptively or generally reflect a deliberate act on the part of the seller,"[30] and therefore the FTC found no reason to seek sanctions against the speaker. Any other approach to analyzing the effects of omitted information, said the FTC, would expand the definition of a deceptive act "virtually beyond limits,"[31] given the almost infinite range of possible interpretations by consumers of missing information.

The FTC also has determined that it normally will not be sufficient for the speaker to argue that a consumer should have been smart enough *not* to have relied on the claims made in the commercial message. According to the FTC, the test is whether a consumer's interpretation of the message, broadly speaking, is a reasonable one. Reasonableness, says the FTC, is determined by an analysis of the totality of the message. However, the FTC has held that it is unreasonable for the receiver of a commercial speech message to either read interpretations into a message that are silly or bizarre or to be deceived by any claims that would inherently be unbelievable to the average viewer or listener. If it is reasonable for a consumer to interpret the message in two ways, one deceptive and one not, the FTC generally will hold the speech to be deceptive.

Commercial claims directed to more vulnerable members of the audience, like children, older adults, and those suffering from illness, may be judged deceptive based on the likelihood that the members of that segment of the audience might be deceived. Thus, claims that a toy oven "Means You Can Bake Bread Just Like Your Mom and Dad," advertisements not disclosing that more parts are needed to equal what the child sees in an advertisement, or failing to mention that calling 900 numbers creates phone charges could run afoul of the FTC's prohibitions on deceptive claims, although no reasonable, normally functioning adult would likely be deceived by such claims.

In almost all cases, straightforward express claims will be considered "material" and contain the potential for deception on their face. In less straightforward situations, the FTC may rely on consumer research to determine such things as the nature and extent of the deception, the importance of the claim to the decision to purchase or use the product, or the reasonableness of interpretation. Research techniques favored by the FTC include public opinion polls, focus groups, and content analyses.

THE FTC'S REQUIREMENT FOR PRIOR SUBSTANTIATION

By far, the most common complaints about false or deceptive commercial speech focus on the failure of the touted products or services to live up to the claims made for them. To discourage such practices, the FTC has implemented a policy of requiring commercial speakers to be ready to provide evidence that all of the material claims made in their commercial speech have been substantiated in advance.

The policy has its origins in the FTC's 1972 decision in *In re Pfizer Inc.*[32] Pfizer claimed in its advertising for Un-Burn, a sunburn remedy, that the product "anesthetizes nerves in sensitive sunburned skin," and that it "relieves pain fast."[33] A complaint to the FTC resulted in an action for issuance of a cease-and-desist order on the basis that Pfizer had failed to back up its claims with "well-controlled scientific studies or tests prior to the making of such statements."[34] Although the FTC eventually dropped its investigation of Pfizer, it informally adopted a prior substantiation rule on the basis that a "consumer . . . cannot make the necessary tests or investigations to determine whether the . . . claims made for a product are true."[35]

The FTC, noting the unequal status between those making claims for a product and those potentially making use of it, added that "it is more rational, and imposes far less cost on society, to require a manufacturer to confirm his affirmative product claims rather than impose . . . [that] burden upon each individual consumer to test, investigate, or experiment for himself. . . ."[36]

The FTC upheld and refined its prior substantiation rules in a series of subsequent cases. By 1976, just 3 years after *Pfizer*, the FTC, in *In re National Commission on Egg Nutrition*,[37] could describe its rules requiring "substantiation" of product claims as established policy. The FTC explained that, "The justification for such a requirement is . . . [that] consumers are likely to assume that when a product claim is advanced which is in theory subject to objective verification, the party making [the claim] possesses a reasonable basis for so doing. . . ."[38] The FTC concluded that consumers have a right to expect that "advertising claims couched in objective terms are not merely statements of unsubstantiated opinion."[39]

The 1984 Policy Statement on Advertising Substantiation[40] codified these decisions. The policy expressly stated that those seeing or hearing claims of a factual nature about a product can reasonably expect that such claims are based on objective evidence. If reference is made to specific tests or experiments, consumers should legitimately be able to depend on the claims being substantiated to the degree claimed in the message.

To inhibit commercial speakers from gambling on the mere possibility that their claims may be substantiated, the FTC has held that the burden of proof rests with those making commercial speech claims to demonstrate that the claims have been substantiated prior to publication.[41] This means that the FTC may act to regulate commercial speech where there is an objective material claim made for a product or service, even if it eventually turns out that there is no demonstrably false statement of fact in the speech. For example, if a claim were made that a product increased the speed of operation by 30% compared with a rival product, the FTC might take action if the claimant could not substantiate the claims when they were made, even if subsequent research conducted after the claim was challenged might prove the statements to be true.[42]

Not all claims require the same degree of prior substantiation, however. The FTC requires the highest levels for statements that readers or viewers reasonably interpret as based on specific levels of proof of objective claims (e.g., "four clinical trials," "the results of two surveys reveal," or other similar evidence, whether stated or implied). In such circumstances, the FTC almost certainly will require the speaker to substantiate such evidence. For example, in *Pfizer*, the FTC noted that the company's testing "consisting of injections of [the drug] benzocaine could not indicate the probable anesthetic effect of a topical application of this substance."[43] The FTC concluded that Pfizer's commercials were unacceptable because they implied clinical trials supporting the claims made for pain relief, and the company in fact "did not conduct adequate and well-controlled scientific studies or tests prior to marketing Un-Burn to substantiate the efficacy claims made for Un-Burn."[44]

Similarly, the actual use of such terms as *scientific proof* and *lab-tested evidence*, although not establishing the amount or specific level of proof, normally will be required to be substantiated with the kinds of evidence those terms would imply to the reasonable consumer. Commercial speech that sets specific standards such as "lasts 20% longer than any other leading brand" or "gets 30 mpg at highway speeds" requires prior substantiation that demonstrates these claims are accurate. An illustration of this heightened prior substantiation requirement for specific claims was provided by the FTC in *Firestone Tire & Rubber Co. v. FTC.*[45] Firestone claimed that its "wide oval" tires stopped "25% quicker" than other tires. Finding that the claims raised a safety issue, the FTC ordered the company to stop advertising such claims unless and until they could be substantiated.

Often, however, the offending commercial speech does not expressly or by implication refer to specific levels or standards of substantiation. In these instances, the FTC has set the prior substantiation requirements for an objectively testable claim at a "reasonableness" level, based on the legitimate expectations of the consumer. Although the FTC has not established a "bright-line test" to determine reasonableness of prior substantiation in such cases, analysis of the evidence used by the speaker in arriving at the claims and the potential harm to consumers relying on these claims normally will be factors contributing to the FTC's evaluation. For example, claims for health-related products most likely will call for more exacting "reasonable" prior substantiation than claims for another kind of product, because of the risks posed for the unwary consumer.

Similarly, a higher standard for reasonableness might be required if the drawbacks to the use of a product were relatively high compared with the advantages the product could provide. The standard for reasonable prior substantiation of objective claims will likely be lower if the product could provide benefits to the potential consumer without much fear of significant downside risk in its use.

Reasonable prior substantiation might also involve analyzing the practices of comparable companies or evidence of industry-wide standards. For example, objective claims for a medical product might be held to a testing-within-the industry standard if the FTC determines there are generally accepted professional standards (e.g., three scientifically controlled tests) established as the norm by the medical community for such products. However, if a product is commonly and widely used, and consumers could easily verify objective claims for themselves, the FTC normally will not require submission of evidence of industry-wide tests to demonstrate the reasonableness of a claim.

The FTC also will give great weight to the findings of other agencies—like the Bureau of Alcohol, Tobacco and Firearms, or the Food and Drug Administration—in accepting arguments for reasonableness of objective claims by commercial speakers.

Weighing the costs of regulation compared with the benefits such regulation might bring to the consumer may also be considered by the FTC in its evaluation of the reasonableness of an objective claim. Setting reasonableness standards at too high a level might discourage the introduction of beneficial new products and services into the marketplace. Recognizing that, because of the inductive logic of scientific testing, critics could almost always argue that additional studies should be conducted, the FTC will normally temper its requirements for prior substantiation by employing an ad hoc cost–benefit analysis. Factors in the balancing process might include an evaluation of (a) the likelihood that additional testing could change the evidence supporting the claim, (b) the cost and time needed to conduct such additional tests, and (c) the degree of risk to the consumer if the objective claims turned out to be false.

"PUFFING"—A SPECIAL PRIOR SUBSTANTIATION PROBLEM

Although objective claims create the problem of evaluating the reasonable prior substantiation of such claims, statements about a product or service—like "It's the Best," "There's No Other One for You," or "No Competing Brand Comes Close"—have forced the FTC to create a workable definition of just what constitutes a nonobjective (or "puffing") statement, compared with an objective claim. *Puffing* has been defined as commercial speech "that is not deceptive [because] no one would rely on its exaggerated claims."[46]

Typically, the FTC and courts are more likely to find a claim to be puffing if the statements in the commercial speech generally refer to a product or service taken as a whole, rather than to any specific attributes of the product or service. The statement "It's a Great Truck" would be more likely to be treated as simple puffery than would the statement "It Gets Great Gas Mileage." Adding the statement "It Gets 5 Miles More Per Gallon at Highway Speeds" would almost certainly turn it into an objective claim requiring prior substantiation. Thus, for example, in *In re Dannon Milk Products, Inc.*,[47] a claim that yogurt was one of nature's perfect foods was termed more than puffing because it was an objective statement about a product's nutritional attributes.

Employing similar reasoning, the FTC and courts usually treat as puffery a company's general claims of superiority for its product or service compared with its competition, but tend to require prior substantiation for specific statements about individual characteristics of its products or services because they are objective claims.

The FTC also looks at the claim to determine whether it can be factually verified. Some statements (e.g., "I Just Feel More Assured Wearing Acme

Shoes") are opinion statements, and are almost always treated as puffery. However, if the statement appears to be based on factual information (e.g., "If You Could See the Results of the Studies I've Seen, You'd Agree That Acme Shoes Are Better"), the statement might be treated as expressing fact. The reader should note that simply placing an "I Believe . . ." or "In My Opinion . . ." in front of a fact statement will not turn that statement into an opinion statement free of a prior substantiation requirement.

Perhaps the most troubling element of its puffing-versus-fact standard from the point of view of the commercial speaker is the FTC's definition of an *average consumer* standard. The FTC's (and the courts') evaluation of the intelligence the "average consumer" displays often differs sharply from the estimations held by commercial speakers. In *In re Matter of Better Living, Inc.*,[48] the court agreed with the FTC that the statement that the company guaranteed "the world's lowest price"[49] was a claim of objective fact requiring substantiation rather than puffery, despite arguments to the contrary that no reasonable consumer would be misled or deceived by such statements. Similarly, in *Gillette Co. v. Wilkinson Sword, Inc.*,[50] the court found that "smoothest, most comfortable shave possible" was "a performance claim for one of the most important characteristics of the product being sold,"[51] although it is open to question whether the "average consumer" would be that easily fooled by such a claim.

The frequent use of the term *new*—as in "New and Improved"—in commercial claims has led the FTC to issue a special policy statement. It states that employing the term *new* for a product or service more than 6 months old would be considered questionable unless the product or service provider was conducting a test-marketing campaign. The FTC indicated that, in such a situation, it would enforce its 6-month policy once the product or service was introduced into the market in its final form.

FTC SUBSTANTIATION STANDARDS FOR COMMERCIAL CLAIMS ABOUT HEALTH/BEAUTY PRODUCTS

Because of a pattern of reoccurring complaints by consumers and consumer groups, the FTC generally looks with special scrutiny at complaints about commercial claims for health care products because of the potential for immediate, serious physical harm that could be caused by such products.

After years of extensive hearings and litigation, the FTC established a requirement that commercial claims for medicines or personal care products that are based directly or indirectly on clinical or scientific evidence must be substantiated by a minimum of two independent clinical tests. The FTC created this standard because it was felt that consumers would likely be deceived by claims allegedly based on clinical trials on the basis that they would expect that such procedures had been conducted, and had been done so "scientifically." Also, the FTC reasoned that the average consumer would be unable to independently evaluate such claims. For example, in *In re Thompson Medical Co.*,[52] the maker of Aspercreme, a topical skin product, claimed that using its product reduced aches and pains due to arthritis as well, if not better, than ingesting regular aspirin. Unfortunately for Thompson, these claims were not based on evidence the FTC considered scientifically valid. Therefore, the FTC ordered the manufacturer to stop making any claims about the pain-relieving qualities of Aspercreme unless it conducted "at least two adequate and well-controlled, double-blinded clinical studies"[53] that met what the FTC felt were the standards of accepted scientific research. There are instances involving nonspecific claims for health care products when the FTC has been content with only one clinical trial. But these are rare and usually involve claims about either attributes of a product not considered potentially harmful or involving physical properties that can be measured by instrumentation.

To meet FTC substantiation requirements, clinical tests and trials normally must be conducted by qualified independent investigators following an acceptable plan of research. At a minimum, this research plan should be specified in advance of the actual clinical trials, and should establish sample sizes, statistical tests, and levels of significance that are recognized as appropriate by experts in the field.

As might be expected, numerous differences in interpretation have arisen between the FTC and commercial speakers over the former's definitions and its implementation of requirements for approved clinical test procedures. Generally, the FTC requires that the investigators be different people and operate independently of each other. In *Thompson*, the FTC affirmed that, "The personnel who administer the test should also be experienced, as well as properly trained and instructed in using the measures involved in the clinical trial."[54]

The FTC has also held that the clinical test procedures should normally include the use of a placebo or its equivalent as a control when comparing two products. Claims of statistical significance must be based on the appropriate statistical procedures and tests, and must be achieved at a level of significance accepted by the scientific community (typically the .05 level of error or less).

Because it is possible for two products to prove virtually identical in everyday use, but to differ when measured by statistical tests, the FTC usually requires claims of superiority for one of the products to be based on both empirical and practical differences. However, the FTC may permit claims that rely on chemical or laboratory test results in lieu of clinical trials if the testing procedures are acceptable within the scientific community. If the commercial speech about a product also involves claims about freedom from unpleasant side effects in its use (e.g., "And It Doesn't Upset Your Stomach"), the FTC normally requires such claims to be substantiated in the same manner as primary claims.

FTC REGULATION OF CONTESTS
AND TESTIMONIALS/ENDORSEMENTS

Although the terms are often used interchangeably by commercial speakers, there are distinct differences among *lotteries*, *contests*, *games of chance*, and *drawings* or *sweepstakes*. Lotteries, unless permitted by statute and conducted by a governmental agency, are banned by law in all states. Generally, a contest is treated as an illegal lottery if contestants must pay money or take any other kind of action that could be considered to be payment of "consideration" (including, in some states, the purchase of a product or service). In addition, a contest risks being judged a lottery if the contestant can win by chance alone, rather than by demonstrating any special skill, and the winners are awarded prizes of economic value.

The FTC has recognized that commercial speech about legal contests, drawings, sweepstakes, and other such promotional techniques presents a risk of deception for potential consumers. In an attempt to minimize this risk, the FTC has published specific guidelines for disclosure of information that apply to games of chance when used by commercial speakers promoting the sale of either food items or gasoline.[55] Those representing these industries would be wise to be in contact with the FTC before creating such contests. The FTC also has used its general supervisory powers to challenge the use of contests and other similar techniques when employed by commercial speakers to promote products or services in other industries.

Although a comprehensive discussion of the wide range of rules covering such techniques is beyond the scope of this text, it would be prudent for a commercial speaker contemplating their use to include clearly written and displayed information in all promotional material about the true chances of winning any prize of value, a description of all prizes (including their value), and the number of prizes to be awarded. Also, the rules and conditions (including any deadlines) for entering the contest or sweepstakes should be included, as should information about who is eligible to be a contestant.

Concerns about the use of testimonials for and endorsement of products and services by celebrities or other noncompany spokespersons caused the FTC to develop a separate policy statement regulating such practices. The Guides Concerning Use of Endorsements and Testimonials in Advertising[56] states that an endorsement is "any advertising message (including verbal statements, demonstrations, or depictions of the name, signature, likeness, or other identifying personal characteristics of an individual or the name or seal of an organization) which message consumers are likely to believe reflects the opinions, beliefs, findings or experience of a party other than the sponsoring advertiser."[57]

Generally, the FTC has held that endorsement statements must meet the same substantiation requirements as other claims that a commercial speaker may make. In *In re Cliffdale Associates, Inc.*,[58] the advertiser of the Ball-Matic Gas Saver Valve claimed that the product was "the most significant automotive breakthrough in the last 10 years," and produced several advertisements with testimonials by alleged users of the product claiming that the valve gave them substantial improvement in miles per gallon of gasoline. The FTC challenged the accuracy of these and other claims for the product. In response, Cliffdale Associates Inc. tried to argue that the consumers providing the testimonials legitimately believed that they had obtained improved gas mileage, and therefore that no other proof was necessary to justify the claims.

The FTC would have none of it. "[C]onsumer tests and testimonials," said the FTC, "are not a recognized way of testing fuel economy."[59] It went on to note that, "irrespective of the veracity of the individual consumer testimonials, use of the testimonials to make underlying claims that were false and deceptive was, itself, deceptive."[60]

In its policy statement, the FTC describes typical examples of endorsements to aid commercial speakers in understanding and following its guidelines. For example, if a celebrity has been a long-term spokesperson for a company or product, the use of the celebrity in commercial speech normally would not constitute an endorsement because consumers likely recognize that the celebrity is speaking on behalf of the company, and not making an endorsement. However, if a popular sports figure or entertainer with no established association with a company is depicted using its product, the FTC considers that an endorsement even if the celebrity never actually makes any overt testimonial statements. Similarly, if statements by critics or reviewers flattering to a product or service appear in commercial speech, the FTC considers them endorsements because of the possible confusion in the mind of the consumer about which are the critics' views and which are the company's.

Companies that use celebrities to endorse their products or services must be able to demonstrate that the endorsements are both genuine and accurate in all important details. For example, in *In re Cooga Mooga, Inc.*,[61] the FTC held that the statements by singer Pat Boone and members of his family endorsing "Acne-Statin," an anti-acne skin product, were false and deceptive. The commercials claimed, among other things, that Boone's daughters had used the product, and that it had produced satisfactory results for them. In finding that most of the health claims for the product were false or exaggerated, the FTC also noted that not all of Boone's daughters had employed the medication, and that the implication that all had done so constituted an additional untrue claim.

In addition, the use of a celebrity endorser must be limited to the time that the celebrity actually uses or testifies for the product or service. Statements to the effect that a celebrity "drives the Terraplane Z6" would constitute false and deceptive claims if the celebrity either never or no longer drives this automobile. The reader should also remember that those employing the celebrity endorser also may be liable for engaging in illegal practices in a Lanham Act cause of action.

Regardless of whether the providers of a testimonial are celebrities or individuals portrayed as typical consumers, the claims they make must reflect what the average consumer of the product or service would experience in normal usage of the product or service. This means that, although the endorser may truthfully testify that he or she experienced a phenomenal response or improvement after using a product or service, such claims may be considered deceptive if scientific or statistical evidence reveals such experiences to be significantly beyond the norm.

One method of possibly avoiding the need to substantiate an endorsement claim is the use of a disclaimer statement. The FTC's guidelines indicate that such a disclaimer—stating the more typical performance record of the product or service, and phrasing and displaying it in such a manner as to be readily understood by the listener or viewer—may be sufficient to satisfy the FTC's requirements for nondeceptive commercial speech. However, simply stating that the endorsement claim "may not be typical" or other similarly worded disclaimers normally are not sufficient. The reader also should note that the more extravagant the claim, the less likely the FTC will accept a simple disclaimer to avoid a charge of deceptive commercial speech.

In addition to celebrities and individuals portrayed as average citizens, commercial speakers often employ professionals described as experts to recommend the speaker's product or service. Not surprisingly, the FTC guidelines on testimonials and endorsements make special provision for such endorsers because of the tendency for consumers to believe such experts and their greater capacity to deceive consumers with their claims. A commercial speaker employing such an expert should be able to demonstrate that the expert has actually evaluated the product or service, and has done so in a manner "as extensive as someone with the same degree of expertise would normally need to conduct in order to support the conclusions presented in the endorsement."[62] When the endorsement contains claims that the product or service is the equal of, or better than, a competitor, the expert endorser similarly must have also evaluated the competitor's product or service.

A claim made by an expert must be based on the standards employed by the industry involved or other experts in the field. Similarly, the credentials of the expert providing the endorsement must demonstrate that the expert is qualified to provide such testimonial endorsement. For example, it would be inappropriate to use a medical doctor in an advertisement endorsing a product if that product is outside the medical specialty of the physician. In *In re Cooper*,[63] astronaut Gordon Cooper, a stakeholder in a company that manufactured and sold the "G-R Gas Saver Valve," was pictured in the company's advertising wearing what appeared to be his space suit, touting the virtues of the product. Cooper was billed as an expert engineer who had performed tests of the valve in his "independent engineering laboratory."[64] The FTC, although not questioning Cooper's credentials as an astronaut with NASA, ordered the company to cease and desist using Cooper as an endorser of the valve in the company's commercial efforts because he was unqualified to serve as an expert in evaluating and recommending automobile products, despite his scientific and engineering expertise.

However, FTC guidelines do not prohibit an expert in one field from endorsing a product in another if it is made clear that the endorsement is merely a personal, rather than a professional, endorsement, and that the endorsement meets the other requirements for testimonials discussed earlier. When the supplier of the testimonial statement is a group or organization, the FTC requires that the statement reflect the overall consensus of its members. It must also be true that such groups or organizations have conducted the appropriate tests or in other ways evaluated the product or service in question if the commercial message states or intimates that they have done so. For example, in *Niresk Industries, Inc. v. FTC*,[65] the FTC ordered the company to stop advertising that its products were endorsed by *Good Housekeeping*'s "Seal of Approval," when, in fact, that organization had not endorsed them.

THE FTC AND RETAIL SALES

Unlike the commercial speech by manufacturers or service providers, commercial speech by retailers usually involves claims about the conditions of the sales situation (e.g., special sales, low prices, or unusual merchandising practices). The FTC, recognizing that such commercial speech can be as equally deceptive to the average consumer as claims for products or services, has published an extensive set of rules governing retail sales. Although a comprehensive review of these rules is beyond the scope of this text, a brief overview of the FTC's efforts in this area may serve to alert retail commercial speakers to the need to familiarize themselves with regulations affecting their activities.

One of the FTC's greatest concerns is potentially deceptive claims involving the pricing of goods and services. To provide retail commercial speakers with guidance in this area, the FTC has formulated its Guides Against Deceptive Pricing.[66] Some of the regulations covered in these and other guidelines involve specific rules describing when speakers legitimately may claim that an item is reduced in price from its "usual" or "regular" price. To meet FTC requirements, such sales claims must be based on a comparison with the normal price charged for the item, or, if no specific dollar amount or percentage of savings is mentioned, the sale price must be low enough to constitute what the average consumer reasonably would consider a legitimate savings. If a commercial speaker claims that its prices are lower than its competitors or are at manufacturer or wholesaler prices, the FTC normally requires such claims to be based on legitimate comparisons with its nearby competitors' normal pricing policies or the usual manufacturers' or wholesalers' prices.

Other FTC guidelines for retailers cover practices like using the terms *Introductory Sale*, *Buy One, Get One Free*, or *Free Gift*, as well as prohibitions on so-called "bait-and-switch advertising," which is defined by the FTC as "an alluring but insincere offer to sell a product or service . . . [for the purpose of switching] consumers from [the advertised item] to . . . something else, usually at a higher price or on a basis more advantageous to the advertiser."[67] Retail commercial speech practices involving mail-order sales and sales of such items as household furniture, electronics, jewelry, and luggage, are the subjects of specific guidelines and industry guides. Readers of this text who engage in commercial speech involving these and related practices should obtain these guidelines from the FTC before making any commercial claims.

The FTC also is charged with monitoring and regulating aspects of commercial speech involving offers of credit extended by retailers to consumers under provisions of the federal Truth-in-Lending Act.[68] The Act, which covers all those who advertise or offer consumer credit—regardless of whether they are actual creditors—calls for nondeceptive commercial speech about the conditions to be met, the actual credit rate the consumer can expect to receive, how any finance charge is computed, and other pertinent information. The Act also covers offers of lease agreements, and requires similar disclosures of terms, conditions, and so forth. The reader engaged in commercial speech involving offers of consumer credit is urged to be in contact with the FTC for guidance to avoid running afoul of its regulations.

ENFORCING FTC REGULATIONS—CORRECTIVE ORDERS

Without the power to enforce its rules and regulations, the FTC's function would be limited to advisory status. To prevent that eventuality, the Federal Trade Commission Act states that the FTC has the power to "issue and cause to be served on such person, partnership, or corporation [in violation of the law] an order requiring such person, partnership, or corporation to cease and desist from using such method of competition or such act or practice."[69] These "cease-and-desist" orders may be imposed by the FTC itself without resorting to the courts for enforcement.

A cease-and-desist order, directed against a party the FTC believes is engaging in false or deceptive commercial speech, is a remedy of last resort. As discussed earlier, almost without exception such an order comes only after a series of negotiations during the investigatory phase of the FTC's preliminary inquiry. If the FTC and the commercial speaker cannot agree on an informal alternative course of action to resolve their disagreements, a more formal complaint and consent procedure can be employed. However, the overwhelming bulk of cases are settled usually as a result of a negotiated, signed consent decree. By agreeing to discontinue the challenged practice, the commercial speaker can save the potential negative publicity of litigation, and need not admit wrongdoing.

Given the normally short shelf life of most commercial speech, such a remedy often satisfies all parties. However, commercial speakers may object to signing such a consent decree if they feel it is unjustified or would seriously interfere either with an ongoing or planned commercial campaign. In that eventuality, typically the next step is a hearing before an ALJ. The ALJ is empowered to obtain evidence through subpoena, and in many respects the hearing is like a trial. At its termination, the judge must render a decision within 90 days. The ALJ may find that a cease-and-desist order be entered, some other remedy is called for, or may decide in favor of the party charged with violating the law. If it is the judge's decision that a cease-and-desist order should be issued, and the FTC is in accord with that judgment, the party against whom the order is issued must file a compliance report within 60 days spelling out how the order is being complied with. If the FTC disagrees with the ALJ, it may elect to overrule the decision and impose its own sanctions. Rather than comply with the FTC, the party against whom the order is entered may elect to appeal the FTC's actions in the federal appeals court system.

In its simplest form, the purpose of a cease-and-desist decree is to remedy the problem by ordering the offending commercial speaker to stop. However, the FTC is not limited to such a remedy if, in its opinion, additional steps are needed to correct the existing problem or to prevent similar problems from reoccurring. In such instances, the FTC may also employ such remedies as issuing a broad order that covers both commercial speech claims it has already found to be false or deceptive and claims for other products or services as well. These so-called "fencing-in" orders, extending to commercial speech about products or services the offending organization provides other than those specifically complained of, are the FTC's method of ensuring that the organization does not make deceptive claims in future commercial speech.

These more inclusive "fencing-in" cease-and-desist orders may extend to some or all of the products or services a company provides, or they may be applied to some or all of the claims made for a particular product or service. Normally the FTC only expands its cease-and-desist order to fence in a commercial speaker in circumstances in which there is evidence that the offending speaker has both a history of deceptive commercial speech claims and when there is a future "likelihood of . . . committing the sort of unfair practice"[70] complained of in the present case.

In more extreme cases, the FTC may ban future commercial speech about a product or service unless affirmative disclosures accompany the speech. Perhaps the best-known example of such an affirmative disclosure order is the agreement reached by the FTC with cigarette manufacturers to include the Surgeon General's warning label in all commercial speech about their products.[71]

When the FTC finds a pattern of long and persistent publication of false and deceptive speech, it may also take the additional step of requiring a commercial speaker to publish corrective information. Although the line between affirmative disclosure and corrective information is not well drawn, the triggering mechanism for FTC action appears to be the longevity of the party's advertising or other commercial speech campaign, the nature and extent of the claims the FTC finds to be false and deceptive, and the hypothesized continuing effects the prior speech might have on the decisions by consumers in the future.

In one of the more notable corrective commercial speech cases, a federal appeals court, in *Warner-Lambert Co. v. FTC*,[72] upheld the FTC's directive to include corrective information in future advertisements for Listerine. The claim that Listerine somehow could prevent colds and related symptoms had been a part of the product's advertising and marketing campaigns for decades. The FTC's remedy was to require Warner-Lambert to insert information clearly refuting such claims in each future advertisement until the company had spent as much money correcting its advertising as it had spent on all its advertising during the preceding 20 years (approximately $10 million). The court agreed with the FTC that such a drastic remedy was justified on the basis that the "deceptive advertisement[s] . . . played a substantial role in creating or rein-forcing in the public's mind a false and material belief which lives on after the false advertising ceases."[73]

THE FTC AND THE COURTS

In addition to its own sanctions, the FTC can turn to the courts to remedy false or deceptive commercial speech claims. For example, the FTC may seek a temporary court order to halt an immediate violation of the law. Although the normal standard for imposition of such an order is a finding that a violation will cause immediate and irreparable harm, at least one court has held that deference by the judiciary to rulings by the FTC means that the FTC only needs to meet a general public interest standard. A court-ordered temporary injunc-tion could become permanent if the court finds that the public would best be served by following this course of action.[74]

If it believes the situation warrants it, the FTC could ask a court to find a commercial speaker guilty of a criminal misdemeanor. Typically this would involve cases of commercial speech claims for medicines or health-related products when an average consumer, believing in the claims for the product, could be seriously harmed by product purchase and use, and the offending party has ignored earlier warnings or orders by the FTC. Typically, when a cease-and-desist order has been ignored or disobeyed, however, the FTC is more likely to seek a civil-law remedy from the courts by invoking Section 45(m) of the Federal Trade Commission Act.[75] This section permits a court to impose stiff financial penalties for each day the defendant is in violation of the order. For example, in *United States v. Readers Digest Association*,[76] the court assessed a 10 cent penalty for each simulated sweepstakes check the publication had disseminated. Unfortunately for Readers Digest, the total number of checks reached more than 17 million—resulting in a fine of $1,750,000.

The reader should also note that the FTC similarly may prevail in civil suits involving commercial speech claims against manufacturers of products or providers of services who are not the subjects of specific FTC cease-and-desist orders, but who nonetheless know that their commercial speech claims would be in violation of such orders issued to prohibit similar claims by competitors.

Not surprisingly, the use and scope of the FTC's remedial powers have created a large percentage of the disputes between the FTC and commercial speakers. A substantial part of this litigation has come from challenges to the scope of cease-and-desist orders. In *Chrysler Corp.*,[77] the FTC ordered the auto-mobile manufacturer to not only cease potentially deceptive claims for the fuel efficiency of its products, but to avoid misrepresenting the results of any tests or other research in its advertising. A federal court of appeals[78] in the District of Columbia approved the FTC's general order, but found that it had over-reached itself in regard to the extent of the order limiting discussion of tests and research results. The court noted that such a prohibition was "potentially limitless"[79]—that Chrysler's infractions "were unintentional and non-continuing," and that the offending speech had appeared in only "two out of a campaign of fourteen advertisements. . . ."[80]

Similarly, in *ITT Continental Baking Co. v. FTC*,[81] a federal appeals court struck down the FTC's limitations on the company's comparative advertising claims as overbroad, in large measure because the company's statements about the nutritional value of its products were found to be accurate in 11 of the 12 cases discussed. In *American Medical Association v. FTC*,[82] a federal court of appeals in the second circuit modified the FTC's cease-and-desist order directed against the AMA by limiting it to a simple requirement that the association add the words *respondent reasonably believes* to its medical advertising.[83]

Sometimes courts disagree with the scope of the FTC's orders when the offending commercial speaker has discontinued the disputed practices prior to the FTC's investigation and issuance of the cease-and-desist mandate. However, if the cessation occurs after an investigation is initiated, courts generally are reluctant to overturn or modify the FTC's rulings.

THE FTC AND COMMERCIAL SPEAKERS: WHO IS LIABLE FOR WHAT?

The FTC's regulations and enforcement procedures apply both to independent commercial speakers, like advertising or public relations agencies, and to the original manufacturers or providers of the products or services for which allegedly false and deceptive claims are made. Independent agencies are typically excused from liability for violations of the law if they can demonstrate that they have made good-faith efforts to ensure that the claims made for their clients' goods and services are truthful. These good-faith efforts usually can be satisfied if an agency has reasonably relied on information supplied by the client, and if the agency has no cause to believe that such information is untrue or deceptive.

Agencies are liable, however, if the claims made in the commercial speech questioned by the FTC are the product of the creative efforts of the agency, regardless of whether such claims are express or implied. Agencies also have an affirmative duty to modify commercial claims if they acquire new information about the products or services from their clients or other sources. This duty extends to being in compliance with FTC regulations or orders directed against other providers of products or services in the competitive industry. The FTC generally presupposes that an agency is responsible for the claims made for a product or service, and therefore carefully scrutinizes arguments made by an agency that it had no reason to question whether the information supplied by the agency's clients was false and deceptive.

If an agency is held liable, it can be subjected to the same remedies as its client. Of particular concern have been attempts by the FTC, some successful and some not, to extend its "fencing-in" requirements to all of the commercial speech an agency creates for all of the products and services of any and all clients the agency represents. Agencies may also be liable for fines up to $10,000 per day for each violation of an FTC cease-and-desist order.

CONCLUSION

Although the degree of zeal the FTC displays in aggressively policing commercial speech in the near future depends, in large measure, on the "regulatory climate" of Washington, DC, commercial speakers would be well advised not to engage in a confrontation with the FTC. The most prudent course of action for those engaged in commercial speech is to be familiar with the guidelines, regulations, and cases interpreting FTC policies before making claims for products or services. As discussed earlier, the FTC produces a number of publications discussing its policies, and often answers specific questions as well.

In trying to determine the likelihood that speech claims will attract the attention of the FTC during the creative phase of commercial message preparation, the speaker should be especially careful if commercial claims are to be directed toward a target audience the FTC might consider especially vulnerable (e.g., children, the elderly, or the infirm), or if the speech appeals to the audience based on claims related to health or some other aspect of physical well-being. Similarly, the speaker would be wise to be wary of making claims that are almost sure to raise the ire of competing companies (e.g., comparative or negative claims), consumer or special-interest groups opposed to the product or service that is the subject of the commercial speech, or the FTC or other governmental agencies because of complaints about similar claims in the past.

The FTC has been unusually aggressive recently in raising and investigating complaints about commercial claims involving so-called "green" issues. In its *Guides for the Use of Environmental Marketing Claims*,[84] the FTC has provided guidelines for "environmental claims . . . about . . . the attributes of a product or package in connection with the sale . . . or marketing of such product or package" to individuals and commercial enterprises.[85] The FTC is especially concerned with the use of such terms as *recyclable, biodegradable,* and *environmentally friendly*. It has created guidelines that detail the degree of prior substantiation for such claims, as well as how and when they may be employed by commercial speakers. Because the FTC appears to be ready to stringently enforce its guidelines through regulation, the commercial speaker making such environmental claims should be careful to be informed about, and to follow, current FTC guidelines and rulings.

The FTC appears to be equally concerned with commercial messages presented by experts or "typical" consumers acting as spokespeople. Those creating such messages should be prepared to substantiate any material claims. This also is true of claims based on "staged" presentations of product effectiveness or performance. Generally, it is still prudent practice to (a) analyze all express or implied claims that could influence a potential consumer to purchase a product or service, and (b) ensure that the claims can be substantiated and only those claims intended by the speaker are present in the commercial message. Similarly, the speaker should satisfy him or herself that a reasonable segment of the audience will not perceive the claims in the commercial message in a way not intended, and that the absence of information will not create material errors of omission, causing significant parts of the message to be misperceived.

If claims could be misconstrued, those creating such claims should evaluate possible disclaimers to ensure that they are effective from the point of view of the target consumer. Additionally, the commercial speaker should evaluate the harm an FTC investigation and possible actions could have on the life of the commercial campaign and the reputation of both the product or service and the organization.

The SEC, the FDA,
and Other Federal Agencies

Although the Federal Trade Commission (FTC; discussed in chap. 4) is the agency that exercises the most pervasive, day-to-day regulation of commercial speech, numerous other governmental agencies, commissions, and boards retain limited jurisdiction over commercial speech dealing with specific products or services. These include the Securities and Exchange Commission (SEC), the Food and Drug Administration (FDA), and the Department of Housing and Urban Development (HUD), as well as a variety of official offices and agencies at the state level.

THE SECURITIES AND EXCHANGE COMMISSION

The workings of the SEC, which oversees the financial regulation of stock markets, as well as the companies and investors that trade securities in these markets, are of vital concern to large segments of both advertising and public relations professionals.

The SEC traces its origins to early attempts to regulate the buying and selling of securities, beginning in the late 1880s. Prior to that time, a pattern of financial good times was invariably followed by economic chaos and a major depression. This recurring cycle of boom-or-bust eventually brought calls for reform of the nation's economic system. Initial efforts at regulation both at the federal and state levels (a discussion of state so-called "Blue Sky" laws is found later in this chapter) proved ineffective, however. It was not until the financial crises that led to the Great Depression in the early 1930s that real reform was accomplished. This began with passage of the Securities Act of 1933[1] and the Securities Exchange Act of 1934.[2] The latter act established the SEC and charged it with the responsibility of ensuring that timely, complete, and truthful information be made available to the public about publicly traded securities.

Until the 1960s, the SEC largely went about its business of enforcing existing regulations involving disclosure of information. However, revisions in 1964 of the Securities Exchange Act,[3] coupled with a greater willingness by the SEC's staff to initiate investigations of investment companies, set the SEC on a collision course with many existing business practices in the 1960s and 1970s. This eventually led to a number of further reforms in financial marketplace activities. Although the 1980s brought a lessening in the SEC's aggressiveness, it nonetheless remains a major player in maintaining the stability of the securities market.

The SEC is composed of five commissioners appointed for 5-year terms by the president with the concurrence of the Senate. One of these appointees is selected by the president to chair the SEC. To reduce partisanship, no more than three commissioners may be members of the same political party. Headquartered in Washington, DC, the SEC has eight regional offices across the country. The SEC's professional staff is composed of securities analysts, accountants, attorneys, and various regulatory and enforcement personnel. The SEC's activities are segmented into divisions. The most important for commercial speakers is the Division of Corporation Finance. This division, among other duties, oversees corporate registration statements, annual and quarterly reports, and other corporate financial communication activities.

SEC Regulation of First-Time or Additional New Offerings of Securities

According to the SEC, the primary purposes of the 1933 Securities Act were to "provide investors with material financial and other information" and "to prohibit misrepresentation, deceit, and other fraudulent acts and practices in the sale of securities generally. . . ."[4] The Supreme Court of the United States, in *Ernst and Ernst v. Hochfelder*,[5] characterized the purpose of the statute as providing "full disclosure of material information concerning public offerings . . . to protect investors against fraud and, through the imposition of specified civil liabilities, to promote ethical standards of honesty and fair dealing."[6]

The Act's definition of a *security* includes "any note, stock, treasury stock, bond, . . . certificate of interest or participation in any profit-sharing agreement, . . . investment contract, . . . certificate of deposit for a security, fractional undivided interest in oil, gas, or other mineral rights, or, in general, any interest in an instrument commonly known as a 'security' . . . or guarantee of, or warrant or right to subscribe to or purchase any of the foregoing. . . ."[7]

With the exceptions of offerings that are sold completely within one state (and therefore subject to state rather than federal regulation) and those that are for small amounts (generally less than $500,000), Section 5 of the Act specifies that, before a security can be offered for sale, a "registration statement" must be formally filed with the SEC. Prior to the filing of this statement of registration, the law mandates that no press releases, news conferences, mass media advertising, or sales promotions issued with the intent or effect of encouraging the sale of the company's securities are permitted. For this reason, commercial speakers must be extremely wary of disseminating any information that the SEC might interpret as promoting the sale of new securities (such as disseminating information about the price of new securities or claims for the safety or benefits of investing).

After the required registration statement is filed with the SEC, the Securities Act ensures a 20-day waiting period, during which the party offering the securities for sale may communicate information about the issuance of the securities. Typically this is done by means of a formal preliminary "prospectus." During the waiting period, the company offering the securities may promote their sale, but no actual purchase offers can be accepted until the waiting period expires. The preliminary prospectus must conform to the format and contain the copious detailed information specifically called for by the Act to meet SEC approval.

The Securities Act provides an exception to its no-advertising policy during the formal waiting period for "tombstone advertisements," so called because their appearance is strictly curtailed by the SEC's rules. Such advertisements are generally limited to a straightforward presentation of information about the price of a security, who is offering it for sale, and how it may be purchased.[8]

Disregard of the no-promotional-activities strictures in the Securities Act by commercial speakers can lead to unfortunate results. In *SEC v. Arvida Corporation*,[9] a press release issued by the brokerage firm of Loeb, Rhoades & Co. touted the virtues of the stock offered by a new company, the Arvida Corporation, describing the company's financial stability and the extensiveness of its land holdings. Unfortunately for Arvida, the news release was issued and distributed to the nation's leading financial publications before the formal processes mandated by the Act had been completed, causing the SEC to determine that the requirements for a formal registration statement had been breached.

In a companion action, *In re Carl M. Loeb, Rhoades & Co.*,[10] the SEC challenged the issuance of the press release as a violation of Section 5 of the Securities Act on the basis that it had "set in motion the processes of distribution . . . by arousing and stimulating investor and dealer interest in Arvida securities."[11] Loeb, Rhoades argued that the news release was exactly that—news—and therefore could not be grounds for a Section 5 violation. The SEC disagreed, holding that "astute public relations activities" had created the "news," and that this was "precisely the evil which the Securities Act seeks to prevent."[12] The SEC concluded that, "Although it appears that defendants acted in good faith . . . and although [they] continue to deny [liability] . . . nevertheless the Court finds that defendants violated Section 5(c) of the Securities Act."[13]

SEC Regulation of the National Securities Marketplace

Congress passed the Securities Exchange Act of 1934 to regulate the ongoing trading of securities (after the first-time offering for sale) in stock exchanges and by brokers. Like the Securities Act, the Securities Exchange Act's basic purpose is to ensure that investors are assured of full disclosure of all timely and pertinent information necessary to make a reasoned and informed decision about selling or purchasing a security. A second, and related, purpose is to prevent "any manipulative or deceptive device or contrivance"[14] that could lead to fraud in the securities market, including false or deceptive advertising or other commercial speech.

To provide potential investors with the accurate and truthful financial information they need, the SEC enforces the Securities Exchange Act's requirements for full disclosure by requiring companies offering their stock for sale to the public—in a stock market or through a broker—to provide periodic reports that detail the state of the company, its future plans, and other similar financial information. Every publicly traded company (except for small or intrastate corporations) must keep a registration statement on file with the SEC that provides information similar to the statement required under the Securities Act. In addition, they are required to file an annual comprehensive report (Form 10-K), quarterly updates, and various other reports as needed to meet the SEC's regulations for timely disclosure of new information about a company's financial status, such as changes in senior management or board of directors, initiation of bankruptcy proceedings, or any other "material" event.

In addition to these normal reporting requirements, in 1968 Congress enacted the Williams Act,[15] that mandated that a company proposing to take control of another company by acquiring a majority of outstanding shares from current stockholders (a so-called "tender offer") must disclose (a) detailed information to the SEC, the target company, and current shareholders about the take-over company; (b) the reasons behind the tender offer; and (c) what the purchaser plans to do with the acquired company. If such disclosure is not complete, or if the SEC finds that the information provided is either false or misleading, the SEC can initiate legal action to ensure compliance.

Because tender offers often are made via the mass media or other publicity techniques, public relations and advertising professionals should be aware of SEC rulings about what constitutes the actual commencement of an official tender order. Otherwise, making statements in advertisements or other forms of publicity that the SEC might consider as sufficient to create such an order could trigger requirements that the tender offeror submit the requisite copious financial information on appropriate forms and within specified time limits or risk legal sanction by the SEC.

Under SEC Rule 14(d) of the Act, for example, publicity about the possible or impending purchase of another company has been held to create a tender offer if it is published in newspaper advertisements or disseminated to security holders or investors by other means. If such publicity is interpreted as creating a tender offer, Section 14(e) of the Act mandates that the communication must include everything from the identity of the bidder to a statement that stockholder lists are being used to reach securities holders. Also, it must include the expiration date of the offer, the degree to which the offer will result in control of the target company by the bidder, and how securities holders may obtain information from the bidder.

SEC Regulation of False or Deceptive Commercial Speech

The SEC's enabling legislation and regulations demand that commercial speech involving securities must be truthful, nondeceptive, and comprehensive. For example, the SEC's interpretation of Rule 14(a), that broadly defines deceptive information involving tender offers, was upheld in *Gillette Company v. RB Partners*.[16] In that case, a chart in a newspaper advertisement was judged to misrepresent the conditions of the offer, despite the fact that all of the information presented was true. The problem, said the SEC, was that the design of the chart made it appear that foreign parties predominated in the group seeking to make the offer when such was not the case.

The extent of the SEC's reach in regulating commercial speech involving tender offers and proxy solicitations is exemplified by the case of *Long Island Lighting Company (LILCO) v. Barbash*.[17] In *LILCO*, a coalition of politicians and activists initiated a proxy fight to change the utility's board of directors and forestall the construction of a nuclear power plant. As part of this campaign, those opposed to the current operation of the utility purchased a newspaper advertisement urging stockholders to vote for replacing management and in favor of turning the utility into a municipally run company. The utility, challenging the advertisement as false and misleading, sought an injunction to prohibit "solicitation" of the company's shareholders "until the claimed false and misleading statements had been corrected" and information to that effect had been filed with the SEC.[18] The company argued that the purpose of the advertisements was to "influence the exercise of proxies by LILCO shareholders," and that the statements were "false and misleading in numerous respects relating to alleged advantages for ratepayers. . . ."[19]

A federal district court judge[20] dismissed the complaint, holding that the SEC's rules about the permissible use and content of commercial speech involving proxy solicitations did not apply because the advertisement in question was not specifically directed toward shareholders. The judge also noted significant constitutional concerns because "Allowing injunctive relief on the ground that the advertisement constitutes an improper proxy solicitation would pervert the legitimate protective function of the regulation into an unconstitutional licensing of political speech."[21] However, the Second Circuit Federal Appeals Court overruled the lower court, holding that the SEC's rule could apply even when there was no direct appeal to shareholders.[22]

The rules apply, said the appeals court, "not only to direct requests to furnish, revoke or withhold proxies, but also to communications which may indirectly accomplish such a result or constitute a step in a chain of communications designed ultimately to accomplish such a result."[23] According to the court, "[d]etermination in every case is whether the challenged communication, seen in the totality of circumstances, is 'reasonably calculated' to influence the shareholders' votes."[24] Noting that SEC rules require that "solicitations in the form of 'speeches, press releases, and television scripts' be filed with the SEC,"[25] the court agreed with the SEC's brief in favor of LILCO's position that "it would 'permit easy evasion of the proxy rules' to exempt all general and indirect communications to shareholders,"[26] including the advertisement in question, even if the information it contained also concerned matters of general public interest.

A case that illustrates the problems that public relations and advertising professionals face in determining the kinds of information a company can and should make public (if that information could impact the trading of its securities), as well as when that information should be released and the ramifications of either carelessness or deliberate deception in the information-dissemination process, is *Securities and Exchange Commission v. Texas Gulf Sulphur Co.*[27]

The case began in the early 1960s when Texas Gulf Sulphur's geophysical surveys revealed the possibility of significant deposits of copper, zinc, and other valuable ores in land owned by the company in eastern Canada. Testing at the site confirmed that the possibility was high that a valuable strike had been located. This information was kept strictly confidential so that Texas Gulf Sulphur would be able to acquire additional lands adjoining its holdings. Further chemical testing convinced the company's scientists and senior management that, if anything, the initial estimates of the worth of the discovery had significantly underestimated its value.

Approximately 6 months later, with most of its land acquisition complete, the company again began to drill into the ore to obtain additional samples. During this time, a number of Texas Gulf Sulphur's management officials and persons said to have received tips from these officials about the value of the discovery purchased significant amounts of the company's stock. In addition, the company issued stock options to its highest paid employees, several of whom knew about the findings revealed by the analysis of the samples from the Canadian site.

With exploratory drilling underway, rumors of a potentially valuable discovery by Texas Gulf Sulphur began to circulate in the financial community. Concerned that the company's strategic and tactical plans for announcing the findings could be compromised, the company, with the help of a public relations consultant, drafted a press statement that was released to major daily newspapers. The statement announced that, although a strike had been made and early results appeared favorable, the rumors of a major discovery exaggerated "the scale of operations and mention plans and statistics . . . that are without factual basis. . . ." According to the release, "[t]he work done to date [on the Canadian site] has not been sufficient to reach definite conclusions and any statement as to size and grade of ore would be premature and possibly misleading."[28]

In the SEC's opinion, the statements both made or implied in Texas Gulf Sulphur's press release and the omission of information known to the company, but not included in the release, involved "material" facts. This satisfied the legal requirement, specified by the Securities Exchange Act, that before a company's commercial speech can be challenged under Rule 10(b)(5)[29] as fraudulent it must contain information that allegedly could have influenced investors or shareholders to purchase, dispose of, or fail to trade in a company's stock (or how to vote in a proxy dispute).

Although the extent of actual detriment to investors and shareholders by reliance on the information contained in the press release was questioned by both the federal district court and the federal appeals court that subsequently heard the case on an appeal by the company, both concluded that the SEC and aggrieved investors and shareholders had sufficient evidence to pursue suits that eventually cost the company hundreds of thousands of dollars and much negative publicity.

Texas Gulf Sulphur illustrates a number of important issues for those engaged in communication activities involving securities transactions or proxy issues. The courts noted that there was nothing wrong with withholding information about the potential value of the discovery until additional land purchases were completed. However, Texas Gulf Sulphur had an affirmative duty to disclose the information promptly once the acquisitions were completed and drilling had resumed, or it would risk violating the SEC's rules requiring timely disclosure of material information, which the company had, in part, satisfied.

Although the courts found that the company had partly satisfied the requirement for timely disclosure, they also found that the SEC's rules mandating that the dissemination of material information be made so as to give the information wide distribution had been violated. In defending themselves against accusations of fraud, several of Texas Gulf Sulphur's corporate officials involved in the case argued that the information about the strike was already public, based on limited publication by Canadian media. The court gave short shrift to this argument, finding that, "rumors and casual disclosure through Canadian media, especially in view of the [earlier] 'gloomy' . . . release denying the rumors . . . hardly sufficed to inform traders on American [stock] exchanges. . . ."[30]

Although ultimately not a factor in the outcome, the efforts of the company's outside public relations counsel in drafting the fraudulent press release also could have subjected the public relations agency to legal liability if a court determined that the agency either knew or should have known that false or misleading material statements of fact were being disseminated. Additionally, although the courts held that Texas Gulf Sulphur had no duty to correct speculation or misstatements made by the financial press to which the company made no contribution, such a duty could arise if misinformation began to circulate based on the company's own statements, unless the company's clearly articulated message was simply misquoted or misunderstood by the media.

Finally, although the focus of the SEC and the courts was on the content of the communication, and not its form, it seems likely that Texas Gulf Sulphur would have been found equally liable for disseminating misleading information if the information had been conveyed by an internal newsletter, in-person briefing, news conference, quarterly or annual report, or other public relations tactic, so long as there was evidence that the information was "material" and that investors or shareholders learned of it and relied on it to their detriment.

Yet another issue of importance to advertising and public relations professionals present in *Texas Gulf Sulphur* is the possibility of violating a fiduciary relationship through "insider trading" or "tipping."[31] The primary duty of those who oversee the management of a corporation is to represent the best interests of the company's shareholders. Thus, using nonpublic information about a company's financial status to trade in a company's securities or engage in stock option plans without first disclosing such information might constitute a breach of fiduciary responsibility that could subject the company and individual officials—including those who manage the company's communication efforts—to legal liabilities.

Similarly, it is considered a violation of fiduciary trust to "tip off" confidants or financial consultants about nonpublic material information that could influence trading in a company's securities. As the appeals court in *Texas Gulf Sulphur* noted, the SEC's regulations are "also applicable to one possessing the information who may not be strictly termed an 'insider' within the meaning of [the Act]. Thus anyone in possession of material inside information must either disclose it to the investing public or, if he is disabled from disclosing it in order to protect a corporate confidence . . . must abstain from trading in or recommending the securities concerned. . . ."[32] Clearly, such requirements would apply to public relations or advertising counsel. Violations of the anti-tipping rules could subject both those who pass along the information and those who profit from it to legal sanctions. For example, the court in Texas Gulf Sulphur concluded that, "all transactions in TGS stock or [stock option] calls by individuals apprised of the drilling results . . . were made in violation of [SEC] Rule 10(b)(5)."[33]

Perhaps the best-known incident involving communication professionals and insider trading involved Anthony Franco, who, at the time of the incident, was president of the Public Relations Society of America (PRSA). According to the SEC, Franco was guilty of a violation of fiduciary trust for allegedly purchasing stock in a company to which he was a consultant based on insider information that the company would soon be acquired by another corporation. Although formally admitting no wrong doing, Franco was eventually forced to resign the PRSA presidency and pledge not to act on insider information in the future.

The Franco incident raises yet another concern for those engaged in commercial speech. Even when not officially acting as an agent or consultant to a company (and therefore technically with no fiduciary responsibility to its shareholders), advertising and public relations professionals may learn of material information about a company's financial status. The SEC and the courts have held in a number of instances that there is a duty for these "market" insiders, as well as for those actually inside the company, to divulge such information or forego trading in the securities at the risk of being found in violation of Rule 10(b)(5).

In *Carpenter v. U.S.*,[34] the Supreme Court of the United States refused to overturn a finding of fraud by a financial columnist for the *Wall Street Journal* who was convicted of using information learned "on the street" for his own gain, as well as tipping off investors in advance about companies he would tout or condemn in his column. Although the columnist was judged not to possess any fiduciary relationship to the companies mentioned in his column or to the market, he nonetheless was held liable under SEC rules prohibiting fraud.

Enforcement of SEC Regulations

Congress has given the SEC civil and criminal remedies for violations of the securities laws and regulations. In addition, the courts have interpreted the securities laws as providing private citizens with the right to go to court to seek money damages from companies and individuals who have, through omission or misrepresentation of material information, induced the investors to buy or sell securities to their disadvantage.

The *Texas Gulf Sulphur* case provides illustrations of how these sanctions may be imposed. After finding that the press release downplaying the magnitude of the ore deposit discovery was misleading to stockholders and investors, and that actions by the company's senior officials and their friends acting on their tips constituted illegal insider trading, the federal appeals court turned its attention to establishing liability and assessing damages. The court found that, contrary to the lower court's opinion, Texas Gulf Sulphur could be subjected to an injunction sought by the SEC to desist from future insider trading. The court remanded the case to the district court for further action on this issue.

Similarly, the appeals court sent back for further proceedings the assessment of liability for the company officials who had violated Rule 10(b)(5), either by insider trading or by exercising stock options during the period before full public disclosure was made. The court also opened the door to later civil suits by stockholders and traders who could demonstrate that they had been materially misled by the fraudulent activities of both the company and its managers.

In a series of subsequent cases, the lower courts decreed that the individuals within the company who had purchased stock based on insider information would be enjoined from future insider trading practices and be forced to disgorge their profits from such purchases. Although it was judged that the company could be the subject of the injunction sought by the SEC if there was evidence of continuing or probable future wrong doing, more troubling for the company was the filing of more than 100 civil cases by disgruntled investors against the company and its management. Depending on how the value of the shares traded based on the misrepresentation of material information by the company was determined, at one point the damages claims against the company ranged from roughly $80 million to as much as $390 million—a figure more than the total worth of the company.

The lessons to be learned for advertising and public relations professionals are clear. It would be prudent to be extremely careful in counseling senior management about the need for a company's broad and timely disclosure of securities information, as well as to create a system of checks and balances within the department or agency by instituting a "disclosure compliance program."[35] Such a program could help forestall the risk of inadvertently publishing information or running afoul of other provisions of the securities laws that could lead to violations of SEC regulations and possibly subject the company or client to crippling lawsuits.

Additionally, advertising and public relations professionals should be wary of capitalizing on material information they acquire by virtue of their status as company or marketplace insiders by trading in securities, passing along tips to friends or brokers, or acting on such tips themselves. It would be wise to pursue such efforts only after seeking sound investment advice from financial consultants knowledgeable about the most up-to-date rulings by the SEC regarding the obligations and legal liabilities of those who engage in such trading practices.

THE FOOD AND DRUG ADMINISTRATION

In contrast to the activities of the SEC, which, of necessity, must be of concern to a variety of commercial speakers, the focus of commercial speech regulation by the Food and Drug Administration (FDA) is much more limited. The FDA is part of the larger U.S. Department of Health and Human Services. Headquartered in the Washington, DC, area, the FDA employs more than 7,000 people in Washington and in 10 regional offices across the country. Its missions include: (a) approving new drugs, medical devices, and certain food additives for safety and, in some cases, effectiveness; (b) setting standards for foods and the labeling of foods, and then ensuring (via testing) that such foods meet these standards; (c) inspecting sites where drugs, cosmetics, medical devices, and foods are produced to ensure these products meet the FDA's public safety standards; and (d) issuing public warnings or taking legal action when unsafe products threaten the public welfare. The FDA's professional staff consists mainly of biologists, chemists, nutritionists, pharmacologists, attorneys, and other compliance personnel and consumer-affairs officers.

Although its name might imply a wider jurisdiction, for the most part the FDA's direct interest in commercial speech is limited to regulating information about the contents and safety of prescription drugs advertised or promoted via the mass media. Although the FDA retains jurisdiction over the labeling of over-the-counter drugs, cosmetics, and food stuffs, Sections 5 and 12 of the Federal Trade Commission Act (discussed in chap. 4) give regulatory power over commercial advertising and other forms of nonlabel commercial speech involving these products to the FTC.

Although normally the FTC will follow its own guidelines for regulation of such commercial speech, including requirements for prior substantiation and appropriate clinical trial, the two agencies usually work closely together in determining what will be considered false or deceptive commercial speech. For example, the FDA publishes guidelines that discuss appropriate labeling requirements. These specify uses and levels of effectiveness for many over-the-counter medications and health claims related to food that the FTC may take into account in determining its regulations of commercial speech involving such products.

The Federal Food, Drug and Cosmetic Act[36] defines a *prescription drug* as a drug "not safe for [human] use except under the supervision of a licensed practitioner"[37] because of potential harm to the consumer either as the result of its use or from employing the methods necessary for its use. Alternatively, a *drug* may be defined as a "prescription drug" following the FDA's policy of labeling all new drugs as initially needing "the professional supervision of a practitioner licensed by law to administer such drug[s]"[38] unless the Agency is satisfied that the new drug can be safely introduced and sold over the counter without this requirement.

The FDA's jurisdiction over prescription drug-related commercial speech emanates, in part, from its original grant of power to regulate "labels and any written, printed or graphic matter (1) upon any article [drug] or any of its containers or wrappers, or (2) accompanying such article."[39] Although the statute does not specifically define what is meant by "printed or graphic matter . . . accompanying such [an] article," the FDA and the courts have treated this language as authorizing broad authority over commercial messages that are part of a promotional campaign, including retail sales promotion materials and direct mail pieces.

The FDA's authority to regulate commercial speech was made more explicit by a series of amendments to the Food, Drug and Cosmetic Act, beginning in the 1960s, that specifically gave the FDA jurisdiction over commercial speech involving prescription drugs while reserving the power to regulate nonprescription drug commercial speech to the FTC.

Usually the FDA will treat commercial speech as falling specifically within its regulatory authority if the prescription drug information is disseminated through broadcast or print commercials, or through public relations activities aimed at the mass media. FDA jurisdiction over nonmedia promotional techniques is neither expressly defined nor directly suggested by the statute. However, in *Nature Food Centres, Inc., v. U.S.*,[40] a series of lectures touting the alleged virtues of a dietary supplement was permitted to be entered as evidence on the question of whether the supplement was mislabeled.

In *U.S. v. Articles of Drug, etc.*,[41] and *U.S. v. Guardian Chemical Corp.*,[42] courts held that printed brochures and pamphlets need not directly accompany a drug to be considered part of the drug's "label," and therefore subject to FDA regulation. Similarly, in *U.S. v. Diapulse Mfg. Corp. of America*,[43] the court ruled that the sending of reprints of medical journal articles constituted "labels" accompanying a medical device. However, despite these rulings, public relations and marketing campaigns, such as direct contact with physicians or news conferences announcing the creation or availability of new drugs, may not be within the FDA's regulatory reach.

FDA Content-Based Regulation of Prescription Drug Commercial Speech

The specific regulations promulgated and enforced with respect to the content of commercial speech within the FDA's jurisdiction are primarily designed to ensure consumer safety. Such content-based regulation would appear to be constitutional under *Virginia State Board of Pharmacy*[44] (discussed in chap. 2) if the commercial speech in question falls within the "untruthful speech," which the Supreme Court of the United States defined as "false or misleading." As the Court noted, "Obviously, much commercial speech is not provably false, or even wholly false, but only deceptive or misleading. We foresee no obstacle to a State's dealing effectively with this problem."[45]

The government does not have a totally free hand to regulate commercial speech just because it involves prescription drugs, however. In *Oregon Newspaper Publishers Assoc. v. Peterson*,[46] the newspaper organization was permitted to go ahead with its challenge to a state law regulating prescription drug advertising. It did so despite the state's arguments that the FDA's regulations made the plaintiff's case meaningless because the state law effectively went beyond federal law by banning such advertising, rather than simply making it conform to federal regulations.

FDA regulations normally require that a detailed list of the ingredients contained in a prescription drug appear in any commercial advertisement or other speech in a prominent and readable manner. Additionally, the message must indicate the percentage of each ingredient, and the list of ingredients must follow the same order as found on the prescription drug's label. Beginning in the early 1960s, the FDA also mandated that the commercial advertising must contain the prescription drug's generic name each time the brand name of the product is mentioned.

As might be imagined, the requirement that the generic name accompany the brand name proved onerous for copywriters and designers who were attempting to use advertisements, brochures, and other communication vehicles to build brand loyalty for a company's product among physicians. The regulation eventually was challenged in federal court by the pharmaceutical industry in *Abbott Laboratories v. Celebrezze*.[47] The case was eventually settled when the FDA agreed to modify its requirements; the generic name now needs to appear in conjunction with the brand name when the brand name is "featured" in the advertisement, but not when subsequently appearing in body copy on the same page of the advertisement. However, it is necessary to include the generic name with the brand name in statements specifying benefits of the drug or detailing side effects.

When the generic name appears, the FDA's regulations require it to be visually or aurally prominent, and it must be located physically close to the brand name in the text of the advertisement. Typically this may be accomplished by placing the generic name in brackets after the brand name, or by adding such wording as "... a brand of (generic name)." The regulations also specify that the generic name must be set in type that is at least half the size of the brand name.

FDA Requirements for a "True Summary" of Side Effects and Effectiveness

The Food, Drug and Cosmetic Act mandates that each commercial message promoting a prescription drug must include a "summary" of specified information about its safety and effectiveness.[48] FDA regulations specify that the information within this summary must reflect the wording accepted by the FDA for the drug's package labeling, including a description of all the specific side effects and "contraindications" that could result from taking the drug, as well as any warnings or cautions for its use.[49]

The regulations prescribe that the requirements for a truthful summary apply to the entire advertisement, and that "untrue or misleading information in [one part] of the advertisement"[50] will not be corrected by inclusion of correct information in another. However, even if part of the advertisement "would make the advertisement false or misleading by reason of the omission of appropriate qualification," the overall advertisement still will be in compliance if a "prominent reference [is included] of a more complete discussion of such qualification or information."[51]

The requirements for information about effectiveness and side effects are limited to information about the purposes for which the drug is intended as promoted in the commercial message. Therefore, the FDA does not require an advertisement for a prescription drug that promotes a specific use for the drug to contain statements of side effects or effectiveness for all the other possible purposes for which a drug might be adopted or recommended by the medical or pharmaceutical communities. However, the FDA has ruled that it is impermissible to group a number of side effects or contraindications together under one general warning unless the language of the warning conforms with the FDA's previously approved language. Also, specific information about possible side effects must be included for each "contraindication" or claim.

Commercial speakers need to beware of inadvertently suggesting uses for drugs that have not been given prior approved by the FDA, for fear the commercial claims may cause the drug to reclassified as a "new drug" under FDA rules. Uses for a drug that are "generally recognized as safe and effective among experts qualified by scientific training and experience to evaluate the safety and effectiveness,"[52] for which evidence exists of well-conducted clinical evaluations, or which are documented in medical literature as safe and effective generally will not be seen as creating a "new drug."

FDA regulations detailing the kinds of information or omissions of information the agency might find to be false or misleading are extensive. Clearly, commercial speech about prescription drugs that (a) fails to indicate possible side effects, (b) exaggerates the effectiveness of a drug compared to its drawbacks, (c) neglects to specify the negative effects of long-term usage, (d) contains "a representation . . . not approved or permitted for use in the labeling, that a drug is better, more effective, [or] useful in a broader range of conditions or patients" than can be justified by at least two appropriate clinical trials,[53] or (e) claims that a drug is safer than a competitor's product without appropriate scientific evidence generally are judged false and deceptive.

Additionally, a number of FDA regulations specifying the kinds of commercial speech claims the agency might find to be false or deceptive are concerned with the inappropriate use of statistical tests, sample sizes, and levels of statistical significance. Examples include statements such as "pooling data from various insignificant or dissimilar studies"[54] in such a way as to incorrectly suggest statistical significance, erroneously using a statistical finding of "'no significant difference' . . . to deny or conceal . . . real clinical difference,"[55] or employing "reports or statements represented to be statistical analyses . . . that are inconsistent with or violate the established principles of statistical theory."[56]

A third general category of potentially misleading statements involves misrepresentations about subjects in clinical trials. For example, it is false and deceptive to study "normal individuals without disclosing that [they] are normal"[57] unless the drug is being marketed to such individuals. Similarly, commercial messages that fail to disclose the potential side effects of a drug when administered to a "selected class" of subjects for whom the drug is actually intended would likely draw the FDA's fire. So too would claims for a drug's effectiveness when the test data are "derived with dosages different from those recommended in approved or permitted labeling,"[58] or when they "represent or suggest that drug dosages properly recommended for use in the treatment of certain classes of patients . . . are safe and effective for the treatment of other classes of patients . . . when such is not the case."[59]

A fourth category involves inclusion or reference to literature that either is false or could be construed in a misleading way. For example, commercial speakers should be careful not to publish testimonials about a drug's effectiveness that exceed the product's actual tested effectiveness, or that have been made questionable by scientific studies published more recently than those cited in the testimonials. Additionally, studies that claim a drug's effectiveness that could be attributed to either a combination of drugs or to the psychological "placebo effect" of taking any medication may run afoul of FDA regulations.[60]

The FDA also might find problems with the manner in which commercial information is presented. For example, false or misleading statements may arise from a failure "to present information relating to side effects ... with [appropriate] prominence and readability ... taking into account ... [such] factors as typography, layout, contrast headlines ... [and] white space. . . ."[61] Similar concerns also could arise in broadcast advertisements.

The FDA has recognized a number of limited exceptions to its "brief summary" requirements for prescription drugs. Commercial speech that simply "reminds" providers or consumers of a drug by mentioning its name and/or the costs of such a drug need not provide information on side effects, "contra-indications," or ingredients. Similarly, advertisements for sale of drugs in bulk to be repackaged or relabeled, or advertisements intended for pharmacists to be used by them as ingredients of prescriptions they create for their clientele are exempt, as long as the advertisements do not contain claims for a drug's safety or effectiveness.[62]

A more general exception to the FDA's commercial speech content-based prescription drug regulations has been created to provide a means to disseminate information about new drugs or new uses for existing drugs through scientific colloquia and professional conferences. Even when a new drug has not officially passed FDA standards, the agency will usually permit information about the existence and properties of the drug to be communicated so long as such meetings are conducted under the auspices of disinterested parties (such as scientific societies or universities) and the information presented is factually correct and balanced. However, although there has been little litigation on this issue to date, the FDA may not be as willing to forego its information requirements for new drugs if the information is communicated by means of manufacturer-sponsored conventions, press conferences, news releases, or other public relations techniques.

Enforcement of FDA Prescription Drug Advertising Regulations

Although the FDA's enabling legislation provides for a number of legal remedies by which the agency may enforce its regulations of prescription drug-related commercial speech, for the most part these remedies remain weapons for threatening legal action, rather than for actual use. This is because the mere threat of legal action has proven to be a virtual guarantee that the offending party will voluntarily take the steps necessary to bring the criticized commercial speech within FDA guidelines.

The Food, Drug and Cosmetic Act provides the FDA with the power to seek injunctive relief, seizure of offending products, and/or criminal penalties for prescription drugs the FDA believes have been "misbranded" (including violations of the Agency's prescription drug advertising policies).[63] However, the offending party must notify physicians or others to whom the communication has been addressed if the information or omission of information the FDA feels is necessary is to be accepted and implemented by the drug's manufacturer or its commercial speech representative.

REGULATION OF COMMERCIAL SPEECH
AND THE FEDERAL FAIR HOUSING ACT

The Federal Fair Housing Act of 1968[64] makes it illegal to discriminate in the sale or rental of housing. Section 804(c) of the Act also "prohibits the making, printing, and publishing of advertisements [or other commercial speech] which state a preference, limitation or discrimination on the basis of race, color, religion, sex, handicap, familial status or national origin. The prohibition applies to publishers, such as newspapers and directories, as well as to persons and entities who place real estate advertisements."[65]

Practices that have run afoul of provisions of this statute, or of the regulations promulgated by the Department of Housing and Urban Development (HUD), the federal agency charged with enforcing fair housing laws, include (a) exclusively employing White models in photographs or illustrations accompanying advertisements depicting potential clients in marketing campaigns for housing developments, (b) showing only adult couples in brochures describing rental property, or (c) specifying preferences for gender ("males preferred") or religion ("a Christian community") in advertising copy. Classified advertisements by individuals seeking roommates are exceptions.

Advertising and public relations professionals should be alert to possible trouble when using terms such as *exclusive* or *private, mature* or *adult, no children* or *couple preferred (or only),* and *Only kosher meals served* or *close to (named denominational) church* in commercial speech related to the sale or rental of housing properties. Exceptions are recognized for commercial speech related to housing that is specifically designed for the elderly or the physically challenged, or is restricted to members of a religious sect, although such speech cannot discriminate by race or other characteristic unrelated to the specific exemption.

HUD's expansive interpretation of the Federal Fair Housing Act's regulation of discriminatory commercial speech has been ratified by the courts. In *Ragin v. New York Times,*[66] a second circuit federal court of appeals in New York upheld the viability of a discrimination claim based on the failure to use minorities as models in housing advertisements that, the plaintiffs said, indicated a preference for Whites as purchases or renters in certain neighborhoods and rental complexes. Finding that such evidence might cause a jury to conclude that the *New York Times* had violated the Fair Housing Act's provisions against discrimination, the court remanded the case for further consideration. The Supreme Court of the United States elected not to hear the newspaper's appeal.

REGULATION OF COMMERCIAL SPEECH
BY OTHER FEDERAL LAWS AND AGENCIES

Simply listing the federal statutes and regulations governing commercial speech that exist, in addition to those involving the FTC, the FDA, the SEC, and other departments and agencies already discussed in this and earlier chapters, could take up much of the rest of this book. For example, there are more than 800 federal statutes affecting commercial speech about everything from atomic energy to Woodsy Owl, including burial of veterans, currency usage in advertising, eavesdropping devices, foods (beef to watermelons), use of insignia of the Girl Scouts and the Olympics, railroads, the Swiss Federation coat of arms, and water hyacinths (transportation thereof).

In addition, more than 4,000 federal regulations cover these subjects in more detail, as well as specify procedural and technical requirements for satisfying these regulations. Prudent advertising and public relations professionals would be wise to review the list of these laws and regulations to determine which pertain to their commercial speech efforts.

Nonetheless, there are a number of subjects covered by federal statutes and regulations that deserve brief special mention because of the problems they might cause for significant numbers of those engaged in commercial speech. These include commercial speech about employment, banking, billboards, and alcoholic beverages.

Various civil rights statutes make discrimination by race, age, and other characteristics illegal in employment practices. These same strictures often apply to commercial speech publicizing these subjects. The Civil Rights Act of 1964[67] forbids employment notices that appear to discriminate by race or sex, and gives those harmed by such advertising the right to file civil suits seeking money damages both against those who place the notices and, in some cases, against those who publish them.

For example, in *Hailes v. United Air Lines*,[68] a federal appeals court upheld a claim that an employment notice seeking women for flight attendant positions had reasonably been interpreted by a man as discouraging his application for such a position. In *Pittsburgh Press v. The Pittsburgh Commission on Human Relations*[69] (discussed in chap. 2), the Supreme Court of the United States found that the newspaper's help-wanted advertisements, segregated by male and female headings, were not protected by the First Amendment. Congress enacted similar restrictions against discrimination by age in the Age Discrimination in Employment Act of 1967[70] and against physical and mental disabilities in the Americans with Disabilities Act of 1990.[71]

Complaints about discrimination involving these characteristics are often generated by use of terms in commercial speech employment notices, such as *young, recent college graduate*, or *able-bodied*. Advertising and public relations professionals should also be alert to terms such as *junior assistant* or *first-time beginner* in describing the position level that is the subject of the commercial speech.

Of more potential concern for those engaged in commercial speech about employment opportunities are the sections of federal laws banning activities indicating "any preference . . . based on race," including advertising and other publicity. Until *Ragin* (discussed earlier), most authorities had agreed with the logic of the court in *Housing Opportunities Made Equal v. Cincinnati Enquirer, Inc.*[72]—that civil rights claims should be limited to statements constituting a "campaign of discrimination," or indicating a "preference, limitation, or discrimination based on race, color . . . or national origin. . . ."[73] The expansive interpretation by the federal court in *Ragin*, however, should be a warning signal for advertising and public relations professionals to take a second look at common practices or thoughtless actions that could be considered discriminatory, particularly when viewed through the eyes of groups that historically have experienced the effects of discrimination.

Banking advertising and public relations are closely regulated by a variety of federal agencies. Both the Federal Reserve System and the Federal Deposit Insurance Corporation set policies for the operation of member banks and financial institutions, including regulations involving commercial speech. Similarly, the Federal Home Loan Bank Board and the Federal Savings and Loan Insurance Corporation regulate the commercial speech of federal thrift and nonfederally chartered thrift institutions, respectively, while the National Credit Union Administration oversees federal credit unions.

Each of these federal agency's concerns with commercial speech arises primarily with enforcement of various provisions of the federal "Truth In Lending Act,"[74] which regulates commercial speech involving offers of consumer credit. Both regulatory agencies and the courts have broadly defined commercial speech under the Act, including, for example, media advertising, direct mail solicitations, and messages accompanying loan applications or checking account statements. The Act forbids commercial speech designed to encourage offers of credit that are not of a "usual and customary" nature, such as offers of low interest that actually are unavailable to the consumer.[75]

The statute also requires commercial speakers to include "disclosures" in a "clear and conspicuous" manner about actual finance charges and other charges not specified in the finance program (such as membership fees and annual percentage rates) if the subject of the speech is the offer of a credit card or charge plan that entails continuing offers of credit at a specified rate of interest. Terms that may "trigger" these disclosures include promotional come-ons like "6 months at no interest, then a small monthly charge," "no money down," and "easy credit terms available."[76]

Those engaged in commercial speech involving financial institutions also should be aware of the provisions of the Federal Consumer Leasing Act,[77] which regulates the offering of leases on personal property such as automobiles, and the antidiscrimination provisions of the Equal Credit Opportunity Act[78] and the Federal Deposit Insurance Corporation,[79] which make it illegal to deny credit or provide loans based on such characteristics as race, gender, or age.

Although most laws regulating outdoor advertising are state laws, several federal statutes and regulations—such as the Federal Highway Act and the Highway Beautification Act—limit the location and size of billboards along federal highways. Because billboards and other signage often run afoul of community or environmental groups on aesthetic grounds, there have been frequent efforts to limit or ban such signs, either by zoning regulations or laws forbidding all outdoor advertising. Objections to such laws and regulations based on a First Amendment rationale have met with mixed results.

In *Metromedia, Inc. v. City of San Diego*[80] (discussed in chap. 2), the Supreme Court of the United States rendered a mixed opinion regarding the constitutionality of the city's efforts to limit billboards for safety and aesthetic reasons, but held that efforts to limit otherwise protected commercial speech must serve an important governmental purpose and be no more extensive than necessary to carry out the government's legitimate interests. As more outdoor advertising signs are erected, complete with eye-catching graphics and electronic displays, the question of whether purely aesthetic reasons for governments to ban or limit billboards will suffice to meet constitutional objections is yet to be determined.

Unlike billboard advertising, commercial speech involving alcoholic beverages has historically been the subject of extensive federal and state regulations. Because of the controversial nature of the effects of drinking alcoholic beverages, regulations involving its production, consumption, and promotion date back two centuries. Although a complete discussion of the myriad laws and rules regulating commercial speech about alcohol is beyond the scope of this text, advertising and public relations professionals involved with this product should be made aware of the more significant federal statutes and Bureau of Alcohol, Tobacco and Firearms (BATF) regulations that impact the promotion of alcoholic beverages.

Because the federal government acquired unique control over alcohol through the passage of the 21st Amendment,[81] the status of the constitutional protection for commercial speech involving intoxicating beverages is somewhat muddled. Although the *Central Hudson*[82] four-part test (discussed in chap. 2) normally would be applicable to such commercial speech, those wishing to regulate speech promoting alcoholic beverages typically argue that, by definition, the government's interest in regulating such speech outweighs the First Amendment interests of the commercial speaker. Short of laws or regulations that completely ban such speech, these antialcohol speech arguments have often been found to be persuasive by courts hearing such cases.

Two recent federal cases indicate the unresolved nature of constitutional protection. In *Adolph Coors Co. v. Bentsen*,[83] the Supreme Court of the United States invalidated restrictions on statements about the alcoholic content of malt beverage labels on the basis that the record was devoid of evidence that truthful information would lead to "strength wars" among brewers. However, in *Anheuser-Busch, Inc., v. Mayor and City Council of Baltimore*,[84] a federal district court upheld the city's rationale for regulating outdoor advertising of alcoholic beverages based on concern about the "welfare and temperance of minors."[85] The court agreed with the assumption that there is a direct link between advertising and consumption, rejecting the plaintiff's arguments that less restrictive means were available. (Similarly, in *Penn Advertising of Baltimore, Inc., v. Mayor and City Council of Baltimore*,[86] a different district court upheld a city ordinance restricting the use of billboards to advertise cigarettes because of concerns about exposure of the commercial message to minors.)

The federal government's regulation of commercial speech about alcoholic beverages is administered by the BATF—an agency of the Department of the Treasury. The Bureau, which has different specific sets of regulations for distilled, brewed, and fermented beverages, generally requires that all alcoholic beverage commercial speech contain certain kinds of information, and forbids the inclusion of statements it considers unacceptable. Required information includes (a) government warnings about the effects of consumption, (b) the company that has produced the product and paid for the speech, and (c) whether the beverage is considered to be a malt beverage, wine, or distilled spirit. Prohibited statements include disparagement of a competitor's product, claims of a health or medicinal nature, and messages considered false, misleading, or indecent.

In addition, the BATF strictly regulates such marketing activities as cooperative advertising schemes and the purchase of advertising in publications produced by retailers. The BATF also has interpreted an Internal Revenue Service ruling as prohibiting the use of athletes in distilled liquor commercial speech, and limits their use in wine or beer promotions.

OVERVIEW OF STATE REGULATION
OF COMMERCIAL SPEECH

Because of the federal constitutional First Amendment issues inherent in governmental attempts to restrict commercial speech, as well as the prominence of federal regulatory agencies like the FTC and SEC, many of those working in advertising or public relations lose sight of the role that state statutes and regulations play in the overall regulation of commercial speech. However, in the same way that much of the law that impacts our everyday existence is found at the state level, state regulation of commercial speech is both comprehensive and extensive.

Many of these laws and regulations are discussed in other parts of this text. However, a number of state statutes and administrative regulations deserve special mention here because of their impact on advertising and public relations professionals, and because they parallel the federal regulations discussed in this and the preceding chapter.

False, Unfair, or Deceptive Commercial Speech:
The State Approach

Chapter 2 noted that, beginning in the early 1900s, states tried to regulate the negative effects of wildly extravagant advertising claims by passing so-called "Printers' Ink" statutes. However, these efforts proved ineffective because they neither allowed consumers or competitors to bring private causes of action nor established effective state agencies or commissions to oversee and enforce the law. Instead, most of these early state laws left it to the discretion of local prosecutors to instigate criminal proceedings against those accused of violating commercial speech statutes—a process that proved cumbersome because of the long and detailed procedures necessary to carry out criminal investigations and prosecutions.[87]

Therefore, it was not surprising that federal regulation, either by federal laws or federal agency rules, became the method of choice by those who wished to regulate commercial speech. The development of federal statutes and regulations, however, did not mean that states surrendered complete control of commercial speech to the federal government. Today, all 50 states have their versions of "mini" Federal Trade Commission/Lanham Acts that prohibit various deceptive commercial speech practices, although generally without the provisions for separate regulatory commissions or agencies. In addition, a myriad of state statutes, common laws, and administrative rules regulate many specific products, occupations, and services, either co-extensively with federal law or in addition to federal regulation.

Sorting out exactly who has jurisdiction in a commercial speech case, or whether and in what circumstances both the federal and state legal systems can each have a hand in regulating a commercial speaker's efforts, creates the kinds of problems that form the bases of final exams in law schools. Generally, federal law prevails if Congress either has exclusive jurisdiction conferred on it by the constitution (e.g., the power to determine the copyright status of an original creative work), or if a congressional statute specifically or implicitly is meant to reserve regulation for the federal government (e.g., various federal statutes regulating over-the-air broadcasting).

In those areas in which both the federal government and a state may regulate commercial speech, the federal rules will exclusively apply if the state regulation conflicts with an express federal statutory provision. Although conflicts of a jurisdictional nature might help a defendant in the procedural development of a lawsuit claiming that the plaintiff's injury was suffered because of false or deceptive commercial speech, perhaps the wisest course of action for advertising and public relations professionals is to (a) be familiar with both state and federal regulations, (b) assume that both apply, and (c) act accordingly.

The overwhelming majority of state statutes mimicking the Federal Trade Commission/Lanham Acts' provisions regulating false, unfair, or deceptive commercial speech practices allow competitors to pursue private lawsuits in state courts, in addition to suits brought under the appropriate federal statutes. This reflects the historical antecedents of much of state regulation of commercial speech in English common law, which prohibited one manufacturer from "passing off" his or her goods as the product of another. Often called "unfair competition" or "palming off," statutes regulating commercial speech in relation to charges of the "passing off" of goods almost always involve speech that negligently or intentionally misrepresents a product in ways that have a tendency to cause confusion on the part of a potential consumer.[88]

State statutes against "passing off" normally require a complainant to show that the defendant has actively and directly engaged in some action designed to mislead. Interestingly, although such efforts may run afoul of other state laws, using "trade dress" (distinctive design or packaging) that resembles another product is usually not considered "passing off." Similarly, removing a label from one's own product or simply failing to label a product normally do not invoke the provisions of state anti-"passing off" statutes.

In addition to laws and regulations prohibiting "passing off," a significant number of states today have either modified existing statutes or passed additional laws to permit private lawsuits by consumers and, in some instances, competitors. These statutes, often referred to as "consumer protection" or "consumer fraud prevention" acts, usually are based on claims of harm other than "passing off" that allegedly result from detrimental reliance on false, unfair, or deceptive commercial speech. A number of states also permit the filing of class-action suits in such cases by consumers. In many states, these consumer-oriented statutes authorize the state's attorney general or other state official to bring suit to prevent false or deceptive commercial speech practices, either as a representative of consumers or competitors, or on their own initiative.

Variations in these laws from state to state make it difficult to summarize them in any meaningful manner. For example, some states require that suits can only be brought by those directly connected with defendants (sometimes referred to as "privity of contract"), either by being in actual competition with the defendants or by being the recipient of their false or deceptive commercial speech. Other states permit suits as well by those only indirectly related to or affected by the defendant's disputed commercial speech practices. Wise advertising and public relations professionals should both take note and seek interpretation of the applicable statutes in the states in which they practice to minimize unpleasant legal encounters with disgruntled state officials, consumers, or competitors.

Perhaps not surprisingly, many state courts, faced with adjudicating cases under state laws prohibiting false, unfair, or deceptive commercial speech, look to the interpretations of the FTC or the federal courts for guidance in defining these terms so as not to produce a jumble of confusing and possibly conflicting decisions. Similarly, state courts often take their cue for determination of "unfairness" from cases involving interpretation of FTC regulations. For example, numerous state courts follow the lead of the Supreme Court of the United States, in *FTC v. Sperry & Hutchinson Co.*[89] In this case, the Court approved of a definition of *unfairness* that looked at the extent of harm to those relying on commercial speech claims that are either offensive to public policy or in violation of some legal definition of immoral activity.

Although federal regulatory agency and commission interpretations are influential when it comes to the definition of terms, state courts normally do not incorporate federal policy requirements (e.g., the FTC's prior-substantiation doctrine; see chap. 4) into the substantive language of state mini-FTC/Lanham Act statutes.

State Remedies for False, Deceptive, or Unfair Commercial Speech: "Passing Off"

Remedies provided by state statutes for those who have been harmed by false, deceptive, or unfair commercial speech that cause consumer confusion about a product or service include the possibility of injunctive relief, money damages for actual or statutorily defined harm, and/or court costs and attorney fees. (The possibility of remedies in state law for other kinds of injuries from false or deceptive commercial speech are discussed elsewhere in this text.)

Injunctions or court orders prohibiting or limiting commercial speech are inherently suspect because of First Amendment issues. However, these concerns may be overcome in situations in which states have passed statutes that make it a criminal offense to "pass off" goods. In such cases, the normal requirements for injunctive relief normally would apply (i.e., the threat of irreparable injury and the unavailability of other remedies that might prove effective to provide the relief sought by the plaintiff). Injunctive relief in other circumstances may be available if not directed toward actual commercial speech, but rather directed at general business practices so as to prohibit a product or service provider from linking its product or service to that provided by the plaintiff.[90]

Although it is common to compensate with money damages any plaintiff who can demonstrate an injury caused by the actions of the defendant, such remedies are frequently unavailable in cases in which plaintiffs are alleging harm amounting to "passing off" of products or services based on false or deceptive commercial speech. The problem lies in the difficulty of establishing the causal relationship between the defendant's actions and the plaintiff's claimed losses. Almost all states require evidence that either the economic loss by the plaintiff or the monetary gain by the defendant claimed by the plaintiff could not have been caused by anything other than the defendant's false or deceptive commercial speech. Short of providing testimony by individuals who purchased products or services from the defendant that they had been deceived into making their purchasing decisions solely on the basis of the defendant's commercial claims, the burden of convincing a court to award damages in a "passing off" case often is too difficult for plaintiffs to meet.

Most state courts have the power to award the costs of attorney fees and other financial burdens associated with bringing a cause of action against the defendant. The possibility of such awards (often substantial), coupled with the possibility of injunctive relief, often provide a strong deterrent or measure of punishment for those guilty of using commercial speech to pass off a product or service as that of another, and should be sufficient to caution the prudent public relations or advertising professional to avoid the possibility of such practices.

FOUR EXAMPLES OF STATE REGULATION
OF COMMERCIAL SPEECH

To fully discuss the statutes, rules, and regulations that control commercial speech in each state would require an additional chapter for each state. Although many of these state regulatory schemes look similar because they mirror their federal counterparts, almost every state statute or rule is worded slightly differently from those of its neighbors, creating nuances requiring state-by-state legal interpretations of how such laws apply. Four examples of commercial speech regulation at the state level involving controversial, tightly controlled, or currently socially relevant products or services that are also regulated by the federal government (and discussed in this and the preceding chapter) are discussed next to illustrate the breadth and complexity of such state regulatory efforts.

State Regulation of Environmental Advertising

During the past 2 decades, environmental issues ranging from a diminishing ozone layer to reports of the accumulating garbage in dumps and landfills, and the resulting problem of what to do with this increasing waste, have served as the basis for extensive public debate and discussion. Partially in response to these problems, environmental activists and others have pushed for the adoption of environmentally friendly policies by commercial providers of products and services.

Fortunately, many of these companies have found that significant numbers of consumers are more prone to purchase items if they are publicized as environmentally safe. Additionally, consumers can be persuaded to recycle containers (as long as it is not too expensive or inconvenient) and will participate in programs to reuse or recycle packaging materials. These findings have led companies to provide environmentally friendly products and services, and to make such efforts part of their advertising and public relations campaigns as well.

Using the environmental angle as a product or service benefit, however, can create negative legal repercussions if the dissemination of information about environmentally friendly practices does not comport with various state statutes that spell out how, and in what circumstances, such claims may be made. Even neighboring states may differ considerably in how they regulate commercial speech regarding environmental issues, including, for example, the legal definitions of key terms used to describe a product, such as *environmentally friendly* or *recyclable*.

Compounding the problem is the inability of states to agree on a common set of standards or procedures for solving environmental problems. This has led to confusion in the enforcement of regulations regarding environmental issues and the packaging and advertising of a product. For example, the bottom of most plastic containers features a triangle of recycling arrows with a number in the middle. This number refers to the ingredients in that type of plastic, and also provides a grouping number for those sorting the containers so that they can ascertain which plastics can be melted together for recycling. However, not all states recycle all types of plastic. The result is that in Oregon, for example, marketing a detergent as bottled in a recyclable container may be truthful and nondeceptive, whereas an identical advertisement in Tennessee for the same product in the same container with the same environmental claim might be judged as an example of deceptive commercial speech.

Concerns about such commercial speech-related environmental issues have inspired a number of states to prepare guidelines for companies that wish to tout the environmental benefits of their products or services. For example, Minnesota's guidelines state that:

(1) Marketers should be wary of tie-ins with environmental groups because their long-term aims may not be compatible;

(2) Marketers should distinguish between green claims for products and those for packaging;

(3) Marketers should not make an environmental claim unless the claim covers all their products; and

(4) Marketers should avoid generalizations and half-truths in claims.[91]

Because such efforts are fairly new, state statutes and rules involving commercial speech and environmental issues are still awaiting final enactment or interpretation by the courts in most states adopting such regulations. Perhaps the safest policy for advertising and public relations professionals is to double-check the current status of environmental regulations in the states in which marketing or other communication campaigns are planned to confirm that contemplated commercial speech claims involving environmental issues do not run the risk of being judged as false or deceptive.

State Regulation of Securities Advertising

Mention was made earlier that the origin of the SEC could be found in early attempts to regulate such speech at the state level under so-called "Blue Sky" laws. The term *blue sky* came from the get-rich-quick schemes of fraudulent promoters whose "speculative schemes . . . have no more basis than so many feet of blue sky."[92] Many times the only information consumers received about securities came from a promoter's commercial speech. Because investments and securities are, for the most part, intangible products, promoters found it easy to twist information, leave out some information, or otherwise deceive gullible buyers all too ready to believe claims of easy money to be made through investments.

Eventually, state "Blue Sky" laws were enacted to provide at least some protection for consumers from the more outrageous examples of fraudulent or deceptive commercial speech practices involving securities. Today, although federal regulation of commercial speech about the offering or trading of securities overshadows efforts at the state level, "Blue Sky" laws still make a substantial impact on the commercial speech practices of advertising and public relations professionals.

Although in the past individual state "Blue Sky" laws varied considerably, most such regulatory schemes involved one or more of three methods for preventing false or deceptive commercial speech related to offering or trading securities. These were: (a) creating a regulatory scheme to regulate who can deal in securities, (b) requiring registration for those who sell or offer securities within a state, and (c) requiring that securities be registered before being offered to the public. As may be imagined, determining which state had adopted any of the three methods and exactly how each was interpreted by an individual state became extremely taxing for commercial speakers engaged in communicating on a regional or national level. Recognizing this difficulty, and to "avoid the complexities involved in satisfying the varying requirements of several states when offering securities for sale,"[93] the model Uniform Securities Act was developed in 1956.[94]

The Act, which provides for variations on all three methods mentioned above, provided states with a pattern from which to mold and shape their individual approaches to securities regulation. The popularity of the Act "resulted in its adoption in some form in most jurisdictions."[95]

Advertising and public relations practitioners should note that, although most states now base their statutes regulating securities-related commercial speech on Section 403 of the Uniform Securities Act, there still remain individual variations in state law that need to be understood before disseminating securities information in a particular state. For example, some states—such as Alaska, Colorado, Montana, North Dakota, and Washington—require a filed notification 5 days prior to the publication of any commercial speech regarding securities. Other states may also require prior notification, but the filing deadline differs from state to state. In addition, the steps that need to be followed in each state during this filing period may vary considerably. In Alaska, for example, the law requires that a copy of the material to be distributed must be submitted for approval. In Montana, the 5-day filing period is often waived. In Washington, the 5-day filing period does not apply to all types of commercial speech, such as reports to shareholders, tombstone advertising, or some other kinds of sales literature.

Advertising and public relations practitioners should be alert to these nuances in state law before engaging in securities-related commercial speech practices or risk unpleasant legal sanctions.

Lotteries, Sweepstakes, and Games of Chance

A few states, like Nevada and New Jersey, have legalized casino-style gambling that allows betting on games of chance. Significantly more states allow supervised betting on sporting events. Some states have begun to get in on the action by creating state-run lotteries. In all cases, however, gambling is a highly controlled activity with detailed state laws specifying who can own or run gambling establishments, how wagers are placed or lottery tickets purchased, and so forth.

It is common for providers of products and services to use contests such as lotteries, sweepstakes, or games of chance as a marketing promotional technique. For example, offering incentives in advertising or as part of marketing special events attracts potential consumers by suggesting that a prize may accompany a purchase. The focus of the commercial speech is not on a benefit of the product or service, but rather on the possible gain the purchaser might realize by winning a contest. Advertising and public relations professionals must be extremely careful about how such contests are presented, or legal action by state regulatory agencies could quickly put an end to the game.

All 50 states prohibit private lotteries. However, many types of contests, sweepstakes, and other promotional devices may be legal if they follow the rules established by individual state legislatures. As discussed in chapter 4, three key elements help determine if a promotional device is a lottery: (a) if there is "consideration" or an effort made on the part of the consumer (interpreted as everything from buying a product to traveling to a destination to pick up a contest application), (b) if a prize is awarded, and (c) if winning is based on chance (as opposed to a demonstration of at least some level of skill). If a proposed promotion or contest contains these elements, an advertising or public relations professional would be wise to seek advice from competent legal counsel before proceeding with the commercial campaign.

Like commercial speech about environmental issues and the offering or selling of securities, definitions of key terms in commercial speech about promotions vary from state to state, and between the various states and the federal government. Some of these terms include *promotional device, chance, prize,* and *consideration.* Additionally, most states have specific statutes or rules regulating games of chance. For example, Arkansas and Alabama allow promotional lotteries as long as the chances of winning or the prizes awarded do not depend on the payment of money or purchase of products by contest participants. Virginia has specific instructions about the information that must be disclosed to conduct a promotional contest, including the number of prizes to be awarded, odds of winning, and the retail value of the prizes. Nevada prohibits gasoline and other motor vehicle fuel dealers and sellers from sponsoring games of chance or contests as a means of promotion. Although lotteries, sweepstakes, and games of chance are popular promotional and advertising tools, advertising and public relations professionals should be familiar with the regulations imposed on such contests in each state where their commercial speech may be disseminated, and should tailor their messages accordingly.

Commercial Speech About Alcoholic Beverages

As noted earlier, the manufacture and sale of alcoholic beverages historically have raised important social issues as illustrated by the enactment and ultimate failure of Prohibition in the 1920s. State laws regulating commercial speech about alcoholic beverages differ widely because of many factors, including the drinking age recognized by the state, rules about the sales of alcohol, and statutes punishing drinking and driving.

At present, Alaska and Nevada are the only states that do not have restrictions on commercial speech involving alcoholic beverages. Eighteen states handle the sale and distribution of alcohol within their borders (with the exception of bars and restaurants). The remaining states allow alcoholic beverages to be sold by private enterprises, but under control by state commissions or agencies. Although for the most part state regulations parallel federal regulations, details of such regulation vary widely. Advertising and public relations professionals involved in disseminating commercial speech about alcoholic beverages might consider obtaining a copy of the guide to state standards for commercial speech involving alcoholic beverage standards published by the Distilled Spirits Council of the United States.[96]

CONCLUSION

Add together federal and state regulations, rules, and statutes ranging from the Federal Trade Commission Act to state laws regulating commercial speech about everything from automobiles to zoological parks and it is clear that even prudent advertising or public relations practitioners face formidable challenges in acting to fulfill their professional obligations. Although the task may appear daunting, only the irresponsible practitioner would respond by claiming it is all just too complicated and trust only luck to avoid legal entanglements. The appropriate way to meet these challenges is to understand the need to check the applicable state and federal laws and regulations, and to be able to identify when it is necessary to seek the advice of legal counsel. This knowledge should sharply reduce the chances of accidently running afoul of legal restrictions on commercial speech that could injure both clients and professional careers.

III

PRIOR RESTRAINTS ON ADVERTISING, PUBLIC RELATIONS, AND COMMERCIAL SPEECH

6

Deceptive, Fraudulent, and Unfair Advertising

In 1995, American newspapers had another record breaking year in advertising revenue—$36.05 billion, according to the Newspaper Association of America.[1] Magazine revenue in 1994 rose almost 11% over 1993, tallying $8.5 billion, according to the Publishers Information Bureau.[2] A 30-second commercial on FOX-TV during the 1996 Super Bowl cost between $1.2 to $1.3 million—a record for a television network program.[3] Before 1996 had ended, the network had sold every single spot. In 1994, U.S. advertising in all media reached $159 billion.[4]

With stakes this high, no one should be surprised that some unscrupulous individuals and corporations will be tempted to go beyond the law by engaging in false, deceptive, unfair, misleading, and even fraudulent advertising. Others may comply with the letter of the law, but step over the ethical line. Most forms of deception, unfairness, and fraud, when detected, typically lead to punishment or at least an agreement to halt the practice under threat of penalties. Falsity, however, is often a different matter, especially if it is in the guise of puffery.

Suppose a television manufacturer makes these claims in its advertising:

1. MFC (Moore–Farrar–Collins) TVs reproduce colors and sound so realistic you'll never buy another that isn't made by MFC.
2. Buy an MFC set 32 inches or larger before the end of this month, and you'll get a $50 rebate direct from MFC.
3. MFC offers the longest and most comprehensive warranty in the industry.

As the head of your state Consumer Protection Division, you respond to consumer complaints about MFC sets and launch an investigation. Your investigation reveals that (a) MFC has no evidence that consumers quit buying other brands after owning an MFC set—no surveys have been conducted, and no other evidence is offered to substantiate the claim; (b) MFC is actually making a $100 rebate, but consumers do not know this until they get the larger check; and (c) The MFC warranty is not unique—it is the same warranty as that of the second and third largest TV manufacturers, but it is longer and more comprehensive than the warranties of all other major brands. Are these claims illegal and/or unethical? This question is tackled during the rest of this chapter as each assertion is examined.

DECEPTIVE ADVERTISING

If a list were compiled of every complaint filed by a state or federal agency against a business for deceptive advertising during the last 10 years, it would probably occupy as much space as a chapter in this book. This chapter looks at some representative cases. As will be seen, the government nearly always wins, although occasionally a business may win a partial victory. Traditionally, the courts defer their judgment to governmental agencies such as the Federal Trade Commission (FTC) because these agencies have the necessary expertise to make such decisions. In other words, the courts avoid second-guessing the decisions of state and federal agencies.

Some advertising and marketing practices are inherently unethical, and thus universally accepted as deceptive. Probably the best-known example is bait and switch—a scheme in which a business advertises a specific product at a low price and then, once the consumer takes the bait and enters the store, the salesperson attempts to switch the customer to a higher priced model of the same product under the premise that the lower priced model has been sold out or is of poor quality. Although the federal government and every state outlaw this practice, most consumers have been subjected to bait and switch at some time. Other schemata may be characterized as deceptive or simply shrewd, depending on the particular state or federal statutes, or on the circumstances in the case.

In late 1996, the FTC announced that Van Den Bergh Foods Co., one of the largest marketers of margarines and spreads in the United States, had signed a consent order, in which it agreed to halt its national advertising campaign for Promise margarine that used the slogan "Get Heart Smart" and included heart-shaped pats of Promise on food items. The FTC alleged that the ads implied that eating Promise helped cut the risk of heart disease and that the ads made false claims regarding low fat. Under a *consent order*, a government agency such as the FTC agrees to take no further action against a business that the government believes has engaged in an illegal activity if the company agrees to immediately halt the activity. Under the consent decree, the company does not admit guilt, but a violation can be punished. According to the FTC, Van Den Bergh did not adequately substantiate its claims.[5] Van Den Bergh is a division of Conopco, a subsidiary of Unilever United States.

In 1995, the FTC issued its final order in a settlement with the Häagen-Dazs Company, in which the ice cream manufacturer agreed to immediately halt its advertising claims that its frozen yogurt was "low fat" and "98% fat free," and that its frozen yogurt bars had only 100 calories and one gram of fat.[6] The ads included a disclaimer in small type, noting that the claims were for frozen yogurt and sorbet combinations. The FTC claimed only two of the nine frozen yogurt flavors actually had three grams of fat or less per serving, and thus were low fat as defined by the Food and Drug Administration (FDA). Some of the flavors had as many as 12 grams of fat, and three had as many as 230 calories.[7] As usual, the two sides lined up. The acting director of the FTC Bureau of Consumer Affairs contended that such a disclaimer does not solve the problem when the ad taken as a whole is deceptive. However, a company spokesperson clarified that there had never been any intent to mislead, although the ads would be killed anyway.[8]

In 1995, the FTC filed a complaint against Third Option Laboratories, Inc. for claiming that its drink called "Jogging in a Jug" acted "like a natural solvent for the body, cleaning crystal deposits that are the base of clogged arteries and arthritis." In a $480,000 settlement that same year, the company agreed to stop making false or unsubstantiated claims for any food, drug, or dietary supplement, and to notify its distributors for the last 2 years as well as consumers who ordered the drink directly from the company about the settlement.[9]

In mid-1995, the Federal Communications Commission (FCC) issued a set of revised administrative regulations that clamped down considerably on slamming by long-distance phone carriers. This practice, by which an individual's preferred long-distance carrier is switched without that person's knowledge, had drawn extensive complaints from both consumers and some of the carriers, particularly AT&T, which has by far the largest share of the market. Most of the complaints centered on the manner in which companies attract new customers through contests and other promotions, in which the consumer signs a form such as a prize entry or a simulated check that is really an authorization to switch carriers. One of the provisions of the revised rules requires the carrier to provide a separate form for the authorization, rather than combining an authorization form with another form such as a contest entry.

Although the U.S. Supreme Court has rendered a relatively long line of decisions involving advertising, the vast majority of these has involved the commercial speech doctrine, as discussed in the previous three chapters. Only rarely does the Court decide cases involving false and deceptive advertising. In 1965, however, the Court rendered a decision that has become a classic in this area. In the *Federal Trade Commission v. Colgate-Palmolive Company*,[10] the Court held that it was "a material deceptive practice" for the manufacturer of Rapid Shave shaving cream to make "undisclosed use of Plexiglas" in three 1-minute television commercials claiming that Rapid Shave could soften sandpaper. The FTC filed a complaint against Colgate-Palmolive, alleging that the ads were false and deceptive because (a) the type of sandpaper used in the commercials required about 80 minutes of soaking to soften, a fact not disclosed in the advertising; and (b) the commercials did not use sandpaper anyway, but instead used a mock-up of Plexiglas and sand. A hearing examiner dismissed the complaint on the ground that neither misrepresentation—the soaking time nor the use of sand and Plexiglas—was a material misrepresentation that would mislead consumers.[11] The FTC overruled the hearing examiner, holding that the company had misrepresented the moisturizing abilities of the shaving cream because it could not shave sandpaper within the time indicated in the commercials. The FTC also held that the Plexiglas ploy was a separate deceptive act, and issued a *cease-and-desist* order forbidding the future use of undisclosed simulations in TV commercials. Under such an order, the company is prohibited from committing the particular act against which the order has been issued.

The Supreme Court agreed with the FTC and rejected Colgate-Palmolive's argument that such simulations were really no different from the practice of substituting a scoop of mashed potatoes for what appears to be ice cream in a commercial, which the FTC had permitted. According to the Court:

> We do not understand this difficulty [making a distinction between the two practices]. In the ice cream case the mashed potato prop is not being used for additional proof of the product claim, while the purpose of the Rapid Shave commercial is to give the viewer objective proof of the claim made. If in the ice cream hypothetical the focus of the commercial becomes the undisclosed potato prop and the viewer is invited, explicitly or by implication, to see for himself the truth of the claims about the ice cream's rich texture and full color, and perhaps compare it to a "rival product," then the commercial has become similar to the one now before us. Clearly, however, a commercial which depicts happy actors delightedly eating ice cream that is in fact mashed potatoes or drinking a product appearing to be coffee but which is in fact some other substance is not covered by the present order.[12]

Suppose you see the following ad in your local newspaper:

$49.00 OVER FACTORY INVOICE*
EVERY NEW CAR ON OUR LOT
MFC MOTORS
MAIN STREET
HOMETOWN, HOMESTATE
*Dealer invoice may not reflect dealer cost.

If you visited the dealership, what price would you expect to pay for a new car? $49.00 more than the dealer paid for the car from the distributor? $49.00 more than the base vehicle price? $49.00 above the base vehicle price plus the dealer's cost for accessories? Suppose the disclaimer (the asterisk material) said instead: "*Invoice price indicates the amount dealer paid distributor for car. Due to various factory rebates, holdbacks, and incentives, actual dealer cost is lower than invoice price." Does the latter disclaimer give you a better idea of how to determine how much you would pay for the car in relation to the "actual dealer cost"?

A Fifth Circuit U.S. Court of Appeals tackled these questions in 1994 in *Joe Conte Toyota Inc. v. Louisiana Motor Vehicle Commission.*[13] The Louisiana Motor

Vehicle Commission, which has the authority to regulate automobile dealer advertising in the state, promulgated a set of rules and regulations under which the use of the term *invoice* is banned from any ad for the sale of a motor vehicle. The regulation was designed to stop misleading ads. In 1985, the New Jersey Supreme Court upheld a similar ban on the use of *invoice* and *dealer invoice* in that state.[14] Joe Conte Toyota sought unsuccessfully in U.S. District Court to have this particular provision (Section 20) declared a violation of its First Amendment rights. It should be noted that the Toyota dealer did not carry any ads that violated the rules, but instead was seeking to have the ban declared unconstitutional so it could, if it so chose, include *invoice* in its ads. Joe Conte submitted a proposed ad, similar to the first one shown previously, and an alternate proposed ad that had a disclaimer like the second one.

Under the first prong of the *Central Hudson* test for commercial speech, a court must first determine that the expression concerns lawful activity and is not misleading before applying the next three prongs of the test. If the expression is misleading, it simply does not have First Amendment protection. The trial court dismissed the complaint filed by Joe Conte Toyota on the grounds that the term *invoice* was inherently misleading in the context of both of the proposed ads. The testimony in the district court did little to bolster the dealer's complaint. One car dealer with 10 years in the business indicated that *invoice* had little meaning because *invoice price* changed over time and from dealer to dealer. Another dealer said *$49.00 over invoice* was basically meaningless for the consumer. Even a sample invoice from Joe Conte Toyota itself had four different invoice prices: "[A] base vehicle price at dealer's cost of $14,190.00, a base vehicle price with accessories at dealer's cost of $16,407.30, a total vehicle price with advertising expense, inland freight and handling at dealer's cost of $16,929.30, and a net dealer invoice amount of $16,860.00."[15]

The U.S. Court of Appeals apparently had little trouble deciding the case, upholding the constitutionality of the Commission's regulation, and thus affirming the judgment of the lower court. Noting that it agreed with the reasoning of the New Jersey Supreme Court in its 1985 decision, the court said:

> . . . We are satisfied that the proposed advertising copy with the suggested alternative disclaimers is inherently misleading.
>
> Because there is ample evidence on the record to support the district court's finding that the use of the word "invoice" in automobile advertisement [sic] is inherently misleading, its conclusion that the commercial speech in question fell beyond First Amendment protection was not in error. Consequently, there was no need for the court to consider the remaining prongs of the *Central Hudson* test.[16]

Under this test, is the claim of our fictitious MFC TV sets that "you'll never buy another that isn't made by MFC" deceptive? The appellate court in *Joe Conte Toyota* never really adequately defined *deceptive* or *misleading*, but instead relied on the Supreme Court of the United States' assertion in *In re R.M.J.*[17] that states may restrict advertising that is "inherently misleading or when experience has proved that in fact such advertising is subject to abuse. . . ."

According to the Fifth Circuit Court, the Supreme Court "suggested" that inherently misleading ads can be banned entirely while "potentially" misleading ads may be restricted but not barred outright. The circuit court also cited the plurality opinion in *Peel v. Attorney Registration and Disciplinary Commission of Illinois*.[18] The court then concluded that "a statement is actually or inherently misleading when it deceives or is inherently likely to deceive."

It appears that the court was having difficulty pinning down precise definitions of *misleading* and *deceptive*. Thus, the MFC claim could be characterized as deceptive or puffery, depending on whether it actually misleads consumers or is likely to mislead.

Traditionally, courts defer to governmental agencies in determining whether ads are misleading or deceptive, as both the Supreme Court of the United States and the Fifth Circuit did in the two major cases discussed so far. The Ninth Circuit U.S. Court of Appeals demonstrated such deference in 1994 in *Association of National Advertisers v. Lungren*.[19] In 1990, California enacted a statute that made it illegal for any manufacturer or distributor of consumer goods to claim its products were "ozone friendly," "biodegradable," "photodegradable," "recyclable," or "recycled" unless the products complied with specific definitions in the statute. Two years later, the various trade associations in California, including the Association of National Advertisers, sued the state to have the statute declared unconstitutionally vague and to seek a permanent injunction against its enforcement. The U.S. District Court for the Northern District of California conducted a full-scale *Central Hudson* analysis, and held that the statute met all four prongs of the test—more specifically, that the law was sufficiently tailored to further substantial state interests in ensuring truthful environmental advertising and encouraging recycling. The trial court applied an intermediate level of scrutiny, which the trade associations contended, among other points on appeal, should have been a higher level of scrutiny, known as strict scrutiny, traditionally reserved for speech that has First Amendment protection or that is intertwined with such speech.

The appellate court conducted its own *Central Hudson* analysis, and affirmed the decision of the district court, rejecting each of the major arguments asserted by the trade associations. The messages throughout the majority opinion are that (a) "finely calibrated determinations" are not necessary in determining whether the fourth prong of the *Central Hudson* test (whether the restriction is more extensive than needed to serve the substantial government interest) is met, and (b) courts should not second-guess legislative decisions involving commercial speech. In this case, the legislature had determined that these terms were potentially misleading, and thus warranted more precise definitions. *Recycled*, for instance, meant "that an article's contents contain at least 10 percent, by weight, postconsumer material. . . ."[20]

Suppose that, in the prior hypothetical, that the state statute requires a seller, manufacturer, or distributor to substantiate any specific claims in an ad—in this case, "longest and most comprehensive warranty." Has MFC run afoul of the law because its warranty is the same as the other leading manufacturers?

Under the reasoning in *Association of National Advertisers*, the state could successfully prosecute MFC, particularly if the statute has the appropriate language regarding warranty claims.

The FTC has been at the forefront for many years in the clamp-down on deceptive and misleading advertising. The discussion regarding the agency's structure and authority is deferred until later; this chapter looks at some typical examples of FTC rulings in this area. Under the Federal Trade Commission Act of 1914, including the 1938 Wheeler-Lea Amendment and the 1975 Magnuson-Moss Act, the FTC has the authority to police unfair and deceptive acts and practices, and to adopt trade regulation rules that provide specific prohibitions on certain practices that are binding on all businesses for whom the rule was designed.

The FTC Bureau of Consumer Protection's Division of Advertising Practices and the Division of Service Industry Practices have been particularly active in cracking down on misleading and deceptive advertising. The most recent edition of the Commission's booklet, *A Guide to the Federal Trade Commission*, notes that Advertising Practices' law enforcement activities have focused on tobacco and alcohol ads, claims for food and over-the-counter drugs, performance and energy-saving claims for energy-related household and automotive products, environmental performance claims for consumer products, infomercials (long-form TV commercials), and other ads, especially those touting specific claims that are hard for consumers to evaluate. These have been hot areas for litigation for some time. Before highlighting a few representative FTC cases, this section looks at how the FTC defines *false advertising*.

Under the FTC Act, *false advertising* is defined as "an advertisement, other than labeling, which is misleading in a material respect. . . ."[21] The definition goes on to note that factors to be taken into account in determining whether an ad is false include representations made and the extent to which the ad does not reveal facts material to the representations.

In 1974, the FTC took on the egg industry, which had launched an extensive advertising and public relations campaign designed to counter much of the adverse publicity surrounding the cholesterol content of eggs. The newspaper ads claimed there was no scientific evidence that consumption of eggs increased the risk of heart and circulatory disease, and that eating eggs does not increase blood cholesterol in normal people. The FTC staff filed a complaint against the National Commission on Egg Nutrition (NCEN), which had placed the ads, and its advertising agency. The complaint was upheld by an administrative law judge (ALJ), who recommended a *cease-and-desist order*. (A cease-and-desist order is legally enforceable and prohibits the individual or company from committing the particular act against which the order has been issued.) On appeal, the full Commission upheld the ALJ recommendation, but with some modifications, and the industry group and its ad agency appealed to the Seventh Circuit U.S. Court of Appeals. The final FTC order required NCEN to identify itself as a trade association. NCEN did not challenge this requirement nor any of the other findings of the FTC, except that the claim by NCEN—that no scientific evidence exists to link egg consumption with increased heart and circulatory disease—was false and misleading.

In *National Commission on Egg Nutrition v. Federal Trade Commission*,[22] the Seventh Circuit Court modified the FTC order somewhat, but essentially upheld the FTC's findings, including the conclusion that the statements in the ads regarding the lack of scientific evidence were false and misleading. The appellate court ruled that the order did not violate the First Amendment, and that it was not unconstitutionally vague. The FTC order had also directed NCEN to include a corrective statement to the effect that many experts believe increased consumption of dietary cholesterol can increase the risk of heart disease when NCEN ads mentioned any relationship between egg consumption and heart and circulatory disease. The court modified this provision to require such corrective advertising only when NCEN made statements about the status of current evidence on the link. It may sound initially as if the court was splitting hairs, but the judges felt the original requirement was broader than necessary to prevent future violations. In its reasoning, the appellate court cited the fact that, unlike in *Warner-Lambert v. FTC*, discussed later in this chapter, there had been no long history of deception that had "permeated the consumer mind." In other words, the court here is saying that NCEN can present its side of the story so long as it indicates that experts differ, and it need not engage in any kind of detailed discussion of the other side. The impact on the average consumer would probably be the same because both approaches would at least alert the viewers or readers to the controversy. NCEN appealed the circuit court decision to the Supreme Court of the United States, but in 1978 the Court denied certiorari.[23]

In 1978, in *Standard Oil Company of California v. Federal Trade Commission*,[24] the Ninth Circuit U.S. Court of Appeals upheld an FTC decision that, in 1970, Standard Oil Company of California had broadcast three false, misleading, and deceptive TV commercials that violated Section 5 of the FTC Act.[25] However, the court ruled that the FTC's cease-and-desist order was not justified because it was overly broad. Each ad promoted the benefits of F-310 gasoline additive, which supposedly reduced "exhaust emissions from dirty engines." In one commercial, a clear balloon was attached to the exhaust pipe of a car engine before using Chevron F-310 and then again after the car had been run on six tanks of the gasoline. The "before" demonstration showed the balloon inflating with a black vapor while the "after" shot had a balloon filling with a clear vapor. Another commercial was similar to the first, except the car was enclosed in a clear bag. A third commercial featured a dial with a scale from 0 to 100 that registered 20 for the "before" view and 100 with the "after" shot.

The FTC notified the oil company that it objected to the ads because they did not indicate whether the car used had been driven with a special gas designed to increase carbon deposits. The FTC also had problems with the lack of any notice in the commercials that improved mileage and emissions reduction could vary by the condition of the engine and other factors. As a result, the company signed an *assurance of voluntary compliance* (AVC), in which it agreed in future ads to superimpose disclaimers such as "Very dirty engine purposely used to provide severe test" and "Degree of improvement in your car depends upon condition of engine." An AVC is an agreement reached between the FTC and the company, in which the company signs an affidavit to halt further advertising of the type in dispute. The AVC is an agreement only, not an order, and thus the company cannot be punished for contempt for violating it, although the FTC could reopen the investigation if a subsequent violation occurs.

In a somewhat unusual move, the FTC filed a complaint against Standard Oil and its ad agency for the ads that had been aired *before* the AVC took effect. An ALJ ruled in favor of the oil company, holding that there was evidence to support the claims for the additive, and that the commercials were accurate. The FTC agreed with the ALJ that the product did reduce air pollution, but held that some of the more specific claims or implications in the commercials were false, including that: (a) F-310 could completely reduce pollutants, (b) all cars would be improved as much as that portrayed in the commercials, (c) the additive would reduce all types of emissions, and (d) there would be an 80% reduction as shown in the third ad. As noted earlier, the appeals court struck down the cease-and-desist order as too broad because it pertained to any advertising of any product by Standard Oil or the ad agency that could mislead consumers through the use of tests or demonstrations, and because the oil company had never previously been accused of false advertising and the ad agency had signed only one previous consent order with the FTC. Thus, the court modified the order to apply only to future advertising of F-310.

Under this reasoning, would the third claim in the hypothetical MFC TV commercials be considered false and misleading? In all likelihood, it would be. After all, would not a reasonable or average consumer assume that "longest" means *longer* than anyone else, not simply longer than all but the two other leading brands? Could not the same be said for "most comprehensive warranty"? What if MFC agrees to halt such advertising, claiming instead that "No other manufacturer offers a longer nor more comprehensive warranty"? Is this factually or materially correct, or would the typical consumer still assume that MFC had a longer and more comprehensive warranty after hearing this phrase?

Everyone at one time or another has probably received an entry form for a sweepstakes such as those offered by *Reader's Digest* and Publishers Clearinghouse. In 1971, the Reader's Digest Association signed a consent order with the FTC agreeing not to use simulated checks or currency nor "any confusingly simulated item of value" in any of its sweepstakes promotions. Two years later, however, the publisher distributed a "Travel Check" and a "Cash Convertible Bond" in its sweepstakes packets. As described by U.S. District Court Judge Latchum: "The Travel Check is printed on light green and blue paper, is approximately the same size as a real traveler's check, has traditional check-style borders, and purports to be for '100 Dollars a Month for Life.' "[26]

The FTC imposed civil penalties of $1.75 million against Reader's Digest for violating the consent order, and the company then appealed the decision. The U.S. District Court judge for the District of Delaware upheld the FTC decision, rejecting the publisher's argument that the First Amendment requires a government agency in such a case to demonstrate that the alleged violation actually caused consumer confusion. The trial court contended that the government's interest in preventing deception outweighed any First Amendment rights because the prior restraint involved affected the *form* of the advertising, not the content. On appeal, the Third Circuit U.S. Court of Appeals affirmed the trial court decision, noting that so long as the steps taken by the FTC were "reasonably necessary" to halt future violations, the agency was not acting unconstitutionally.[27]

The Fourth Circuit U.S. Court of Appeals used a similar analysis in 1984 in upholding the FTC Funeral Rule, which requires funeral directors to disclose prices, purchase options, consumer rights, and other information about their goods and services. In *Harry & Bryant Co. v. FTC*,[28] the appellate court found the rule reasonably necessary to prevent misleading and deceptive practices that had existed in the industry for some time. Such prophylactic measures are generally easier for the government to justify when there has been a pattern of prior bad conduct, either on the part of a specific party or an entire industry. This may explain the different manner in which the courts dealt with Standard Oil than with Reader's Digest and Harry & Bryant Co. Even under the commercial speech doctrine, courts will naturally be reluctant to impose prior restraint when a party had previously had clean hands (i.e., no record of offenses).

CORRECTIVE ADVERTISING

Corrective advertising, ordered as a means to correct previous advertising that was misleading or deceptive, is rarely used by the FTC and other government agencies, and is even more rarely approved by the courts. The classic case is *Warner-Lambert Co., v. FTC*,[29] the first FTC corrective advertising order challenged in the courts. Since at least 1921, Listerine Antiseptic Mouthwash ads claimed it could "kill germs by the millions on contact," and that it could cure or help the common cold. After 4 months of hearings that produced 4,000 pages of documents and 46 witnesses, in 1972 an ALJ determined that, based on scientific evidence, although Listerine might kill germs by the millions on contact, it did not affect the apparent cause of colds—viruses. In 1975, the FTC affirmed the ALJ decision and issued an order requiring the company that distributed the mouthwash, Warner-Lambert, to include the statement, "Contrary to prior advertising, Listerine will not help prevent colds or sore throats or lessen their severity," in the next $10 million in advertising for the product. Warner-Lambert appealed the FTC decision on the grounds that the agency lacked the authority to issue such corrective advertising. The U.S. Court of Appeals for the D.C. Circuit held that the FTC had such authority under previous court decisions granting the government the right to regulate false or misleading advertising. But the court said corrective advertising was permitted only when "the restriction inherent in its [the FTC's] order is no greater than necessary to serve the interest involved."[30] The court ruled in favor of the FTC, except that the company would not have to carry the initial four words—*Contrary to prior advertising*—because this phrase would accomplish little more than humiliating the company. The court made it clear that $10 million in advertising was by no means an unjustified burden on a company that had misrepresented the effectiveness of its product for decades. The circuit court relied heavily on the reasoning in the Supreme Court of the United States' decision in *Virginia State Board of Pharmacy v. Virginia Citizens Consumer Council*[31] and *Bates v. State Bar of Arizona*,[32] decided earlier in the same year as *Warner-Lambert*. Both Supreme Court decisions said that false, misleading, or illegal advertising can be regulated. The Supreme Court of the United States denied certiorari in 1978.

The circuit court in *Warner-Lambert* iterated that Section 5 of the Federal Trade Commission Act imposes two requirements for corrective advertising: (a) the ads must have played "a substantial role in creating or reinforcing in the public's mind a false belief about the product," and (b) the belief "linger[s] on after the false advertising ceases." The motivation behind corrective advertising is to offset false impressions created over time by an advertiser. Courts generally look to see if the deception is cumulative—one-shot deals may result in fines and other punishment, but they usually do not lead to corrective advertising.

In a case somewhat similar to the *National Commission on Egg Nutrition* case, discussed earlier, the FTC settled a 1994 complaint it had filed against Eggland's Best for false advertising (i.e., for claiming that clinical studies had shown that consuming a dozen of its eggs each week would not significantly increase an individual's serum cholesterol). The company agreed to place the following statement on its egg packages for a year: "There are no studies showing that these eggs are different from other eggs in their effect on serum cholesterol."

THE LANHAM ACT

In 1946, Congress passed the Lanham Act, named after Representative Fritz G. Lanham; the Act substantially revised the Trademark Act of 1905. The Lanham Act, also known as the Trademark Protection Act of 1946, took effect in 1947, and had the support of special interest groups such as the American Bar Association and the National Association of Manufacturers. The primary purpose of the federal statute is to provide a means for registering trademarks and remedies for the disparagement of products and services and their trademarks and service marks. Section 43(a) of the Act says that, "any person who believes that he is or is likely to be damaged by the use of any such false description or representation" can sue for damages.

At least two courts of appeals have ruled that "any person" does not include consumers. The first appellate court to rule on this interpretation was the Second Circuit in 1950 in *Colligan v. Activities Club of New York, Ltd.*[33] The case arose when two parochial school children sued an interstate ski tour service for damages suffered when a ski weekend for 153 students was cut short because of various problems, such as a shortage of skis and boots. The court rejected the students' argument that " 'any person' is so unambiguous as to admit of no other construction than that of permitting consumers the right to sue under its aegis [section 43(a)]." According to the court, "Our analysis requires that the manner in which this issue be posted is precisely the reverse: had Congress contemplated so revolutionary a departure implicit in appellants' claims, its intention could and would have been clearly expressed."[34]

In 1988, Congress passed The Trademark Law Revision Act,[35] which became effective in November 1989. The Act made the inclusion of false advertising much more explicit: "any false designation of origin, false or misleading description of fact, or false or misleading representation of fact."[36] The phrasing, "any person who believes that he or she is or is likely to be damaged by such act," remained in essentially the same form in the new Act. However, the statute was amended in 1992 to define *any person* as "any State, instrumentality of a State or employee of a State or instrumentality of a State acting in his or her official capacity."[37]

In 1993, the Third Circuit U.S. Court of Appeals, in a case involving lawsuits brought by consumers for ads promoting premium gasoline and rust inhibitor for cars, said the intent of Congress in approving the Act was to provide a remedy for competitors, not for consumers, noting that the wording *including a consumer* was originally proposed to be included in the Act, but then dropped from the final draft.[38] There is a long series of cases in which businesses have challenged competitors in civil action under the Lanham Act. Many of these suits fall under trademark infringement, product disparagement, and appropriation.

COMPARATIVE ADVERTISING

An area that has received particular attention is comparative advertising, which is even mentioned in the Standards of Practice of the American Association of Advertising Agencies (AAAA). The AAAA Code says, "Comparative advertising shall be governed by the same standards of truthfulness, claim substantiation, tastefulness, etc., as apply to other types of advertising."[39] This form of advertising became particularly prevalent in the 1970s and 1980s, when the national economy created a more competitive marketplace, and restrictions imposed by the major television and radio networks and the FTC on comparative ads were eased. The classic case in this area is *American Home Products Corp. v. Johnson and Johnson.*[40]

The leading makers of over-the-counter (OTC) pain relievers were locked in a battle over market shares in the mid-1970s. Primarily through heavy advertising, Anacin knocked out the former best seller, Bayer Aspirin, but a few years later Tylenol took over the top spot. To counter its loss, American Home Products, the maker of Anacin, launched a network television and national magazine advertising campaign that claimed Anacin was more effective than other OTC analgesics such as Datril and Tylenol. The magazine ads said that, "Anacin can reduce inflammation that comes with most pain. Tylenol cannot." The two 30-second TV ads shown on CBS and NBC had a spokesman saying, "Your body knows the difference between these pain relievers [other products shown at this point] and Adult Strength Anacin." The commercials also claimed that Anacin reduces inflammation and relieves pain fast while the others did not. McNeil Labs, the maker of Tylenol, complained to the networks, magazines, and the National Advertising Division of the Better Business Bureau, a self-regulatory organization, but to no avail.

As a result, American Home Products filed suit in U.S. District Court, asking for an injunction to bar McNeil from interfering with the dissemination of the ads. McNeil filed a countersuit under Section 43(a) of the Lanham Act, claiming that four of the claims made in the ads were false, including that Anacin was superior to Tylenol, that it was effective against inflammation, that it provided faster relief than Tylenol, and that it did not harm the stomach. The trial court judge determined that the first two claims were false, but he could not determine from the evidence presented, which included consumer surveys and clinical tests, whether the third claim was false. He ruled, however, that because the three claims are "integral and separable, the ads as a whole make false representations for Anacin . . . ,"[41] and he granted an injunction barring American Home Products from discussing any anti-inflammatory qualities of Anacin in any comparative ads. The Second Circuit U.S. Court of Appeals upheld the decision of the trial court, including the injunction, noting that, "on the basis of the evidence introduced at trial, the judge was justified in holding that he could not determine whether Anacin, at OTC dosages, reduces inflammation in the conditions listed in the advertisements."[42]

The two companies locked horns again years later in another comparative advertising case, and a U.S. District Court judge in 1987 ruled that the advertising of both violated Section 43(a).[43]

Comparative advertising has mushroomed over the last two decades. But legal challenges either from a regulatory agency or from a competitor are fairly uncommon, primarily because the evidentiary burden lies with the plaintiff in demonstrating that the advertising is false and misleading.[44]

UNFAIR ADVERTISING

The concept of "unfairness" in advertising has been rather controversial over the years, primarily because it encompasses the idea that advertising that is neither untruthful nor deceptive can nevertheless be unfair. For example, for about 2 years in the early 1980s, the FTC had its authority to deal with unfair advertising taken away by Congress. In fact, in 1980 the FTC had to shut down for one day and then reopen the next day, thanks to an emergency appropriation granted by Congress.[45] Until 1994, the FTC was funded from year to year because of the controversy over the regulation of unfair ads. The agency was finally reauthorized after an agreement between the House and the Senate that the FTC could not regulate an "unfair" act or practice unless it "causes or is likely to cause substantial injury to consumers that is not reasonably avoidable by consumers themselves and not outweighed by countervailing benefits to consumers or to competition."[46]

This is a rather tough standard to meet, and thus it is likely there will be fewer and fewer complaints filed by the FTC for unfair advertising, especially advertising that is truthful. In 1993, FTC staff recommended that the agency ban ads for Camel cigarettes that included the character "Old Joe" or "Joe Camel." Studies have shown that even young children associate the character with Camels.[47] Within 3 years after Joe appeared, the illegal sale of Camels to children under 18 reportedly rose from $6 million to a whopping $476 million a year.[48] According to a study in 1993 by the U.S. Centers for Disease Control and Prevention in Atlanta, the three most heavily advertised brands—Marlboro, Camel, and Newport—controlled 86% of the market share for smokers ages 12 to 18, compared with only 33% of the U.S. market share overall. (Marlboro had 60% while Camel and Newport each had 13%.)[49] According to the Centers for Disease Control (CDC) survey, 3 million adolescents smoke 1 billion packs of cigarettes each year.[50] A study published in the February 23, 1994, *Journal of the American Medical Association* found that the Virginia Slims "You've Come a Long Way, Baby" campaign persuaded 11- to 17-year-old girls to smoke. In June 1995, Philip Morris, Inc., signed an agreement with the U.S. Attorney General's Office to quit putting ads for Marlboros and other brands in stadiums and arenas that appear during telecasts of professional sports.[51] The agreement came after the federal government accused Philip Morris of skirting the 1971 ban on television ads for tobacco products with the use of the ads. The company will still be able to have ads in stadiums and arenas, but only where they would get minimal television exposure.

In early 1994, the FTC launched a much-heralded investigation of the "Joe Camel" advertising campaign for Camel cigarettes, which are manufactured by the R.J. Reynolds Tobacco Company. In 1993, Reynolds spent $42.9 million in major market advertising for Camel.[52] In June of the same year, the FTC formally announced it was ending the investigation, saying there was no evidence to support claims that children were lured to smoke by the campaign, thus accepting the arguments of the tobacco industry. However, R.J. Reynolds was by no means off the hook. In November 1994, the Supreme Court of the United States denied certiorari in an appeal from Reynolds seeking to halt a suit filed against it by San Francisco lawyer Janet Mangini in a California trial court.[53] Mangini sought a permanent injunction against Joe Camel ads, and sought to force the company to pay for a national antismoking campaign for children. The tobacco firm argued in its appeal that federal law preempted state law in such a case.

In mid-1996, one of the largest billboard firms in the country, 3M Media, decided that it would no longer carry cigarette advertising on its billboards. President Clinton immediately praised the new policy of the company, which is a subsidiary of the huge 3M Corporation, whose products include medical supplies.[54]

In late 1995, an antismoking organization, the Campaign for Tobacco-Free Kids, began purchasing ads in major newspapers such as *The New York Times*, the *Washington Post*, and *USA Today*. One ad featured a close-up photo of a young girl with pigtails and a cigarette in her mouth and a message in large type that read: "The Tobacco Industry Can't Be Trusted With America's Children."[55] According to the organization, now known as the National Center for Tobacco-

Free Kids, 3,000 children begin smoking each day and the tobacco industry annually spends more than $6 billion in advertising and marketing.

In May 1996, antitobacco forces suffered a major setback when the 5th U.S. Circuit Court of Appeals reversed a U.S. District Court decision certifying *Castano v. The American Tobacco Company*[56] as a class action.[57] The plaintiffs' lawyers subsequently began the process of filing class action suits in all 50 states.

In 1997, tobacco companies suffered several major setbacks, including: (a) a ruling by U.S. District Court Judge William Osteen of Greensboro, NC, that the U.S. Food and Drug Administration could regulate cigarettes, smokeless tobacco, and other tobacco products as drug delivery devices, but that it could not restrict tobacco advertising and promotion, and (b) an announcement by the FTC that it planned to reverse its earlier decision and issue a complaint against the Reynolds Tobacco Co. for unfair advertising for its Joe Camel ads.

Alcohol advertising has also attracted controversy for a long time for its alleged unfairness, including its impact on young people. The Federal Alcohol Administration Act (FAAA) of 1935, enacted by Congress after Prohibition died and "strength wars" started among brewers, prohibits brewers from including the percentage of alcohol on beer labels unless required by state law.[58] In 1987, Coors Brewing Company applied to the federal Bureau of Alcohol, Tobacco and Firearms (BATF) of the Department of Treasury, which administers the Act, for approval of proposed labels and ads that included the percentage of alcohol in its beer. Coors expressed concern about rumors that its beer was weaker than other national brands. The BATF turned down the request on the grounds that it would violate the FAAA, and that such advertising and labeling would lead to "strength wars" in which brewers would compete to have the highest alcohol content. The government also argued that such competition would result in more drunkenness and alcoholism, and thus more deaths and injuries from drunken driving. Coors then filed suit in U.S. District Court for the District of Colorado, seeking a declaratory judgment that certain provisions of the FAAA violated the First Amendment and an injunction against enforcement of the provisions regarding labeling and advertising of alcohol content. The district court granted Coors' requests, but the Tenth Circuit U.S. Court of Appeals reversed the decision and remanded it to the trial court.[59]

Although the appellate court determined that, under the *Central Hudson* test, the government had shown a substantial interest in suppressing strength wars, there had been insufficient evidence presented to determine whether the ban would directly advance the interest. Thus, the appellate court remanded the case back to the district court. The district court upheld the ban on alcohol content ads, but struck down the ban on labels. On appeal, the appellate court affirmed,[60] and the case was appealed to the Supreme Court of the United States, which granted certiorari. In a unanimous decision written by Associate Justice Clarence Thomas, with a separate concurring opinion by Justice John Paul Stevens, the Supreme Court of the United States held in *Rubin v. Coors Brewing*[61] that the statutory provision was unconstitutional. Although the Court agreed with the government that its interest in curbing "strength wars" was sufficiently substantial to meet the *Central Hudson* test, the Court said the ban failed the third and fourth prongs of the test. The Court concluded that the statutory provision "cannot directly and materially advance its [the government's] asserted interest because of the overall irrationality of the Government's regulatory scheme."[62] The Court noted that, although the provision prohibits disclosure of alcohol content on labels unless state law requires it, federal regulations regarding advertising ban statements about alcohol content only in the 18 states that specifically prohibit such advertising content.

In other words, the laws regarding labels are at odds with those regarding advertising. As the Court saw it, "There is little chance that 205(e)(2) [the labeling ban provision] can directly and materially advance its aim, while other provisions of the same act directly undermine and counteract its effects."[63] The Court's opinion called the government's evidence "anecdotal" and "educated guesses" regarding the strength wars that would supposedly be fought if the ban were lifted. On the fourth prong of the *Central Hudson* test, the Court said the regulation was not sufficiently tailored to meet the government's goal. Other options, according to the Court, include directly limiting the alcohol content of beers, banning ads that emphasize high alcohol strength, or limiting the label ban to malt liquors (the market the government believes has the greatest chance of a strength war). Note that the Court is suggesting that less intrusive forms of the ban might be permitted, although the information being disseminated on the labels and advertisements is truthful information.

In 1996, the Supreme Court of the United States handed down a decision in a case that had the potential to demonstrate just how far the Court was willing to go in protecting truthful commercial speech. Unfortunately, in *44 Liquor Mart v. Racine*,[64] the Court muddied the waters a bit. The case concerned the constitutionality of two Rhode Island statutes.[65] The first law banned the advertising prices of alcoholic beverages except at the place of sale if sold within the state and so long as the prices were not visible from the street. The second law included a ban on the publication or broadcast of any advertisements with prices of alcoholic beverages, even if the ads were for stores in other states. The purpose of the statutes is to (a) discourage the consumption of alcohol, and (b) maintain control over the traffic in alcoholic beverages. 44 Liquormart, Inc. and Peoples Super Liquor Stores, Inc.—supported by the Rhode Island Liquor Stores Association—successfully challenged the statutory provision in the Rhode Island U.S. District Court, which held it was a violation of the First Amendment.

The case began in 1991, when 44 Liquormart had to pay a $400 fine for a newspaper ad that did not include the prices of alcohol, but instead included the word *WOW* in large letters next to some pictures of vodka and rum. Because the ad also featured low prices for peanuts, potato chips, and mixers, the Rhode Island Liquor Control Administrator, who is charged with enforcing the statutes, ruled there was an implied reference to bargain prices for alcohol, and thus the law had been violated.

The lower court determined there was "no empirical evidence that the presence or absence of alcohol price advertising significantly affects levels of alcohol consumption."[66] On appeal, the First Circuit U.S. Court of Appeals reversed, contending that the state's action was reasonable, and that "[a]dvertising must be generally productive, or so much money would not be spent on it." The court also noted:

> . . . there would seem to be inherent merit in the State's contention that competitive price advertising would lower prices, and that with lower prices there would be more sales. We would enlarge on this. There are doubtless many buyers whose consumption is sometimes measured by their free money. If a buyer learns that plaintiffs charge less, is he not likely to go there, and then to buy more? Correspondingly, if ignorant of lower prices elsewhere, will he not tend to buy locally, at the higher price, and thus buy less?[67]

The Supreme Court of the United States unanimously reversed, concluding in an opinion written by Justice Stevens that the state had "failed to carry its heavy burden of justifying its complete ban on price advertising."[68] Thus, the two statutes and an accompanying state Liquor Control Board Administration regulation violated the First Amendment as applied to the states through the Due Process Clause of the Fourteenth Amendment. Unfortunately, there was no agreement among the justices regarding the appropriate test for making this determination. A plurality of the justices—Stevens, Kennedy, Souter, and Ginsburg—agreed that the *Central Hudson* was the correct test. The plurality agreed that Rhode Island had a substantial government interest in promoting temperance, although there was some confusion over what the state meant by *temperance*. The four justices also agreed that even common sense supported the state's argument that a ban on price advertising would elevate prices, and that consumption would be somewhat lowered as a result. However, they saw no evidence to support the state's contention that the price advertising ban would significantly advance its interest in reducing alcohol consumption. Furthermore, the justices said, the state could not satisfy the *Central Hudson* requirement that the restriction be no more extensive than necessary.

Chief Justice Rehnquist and Justice Thomas concurred with the judgment of the Court. However, in a separate concurring opinion, Justice Thomas argued that the *Central Hudson* balancing test should not be applied in commercial speech cases such as this one, when "the asserted interest is one that is to be achieved through keeping would-be recipients of the speech in the dark."[69] Later in his opinion, he noted that "all attempts to dissuade legal choices by citizens by keeping them ignorant are impermissible."[70] Justice Thomas instead endorsed the *Virginia State Board of Pharmacy* test: "rather than continue to apply a test [*Central Hudson*] that makes no sense to me when the asserted state interest is of the type involved here, I would return to the reasoning and holding of *Virginia Pharmacy Bd.*"[71]

The Chief Justice said that he shared Justice Thomas' "discomfort with the *Central Hudson* test." However, he went on to note, "Since I do not believe we have before us the wherewithal to declare *Central Hudson* wrong—or at least the wherewithal to say what ought to replace it—I must resolve this case in accord with our existing jurisprudence."[72] Thus, he clearly was accepting the application of *Central Hudson* only for now. If the Court were to accept Justice Thomas' analysis in future commercial speech cases, although there is no indication at this point that such is likely to happen, there could be a new era for protection for commercial speech, especially that involving truthful speech.

Such a change in direction would be particularly interesting in light of *Florida Bar v. Went for It*.[73] In *Florida Bar*, the Court upheld the constitutionality of Florida Bar Association rules that prohibited personal injury attorneys from sending direct mail solicitations to victims and their families during the 30 days after an accident or disaster. The Court applied the intermediate level of scrutiny from the *Central Hudson* test, and concluded that the bar association had substantial state interests in protecting (a) the privacy of victims and their families from the intrusion of unsolicited contact by lawyers, and (b) public confidence in the legal profession. If you try to fit *44 Liquor Mart* and *Rubin v. Coors* with *Florida Bar v. Went for It*, you quickly realize that the Court continues to have a split personality when it comes to truthful commercial speech. When the Court is presented with strong scientific evidence—whether surveys or other rigorous scientific research—to demonstrate both a substantial state interest and the effectiveness of the particular law, it is more likely to side with the government.

On November 7, 1996, the U.S. liquor industry formally announced that it was ending a longtime self-imposed ban on the advertising of so-called "hard liquor" (vodka, whiskey, gin, rum, etc.) on television and radio.[74] According to a *Wall Street Journal* story several months earlier, the Seagrams Co. officials had debated internally whether to end the voluntary ban by making a big "splash" (a high-profile TV commercial for its Absolut vodka) or an unannounced "creep" (a series of ads on cable networks or local stations).[75] Seagrams opted for the "creep" approach.

Predictably, FCC Chair Reed Hundt condemned the liquor industry's decision, as did President Bill Clinton. The four major commercial TV networks—ABC, CBS, NBC, and FOX—immediately announced that they would not rescind their policies against accepting liquor ads.[76] However, at least one major cable firm, Continental Cablevision, Inc., adopted a new policy allowing its five regional operating regions to decide whether to accept liquor ads.[77] Several cable companies, including Tele-Communications, Inc., and Time-Warner Cable, refused to accept hard liquor ads.[78]

The industry association responsible for the initial ban, the Distilled Spirits Council of the United States (DISCUS), said it would continue its bans against the use of children's cartoon characters and any claims of "sexual prowess" from alcohol consumption.[79]

Continental said it would maintain a "safe-harbor" (usually late night) period for its ads,[80] but the DISCUS policy imposes no time constraints on liquor advertising.[81]

In November 1996, the U.S. Court of Appeals for the Fourth Circuit reaffirmed a decision it had rendered prior to *44 Liquor Mart v. Rhode Island*[82] in which it had upheld a Baltimore provision prohibiting ads for alcoholic beverages in some areas of the city.[83] The appellate court distinguished *44 Liquor Mart* by asserting that the Baltimore law was a reasonable time, place, and manner restriction, in contrast to the blanket ban in Rhode Island (*44 Liquor Mart*). Baltimore had the right, according to the court, to protect children from alcohol. In April 1997 the Supreme Court of the United States denied certiorari, thus allowing the Fourth Circuit decision to stand.

In the previous hypothetical, MFC Corp. clearly engaged in false advertising when it touted a $50 rebate but was actually sending out a $100 rebate. But is this false advertising unfair or deceptive? This situation represents the other side of the question of "fair" advertising—false advertising itself is not necessarily unfair or deceptive, just as truthful advertising is not inherently fair. The consumer or purchaser in this case gets a positive benefit from responding to the advertising. What if a manufacturer consistently advertises a product at one price, but it always sells at a lower price? Suppose the advertised price is generally twice the actual retail price? Once again, it would be difficult for the government to substantiate a negative impact on consumers. Why then are not lower prices desirable even for alcoholic beverages? Most liquor purchasers are responsible drinkers; only a minority abuse alcohol. Why then should not the state encourage liquor stores to compete on price?

PUFFERY

The FTC and other agencies have been quite tolerant of puffery, a common advertising technique in which evaluative claims are made such as "brightest," "best," "freshest," and "best tasting," so long as such puffing does not cross the line and become factual statements that could materially affect a consumer's decision to buy the product or service. The idea is that consumers do not take such hype seriously. Although puffery can clearly influence consumer behavior, in its traditional form, it has become an accepted advertising technique. Consumers presumably suffer no real harm, but they gain little useful information. There have been relatively few suits involving puffery, and the decisions have gone both ways. The general rule is that the more vague the exaggeration, the less likely it can be substantiated, and thus be actionable. The courts are also more likely to permit the puffing if it is unlikely that a rational consumer would rely on the claim.[84]

STATE REGULATION OF FALSE, DECEPTIVE, AND UNFAIR ADVERTISING

Although the FTC gets much of the attention regarding false, deceptive, and unfair advertising, there are other federal agencies and state governmental bodies that are charged with regulating such advertising. For example, the FDA shares jurisdiction over food product claims with the FTC: The FTC handles advertising and the FDA regulates food labels. Because there were some differences in the standards applied by the two agencies for health and nutrition claims, they reached an agreement in 1994 to coordinate their regulations: The FTC agreed to adopt essentially the same standards for advertising that the FDA has for labels under the Nutrition Labeling Act of 1990.[85]

Every state has some form of a statute regulating false, deceptive, and unfair advertising, but there is generally little uniformity from state to state on the standards to be applied and the specific acts or types of advertising that are prohibited. These laws are sometimes modeled after the FTC Act, and thus are sometimes known as "little FTC Acts." Other statutes are known as "Printer's Ink" statutes, named after a model law, first published in 1911, that makes false, deceptive, or misleading advertising a misdemeanor.

LIABILITY OF ADVERTISING AGENCIES IN DECEPTIVE, FRAUDULENT, AND UNFAIR ADVERTISING

Advertising agencies can be held vicariously liable as defendants in product liability suits, such as when an advertised product harms a consumer, but they can also be held liable for false, misleading, or deceptive advertising created for clients. As noted in the *National Commission on Egg Nutrition* and the *Standard Oil* cases, discussed earlier in this chapter, the FTC held both the advertiser and its ad agency liable. In *Standard Oil*, the FTC issued its cease-and-desist order against both the oil company and its advertising agency—Batten, Barton, Durstine & Osborn, Inc. (BBD&O)—for broadcasting the F-310 commercials. The U.S. Court of Appeals upheld the FTC decision, but modified the order to include only future ads for F-310, rather than misleading ads for *any* product. The Ninth Circuit U.S. Court of Appeals made it clear that an ad agency can be held liable:

> BBD&O contends the Commission acted improperly in holding it liable under section 5. The standard of care to be exercised by an advertising agency in determining what express and implied representations are contained in an ad and in assessing the truth or falsity of those representations increases in direct relation to the advertising agency's participation in the commercial project. [cites omitted] The degree of its participation is measured by a number of factors including the agency's role in writing and editing the text of the ad, its work in creating and designing the graphic or audio-visual material, its research and analysis of public opinions and attitudes, and its selection of the appropriate audience for the advertising message. Precisely these factors were weighed in reaching the conclusion that BBD&O knew or should have known of the deceptive nature of the F-310 advertising.[86]

Thus, the two factors to be considered by the FTC and the courts in determining whether the advertising agency will be held liable are: (a) whether the agency "knew or should have known of the deceptive nature" of the ad, and (b) the degree to which the agency participated in the creation of the ad. The second factor is probably weighed the most in the determination. An agency that has knowledge of an attempt by a client to deceive the public, or which would have known if it had acted in a reasonable matter by exercising appropriate diligence, is going to have a difficult time convincing a regulatory agency and the courts that it should not be held jointly liable with the advertiser. Active participation by the ad agency in the creative process is probably going to be sufficiently strong evidence that the agency had actual or constructive knowledge of the deception.

Suppose, unknown to viewers, that a popular prime-time network television show strikes a deal with advertisers that it will "place" name-brand products on the show for a fee. For example, the main characters are shown watching TV on an MFC set. The MFC brand is highly visible on the set, and one of the characters even remarks that, because she bought the MFC set, she will never buy another brand of TV. Is this unfair or deceptive advertising? Most viewers have no knowledge that the reference to the MFC television is actually a commercial plug for which the production company receives compensation.

If it is deceptive or unfair, neither the FTC nor the FCC is convinced because this is precisely what is already occurring on television. Theatrical movies have been doing this for years, but it is a relatively new phenomenon for television shows. In fact, a cottage industry has been created, known as the "product-placement business." One such company is Keppler Entertainment, which has placed KitchenAid appliances on many shows, including a KitchenAid blender on "Seinfeld" and other appliances on "Frasier" and "The Nanny."[87] Apple computers have also been placed by another firm on several television shows.

CONCLUSION

Deceptive, fraudulent, and unfair advertisements have received extensive regulatory attention at both the federal and state levels, especially since the 1970s. Fraudulent advertising has often been the most difficult to prosecute, not because of the lack of tough statutes (which are on the books), but because of the savvy and shrewdness of the fraudulent marketers. Deceptive ads have attracted a lot of attention from the FTC and other regulatory agencies. As the *Colgate-Palmolive, Joe Conte Toyota, Association of National Advertisers, National Commission on Egg Nutrition* (NCEN), *Reader's Digest*, and *Standard Oil* cases illustrate, the courts, including the Supreme Court of the United States, give the regulatory agencies substantial leeway in imposing prior restraint and in punishing advertising considered deceptive. The *Central Hudson* test, which has been bolstered by subsequent Supreme Court decisions, makes it clear that misleading commercial speech generally does not enjoy First Amendment protection. As the *Standard Oil* and *NCEN* cases demonstrate, courts will sometimes modify FTC and other agency orders when their prior restraint is too broad (i.e., when they are out of line with the fourth prong of the *Central Hudson* test).

Corrective advertising is also a powerful tool for government agencies to employ, but it is rarely used. Under the Lanham Act, false and misleading advertising, including comparative advertising, can be actionable, although remedies under the Act have been restricted to competitors and governmental agencies, with consumers left out of the picture. In fact, two U.S. Courts of Appeals have held that "any persons" does not include individual consumers.

The concept of *unfairness* in advertising has been controversial, especially when it includes advertising that is neither deceptive nor false. Cigarette advertising, as illustrated by the Joe Camel campaign, is a prime example of this controversy, as is alcohol advertising. Thus far, the decisions regarding alcohol have been mixed, although the Supreme Court of the United States handed the industry major victories in *Rubin v. Coors* and *44 Liquormart v. Rhode Island*. In the Coors case, the Court held that the federal statute forbidding the advertising of the percentage of alcohol in beer did not pass the *Central Hudson* test. In *44 Liquormart*, the Court unanimously held that it is a violation of the First Amendment for states to ban advertising prices for alcoholic beverages, but the justices could not agree on whether *Central Hudson* was the appropriate test. In 1995, in *Florida Bar v. Went for It*, however, the Court upheld a 30-day ban on direct mail solicitation of the victims and families of victims of disasters and accidents by attorneys.

7

Professional Advertising and Promotion

When Warren E. Burger, former Chief Justice of the United States, died in late June 1995, one of the legacies recounted by the news media in his obituary was that, during his 17-year tenure, the Supreme Court of the United States had recognized that advertising and other forms of commercial speech had some First Amendment protection. Burger served as Chief Justice from 1969 to 1986. During his term, the Court handed down *Pittsburgh Press* (1973), *Bigelow* (1975), *Virginia State Board of Pharmacy* (1976), *Linmark Associates* (1977), *Hugh Carey* (1977), *Bates* (1977), *First National Bank of Boston* (1978), *Central Hudson* (1980), *Bolger* (1983), and *Posadas* (1986). This is certainly an impressive record, but it is marred by glaring inconsistencies in the manner in which commercial speech has been treated. There is no better illustration of the Court's contradictory approach than in the cases dealing with professional advertising and promotion. As is seen here, the inconsistencies have continued with the Rehnquist Court, despite the fact that only three of the justices on the Court when Burger retired are still on it. This chapter looks first at advertising by media corporations, followed by nonmedia corporations, and then professionals. Finally, it looks at advertising for products and services.

Overall, media corporations have probably made the strongest headway in obtaining protection for commercial speech, although they do not have a perfect win–loss record. Of the categories considered here, nonmedia corporations have received the most attention from the courts, especially the Supreme Court of the United States. Nonmedia corporations have made some progress despite some surprising setbacks, but the limits of First Amendment protection for commercial speech have been tested the most by professionals, particularly lawyers, who have had mixed results. The general trend continues to be somewhat broader protection for commercial speech, but with twists and turns that often defy logic.

MEDIA CORPORATIONS

There have been only three major decisions by the Supreme Court of the United States in the last 25 years that deal specifically with advertising rights of media outlets, and all of them came from relatively small corporations. The first two cases, which were handed down within 2 years of one another, are *Pittsburgh Press Company v. The Pittsburgh Commission on Human Relations*[1] and *Jeffrey Cole Bigelow v. Virginia*.[2] Both cases were introduced in chapter 1 of this book within the context of the development of the commercial speech doctrine. The third case, *City of Cincinnati v. Discovery Network, Inc.*,[3] was decided in 1993.

This chapter focuses on whether the status of the defendants as media outlets may have affected the outcomes of the cases on appeal. The landmark decision in *New York Times v. Sullivan*,[4] which established the "actual malice" requirement for public officials suing media defendants for libel, concerned an advertisement. In the case, which is discussed in considerable detail in chapter 12, the Supreme Court of the United States made it clear that it considered the political ad *not* to be commercial speech for purposes of the decision because: "It communicated information, expressed opinion, recited grievances, protested claimed abuses, and sought financial support on behalf of a movement whose existence and objectives are matters of the highest public concern. That the *Times* was paid for publishing the advertisement is as immaterial in this connection as is the fact that newspapers and books are sold."[5]

New York Times v. Sullivan is a landmark decision, but it says little about commercial speech other than establishing that the Supreme Court of the United States will, when warranted, characterize advertising as editorial content. In *Pittsburgh Press*, the Court handed the media a significant loss, but 2 years later *Bigelow* helped soothe the pain. The surprise in *Pittsburgh* was that the split 5–4 majority included two of the staunchest supporters of the First Amendment—Justices William Brennan and Thurgood Marshall.

In the late 1960s, the city of Pittsburgh enacted an ordinance that forbid discrimination based on race, color, religion, ancestry, national origin, place of birth, or gender by employers, "except where based upon a bona fide occupational exemption certified by the Commission [the Pittsburgh Commission on Human Relations, charged with implementing the ordinance]." The ordinance included a clause that made it illegal "[f]or any person, whether or not an employer, employment agency or labor organization, to aid . . . in the doing of any act declared to be an unlawful employment practice. . . ."[6] This clause was interpreted by the Commission to include the press. A complaint was filed against the Pittsburgh Press Co., the publisher of the *Pittsburgh Press* newspaper, by the National Organization for Women (NOW), which alleged that the paper had violated the law by publishing classified ads labeled "Jobs—Female Interest," "Jobs—Male Interest," and "Male–Female." After a hearing, the agency issued a cease-and-desist order against the newspaper, which was upheld by the state trial court, but modified by the intermediate state appellate court to exclude ads in gender-designated columns, which were exempt from the ordinance. (The Commission order had banned all classified ads that referred to gender.)

As both the majority opinion and the dissenting opinion of Chief Justice Burger pointed out, the newspaper included the following "Notice to Job Seekers" before each column heading:

> Jobs are arranged under Male and Female classifications for the convenience of our readers. This is done because most jobs generally appeal more to persons of one sex than the other. Various laws and ordinances—local, state and federal, prohibit discrimination in employment because of sex unless sex is a bona fide occupational requirement. Unless the advertisement itself specifies one sex or the other, job seekers should assume that the advertiser will consider applicants of either sex in compliance with the laws against discrimination.[7]

The majority of the Supreme Court justices agreed with the lower courts and the Commission that "the practice of placing want ads for non-exempt employment in sex-designated columns did indeed 'aid' employers to indicate illegal sex preferences."[8] The newspaper argued that it was exercising editorial judgment in deciding whether to allow an advertiser to select a gender-designated column, and thus the ads were like the advertising editorial in *New York Times v. Sullivan*. The Court considered this argument but rejected it. It also rejected the argument that, if the ads were commercial speech, they should nevertheless be given a higher level of protection than that provided in *Valentine v. Chrestensen* (see chap. 1). "Discrimination in employment is not only commercial activity, it is *illegal* commercial activity under the Ordinance,"[9] the Court said, in noting that gender-discrimination ads are no different than ads for narcotics or prostitution. The reasoning of the Court in this case is that this type of activity by the press falls within one of the few exceptions to the First Amendment ban on prior restraint:

> ... This is not a case in which the challenged law arguably disables the press by undermining its institutional viability. As the press has evolved from an assortment of small printers into a diverse aggregation including large publishing empires as well, the parallel growth and complexity of the economy have led to extensive regulatory legislation from which "[t]he publisher of a newspaper has no special immunity." [cites omitted][10]

Although the dissenters in the case—Chief Justice Burger and Associate Justices Stewart, Douglas, and Blackmun—did not win the day, their points may be the most telling. Chief Justice Burger called the majority decision "a disturbing enlargement of the 'commercial speech' doctrine," and noted that it "also launches the courts on what I perceive to be a treacherous path of defining what layout and organizational decisions of newspapers are 'sufficiently associated' with the 'commercial' parts of the papers as to be constitutionally unprotected and subject to governmental regulation."[11] Justice Stewart, joined by Justice Douglas, said, "So far as I know, this is the first case in this or any other American court that permits a government agency to enter a composing room of a newspaper and dictate to the publisher the layout and the makeup of the newspaper's pages."[12]

In *Bigelow v. Virginia*, a 7–2 majority gave the press a victory that in many ways overshadowed the defeat in *Pittsburgh Press*. Jeffrey C. Bigelow, director and managing editor of *The Virginia Weekly* of Charlottesville, Virginia, home of the prestigious University of Virginia, carried an advertisement in his newspaper for a New York abortion referral service—the Women's Pavilion. At that time, 1971, abortions were illegal in Virginia, but legal in New York. (The Supreme Court of the United States' decision in *Roe v. Wade*,[13] which recognized women's constitutional right to have abortions under certain conditions, did not arrive until 1973.) The ad contained detailed information about abortions in New York, including that New York State residency was not a prerequisite:

UNWANTED PREGNANCY
LET US HELP YOU
Abortions are now legal in New York.
There are no residency requirements.
FOR IMMEDIATE PLACEMENT
ACCREDITED
HOSPITALS AND CLINICS AT LOW
COST
Contact
WOMEN'S PAVILION
515 Madison Avenue
New York, N.Y. 10022
or call any time
(212) 371-6670 or (212) 371-6650
AVAILABLE 7 DAYS a WEEK
STRICTLY CONFIDENTIAL.
We will make all arrangements for you and help you
with information and counseling.[14]

As you can see, the ad was clearly aimed at encouraging Virginia women, including university students, to obtain abortions in New York, even mentioning that Women's Pavilion could assist a woman in getting "immediate placement in accredited hospitals and clinics at low cost," and that all arrangements were "strictly confidential." The advertisement appeared on February 8, 1971: slightly more than 3 months later, Bigelow became the first person apparently ever prosecuted under the 1878 statute, which read: "If any person, by publication, lecture, advertisement, or by the sale or circulation of any publication, or in any other manner, encourage or prompt the procuring of abortion or miscarriage, he shall be guilty of a misdemeanor."[15]

The editor was tried and convicted, first by the county court and then by the circuit court in a bench trial, and fined $500, with $350 suspended if there were no further violations. The Virginia Supreme Court affirmed on appeal, but the Supreme Court of the United States reversed in a resounding 7–2 decision. Citing *Pittsburgh Press Company* and *New York Times v. Sullivan*, the Supreme Court of the United States in *Bigelow v. Virginia* rejected the argument by the Virginia Supreme Court that the First Amendment did not protect paid commercial ads. According to the Court, "The fact that the particular advertisement in appellant's newspaper had commercial aspects or reflected the advertiser's commercial interests did not negate all First Amendment guarantees. The State was not free of constitutional restraint merely because the advertisement involved sales or 'solicitations,' . . . [cites omitted] or because appellant was paid for printing it, . . . [cite omitted] or because appellant's motive or the motive of the advertiser may have involved financial gain. . . . [cite omitted]"[16] The Court distinguished the abortion ad from the gender-discrimination ads in *Pittsburgh Press Company* by noting that the *Pittsburgh Press* classifieds were promoting an illegal act, whereas the *Bigelow* ads were for an activity that was legal in New York at that time.

The Court also pointed out:

Viewed in its entirety, the advertisement conveyed information of potential interest and value to a diverse audience—not only to readers possibly in need of the services offered but also to those with a general curiosity about, or genuine interest in, the subject matter or the law of another State and its development, and to readers seeking reform in Virginia. The mere existence of the Women's Pavilion in New York City, with the possibility of its being typical of other organizations there, and the availability of the services offered, were not unnewsworthy. Also, the activity advertised pertained to constitutional interests.[17]

In *New York Times v. Sullivan*, the Supreme Court did not directly refer to newsworthiness, but instead characterized the ad as an "editorial advertisement." How does an ad become newsworthy? Is newsworthiness alone sufficient to attain full First Amendment protection for an ad, or is it to be considered in light of other factors? Would the ad have been protected if it had been little more than the name, address, and phone number of the Women's Pavilion under the heading "Abortion Referral Service"? That is, does an advertisement enjoy First Amendment protection because of the newsworthy information it conveys?

Near the end of the majority opinion, the Court indicated the particular importance of the status of the appellant:

The strength of the appellant's interest was augmented by the fact that the statute was applied against him as publisher and editor of a newspaper, not against the advertiser or a referral agency or a practitioner. The prosecution thus incurred more serious First Amendment overtones.

If application of this statute were upheld under these circumstances, Virginia might exert the power sought here over a wide range of national publications or interstate newspapers carrying advertisements similar to the one that appeared in Bigelow's newspaper or containing articles on the general subject matter to which the advertisement referred. [footnote omitted] Other States might do the same. . . .[18]

Notice how the Court stresses the potential chilling effect on similar publications. As indicated earlier in this chapter, in *Pittsburgh Press* the Court said, "This is not a case in which the challenged law arguably disables the press by undermining its institutional viability."[19] Are the two cases really that different? What if the ads in the *Pittsburgh Press* had been for jobs in states that did not bar gender discrimination? Would the decision have been different? What if the ads in *Bigelow* were for organizations in Virginia *promoting* abortion, but not actually *performing* abortions? In other words, what if the organizations were advocating disobeying the law, but not actually providing a means for doing so? No matter how hard one tries, it is impossible to fully reconcile *Pittsburgh Press* with *Bigelow*. Both involved the press, and both ads promoted activities that were illegal in the states in which the ads were published. One thing was clear, however. A majority of the justices were seeking a means to recognize broader protection for at least some forms of commercial speech, especially those involving public interest.

Eighteen years after *Bigelow*, the Supreme Court of the United States added icing to the cake when it struck down a city ordinance that barred the distribution of commercial handbills in newsracks, but that imposed no such ban on advertising for traditional newspapers. In *City of Cincinnati v. Discovery Network, Inc.*, the Court affirmed a ruling of the Sixth Circuit U.S. Court of Appeals that the ordinance failed the *Central Hudson* four-prong test, including the fourth prong's requirement that the regulation be no more extensive than necessary to advance the government's interest. The 6–3 majority opinion written by Justice Stevens said the city had a significant interest in preventing littering, which had become a problem near such newsracks. But, the Court contended, the city was not justified in making a distinction between publications that were predominantly advertising and more traditional publications, especially in light of the Court's earlier decision in *Board of Trustees of the State University of New York v. Fox*.[20]

The Supreme Court of the United States held that the fourth prong of the *Central Hudson* test imposes a burden of proof on the government in demonstrating a "reasonable fit" between the ends and means chosen to further the substantial government interest. This "reasonable fit" had not been shown by the City of Cincinnati, according to the Court, because the city had focused on the content of the handbills, rather than its effect in achieving the city's goal of reducing litter. The Court was clearly bothered by the inappropriate distinction the city made between commercial and noncommercial speech. As the majority opinion noted, "In our view, the city's argument attaches more importance to the distinction between commercial speech and noncommercial speech than our cases warrant and seriously underestimates the value of commercial speech."[21] As the Court pointed out, there was no evidence presented by the city that the newsracks for handbills contributed more to the litter problem than other newsracks. The dissenters—Chief Justice Rehnquist, joined in his opinion by Justices White and Thomas—strongly disagreed with the majority's reasoning, arguing that the ordinance "burdened less speech than necessary to fully accomplish its [the city's] objective of alleviating the problems caused by the proliferation of newsracks on its street corners."[22]

Cincinnati v. Discovery Network seems to be at least a slight broadening of the concept of "reasonable fit" under *SUNY v. Fox*, although the precise boundaries are by no means clear. The handbills or free circulation publications, as they are sometimes known, do appear to have been considered the press for purposes of the First Amendment, as indicated by the criticism by the court of the City of Cincinnati for its distinction based on content in enforcing the ordinance. This may at least partially explain why the government lost in a case that, for all practical purposes, involved traditional advertising, rather than public interest commercial speech, such as that in *Bigelow*. The decision undoubtedly would have been different if the racks had sold baseball collector cards. But are collector cards really different from advertising circulars or even the daily newspaper, which must be purchased with coins deposited in the newsrack? What if the cards dealt with controversial issues such as drugs, politics, or religion?

NONMEDIA CORPORATIONS

There have been at least seven major Supreme Court of the United States decisions dealing with the First Amendment rights of nonmedia corporations. Each is reviewed here to see how they fit into the constitutional scheme. *Central Hudson Gas & Electric Corporation v. Public Service Commission of New York*,[23] already discussed in some detail in chapter 2, is by far the most important decision handed down by the Court in this area, and probably the most significant commercial speech case ever decided by the Court. The *Central Hudson* test for commercial speech enunciated by the justices has already been thoroughly analyzed in this book, and thus is not reiterated here. Instead, this chapter focuses on whether the utility's status as a nonmedia corporation was a factor in the case's outcome.

In its decision in *Central Hudson*, upholding the rulings of the state trial and intermediate courts, the New York Court of Appeals (the state's highest appellate court) reasoned that, because Central Hudson Gas & Electric had a monopoly on the sale of electricity in its service area, its advertising was of no benefit to consumers. Thus, the court felt such commercial speech had no First Amendment protection. In other words, the court implied that if the information is of little or no use to the consumer, it escapes constitutional protection.

The Supreme Court of the United States had considerable difficulty with that line of reasoning:

> Even in monopoly markets, the suppression of advertising reduces the information available for consumer decisions and thereby defeats the purpose of the First Amendment. The New York court's argument appears to assume that the providers of a monopoly service or product are willing to pay for wholly ineffective advertising. Most businesses—even regulated monopolies—are unlikely to underwrite promotional advertising that is of no interest or use to consumers. Indeed, a monopoly enterprise legitimately may wish to inform the public that it has developed new services or terms of doing business. A consumer may need information to aid his decision whether or not to use the monopoly service at all, or how much of the service he should purchase. In the absence of factors that would distort the decision to advertise, we may assume that the willingness of a business to promote its products reflects a belief that consumers are interested in the advertising. Since no such extraordinary conditions have been identified in this case, appellant's monopoly position does not alter the First Amendment's protection for its commercial speech.[24]

The Court appears to be saying that even regulated monopolies may have a need to advertise and promote their services and products, and such advertising generally enjoys First Amendment protection. This protection is by no means absolute. As the Court notes, there may be "extraordinary conditions" under which such advertising and promotion could be regulated. For purposes of this case, however, the Court saw no such conditions, and thus sided with the nonmedia corporation. The Court is effectively treating the utility company as a media organization.

In his dissent, Justice Rehnquist argued that a state-created monopoly of this type had no First Amendment protection. As he saw it, the decision should have turned on this issue, as well as the fact that a state could impose economic restrictions on such an entity. However, Justice Stevens concluded in his concurring opinion that *Central Hudson* was not a commercial speech case at all. He noted that the Court has formulated two definitions of *commercial speech*: (a) "expression related solely to the economic interests of the speaker and its audience," and (b) "speech proposing a commercial transaction." According to Justice Stevens, the first definition "is unquestionably too broad" and the second definition should not include "promotional advertising."[25] Is either Justice Rehnquist or Stevens correct?

On the same day the *Central Hudson* decision was handed down, the Court also announced its decision in *Consolidated Edison Company of New York v. Public Service Commission of New York*.[26] This case was overshadowed by *Central Hudson*, primarily because *Central Hudson* presented, for the first time, the Court's four-prong First Amendment test for commercial speech. Nonetheless, this is an important case. In its 7–2 decision, the Court did not emphasize that the speech involved arose from a public utility as much as it had in *Central Hudson*, although this clearly played a role in the ruling. The case began in 1977, when the New

York Public Service Commission (PSC), the same agency as in *Central Hudson*, issued an order barring all public utilities from "using bill inserts to discuss political matters, including the desirability of future development of nuclear power." The order came after a complaint was filed with the PSC by the Natural Resources Defense Council (NRDC), a consumer group strongly opposed to nuclear energy, when Con Ed turned down its request to include a written rebuttal to a pronuclear power insert in customers' bills the previous month. The commission rejected NRDC's appeal that it order the utility to offer space in the monthly inserts to opposing views in controversies in which the utility had gotten involved. Instead, the PSC adopted a policy of prohibiting public utilities from discussing any public controversies.

On appeal from the New York Supreme Court (an intermediate appellate court), the New York Court of Appeals held that the order was a reasonable time, place, and manner restriction designed to serve a legitimate state interest—individual privacy or the right not to be bombarded with utility propaganda. The Supreme Court of the United States reversed, with Justices Blackmun and Rehnquist dissenting, holding that the ban was *not* "(i) a reasonable time, place and manner restriction, (ii) a permissible subject matter regulation, or a narrowly tailored means of serving a compelling state interest."[27] The Court also rejected the rationale that the ban protected consumers' privacy rights: "The customer of Consolidated Edison may escape exposure to objectionable material simply by transferring the bill insert from envelope to wastebasket."[28]

The Court also rejected the argument that a public utility was similar to a broadcast station for purposes of the First Amendment, and thus could be regulated in the same manner as the Court had approved in 1969 in upholding the Fairness Doctrine in *Red Lion Broadcasting v. Federal Communications Commission*.[29] The airwaves are a limited public resource, said the Court, but utility inserts are not. Once again, as it did in *Central Hudson*, the Court ascribed public utility publications the status of media outlets with First Amendment rights, although the Court did hint that public service commissions could force utilities to exclude the costs associated with such communications from its base rate. Such an imposition on the traditional press would, of course, not be constitutional.

In 1977, the Supreme Court of the United States issued three decisions dealing directly with commercial speech, two of which are discussed in this section. The third, *John R. Bates and Van O'Steen v. State Bar of Arizona*,[30] is deferred until the next section because it dealt with lawyer advertising. *Linmark Associates, Inc. and William Mellman v. Township of Willingboro*[31] and *Gerald Daly and Hugh Carey v. Population Services International*[32] were announced by the Court in 1977 within 3 weeks of one another. In *Linmark*, the Court held 8–0 (with Justice Rehnquist not participating) that a local ordinance banning the posting of "For Sale" and "Sold" signs on the lawns of all homes, except model homes, violated the First Amendment. The ordinance was passed by the Township Council, apparently with strong public support, but over the opposition of real estate agents and agencies. Noting that there was no evidence that Whites were leaving the town *en masse* because of "For Sale" signs, the district court declared the ordinance unconstitutional. The Court of Appeals reversed in a divided opinion, pointing out that the town had suffered "incipient" panic selling, and that a "fear psychology" was present. The Supreme Court of the United States reversed in an opinion written by Justice Marshall. The Court held that, although the goal of preventing "panic selling" by Whites who feared that the township was becoming all African American may have been noble, the town had not demonstrated that such a ban was necessary or justified under the circumstances. According to the Court, "If dissemination of this information can be restricted, then every locality in the country can suppress any facts that reflect poorly on the locality, so long as a plausible claim can be made that the disclosure would cause the recipients of the information to act 'irrationally.' "[33]

Linmark was decided, of course, 3 years before *Central Hudson*, and thus the four-prong test was not applied. Instead, the Court resorted to its reasoning in *Bigelow* and *Virginia State Board of Pharmacy*, which follows later in this chapter. The justices specifically rejected the town's argument that the ban was merely a reasonable time, place, and manner restriction, noting that the ordinance focused on real estate advertising (specific content), and the government had apparently not availed itself of alternative means of communication for achieving its goal of preventing White flight. Although in a sense the Court was recognizing the First Amendment rights of real estate agents, because they were singled out in the statute, the Court also referred to the rights of homeowners to advertise. "Persons desiring to sell their homes are just as interested in communicating that fact as are sellers of other goods and services."[34] It should be noted here that the case did not directly involve the rights of individual homeowners—Linmark and Mellman, who challenged the law, were the corporation that had the property for sale and the real estate agent, respectively.

Carey involved a New York statute making it illegal to sell or distribute nonprescription contraceptives to minors younger than 16, and to advertise or publicly display such contraceptives. Seven of the justices, headed by Justice Brennan, applied a "strict scrutiny" test to find that the ban on the distribution of contraceptives violated the due process clause of the Fourteenth Amendment, but the justices split on whether such a ban applied to minors was permissible. The majority did agree that the advertising restrictions violated the First Amendment, noting that there is no real constitutional difference between contraceptive ads and those for prescription drugs, abortion, and real estate. Justice Brennan was concerned in his opinion with privacy rights, which a split court had struggled with 12 years earlier in *Griswold v. Connecticut*.[35] By limiting the distribution of nonprescription contraceptives to licensed pharmacists, Brennan said, "a significant burden" is imposed "on the right of the individuals to use contraceptives if they choose to do so." The opinion also countered the argument of the state—that the advertising could be banned as offensive and embarrassing with the contention that, unless the information is determined to be legally obscene, "the fact that protected speech may be offensive to some does not justify its suppression." Some critics would say, perhaps with justification, that the fractured opinion does not represent much on the issue of commercial speech, but it is notable that the justices were significantly more in agreement on the protection afforded advertising in the case than they were with the rights of distribution.

One year later, a divided Court struck down as unconstitutional a Massachusetts statute that barred banks and other businesses from attempting to exert direct influence on public opinion unless the issue involved directly and materially affected its business. In *First National Bank of Boston v. Francis X. Bellotti*,[36] the Court tackled the issue directly over whether nonmedia corporations enjoyed First Amendment rights. The case arose when the bank decided to spend money to publicize its opposition to a proposed state constitutional amendment that would have allowed the legislature to enact a graduated income tax. Before launching the publicity campaign, however, the state's attorney general told the bank that he would take action against it as permitted under the statute if the bank spent the money. The bank faced a possible fine of up to $50,000, and its officers, directors, or agents faced a potential fine of up to $10,000 and/or imprisonment for up to 1 year. The bank then filed suit with the Supreme Judicial Court of Massachusetts to have the statute declared unconstitutional. In an expedited review, the state appellate court upheld the statute on the grounds that the due process clause of the Fourteenth Amendment and the First Amendment rights of free speech applied to corporations "only when a general political issue materially affects a corporation's business, property or assets." The statute specifically singled out questions submitted to voters solely regarding income, property, or individual taxes as not "deemed materially to affect the property, business or assets of the corporation." The state supreme judicial court saw no problem with this provision. The court did acknowledge that business corporations had some First Amendment rights, but those rights, according to the court, were not as broad as individuals' First Amendment rights.

In an opinion written by Justice Powell (joined by Chief Justice Burger and Justices Stewart, Blackmun, and Stevens), a 5–4 Supreme Court of the United States majority reversed the state appellate court decision. The Court noted that the state appellate court had not even posed the right question in its decision:

> The court below framed the principal question in this case as whether and to what extent corporations have First Amendment rights. We believe that the court posed the wrong question. The Constitution often protects interests broader than those of the party seeking their vindication. The First Amendment, in particular, serves significant societal interests. The proper question, therefore, is not whether corporations "have" First Amendment rights and, if so, whether they are coextensive with those of natural persons. Instead, the question must be whether § 8 abridges expression that the First Amendment was meant to protect. We hold that it does.[37]

The Court went on to note that the real question is whether status as a corporation ("corporate identity") deprives the speaker of protection for speech that would otherwise be protected. The Court was particularly critical of the suggestion by the state that First Amendment rights generally applied "only to corporations engaged in the communications business or through which individuals express themselves."[38] As the lower court saw it, by allowing business corporations to speak out on issues "materially affecting" them, the statute put business corporations in the same position as media corporations for purposes of the First Amendment. However, the Supreme Court of the United States did not buy this argument:

> It is true that the "materially affecting" requirement would have been satisfied in the Court's decisions affording protection to the speech of media corporations and corporations otherwise in the business of communication or entertainment, and to the commercial speech of business corporations. . . . In such cases, the speech would be connected to the corporation's business almost by definition. But the effect on the business of the corporation was not the governing rationale in any of these decisions. None of them mentions, let alone attributes significance to the fact, that the subject of the challenged communication materially affected the corporation's business.[39]

The majority went on to point out that, although the press has a "constitutionally recognized role . . . in informing and educating the public, offering criticism, and providing a forum for discussion and debate . . . the press does not have a monopoly on the First Amendment or the ability to enlighten."[40] The Court rejected other arguments made by the state and/or the lower court, including that the electoral process could be harmed by the undue influence corporations could exert if allowed to speak out, and that the statute protected the interests of shareholders.

If this case stands for anything, it is the idea that nonmedia corporations have First Amendment rights comparable to those of the press when their speech falls within the realm of speech that would be otherwise protected. In his concurring opinion, Chief Justice Burger pointed to a question yet to be directly answered by the Court—whether the Press Clause of the First Amendment granted special protection to the "institutional press." The Chief Justice argued that it did not: "Because the First Amendment was meant to guarantee freedom to express and communicate ideas, I see no difference between the right of those who seek to disseminate ideas by way of a newspaper and those who give lectures or speeches and seek to enlarge the audience by publication and wide dissemination."[41] As Chief Justice Burger saw it, the idea behind the First Amendment was to protect the liberty to express ideas and beliefs (Speech Clause) and to "disseminate expression broadly" (Press Clause). Burger was particularly bothered by the trend toward conglomerate ownership of the media, and by the involvement of media corporations in a wide range of activities beyond traditional publishing. Indeed he noted that media corporations may pose a more serious threat to the electoral process than that ascribed to nonmedia corporations by the state of Massachusetts in its arguments supporting the statute.

The last two cases in this area were decided after *Central Hudson*, and thus have the advantage or disadvantage, depending on one's perspective, of the four-prong test. The question facing the Supreme Court of the United States in *William F. Bolger v. Youngs Drug Products Corporation*[42] was whether there is a First Amendment right to mail unsolicited advertising for contraceptives. The surprising answer in a unanimous decision (with Justice Brennan not participating) was "yes." Youngs Drug Products, one of the largest manufacturers of condoms, planned to mail unsolicited advertising, including a drug store flyer and two pamphlets entitled "Condoms and Human Sexuality" and "Plain Talk about Venereal Disease." The U.S. Postal Service notified the company that such mailings would violate a federal statute providing that "any unsolicited advertisement of matter which is designed, adapted, or intended for preventing conception is nonmailable matter."[43] When the U.S. Postal Service denied its request for a permit to mail the materials, the drug company sought a declaration that the statute was unconstitutional and an injunction to halt its enforcement by the U.S. Postal Service. The U.S. District Court for Washington, DC, granted the company's requests, and the U.S. Postal Service appealed to the Supreme Court of the United States, which upheld the lower court ruling.

The threshold question was whether the speech was commercial or noncommercial. The Court opted to characterize the pamphlets as commercial. Although the publications were informative, the majority opinion written by Justice Marshall said:

> Most of the appellee's mailings fall within the core notion of commercial speech—"speech which does no more than propose a commercial transaction" [citing *Virginia State Board of Pharmacy*]. Youngs' informational pamphlets cannot be characterized merely as proposals to engage in commercial transactions. Their proper classification as commercial or non-commercial speech thus presents a closer question. The mere fact that these pamphlets are conceded to be advertisements clearly does not compel the conclusion that they are commercial speech [citing *New York Times v. Sullivan*, discussed in chap. 9]. Similarly the reference to a specific product does not by itself render the pamphlets commercial speech. Finally, the fact that Youngs has an economic motivation for mailing the pamphlets would clearly be insufficient by itself to turn these materials into commercial speech [citing *Bigelow*]. The combination of all these characteristics, however, provides strong support for the District Court's conclusion that the informational pamphlets are properly characterized as commercial speech.[44]

Having determined that the pamphlets were commercial speech, the Court then applied the *Central Hudson* test. Although the federal government was involved in this case, rather than a state, the four-prong test is still the same. First, the Court ruled that the advertising was neither misleading nor concerned with illegal activities. The Court also determined that the advertising promoted "substantial individual and societal interests," such as family planning and the prevention of sexually transmitted diseases. It rejected the U.S. Postal Service's contention that the federal statute served a substantial government interest in preventing interference with parents' attempts to discuss birth control with their children. "We can reasonably assume that parents already exercise substantial control over the disposition of mail once it enters their mailbox,"[45] the Court noted. The opinion then concluded that the statute was overly broad in achieving its objective. Arguing that unsolicited mailings were "entirely suitable for adults," the Court said that the "level of discourse reaching a mailbox cannot be limited to that which would be suitable for a sandbox."[46]

Justice Rehnquist (joined by Justice O'Connor) filed a separate, but concurring, opinion that recognized the government interest as substantial. But he noted his agreement with the majority that the statute was too broad in light of the limited intrusion involved. Justice Stevens also filed a separate, concurring opinion, in which he said that the statute "censors ideas, not style. It prohibits appellee from mailing any unsolicited advertisement of contraceptives, no matter how unobtrusive and tactful; yet it permits anyone to mail unsolicited advertisements of devices intended to facilitate conception, no matter how coarse or grotesque."[47]

One of the most troublesome commercial speech cases from a First Amendment perspective was handed down by the Supreme Court of the United States 3 years after *Bolger*. In *Posadas de Puerto Rico Associates v. Tourism Company of Puerto Rico*,[48] as discussed in chapter 2, the Court held that, under the *Central Hudson* test, the Puerto Rican government's restrictions on advertising for legalized gambling directed at its own citizens did not violate the First Amendment. The impact of the case on commercial speech was already examined in chapter 2, and thus the discussion in this section focuses on the status of the plaintiff/appellant in the case, Posadas de Puerto Rico Associates. The 5–4 majority, headed by Justice Rehnquist, had no problem characterizing the speech as "pure commercial speech which does no more than propose a commercial transaction." As such, the ads sailed right through the *Central Hudson* test. Unlike *Bigelow, Bolger,* and *Bates* (discussed in the next section of this chapter), which granted First Amendment protection to truthful commercial speech, *Posadas* stands for the principle that even commercial speech that concerns legal activities and is truthful and not misleading can still be banned. The status of the speaker in this case, the owner of the Condado Holiday Inn, was not at issue as far as the Court was concerned.

What if the hotel had purchased air time and newspaper space to oppose the statute, rather than to encourage gambling? Presumably the status of the hotel would have changed to a speaker within the meaning of the First Amendment if *Central Hudson* and *Consolidated Edison* are to be followed. After all, in both of these cases, the advertising at least indirectly proposed a commercial transaction—the use of electricity. Nevertheless, *Posadas* makes it rather clear that *Valentine* is still alive and well when it comes to what the Court considers purely commercial speech. Indeed, the *Posadas* rationale could probably be used to ban or restrict advertising for a wide range of other legal products and services, including that for alcohol and cigarettes.

PROFESSIONALS

The vast majority of both Supreme Court of the United States and lower court decisions dealing with advertising by professionals have involved lawyers, but other professions have not been immune from the scrutiny of the courts. This section begins with the profession that has attracted the most attention from the judiciary.

The 1994 to 1995 term of the Supreme Court of the United States was marked by some mild and some not-so-mild surprises in the First Amendment arena. One of the "mild" surprises came in *Florida Bar v. Went For It, Inc.*,[49] which the Court handed down on June 21, 1995, near the end of its term. In a 5–4 opinion written by Justice O'Connor (joined by Chief Justice Rehnquist and Associate Justices Scalia, Thomas, and Breyer), the Court held that Florida Bar rules that prohibit personal injury attorneys from sending targeted direct mail solicitations to victims and their relatives for 30 days after an accident or disaster do not violate the First and Fourteenth Amendments to the Constitution.

In 1990, the Florida Supreme Court approved with some revisions the state bar association's proposed amendments to the Rules of Professional Conduct that involve advertising.[50] The bar association made the proposals after a 2-year study, which included hearings, surveys, and public comments about lawyer advertising. An attorney[51] and his wholly owned lawyer referral service, Went For It, Inc., challenged two of the rules[52] in the U.S. District Court for the Middle District of Florida as unconstitutional because, taken together, they imposed a 30-day blackout after an accident or disaster in which attorneys could not directly or indirectly target victims or their relatives for solicitation of business. Prior to the enactment of the rules, the attorney had regularly mailed targeted solicitations to victims or their survivors, and had referred potential clients to other attorneys within the 30 days. His suit for declaratory and injunctive relief asked that he be allowed to continue this practice. Both sides asked for a summary judgment in their favor. A magistrate judge to whom the district court referred the case recommended that summary judgment be granted to the Bar. The district court rejected his recommendation, and issued a summary judgment instead for the plaintiffs.[53] Citing *Bates* and its progeny, which had also been cited by the trial court, the Eleventh Circuit U.S. Court of Appeals reluctantly affirmed in 1994.[54] The Supreme Court of the United States acknowledged in the majority opinion that *Bates* had laid the "foundation" for nearly two decades of cases, and that "[i]t is well established that lawyer advertising is commercial speech and, as such, is accorded a measure of First Amendment protection."[55] However, that measure of protection is limited, the Court said, noting that *Central Hudson* requires an intermediate level of scrutiny of restrictions on commercial speech.

Applying the *Central Hudson* test, the Court found: (a) without question that the speech being regulated did not concern unlawful activity nor was it misleading; (b) with "little trouble" that the state bar had a "substantial interest in protecting the privacy and tranquility of personal injury victims and their loved ones against intrusive, unsolicited contact by lawyers" and a substantial interest in protecting "the flagging reputations of Florida lawyers by preventing them from engaging in conduct that, the Bar Association maintains, 'is universally regarded as deplorable and beneath common decency . . .' "; (c) based on extensive studies and other evidence (including news stories and editorials), that the harms targeted by the rules are "far from illusory"; and (d) "[t]he palliative devised by the Bar to address these harms is narrow both in scope and in duration."[56]

The majority opinion in *Florida Bar* cited most of the lawyer advertising cases it had decided prior to the decision. This section looks at each of these cases, as well as the Court's rulings involving advertising by other professionals. The Court distinguished *Virginia State Board of Pharmacy* by pointing out that it had limited its holding in the case to advertising by pharmacists, and that it had noted in the case that physicians and lawyers are different from pharmacists because the former two "do not dispense standardized products; they render professional services of almost infinite variety and nature, with the consequent enhanced possibility for confusion and deception if they were to undertake certain kinds of advertising."[57] As noted earlier, the Court cited *Bates* for the principle that commercial speech had limited First Amendment protection. In *Bates*, the Supreme Court, in a 5–4 decision, struck down as a violation of the First Amendment an Arizona State Bar rule prohibiting the advertising of routine legal services. In that case, the Court made it clear that its holding was applicable only to the specific type of advertising involved; it also went to unusual lengths to distinguish permissible from impermissible forms of advertising. As Justice O'Connor pointed out in the majority opinion in *Florida Bar*, "Expressing confidence that legal advertising would only be practicable for such simple, standardized services, the Court [in *Bates*] rejected the State's proffered justifications for regulation."

Bates, of course, was decided before *Central Hudson*, as were two other lawyer solicitation cases—*Ohralik v. Ohio State Bar Association*[58] and *In re Primus*,[59] both issued in 1978. In *Ohralik* and *Primus*, the Court began the process of determining the extent to which states may regulate lawyers' solicitations of potential clients, which culminated in the ruling in *Florida Bar*. In *Ohralik*, the justices upheld the suspension of an attorney by the Ohio Bar Association for his inperson solicitation of two 18-year-old women shortly after they had been in a car accident. Both victims signed contingent fee agreements with the lawyer, and the bar association suspended his license, although it did not demonstrate any harm to the women from the contracts. The majority opinion, written by Justice Powell, distinguished this type of solicitation from the advertising in *Bates*. According to Powell, the state had a "legitimate and indeed 'compelling' " interest in "preventing those aspects of solicitation that involve fraud, undue influence, intimidation, overreaching, and other forms of 'vexatious conduct.' "[60]

The majority opinion in *Florida Bar* cited *Ohralik* three times, but did not discuss the case. Instead, the Court used it to support the notion that commercial speech is to be treated differently for purposes of the First Amendment from "speech at the First Amendment's core," which, of course, enjoys full protection of the Constitution. *Ohralik* was also cited to bolster the idea that states have a "compelling interest" in regulating professions, such as law "to protect the public health, safety, and other valid interests."

Primus is cited only once in the majority opinion—in the conclusion as an example of "circumstances in which we will accord speech by attorneys on public issues and matters of legal representation the strongest protection our Constitution has to offer."[61] In *Primus*, a volunteer American Civil Liberties Union (ACLU) attorney in South Carolina sent a letter to a former patient to solicit her as a potential plaintiff in a suit against a physician. The attorney believed the doctor had sterilized pregnant women who were allegedly told they would no longer receive Medicaid care unless they agreed to the surgery. Justice Powell, who once again wrote the majority opinion, set aside the public reprimand handed down to the attorney on the grounds that the First Amendment's right to freedom of speech protected this form of political expression because there was no evidence of "undue influence, overreaching, misrepresentation, or invasion of privacy." In other words, the Court saw the attorney's actions as political, not commercial, speech. In contrast, Ohralik had been involved in a commercial transaction. In his dissent, Justice Rehnquist said he saw "no principled distinction" between the two cases in which "'ambulance-chasers' suffer one fate and 'civil liberties lawyers' another? . . . I believe that constitutional inquiry must focus on the character of the conduct which the State seeks to regulate, and not on the motives of the individual lawyers or the nature of the particular litigation involved."[62] Although he did not write the majority opinion in *Florida Bar*, but instead assigned it to Justice O'Connor,[63] Chief Justice Rehnquist clearly made his imprint on the decision. Much of the reasoning in the majority opinion in *Florida Bar* is similar to that offered in Justice Rehnquist's dissent in *Primus*, especially the Court's concern with the impact of such conduct on public perceptions of the legal profession. Privacy was also a major concern, as discussed shortly.

Three post-*Hudson* lawyer advertising cases are cited in *Florida Bar*—*In re R.M.J.*,[64] *Zauderer v. Office of Disciplinary Counsel*,[65] and *Shapero v. Kentucky Bar Association*.[66] *R.M.J.* involved a new series of professional ethics rules adopted by the Missouri bar after the Supreme Court of the United States handed down its decision in *Bates*. The rules were rather strict, as Justice Powell pointed out in the only unanimous opinion issued so far dealing with lawyer advertising. *R.M.J.* was reprimanded for violating several of the rules, including restrictions on information about areas of practice, announcements about office openings, and jurisdictions in which he was admitted to practice. In fact, the rules were so restrictive that only 23 specific terms could be used to describe areas of practice. For example, *R.M.J.* was punished for using *real estate* instead of *property* in his advertisement, and for listing *contracts* and *securities* as areas of practice. He also ran afoul of the rules by mailing out cards announcing the opening of his office to individuals who were not included in approved categories, and for truthfully indicating that he was a member of both the Missouri and Illinois bars, and that he had been admitted to practice before the Supreme Court of the United States.

The Court noted that the state bar association did not claim the ads were in any way misleading or inaccurate, and thus had demonstrated no substantial government interest in enacting the rules. According to the Court, about all the state had shown was that the ads may have been in bad taste. The Court had a little trouble with R.M.J.'s claim—in large, boldfaced type in the ad—that he was a member of the Supreme Court of the United States bar. Under Rule 5 of the *Rules of the U.S. Supreme Court*, any attorney can be admitted to practice before the Court if the attorney has been admitted to practice in the highest court of a state, territory, district, commonwealth, or possession for at least 3 years, and if the individual "appears to the Court to be of good moral and professional character." After an application is filed and a fee paid, the attorney is sworn in. Thus, the vast majority of attorneys are either a member or eligible to be a member of the Supreme Court bar. The Court felt R.M.J.'s use of this information "could be misleading to the general public unfamiliar with the requirements of admission to the bar" of the Supreme Court. Nevertheless, the justices found that this and the other violations were not actually misleading, and thus were protected by the First Amendment.

R.M.J. is cited only once in *Florida Bar*—to lend credence to the principle that lawyer advertising is commercial speech that enjoys some First Amendment protection. *Zauderer* and *Shapero* are cited in the same context, but the Court went on to extensively cite *Shapero*, as discussed shortly. The Court cited *Zauderer* once and then simply dropped it. If public perceptions about the legal profession are as significant as the Court claimed in *Florida Bar*, then *Zauderer* is clearly relevant. *Zauderer* involved a Columbus, Ohio, attorney who was disciplined by the Ohio Office of Disciplinary Counsel for publishing a newspaper advertisement in violation of the bar disciplinary rules. The ad said he was willing to handle on a contingency fee basis cases involving women who had been injured by an intrauterine contraceptive device (IUD) known as the Dalkon Shield. The ad, which said clients would pay no fees unless they won damages, included a drawing of the IUD. Both the "no fees" assertion and the illustration clearly violated the state bar rules. The top portion of the ad, in all capitals and boldface, said: "DID YOU USE THIS IUD?" The line drawing was along the side. The ad also noted, "Our law firm is presently representing women on such cases."

The disciplinary counsel punished Zauderer on the grounds that he was soliciting business, had engaged in deceptive advertising, and had included an illustration in an ad. The Ohio Supreme Court upheld the state's action, but the Supreme Court of the United States, in a 5–3 decision written by Justice White, ruled that the Ohio rule regarding solicitation violated the First Amendment because it applied to both deceptive and nondeceptive advertising. The Court said that if it accepted the state's argument in the case that such solicitations were inherently misleading, and therefore should be banned, "we would have little basis for preventing the Government from suppressing other forms of truthful and nondeceptive advertising simply to spare itself the trouble of distinguishing such advertising from false or deceptive advertising."[67] All eight of the justices voting found the ban on illustrations unconstitutional, but six of them agreed that the attorney could be disciplined for the claim that "no fees would be owed by the client" because he failed to disclose that the client could be held responsible for court costs even if the client loses. Although states permit attorneys to represent clients at no charge, and even encourage attorneys to act *pro bono* for indigents, courts and state codes of professional conduct do not permit attorneys to pay court costs for clients. However, judges usually have the discretion to waive such expenses when warranted. The Ohio rules required full disclosure of information about contingency fees—a constitutionally sound provision, according to the Supreme Court of the United States.

It is interesting that, except for the one cite, the Court ignores *Zauderer* in *Florida Bar*. Granted, *Zauderer* involved a newspaper ad, whereas *Florida Bar* concerned mail solicitation. But both were targeted to victims of unfortunate circumstances, and both arguably could bring disrepute to the profession.

Shapero is a different story. It is discussed throughout *Florida Bar*, primarily because the federal appellate court, in striking down the ban, determined that the case was governed by *Shapero*. Clearly, *Shapero* shares several similarities with *Florida Bar*. Kentucky attorney Richard D. Shapero's case began when he requested the Attorneys Advertising Commission, a three-member body created by the Kentucky Supreme Court "to aid lawyers to ethically advertise and to protect the public," to approve a letter he wanted to send to potential clients he believed were facing foreclosure on their home mortgages. The proposed letter urged the recipient to "call my office . . . for *FREE* information on how you can keep your home. Call *NOW*, don't wait. It may surprise you what I may be able to do for you."[68] At that time, attorneys were barred from mailing letters or advertisements to potential clients who might need legal assistance because they had experienced a change of personal circumstances, such as a divorce, a death in the family, or foreclosure. The Commission rejected Shapero's proposed letter as a direct solicitation in violation of the state rules of professional conduct. On appeal, the Kentucky Supreme Court affirmed.

In a 6–3 decision written by Justice Brennan, the Supreme Court of the United States reversed the state appellate court, holding that the rule violated the First and Fourteenth Amendments because it imposed a blanket ban on both deceptive and nondeceptive mail advertising. The state bar association argued that the ban was needed to prevent lawyers from having undue influence on or abusing individuals by taking advantage of them while they were facing serious legal problems. According to the majority opinion of the Supreme Court of the United States, however, the potential for undue influence and fraud was significantly less than inperson solicitation, which the Court had held could be barred in *Ohralik*. Justice Brennan noted, "Unlike the potential client with a badgering advocate breathing down his neck, the recipient of a letter and the reader of an advertisement can effectively avoid further bombardment of his sensibilities simply by averting his eyes."[69]

Justice Brennan was unable to convince a majority of the Court to go along with him on one portion of his opinion—Part III, in which he said that even the use of underlined, capital letters and hyped claims was protected by the First Amendment. According to Brennan, joined only by Justices Marshall,

Blackmun, and Kennedy, "[A] truthful and nondeceptive letter, no matter how big its type and how much it speculates can never shout at the recipient or grasp him by the lapels, as can a lawyer engaging in face-to-face solicitation."[70] Justices White and Stevens, who had joined Justice Brennan on Parts I and II, dissented on Part III, contending that the determination of whether this content was permissible should be left to the state courts.

How could the Court, 7 years later, appear to take the opposite stance without explicitly overruling *Shapero*? One reason may be that the composition of the Court changed significantly during the interval. All three of the dissenters in *Shapero*—Justices O'Connor, Rehnquist, and Scalia—were still on the Court when *Florida Bar* was decided, but only one of the four justices—Justice Kennedy, who was a member of the plurality that signed on to all three parts of Justice Brennan's opinion—was still on the Court. Justice Brennan was replaced by Justice Souter, a moderate who voted on this issue undoubtedly the way Justice Brennan would have done—with the dissent. Justice Breyer, who voted with the majority in *Florida Bar*, replaced Justice Blackmun. Finally, Justice Thomas, a strong conservative who, as expected, voted with the majority that upheld the constitutionality of the 30-day restriction in *Florida Bar*, replaced Justice Marshall, a staunch liberal. Not surprisingly, Justices O'Connor, Rehnquist, and Scalia were in the majority as well. Justice Kennedy, of course, wrote the dissenting opinion in *Florida Bar*, whereas Justice O'Connor wrote the majority opinion. First Amendment protection for mail solicitation by attorneys had now come almost full circle.

The majority in *Florida Bar* chose to distinguish the case from *Shapero* and *Edenfield v. Fane*[71] (in which the Court had ruled that a ban on inperson solicitation by Certified Public Accountants [CPAs] was unconstitutional), rather than overrule them, which the Court could easily have done, using the rationale in *Florida Bar*. The Court said that the State Board of Accountancy in *Edenfield* had not demonstrated any "studies that suggest personal solicitation of prospective business clients by CPAs creates the danger of fraud, overreaching, or compromised independence that the Board claims to fear."[72] Thus, the state had not shown sufficient evidence to prove that the challenged regulation would advance the government's substantial interest (Prong 2 of the *Central Hudson* test).[73] As the Court indicated, once again quoting *Edenfield*, the burden on the government in proving this prong: "is not satisfied by mere speculation and conjecture; rather a governmental body seeking to sustain a restriction on commercial speech must demonstrate that the harms it recites are real and that its restriction will in fact alleviate them to a material degree."[74]

Interestingly, Justice Kennedy wrote the majority opinion in *Edenfield*, whereas Justice O'Connor wrote the sole dissent in the case, in which she said *Ohralik* and *Edenfield* were the same because both harmed public perceptions about their respective professions. It appears that Justice O'Connor may have simply been unable to form a majority coalition in *Florida Bar* to overturn *Edenfield* and *Shapero*. Even Chief Justice Rehnquist and Justices Thomas and Scalia had voted with Justice Kennedy in *Edenfield*.

The majority in *Florida Bar* acknowledged that, "[w]hile some of Shapero's language might be read to support the [Eleventh] Circuit Court of Appeals' " determination that "a targeted letter [does not] invade the recipient's privacy any more than does a substantively identical letter mailed at large."[75] According to the Court, however, the ban in *Shapero* was much broader, and the intrusion the Florida Bar wanted to regulate involves "the lawyer's confrontation of victims or relatives . . . while wounds are still open, in order to solicit their business."[76] The Court also distinguished the case from *Bolger* because, in that situation unlike this one, "Citizens have at their disposal ample means of averting any substantial injury inhering in the delivery of objectionable contraceptive material."[77] (Recall from the discussion earlier in this chapter that, in *Bolger*, the Court said that it was unconstitutional to ban the mailing of contraceptive ads and information.)

Two Supreme Court of the United States' cases that are surprisingly not mentioned in either the majority opinion or the dissent are *Ibanez v. Florida Department of Business and Professional Regulation, Board of Accountancy*[78] and *Peel v. Attorney Registration and Disciplinary Commission of Illinois*.[79] *Peel* may not have been cited because it was a plurality opinion, but it did involve lawyer advertising in the form of a letterhead. The Supreme Court of the United States in a 5–4 vote, reversed the decision of the Illinois Supreme Court, upholding the Commission's finding that an attorney should be publicly censured for acting improperly by including "Certified Civil Trial Specialist by the National Board of Trial Advocacy" (NBTA) on the letterhead of correspondence that he sent to two clients. The letterhead also listed the three states in which he was licensed. The plurality opinion written by Justice Stevens (joined by Justices Brennan, Blackmun, and Kennedy) rejected the state supreme court's contention that advertising a lawyer's certification as a trial specialist by a non-bar association was not protected speech under the First Amendment. The state court felt the public could wrongly believe that an attorney "may practice in the field of trial advocacy solely because he is certified by the NBTA," and that the public might confuse "certified" with "licensed." The NBTA "certifies" attorneys who have at least 5 years of civil trial practice, have been lead counsel in at least 15 civil cases, and pass a full-day exam. NBTA is a private organization not affiliated with any government. Justice Stevens compared NBTA certification to that of a trademark, and disagreed with the state court's contention that "certified" was so close to the listing of the states in which he was licensed that it would confuse consumers. Any potential for misleading the public in this case, Justice Stevens said, was overridden by the heavy burden borne by the state in justifying its ban. Peel had violated a provision of the state Code of Professional Responsibility: "A lawyer shall not hold himself out publicly as a specialist, except as follows: patent lawyer, trademark lawyer, admiralty lawyer."

In his concurring opinion, Justice Marshall (joined by Justice Brennan) said the Illinois ban was unconstitutional because it went too far. The letter was potentially misleading, he said, but there were less restrictive ways to avoid this problem than a total ban. Justice White dissented, as did Justice O'Connor, who was joined by Chief Justice Rehnquist and Justice Scalia. In a slight preview of her opinion in *Florida Bar*, Justice O'Connor said states should be given greater leeway in regulating speech that is "inherently likely to deceive," especially given the "public's comparative lack of knowledge" and "the limited ability of the professions to police themselves."[80]

In *Ibanez*, the Court held, in the first majority opinion written by Justice Ginsburg, that a Florida ban on lawyers advertising that they are also CPAs and Certified Financial Planners (CFPs) was a violation of the First Amendment. This case had a new twist: The prohibition was placed by the state Board of Accountancy, which licenses and regulates CPAs, rather than the state bar. Silvia Ibanez had placed the initials CPA and CFP in her yellow pages listing, on her business cards, and on law office stationery. CPA designates Certified Public Accountant, indicating board licensing, and CFP stands for Certified Financial Planner, which is granted after an approved course of study and passing an exam administered by the Certified Financial Planner Board. On appeal, the Board of Accountancy argued that the designation "CPA" by Ibanez was misleading because, as she had admitted at her hearing, she was practicing law, not accounting. The Board also contended that the "CFP" designation was misleading because, in conjunction with CPA, it implied state approval and recognition.

The Court unanimously held that "CPA" was not misleading because Ibanez continued to hold her CPA license, and thus the Board was punishing her for disseminating truthful commercial speech. No deception and no harm to the public had been demonstrated. Although the Board of Accountancy had reprimanded her for engaging in "false, deceptive, and misleading" advertising, it did not revoke her CPA license or her CFP authorization. All but Chief Justice Rehnquist and Justice O'Connor believed the "CFP" designation was neither misleading nor harmful. However, the latter two justices contended that the Board could take action against Ibanez for not putting a required disclaimer with "CFP" to indicate that the CFP board is not affiliated with the state. Of course, Chief Justice Rehnquist joined Justice O'Connor's majority opinion in *Florida Bar*. Justice Breyer, who also joined the majority, had replaced Justice Blackmun in the 1-year interim between *Ibanez* and *Florida Bar*.

Ibanez was and continues to be a sound victory for commercial speech. Licensing agencies remain free to impose limits on advertising, but such restrictions must meet the *Central Hudson* test. Under this standard, the state may ban advertising only if it is false, deceptive, or misleading. It may restrict it only if it can show the restriction directly and materially advances a substantial interest in a manner no more extensive than necessary to advance that interest. As the Court noted, "The State's burden is not slight. . . . '[M]ere speculation or conjecture' will not suffice; rather the State 'must demonstrate that the harms it recites are real and that its restriction will in fact alleviate them to a material degree.' "[81]

States will undoubtedly continue to try to hold onto restrictions already in place, and to impose new restrictions when perceived problems arise. But the

Court is making it more difficult for most restrictions to survive First Amendment hurdles. In particular, state bars have become more sensitive to public concerns about lawyers as the perceptions about the profession continue to decline. In a November 1993 Gallup poll of American Bar Association (ABA) members, 87% of the respondents said advertising has a negative effect on perceptions about attorneys, compared with 3% who said the effect was positive.[82] Sixty-one percent said their firms use some form of advertising, but only 2% use television and only 12% use direct mail. The ABA has been conducting public hearings, and is in the process of making recommendations to the ABA Board of Governors, which could, in turn, set guidelines for state bars. The ABA has no power to regulate lawyer ads. Iowa has by far the toughest restrictions of any bar association, and it is seeking ABA endorsement. The state's restrictions are so severe that ABA Staff Counsel William E. Hornsby said, "There is no electronic advertising for lawyers in Iowa."[83] Could such a ban be justified under the reasoning set forth in *Florida Bar*? Probably not, because the Court was not prepared to overturn *Shapero* or *Edenfield*.

Justice Kennedy's dissent in *Florida Bar* is notable because it demonstrates how thin the majority was in the case, and because he minces no words regarding the obvious disdain he has for the majority opinion. His blistering attack, to which Justices Stevens, Souter, and Ginsburg signed on, criticized the document ("Summary of Record") that the majority relied on in supporting the claim that the government had a substantial interest:

> This document includes no actual surveys, few indications of sample size or selection procedures, no explanations of methodology, and no discussion of excluded results. There is no description of the statistical universe or scientific framework that permits any productive use of the information the so-called Summary of Record contains. The majority describes this anecdotal matter as "noteworthy for its breadth and detail" . . . but when examined, it is noteworthy for its incompetence.[84]

His dissent went on to say, "Our cases require something more than a few pages of self-serving and unsupported statements by the State to demonstrate that a regulation directly and materially advances the elimination of a real harm when the state seeks to suppress truthful and nondeceptive speech."[85] The opinion also noted that the ban created by the bar association rule is much too broad: "Even assuming that interest [the state's interest] were legitimate, there is a wild disproportion between the harm supposed and the speech ban enforced."[86]

Justice Kennedy's other arguments included: (a) mail is not sent to a "captive audience"—it can simply be thrown away; (b) there is no justification for assuming, as the majority does, that the information provided in direct mail solicitations is "unwelcome or unnecessary" during the 30-day ban; and (c) the ban cuts off information at a time when "prompt legal representation" could be essential. He also noted that, "[p]otential clients will not hire lawyers who offend them" and that a "solicitation letter is not a contract." According to

Justice Kennedy, "It is most ironic that, for the first time since *Bates v. State Bar of Arizona*, the Court now orders a major retreat from the constitutional guarantees for commercial speech in order to shield its own profession from public criticism."[87]

Justice Kennedy concluded:

> Today's opinion is a serious departure, not only from our prior decisions involving attorney advertising, but also from the principles that govern the transmission of commercial speech. The Court's opinion reflects a new-found and illegitimate confidence that it, along with the Supreme Court of Florida, knows what is best for the Bar and its clients. Self-assurance has always been the hallmark of a censor. That is why under the First Amendment the public, not the State, has the right and the power to decide what ideas and information are deserving of their adherence. . . .[88]

State appellate courts and the U.S. Court of Appeals have generally been liberal in what and how they permit lawyers to advertise and otherwise promote, and typically they have their way because the Supreme Court of the United States usually denies certiorari in such cases. There have been a few exceptions, especially when the advertising is clearly deceptive or misleading, or the conduct vexatious, such as in 1992 when the New Jersey Supreme Court ruled that an attorney could be punished for sending a direct mail solicitation to the family of a plane crash victim 2 weeks after he had been killed.[89] After *Florida Bar*, the trend toward liberalization of restrictions may slow down. *Florida Bar* is probably not the last word on lawyer advertising unless the Court refuses to hear any cases from the flood of appeals likely to come from the lower courts as more restrictions emerge and are challenged. On September 22, 1995, 3 months after the Supreme Court of the United States handed down *Florida Bar*, the Eleventh Circuit U.S. Court of Appeals reversed the district court's summary judgment for the plaintiff, and remanded the case back to the district court for further proceedings.[90]

OTHER PROFESSIONS

Except for *Ibanez* (which involved a lawyer-accountant), *Virginia State Board of Pharmacy* (which involved pharmacists, although a consumer group, not the pharmacists, challenged the restriction on advertising prescription drug prices), and *Edenfield* (which involved accountants), the Supreme Court of the United States has only issued two other decisions in the last two decades dealing directly with advertising by licensed professionals. In *Friedman v. Rogers*,[91] the Court held 7–2 that Texas could prevent optometrists from practicing under a trade name because the state had a "substantial and well-demonstrated" interest in protecting consumers from the deceptive and misleading use of optometrical trade names. According to the Court:

> A trade name is . . . a significantly different form of commercial speech than that considered in *Virginia Pharmacy* and *Bates*. In those cases, the State had proscribed advertising by pharmacists and lawyers that contained statements about the products or services offered and their prices. These statements were self-contained and self-explanatory. Here we are concerned with a form of commercial speech that has no intrinsic meaning. A trade name conveys no information about the price and nature of the services offered by an optometrist until it acquires meaning over a period of time by associations formed in the minds of the public between the name and some standard of price or quality. Because these ill-defined associations of trade names with price and quality information can be manipulated by the users of trade names, there is a significant possibility that trade names will be used to mislead the public.[92]

In 1982, the Supreme Court of the United States affirmed without opinion a decision by the U.S. Court of Appeals for the Second Circuit that upheld with minor changes an FTC order prohibiting the American Medical Association (AMA) from promoting unfair competition by banning advertising by its members, including prices.[93] The order does not prevent the AMA nor the states from regulating deceptive, unethical, or unfair advertising. The FTC issued a similar order with the American Dental Association (ADA).

Other licensed professionals simply have not attracted the attention of the Supreme Court of the United States in their advertising, although the U.S. Court of Appeals occasionally gets involved. For example, in 1982, the Fifth Circuit upheld a Texas statute that prohibited osteopaths from using "MD" after their names.[94] In 1987, the Sixth Circuit struck down a Kentucky provision that prevented dentists not licensed as specialists from using the name of a specialty or words implying a specialty in advertising. It did so because such information is truthful, in that nonspecialists are allowed to offer specialized services such as *orthodontics* (one of the banned words).[95]

CONCLUSION

Generally, licensed and, to some extent, other professionals are still relatively free to truthfully advertise, so long as the advertising is not inherently deceptive, unfair, or misleading. They are also allowed to engage in promotional activities such as soliciting via mail or in person, so long as such conduct is not vexatious. But *Florida Bar*, despite the 5–4 vote, makes it clear that the Court will look to uphold state actions against professionals, particularly lawyers, who take steps to further erode public perceptions, and that may encroach on personal privacy at a time when individuals are possibly vulnerable, such as during disasters and accidents. *Central Hudson* appears to be alive and fairly well, but its tests for finding a significant government interest and the extent to which the restriction will advance that interest have been significantly eased. More than anything else, *Florida Bar* may signal a turn toward the days when commercial speech for professionals entailed limited First Amendment rights.

Products Liability

Products liability, as the name suggests, refers to the legal responsibility of manufacturers and sellers to compensate buyers, users, and even innocent bystanders for injuries or damages that result from defects in the goods that were purchased. Although the responsibility for flawed products falls primarily on the manufacturer, liability may be imposed on the retailer, wholesaler, some other middleman, or even, as is discussed herein, the advertising and public relations people who provide information to the consumer public about the products.

In this context, the law affecting liability for product-related injuries and damages has changed dramatically. "Let the buyer beware" (caveat emptor), a phrase mentioned frequently in these pages, is being replaced in products liability cases by "strict liability" (i.e., liability even without the showing of negligence). This means that the seller might be held responsible in the eyes of the law for any and all defective or dangerous products that unduly threaten a consumer's safety.

An illustration can be found in the *Restatement of Torts*:

> A manufactures automobiles. He advertises in newspapers and magazines that the glass in his cars is "shatterproof." B reads this advertising, and in reliance upon it purchases from a retail dealer an automobile manufactured by A. While B is driving the car, a stone thrown up by a passing truck strikes the windshield and shatters it, injuring B. A is subject to strict liability to B.[1]

Products liability is one of the fastest growing areas of contemporary American law. More than a million claims for product-caused injuries are made a year, and half of these involve litigation.[2]

Most of these cases do not concern advertising, public relations, and media people, but some cases do. Vicarious liability (imposing responsibility on one person arising out of the actionable conduct of another, based on a relationship between them) can involve those individuals who simply provided information in products liability cases—communications messages about the products—that somehow proved harmful. Products liability cases can become especially important to public relations practitioners engaged in crisis management.

Some critics believe that products liability litigation has moved too far too fast. They tell horror stories of seemingly bizarre cases, such as a $2.9 million award given in 1994 (it was later reduced) to a fast-food restaurant customer who was burned when the coffee she spilled on herself was thought to be unreasonably hot. Critics argue that outlandish verdicts such as this could destroy American business competitiveness. On the other side of this debate are those who defend products liability litigation as a means of recovery against what they regard as careless, profit-hungry manufacturers who flimflam the American public with dangerous products that should not be on the market. These larger issues and their implications are discussed later in this chapter. First, this chapter examines some aspects of this type of liability as they specifically apply to the advertising media.

RESPONSIBILITY OF THE ADVERTISING MEDIA: INNOCENT MISTAKES

Historically, the mass media have been shielded from liability when an advertising message that is published or broadcast turns out to be wrong, or even if the product or service being promoted is somehow defective. As one court put it, the advertisement is "simply an announcement by the advertiser that he is opening negotiations."[3] Said another: "The price quoted in an advertisement is a mere announcement of what money value the merchant has placed upon his merchandise, and it, too, is not a legal offer to sell at that figure."[4]

Because the merchant is not required by law to sell at the advertised price, a typographical error—no matter how awkward or embarrassing it might be—does not cost the advertiser any actual damage unless the advertiser voluntarily decides to honor the mistaken price as a gesture of goodwill toward his or her customers. Accordingly, the newspaper or broadcaster has no legal obligation to cover the costs for such errors. However, in most cases, good will-conscious media owners will print or broadcast corrections promptly and for free. Some newspapers warn in their advertising rate cards that the publication will assume no responsibility for errors. In other cases, newspapers will limit their own liability to the actual cost of the ad itself, not to any damage that might be caused by mistakes in it.

As an example, a newspaper ad for a department store in a Georgia city mistakenly quoted the price of a $15 scarf at $5. The store owner, probably through gritted teeth, sold a number of the scarfs at the misprinted price of

$5, but then sued the newspaper for damages to recover the loss he had absorbed. The court rejected the store owner's claim.[5] In that same vein, a Mississippi merchant ordered two full-page ad layouts from the local newspaper. One ad, scheduled to run on December 15 of that year, promoted gift ideas for Christmas shoppers. At the same time, the merchant scheduled a "clearance sale, one-half off" ad to be run early in January. The newspaper mixed up the two, mistakenly publishing the "one half off" ad just in time to catch bargain-hungry Christmas shoppers in a buying mood. The store owner honored the deep discounts anyway, although he lost thousands of dollars in profits by doing so. He sued the newspaper for recovery, and a sympathetic local jury awarded him $4,000 in damages. The state appeals court reversed the verdict, however, holding that, although the newspaper was clearly negligent, it was not liable. The advertisement was only an invitation to the public, the court ruled, and if the store elected to sell at the erroneous prices, it must accept the loss.[6]

Thus, advertising media are protected from mistakes—even stupid mistakes—in the advertising they carry so long as the mistakes are innocently made. The California state *Business and Professional Code* statute, using language widely adopted throughout the country, declares that false advertising liability does not apply to any mass communication that "broadcasts or publishes an advertisement in good faith, without knowledge of its false, deceptive, or misleading character."[7]

The general principle is that a publication or broadcaster is not responsible for fraud in an advertising message unless the publisher or broadcaster knew in advance that the advertisement was fraudulent—a difficult thing to prove. Most mass communications media managers head off potential problems with errors of this type simply by submitting proofs of the ad copy to the clients and obtaining their approval before the advertising message is published or broadcast. The advertiser is ultimately responsible for his or her advertisements. Publishers and broadcasters have vested interests in the credibility of the advertising messages they carry, of course, knowing that false or misleading ads make them no friends among their clients or audiences.

RESPONSIBILITY OF THE ADVERTISING MEDIA: ADS THAT HARM

Should the media of mass communications be held accountable for harm resulting from an advertising message? Consider this example: X, seeking assistance in undertaking a criminal act, purchases advertising space in a magazine, Y. Reader Z notices the ad, contacts X directly, and conspires with X to perform the criminal act. Obviously Z, the originator, and X, the perpetrator, broke the law and should be punished. But what about Y? The magazine neither conceived the ad nor participated in the criminal act. Should the magazine be punished simply for accepting and publishing the advertisement that brought two culprits together? Two recent cases, each involving *Soldier of Fortune* magazine, address this issue.

The first of these began with an advertisement that John Wayne Hearn and another ex-Marine ran in the magazine, which focused on mercenary activity and military affairs: "EX-MARINES—67–69 'Nam Vets, Ex-DI, weapons specialist—jungle warfare, pilot, M.E., high-risk assignments, U.S. or overseas. (404)991-2684." Hearn would later testify that "DI" stood for "drill instructor" and "M.E." referred to multiengine airplanes, and that he intended "high-risk assignments" to mean bodyguard work for top executives. He and his partner hoped to land work as security guards or in training troops in South America. But most of the callers who responded to the ad sought to engage the pair in kidnappings, jailbreaks, bombings, or murders. Hearn's partner balked at these overtures, and soon quit the venture.

Hearn, however, stayed with it and accepted at least two commissions. One of them, quite legal, was to place seven bodyguards with an oil company conglomerate office in Lebanon. The other transaction, which he undertook personally, was for $10,000 to kill a Bryan, Texas, woman, Sandra Black, at the behest of her husband, Robert. By the time he had done so, on February 21, 1985, Hearn had already killed two of Mrs. Black's friends who had learned of his intentions. Hearn was soon arrested, tried, convicted, and sentenced to concurrent life sentences for the murders. Sandra Black's son and her mother, Marjorie Eimann, sued *Soldier of Fortune* for its part in the affair. The specific accusation was negligence: that the magazine knew, or should have known, from the content that the ad was, in fact, an offer to perform illegal acts. The trial court jury agreed that the ad amounted to criminal solicitation and awarded $9.4 million to the plaintiffs.

On appeal, the judgment was reversed. The court held that the magazine "owed no duty to refrain from publishing a facially innocuous classified advertisement when the ad's context—at most—made its message ambiguous." The ad revealed no identifiable offer to commit a crime, the appeals court ruled, and thus to find it actionable would not

> ... strike the proper balance between the risks of harm from ambiguous advertisement and the burden of preventing harm from this source under these facts. ... Hearn's ad presents a risk of serious harm. But everyday activities, such as driving on high-speed, closed access roadways, also carry definite risks that we as a society choose to accept in return for the activity's usefulness and convenience. To take a more extreme example, courts have almost uniformly rejected efforts to hold handgun manufacturers liable under negligence or strict liability theories to gunshot victims injured during crimes, despite the real possibility that such products can be used for criminal purposes.[8]

Shortly thereafter, *Soldier of Fortune* was involved in another, yet strikingly similar, case, and this time the magazine would ultimately lose. The ad ran as follows: "GUN FOR HIRE: 37-year-old professional mercenary desires jobs. Vietnam Veteran. Discreet and very private. Body guard, courier, and other special skills. All jobs considered [telephone and box numbers]." The ad was placed by Richard Savage, then living in Tennessee, and it drew well—30 or more responses per week, many of them involving proposals for criminal activity. This amounted to more heavy work than one man could handle, so Savage hired Sean Trevor Doutre, who had also seen the ad in *Soldier of Fortune* and had traveled from Canada to help service Savage's growing business clientele. Savage put him to work as a contract killer. Doutre had already murdered at least two persons for Savage before he accepted a contract to kill Richard Braun, who was the unfortunate business associate of another of Savage's customers. On August 25, 1985, as Richard Braun and his 16-year-old son, Michael, were leaving Braun's home in suburban Atlanta, Doutre stepped in front of Braun's car and fired bullets into the car from an automatic pistol. Richard Braun and young Michael, both wounded, rolled out of the car on separate sides of the driveway. Doutre fired two more shots into Richard Braun's head, then walked over to Michael Braun, who had been wounded in the thigh, aimed the pistol at Michael, but did not fire. Instead, he put his finger over his lips, signaling the boy to be quiet, and ran into the woods.

In 1990, Michael Braun and his brother sued *Soldier of Fortune*, contending that the magazine was liable for the death of their father for publishing an advertisement that had created an unreasonable risk of soliciting violent criminal activity. The jury agreed, awarding $2 million to the Brauns for the wrongful death claim, $375,000 to Michael for emotional distress (he had watched his father die), and $10 million in punitive damages against the magazine. "It is apparent," the appeals court said, "that the jury did not believe that *Soldier of Fortune* was unaware of the risks associated with running an ad such as the one placed by Richard Savage." The court said that specific phrases in the ad—"gun for hire," "discreet and very private," and "all jobs considered"—could be reasonably construed as an offer to perform illegal acts: "A risk becomes unreasonable when its magnitude outweighs the social utility of the act or omission that creates the risk. The risk in the Savage ad was the risk of murder or serious, violent crime." However, the court did reduce the total to $2.375 million, finding that the additional $10 million in punitive damages would be excessive.[9]

In *Eimann*, the court found that the ad in *Soldier of Fortune* presented no clear and present danger to law and order. In *Braun*, the court found that a similar, although somewhat more specific and sinister, ad in the same magazine did present such a threat. The urgent message to the communications media is that the publisher has a duty to screen out advertising that poses a threat of leading to the commission of a crime. Reasonable precaution in accepting dubious-appearing ads manifestly is necessary. The Supreme Court of the United States has not yet ruled in this murky area, where First Amendment freedoms clash with negligence and personal injury claims. There will likely be more such lawsuits in the years ahead, testing the advertising/media role in promoting antisocial behavior.

For example, in 1990, a woman in Texas sued *Boy's Life* magazine, charging that an advertising supplement ("Aiming for Fun") in that magazine prompted some boys to play with a rifle that accidently discharged, killing her 12-year-old son. The court found that the advertising was not inciteful and the magazine was not at fault.[10] Similar claims have met with little success in the courts thus far, perhaps because the courts are apprehensive about opening a door, through advertising restraints, to a climate in which the First Amendment might be severely curtailed. As one Mississippi court put it: "The commercial speech doctrine would disappear if its protection ceased whenever the advertised product might be used illegally. Peanut butter advertising cannot be banned just because someone might someday throw a jar at the presidential motorcade."[11]

INDIRECT INVOLVEMENT:
TOBACCO ADVERTISING

In 1988, after 5 years of litigation, including a 6-month trial, a New Jersey jury awarded $400,000 to Antonio Cipollone for the death of his wife, Rose Cipollone. A cigarette smoker since 1942, Mrs. Cipollone died of lung cancer in 1984. The Cipollone suit alleged that the tobacco company's advertising provided a warranty of sorts, portraying cigarette smokers as attractive and healthy and happy persons. The ads failed to provide sufficient alerts to the hazards of smoking. Tobacco advertising that pictures a healthy smoker, in short, might be interpreted as an express warranty. In a deposition taken shortly before her death, Rose Cipollone testified that she smoked because she saw people smoking in advertisements and because she came to regard smoking as something "cool, glamorous, and grown up to do." Although the federally required warnings ("Smoking may be hazardous to your health") may appear in the ads, she contended, the larger context of the advertising was so idyllic as to neutralize the warning altogether. The jury agreed, and for the first time found a tobacco company liable for injuries due to cigarette smoking.

The verdict was seen as a breakthrough of startling proportions by some industry leaders, consumer affairs advocates, and legal experts. This case, one legal scholar proclaimed, presented "the legal theory that finally pierced the tobacco industry shield . . . a breach of express warranties created by cigarette advertisements."[12] Some legal scholarship predicted that future courts could thus have the opportunity to give breach of warranty recoveries to older smokers who saw advertisements a generation ago, as well as to younger smokers viewing and relying on today's advertisements.[13]

However, the rejoicing may have been premature. An appeals court reversed the Cipollone award and dismissed the majority of the claims against the tobacco company. Fraud (on the part of the tobacco industry) would require the establishment of knowing, willful misconduct. The court held that an express warranty requires explicit health claims. By continuing to smoke, Rose Cipollone reflected behavior that made her partly to blame. Indeed, the terms *assumption of risk* and *contributory negligence*—the degree to which victims might be responsible for their own misfortunes—were used by the court in justifying the reversal. The case was heard again, and a subsequent appeals court ruled that Mrs. Cipollone voluntarily encountered a known danger by smoking, and thus held her 80% responsible for her own fate. The door was left open for Cipollone to try yet again, for partial damages this time, but he had had enough and elected to drop the case altogether.[14]

The tobacco companies are powerful adversaries, prepared to litigate vigorously despite great expense, and few plaintiffs have the staying power to prevail against them.[15] Even so, the growing number of claims (more than 300 cases comparable to Mrs. Cippolone's have been filed against the tobacco companies, although most have been dismissed), the accessibility to trial lawyers (through contingency fee arrangements), and the enormous stakes involved would seem to indicate much more activity in this field in the years to come.

The impact on the advertising and mass media communities could be substantial. Tobacco advertising no longer appears on radio or television, but the annual expenditure for tobacco advertising means many millions of dollars each year to magazines, newspapers, and outdoor advertising companies. In the mid-1990s, however, advertising people would seem to have a relatively free creative hand in developing tobacco ads for the print media, particularly if the ads are not overly factual and specific. There could be some danger in advertising for filter and low-tar cigarettes, which might qualify as express warranties, and in health claims made by public relations representatives of tobacco companies.[16]

THE LARGER CONTEXT: CHANGE AND GROWTH

Despite the frequent mention throughout this book of "caveat emptor," manufacturers of faulty products throughout much of American legal history have often been held accountable for the harm those products may have caused to those who purchased them. But in earlier claims, only the actual purchasers could recover; the public at large historically was not a factor. As one important 1852 New York Appeals Court opinion put it:

> If A. builds a wagon and sells it to B., who sells it to C., and C. hires it to D., who in consequence of the gross negligence of A. in building the wagon is overturned and injured, D. cannot recover damages against A., the builder. A.'s obligation to build the wagon faithfully arises solely out of his contract with B. The public have nothing to do with it. Misfortunes to third persons, not parties to the contract, would not be a natural and necessary consequence of the builder's negligence. . . .[17]

However, this narrow interpretation was to be greatly expanded early in this century. A leading case in this regard, *MacPherson v. Buick Motor Co.*, involved the sale of an automobile to a retail dealer in New York. The dealer then sold the car to MacPherson. While he was driving his new machine, a wheel came off, causing the car to crash. MacPherson was thrown clear, but injured. The wheel later proved to have been made of defective wood and its spokes crumbled. The wheel was not manufactured by Buick, but bought from a subcontractor. However, the court found that the defects in the wheel could have been discovered by reasonable inspection. MacPherson sued the manufacturer, Buick; Buick argued that its responsibility ended with the sale of the car to the dealer. The court disagreed. In a ringing opinion, written by New York Appeals Court Justice Benjamin Cardozo, the court held:

> If the nature of a thing is such that it is reasonably certain to place life and limb in peril when negligently made, it is then a thing of danger. . . . There must also be a knowledge that in the usual course of events the danger will be shared by others than the buyer. Such knowledge may often be inferred from the nature of the transaction. . . . We have put aside the notion that the duty to safeguard life and limb, when the consequences of negligence may be foreseen, grows out of contract and nothing else.[18]

This strict liability philosophy is now in effect in most jurisdictions throughout the United States. As the *Restatement of Torts* explains it:

> . . . the justification for the strict liability has been said to be that the seller, by marketing his product for use and consumption, has undertaken and assumed a special responsibility toward any member of the consuming public who may be injured by it; that the public has the right to and does expect, in the case of products which it needs and for which it is forced to rely upon the seller, that reputable sellers will stand behind their goods; that public policy demands that the burden of accidental injuries caused by products intended for consumption be placed upon those who market them. . . .[19]

Currently, then, products liability cases can cover various kinds of harm to various categories of persons connected to, or affected by, the product. Purchasers can sue, but so can users or consumers, and even bystanders who have become involved (e.g., a third person injured in a wreck caused by a manufacturing flaw in a vehicle). Others besides the manufacturer might be sued: employees and subcontractors who helped design and build the product, retailers who sold the product, packagers who labeled the product, and even those advertising and public relations people who provided information about the product.

THE ROLE OF INFORMATION

At one time, most selling was done face to face. Now, with highly developed mass communications networks, selling is often impersonal. Indeed, many customers who enter a store are already presold, through advertising, and the only employee the customer may encounter in the store is the cashier at the checkout stand, who takes the money for a purchase largely made possible through advertising. Advertising's vital importance to commerce is recognized by the law as well. The *Restatement of Torts* defines advertising's legal responsibilities in products liability this way:

> One engaged in the business of selling chattels [items of personal property] who, by advertising, labels, or otherwise, makes to the public a misrepresentation of a material fact concerning the character of quality of a chattel sold by him is subject to liability for physical harm to a consumer of the chattel caused by justifiable reliance upon the misrepresentation, even though (a) it is not made fraudulently or negligently, and (b) the consumer has not bought the chattel from or entered into any contractual relation with the seller.[20]

Increasingly, state and federal governments are requiring more information to be provided to potential purchasers. The stated objective of the 1968 Truth-in-Lending Act, as an example, is "to assure a meaningful disclosure of credit terms so that the consumer will be able to compare more readily the various credit terms available to him and to avoid the uninformed use of credit. . . ."[21]

Hence, the specific statements in such advertising must be accurate. Advertising and public relations people, although they might work in an outside agency and serve as an independent contractor to the seller, should be able to verify specific assertions and prove their claims. Additionally, there can be trouble if marketing messages fail to provide adequate instructions for the safe use of the product or warn of possible dangers associated with it.

Essentially, warranties[22] provide assurances about the quality or character of products, or about their fitness for the purpose for which they were bought. An express warranty is a promise made about the goods by the seller (or his or her representative, such as an advertising agency) to induce the sale. Such promises often become "the basis of the bargain" (i.e., a key part of the transaction), and as such they are held to be express warranties. One example is the description of the goods ("One-year guarantee on parts and labor"). The words *guarantee* or *warranty* might not even be used; an affirmation of benefits of using the product (as with the tobacco advertising cited earlier in *Cipollone*, which was merely interpreted in context to present cigarette smoking as not only unharmful, but "cool") could be interpreted as an express warranty.

Implied warranties are of less concern here because they chiefly involve manufacturers and retailers. An *implied warranty of merchantability* means that the products are suitable for the ordinary purposes for which such goods are sold. Understood, if not specifically stated, is that a reasonable standard of safety has been met (e.g., the sale of food products at restaurants or grocery stores). An *implied warranty of fitness* means that when the seller knows, or should know, the particular purpose for which the product is sold, the product is indeed fit for that purpose (e.g., a spreadsheet computer program or a heavy-duty pipe wrench). As the name suggests, implied warranties need not be stated, but may be presumed.

Note that warranties are based on facts, not opinions. High-flown sales rhetoric, so long as it remains the opinion of the seller (or advertiser), does not constitute a warranty. As the Uniform Commercial Code puts it, "an affirmation merely of the value of the goods or a statement purporting to be merely the seller's opinion or commendation of the goods does not create a warranty."[23] Thus, the topic of "puffery," already discussed at length elsewhere in this chapter, applies to products liability questions as well.

The Federal Trade Commission's (FTC's) enforcement activities in monitoring advertising are also treated at length, especially in chapters 4 and 6. They are summarized again here for their role in products liability advertising. The FTC's mission is to deal with unfair competition in: (a) advertising claims, particularly those relating to safety or effectiveness, for food and drugs sold over the counter; (b) performance and energy-savings claims for solar products, furnaces, storm windows, residential siding, wood-burning products, gas-saving products, motor oils, and other products that are marketed by emphasizing their energy conservation features; (c) advertising directed at children; and (d) cigarette advertising, which includes monitoring for deceptive claims; operating a tobacco-testing laboratory to measure tar, nicotine, and carbon monoxide content of cigarettes; and reporting to Congress annually on cigarette labeling, advertising, and promotion.[24]

DEFENSES: ASSUMPTION OF RISK
AND FORESEEABILITY

Contributory negligence is not generally regarded as a defense if the negligence involves failure to discover the flaws in a product or to protect against the dangers of those flaws. Courts have recognized "misuse" of the product as a defense (e.g., a residential fire caused by the homeowner's using gasoline to clean tile floors). However, a defense that has been widely recognized is the assumption of a foreseeable risk. If the victim of a product-related accident voluntarily decided to take on a known danger, then the courts will normally expect the victim to bear responsibility for the consequences.

A number of lawsuits against the tobacco companies have been decided on these grounds; smokers were aware of the danger and continued to smoke anyway. Even then there could be complications, as a noted California case suggests. The case arose when a driver sued General Motors after his GM-imported Opel crashed on the Harbor Freeway in Los Angeles. The jury, noting that the driver had been driving up to 70 miles per hour in a state of intoxication and not using his seat belts or automatic door locks, found in GM's favor. But on appeal, the finding was reversed; the court took seriously the question as to whether a design flaw in the Opel had diminished the car's "crashworthiness."[25] But if the consumer discovers the defect, is aware of the danger, and proceeds accordingly, then recovery is unlikely. As a Nebraska court explained:

In the law of products liability, misuse is use of a product in a way not reasonably foreseeable by the supplier or manufacturer, while assumption of risk is a user's willingness or consent to use a product which the user actually knows is defective and appreciates the danger resulting from such defect.[26]

In a Texas case, Ronald Wayne McGuire, an admitted alcoholic, brought suit against Joseph E. Seagrams & Sons seeking damages he said were created by his long-term consumption of Seagrams' products. While holding that the dangers of alcohol were commonly known, the Texas Supreme Court conceded that Seagrams' massive campaign to advertise consumption of beverage alcohol "as a particularly positive activity" may have diluted the impact of the community's warnings about alcohol abuse.[27] In similar cases, variously involving the Stroh, Pabst, and Miller Breweries, courts have acknowledged that their advertising's impact had at least partially undermined public understanding of the grave risks involved in excessive use of the product. For example, in *Maguire v. Pabst Brewing Co.*, the plaintiff argued that advertising for Pabst Blue Ribbon beer was "an invitation to excess through exaltation of hedonistic tendencies over good judgment." But the Iowa Supreme Court rejected the argument, critical to the specific case, that Pabst advertising produced "a danger to highway safety."[28] The foreseeability factor cuts both ways, however. Suppose a small child opens a can of her mother's oven cleaner and drinks it down. The manufacturer of the oven cleaner may well be found to have a duty to design the product in such a way as to minimize the possible misuse.[29]

RICO, MAIL FRAUD, AND PRODUCTS LIABILITY ADVERTISING

The federal mail fraud statute prohibits "any scheme or artifice to defraud or for obtaining money or property by means of false or fraudulent pretenses, representations, or promises. . . ." Obviously fraudulent or otherwise illegal advertising would qualify—and has qualified—for prosecution on those grounds, especially in cases involving the peddling of obscene materials. An ominous move in the late 1980s was to invoke the federal Racketeer Influenced and Corrupt Organizations (RICO) act as a weapon against what was alleged to have been fraudulent advertising in a products liability context. Civil liability under RICO, which does not depend on a prior criminal conviction, allows the successful plaintiff to recover treble (triple) damages as well as attorney's fees. Many states have enacted RICO statutes as well. Indeed, the North Carolina RICO statute was found to be applicable to Jim Bakker, a prominent television evangelist, during the late 1980s.[30]

Also in the late 1980s, the first RICO-inspired false advertising products liability cases were filed. The basic charge behind the RICO claims was that the advertiser committed acts of mail and wire fraud as part of an ongoing scheme to run false advertising in the media. By reinvesting the income derived from the alleged mail and wire fraud activity, the advertiser thereby perpetuated the false advertising scheme, which in turn increased sales—thus qualifying for a charge of racketeering.

In one such case, *In re: Suzuki Samurai Products Liability Litigation*, several disgruntled purchasers of Suzuki Samurai vehicles alleged that Suzuki advertising and public relations firms made false claims that the Samurai was "suitable and safe for on and off road use" when, in fact, the vehicles allegedly tended to tip over on turns. The plaintiffs contended that the defendants, including the advertising and public relations people, used the mails in connection with these messages and reinvested the income derived from them. The court dismissed the case in a brief, unpublished opinion.[31]

However, other cases have been allowed to go to trial. In one of these, a Pennsylvania court permitted consumers to sue the Ralston Purina Co., charging that the company's advertising falsely claimed that Purina Puppy Chow was helpful in preventing canine hip dysplasia, a disabling disorder caused by bone and cartilage degeneration. This particular advertising campaign had stopped following a Food and Drug Administration (FDA) regulatory letter that ordered Ralston to quit making its claims and to run corrective advertising messages stating that Puppy Chow does not affect the onset of canine hip dysplasia. The class-action RICO lawsuit was ultimately settled, with Ralston creating a substantial fund providing for coupons offering cash discounts on subsequent purchases of its products.[32] Thus far, cases such as this have remained infrequent, but a major court victory against an advertiser in a RICO-inspired case might lead to a spate of products liability litigation in the future.

PLAIN LANGUAGE LAWS: A PUBLIC RELATIONS CHALLENGE

Another problem for consumers and consumer affairs officers is that many messages to the public are so fraught with legalese that nonlawyers have difficulty fathoming what is meant by them. Ponder the following, from a credit card company, explaining how finance charges would be computed:

> The average daily balance will equal the sum of the principal amounts of purchases included in the previous balance shown on your statement that are unpaid each day of such statement's billing period, divided by the number of days in such period. Such daily unpaid principal amounts will be determined by deducting from the principal amount of such purchases unpaid as of the beginning of a day all payments and other credits made or received as of that day which were applied to reduce such unpaid principal amount; however, if a previous balance is shown on your statement and the amount of payments and credits shown on such statement does not equal or exceed such previous balance, there will be added to such unpaid principal amount for each day all purchases or debits posted to your account as of that day.[33]

As a result of such impenetrable writing, a number of states have enacted what are called "plain language laws." The New York statute, for example, requires that consumer contracts be "written in a clear and coherent manner using words with common and every day meanings" and "appropriately divided and captioned by its various sections."[34] The federal Magnuson–Moss Act of 1975 was intended to make warranties on consumer products more understandable to consumers, and it authorized the FTC to interpret and implement the law's provisions. Public relations experts are frequently brought in to assist in these efforts to clarify and simplify communications messages to the public.

Advertising and salesmanship are the primary devices for prompting consumers to buy and sell. When the seller, or the advertiser, engages in false or misleading statements or practices, the consumer may embark on a transaction very different from the one he or she contemplated.[35] Thus, it is important to communicate advertising and public relations messages so they are honest, straightforward, clear, and understandable.

THE FUTURE: AN EXPANDED ROLE
FOR COMMUNICATORS?

The earlier products liability cases were characterized by a strong tradition that business should be protected as much as possible from overly broad awards that could cripple American commerce. When they were challenged, the manufacturers fought back fiercely and with tenacity. For example, consider this internal tobacco industry memorandum for what it reveals about legal strategy and tactics:

> The aggressive posture we have taken regarding depositions and discovery in general continues to make these [products liability] cases extremely burdensome and expensive for plaintiffs' lawyers, particularly sole practitioners. To paraphrase General Patton, the way we won these cases was not by spending all of [RJR's, a tobacco company's] money, but by making that other son of a bitch spend all of his.[36]

But faulty and dangerous products do create legitimate victims, too, and increasingly the courts and consumer protection agencies have befriended them. Thousands of products liability cases are filed each month, the victims represented by forceful trial lawyers determined to protect citizens' rights and punish corporate wrongdoing. Sympathetic juries award huge judgments to persons who were injured by faulty products they purchased or used, or were somehow injured as innocent spectators. During the 1980s and early 1990s, some of the momentum shifted to the victims.

In the mid-1990s, however, following a decade or more of enormous jury awards, the country seemed ready to move back in the other direction. The medical, insurance, and manufacturing communities flexed their considerable political muscle, putting pressure on Congress for massive changes in the laws affecting products liability. American business and medicine had become intimidated by threats of malpractice and products liability litigation, reformists argued; as a result, innovations were discouraged, and products and services had become far more expensive than necessary. Any savings, proponents of the damage caps said, would be passed on to consumers in the form of less expensive products. A "Products Liability Fairness Bill" introduced in Congress was designed to limit the kinds and amounts of damages that could be awarded to victims, among much else. The bill was defeated in 1994. But later that same year, a Republican majority was voted into both houses of Congress. A products liability reform act, reflecting proposed damage caps on jury awards, was an integral part of the Republican "Contract With America" platform that year. The entire field of products liability law may well undergo drastic change in the near and midrange future.

Even so, the complexities of modern society will certainly create new innocent victims, and products liability traditions will not ignore those who have been unfairly harmed. (It is very difficult to blame nonsmoking secretaries for having continued to work in smoky offices, for example, or an 8-year-old girl who suffers brain damage and blindness because of a defective medication administered to her.) The next wave of products liability cases[37] may be intended not to make trouble for manufacturers, but to obtain justice for those who have been injured. In the process, advertising and public relations may well assume a larger role: The consumer protection cases and others involving industry's fraudulent behavior may not only cause that behavior to stop, but may also create a substantial fund for corrective advertising. Thus, the advertising and public relations communities, whose messages might make or break a products liability claim, could ultimately play an expanded role in the resolution of such claims in the years to come.

9

Defamation and Product Disparagement

The First Amendment to the Constitution declares that Congress "shall make no law ... abridging the freedom of speech, or of the press." That sounds absolute. It is not. A business executive might criticize the government, but had better not advocate the violent overthrow of it. A citizen is privileged to yell "Phooey!" or worse at a political rally, but not "Fire! Fire!" in a packed movie house. Advertising agencies and business corporations have extensive liberty to print and broadcast messages promoting products and services, but not to falsely and unfairly damage a competitor's good name. The Supreme Court has described the limits this way:

> All men have a right to print and publish whatever they deem proper unless by doing so they infringe upon the rights of another. For any injury they may commit against the public or an individual, they may be punished. . . . The freedom of speech and the press does not permit the publication of libels . . . or other indecent articles injurious to morals or private reputations.[1]

Defamation is the most common, and perhaps the most serious, legal problem currently facing the mass communications industry. Although much libel litigation arises out of news-gathering activities, defamation is still of concern to the public relations and advertising professions. Corporations, products, services, and business reputations can be defamed, as is shown here, in advertising messages and other types of business communications. Moreover, public relations specialists have the responsibility to inform their clients about the possibly far-reaching consequences of libel suits; each court appearance or motion could expose their clients to further potentially adverse coverage. Public relations practitioners should also help their clients understand that fair and accurate accounts of trials, legislative sessions, and government actions are insulated from defamation suits. Thus, unfavorable or even damaging statements, in certain contexts, are protected speech under current libel law.[2]

Because of that, and because all of society, and not only mass communications and its related industries, has a profound stake in freedom of expression, the subject of defamation is examined in some detail. The purpose of this chapter is not to provide a definitive treatment of this complex topic, which also includes product disparagement and trade libel, but rather to suggest some of the legal dilemmas that mass communicators might encounter while promoting goods and services. You will also see how the courts, when forced to make tough choices in this area—either to uphold freedom of expression or protect a private, corporate, or product reputation—have reacted.

TERMINOLOGY

Defamation is commonly defined as that which exposes a person to hatred or contempt, lowers that person in the esteem of friends and associates, or hurts his or her business. Printed defamation is referred to as *libel*, and spoken defamation is called *slander*.

Which of these describes broadcast defamation? If the offending statements came from a script, they likely would be regarded as libelous. If they were ad libs—spontaneous comments, broadcast live—they would probably be classified as slander. Courts tend to regard libel as more serious than slander.

Although there have been penal laws against defamation enacted by legislatures in every state, the overwhelming majority of libel and slander cases are handled as civil wrongs, or torts—matters to be settled between individuals (such as contract disputes, determinations of negligence in medical malpractice cases, and so on). Criminal libel, in which the prosecuting attorney and the police get involved, is exceedingly rare. Thus, one who loses a libel suit in court is not "found guilty" of libel, but is simply held liable for libel.

Nearly every press release, news article, or advertisement holds the potential for a libel suit. Although there have been a number of defamation actions arising out of major advertising campaigns or momentous news stories, most libel suits are prompted by small messages that seem minor and are, for that reason, carelessly handled.

Libel suits are expensive, time-consuming, and fatiguing for both sides. The person instigating the action, the plaintiff, seeks damages (i.e., a monetary award) to pay for restoring what he or she believes to be a sullied individual or business reputation. Judges and juries are hard pressed to place precise dollar values on an individual, organization, or product's reputation, much less on the depreciation of it caused by a defamatory remark. As a result, libel suits often end in frustration for everyone concerned. Many who bring suit for libel may be less interested in obtaining money than in moral vindication—in having some official organization, such as a court of law, put a stop to an unfair advertising campaign, or in proclaiming to one and all that a wrong has been committed.

Former Chief Justice Warren Burger and others have urged the government and the legal profession to develop mechanisms outside the judicial system for handling a share of civil disagreements. This search for what is called *alternative dispute resolution* has led to the creation of advertising review boards and other mediation services.[3] For now, however, and probably for the future as well, defamation questions are ultimately resolved in courts, and when plaintiffs win they are usually awarded a sum of money. This may seem a crude and inappropriate means to restore so intangible a thing as a reputation, but it appears to have worked over time. If nothing else, cash does translate the harm into a language everybody can understand. This chapter looks at injurious falsehood, which includes product disparagement and trade libel. It begins with an overview of the broader issue of defamation.

THE ELEMENTS OF LIBEL

Before a plaintiff can expect to win a libel suit, he or she must establish at the outset that (a) the offending statement has been published; (b) the plaintiff, or person bringing the action, has been identified in the statement; (c) the statement is defamatory; and (d) it appeared because the defendant—the one being sued (in this case, the publication, broadcaster, advertising, or public relations company)— was somehow at fault. Let us take a closer look at each of these points in turn.

Publication

The offending words must reach an audience, if only a small one. Technically, publication can occur the moment a third person has seen the communication. In *Dun & Bradstreet v. Greenmoss Builders, Inc.*, the Supreme Court affirmed a substantial judgment against a credit reporting company for publicizing false and defamatory information, although only five copies of the report had been sent to subscribers.[4] In 1982, the Alton, Illinois, *Telegraph* was hit with a $9.2 million libel judgment (enough to force the paper into bankruptcy, although the suit was eventually settled for $1.4 million) stemming from a note that never even got into the newspaper. It was an internal memorandum written by two of the paper's reporters who accused a local contractor of having ties with a savings and loan institution that seemed, to the reporters, at least, connected to organized crime. If a written communication circulates, publication has occurred.

Identification

If the audience, or even a tiny portion of it, believes that the defamatory statements refer to the plaintiff, then that person has been identified. Identification need not be by name; veiled references may be enough for readers to know, or think they know, whom the story concerned. Identification of group members, for libel purposes, is more difficult. A statement such as "students at Siwash State are deep into booze and drugs" may be hurtful to you if you are enrolled at Siwash State, but the courts would almost certainly decide that the student body is too large for any single member to suffer harm from it. However, those who do belong to small groups, about 25 members or fewer, may sue and collect, even if they are not personally identified in a defamatory communication. Two racy paragraphs from a 1952 book, *U.S.A. Confidential,* by Jack Lait and Lee Mortimer, illustrate this point. Breathlessly revealing "inside" information turned up in their travels, the two writers had this to say about employees in a chic specialty store in Dallas:

> He [Stanley Marcus, president of the Nieman-Marcus Company] may not know that some Nieman models are call girls—the top babes in town. The guy who escorts one feels in the same league with the playboys who took out Ziegfield's glorified. Price: a hundred bucks a night.
>
> The sales girls are good, too—pretty, and often much cheaper—twenty bucks on the average. They're more fun, too, not as snooty as the models. We got this confidential, from a Dallas wolf.[5]

In the inevitable lawsuits that followed, the court found that the models—there were only nine of them—indeed had been identified. But 30 sales girls, acting on behalf of the 382 then working at Nieman-Marcus, were not. The court held that this group was too large to permit individual identification.

Defamation

Here the plaintiff must show that the words did in fact hurt business or a reputation. Some words may be libelous per se (i.e., in and of themselves). *Swindler, cheat, blackmailer, prostitute, forger, criminal, murderer, crook*—these words and many others can cause a jury to believe that an individual who has been so characterized is diminished in the eyes of fellow citizens. Libel *per quod* means the words might not be libelous, but the way they are used makes them so. Suppose the following item appears in a company house organ for employees: "Mr. and Mrs. L. Q. C. Lamar III last week became the parents of twins." The item is incorrect; the company publication misidentified the new parents. Have the Lamars been defamed? Quite possibly, if some readers knew that the couple got married only a month ago. In this situation, the knowledge the readers brought into their reading of the story—extrinsic circumstances—made the item defamatory.

Defendant Fault

In addition to publication, identification, and defamation, the person bringing the libel suit must show that the person being sued was in some way remiss, or at fault, in permitting the offending material to be published or broadcast. The extent of the fault that must be shown depends on whether the person or corporation bringing the suit is, in the eyes of the court, a "private" or "public" figure. Current libel law is far more protective of private citizens. Public figures—persons who hold elective office, are celebrities, or attempt to influence public issues—according to the law have less protection in defamation actions. Public figures seek public attention, and according to the law are largely able to take care of themselves when they get it. Many business corporations, especially those with substantial advertising budgets and public relations departments, are likely to be classified as public figures.

Private persons often need only to show that the offending material is false and that it was published because the defendant was careless. Thus, an accidental mistake (e.g., sloppy editing) may constitute fault where a private person is concerned. There is no national standard for determining negligence in matters such as this; each state can establish its own level of proof that it will require. But the reputations of private individuals can be fragile indeed, and current libel law affords them protection by making it easier to win a defamation case when a private person is unjustly maligned.

In contrast, public persons face a much tougher task. They must establish that the offending words were published with actual malice—in other words, that the defendant published a deliberate lie or, alternatively, showed a reckless disregard for the truth in handling the communication. Where defamation is concerned, the term *malice* does not refer to hatred or spite in the usual way; malice is *shown* against individuals or corporations by deliberately or recklessly publishing untruths about them.

Actual malice is hard to prove; as a result, most public figures who bring libel suits ultimately lose. The defense lawyers need not show that the offending statements are true, only that their clients believed them to be true at the time they were published or broadcast. Efforts to determine what writers and editors believed before publishing a controversial article, advertisement, or press release have prompted libel lawyers to probe the writers' "state of mind," as reflected in private conversations, notebooks, internal memoranda, and other means. For the most part, such inquiries have not turned up widespread, pervasive evidence of a reckless disregard for the truth, much less a penchant for printing deliberate lies. Unless the communicators have been flagrantly unprofessional and reckless in handling a communication about a public figure, they will find sympathetic treatment from the courts (at the appeals level, at least) where defamation is concerned. Such has been the letter and spirit of defamation law since 1964, when the Supreme Court of the United States handed down its far-reaching decision in *New York Times v. Sullivan*.

NEW YORK TIMES V. SULLIVAN

This controversy arose out of a full-page advertisement that appeared in the *Times* on March 29, 1960, in an attempt to raise money to support civil rights crusades in the South. The ad called attention to the leadership of a dynamic young minister, Dr. Martin Luther King, Jr., who was resisting racial segregation policies in Montgomery, Alabama. Sixty-four celebrities, including Marlon Brando, Sidney Poitier, Sammy Davis, Jr., Nat King Cole, and Mrs. Eleanor Roosevelt, signed the advertisement and paid to have it published.

The ad copy contained harsh statements, many of which later proved untrue, about the treatment accorded African-American leaders and White sympathizers. For example:

In Montgomery, Alabama, after students sang "My Country, 'Tis of Thee," on the state capitol steps, their leaders were expelled from school, and truckloads of police armed with shotguns and tear gas ringed the Alabama State College campus. When the entire student body protested to state authorities by refusing to register, their dining hall was padlocked in an attempt to starve them into submission. . . .

Again and again Southern violators have answered Dr. King's peaceful protests with intimidation and violence. They have bombed his home, almost killing his wife and child. They have assaulted his person. They have arrested him seven times—for "speeding," "loitering," and similar "offenses." And now they have charged him with "perjury," a felony under which they could imprison him for ten years.[6]

These simply were not accurate accounts of events that had transpired in Montgomery. There had been no padlocks and no tear gas, and Dr. King had a far milder arrest record. Thus, when Montgomery city officials sued, the *Times*—which, to its embarrassment, was found not to have verified the assertions in the ad—could not plead as a defense that it was merely printing truth. The first of 11 lawsuits against the *Times* was filed by L. B. Sullivan, one of three elected city commissioners of Montgomery and the man responsible for operating the police department. The trial judge instructed the jury that the statements in the ad reflected adversely on the police department and were libelous per se. The jurors awarded Sullivan $500,000. After this judgment was upheld by the state supreme court, the *Times* carried its appeal to the Supreme Court of the United States.

On March 9, 1964, in a unanimous ruling, the Supreme Court of the United States reversed the judgment against the *Times*. In the process, the Court pronounced a new key for determining the extent and character of the libel of a public official. The newspaper had published the advertisement without malice, the Court held, and in effect was attempting to do a job the press is supposed to do: discuss the public actions of public officials. The majority opinion was written by Justice William J. Brennan: "Thus we consider this case against the background of a profound national commitment to the principle that debate on public issues should be uninhibited, robust, and wide open, and that it may well include sharp attacks on public officials.[7]

Acknowledging that there were errors in the ad copy, the Court rejected the argument that the newspapers had published the errors intentionally. The opinion quoted John Stuart Mill's treatise *On Liberty*: "Even a false statement may be deemed to make a valuable contribution to public debate, since it brings out 'the clearer perception and livelier impression of truth, produced by its collision with error.' "[8] The Court was emphatic in reasserting the right to criticize the government—all aspects of it, down to and including the conduct of the police department in Montgomery, Alabama—so long as the criticism is genuinely meant and not laced with intentional lies. To limit such criticism would diminish what the Court described as "the unfettered interchange of ideas for the bringing about of social changes desired by our people." It also noted that Sullivan, a public official, was not helpless; he had the means to dish out criticism as well as take it. Public officials seek attention by running for office, and heated attacks from the citizenry come with the territory. *Times v. Sullivan* was, in short, a significant victory for freedom of expression.

Later decisions made by the Supreme Court of the United States expanded the *Times v. Sullivan* doctrine to include public figures and public officials. In the eyes of the Court, a *public figure* is an individual well known to be an outspoken participant in civic matters. Political columnist William F. Buckley, Jr., has been held to be such a person, as has Johnny Carson, for his freewheeling comments on his "Tonight Show" television show monologues. Consumer advocate Ralph Nader could be a public figure, as well as "Crossfire" television debaters Michael Kinsley and Patrick Buchanan. Or an individual might become a public figure in certain limited areas of interest.[9] If a person voluntarily stepped into the spotlight in a public debate concerning the legalization of cocaine, or some comparable issue, and while doing so attempted to influence the outcome of it, he or she might be considered a limited public figure for purposes of any libel action arising out of that particular controversy.

THE ORGANIZATION AS PUBLIC FIGURE

As with individuals, corporations and other organizations are classified, for purposes of a libel suit, as public or private figures. In making this important determination, the courts take into account the following factors:

1. *The size of the organization.* Martin Marietta Corp., as an example, was held to be a public figure on the strength of its being the 20th largest defense contractor in the United States, and therefore in a position to influence the outcome of the issues in which it was involved.[10]

2. *The volume and character of the organization's advertising.* Not every organization that advertises is necessarily a public figure,[11] but organizations that attempt to influence events through advertising are likely to forego their private figure status. Organizations that advertise heavily demonstrate that they have ready access to the channels of communication, and that they can readily respond to negative statements about their activities.

3. *The history of the organization insofar as controversy is concerned.* If the organization has previously been involved in a public dispute, then such participation will likely contribute to a decision to classify the organization as a public figure.[12]

4. *Whether the organization is engaged in a heavily regulated industry* (e.g., insurance or broadcasting) *and whether the organization is publicly owned.*[13]

Financial institutions, such as savings and loan companies and banks, are usually classified separately, where injurious falsehoods are concerned, because of the hardships that could occur if public confidence in them is undermined. Corporate libel, in this case, could result in criminal prosecution. For example, the Iowa Code, Section 528.89, contains this language:

> Whoever maliciously or with intent to deceive makes, publishes, utters, repeats, or circulates any false report concerning any bank or trust company which imputes, or tends to impute, insolvency or unsound financial condition shall be

fined not more than $5,000 or imprisoned more than five years in the penitentiary or by punishment by both such fine and imprisonment.[14]

In each case, the court decides whether the person or organization bringing the action is a public or private figure. Much depends on this decision. One is far more likely to win a libel suit as a private figure than as a public figure because the fault requirement is easier to establish. Any journalist, public relations, or advertising professional can make a mistake and handle a communication negligently. But responsible communicators seldom publish or broadcast deliberate lies or, for that matter, act with extreme recklessness in presenting news and advertising messages.

COMMON LAW DEFENSES

Once a libel plaintiff has made a *prima facie* case (i.e., established publication, identification, defamation, and fault), the other side must put on a defense, or argument used in vindication. The traditional, or common law, defenses that have evolved over time include truth, conditional privilege, and fair comment.

Truth is now regarded as a complete defense, the rationale being that no individual or organization's reputation is greater than the truth that can be told about it. But truth is often hard to prove. In reality, it often boils down to one person's word against another's. Thus, one may know, deep down inside, that something is true, but face enormous difficulty proving it before a judge and jury. Information sources who speak fearlessly while a news story or press release is being developed have been known to lose their voices, or their memories, while under oath on the witness stand. Truth is considered a risky defense. But when truth can be proved, it will work.

Absolute privilege is the freedom to discuss certain aspects of the public's business with impunity. Absolute privilege is conferred on members of Congress during debates and hearings, for example. During these proceedings, the men and women who comprise the Congress are accountable to no court for any statement they may make while pursuing their official duties. Prosecuting attorneys, judges, mayors, city council and school board members, and zoning commissioners all must be free to comment fully and freely while performing official duties. If these individuals had to worry about full legal justification for everything they said, they would become too inhibited to get their work done.

Outside the official arena, however, privilege can disappear. During a court trial, a prosecutor might accuse a witness in a criminal case of being a "chronic liar," and nothing can be done about it. If the prosecutor makes the same accusation at a cocktail party, however, he or she has no special privilege and might be sued as an ordinary citizen.

A journalist enjoys a similar immunity, called *conditional* or *qualified privilege*, to report information stemming from someone who has absolute privilege. Suppose Senator McNoise, on the floor of the state legislature, delivers an angry speech, in which he refers to several prominent bankers by name and accuses them of being "loan sharks who gouge their customers with illegal interest rates."

So long as his comments are made as part of his official duties, Senator McNoise enjoys absolute privilege. The journalist covering the legislature for a newspaper or broadcast station can report what the senator said, provided the account is fair and accurate, because in this context the journalist enjoys conditional privilege. This is an important freedom: It lets reporters and editors tell society what public servants such as Senator McNoise are saying. The journalist is not personally agreeing or disagreeing with the assertion that the bankers are loan sharks; that is beside the point. The immediate concern is to keep voters informed about what goes on in government meetings.

Conditional, or qualified, privilege extends to many (but by no means all) public records as well. Journalists and other citizens can quote from privileged documents without fear of libel suits or criminal prosecutions—again, so long as the published or broadcast accounts remain essentially fair and accurate.

Other common law forms of privilege may apply, especially where commercial speech is concerned. First, a competitor is conditionally privileged to make boastful, embellished comparisons of its own products, property, or services offered with those of the competition—even if it does not personally believe its own things are superior to the competition—so long as the comparison does not contain false, specific factual assertions.[15] In short, *puffery,* defined here as exaggerated praise of one's own goods or services offered for sale, is not considered defamatory, even if it is sharply critical of the competition, so long as the boasting is couched in general, unspecific terms. A corporation can advertise that its product is far superior to that of a rival company. However, if the corporation claims its product is superior because the competitor builds with substandard material, the statement has become specific, capable of being proved or disproved, and would no longer be covered by this privilege.[16]

Second, a defendant has interest privilege. This may be used to allow a reply to communications to serve one's own interests—in other words, to defend against the defamation of another, even if the reply may be defamatory. However, this does not mean that the response can be a deliberate lie or reflect a reckless disregard for the truth.[17] These and other conditional privilege defenses manifest the general belief that limits on public discussion should be imposed as sparingly as possible. But deliberate, specific untruths constitute an abuse of privilege, and such statements are not protected.

Third, fair comment gives journalists and others the right to express opinions about anything that is offered to the public for acceptance or rejection. A politician's record, a concert pianist's keyboard technique, an actor's stage presence, an architect's creativity, and a restaurant's menu are all examples of acceptable targets for public discussion, although such adverse criticisms might hurt the "business" or the professional reputation of the individual or organization. The classic example is a review written in 1901 for a Des Moines newspaper about a vaudeville act, the Cherry Sisters:

> Effie is an old jade of 50 summers, Jessie a frisky filly of 40, and Addie, the flower of the family, a capering monstrosity of 35. Their long, skinny arms, equipped with talons at the extremities, swing mechanically, and anon waved frantically at the

suffering audience. The mouths of their rancid features opened like caverns, and sounds like the wailing of damned souls issued therefrom. They pranced around the stage with a motion that suggested a cross between the *danse du ventre* [belly dance] and the fox trot—strange creatures with painted faces and hideous mien. Effie is spavined, Addie is stringhalt, and Jessie, the only one who showed her stockings, has legs with calves as classic in their outlines as the curves on a broom handle.[18]

Such withering prose must have severely tested the outer limits of fair comment. But when the Cherry Sisters, understandably miffed at the review, brought a defamation suit, the judge held that the comments were not libelous. "Fitting strictures, sarcasm, or ridicule, even, may be used," he wrote, "if based on facts, without liability, in the absence of malice or wicked purpose."[19] Thus, so long as the writer confined the remarks to that portion of the Cherry Sisters that was offered to the public—the performance, not their private lives—the comments were defensible.

More recently, the courts have gone even further. In another famous libel case, *Gertz v. Welch*, the Supreme Court commented: "We begin with the common ground. Under the First Amendment there is no such thing as a false idea. However pernicious an opinion may seem, we depend for its correction not on the conscience of judges and juries, but on the competition of other ideas."[20] Opinions, then, are protected by law. In and of itself, an opinion cannot be verified. However, when opinions are bolstered by "facts," or dubious assertions presented as facts, problems can arise. A music critic might write that the conductor of the local philharmonic is a lousy musician, and that would be fair comment, protected opinion. But if the critic writes, "He is a lousy musician and none of his own orchestra members can stand him," the statement takes on a different character; it can be verified.[21] In general, the courts have given wide latitude in the area of fair comment. Mass communicators find it a valuable defense as they attempt to interpret ideas, products, and events for their audiences.

OTHER DEFENSES

In addition to truth, privilege, and fair comment, there are secondary defenses, often called *defenses in mitigation*, or *incomplete defenses*. One of these is retraction. A voluntary retraction can show good faith on the part of the communicator— an attempt to set the record straight and atone for a wrongful statement. For the court to find it persuasive, the retraction should be timely, prominent, and complete. (In an angry political ad, your client mistakenly accuses a prominent businessman of tax evasion. To be effective, your retraction should not say, "We are *sorry* that he is a tax dodger," but rather, "He is *not* guilty of tax evasion.") Another secondary defense is to offer the offended persons the right of reply (i.e., to provide space to let those who have been wronged, or think they have been, to tell their side of the story).

Neither a retraction nor a right of reply can be imposed. The courts recognize the rights of publishers to control the content of their publications.[22] Corrections, retractions, and rights of reply are all provided voluntarily, when they are provided at all. Even then, secondary defenses do not afford full protection. But they can lessen the blow of an adverse libel judgment by lowering the amount of money a court might award, chiefly by lessening the threat of punitive damages.

NEUTRAL REPORTAGE

A few jurisdictions have begun to recognize a highly controversial doctrine called *neutral reportage*, which means that certain newsworthy statements, although defamatory, have news value and the general public should know about them. An important case in this regard was *Edwards v. National Audubon Society, Inc.* The dispute arose from a *New York Times* article that quoted an Audubon publication, charging that some scientists were being paid to lie about the effects of the pesticide DDT on the bird population. The *Times* reporter asked for, got, and published the names of five scientists to whom the Audubon Society was referring. In the lawsuit that followed, the Sixth U.S. Circuit Court of Appeals held that an accurate report of this nature deserved constitutional protection:

> At stake in this case is a fundamental principle. Succinctly stated, when a responsible, prominent organization like the National Audubon Society makes serious charges against a public figure, the First Amendment protects the accurate and disinterested reporting of these changes, regardless of the reporter's private views regarding their validity. . . . What is newsworthy about such accusations is that they were made. We do not believe that the press may be required under the First Amendment to suppress newsworthy statements merely because it has serious doubts regarding their truth. . . .[23]

As defined by *Edwards* and a handful of other cases,[24] the defense of neutral reportage can only work when: (a) the defamed person is a public figure, (b) who is involved is in an existing public controversy, (c) the defamatory charges are made by a prominent person or organization, and (d) the charges are reported accurately and without comment. Even then, the doctrine of neutral reportage has not been widely accepted throughout the country, and a number of jurisdictions have specifically rejected it.

INJURIOUS FALSEHOOD:
PRODUCT DISPARAGEMENT

Much like defamation, the tort of product disparagement involves injurious falsehood—in this case, the publication of material that disparages property or the quality of a product or service without injuring the reputation of a company. The common law criteria for establishing product disparagement are: (a) The statement must be published, or be intended for publication; (b) the statement must be false; (c) the statement must result in financial damage, or be likely to do so, to the interests of another; and (d) the person making the offending statement must know that the statement is untrue or act with reckless disregard as to whether the statement is true or not.[25] Thus "actual malice," not mere negligence, must be shown in *all* product disparagement cases, not just those involving a "public figure," as in defamation. The burden of proof, of showing falsity, is on the person bringing the suit. (By the same token, if the defendant can demonstrate that the statement is true, the defendant will win.)

Representations as to value, quality, and the like are generally interpreted by the courts as being statements of opinion. Thus, broad, vague criticisms of a product, service, or piece of property may not, in and of themselves, constitute product disparagement. In deciding whether a statement is an opinion or a misrepresentation of facts, the courts may examine the background, expertise, and vested interests, if any, of the person making the offending statement and the person who is offended by it. One is usually more justified in relying on the statement of a neutral person, especially if that person is believed to have special expertise in the subject at hand. Product disparagement statements may be written or oral, or may even be implied from conduct and not expressed in words.[26]

Defamation and product disparagement represent concern over somewhat different interests, but at times they may overlap. For example, in *Steaks Unlimited, Inc., v. Deaner*, a false advertising charge was made by a local TV newscast concerning the value of meat sold by the plaintiff. The court found there was both product disparagement and corporate defamation. If the statement reflects merely on the quality of what the plaintiff is selling or solely on the character of the business, it is injurious falsehood alone. But if it is alleged that the plaintiff is not honest, lacks integrity, or is defrauding the public by selling something known to be defective, then personal defamation may also be found. Action may be brought in the same lawsuit to cover both torts, so long as the damages are not duplicated.[27] Another type of injurious falsehood, called *false light*, may also be found to be an invasion of privacy.

INJURIOUS FALSEHOOD: TRADE LIBEL

The term *trade libel*, an ancient one, was coined to describe written defamations of the quality of commercial goods and services. Casting aspersions on the quality of goods and services was likened to personal defamation. In recent years, the expansion of the concept of "injurious falsehood" has left trade libel a rather narrow affair. However, trade libel is different from defamation in several respects. In trade libel:

1. Special harm—actual damages, pecuniary losses resulting from the offending statements—must be proved.
2. Actual malice—publishing a lie or with reckless disregard for the truth— usually must be shown. In any event, proof of fault must be established, and the degree of fault required is greater than simple negligence.
3. Under certain conditions, it is possible to obtain an injunction to stop the trade libel (e.g., in a continuing advertising campaign), whereas in personal defamation such speech cannot be enjoined.[28]

In some states, trade libel laws are referred to as "slander of goods" or "slander of title." In injurious falsehood, the defenses, burden of proof, and functions of the court and jury are generally the same as they would be for defamation actions.

In recent years, many product disparagement claims, if they involve charges of false advertising, have been brought under the Lanham Act, which permits recovery for "any person who is or who believes he or she is likely to be damaged by a misrepresentation of the nature, characteristics, qualities, or geographic origin of his or her or another person's goods, services, or commercial activities." The provisions of the Lanham Act are discussed more fully elsewhere in this book.

WHO IS LIABLE?

In the eyes of the law, "tale bearers are as bad as tale tellers." Put another way, anyone who passes along a defamatory statement is as answerable to the court as the person who originated it. Suppose a press release, issued by a public relations agency, quotes a business executive as claiming that a competitor's construction standards are resulting in unsafe buildings. Attributing the statement to the business executive does not provide immunity for the public relations writer or the client, nor would such qualifying terms as the *alleged* inside trader or the *reported* corporate embezzler. These republish a libel.

Where defamation, product disparagement, and trade libel are concerned, each repetition of the offending statement may be regarded as a separate publication for which damages may be recovered. Every person who had a hand in the publication could, in theory at least, be sued. Specifically, defamation defendants can be categorized as:

1. *Primary publisher.* The owner of a newspaper or television station carrying a defamatory statement is considered a primary publisher, and thus is held accountable for that message to the same extent as the author or speaker might be. Everything that appears in print or on the air—including letters to the editor, advertising messages, and other communications that originate from the outside—becomes the responsibility of the publisher. Reporters, editors, and advertising and public relations copywriters who actually prepared the defamatory messages may well be named as co-defendants, although in actual practice the publisher or station manager will usually finance the defense for the employees/subcontractors involved.

2. *Republisher.* Anyone who repeats or passes along a defamatory statement would be held accountable on the same basis as the primary publisher, even if the person repeating the libel makes it clear that he or she does not believe it.

3. *Secondary publisher.* One who helps circulate the materials that might be defamatory (such as the person who sells or delivers the newspaper, or who plays a defamatory videotape). These individuals, however, are accountable only if they knew, or should have known, of the defamatory content.[29]

IV

COMMERCIAL SPEECH TORTS

10

Appropriation and the Right of Publicity

In the final years of the 20th century, individuals find it difficult to live out their lives in isolation. Our culture bristles with computers, databanks, electronic eavesdropping devices, powerful telephoto lenses, and a whole arsenal of high-tech equipment for gathering, storing, and retrieving personal and professional information about us. If all the federal government's databanks were linked up to pool income tax return information with census, Social Security, and other information in the files, it would be quick and easy to compile a dossier of an estimated 20 pages or more on every man, woman, and child in America, and no record would take more than a few seconds to locate. Commercial databanks possess salary, employment, credit, home mortgage, medical insurance, and other personal information that may be even more sensitive. The ever-present mass media are capable of disseminating a great deal of information about us, including our physical likenesses, although we may urgently wish them not to do so.

Although only a fraction of today's invasions of privacy concern advertising and the mass media, it was the unrestrained, sensational press coverage of a century ago that prompted legal scholars to advocate our first privacy laws. The lurid era of yellow journalism found reporters prying feverishly into the personal affairs of the rich and famous. An aristocratic Boston lawyer and businessman, Samuel Warren, was particularly offended by what he regarded as steamy, voracious press attention paid to the forthcoming wedding of his daughter.[1] Because no remedies were available under existing law to deal with such journalistic excesses, Warren declared that a different approach was needed. In collaboration with his former law partner, Louis Brandeis, Warren pounded out an angry, sweeping article for the *Harvard Law Review*. They proposed that the legal system recognize a new principle, which they described as an individual's right to privacy:

The press is overstepping in every direction the obvious bounds of propriety and decency. Gossip is no longer the resource of the idle and of the vicious, but has become a trade, which is pursued with industry as well as effrontery. . . . To occupy the indolent, column upon column is filled with idle gossip, which can only be procured by intrusion upon the domestic circle. The intensity and complexity of life, attending upon advancing civilization, have rendered necessary some retreat from the world, and man, under the refining influence of culture, has become more sensitive to the individual; but modern enterprise and invention have, through invasions upon his privacy, subjected him to mental pain and distress, far greater than could be inflicted by mere bodily injury.[2]

The courts and legislatures did not react immediately to provide citizens, in the Warren and Brandeis phrase, "some retreat from the world," but clearly the privacy thesis struck a responsive chord within the legal profession. Several privacy invasions were alleged in lawsuits, although the first recovery for damages would not be allowed by a court for 15 years. Privacy law has been evolving, in fits and starts, ever since, responding—sometimes slowly, often inconsistently—to technological and social change.

Currently, the law recognizes that an individual's privacy may be invaded in any of four major ways: (a) unreasonable intrusion on one's physical solitude, (b) unreasonably placing an individual in a false light before the public, (c) unjustified publication of embarrassing facts, and (d) commercial appropriation of one's name, identity, or likeness. The fourth tort, appropriation, is the focus of this chapter. It also covers a newer, but closely related, area—the right of publicity.

APPROPRIATION

When Warren and Brandeis were advancing their radical ideas for the *Harvard Law Review*, they probably were not thinking in terms of commercial appropriation as a factor in their proposed right of privacy. Yet appropriation cases were among the first to be presented as invasions of privacy. Over the years, such commercial exploitation has become a major aspect of the ever-evolving laws of privacy and publicity.

Although the specifics of it are defined somewhat differently from state to state, generally commercial appropriation is the unauthorized use of a person's name, likeness, or voice for purposes of trade or advertising. Commercial appropriation can come in two forms. First, the traditional right of privacy—to be left alone—refers to the damage to a private person's feelings at being commercially exploited for the profit of another. Second, the newer claim made by celebrities—persons who otherwise *seek* public attention—for a violation of what they believe to be their hard-won right of publicity. This latter concept— that of publicity as a property right as it began to evolve some 50 years afterward—is discussed later in this chapter.

The first attempts to recover monetary damages in appropriation cases were not successful, although one plaintiff, an actress, was able to stop publication of a picture of her in a costume she thought to be scandalous.[3] Among the most famous of the early appropriation cases was that of Abigail Roberson of Albany, New York, whose picture, published without her consent, appeared in 1902 on thousands of posters advertising Franklin Mills Flour. The attractive young woman, mortified at seeing pictures of herself splashed across the city, and with the accompanying copy describing her as "the flour of the family," brought suit for what she regarded as an invasion of her privacy. But the New York Appeals Court, in a 4–3 decision, rejected the arguments that had been advanced by Warren and Brandeis, and issued a majority opinion insisting that the right of privacy did not exist. Recognizing such a right, the justices held, would create an entirely new set of legal issues, bring on a barrage of similar lawsuits, and impinge on freedom of the press:

> . . . an examination of the authorities leads us to the conclusion that the so-called "right of privacy" has not yet found an abiding place in our jurisprudence, and, as we view it, the doctrine cannot now be incorporated without doing violence to settled principles of law by which the profession and the public have long been guided.[4]

This ruling, allowing Miss Roberson no relief for what had clearly been commercial exploitation of her, touched off a firestorm in the next session of the New York Legislature, and in 1903 led to the passage of a statute making it both a criminal offense (a misdemeanor) and a civil wrong to make use of the name or likeness of an individual for "advertising purposes or for the purposes of trade" without first obtaining written consent. The new law permitted the person whose privacy had been invaded to seek monetary damages as well as an injunction to halt further publication of the offensive material. This statute, which later became part of the New York Civil Rights Law, was the first ever to deal with the right of privacy, and it remains on the books today.

The first common law acceptance of the right of privacy came 2 years after *Roberson* by the Georgia Supreme Court in 1904. An insurance company's advertising featured the name and picture of an Atlanta artist, Paolo Pavesich. The ad copy also presented a spurious testimonial from him as to the value of having a sound insurance portfolio. He sued for $25,000 and won. The Georgia Supreme Court expressly rejected the New York decision regarding Abigail Roberson, and endorsed the earlier views of Warren and Brandeis:

> The form and features of the plaintiff [Pavesich] are his own. The defendant insurance company and its agents had no more authority to display them in public for purposes of advertising . . . than they would have had to compel the plaintiff to place himself upon exhibition for this purpose.[5]

Once the right of privacy was accepted in *Pavesich*, most other jurisdictions—but by no means all—began to follow suit. For example, a Pennsylvania court came down hard on an advertiser who used a customer's name as an endorsement without permission: "Nothing so exclusively belongs to a man or is so personal and valuable to him as his name. . . . Others have no right to use it without his express consent, and he has the right to go into any court at any time to enjoin or prohibit any unauthorized use of it."[6] The key here is commercial use—exploitation by another for purposes of trade or other financial benefit. The injury is personal. Defamation damages reputation and one's standing in business or in the community, whereas privacy damages feelings. Invasions of privacy cause humiliation, embarrassment, and emotional distress.

Beyond that, in appropriation cases, the right of privacy also recognizes that one's name and likeness have value, in the nature of property rights, and can be protected from unauthorized exploitation (e.g., unauthorized endorsements of products or services, or unauthorized use of one's name or likeness in promotional materials, product manuals, recruiting films, advertising messages, or even shop windows). Truth is not a defense in appropriation cases. Consider two examples. First, Joe Piscoonyak is indeed a substantial consumer of Old Sandlapper beer. Without his knowledge, you take a photograph of him headed for the checkout stand in a local supermarket, his shopping cart filled with cartons of Old Sandlapper, and publish the photo in an advertisement. Although the photograph truthfully depicts his enthusiastic choice of brews, you have nevertheless invaded his privacy. Second, Sally Sunshine's engagement picture, a splendid photographic portrait, is displayed, without her knowledge and consent, in the window of the photographer as an example of the superior quality of work done by that studio. The work is indeed of admirable quality, yet Miss Sunshine's privacy has been invaded.

At issue in appropriation cases is an identity, not merely a name. There are many persons who look alike (as the Elvis Presley impersonators can attest), and a great many individuals are named Joe Jones. But it is when someone makes use of another's name or likeness to pirate that person's identity for some monetary advantage that appropriation occurs.

NEWSWORTHINESS
AS A DEFENSE

Persons cannot prevent publication of their names when they take part in or become involved in the news or a public event. In matters "concerning newsworthy events or matters of public interest,"[7] the news media's right to inform the public will take precedence over an individual's right to privacy. A Kentucky resident, an innocent bystander at the scene of a brutal knife assault, sued when a local newspaper published a photograph of the incident. The Kentucky Supreme Court held that the man's privacy had not been unjustly violated:

The right of privacy is the right to live one's life in seclusion, without being subjected to unwarranted and undesired publicity. In short, it is the right to be left alone. . . . There are times, however, when one, whether willing or not, becomes an actor in an occurrence of public or general interest. When this takes place, he emerges from his seclusion, and it is not an invasion of his right or privacy to publish his photograph with an account of such occurrence.[8]

Thus, a name or photo of a person involved in a newsworthy situation may be used without that person's permission. This holds true despite that most newspapers, magazines, and broadcast stations are, in fact, commercial enterprises attempting to make a profit. The primary consideration in newsworthiness is the attempt to inform the public about matters of general interest. The profit motive—that of selling newspapers or increasing market share for advertising purposes—is regarded as secondary. The *Restatement of Torts* put it this way:

> The value of the plaintiff's name is not appropriated by mere mention of it, or by reference to it in connection with legitimate mention of his public activities. . . . The fact that the defendant is engaged in the business of publication, for example of a newspaper, out of which he makes a profit, is not enough to make the incidental publication a commercial use of the name or likeness.[9]

Much depends on how the material is used. A photograph might be newsworthy in one context, but appropriation in another. For example, a Page 1 photograph of a victim of a hit-and-run driver would obviously be considered newsworthy. However, that same photo used in an advertisement to promote the newspaper's photographic talent, as a reason to subscribe to the paper, might well invade the victim's privacy. Consider two other examples. First, a Sunday supplement news feature on spring styles, accompanied by photos of fashion models, would likely be newsworthy. The same photos in trade advertisements would not be protected. Second, a spectacular photograph taken in Times Square of a sailor kissing a nurse on V-J Day could safely appear in *Life* magazine as being newsworthy. The same photo, reproduced and sold as a poster, would not.[10]

From the beginning of privacy law, courts have recognized the conflict between an individual's desire for privacy and the public's concern about being informed. In the landmark *Pavesich* case, the Georgia Supreme Court held that it believed the right of privacy to be a natural right, recognized by "the law of nature." But it also warned that enforcing an individual's right of privacy could "inevitably tend to curtail the liberty of speech and of the press," which, the court said, is also a natural right. "It will therefore be seen," the court predicted, "that the right of privacy must in some particulars yield to the right of speech and of the press." This has proved to be the case.[11]

Traditionally, the news media's most useful defense against an invasion of privacy lawsuit has been the concept of "newsworthiness." But news reports and advertising and public relations messages may be very different, insofar as privacy laws are concerned, and newsworthiness as a defense may well prove of no benefit whatever to an advertiser threatened with an invasion of privacy lawsuit.

INCIDENTAL USE

As a general rule, use of names and likenesses in news contexts are protected, whereas use of names and likenesses in press releases, promotional materials, and advertising messages may not be. Sometimes the distinctions are blurred. Professional football legend Joe Namath brought suit in 1976 against *Sports Illustrated* for using his photograph, which had been on the magazine's cover, in advertising and promotional materials to attract new subscribers. But the New York Jets quarterback's claim was rejected when the court held that this was "incidental use" of his photograph to illustrate the "quality and content" of the publication, and that this was a "necessary and logical extension" of the otherwise newsworthy photograph.[12] However, if the photograph had been used in a manner to suggest that Namath was personally endorsing the magazine, the photograph would likely have been found to be appropriation—an invasion of his privacy. The same reasoning applies to public relations messages, particularly in the preparation of employee publications.

Another factor to be considered in determining incidental use is whether the use of an individual's photo is sufficiently germane to the advertisement as to constitute appropriation. For example, a crowd shot to illustrate an advertisement may indeed have identifiable faces in it. But if these faces are merely that—faces, and otherwise immaterial to the selling message—then it is not likely that an appropriation action could be won by any of the individuals depicted in the photo. Again, it is the identity of the individual, not merely the incidental use of it, that must be appropriated. So long as these persons are not shown as specifically endorsing the product in the ad, and so long as their presence is incidental to, not directly supportive of, the selling message, an action for invasion of privacy would likely not succeed.

De minimis (or trivial) uses of names or likenesses do not normally constitute invasions of privacy. Still, if there is any doubt about using an advertising photograph showing a number of identifiable likenesses, it may be a good idea to find another way to illustrate the ad. Either that or obtain consent to use the names and/or likenesses in this commercial context. Consent provides protection, but only if the consent is properly obtained and utilized.

CONSENT AS A DEFENSE

New York's pathbreaking Right of Privacy law says, in part:

> Any person whose name, portrait or picture is used within this state for advertising purposes or for the purposes of trade without . . . written consent . . . may

maintain an equitable action in the supreme court of this state against the person, firm or corporation so using his name, portrait or picture, to prevent and restrain the use thereof, and may also sue and recover damages for an injuries by reason of such use. . . .[13]

Experienced photographers, public relations practitioners, and advertisers know the value of obtaining signed consent (release) forms from their subjects. Photographs used purely for news reporting purposes, as was noted, do not require consent. However, if the photo could be reprinted later for use in advertising or promotional materials, the newsworthiness defense may not apply, and some additional protection—in the form of a signed consent—may be necessary. In any case, a photographer attempting to freelance a picture will find that a signed release to accompany the photo will make the photograph more marketable.

An example of a tightly drawn sample model release is shown in Appendix C. Most professional photographers routinely carry around pads of such blank release or consent forms to use as needed. Other, simpler versions of a release form may also be used; there is no single, uniform model release.

The consent form allows the person who is being used for advertising purposes to decide how much right of privacy to give up and on what terms. Even so, problems with consent can arise. The following are ways to avert some of them. The consent should be written. A number of states do not recognize verbal agreements or handshakes where appropriation lawsuits are concerned. The person giving the consent must be a competent adult. Minors—persons under 18 years of age—cannot sign consent forms that are legally binding; a parent or guardian must sign the consent form on their behalf. This point was sorely tested in prolonged litigation in New York by the actress, Brooke Shields, and her mother during the 1980s. At the age of 10, Miss Shields posed nude for a picture story that appeared in a Playboy Press book, *Sugar and Spice.* Her mother had signed the appropriate consent forms. Five years later, however, Miss Shields, by then a promising young actress, had attained a measure of notoriety, and the owner of the consent forms marketed the photos to other magazines, at least one of which published them with the caption, "Brooke Shields Naked." Mrs. Shields sued and, in a complex series of trials, ultimately lost: The consent forms she had signed took away her rights to recovery.[14]

In some cases, the consent may become invalid. In a 1961 Louisiana case, a health spa owner had obtained written consent to use photographs of a customer, Cole McAndrews, to illustrate the before-and-after effects of a rigorous exercise program. However, the health spa owner waited for 10 years before deciding to use the photos. During that time, the physical condition of the model, McAndrews, had deteriorated more than somewhat. He presumably resembled the "before" rather than the "after" photos. Thus, the health spa ads featuring his photos subjected him to a certain amount of embarrassment and he sued. The trial judge was sympathetic, noting that, under the circumstances, the permission forms McAndrews had signed should have been renewed.[15]

If there is no consideration—something of value given in return for the consent—the consent can be withdrawn before the photographs are published. The consideration may be payment of as little as $1, or it may be something else of value. Without "valuable consideration," a consent form, as with other types of contracts, can be difficult to enforce.

Finally, if the photos are altered, or the context in which they are used is materially changed from what the model thought it would be, the consent may not be binding. Retouching the photo, changing the background scene, and using the photo to advertise one product when the model believed it to be another can effectively undermine a consent agreement. In an era when digital imaging makes it possible to alter photographs easily, this point becomes especially pertinent.

The American Magazine Photographers Association offers its members this useful nuts-and-bolts advice:

1. Get a release whenever possible.
2. If you do not have a release, and if a person could be recognized by anyone, retouch the face and/or figure to eliminate all possibility of recognition when people might appear in: (a) paid ads, (b) promotional matter, or (c) any published use that could be deemed embarrassing or in incorrect context (no matter how remote).[16]

PROPERTY RELEASES

It is also a good idea to obtain a release from the owners of buildings and other real estate that might be used in photographs for advertising or other trade purposes. These owners do not have a "right of privacy," as such, to be invaded by such photos, but courts have determined that there are property rights that cannot be unjustly exploited for commercial purposes. Property releases, signed by the owners or agents for the owners, may be needed for photographs of such places.

If the building is merely incidental or part of the background (a photograph of a street scene or other public gathering place), a property release probably is not necessary. Although most buildings in public places can be safely photographed and used in advertisements, there have been instances where claims have been successful that the photographs of an identifiable building in a public location in an advertisement constituted a legal infringement of the owner's property rights. Property rights can be, and have been, extended to owners of animals when the animals have been photographed for purposes of trade without the owner's consent. Again, specific consent forms signed by the owners should be obtained.[17]

THE RIGHT OF PUBLICITY

Although the right of privacy is designed to protect everyone, the right of publicity has evolved to protect celebrities' hard-won fame—as reflected in their names, likenesses, and voices—from unauthorized exploitation.

The right of publicity is much younger than the right of privacy. Publicity as a property right was first recognized in 1953, when a court used the term to describe the rights of professional athletes to protect their likenesses from unauthorized use on chewing gum cards.[18] Since that time, the mass media and society have conferred celebrity status on vast numbers of persons: film and TV stars, rock singers, ballplayers, authors, fashion designers, and a great many others. To these individuals, celebrity status has profound economic implications; unfair use of one's celebrity status is, in effect, a form of thievery. Although the police and prosecutors are unlikely to get involved in such cases, private attorneys can and do file lawsuits to protect their celebrity clients' interests. This fast-moving area of the law, pursued with vigor by celebrities (and their agents), has important consequences for advertisers, public relations specialists, and promoters. Increasingly, courts are willing to entertain claims based on the unauthorized use of a celebrity's likeness, even where the person's photograph has not been used or might previously have been thought to be unrecognizable—in other words, a perception that the likeness is that of a Michael Jackson, a Muhammad Ali, or a Madonna.

Beyond an infringement of the right of publicity, or an invasion of privacy (appropriation), such unauthorized use may be regarded as *deception*—a violation of the Lanham Act, which prohibits unfair competition. In one such case, a court found that the likeness of a model used in promoting a video rental store looked enough like Woody Allen to cause confusion in the minds of customers, implying that Woody Allen was in some fashion involved with the video rental operation or endorsing it. Indeed, as New York's Chief Justice Motley wrote, the imitation in the advertising photograph was highly specific, portraying

> a customer in a National Video Store, an individual in his forties, with a high forehead, tousled hair, and heavy black glasses . . . his face, bearing an expression at once quizzical and somewhat smug, is learning on his hand. . . . The features and pose are characteristic of the plaintiff. The staging of the photograph also evokes associations with plaintiff. Sitting on the counter are videotape cassettes of *Annie Hall* and *Bananas*, two of plaintiff's best-known films, as well as *Casablanca* and *The Maltese Falcon*. The latter two are Humphrey Bogart films of the 1940's associated with plaintiff primarily because of his play and film, "Play It Again, Sam," in which the spirit of Bogart appears to the character played by Allen and offers him romantic advice. In addition, the title "Play It Again, Sam" is a famous, although inaccurate, quotation from *Casablanca*.
>
> The individual in the advertisement is holding up a National Video V. I. P.

Card, which apparently entitles the bearer to favorable terms on movie rentals. The woman behind the counter is smiling at the customer and appears to be gasping in exaggerated excitement at the presence of a celebrity.

Allen's objections, the judge decided, were well founded. The comedian/film star/writer/director seemed to be personally offended. In Judge Motley's words, Allen, "to paraphrase Groucho Marx, wouldn't belong to any video club that would have him as a member."[19] More to the point for our purposes, Allen's right of publicity had been well and truly violated.

ORIGINS AND SCOPE
OF PUBLICITY RIGHTS

The right of publicity has developed as an offshoot of the law of privacy (appropriation), the law of unfair competition, and property rights. About half of the states expressly recognize the right of publicity while at least 14 others have accepted it as a part of the common law. In some states, the rights of privacy and publicity are merged, to protect private citizens and celebrities alike, under one common law tort of "appropriation of name or likeness."[20] (Violations of publicity rights can also constitute deception, as detailed in the Lanham Act, as well as infringe on copyrighted material. These possibilities are discussed at length elsewhere in this book.)

The landmark ruling in publicity law was *Haelan Laboratories v. Topps Chewing Gum*. This 1953 case involved some major league baseball players who had consented to "an exclusive license" to a bubble gum company to publish their photographs on baseball cards. When a second company wanted to use some of the same players' photos, a lawsuit ensued. At issue was whether the players' rights to privacy could be assigned to a third party. The court of appeals held that the rights, under these circumstances, had economic value and could be protected as such. Judge Jerome Frank, in writing the opinion, described this unique characteristic as "the right of publicity."[21]

In numerous cases since that time, the right of publicity has become more clearly defined. Although much like privacy, it is different in a number of respects:

1. *The nature of the damages*. In privacy, the damage is personal; it results in humiliation, embarrassment, indignity, or emotional distress. Celebrities have feelings too, of course, but in rights of publicity cases, the damage is largely economic. Not unlike copyright or patent law, the right of publicity allows these individuals to reap the rewards of their endeavors. The right of publicity has little to do with embarrassment, but a great deal to do with protecting one's commercial interests as a celebrity.

2. *Descendability*. The right of privacy is essentially an individual matter, whereas the right of publicity is recognized in some jurisdictions as having a

commercial life even after the death of the celebrity. In other words, the estate/heirs can recover for unauthorized use of a celebrity's name or likeness, whereas right to privacy is limited to living persons.[22]

NAMES, LIKENESSES, AND LOOK-ALIKES

To win a right of publicity case, a celebrity must convince a court that the defendant has benefited financially from the association with the celebrity. The association need not always be explicit, but perhaps only implied. In *Cher v. Forum International, Ltd.*,[23] the singer won a substantial judgment on the basis of an interview article that was promoted as her personal endorsement of the magazine.

The article, developed by a freelancer, was originally planned for *Us* magazine. But Cher, who had stipulated before granting the interview that she wanted to approve any additional uses of the material, was unhappy with the way the interview had gone, and requested the editors of *Us* not to use it. When the editors agreed, the freelancer then sold copies of the tape-recorded interview to *Forum* and to a supermarket tabloid, *The Star. Forum* quickly used the tape to prepare a cover story about Cher, and promoted the article with advertising that said, "There are certain things that Cher won't tell *People* and would never tell *Us*." The copy also urged audiences to "join Cher and *Forum's* hundreds of thousands of other adventurous readers today." When Cher sued, the court agreed with her that the advertising copy could reasonably be interpreted as being Cher's personal endorsement of the magazine, and thus a violation of her right of publicity.

Even a nickname can be protected if the person associated with it can prove that someone else was using it for commercial gain, as the former Wisconsin and professional football star, "Crazy Legs" Hirsch, proved in a lawsuit against the maker of "Crazy Legs" pantyhose.[24] Muhammad Ali, the former heavyweight boxing champion, won an injunction to halt further publication in *Playgirl* magazine of a frontally nude black male sitting in a corner of a boxing ring. This was a drawing, not a photograph, but the face resembled that of Ali and the accompanying text referred to the figure as *The Greatest*—a term Ali had often used to describe himself in promoting boxing matches. In this context, the court held, the nickname and likeness were indeed identified with Ali in the public mind, and thus could be protected from unauthorized use.[25]

In *Onassis v. Christian Dior-New York, Inc.*, a court found that an advertising photograph of a fictional wedding scene, where some of the guests were real celebrities, featured a model who too-closely resembled Jacqueline Kennedy Onassis. She was able to get the advertisement stopped. Particularly hurtful to the defendant's case was the fact that the fashion photographer had specifically asked the modeling agency for a Jackie Kennedy look-alike. When photographed with the real-life celebrities, the model created for the advertisement a persuasive illusion of authenticity. The court was not impressed. Justice Edward J. Greenfield wrote:

> Defendants knew there was little or no likelihood that Mrs. Onassis would ever consent to be depicted in this kind of advertising campaign for Dior. She has asserted in her affidavit, and it is well known, that she has never permitted her name or picture to be used in connection with the promotion of commercial products. . . .

The woman who had posed for the picture, a secretary named Barbara Reynolds, argued that she could not be prevented from using her own face. But the court held otherwise: "Where, however, that use (of one's own face) is done in such a way as to be deceptive or promote confusion, that use can be enjoined."[26]

FURTHER POSSIBILITIES

Advertisers may also violate a celebrity's right of publicity in ways other than unauthorized use of a name or likeness. Recent court decisions have found advertisers liable for damages in connection with the unauthorized use of a particular expression associated with the celebrity, or a voice, a character created by the celebrity, or even, in *Motschenbacher v. R. J. Reynolds Tobacco Co.*, for authorized altering of the unusual decorations used by the owner of a racing car. The opinion noted:

> . . . plaintiff [Lothar Motschenbacher] has consistently "individualized" his [racing] cars to set them apart from those of other drivers and to make them more readily identifiable as his own. Since 1966, each of his cars his displayed a distinctive narrow white pinstripe appearing on no other car. This decoration has adorned the leading edges of the cars' bodies, which have uniformly been solid red. In addition, the white background for his racing number "11" has always been oval, in contrast to the circular background of all other cars.[27]

When these were altered slightly, and the cigarette brand name "Winston" was added to the markings of the car, the court found the driver's right of publicity had been violated.

In *Carson v. Here's Johnny Portable Toilets*,[28] the talk show host and comedian Johnny Carson objected to the phrase, "Here's Johnny!" as the name for a line of portable toilets. Carson, who was not asking for monetary damages, but instead to have the company adopt another name for its product, argued that he had been introduced for many years to the national television audience of the NBC "Tonight Show" with that phrase, and that the public associated it with him. Additionally, Carson owned stock in a line of clothing that used "Here's Johnny!" in its advertising. The manufacturer of the "Here's Johnny!" portable toilets countered with the argument that "john" and "johnny" had been used by the public for years to describe restroom facilities, but admitted that he did indeed have Carson in mind when he named his portable toilet. In advertising the product, he referred to his company as "The World's Foremost Commodian." But the majority of a divided court sided with Carson, holding that he had been unfairly capitalized upon, that the phrase had indeed become a part of his identity, and thus he should be permitted to control its use.

Another court determined that unique characters developed by actors can be protected—in this case, the characters of Groucho, Chico, and Harpo, creations of the Marx Brothers. But the mere portrayal of a role does not give the actor publicity rights to it, as the heirs of Bela Lugosi learned when they attempted to control the character of Count Dracula. Tartly, the court noted that Lugosi did not have exclusive rights to Dracula any more than Charlton Heston might have to Moses.[29]

Bert Lahr, the comedian and film actor, and Bette Midler, the singer, among others, have been able to recover damages (in Miss Midler's case, $400,000) for unauthorized imitations of their voices. Lahr, who had been the voice of the Cowardly Lion in *The Wizard of Oz*, sued over an imitation of his voice in an advertisement; the court agreed with Lahr, noting that the advertisement "had greater value because its audience believed it was listening to him."[30]

In Miss Midler's case, the advertising agency of Young & Rubicam had invited her to sing one of her hit recordings, "Do You Want to Dance?", in commercials for the Ford Motor Company. When she declined, the agency hired one of her former backup singers to imitate her voice, which she did, highly successfully. Miss Midler sued, and the federal court found in her favor, commenting that "the human voice is one of the most palpable ways identity is manifested," and the unauthorized imitation was a violation of her right of publicity.[31] In 1990, a federal jury in Los Angeles found that a sound-alike commercial violated the publicity rights of Tom Waits and awarded the singer nearly $2.5 million in damages.[32]

In these and other decisions, the right of publicity, still in its relative infancy, has already been stretched to the point that it could muzzle certain aspects of freedom of expression where advertising and promotion are concerned. In the wake of the Bette Midler ruling, an advertising executive was quoted in the *New York Times*: "If you're forced to go to extremes to avoid infringing on a singer's rights, that affects creativity."[33] Legal scholar Christopher Pesce warned, "Allowing celebrities to recover in cases where advertisers loosely imitate limited aspects of their 'personae' protects interests unworthy of the status of property, chills creative endeavor, and creates an unpredictable standard of recovery."[34] Richard Kurnit, whose Manhattan law firm represents a number of publishers and advertising agencies, put it this way: "The idea that entertainment properties are akin to explosives—if you hit someone you are strictly liable—is particularly frightening when you consider that publicity claims result in uncontrollable damage awards for emotional distress and punitive damages at the whim of a jury."[35]

A FIRST AMENDMENT THREAT?

Beyond the hazards, real or imagined, posed by the right of publicity to creative people in the advertising and public relations field, there has emerged some First Amendment concern as well. A traditional defense in privacy cases—and, by extension, cases involving the right of publicity—has been newsworthiness. Courts have allowed the use of a person's identity in news and feature reports (and even, as in *Namath*, some incidental use in advertising and promotional material for the news media). But a bizarre case, *Zacchini v. Scripps-Howard Broadcasting*,[36] blurred the distinction between commercial and noncommercial use and, in effect, changed the nature of appropriation law.

Hugo Zacchini, billed as "the human cannonball," earned his living at carnivals and county fairs by allowing himself to be blasted from a huge cannon into a safety net some 200 feet away. His act, in its entirety, took only a few seconds. One evening, as Zacchini was about to perform in the Cleveland area, a TV news crew showed up and, over his protests, filmed the act, all 15 seconds of it, and showed the segment on the late evening news. Zacchini sued, claiming this showing violated his right of publicity and cost him thousands in lost revenue. Once his entire act had been shown on television, he argued, few persons would be willing to pay money to watch him perform in person.

The TV station, for its part, argued that Zacchini's act had legitimate news value, and that newscasts were securely protected by the First Amendment. Also, the station contended, the Zacchini segment represented only a tiny fraction of the newscast, and that the station did not realize any revenue, directly or indirectly, from reporting this particular news story. The Supreme Court of the United States ultimately agreed, but in a tortured, 5–4 decision, sided with Zacchini anyway. In Justice White's opinion,

> The broadcast of petitioner's [Zacchini's] entire performance, unlike the unauthorized use of another's name for purposes of trade or the incidental use of a name or picture by the press, goes to the heart of petitioner's ability to earn a living as an entertainer. Thus in this case, Ohio has recognized what may be the strongest case for a "right of publicity"—involving not the appropriation of an entertainer's reputation to enhance the attractiveness of a commercial product, but the appropriation of the very activity by which the entertainer acquired the reputation in the first place.[37]

The *Zacchini* decision, the first ruling ever by the Supreme Court of the United States in this sector of the law, could lead to further confusion in determining what is commercial exploitation and what is simply news. Some months after *Zacchini*, the ABC television network began to prepare a docudrama on the life of the celebrated actress, Elizabeth Taylor. Miss Taylor objected on the grounds that her life story was her own, and that she might one day write her autobiography. A movie about her life now, she contended, might take away income that should be hers. Rather than risk a court suit, ABC decided to shelve the project.[38]

Because of the zany facts of the *Zacchini* case—few celebrities will find their total act being filmed for a newscast—it is unlikely that the case will have much in the way of direct influence on the rapidly emerging law of publicity. To the extent that it represents a judicial propensity to protect celebrity right of publicity, however, *Zacchini* might well be regarded as an important case indeed. The dynamic growth of advertising and the mass media industry in recent years has given publicity new status with society and in the law. Mass media coverage and advertising and public relations messages have helped create thousands of celebrities, although many of them, obviously, may enjoy only a few fleeting moments of fame. But during that time in the spotlight, they understandably wish for some authority to protect their professional personalities from unauthorized exploitation. To an ever-increasing degree, the courts seem inclined to grant that protection to them.

11

Public Disclosure of Private Facts

On September 11, 1975, less than a generation after the assassination of President John F. Kennedy, the life of another U.S. President was suddenly and dramatically placed in jeopardy. The president: Gerald R. Ford. The would-be assassin: a deeply disturbed young woman named Sara Jane Moore. The episode occurred at Union Square in San Francisco, where the president was to make a speech. As President Ford worked through the crowd, shaking hands with onlookers and well wishers, neither he nor his Secret Service bodyguards spotted the revolver in the hands of Ms. Moore, who had edged her way toward the front rank of spectators, and was by now only a few feet from the president. But a man standing nearby, Oliver W. Sipple, did. Just as she raised the pistol to fire, Sipple dived at the woman, grabbing her arm and causing the bullet to miss. This valiant, selfless effort almost certainly saved the president's life. Sipple was hailed as a hero and, inevitably, subjected to massive local and national publicity, although, as things turned out, he would greatly have preferred no publicity at all.

Within hours, popular local columnist Herb Caen published an item in the San Francisco *Chronicle* column suggesting that Sipple was homosexual:

> One of the heroes of the day, Oliver "Bill" Sipple, the ex-Marine who grabbed Sara Jane Moore's arm just as her gun was fired and thereby may have saved the President's life, was the center of midnight attention at the Red Lantern, a Golden Gate Ave. bar he favors. The Rev. Ray Broshears, head of Helping Hands, and Gay Politico, Harvey Milk, who claim to be among Sipple's closest friends, describe themselves as "proud—maybe this will help break the stereotype."

An article the next day in the *Los Angeles Times* theorized that President Ford's failure to promptly thank Sipple for his heroism was a direct result of Sipple's sexual orientation:

A husky ex-Marine who was a hero in the attempted assassination of President Ford emerged Wednesday as a prominent member of the gay community.

And questions were raised in the gay community if Oliver (Bill) Sipple was being shunned by the White House because of his associations.

Sipple, who lunged at Sara Jane Moore and deflected her revolver as she fired at the President, conceded that he is a member of the "court" of Mike Caringi, who was elected "emperor of San Francisco" by the gay community.

A column item in a morning newspaper [the piece by Herb Caen in the San Francisco *Chronicle*, just referred to] here strongly implied that Sipple is gay. . . .

Harvey Milk, a prominent member of this city's large homosexual community and a long-time friend of Sipple, speculated Wednesday that the absence of a phone call or telegram of gratitude from the White House might not be just an oversight. . . .

In these articles, Sipple said, his parents, brothers, and sisters learned for the first time of his sexual orientation. As a result, he had been abandoned by his family and exposed to contempt and ridicule, causing him mental anguish, embarrassment, and humiliation. He sued the *Chronicle*.[1]

Another California invasion of privacy case, from many years earlier, also dealt with the public disclosure of private facts. A woman named Gabrielle Darley, who earned her living by being a prostitute, was charged with murder, and the trial was highly publicized. Miss Darley was acquitted. Afterward, she forsook her old ways, moved to a different community, and became a model citizen. She then married and settled into a totally respectable existence among new friends who knew nothing of her previous lifestyle.

Seven years later, however, someone who did know about it used the Darley case as the basis for a sensational movie, *The Red Kimono*. The motion picture provided an essentially true account of the murder trial, using the name of Gabrielle Darley for the central character. When the movie was released, Miss Darley, who was by now an upright, highly principled matron, Mrs. Melvin, found her steamy past exposed and her new life ruined. She sued the movie producer.[2]

These cases illustrate the kinds of pain and humiliation that can follow the public disclosure of facts that those most affected by them had desperately hoped to keep secret—secret, at least, in certain communities. Total secrecy, of course, would be impossible: Some details of Miss Darley's previous career had surfaced in the public trial in which she was acquitted of a murder charge, but that trial was at a different town in a different time. Mr. Sipple's membership in the local gay community was known in San Francisco, and he did not worry about that; what he did worry about, however, was news of his sexual orientation being reported in the Midwest, where his parents, brothers, and sisters lived. Both Ms. Darley/Melvin and Mr. Sipple hoped to define the realm of secrecy—to control the information publicized about themselves. But such controls are not easily permitted in a free and open society, lest they become a chill on the First Amendment.

If the conflicts between liberty of expression and an individual's desire to hide embarrassing personal facts are delicate and difficult, they can also be murky and inconsistent. Mr. Sipple lost his privacy lawsuit against the San Francisco *Chronicle*, whereas Mrs. Melvin won her case against the producers of the *Red Kimono* film, although more recent interpretations by the courts might well produce a different result today. The unpredictability of this aspect of privacy law is unsettling. "One steers clear of a barbed wire fence," a distinguished scholar has noted in a law review article on this subject. "He stays even farther away if he is not exactly sure where the fence is."[3] It is this fence, which skirts the edges of the territory wherein private facts can become public knowledge, that is surveyed in the pages that follow.

CURRENT CRITERIA

A disclosure of a private fact occurs when someone—usually, for our purposes, in one of the mass media—reveals personal information involving an individual who did not want the information to be public. When Samuel D. Warren and Louis D. Brandeis wrote their famous *Harvard Law Review* article calling for the recognition of an individual's right to privacy (see chap. 10), it was this offense, in particular—publicizing information that may be nobody's business but those immediately and directly concerned—they had in mind. "Gossip," they wrote, ". . . has become a trade, which is pursued with industry as well as effrontery."[4] But when does idle gossip become a matter of permissible public concern? It might be embarrassing to a prominent industrialist to see details of his conviction on a charge of shoplifting reported by the news media. But if he were able somehow to have this report suppressed—the truthful report of a decision arrived at in a court of law—then the local news media would have a credibility problem, and the liberty of expression promised by the First Amendment would be seriously impaired.

So embarrassing facts about an individual may be, and often are, safely publicized without violating the person's right to privacy. But two conditions must be met: A reasonable person would not be offended by the disclosure, and the disclosure pertains to a matter of public concern. If those conditions are not met, then it is entirely possible the disclosure would constitute an invasion of personal privacy. According to the *Restatement of Torts*:

> One who gives publicity to a matter concerning the private life of another is subject to the other for invasion of his privacy, if the matter publicized is of a kind that
> (a) would be highly offensive to a reasonable person, and
> (b) is not of legitimate concern to the public.[5]

Disclosure of private information is one of the few media-related situations in which truth is not an absolute defense. The key phrases, again, are *highly offensive* and *legitimate public concern*. Both are tough to define. Some cases are examined to help place these terms in context.

SEXUAL MATTERS

In a scathing investigative report that charged misconduct at a county home in Iowa, the *Des Moines Register* in the mid-1970s revealed that an 18-year-old woman had been involuntarily sterilized some years previously. The woman's name was given, although the incident was not mentioned until well into the story:

> The *Register* also learned that an 18-year-old woman sterilized in 1970 was not retarded nor mentally disabled, but an "impulsive, hair-triggered young girl," in the words of Dr. Roy C. Sloan, the home's psychiatrist.
>
> He said the decision to sterilize the resident, Robin Woody, was made by her parents and himself. He does not recall whether Woody agreed to the operation, but a woman who was a nurse at the home at the time said "she didn't want it at all."
>
> Forced Sterilization
>
> "For two or three weeks when I came to work she was crying," said Collene Blakeley of Newton. "She was told the only way she could be dismissed from the home is if she would agree to be sterilized."
>
> Dr. Sloan denied that, saying, "We don't think in terms of punishment. That child—she was a young girl—was a very explosive, impulsive young girl largely without controls over her aggressive and, at times, irrational behavior."
>
> He said she was sterilized because "she would be a very questionable risk as far as having and rearing a baby. The people who hold on that way are those who move on to child abuse. . . ."

Miss Howard sued the *Register* for what she regarded as unreasonable publicity about her private life. The trial court sided with the newspaper, holding that the incident, including the use of Miss Howard's name, was a matter of legitimate public interest. The appeals court agreed, noting that the use of the name lent authenticity to the newspaper report, adding: "We do not say it was necessary to do so [use the name of the defendant], but we are certain they had a right to treat the identity of victims of involuntary sterilization as matters of legitimate public concern."[6]

"Legitimate public concern" also was an issue in the matter of Toni Ann Diaz, who in the early 1980s was elected to be the first woman president of the student body at the College of Alameda, in the San Francisco Bay area. Newsworthy? Possibly. But an *Oakland Tribune* columnist, Sidney Jones, found out there was another aspect to the story, and he passed it along to his readers:

> More Education Stuff: The students at the College of Alameda will be surprised to learn their student body president Toni Diaz is no lady, but is in fact a man whose real name is Antonio.
>
> Now I realize, that in these times, such a matter is no big deal, but I suspect his female classmates in P.E. 97 may wish to make other showering arrangements.

Ms. Diaz sued the *Tribune*, arguing that, although the account of her sex-change operation was true, it was nevertheless a private matter, not of legitimate public concern, and might be offensive to many persons. The jury agreed, and awarded her $775,000 from the paper and $25,000 from the columnist. The judgment was appealed and, largely for technical and procedural reasons, the case was retried. As it sent the case back for retrial, the court said the decision as to the newsworthiness of Ms. Diaz and her sex-change operation "depends on contemporary community mores and standards of decency," an assessment best made by a jury.[7] Ultimately the case was settled out of court, with Ms. Diaz reportedly receiving between $200,000 and $300,000.

In another context, but in connection with a similarly delicate case, an appeals court in Iowa said much the same thing: "In determining whether an item is newsworthy, courts cannot impose their own views about what should interest the community. Courts do not have license to sit as censors."[8]

In recent years, however, when an individual's right to privacy conflicts with the public's right to be informed, the right to privacy has tended to lose out—if not with a jury, then in the appeals process. *Cape Publications, Inc., v. Bridges* underscores the difficulty plaintiffs have winning privacy cases against media defendants when a key element is "legitimate public concern." In *Bridges*, a young woman was kidnapped by her estranged husband and taken to an apartment where she was held hostage. He forced her to undress, then beat her. As police—and the press—arrived on the scene, the husband committed suicide. Police hurriedly removed the nude woman from the apartment; she was able to grab a dishtowel, which only partially covered her. As she left the building, a newspaper photographer shot a picture of her that was published in *Cocoa Today*.

She sued, arguing that the photo was offensive, caused her extreme embarrassment, and exceeded the boundaries of newsworthiness. A sympathetic jury found in her favor, awarding her $1,000 in actual damages and $9,000 in punitive damages from the newspaper. But on appeal, the judgment was reversed. In the court's opinion:

> Just because the story and photograph may be embarrassing or distressful to the plaintiff does not mean the newspaper cannot publish what is otherwise newsworthy. At some point, the public interest in obtaining information becomes dominant over the individual's right of privacy.[9]

But a South Carolina case suggests that the public interest in a news story might take a back seat to protecting the privacy of an individual under certain circumstances. In a lengthy story dealing with teenage pregnancies, the *Greenville News* interviewed a high school student who had been identified—by the mother—as the father of her illegitimate baby. The young man said he had been led to believe he was talking to a data gatherer for a research study of teen pregnancies, not to a newspaper reporter, and that he had no idea his statements, including his identification by name and his admission that he fathered the child, would appear in the newspaper. When the article was printed by the newspaper, the young man sued. The newspaper argued that the information was newsworthy and of legitimate public concern. The South Carolina Supreme Court, however, determined that this was a matter for a jury to decide. The jury found the name of the father was not of great public concern, and decided on a substantial judgment against the newspaper.[10]

EMBARRASSING MATERIAL

In a lengthy, sympathetic feature on special education classes in its county, the *Delta Democrat-Times* of Greenville, Mississippi, published photographs and names of at least four members of one class, describing the children as "retarded" and "trainable mentally retarded." The families sued in behalf of the children, claiming that, by being characterized as retarded, their privacy was violated and so was their "right to the pursuit of happiness." The newspaper argued that the children were in a public school, and that classroom assistance to retarded children was a matter of legitimate public interest. The court conceded that the special education class may be newsworthy. But, in finding in favor of the children, the court held:

> ... the publication of the names and photographs of the children involved casts the issue into a different legal perspective. It is difficult to conceive that any information can be more delicate or private in nature than the fact that a child has limited mental capabilities or is in any sense mentally retarded. Simply enrolling in a public school does not make one a "public figure" or "personage" to the extent that such person has no right to privacy concerning his mental capabilities or lack of such. Reasonable limitations applied to the right of a free press to expose facts of private concern to individuals do not infringe upon the right of the people to be informed of matters properly in the public domain.[11]

Another photograph, this one taken at a county fair in October 1961, got the Cullman, Alabama, *Daily Times Democrat* in an invasion of privacy lawsuit. The plaintiff was Mrs. Flora Bell Graham, then 44, the wife of a chicken farmer, mother of two pre-teen sons, and a woman active in church and community affairs. She took her young sons to the county fair, where they urged her to accompany them through what was called "the fun house." She had not been through a fun house previously, and did not know that lurking inside the facility was a device that blew jets of air up from the floor of the exit. As she emerged from the fun house, a sudden blast from the air jet blew her dress up over her shoulders; while she desperately attempted to pull it down, she was nevertheless exposed and humiliated in her underpants. At that moment, a photographer from the local daily snapped a picture of her, which, the editor thought, caught the spirit of the fair. The photo soon appeared on the front page of the *Daily Times Democrat*.

As a result, Mrs. Graham was embarrassed and became self-conscious, and on several occasions afterward burst into tears. She sued the paper. The newspaper contended that the photo was taken in a public place and that it was newsworthy.

The trial court found in Mrs. Graham's favor, awarding her $4,166 in damages. The appeals court upheld the verdict: "Not only was this photograph embarrassing to one of normal sensibilities, we think it could properly be classified as obscene, in that 'obscene' means 'offensive to modesty or decency.' "[12]

More recent court definitions of obscenity are considerably more stringent, and the argument could be made that the photo of Mrs. Graham was intended to be good-natured, rather than outrageously offensive. Still, the embarrassment by this publication was sufficient for the trial court to sustain the invasion of privacy charge. The Alabama Supreme Court upheld the judgment, and quoted Dean William L. Prosser, an eminent authority, on this point: "It may nevertheless be suggested that there must be yet some undefined limits of common decency as to what can be published about anyone; and that a photograph of indecent exposure, for example, can never be legitimate 'news.' "[13]

Yet the limits are not always clear, nor the trial outcomes consistent, where embarrassing facts are concerned. A *Dallas Times-Herald* article about a prison guard who had been held hostage during a riot cost the paper a substantial invasion of privacy judgment. The guard, talking with a friend in his hospital room, told of having been beaten, stabbed, and sexually assaulted by prisoners. A reporter from the paper overheard the conversation and printed the details, also disclosing that the guard and his wife were living in near poverty. Upset by the *Times-Herald* story, which the guard said was not only embarrassing but obtained thorough eavesdropping, the guard sued and was awarded a $200,000 judgment.[14]

In *Barber v. Time*,[15] a young woman won her case by proving that the details of her privacy were highly offensive, although they were both true and newsworthy. Dorothy Barber suffered from a rare metabolic disease; although she ate constantly, she continued to lose weight. Eventually she was hospitalized for treatment. The case was something of a medical curiosity, and several news media, including *Time* magazine, decided to do a piece about it. Bursting into her Kansas City hospital room, a news service photographer got a picture of Mrs. Barber, which, when it later appeared in *Time*, portrayed the unfortunate young woman in terms not unlike those that might be used to describe a freak: "Insatiable Eater Barber" read the caption accompanying the photograph. In the piece, she was referred to as "Starving Glutton" and "she eats for ten." This article prompted Mrs. Barber to sue. The court agreed that, although the story might well be newsworthy, the specific identification of her by name and the way she and her medical problem were characterized were so odious as to represent an invasion of her privacy. Barber won the case.

In contrast, a newspaper reported that a state university basketball team was in trouble because four players, identified by name, were on academic probation and at risk of flunking out of school. One of the players sued, but the case against the newspaper was dismissed.[16]

Does "newsworthiness" extend to publicizing private details in the life of a *public* person? The courts explored this question in *Virgil v. Time Inc.*,[17] a 1975 case arising from a lively profile of a famed body surfer, Mike Virgil, as it appeared in *Sports Illustrated*. Described as the most fearless member of a daredevil band of surfers at The Wedge, dangerous waters near Newport Beach, California, Virgil was comparably uninhibited on dry land as well. During interviews with Curry Kirkpatrick of *Sports Illustrated*, Virgil spoke freely about his private life. He recalled that he had devoured insects and spiders; extinguished a lighted cigarette inside his mouth; won a bet by burning a hole through a dollar bill with a lighted cigarette, with the dollar bill resting on the back of his hand; that he had never learned to read; had dived down a flight of stairs at a ski resort "to impress these chicks"; and had contrived to injure himself: ". . . dive off billboards or drop loads on myself so that I could collect unemployment compensation so that I could surf at The Wedge."

Afterward, when a fact-checker from the magazine telephoned to verify these assertions, Virgil developed second thoughts about the article and asked *Sports Illustrated* not to print anything connected with his private life. The magazine published the piece anyway, details and all, and Virgil sued for invasion of privacy. He lost.

In this context, the court ruled, the details of Virgil's private life were newsworthy because they "were revealed in a legitimate journalistic attempt to explain his extremely daring and dangerous style of bodysurfing." Given a different situation, if the story had been written about an ordinary person, publicizing such details might have been actionable. But in a profile of a daredevil bodysurfer, the details became a significant part of the story. These private-life tidbits were not published for their own sake, the court held, adding that, under those circumstances, reasonable jurors would not find the story highly offensive.

The following year, 1976, found *Sports Illustrated* involved in another invasion of privacy suit—this one prompted by a photograph. A noisy band of Pittsburgh Steeler fans, celebrating before the start of what they were certain would be a victory by their pro football heroes, urged a photographer to take pictures of them atop the team dugout. The photographer did so, and the photo selected for publication featured one fan with his pants unzipped. Claiming the photo caused him humiliation, the fan sued the magazine for invasion of privacy. The photograph was not revealing, anatomically, but the fan who sued objected to his boisterous behavior being so prominently displayed. The trial court dismissed the case, noting that the photo was taken in a public place, and thus was already public knowledge, not private information.[18] In this and a number of comparable cases, courts have ruled that before there can be an invasion of privacy, it must be shown that the information publicized was in fact private.

DREDGING UP THE PAST

Is there a point in which one's past can be safely buried? Does the law's concept of rehabilitation—as, for example, with convicts who, on being released from prison, are said to "have paid their debt to society." Or does one's private life, once made public, remain public forever? Again, the law is not clear.

For example, consider the case of Marvin Briscoe, who once hijacked a truck. He was subsequently arrested and convicted, and served time in prison. Thereafter, in his lawyer's words, Mr. Briscoe "abandoned his life of shame and became entirely rehabilitated and thereafter lived an exemplary, virtuous, and honorable life ... he has assumed a place in respectable society and made many friends who were not aware of the incident in his earlier life."

But a magazine writer was aware of it, and he used the unfortunate Mr. Briscoe's criminal example to illustrate a piece later published by the *Reader's Digest*, "The Big Business of Hijacking." At one point, the article read: "Typical of many beginners, Marvin Briscoe and [another man] stole a 'valuable looking' truck in Danville, Ky., and then fought a gun battle with the local police, only to learn they had hijacked four bowling-pin spotters."

Although the account was truthful, there was nothing in it to suggest that the incident had happened 11 years previously. Mr. Briscoe, who had since moved to California, found himself "scorned and abandoned" by his friends; his 11-year-old daughter learned of her father's conviction from the publication. He sued. The trial court decided Mr. Briscoe had no cause of action, and effectively dismissed the case. On appeal, however, the California Supreme Court reversed this decision and sent the case back for trial. Mr. Briscoe's claim that he had been rehabilitated, the appeals court said, should be examined seriously by a jury:

> In a nation of 200 million people there is ample opportunity for all but the most infamous to begin a new life.
> Plaintiff is a man whose last offense took place 11 years before, who has paid his debt to society, who has friends and an 11-year-old daughter who were unaware of his early life—a man who has assumed a position in "respectable" society. Ideally, his neighbors should recognize his present worth and forget his past life of shame. But men are not so divine as to forgive the past trespasses of others, and plaintiff therefore endeavored to reveal as little as possible of his past life. Yet, as if in some bizarre canyon of echoes, petitioner's past life pursues him through the pages of *Reader's Digest*, now published in 13 languages and distributed in 100 nations, with a circulation in California alone of almost 2,000,000 copies.

The appeals court opinion held that, although the hijacking story was clearly newsworthy, it could have been effectively told without specifically identifying Mr. Briscoe by name. A trial jury, the appeals court said, "might find that revealing one's criminal past for all to see is grossly offensive to most people in America." Indeed, rehashing Mr. Briscoe's crime so publicly might cause a jury to "find that a continuing threat that the rehabilitated offender's old identity will be resurrected by the media is counter-productive to the goals of this [prison] corrective process."[19]

Mr. Briscoe still did not win. A federal judge in California swiftly found in favor of the *Reader's Digest*: The article did not disclose private facts, the judge ruled. Mr. Briscoe's conviction on the hijacking charge was public knowledge—

in Kentucky, if not necessarily in California—and, perhaps more to the point, the article was newsworthy.[20]

In the public disclosure of private facts, as in much else protected by the First Amendment, the courts presume that the balance is generally weighed in favor of free expression. Only under extraordinary circumstances are the mass media punished for printing truthful reports, even if those reports cause humiliation to those directly affected by them. The appeals court in *Briscoe* warned that public disclosures of delicate private facts, although the disclosures may be protected by law, could still carry grave consequences:

> A publisher does have every reason to know, *before* publication, that identification of a man as a former criminal will be highly offensive to the individual involved. It does not require close reading of *Les Misérables* or *The Scarlet Letter* to know that men are haunted by the fear of disclosure of their past and destroyed by the exposure itself.[21]

Such reasoning is not new. In 1948, two Alabama sisters sued a radio station for broadcasting a report of the disappearance of their father—some 43 years earlier. There had been no additional developments in the story. The sisters lost their case. "The right of privacy is supported by logic and the weight of authority," the trial court acknowledged, "but in the face of legitimate public interest it has to give way."[22]

One of the saddest cases in this area, and one of the most often referred to in determining how much of the past can safely be dredged up, is that of William James Sidis. In 1910, young Sidis was known far and wide for his intellectual prowess. By the time he was 11 years old, he had already become an authority on the subject of four-dimensional bodies, and he lectured to distinguished mathematicians on that and other matters. At 16, and amid much public fanfare, he was graduated from Harvard College.

However, Sidis' youthful genius did not prepare him for later life, and he never seemed comfortable as an adult. He lived as unobtrusively as possible, and soon had become something of a recluse. Twenty years later, the *New Yorker* decided to develop a profile on Sidis, another in its series entitled "Where Are They Now?" The *New Yorker* writer found Sidis living in a hall bedroom in "Boston's shabby south end," and reported in great detail that (a) the room was messy; (b) Sidis had developed a curious and hollow laugh; (c) he had suffered a nervous breakdown; (d) he regarded his former fame with contempt; (e) he was presently employed as an insignificant clerk, a position in which he would never use his astonishing mathematical gifts; (f) his bizarre collection of streetcar tokens; and (g) his consuming interest was now focused on the folklore of the Okamakammessett Indians. As the court would later point out:

> It is not contended that any of the matter printed [in the *New Yorker* profile] is untrue. Nor is the manner of the author unfriendly; Sidis today is described as having "a certain childlike charm." But the article is merciless in its dissection of intimate details of its subject's personal life, and this in company with elaborate

accounts of Sidis's passion for privacy and the pitiable lengths to which he has gone in order to avoid public scrutiny. The work possesses great reader interest, for it is both amusing and instructive; but it may be fairly described as a ruthless exposure of a once public character, who has since sought and has now been deprived of the seclusion of private life.

The *New Yorker* profile proved devastating to Sidis, and he sued the magazine for invading his privacy. However, the trial court found that the unfortunate Sidis, many years later, was still newsworthy. The massive publicity about his childhood, which he may or may not have wanted even at the time, would continue to haunt him so long as audiences remembered him as a one-time celebrity. The court, somewhat reluctantly, found in favor of the *New Yorker*:

> We express no comment on whether or not the news worthiness of the matter printed will always constitute a complete defense. Revelations may be so intimate and so unwarranted in view of the victim's position as to outrage the community's notions of decency. But when focused upon public characters, truthful comments upon dress, speech, habits, and the ordinary aspects of personality will usually not transgress this line. Regrettably or not, the misfortunes and frailties of neighbors and "public figures" are subjects of considerable interest and discussion to the rest of the population. And when such are the mores of the community, it would be unwise for a court to bar their expression in the newspapers, books, and magazines of the day.[23]

NEWSWORTHINESS AS A DEFENSE

The central purpose of the First Amendment, according to the distinguished scholar Alexander Meiklejohn,

> is to give to every voting member of the body politic the fullest possible participation in the understanding of those problems with which the citizens of a self-governing society must deal. . . . Nor . . . is freedom of the press confined to comment upon public affairs and those persons who have voluntarily sought the public spotlight . . . the scope of the privilege thus extends to almost all reporting of recent events, even though it involves the publication of a purely private individual's name or likeness.[24]

Thus, the right to keep information private is bound to collide with the right to disseminate information to the public. Over the years, however, the courts have been quite liberal in defining public interest not as something people necessarily *should* read about, but as something they *do* read about—something in which people are interested.[25]

Those individuals who seek the public limelight, of course, are generally thought to deserve less protection from publicity of private information about them than those individuals who prefer to live out their lives quietly. Private persons often find themselves drawn into an event (i.e., an accident, as the victim of a crime, or simply happening by chance to be, as was Mr. Sipple, the ex-Marine who saved a president's life—in a public place during a newsworthy moment). Thus, there are voluntary and involuntary public figures. The *Restatement of Torts* points out that even involuntary subjects may not always have their privacy protected:

> These persons [involuntary public figures] are regarded as properly subject to the public interest, and publishers are permitted to satisfy the curiosity of the public as to its heroes, leaders, villains and victims, and those who are closely associated with them. As in the case of the voluntary public figure, the authorized publicity is not limited to the event that itself arouses the public interest, and to some extent includes publicity given to facts about the individual that would otherwise be purely private.[26]

In making such determinations on a case-by-case basis, the courts have taken into account such factors as the way the communication was presented, the nature of the information being publicized, the degree of intimacy such disclosure represents, and the value of the disclosure—as measured in newsworthiness—to the general public. What often emerges, as Dean Prosser theorized some years ago, "is something in the nature of a 'mores test,' by which there will be liability only for publicity given to those things which the customs and ordinary views of the community will not tolerate."[27] By whatever criteria that may be used to measure the extent of an embarrassing fact, the courts have generally been most generous to the American media of mass communications in defining "legitimate public concern," thus making newsworthiness a valuable, although not foolproof, defense in privacy actions.

PRIVILEGE AS A DEFENSE

In general, the news media and other communicators are free to publish private facts, taken from judicial, legislative, or other public and official proceedings, without fear of losing an invasion of privacy lawsuit. In privacy actions, as with defamation suits, fair and accurate accounts of statements taken from official records are regarded as privileged, and may be reported to the public.

The landmark case in this regard—the first time the Supreme Court of the United States acted on a true privacy case and affirmed a constitutional privilege in certain privacy matters—came in 1975, with *Cox Broadcasting v. Cohn*. This invasion of privacy case arose out of a far greater tragedy—when 17-year-old Cynthia Cohn was gang-raped in Georgia. During the ordeal, she died. The story was widely publicized at the time, but the identity of the victim was not revealed. Police arrested six youths and charged them with the crime. Eight months later, when their trial began, five of the six pleaded guilty to rape or attempted rape, and the sixth defendant's trial was postponed.

During a recess in these court proceedings, a reporter from WSB-TV, the Cox-owned television station in Atlanta, asked the clerk for copies of the indictments to check the accuracy of the details. The victim's name was listed in the indictments, and the journalist disclosed the victim's name in his televised report that evening. The story was rebroadcast the following day.

The State of Georgia, as with some other states, had on its lawbooks a statute forbidding publication of the identity of a rape victim. Under normal circumstances, only the victim in a disclosure of private information action can instigate the suit. But the Georgia law permitted close relatives of a rape victim to file the suit in her behalf. Additionally, Martin Cohn, the victim's father, brought suit against Cox Broadcasting, claiming that the disclosure of his daughter's name and other information invaded his privacy as well. Georgia trial and appeals courts found in Mr. Cohn's behalf, holding that the publication of a rape victim's name is not a matter of legitimate public concern. The Georgia Supreme Court held that the Georgia statute prohibiting the publication of a rape victim's name was "a legitimate limitation on the right of freedom of expression contained in the First Amendment." Cox Broadcasting appealed to the Supreme Court of the United States, which agreed to hear the case.

At issue was this: Could the news media be punished for publishing facts already on the public records of a court? In an 8–1 decision, the Supreme Court of the United States said "no":

> We are reluctant to embark on a course that would make public records generally available to the media but forbid their publication if offensive to the sensibilities of the supposed reasonable man. Such a rule would make it very difficult for the media to inform citizens about the public business and yet stay within the law. The rule would invite timidity and self-censorship and very likely lead to the suppression of many items that would otherwise be published and that should be made available to the public. At the very least, the First and Fourteenth Amendments will not allow exposing the press to liability for truthfully publishing information released to the public in official court records. If there are privacy interests to be protected in judicial proceedings, the States must respond by means which avoid public documentation or other exposure of private information. Their political institutions must weigh the interests in privacy with the interests of the public to know and of the press to publish. Once true information is disclosed in public court documents open to public inspection, the press cannot be sanctioned for publishing it.[28]

Some court records, such as juvenile proceedings, might not be open to the public. The Court's opinion in *Cox*, written by Justice Byron R. White, avoided addressing any questions on the constitutionality of sealed court records. The thrust of the *Cox* holding was this: If the records are available to the public, then the mass media cannot be restrained from publishing truthful articles based on them.

Essentially the same reasoning prevailed in another Court ruling, *The Florida Star v. B.J.F.* This 1989 case also involved publication of a rape victim's name. A cub reporter for a Jacksonville weekly newspaper, leafing through the Sheriff's Department "beef sheets"—incident reports prepared by officers based on their activities that day—ran across an item in which a woman had complained that she had been raped and robbed. Incident reports are routinely made available to the press by the Sheriff's Department, but in this case there was a lapse: The full name of the rape victim was included. The reporter copied the report and included the story in the "Police Reports" column of The Florida Star. The one-paragraph item disclosed that the assailant had forced the victim to undress and have sexual intercourse with him before he absconded "with her 60 cents, Timex watch and gold necklace." B.J.F.'s full name was revealed in the story.

Much had gone wrong here. The rape victim's name was carelessly included in the report. Even so, there were signs in the press room, where the report was made available, that victims of sex crimes were not to be identified. There was a Florida statute forbidding disclosure of a rape victim's name. Beyond that, The Florida Star's own editorial policy forbade the publication of a rape victim's identity in the columns of the paper.

B.J.F. then sued for invasion of privacy, claiming that the publication caused her emotional distress, provoked at least one harassing telephone call, forced her to change her telephone number, and prompted her to seek psychiatric counseling. At trial, the judge found the newspaper to have been negligent, leaving it to the jury to determine the amount of damages. The jury awarded her $100,000. On appeal, the Florida Supreme Court affirmed the judgment. However, the Supreme Court of the United States reversed it. By a 6–3 vote, the Court ruled that the newspaper should not be punished for publishing truthful information from an official source, even though the information was not part of a court proceeding and the information was obtained by mistake.

In a cautiously written opinion, Justice Thurgood Marshall wrote for the majority:

> Our holding today is limited. We do not hold that truthful publication is automatically constitutionally protected, or that there is no zone of personal privacy within which the State may protect the individual from intrusion by the press, or even that a State may never punish publication of the name of a victim of a sexual offense. We hold only that where a newspaper publishes true information which it has lawfully obtained, punishment may be imposed, if at all, only when narrowly tailored to a state interest of the highest order, and that no such interest is satisfactorily served by imposing liability . . . under the facts of this case.[29]

In a 1982 case, Globe Newspapers v. Superior Court,[30] the Supreme Court of the United States struck down a Massachusetts law under which news media could be barred from attending court trials when the victims were minors. Although acknowledging that some court trials, or portions of trials, might indeed be conducted behind closed doors, the Court said judges would have to make such determinations on a case-by-case basis. But in Globe, the Court held, the names of the victims were already on the public record. In that same vein, during a widely publicized 1991 rape trial in Florida, in which the defendant was William Kennedy Smith, nephew of U.S. Senator Edward M. Kennedy, a supermarket tabloid published the name of the alleged rape victim. Some other news media, including the New York Times and NBC News, then proceeded to identify the alleged rape victim by name, despite that, during the trial, which was televised, the face of the woman was obscured by an electronically generated blur. Although there was widespread public condemnation of the news media for disclosing the alleged victim's name, there were no lawsuits filed against the media for doing so.

These and other cases seem to make it clear that the mass media are generally free to publicize the names of victims of sex crimes if they choose to do so. Usually they do not.

The same is true for disclosing the names of juveniles. In a 1979 case, *Smith v. Daily Mail Publishing Co.*,[31] a West Virginia newspaper was sued for publishing the name of a junior high school student who was accused in the shooting death of a schoolmate on the school grounds. The name of the suspect was not on the public record at the time, but was obtained in interviews with fellow students, the prosecuting attorney, and the police at the scene. The newspaper decided to print the name, despite the fact that West Virginia had on the books a law that forbade disclosing the identities of juvenile offenders. The Court ruled that the West Virginia law was too broad; the juvenile's name was obtained in a lawful manner by the newspaper, using what the Court referred to as "routine newspaper reporting techniques," such as questioning witnesses and police officers. In addition, the newspaper's report concerned "a matter of public significance." Under such circumstances, the Court held, the state law should not be permitted to stifle public discussion about an important local matter. The state's interest in protecting juveniles and encouraging their rehabilitation is important, but not enough to stifle First Amendment protections for the media of mass communications.

In summary, the Court has preserved the right of an individual to sue for disclosure of embarrassing private facts, but has imposed constitutional limits on that right.[32] Truthful reports, based on lawfully obtained information, are most likely to be protected. This is especially true when the information is contained in a public record. As Justice White wrote in *Cox*,

> Public records by their very nature are of interest to those concerned with the administration of government, and a public benefit is performed by the reporting of the true contents of the records by the media. The freedom of the press to publish that information appears to us to be of critical importance to our type of government in which the citizenry is the final judge of the proper conduct of public business. In preserving that form of government the First and Fourteenth Amendments command nothing less than that the States may not impose sanctions on the publication of truthful information contained in official court records open to public inspection.[33]

CONCLUSION

Legal problems arising from the public disclosure of private facts are far more likely to involve news reporters and editors (i.e., journalists) than advertising and public relations people. However, it should be noted that several of the first lawsuits brought in this area were indeed prompted by advertisements: Public notices—one published in a newspaper, another posted prominently on a busy street, a third cried out from the highway—that certain creditors, identified by name, did not pay their debts[34]—allegations that were as embarrassing in 1918, when the first such suit was filed, as they might be today.

Public relations people, especially, would do well to familiarize themselves with this aspect of privacy law for at least two reasons:

1. Public relations writers prepare publicity releases and other types of organizational communications on any number of topics and issues, and some of these messages could easily concern the public disclosure of private facts (e.g., explaining the complexities of a sensitive personnel decision, or backgrounding the issues in a heated proxy fight for control of a corporation). These and numerous other possible scenarios hold the potential for invasion of privacy suits.

2. Public relations persons bear the responsibility of advising their clients about the potential for invasion of privacy suits on the possible implications of communications issued by the client's organization. This responsibility also includes providing advice in response to inquiries from the mass media; and furnishing clients ammunition, as warranted, if their clients' rights are threatened by the potential disclosure of sensitive and embarrassing information that could properly be kept private.

Under current interpretations—again that, unless the private facts disclosed are outrageously offensive and outside the broad realm of legitimate public interest, they may be publicized—disclosure actions are difficult to win. When the public's interest in knowing collides with an individual's claim to privacy, the former usually prevails. The law is so favorable to media professionals, in fact, that editors and broadcast news directors tend to regard privacy as more of an ethical concern than a legal matter. It may be more important, they reason, to win in the court of public opinion than in a court of law.

Still, the right of privacy is very much alive, and the improper disclosure of embarrassing and offensive private information is an ingrained part of it. Mass communicators of all kinds—journalists, advertising and public relations people, and others in the media-related industries—need to be aware of what this aspect of privacy law will allow and what it will punish.

12

False Light Invasions of Privacy

In 1947, when she was 10 years old, Eleanor Sue Leverton of Birmingham, Alabama, was struck by a car, knocked down, and nearly run over. As the injured child was being lifted off the pavement by a woman bystander, a newspaper photographer who happened to be nearby shot a picture of the scene. His powerful, dramatic photograph was published the following morning in a Birmingham newspaper.

Nearly 2 years later, the Curtis Publishing Company, parent company of the *Saturday Evening Post*, used that same picture—it had been purchased from a photo syndicate house—to illustrate a magazine piece on pedestrian carelessness. The article was entitled "They Ask to Be Killed," and underneath Miss Leverton's photograph was this subheading: "Safety education in schools has reduced child accidents measurably, but unpredictable darting through traffic still takes a sobering toll." Beside the title was a box that read: "Do you invite massacre by your own carelessness? Here's how thousands have committed suicide by scorning laws that were passed to keep them alive."

Miss Leverton and her parents resented the implication that her own misfortune should be twisted into something quite different—that is, a near-tragedy brought on by her own carelessness. Indeed, the Birmingham police concluded at the time that Miss Leverton's accident happened not because of her own carelessness, but because the motorist had run through a red light. The Levertons sued for an unwarranted invasion of her privacy and collected, in this case, $5,000. The appeals court agreed that the judgment was appropriate: "The sum total of all this is that this particular plaintiff, the legitimate subject for publicity for one particular accident, now becomes a pictorial, frightful example of pedestrian carelessness. This, we think, exceeds the bounds of privilege."[1] In other words, Miss Leverton had been placed in a false light.

False light invasions of privacy involve portraying individuals as something they are not, and doing so in a way that ordinary persons find offensive—a distortion of a person's personality that results in that person being depicted to the public in a wrongful manner. In some respects, false light privacy is much like defamation, a point we return to later. But there are important differences—enough of them to make false light, in the eyes of most courts, a separate matter entirely.

CURRENT CRITERIA FOR WINNING
A FALSE LIGHT CLAIM

The first successful false light courtroom victory was in 1816, and the winner was Lord Byron, the most colorful of all the English romantic poets. Angry because someone had falsely attributed a mediocre poem to him—one he swore he had not written—Byron persuaded a British court to issue an order halting further publication and circulation of the poem.[2]

More recent false light claims have been in that same vein—that is, publicly ascribing to an individual writings or speech reflecting views he or she did not hold: falsely claiming that someone endorsed a product, would vote for a particular candidate or political party, or supports a certain charity.[3]

Fictionalization, too, can become an invasion of privacy: Inventing dialogue of a living person and using it to illustrate an article, book, or movie can result in false light charges. As was the case with Miss Eleanor Sue Leverton of Birmingham, Alabama, utilizing a person's photograph in a misleading context, claiming the photo illustrated one thing when in fact it depicted something else, is likewise a false light invasion of privacy.

The *Restatement of Torts,* much referred to in this book, attempts to summarize the law in a general area, how the law may be changing, and what direction the authors—who are leading scholars in each field—think the law should take. The *Restatement* defines *false light privacy* this way:

> One who gives publicity to a matter concerning another that places the other before the public in a false light is subject to liability to the other for invasion of his privacy, if
>   (a) the false light in which the other was placed would be highly offensive to a reasonable person, and
>   (b) the actor [perpetrator] had knowledge of or acted in reckless disregard as to the falsity of the publicized matter and the false light in which the other would be placed.[4]

Determining what is "highly offensive to a reasonable person" can be a vague and uncertain business, of course, but it is in this arena that most false light privacy actions are fought. With few clear-cut guidelines to draw on, juries are given broad latitude to define what is "highly offensive," and the results are not always consistent or predictable.

FALSE LIGHT PRIVACY OR DEFAMATION?

Clearly, false light privacy is much like defamation of character (see chap. 9). The similarities include:

1. *Publication*. The offending material must be shown to at least one other person.

2. *Falsity*. Under current defamation law, truth is almost universally a complete defense (although truth may sometimes be awkward or difficult to prove). Logically, the same standard applies in dealing with charges of false light: If the offending statements are indeed true, then obviously no false light has been cast. In other invasions of privacy discussed in chapter 9, appropriation, and in chapter 11, disclosure of private facts, truth is not necessarily a complete defense. Indeed, the very truth of the disclosure might well create the claimed invasion of privacy (e.g., publicizing delicate, embarrassing facts about an individual, or using someone's personality, claiming it as representing a satisfied customer, to promote the sale of a product—disclosures that may be true, but are not authorized and therefore actionable). Where false light charges are concerned, however, truthful statements are not actionable.

3. *Damage*. In both defamation and false light privacy lawsuits, the person bringing the action normally must show that the offending statements were in some way hurtful.

4. *Fault*. As with defamation, false light privacy requires that the offending publication resulted because the person who published the material was at fault. For our purposes, *fault* is defined as an error in judgment or conduct, negligence, or any departure from normal care because of inattention, carelessness, or incompetence. In defamation, the degree of fault often depends on whether the injured person is a private or public person, distinctions developed more fully in chapter 9. For false light privacy, the normal degree of fault is "actual malice" (i.e., the publication of a deliberate lie, or publishing with a reckless disregard as to whether the statement is true).

But false light privacy differs from defamation in at least one important respect: False light privacy can cover more ground. Defamation actions essentially deal only with damage to one's reputation—one's standing in the community or business world. In contrast, false light charges can be brought in response to any statement that injures feelings. A published, erroneous statement about an individual that causes individual emotional distress is highly unlikely to be found defamatory; as a false light invasion of privacy, however, the chances for recovery are better.

The false light statement need not be defamatory—although it often is—but it must be found offensive to a reasonable person. "Offensiveness" in defamation cases may not matter unless it hurts business—a condition not always easy to document. However, "offensiveness" in and of itself can determine the outcome of a false light privacy lawsuit.

OFFENSIVE STATEMENTS

Sue S. Crump, a coal miner in West Virginia, was photographed in 1977, with her permission, to illustrate a newspaper article about women coal miners. Two years later, the same photograph was dug out of the files to illustrate another article, this one about problems facing female coal miners. Entitled "Women Enter 'Man's' World," the article recounted various hazing incidents inflicted on female miners by their male counterparts. Two Kentucky women, the article said, had been " 'stripped, greased and sent out of the mine' as part of an initiation rite"; a Virginia woman miner was physically attacked twice while underground, and a Wyoming woman miner "was dangled off a 200-foot water tower accompanied by the suggestion that she quit her job. She did."

None of these things happened to Ms. Crump, but when friends and associates began questioning her about them, she said the unfavorable attention prompted by the photograph and its context caused her a great deal of embarrassment and humiliation. She sued for both defamation and invasion of privacy. The trial court, focusing on the defamation aspects of the case, ruled against her summarily. But the appeals court reversed, deciding that perhaps Ms. Crump did have a case: Her allegations, the opinion held, were sufficient to raise a genuine issue of material fact for jury consideration. It said, "false light invasion of privacy is a distinct theory of recovery entitled to separate consideration and analysis."[5]

Magazine publisher Larry Flynt, whose strange editorial themes have landed him in more than one courtroom, tested the limits of "offensiveness" in 1977 in an issue of his *Chic* magazine. This particular article featured Mrs. Jeannie Braun, who worked at an amusement park in San Marcos, Texas, among other things doing a novelty act with "Ralph, the Diving Pig." In this performance, Mrs. Braun, while treading water in a pool, would hold out a bottle of milk with a nipple on it and Ralph would dive into the pool to feed from the bottle. A photographer made pictures of this performance, and obtained a signed release from Mrs. Braun; the release promised "that all photographs are to be in good taste and without embarrassment to me and my family."

Later, however, an editor of *Chic* magazine caught Mrs. Braun's act, and obtained photos of it from the amusement park. One picture was used, in the December 1977 issue of *Chic*, with this caption:

SWINE DIVE—A pig that swims? Why not? This plucky porker performs every day at Aquarena Springs Amusement Park in bustling San Marcos, Texas. Acquarena staff members say the pig was incredibly easy to train. They told him to learn quick, or grow up to be a juicy ham sandwich.

But Mrs. Braun found the rest of the magazine to be scurrilous and suggestive. She was shocked, as were others in her hometown of Lockhart, Texas. Her testimony was: "I was really terrified. ... My legs were like jelly, I couldn't untrack. I was petrified. I was raised in a private Catholic school and I had never seen anything like this. I thought something horrible was going to happen to me. . . ."

What offended her was the editorial environment in which her photo was published, and the content of *Chic* magazine in general. The appeals court opinion described the context with clarity and precision:

> On the same page on which Mrs. Braun's picture appeared were stories about "10 Things that P_ _ _ Off Women" with an accompanying cartoon of a woman whose large breasts are partially exposed; a story entitled "Mammaries Are Made of This" about men whose breasts have been enlarged by exposure to a synthetic hormone, with an accompanying cartoon showing a man with large breasts; and a story entitled "Chinese Organ Grinder" about the use of sexual organs from deer, dogs, and seals as a Chinese elixir. On the facing page is a picture showing a nude female model demonstrating jewelry and an article on "Lust Rock Rules" about a "throbbing paean" to sex written by "the Roman Polanski of rock." The cover of the issue shows a young woman sitting in a chair with her shirt open so as to partially reveal her breasts, one hand to her mouth and the other hand in her tightly-fitting, unzipped pants.

The appeals court held that a jury, which had awarded $95,000 in damages, could indeed have found that Mrs. Braun was unfairly cast in a false light by a magazine "devoted exclusively to sexual exploitation and to disparagement of women." (In agreeing to the publication of her photo in *Chic*, Mrs. Braun and the amusement park executives had the distinct, although obviously mistaken, impression that *Chic* was a fashion magazine.) In other words, the editorial content could have qualified, by any reasonable standard, as "highly offensive."[6]

So was the behavior of another Larry Flynt publication, *Hustler* magazine, that same year in handling the photographs of LaJuan Wood—photographs and text that, a court ruled, placed her in a false light.

Mrs. Wood and her husband, Billy, had gone camping at a state park in Texas. While in a secluded wilderness area, the couple went skinny-dipping in a river, and afterward took several photographs of each other while still in the nude. The Woods kept the photographs private, hidden in a drawer in their bedroom. But a neighbor, Steve Simpson, broke into the Woods' duplex and pilfered some of the photos. Simpson and Kelley Rhoades, who was then Simpson's wife, sent one of the photographs of LaJuan Wood in the nude to *Hustler*, for possible use in what the magazine referred to as its "Beaver Hunt" section. They also submitted a phoney "consent form" that authorized use of the photos. Besides forging LaJuan's signature, Kelley also included some bogus personal information, such as claiming that LaJuan's suppressed desire was to be "tied down and screwed by two bikers."

Hustler's editors did not bother to check the authenticity of the consent form very carefully, and printed the photo of LaJuan Wood, identifying her as "a 22-year-old housewife and mother from Bryan, Texas, whose hobby is collecting arrowheads. Her fantasy is 'to be screwed by two bikers.' " The whole thing may have been intended as a practical joke played on the Woods by their neighbors, but neither LaJuan nor her husband was amused, especially when she began receiving obscene phone calls after the issue of *Hustler* was published. Dealing with her feelings of shame and degradation compelled her to undergo extensive psychological counseling. The Woods sued. A trial jury awarded $150,000 to Mrs. Wood and $25,000 to the husband. An appeals court later reversed the award to the husband, holding that his feelings of emotional distress reflected his concern for his wife, rather than personal damage to himself. But the substantial award to LaJuan Wood was affirmed. The judgment was not based on "*Hustler*'s liability for publicly disclosing the highly private, but truthful, fact of her nudity," the court held, but because the context of the photograph had cast her in a false light.[7]

In a milder, but comparable, case, the *Saturday Evening Post* provided what the court found to be a false and offensive context for a photograph it chose to illustrate an article about taxicab drivers in Washington, DC. Entitled "Never Give a Passenger an Even Break," the piece dwelled on what it said was the rude and conniving behavior of cabbies in the nation's capital, characterizing them as "ill-mannered, brazen, and contemptuous of their patrons . . . dishonest and cheating when opportunity arises." Accompanying the *Post* article was a photograph of a cab driver, Muriel Peay, who evidently was neither impolite nor corrupt. She sued, claiming the article and photo placed her in a false light, and she won.[8]

A wrong or misleading context alone, however, may not win a false light privacy suit if the conduct depicted is not found to be offensive. For example, consider the case of Clarence W. Arrington, whose photograph was used on the cover of *The New York Times* magazine in connection with a lengthy article, "The Black Middle Class: Making It." His photograph, published without his knowledge and consent, had been taken of him walking down a Manhattan street wearing an expensive business suit, carrying a briefcase, and, in general, looking prosperous. Indeed, Mr. Arrington was doing well. He had earned an M.B.A. from Columbia University, and at the time his photo was taken he was a financial analyst with General Motors. Still, he resented being associated with the *Times* magazine article: It was a harsh indictment of materialistic and status-conscious African Americans who, the article contended, were becoming less and less concerned about the plight of their less fortunate African-American brothers and sisters.

Mr. Arrington sued the *Times*, claiming that he did not share the theme of the article or the materialistic views of the persons who had been interviewed. He was placed in a false light, he argued, and as a result he was exposed to contempt and ridicule from his friends and suffered emotional distress. The trial court agreed with him. But the appeals court did not, holding that the *Times* article did not depict him personally as being insensitive, nor was he himself portrayed in an offensive manner.[9]

Similarly, Michael Cibenko, a White male transit officer in New Jersey, sued the publisher of a sociology textbook that contained a photograph of him prodding an African-American man with a stick. The caption beneath the picture read:

> The social status of the offender seems to be the most significant determinant of whether a person will be arrested and convicted for an offense and of the kind of penalty that will be applied. In this picture, a police officer is preventing a black male from falling asleep in a public place. Would the officer be likely to do the same if the "offender" were a well-dressed, middle-aged white person?

Mr. Cibenko claimed that the photograph and context portrayed him "in an awkward, ludicrous, and contemptible light, falsely representing him . . . as being unscrupulous and racially prejudiced." The court disagreed, holding "that the picture and caption are not reasonably capable of conveying the offensive meaning or the innuendo ascribed by the plaintiff as the basis for his invasion of privacy claim,"[10] and therefore dismissed the complaint.

Although the court verdicts in this area seem to be sending mixed signals, the lesson for communicators is nevertheless clear: It is important to make certain that a photograph—any photograph—used to illustrate a situation does what it is supposed to do. Avoid using old, unrelated photos to illustrate articles and stories. The public relations employee who is preparing an article for the company magazine about worker carelessness should not simply drag a file photo of one of the employees working on the assembly line. That employee could claim that you are suggesting he or she is careless.[11] The same advice goes for an advertising agency art director who is tempted to illustrate a public service TV spot about kids and handguns using old file footage from a school playground. The resulting impression—that the kids being shown in the TV spot are armed and dangerous—could prove to be false and expensive.

FICTIONALIZATION

Fictitious, according to *Black's Law Dictionary*, is defined as: "Founded on a fiction; having the character of a fiction; pretended; counterfeit. Feigned, imaginary, not real, false, not genuine, nonexistent. Arbitrarily invented and set up, to accomplish an ulterior object." Fictionalization, then, can be any or all of the above, as they relate to wrongfully placing an individual in a false light, and thereby invading his or her privacy. Most commonly, this category of false light privacy involves enhancing a news article, book, play, or movie by inventing additional dialogue, characters, thoughts, and ideas, and attributing them, falsely, to real persons.

Fictionalization is as old as storytelling, of course—that is to say, as old as mankind—and many journalists over the years have been known to embellish a story or fabricate a quote. Indeed, the first attempt at producing a newspaper in the American colonies, Boston's *Publick Occurrences*, was banned by the royal governor because the publisher, Benjamin Harris, among much else, fabricated and printed in his first and only issue a list of then-recent indiscretions by the King of France. Professional and ethical standards are far higher now in the field of mass communications. But some fictionalization still does occur, and, under certain circumstances, a false light invasion of privacy can result.

Cantrell v. Forest City Publishing Co. is such an example. The case began this way. In 1967, the Silver Bridge across the Ohio River near Point Pleasant, West Virginia, collapsed. Forty-four persons were killed, among them Melvin Cantrell. The Cleveland *Plain Dealer* sent Joseph Eszterhas, a reporter, and a photographer to the scene. Eszterhas wrote several powerful, human-interest articles about the disaster. One of these award-winning pieces focused on the funeral of Mr. Cantrell and the impact of the tragedy on his family. Five months later, Eszterhas was sent back to the Point Pleasant area to write a follow-up article. The reporter and photographer visited the Cantrell home and talked with the Cantrell children, but Mrs. Margaret Cantrell, the widow, was not present. The article that Eszterhas developed from his revisit to Point Pleasant, later published in the Sunday magazine section of the *Plain Dealer*, emphasized the family's poverty-stricken condition—the old, poorly fitting clothes the children wore and the deterioration of the family home. At one point, the text read:

> Margaret Cantrell will talk neither about what happened nor about how they are doing. She wears the same mask of non-expression she wore at the funeral. She is a proud woman. Her world has changed. She says that after it happened, the people in town offered to help them out with money and they refused to take it.

Beyond the misleading impression that the reporter had personally inter-viewed Mrs. Cantrell, there were a number of other flaws in the piece. In particular, statements about the Cantrell family's poverty were exaggerated. She sued for false light invasion of privacy, alleging that the *Plain Dealer* article caused her family members to become objects of pity, and that she and her son suffered mental distress, shame, and humiliation. The trial court awarded her $60,000 in damages, but the appeals court reversed. The Supreme Court of the United States, however, agreed to review the case—*Cantrell v. Forest City Publishing Co.* was only the second invasion of privacy case to reach the Court—and ruled in favor of Mrs. Cantrell. "These were calculated falsehoods," the Su-preme Court opinion said of the *Plain Dealer* article, "and the jury was plainly justified in finding that Eszterhas had portrayed the Cantrells in a false light through knowing or reckless untruth."[12]

Celebrities, too, can recover damages for fictionalization, as baseball star Warren Spahn proved when he sued a company that published a fictitious biography of him. Entitled *The Warren Spahn Story*, the book was a highly flattering portrait of the famous left-handed pitcher who won more than 300 games and was a National League fan favorite for many years. Indeed, the "biography" embellished Spahn's life in many ways, adding luster to his World War II record, for example, and including, as the trial court put it, "a host, a preponderant percentage, of factual errors, distortions and fanciful passages."

Spahn's stature as a public figure might allow for some latitude, the court conceded, but in this case "the findings of fact go far beyond the establishment of minor errors in an otherwise accurate biography":

> The free speech which is encouraged and essential to the operation of a healthy government is something quite different from an individual's attempt to enjoin the publication of a fictitious biography of him. No public interest is served by protecting the dissemination of the latter.[13]

Minor fictionalizations (e.g., trivial and clearly unbelievable falsehoods designed to enhance a movie or short story) normally will not justify a false light privacy suit. Incidental use of fictitious quotes from real celebrities in a historical novel, say, would not likely be actionable, so long as reasonable readers are likely to understand that the quotes are used to add color to what is clearly a work of fiction.[14]

Similarly, a bizarre story in *Penthouse*, "Miss Wyoming Saves the World," described a fictional winner of the Miss Wyoming competition who twirled a baton, but whose real talent was in her sexual promiscuity. The fantasy's central character, whose name was Charlene, performed oral sex on her baton coach, causing him to levitate; the awed contest judges promptly chose her "Miss America," whereupon she then became an ambassador to the world of love and peace. At the time the *Penthouse* article appeared, there was indeed an accomplished baton twirler at the University of Wyoming who had, in fact, won a number of beauty titles, including that of "Miss Wyoming." Charging that the *Penthouse* article would cause others to think her life was the inspiration for "Miss Wyoming Saves the World," she sued. A Wyoming jury found massively in her favor, awarding her $1.5 million in actual damages and $25 million in punitive damages—one of the biggest verdicts of its kind in history.

However, by a 2–1 margin, the federal appeals court reversed *Pring v. Penthouse, International, Ltd.*[15] Although the story, written by a PhD English professor at a university in New Jersey, was described by the court as "a gross, unpleasant, crude, distorted attempt to ridicule the Miss America contest and contestants" and "has no redeeming features whatever," the court said it was too obviously fictional to be taken seriously.

A different kind of fictionalization was represented by *Time, Inc., v. Hill*. In this—the first invasion of privacy case ever ruled on by the Supreme Court—a quiet, private family had become the subject of intense and poorly handled mass media coverage because of the crush of events quite out of their control.

The story began with a jailbreak. In 1952, three convicts escaped from a maximum security prison in the Northeast and, rather than head for the Canadian border, they slipped into a peaceful suburb of Whitemarsh, Pennsylvania, taking over a private home and holding the owner, James Hill, and his wife and five children hostage for 19 hours.[16] The family members were not harmed or molested; in fact, they reported that they had been treated with courtesy, despite the tenseness of the situation. But police found out about the hostages and soon had the Hill home surrounded. When the convicts attempted to escape, two of the three were shot and killed in a gun battle with the police. The trauma of this experience, plus the intense media attention surrounding the 19-hour standoff, prompted the Hill family to move to Connecticut, where, they hoped, they could simply be left alone.

The following year, however, a writer named Joseph Hayes published a novel about a family held hostage by three escaped convicts. Entitled *The Desperate Hours*, the novel was inspired by the Hill family drama, although the author drew on other hostage situations as well. The book differed from actual events in several respects. For one thing, the convict characters in the novel, far from being courteous, were mean and abusive, especially toward the daughter of the family. There is no evidence to suggest that the Hill family was distressed by the novel, but the novel was only the beginning.

A few months later, *The Desperate Hours* would become a play. Drawing favorable reviews on its out-of-town performances, *The Desperate Hours* was soon headed for Broadway. Editors at one of the country's leading magazines, *Life*, decided to do a piece about it—but not just another run-of-the-mill advance story on a Broadway-bound drama. Instead, *Life*'s editors elected to dredge up the Hill family's ordeal and contrast it with the fictional treatment depicted in *The Desperate Hours*. "The play," the *Life* article exclaimed, "is a heart-stopping account of how a family rose to heroism in a crisis." One photograph illustrated a scene from the play, in which the son was being roughed up by one of the convicts. Another photo, captioned "daring daughter," showed the daughter in the play biting the hand of a convict, forcing him to drop the pistol on the floor, while still another photo was of the father hurling the pistol out a window. None of these things had happened to the Hill family. But the editor at *Life* who handled the story decided to spice up the text a bit to give it a stronger, if inaccurate, parallel to the real-life drama.

The Hills sued for invasion of privacy. (Their attorney was Richard M. Nixon; after his two terms as vice president and before he was elected president, Mr. Nixon was a practicing lawyer and, by all accounts, a shrewd and effective one.) Their complaint was that the *Life* article placed them in a false light by implying that the fictionalized, sensationalized events shown in the photographs reflected their own experiences as hostages. The trial court jury found in favor of the Hills, awarding them $75,000 in damages. But that victory was only Round 1 in a wrenching, prolonged legal battle that would last for more than 10 years.

An appeals court found the dollar award excessive and ordered a retrial. The Hills won again, but this time the judgment was for $30,000. The award was affirmed by the appeals court, but eventually the case made its way to the Supreme Court of the United States, with *Life* arguing that a constitutional question—freedom of the press to discuss matters that are newsworthy—was involved. It would become one of the first privacy cases ever taken up by the Supreme Court, and the Court did so in the wake of its previous ruling in the related matter of defamation, *New York Times v. Sullivan*. This historic case, discussed in chapter 9, was a sweeping victory for freedom of the press; *Sullivan* opened the doors for full, and even inaccurate, debate of public events and personalities, so long as the discussion was not prompted by malice (i.e., printing a deliberate lie or being unduly reckless with regard to the truth). The connection between a public event and the Hill family's private ordeal struck some observers as tenuous, but the Court made it anyway. Essentially ruling in favor of *Life* magazine, the Court sent the case back for still another trial, holding that the Hill family could win only if actual malice could be proved. *Life* magazine was careless, sloppy, and negligent perhaps, but was its behavior malicious? Actual malice, the Hills knew, is difficult to prove. At this point, they threw in the towel.

The Supreme Court's ruling in *Time, Inc., v. Hill* was a powerful victory for freedom of expression, although, some critics argue, an individual's right to privacy was curtailed somewhat in the process. The majority opinion, written by Justice Brennan (who had also written the opinion in *Sullivan*) said that incidental errors resulting from simple negligence should not be permitted to inhibit discussion of important public events:

> Erroneous statement is no less inevitable in . . . [discussion of other activities, such as a theatrical production] than in the case of comment on public affairs, and in both, if innocent or merely negligent . . . it must be protected if the freedoms of expression are to have the "breathing space" that they "need to survive."[17]

Thus was constitutional protection accorded, for the first time, in a false light privacy matter. Persons like the Hills, who are dragged into the public media against their wishes and depicted in an untruthful manner, would henceforth have to prove that the false light was cast on them deliberately, knowingly, or recklessly. Our society, *Time, Inc., v. Hill* made clear, cherishes privacy, but it cherishes freedom of expression even more.

THE FAULT REQUIREMENT

Again, the two criteria for winning a false light invasion of privacy suit are: (a) that the false light in which the other person is placed would be highly offensive to a reasonable person, and (b) that the person who publicized the false and offensive information knew it was false at the time—either that or acted in reckless disregard of whether the material was true. The latter criterion is called *the fault requirement*. It was first applied by the Supreme Court to false light privacy in 1967, in *Time, Inc., v. Hill*. In *Hill*, the majority opinion held: "Material and substantial falsification is the test. . . . Factual error . . . [is] insufficient to an award of damages for false statements unless actual malice— knowledge that the statements are false or in reckless disregard of the truth—is alleged and proved."[18]

The actual malice standard requires a showing of intent to harm through falsity—a purposeful disregard for the truth. A lesser standard of fault would be simple negligence (i.e., carelessness, unintentional error). The Supreme Court adopted the actual malice standard in defamation cases, where public officials are concerned, in an effort to open up important discussion of civic matters. Such discussions should be wide open and robust, the Court ruled, and the fewer the restrictions placed on them the better. However, this does not mean that deliberate falsehoods should be protected. A person who is proven to have intentionally or recklessly spread lies about someone else is guilty of actual malice.

That is the standard of fault the Supreme Court specified in *Time, Inc., v. Hill* to govern false light privacy cases. However, the Supreme Court has modified its actual malice requirement somewhat in defamation cases. In its 1974 ruling in *Gertz v. Robert Welch, Inc.*,[19] the Supreme Court held that public officials and public figures must prove actual malice, but added that individual states may allow private persons to win a defamation case by proving simple negligence—careless, unintentional error—not actual malice. Whether this distinction will change the law of false light privacy as well remains an unanswered question. In one of its earliest-ever rulings on a case involving false light privacy, *Cantrell v. Forest City Publishing Co.*, the Supreme Court ducked that particular issue. Justice Potter Stewart's majority opinion in *Cantrell* noted that the fabrications by the Cleveland *Plain Dealer* reporter were deliberate:

> Consequently, this case presents no occasion to consider whether a State may constitutionally apply a more relaxed standard of liability for a publisher or broadcaster of false statements injurious to a private individual under a false-light theory of invasion of privacy, or whether the constitutional standard announced in *Time, Inc., v. Hill* applies to all false-light cases.[20]

If the actual malice standard is modified, either by the Supreme Court or individual state action, then the actual malice rule might apply only to public officials and public figures, whereas the negligence rule will apply to everyone else. Some scholars predict this will be done.[21]

INTENTIONAL INFLICTION OF EMOTIONAL DISTRESS

Until fairly recently, the law shied away from protecting an individual's interest in emotional and mental tranquility in and of itself. As late as the mid-1930s, the *Restatement of Torts* declared:

> The interest in mental and emotional tranquility and, therefore, in freedom from mental and emotional disturbance is not, as a thing in itself, regarded as of sufficient importance to require others to refrain from conduct intended or recognizably likely to cause such disturbance.

More recently, however, the law has come to recognize that sometimes mental distress could be so extreme as to bring on physical or mental illness and should have been foreseen by those who caused it. If someone intentionally subjects another person to such intense mental suffering, the perpetrator could be found liable for whatever harm resulted. By 1947, the *Restatement of Torts* carried this language: "One who, without a privilege to do so, intentionally causes severe emotional distress to another is liable (a) for such emotional distress, and (b) for bodily harm resulting from it."[22] In other words, individuals have the right to be free from negligent interference with their physical well-being, and one's physical well-being can be affected by a deliberate effort to upset one's mental tranquility.

Cases alleging intentional infliction of emotional distress, involving outrageous conduct calculated to cause mental anguish, have arisen out of excommunication from a church, religious harassment and religious shunning,[23] hounding for collection of an overdue bill,[24] mimicking a person with a stuttering problem,[25] solicitations to sexual intercourse,[26] and even an unexpected eviction notice.[27] However, a few cases have arisen directly out of mass media-related situations, and thus in recent years intentional infliction of emotional distress has become another tort affecting mass communications litigation.

Intentional infliction of emotional distress refers to the impact of communications to damage one's psyche, as opposed to one's reputation. In some respects, intentional infliction of emotional distress is much like an invasion of privacy. In others, it resembles defamation. Some states have incorporated intentional infliction of emotional distress into their defamation laws, whereas others regard intentional infliction of emotional distress as a separate wrong. In actual practice, lawsuits have been brought alleging all three—defamation of character, invasion of privacy, and intentional infliction of emotional distress—leaving it to the courts to sort out which torts, if any, might apply in a given situation.

Briefly, before awarding a judgment in an intentional infliction of emotional distress lawsuit, the court must be satisfied that: (a) the conduct of the perpetrator must be outrageous or highly offensive to a reasonable person; (b) severe mental distress, resulting in emotional or physical damage, did result; and (c) the perpetrator intended to cause such distress—either by acting deliberately or through a reckless disregard for the risks involved.

Such cases are difficult to win, especially involving a mass media defendant. For example, consider *Hood v. Naeter Brothers Publishing Co.*, tried in Missouri in 1978. *The Southwest Missourian*, a newspaper in Cape Girardeau, published the name and address (accurately taken from police reports) of an eyewitness to a liquor store robbery in which one person was killed—this while the suspects were still at large. Plaintiff Hood sued the newspaper, stating that as a result of the publication he had lived in constant fear, had to change his residence repeatedly, had become suspicious of all African-American persons, and had had to submit to the care of a psychiatrist. He claimed that the newspaper knew, or should have known, that his exposure as an eyewitness while the killers were still at large constituted outrageous behavior, and he sued for intentional infliction of emotional distress. But the trial court ruled in favor of the newspaper, holding that the conduct was not highly offensive. The appeals court agreed:

> The liability [for intentional infliction of emotional distress] clearly does not extend to mere insults, indignities, threats, arrogancies, petty oppression, or other trivialities. The rough edges of our society are still in need of a good deal of filing down, and in the meantime plaintiffs must necessarily be expected and required to be hardened to a certain amount of rough language, and to occasional acts that are definitely inconsiderate and unkind.[28]

The most famous case in this area, *Hustler Magazine v. Falwell*,[29] was decided by the Supreme Court in 1988. The key players were the Rev. Jerry Falwell—a nationally known minister, commentator on politics and public affairs, and leader of The Moral Majority, a conservative action group—and Larry Flynt, publisher of the irreverent and often-raunchy magazine, *Hustler*.

The inside front cover of *Hustler*'s November 1983 issue was what the magazine referred to as a "parody" of a Campari Liqueur advertisement featuring the name and picture of Mr. Falwell; it was entitled, "Jerry Falwell Talks About His First Time." (The format resembled actual Campari ads, in which celebrities recounted their "first times"—of sampling Campari.) In this presentation, however, it was clear that the "first time" had to do with sex, and Mr. Falwell, in an alleged interview, was portrayed as having as his "first time" a drunken, incestuous rendezvous with his mother in an outdoor privy. The *Hustler* presentation depicted Mr. Falwell as a hypocrite who preaches only when he is drunk and his mother as drunken and immoral. The magazine's table of contents listed the inside front cover as "Fiction: Ad and Personality Parody"; in tiny print at the bottom of the offending page was a disclaimer: "ad parody—not to be taken seriously."

Mr. Falwell, however, did indeed take it seriously, firing off a lawsuit for libel, invasion of privacy, and intentional infliction of emotional distress. A Virginia judge summarily threw out the invasion of privacy claim, and the trial jury found against Mr. Falwell on the libel allegation. But the jury did award Mr. Falwell a total of $200,000 on the intentional infliction of emotional distress charge. The Fourth U.S. Circuit Court of Appeals affirmed the judgment.

The U.S. Supreme Court, however, reversed, holding that to punish a media defendant for its parody of a public figure such as Mr. Falwell could effectively silence political cartoonists, satirists, and others who attempt to poke fun at public personalities, and, in the process, curtail the free flow of ideas and opinions on matters of public interest and concern. The unanimous opinion, written by Chief Justice Rehnquist, conceded that the parody of Mr. Falwell was "offensive to him, and doubtless gross and repugnant in the eyes of most," but insisted that the members of the Court "have been particularly vigilant to ensure that individual expressions of ideas remain free from governmentally imposed sanctions. The First Amendment recognizes no such thing as a 'false' idea."

Because of this, public officials and public figures—as defined in *New York Times v. Sullivan* and *Gertz v. Robert Welch* (see chap. 9)—cannot win an intentional infliction of emotional distress lawsuit without showing that the offending statements were published with actual malice and presented as truth. Satire of public figures, then, is clearly exempt.

As Justice Rehnquist pointed out, *Hustler* magazine "is at best a distant cousin [of distinguished political journals] . . . and a rather poor relation at that." But the term *outrageousness* in the area of political and social discourse has an inherent subjectivity about it that would allow a jury to impose liability on the basis of the jurors' tastes or views, or perhaps on the basis of their dislike of a particular expression. *Hustler Magazine v. Falwell* is an important case, limiting as it does the chances for public personalities to recover for intentional infliction of emotional distress. How private plaintiffs will be affected in such cases in years to come remains an open question.

CONCLUSION

As has been seen, false light invasion of privacy occurs when (a) something factually untrue has been communicated about an individual, or (b) the communication of true information carries a false implication. The falsity—either literally or through a wrong context—must be material and substantial, and must reach enough of an audience to constitute "widespread publicity." As such, false light invasions of privacy have been regarded by some as a threat to freedom of expression. "If our aim is to never resort to falsehood," the English philosopher A. J. Ayer observed, "it would be prudent for us to abstain from using language altogether."[30]

Because of the vagueness of the false light tort, and because of the possibility that it could inhibit the free flow of information in our society, some legal scholars argue that the tort should be scrapped. Indeed, at least two states—Missouri and North Carolina—have formally rejected the false light tort altogether. Most injuries from untruths will, and should, be handled as defamation actions, critics of false light argue; those untruths that cannot be considered defamatory are probably too trivial to worry about—either that or they may be protected speech involving matters of legitimate public concern. "False light has proved in practice to illuminate nothing," wrote law professor Diane Leenheer Zimmerman. "From the viewpoint of coherent First Amendment theory, it has served instead to deepen the darkness."[31]

Indeed, the courts seem to be less impressed with false light claims, and with claims of intentional infliction of emotional distress, now than they were a generation ago. Even so, in most jurisdictions, it remains possible to invade one's privacy by presenting the person in a false light. In advertising, public relations, and journalism, two common sense precautions are in order: Do not portray an individual wrongfully, through words, implication, or context. Do not use stock photographs taken for one purpose to illustrate something different. If one is accurate, both literally and figuratively, false light will not become a problem.

V

INTELLECTUAL PROPERTY

Trademarks, Patents, and Trade Secrets

Copyright, trademarks, and patents are typically grouped into an area of the law that has become known as *intellectual property*. Trade secrets are sometimes included in this area as well. Most of this chapter is devoted to trademarks because this is an area of the law that has a substantial impact on advertising and public relations. It also deals briefly with patents and trade secrets. The next chapter focuses entirely on copyright.

The constitutional origins of intellectual property, at least for copyright and patents, can be traced to Article I, § 8, of the U.S. Constitution, which provides, among other powers, that Congress shall have the authority "[t]o promote the Progress of Science and useful Arts, by securing for limited Times to Authors and Inventors the exclusive Right to their respective Writings and Discoveries."[1] Patents and copyrights are regulated almost exclusively by federal statutes (Titles 35 and 17 of the U.S. Code, respectively) because Congress has chosen to invoke the preemption doctrine granted under Article VI of the U.S. Constitution (known as the "supremacy clause"), which provides, in part: ". . . This Constitution, and the Laws of the United States which shall be made in Pursuance thereof; and all Treaties made, or which shall be made, under the Authority of the United States, shall be the supreme law of the Land; and the Judges in every State shall be bound thereby, any Thing in the Constitution or Laws of any State to the Contrary notwithstanding."[2]

Exclusive federal regulation of copyrights and patents is also justified under the "commerce clause" in Article I, § 8 of the U.S. Constitution, which provides that Congress shall have the power "[t]o regulate Commerce with foreign Nations, and among the several States, and with the Indian Tribes. . . ."[3]

In contrast, trademarks and trade secrets involve both state and federal law, as well as common law, although state laws are not permitted to conflict with federal law. Trademark law can be found primarily in Title 15 of the United States Code (known as the "Lanham Act" or the "Trademark Act of 1946"). Trademarks, which identify goods, and service marks, which identify a service, may be registered and have protection under either state or federal statutes. Trade secrets usually are not registered under federal law, except as they relate to a patent application, because registration is ordinarily public record, which would defeat the purpose of the trade secret.

PATENTS, INCLUDING CREATION AND DURATION

The U.S. Copyright Office is an arm of the Library of Congress, whereas the U.S. Patent and Trademark Office (which, as the name indicates, handles both patents and trademarks) is an agency in the Department of Commerce, and is headed by the Commissioner of Patents and Trademarks, an Assistant Secretary of Commerce. Patents, trademarks, and copyright are all forms of exclusive (i.e., monopolistic) control that owners, who can be individuals or companies, can exercise to ensure that others generally cannot market, use, or sell the work, invention, or mark without the owner's consent. Until June 8, 1995, patents generally had protection for 17 years from the date they were issued, after which they passed to the public domain and could be used, marketed, or sold to anyone without consent. In 1989, Congress revised the patent law, including establishing a new 20-year term for protection, measured strictly from the filing date, for any patent filed after June 8, 1995.[4] In some cases, the 20-year period can be extended for a maximum of 5 years when marketing time was lost because of regulatory delay.[5] The 20-year period was chosen because it has been the standard of the rest of the industrialized world for some time. The new law also grants greater authority to the U.S. government to seize imports when they enter the United States when they infringe on patents owned by a U.S. company or citizen, and it creates a means by which a provisional application can be filed while the inventor prepares the regular application, which must be filed within 1 year.

When a patent expires for a popular drug or invention, the impact on the marketplace can be strong, as witnessed by the proliferation of marketers of the artificial sweetener, aspartame, when the Monsato Co.'s patent expired in December 1992. Although the name NutraSweet continued to be protected as a trademark, other companies could and did market aspartame under their own name, or simply as a generic product with approval of the U.S. Food and Drug Administration (FDA), which regulates artificial sweeteners. Securing a patent is typically only the first step in the process. Before the invention can be marketed, approval from other federal and state agencies may be needed. For example, a new food or drug product would probably require a green light from the FDA. Protecting a name under which the invention is to be sold would require compliance with provisions of trademark laws, and probably trademark registration at some point. Unlike the trademark and copyright laws, patent law is incredibly complex, and the process of obtaining a patent is expensive, time-consuming, and complicated. Even most attorneys have a limited knowledge of patent law. The government filing fee alone is $375–$750 (if the company has at least 500 employees), and the costs of a search, which is necessary to establish the novelty of the invention, can add up to thousands of dollars.

In June 1995, new patent rules took effect that allow inventors to file provisional patent applications for a fee of $75, under which the patent is protected from infringement for a year without having to demonstrate that the invention has already been built and used (a requirement for protection under traditional patent law). During the 1-year interim, the person is given the oportunity to market the invention without fear of the idea being stolen.

There are three basic types of patents—utility, plant, and design. Patents on mechanical devices, electrical and electronic circuits, chemicals, and similar items are known as *utility patents*.[6] *Plant patents* apply to the invention or asexual reproduction of a distinct new variety of a natural plant,[7] and *design patents* are issued for new, original, and ornamental designs.[8] In 1994, the U.S. Court of Appeals for the Federal Circuit, which hears all appeals from all decisions in patent infringement suits,[9] ruled that computer software could be patented, although mathematical formulas and algorithms cannot be patented. In *In re Alappat*, the court reasoned that software "creates a new machine, because a general purpose computer in effect becomes a special purpose computer once it is programmed."[10] Under the federal statute, an invention cannot be patented if "the subject matter as a whole would have been obvious at the time the invention was made to a person having ordinary skill in the art. . . ."[11] Many patent applications have failed because the invention was too obvious.

Patent infringement is a serious matter, and can result in extensive damages, as illustrated in the infringement suit filed by Polaroid against Eastman Kodak over instant photography.[12] When the dust settled in 1986, Eastman Kodak was ordered to pay Polaroid more than $1 billion in damages, and was prohibited from further sales of instant photo cameras, film, and related products. The suit was based on patents granted to Polaroid in the 1970s. Because the stakes can be quite high, patent holders for popular inventions rigorously defend their rights even against small-time entrepreneurs and companies. Patents are generally granted on a first-come, first-serve basis, and the race to the finish line can be intense when competitors battle. When two or more claimants apply separately for a patent on essentially similar inventions, the PTO will hold an interference proceeding, complete with motions and testimony, to ascertain the rightful inventor.

TRADE SECRETS

Trade secrets can take many forms, including formulas, plans, processes, devices, and compounds. The distinguishing characteristics of a trade secret include: (a) it has commercial value by virtue of the fact that it gives the owner a business advantage over competitors because they are not familiar with it, and (b) it is known only to those individuals who have a need to know it. Under the state and federal laws governing trade secrets, a trade secret must be kept secret, particularly from competitors or potential competitors, to warrant protection. For example, North Carolina defines misappropriation of a trade secret as the "acquisition, disclosure, or use of a trade secret of another without express or implied authority or consent"[13] unless the trade secret was derived independently, by reverse engineering or from someone who had authority to disclose the secret. The Illinois Trade Secrets Act defines a *trade secret* as "information, including but not limited to, technical or non-technical data, a formula, pattern, compilation, program, device, method, technique, drawing, process, financial data. . . .[14]

Remedies for appropriation of trade secrets include damages and injunctions, whenever appropriate, especially where it is likely that a trade secret will be further disclosed if an injunction is not issued, and that such disclosure would likely result in irreparable harm to the business. For example, Pepsico successfully sought an injunction in a district court in Illinois in 1994 to prevent one of its former officers from assuming a position with Quaker Oats for 6 months and preventing him from forever disclosing trade secrets regarding the company's annual operating plan. The Seventh Circuit U.S. Court of Appeals upheld the injunction.[15] The annual plan ("Strategic Plan") included marketing strategies for Pepsico to position its AllSport drink to compete with Quaker's Gatorade.

Federal statutes, including the Freedom of Information Act,[16] which otherwise requires disclosure of information held by federal agencies, contain exemptions for trade secrets. In fact, the federal Trade Secrets Act,[17] imposes criminal sanctions on federal employees who disclose certain kinds of confidential information disclosed to the government, including trade secrets and confidential statistical data.[18]

The Supreme Court of the United States has decided few cases over the years directly involving trade secrets, probably because the lower federal courts generally are not involved in such cases unless they involve parties from two or more different states ("diversity jurisdiction") or concern federal employees or federal law. Since 1974, in fact, the Supreme Court has decided only six cases focusing on trade secrets. In a 1974 case, *Kewanee Oil Co. v. Bicron Corp.*,[19] the Court held that Ohio's trade secret law was not preempted by federal patent law, noting among other points that the federal patent policy of encouraging invention is not harmed by the existence of other incentives to invention, such as state trade secret statutes. In 1986, in *Dow Chemical v. United States*,[20] the Court held that the U.S. Environmental Protection Agency (EPA) was acting within its authority when it employed a commercial aerial photographer to take photographs from public airspace of a chemical plant after the agency had been denied access by the company for an onsite inspection. The Court said such observations were legitimate even though the company's competitors might be barred from such action under state trade secrets law. The opinion noted that governments generally do not try to appropriate trade secrets from private enterprises, and that state unfair competition laws do not define the Fourth Amendment's provision regarding unreasonable search and seizure. In 1984, in *Ruckelshaus v. Monsanto Co.*,[21] the Court held that, under certain conditions, disclosure of a trade secret by a government agency could constitute a "taking" under the Fifth Amendment, particularly when such disclosure interferes with what the Court called "reasonable investment-backed expectations." Without deciding whether there actually was a Fifth Amendment violation in the case, the Court said that trade secrets that enjoyed protection under state law could constitute "property" for purposes of the Fifth Amendment, despite their intangible nature. The Court pointed out that the EPA had promised confidentiality in exchange for disclosure of the information to the agency that the company had designated as trade secrets at the time of submission.

TRADEMARKS, INCLUDING FEDERAL AND STATE PROTECTION AND RENEWAL

Trademarks are extremely important in advertising and public relations, as witnessed by the fact that trademark battles can be intense and drawn out, with millions and sometimes even billions of dollars at stake. The basic purpose of a trademark is to enable the consumer, which can range from a private individual to a business conglomerate, to identify the origin of a product or service. Identifying the origin does not necessarily mean knowing the specific manufacturer, distributor, or franchise. The idea is that the consumer should be able to have confidence that all goods with a specific trademark are associated with a common source. For example, when a viewer sees a television commercial for Hershey's Kisses, the person can assume that all Kisses come from Hershey's. That does not mean, however, that the consumer can assume that all candy bearing the Hershey's trademark is necessarily actually made by the same company, but simply that Hershey's has given its consent for and presumably imposed its standards on the distribution of the products under its name. In other words, trademarks provide some indication of quality assurance. Through the effective marketing and communication of its trademark, an owner can build up invaluable market good will. Think about the value of trademarks such as Coca-Cola, McDonald's, IBM, Kodak, Xerox, Sony, and Walt Disney. Coca-Cola, which has already celebrated its 100th anniversary, is such a valuable trademark that the corporation has licensed its own line of clothing. Walt Disney licenses or produces thousands of products, including toys, movies, clothes, games, and, of course, its own entertainment complexes throughout the world. Neither Disney nor Coca-Cola actually manufacture the goods bearing their names; instead, they have contracts with other firms granting permission for the use of their marks.

In 1996, some coffee companies who sell their products on the World Wide Web (WWW) got a warning from Sun Microsystems, which owns the trademark

"Java" for its computer programming language. Sun was concerned that its trademark was being infringed on by the use of the term *java* in some of the coffee companies' Internet addresses. According to press reports, there was a bit of irony in that several of the companies had used Sun's Java language to create the sites.[22]

Service marks are essentially the same as trademarks, except that they identify services rather than goods. Famous service marks include Hertz, Avis, Home Box Office, The Movie Channel, Showtime, Citicorp, True Value, and Minit-Lube. To avoid repetition, the term *trademark* is used herein to refer to both trademarks and service marks.

The Patent and Trademark Office (PTO) handles both trademarks and patents, but trademark registration is much different and far less expensive than that for patents. In fact, copyright and trademark registration involve quite similar processes, although they are administered by different federal agencies. But the similarities between trademarks and copyright end there. Unlike copyright and patents, trademarks do not derive their origin from the U.S. Constitution, although the authority of Congress to regulate trademarks and service marks comes from the Constitution—more specifically, the infamous commerce clause mentioned earlier in this chapter. Trademarks and service marks are statutory creations of state and federal government. Because trademark laws vary considerably from state to state, state laws will not be discussed here. However, some trademarks and service marks—those that are not used nor intended to be used in interstate and/or international commerce between the United States and another country—can be registered and protected only under state law. Before a trademark or service mark can be registered under federal law (i.e., the Lanham Act), the owner must either use the mark on goods that are shipped or sold in interstate or international commerce, or have a bona fide intention to use the mark in such commerce.[23]

Until the Trademark Law Revision Act of 1988,[24] which became effective November 16, 1989, a trademark had to have been used in some form of interstate commerce. But the new law permits registration so long as there is a bona fide intent to use it in interstate commerce. Nevertheless, trademarks that are strictly for intrastate use are registered with the Secretary of State in the state where they will be used.

Even colors can be trademarked, under the right circumstances, as demonstrated in a 1995 Supreme Court of the United States decision. In *Qualitex Company v. Jacobson Products, Inc.,*[25] a unanimous Court held that the Lanham Trademark Act of 1946 does allow trademark registration of a color. The opinion, written by Justice Breyer, said that the special shade of green-gold used to identify dry cleaning press pads made by Qualitex had acquired the requisite secondary meaning under the Lanham Act. Jacobson Products, a competitor to Qualitex, had challenged the trademark registration, unsuccessfully arguing that such registration would create uncertainty about what shades of color a competitor could use and that it was unworkable because of the limited supply of colors. Qualitex won in U.S. District Court, but lost in the

Ninth Circuit Court of Appeals. The Supreme Court reversed the appellate court decision.

Even sounds can be registered. In 1978, the Trademark Trial and Appeal Board recognized the combination of the musical notes "G, E, and C" used by the National Broadcasting Company as a valid trademark, while denying the registration of the sound of a ship's bell.[26] The roar of the MGM lion has been registered as a trademark for some time. Harley-Davidson, Inc., which already owns the rights to the word *hog*, applied for a trademark on its engine sound in 1994, but several competitors, including Suzuki, Honda, and Kawasaki, opposed the registration. The final word will come from the PTO after hearings in which the opposition will have its say. In July 1994, before he was acquitted on two murder counts more than a year later, O.J. Simpson applied for registration of the mark "O.J." for use on a series of goods, including clothing, footballs, video games, playing cards, newsletters, and jigsaw puzzles. In August 1995, Simpson's lawyers sued several dozen clothing manufacturers and retail stores for selling goods with Simpson's name or likeness. In 1994, singer/songwriter Bob Dylan sued Apple Computer for trademark infringement, seeking damages and an injunction to stop Apple's use of *Dylan* as a trademark for its new Dynamic Language software. Bob Dylan got his name from poet/author Dylan Thomas.[27] Also in 1994, Microsoft Corporation was finally permitted to trademark *Windows* after the application was first denied amid strong opposition from competitors such as IBM, who eventually dropped their opposition.[28]

The registration process and protection under federal law for trademarks and service marks are the same. (See the appendices for sample registration forms.) Under the Lanham Act, a *trademark* is defined as ". . . any word, name, symbol, or device, or any combination thereof adopted and used by a manufacturer or merchant to identify his or her goods or services."[29] Thus, a trademark can be a slogan, design, or distinct sound so long as it identifies and distinguishes the goods or services from those of others. The key characteristics are identification and distinction.

Among the other changes wrought by the Trademark Revision Act of 1988 is that use prior to registration of the trademark is no longer necessary. Now the trademark owner needs only to have a bona fide intention to use the mark. The new law also cut the term of registration in half—from 20 years to 10 years. Unlike copyrights and patents, which have limited duration, trademarks can last indefinitely if the owner takes appropriate steps to ensure that infringers are prosecuted and that the mark does not go onto the public domain. Protection can also be lost by abandonment. Contrary to popular myth, registration is not necessary for a trademark to have protection. As with copyright, as discussed shortly, there are some important advantages to registration:

1. Provides *prima facie* evidence of first use of the mark in interstate commerce and the validity of the registration.
2. Permits the owner to sue in federal court (U.S. District Court) for infringement.

3. Allows lost profits, court costs, attorneys' fees, criminal penalties, and treble damages, in some cases, to be sought.
4. Serves as constructive notice of an ownership claim, preventing someone from claiming that the trademark was used because of a good faith belief that no one else had claim to it. In other words, once the mark is registered, any potential user has an obligation to check the registry to ascertain that no one else owns the mark.
5. Establishes a basis for foreign registration.

Registration is a fairly simple process, although it is more complicated than copyright registration and much easier than securing a patent. The owner or his or her attorney files (a) an application form (available from the PTO), (b) a drawing of the mark, (c) a $245 filing fee for each class of goods or services for which the owner is applying, and (d) three specimens showing actual use of the mark on goods or services if the mark has been used in commerce. Once the PTO has received the application materials, a Trademark Examining Attorney must decide if the mark can actually be registered. This decision is then sent to the applicant about 3 months after the application is filed. A refusal can be appealed to the Trademark Trial and Appeal Board, an administrative tribunal in the PTO. Further refusal can then be appealed to a U.S. District Court and the U.S. Court of Appeals for the Federal Circuit. The Supreme Court of the United States has jurisdiction to hear further appeals, but rarely does so. Once approval is granted, the mark is published in the *Trademark Official Gazette*, a weekly bulletin from the PTO. Anyone opposing the registration has 30 days after the publication to file a protest with the Trademark Trial and Appeal Board, which acts like a trial court. If there is no opposition, about 12 weeks after the mark is published, the registration then becomes official if the application was based on actual use in commerce. If the application is based on an intention to use the mark in commerce, the trademark owner then has 6 months to either use the mark in commerce or request a 6-month extension. (Once the mark is used, a Statement of Use form must be filed.) As of January 1, 1996, there is a rebuttable presumption that if a trademark is not used for 3 years, it has been abandoned. Under a rebuttable presumption, the owner would have the burden of demonstrating that the trademark was in use in any infringement suit.

Advertising and public relations specialists should be familiar with the registration process because it can play a major role in determining the outcome of an infringement suit or a suit over ownership of the mark. A good start is the PTO booklet, *Basic Facts About Trademarks*.[30] The U.S. Trademark Association, a private organization in New York City, also distributes informative materials, and the American Bar Association's Section on Intellectual Property Law has published a booklet, *What Is a Trademark?*[31]

Grounds on which marks can be excluded from registration include that the mark:

1. Disparages or falsely suggests a connection with people, organizations, beliefs, or national symbols, or brings them into contempt or disrepute.
2. Consists of or simulates the flag, coat of arms, or other insignia of the United States, a state, a city, or any foreign country.
3. Is immoral, deceptive, or scandalous.
4. Is the name, portrait, or signature of a living person unless he or she has given permission.
5. Is the name, portrait, or signature of a deceased U.S. president while his surviving spouse is alive unless the spouse has given consent.
6. Is so similar to a mark previously registered that it would be likely to confuse or deceive a reasonable person.
7. Is simply descriptive or deceptively misdescriptive of the goods or services.

If an applicant can demonstrate that a mark already being used in commerce has become distinctive enough that the public now identifies the goods or services with the mark, it can be registered even if it is merely descriptive. For example, *World's Finest* is a registered trademark of World's Finest Chocolate, Inc.

Trademark registration is not restricted to commercial enterprises. Nonprofit organizations, trade associations, and other groups, as well as individuals, can register trademarks. For example, the Society of Professional Journalists (SPJ) registered its name and logo—along with the name, Sigma Delta Chi—as trademarks in 1991. Trade names such as International Business Machines Corporation and Pepsi-Cola Bottling Company cannot be registered as trademarks under the federal statute, but the name associated with the product or service (i.e., International Business Machines, IBM, Pepsi-Cola, Pepsi, etc.) can be registered, and the corporation name can be filed and registered with the appropriate official (usually the Secretary of State) in each state.

Some of the owners of popular trademarks, such as Xerox, IBM, Kleenex, and Kodak, sometimes purchase ads in professional publications such as *Editor & Publisher, Broadcasting*, and the *Quill* (published by SPJ), informing journalists that their names are registered trademarks and should be identified as such. Many famous former trademarks, such as cornflakes, linoleum, mimeograph, escalator, and raisin bran, went into public domain, and thus lost their protection as trademarks because they were abandoned or the owners did not aggressively fight infringers. Some companies often send out press releases and buy ads in trade publications requesting that their trademarks be used as a proper adjective in connection with their products and services, and not as a verb. Advertisers are particularly irked when news stories mention trademarks without identifying them as such.

The Associated Press Stylebook and Libel Manual notes, in its "trademark" entry, "In general, use a generic equivalent unless the trademark name is essential to the story."[32] The *Stylebook* also says that trademarks should be capitalized when they appear. Some companies have a reputation for notifying newspapers, magazines, and radio and television stations when they believe their trademarks have been used inappropriately. They do this because it is one way to demonstrate a strong effort to protect the marks in case an infringement occurs and they have to counter the claim from a defendant that the mark has become generic, and thus may no longer be worthy of protection. Although a company would have no real basis for claiming infringement simply because a news or feature story made generic use of a trademark, the savvy advertiser and public relations practitioner reminds reporters, editors, and other journalists from time to time that good journalistic practice dictates appropriate acknowledgment of trademarks.

Thousands of court battles have been fought over trademarks over the years about products from beer to cars. Even universities have entered the fray. In 1989, Toyota and Mead Data General fought in U.S. District Court over Toyota's use of Lexus as the trademark for its new line of luxury cars. Mead Data argued that the car line name was so similar to Lexis, the trademark for Mead's computerized information retrieval service, that consumers would be confused. Toyota argued that consumers did not confuse *Pulsar* cars by Nissan with *Pulsar* watches or *Lotus* computer software with *Lotus* autos. Ultimately, U.S. District Court Judge David N. Edelstein agreed with Toyota and permitted the registration, and the Second Circuit U.S. Court of Appeals upheld the decision.[33] In 1990, Toyota also changed the logo for the cars under its own name to a 1 with three ellipses.[34]

In 1989, the PTO Trademark Trial and Appeal Board affirmed the decision of the Trademark Examining Attorney that Churchill Downs, Inc., in Louisville, Kentucky, be allowed to register The Kentucky Derby as a trademark for use on various consumer goods. The registration had been challenged by a gift shop operator who argued that the slogan was merely descriptive or generic. Products licensed include a Derby Pie, a great chocolate and pecan pie that has spawned numerous copycats, none of which can bear the Derby Pie trademark without consent. In the same year, Harvard University became the last Ivy League school to register its name as a trademark. More than 100 colleges and universities have registered their names as trademarks. Usually the schools then license their products through one of the major licensing firms for a set fee and a percentage of the profits from the sale of products. Some registration attempts have been unsuccessful, such as the G. Anheuser-Busch Inc.'s failed effort with the mark, LA, for its low alcohol beer. The Seventh Circuit U.S. Court of Appeals upheld the decision of a U.S. District Court that LA was merely descriptive, and thus had not acquired the requisite secondary meaning, or distinctiveness, as described earlier. According to the court, the common-sense view is: "... that, as a practical matter, initials do not usually differ significantly in their trademark role from the description words that they represent ... [and thus] ... there is a heavy burden on a trademark claimant seeking to show an independent meaning of initials apart from the descriptive words which are their source."[35]

Once the federal registration is issued by the PTO (usually about 6 months after the application is filed if there is no opposition from another party and if the Trademark Examining Attorney gives the OK), the owner gives notice of registration by using (a) the ® symbol; (b) the phrase, Registered in U.S. Patent and Trademark Office; or (c) the abbreviation, Reg. U.S. Pat. & Tm. Off. These registration symbols cannot be used before registration, but the owner is free to use ™ or ℠ as symbols for trademark and service mark, respectively, although he or she is not required to do so. Recall that, under the federal statute, registration is not required for trademark protection, although there are many advantages to registration.

The Trademark Law Revision Act of 1988 made another important change that may have an impact on some nontraditional forms of communication, especially some parodies. The Act permits a trademark owner to recover damages and get an injunction for product or service misrepresentation. The provision only applies to commercial use, not political communication or editorial content, but it appears aimed at specific product disparagement, although some forms may continue to be protected, such as that in *L.L. Bean, Inc. v. Drake Publishers, Inc.*[36] When Drake published a sex catalog parodying L.L. Bean's famous clothing catalog, L.L. Bean filed suit, claiming that L.L. Bean's *Back-To-School-Sex-Catalog* violated Maine's antidilution statute. (Such statutes are aimed at protecting trademarks and similar names from suffering disparagement, and thus having their commercial value chipped away through unauthorized use.) The First Circuit U.S. Court of Appeals ruled that, because the sex catalog was noncommercial use, the antidilution statute could not be used under the First Amendment to prohibit its publication. (L.L. Bean had sought an injunction against the parody.) If the sex catalog had been an attempt to actually market products, rather than simply an artistic endeavor, and had it been published after the new Act took effect on November 16, 1989, the Court would probably have ruled in favor of L.L. Bean. Recall that Larry Flynt's notorious Campari parody with Jerry Falwell, as discussed in chapter 9, had First Amendment protection according to the Supreme Court of the United States. The manufacturer of Campari took no legal action against Flynt, but probably would have been unsuccessful anyway because the ad was editorial content, not commercial speech.

Two common mistakes most people make with trademarks are (a) confusing trademarks with other forms of intellectual property, especially copyright; and (b) failing to recognize trademarks. An example of the first type of error occurred in 1990 in news stories about the new NC-17 rating instituted by the Motion Picture Association of America (MPAA). Several major newspapers and at least one wire service reported that pornographic moviemakers started using the non-copyrighted X rating in the early 1970s, but the new NC-17 rating is copyrighted. The truth is that none of the ratings are copyrighted—instead, they are registered trademarks. As is discussed in the next section, names and titles cannot be copyrighted, but they can become trademarks. Open up the entertainment section of your favorite newspaper and you will clearly see the registered trademark symbol dutifully stationed after the rating of each movie, along with the MPAA symbol, which is also a trademark. The MPAA deliberately chose not to protect the X rating, but it did so by not registering it as a trademark rather than not copyrighting it (which it could not do anyway). The distinction between a *trademark* and a *copyright* is important. Advertising and public relations practitioners should learn the difference before using the terms, just as they would make sure to get the correct spelling of a spokesperson's name before issuing a press release or turning in ad copy to a magazine.

The second type of mistake is certainly the most common. Although a press release is not required to indicate when a term, symbol, or phrase is a trademark, you cannot point a finger at the reporter or editor when your company's trademarks are used generically in the resulting news story. Most national advertisers know the importance of identifying trademarks, especially their own, but it is not unusual for local and regional advertisers to omit the trademark symbol, particularly when referring to the products of competitors, such as in comparative ads.

Trademarks may be big business, but trademark protection is by no means restricted to profit-making enterprises. Olympic and the Olympic symbol (three intertwined circles and five intertwined circles) are registered trademarks of the International Olympic Committee. Indeed, many businesses, including the U.S. Postal Service, Delta Airlines, and United Parcel Service, have paid fees for the use of the Olympic trademarks, and yet *olympic* is often used in news stories as a generic term. In 1987, the Supreme Court of the United States in a 5–4 decision held that the U.S. Olympic Committee had the exclusive right to use the term and symbol, and could therefore bar a homosexual group from using the trademark in a Gay Olympics.[37] On the profit-making side, Star Wars is a trademark, having been registered by Lucasfilm, Ltd., owned by George Lucas and others, during the height of Star Wars mania.

The BBB symbol of the Better Business Bureau is a registered trademark, but the walking fingers logo of yellow page fame is not a trademark. The famous L'eggs package for women's hosiery is now history because the Sara Lee Corporation phased out the containers in 1992 in favor of cardboard packaging that is less harmful to the environment, but both the old and new containers are registered trademarks. (Distinctive packaging can be trademarked.) Sometimes trademarks are changed or even taken off the market at the behest or urging of government, or sometimes because of consumer perceptions. In 1991, the Kellogg Company changed the name of its Heartwise cereal to Fiberwise under pressure from the FDA, which has a policy of discouraging the use of *heart* in a brand name. In the same year, the U.S. Federal Trade Commission (FTC) rescinded its initial approval of Powermaster as a brand name for a beer with a higher than usual percentage of alcohol because it also has a policy of banning brand names of alcohol that promote the alcohol content.

The Procter & Gamble (P&G) Company redesigned its decade-old moon and stars trademark, including eliminating the curly hairs in the man's beard that look like the number "6." Since 1981, the company has filed lawsuits and has repeatedly issued statements attempting to dispel rumors that P&G sup-ported Satan because of the sixes that appeared in the symbol's beard. (The number 666 is mentioned in the *Book of Revelation* in connection with the devil.) The company has continued using the trademark in its revised form, but it also uses two newer symbols—a scriptlike Procter & Gamble and P&G. In 1985, P&G began omitting the moon-and-stars emblem from most of its products. The company continues to use the symbol (in revised form) on buildings, awards, and some stationery.

Even radio and television call letters and sounds can be trademarked. Many stations have registered their calls and distinctive sound identifications to differentiate them in a highly competitive market, in which call letters readily alert listeners and viewers to their favorite channels and frequencies, such as FOX'100, COZY'95, Double-Q, and ROCK'105. When you use a registered slogan, name or symbol in an advertisement, press release, or other publication, be sure to include the registered trademark symbol or the TM designation, as appropriate, even if in small type so you alert the world to the trademark's status.

Two final notes need to be made about trademarks. First, they can last indefinitely so long as they are aggressively protected—to avoid dilution and infringement—and not abandoned. As noted earlier, registration lasts 10 years, but it can be renewed every 10 years by filing a renewal application during the 6 months before the registration ends. (A renewal request can be made only during the 6 months before the last registration expires—not before and not after.) Second, trademarks, like patents and copyrights, can be sold and transferred by a written agreement or contract just as with other types of property. When corporations merge and large companies acquire smaller ones, the trademarks are often among the most valuable assets. Consumers rely heavily on brand names or trademarks in their decisions, which is why a company will pay hundreds of millions of dollars to acquire an already well-established trademark for a brand of candy bar, for instance, rather than market a similar candy bar under a new trademark. The existing brand is a sure winner; a new name could be a huge risk.

CONCLUSION

Trademarks have considerable protection under both state and federal law, but trademark holders must take aggressive steps to ensure that their marks do not become diluted and risk going into the public domain. Most advertisers and other commercial and noncommercial enterprises also constantly monitor the use of their trademarks for possible infringement, while making sure that they treat the trademarks of others with appropriate respect.

14

Copyright

On January 1, 1978, the law of copyright changed dramatically when the Copyright Act of 1976 took effect and the pieces of what was once a colossal mess acquired some long-needed order. Prior to January 1, 1978, copyright was governed principally by a federal statute known as the Copyright Act of 1909, which had been revised on numerous occasions over a period of almost 70 years to accommodate new technologies and unresolved problems. In 1909, there were no computers, compact disks, photocopy machines, satellites, or television broadcasts, and even radio had reached only an experimental stage. Copyright infringement was certainly possible, and authors definitely needed protection, but it was much more difficult then than it is today to make unauthorized use of a person's creative work.

The idea of copyright was not new even in 1909. Copyright laws arose as early as the 1400s in Europe, with the development of movable type and mass printing, but they were largely employed as a mechanism for prior restraint in the form of licensing and not as a means for protecting authors. The first federal copyright statute was enacted by Congress in 1790, one year after the U.S. Constitution was ratified and a year before the Bill of Rights took effect. A two-tiered system emerged, with the federal statute protecting principally published works and state common law governing unpublished works. That system essentially continued with the 1909 law, but was eviscerated by the 1976 statute in favor of a system that made common law copyright unnecessary and theoretically nonexistent.

Congress is often criticized for its laborious, cumbersome, and time-consuming decision making, and some of that criticism may be in order for the deliberations involved in formulating a new copyright statute in the 1970s. But the end result was a well-crafted, albeit imperfect, federal law that differs substantially from the old 1909 scheme. Even the premises of the two are at odds. As Kitch and Perlman noted, "Under the old law the starting principle was: the owner shall have the exclusive right to copy his copies. Under the new the principle is: the owner shall have the exclusive right to exploit his work."[1] The new law is clearly an author-oriented statute that offers tremendous protection to the creators of original works of authorship.

THE OLD VERSUS THE NEW LAW

There are some other major differences that need only be briefly mentioned here because most of them are discussed in more detail later in this chapter. First, the duration of copyright protection was considerably increased, even for works that began their protection under the old law. As discussed later, the general term of protection for most works is now the author's lifetime plus 50 years, compared with two 28-year terms under the old law. Second, under the old law, works could generally claim federal copyright protection only if they were published; publication is not required under the new law. Third, the scope of both "exclusive rights" (rights initially conferred solely on the creator of the work) and the types of works included was considerably expanded. Finally, registration is no longer necessary for protection. There are other differences, but they are not substantial enough to warrant discussion here.

THE NATURE OF COPYRIGHT UNDER THE NEW LAW

Because the Copyright Act of 1976 effectively killed common law copyright, under which states offered perpetual protection for unpublished works, copyright is now strictly a federal statutory matter—more precisely, it arises from Title 17 of the U.S. Code Sections 101–810 and subsequent revisions. Under Section 102, copyright protection extends to "original works of authorship fixed in any tangible medium of expression, now known or later developed, from which they can be perceived, reproduced, or otherwise communicated, either directly or with the aid of a machine or device." This section enumerates seven categories under works of authorship: (a) literary works; (b) musical works, including any accompanying words; (c) dramatic works, including any accompanying music; (d) pantomimes and choreographic works; (e) pictorial, graphic, and sculptural works; (f) motion pictures and other audiovisual works; and (g) sound recordings.[2]

Section 102(b) notes that copyright protection does not extend to "any idea, procedure, process, system, method of operation, concept, principle, or discovery, regardless of the form in which it is described, explained, illustrated, or embodied in such work."[3] As discussed earlier, some of these entities may enjoy protection as trademarks, trade secrets, or patents, but they cannot be copyrighted even though works in which they appear can be copyrighted. Section 103 specifies that compilations and derivative works have copyright protection, but this protection only includes material contributed to the author of a compilation or derivative work. Thus, any preexisting material used in the derivative work or compilation does not gain additional protection, but maintains the same protection it had originally. In other words, you cannot expand the protection a work originally enjoyed by using it, whether in whole or in part, in another work such as a derivative work or compilation. Section 101, which contains definitions of terms in the statute, defines a *compilation* as: "... a work formed by the collection and assembling of preexisting materials or of data that are selected, coordinated, or arranged in such a way that the resulting work as a whole constitutes an original work of authorship."[4] Compilations also include *collective works*, defined as: "... a work, such as a periodical issue, anthology, or encyclopedia, in which a number of contributions, constituting separate and independent works in themselves, are assembled into a collective whole."[5] A *derivative work* is defined as:

> ... a work based upon one or more preexisting works, such as a translation, musical arrangement, dramatization, fictionalization, motion picture version, sound recording, art reproduction, abridgment, condensation, or any other form in which a work may be recast, transformed, or adapted. A work consisting of editorial revisions, annotations, elaborations, or other modifications, which, as a whole, represent an original work of authorship, is a "derivative work."[6]

The key differences between a compilation and a derivative work are that (a) a compilation consists of pulling together separate works or pieces of works already created, whereas a derivative work can trace its origins to one previous work; and (b) the key creative element in a compilation is the way in which the preexisting works are compiled to create the whole (i.e., the new work), whereas the creative dimensions of a derivative work are basically independent of the previous work. An example of a derivative work is the film, *Gone With the Wind*, which was based on Margaret Mitchell's book by the same name. An anthology of poems by Robert Frost, which consisted of poems previously published on their own or in even in other anthologies, is an illustration of a compilation that is also a collective work. With certain exemptions, such as "fair use" and compulsory licensing for nondramatic musical works (both discussed later), the owner, who is usually the creator, of an original work of authorship acquires exclusive rights that only he or she can exercise or authorize others to exercise. "Exclusivity" is an important concept under the current copyright law because copyright owners are essentially granted a monopoly over the use of their works. No matter how valuable a work may be in terms of its scholarship, commercial value, artistic quality, or contribution to society, its copyright owner has the exclusive right to control its use and dissemination during the duration of the copyright. For example, Margaret Mitchell's heirs, who inherited the rights to her novel when she was killed by an auto in 1949, nixed any sequels to the enormously popular book and movie until 1988, when Warner Books paid $4.5 million at an estate auction for the right to publish a sequel, although the estate retained the right to choose the author. A series of sequels, including books and movies, would probably have brought in millions of dollars in royalties, but *Gone With the Wind* devotees dying to learn the fate of Rhett and Scarlett had to wait until 1991, when Alexandra Ripley's *Scarlett: Tomorrow Is Another Day* was published. The 768-page sequel was published simultaneously in 40 countries, with excerpts appearing a month earlier in *Life* magazine. The television movie followed in 1994—all 6 hours plus commercials.

Under Section 106, these exclusive rights are:

(1) to reproduce the copyrighted work in copies or phonorecords;

(2) to prepare derivative works based upon the copyrighted work;

(3) to distribute copies or phonorecords of the copyrighted work to the public by sale or other transfer of ownership, or by rental, lease, or lending;

(4) in the case of literary, musical, dramatic, and choreographic works, panto-mimes, and motion pictures and other audiovisual works, to perform the copyrighted work publicly; and

(5) in the case of literary, musical, dramatic, and choreographic works, panto-mimes, and pictorial, graphic, or sculptural works, including the individual images of a motion picture or other audiovisual work, to display the copyrighted work publicly.[7]

Actual ownership of a work, as opposed to ownership of the copyrights to a work, does not convey any copyrights. For example, if Jan Smurf purchases a videocassette of Walt Disney's (a registered trademark) *Cinderella* (a copyrighted work) at her local Wal-Mart (another registered trademark), she can play the tape to her heart's content in her own home, and even invite her friends for an evening of magic on the big-screen Sony. However, she does not have the right to make a copy of the tape nor even to play it at a neighborhood fundraiser for the homeless, no matter how worthy the cause. She does not even have the right to make her own edited version of the film. In other words, purchasing the cassette merely gave her the right to use it in the form in which it was intended to be used—nothing more. She could, of course, loan the movie to a neighbor or even sell her copy to a stranger, just as she could with a book or other physical object. Thus, her rights are strictly tangible; she has no intangible rights.

CREATION OF COPYRIGHT

Probably the most important difference between the old and new copyright statutes is the point at which copyright protection begins. Under the 1909 federal statute, federal copyright protection generally could not be invoked until a work had been published with notice of copyright. There were a few exceptions to this general rule, but unpublished works were basically protected only under state law, or what was known as *common law copyright*, as mentioned earlier. Common law copyright certainly had some advantages, including perpetual protection for unpublished works. But with each state having its own common law, there was no uniformity. The 1976 Copyright Law solved this problem easily: Copyright exists automatically: "... in original works of authorship fixed in any tangible medium of expression, now known or later developed, from which they can be perceived, reproduced, or otherwise communicated, either directly or with the aid of a machine or device."[8] No registration is necessary. No publication is required. Not even a copyright notice has to be placed on the work for it to be copyrighted. The copyright exists automatically on creation. This is one of the most difficult aspects of copyright for laypersons to understand, including advertising and public relations practitioners. In the copyright workshops for laypersons taught by the first author of this text, the most frequently asked question is, "What do I do to copyright my book (or other creative work)?" The answer is simply "nothing" because the work was copyrighted the very second it was created in a tangible medium. Nothing could be simpler. No hocus-pocus, smoke and mirrors, or other magic. Not even a government form to complete.

The question the person actually wants answered is, "How do I register the copyright for my work?" As discussed shortly, there are some major advantages to registration, but this step is absolutely not essential to secure copyright protection, only creation and fixation in a tangible medium. A work is created under the statute "when it is fixed in a copy or phonorecord for the first time."[9] Thus, a work cannot be copyrighted if it exists only in the mind of the creator; once it is fixed in a tangible medium, the protection begins. When a work is developed over time, the portion that is fixed at a particular time is considered the work at that time. For instance, the copyrighted portion of this textbook at the time these words are being written on the word processor is everything written thus far to the end of this sentence. If a work is prepared in different versions, each version is a separate work for purposes of copyright. Thus, the first edition of this book is considered a separate work from the second edition and so on.

When is a work actually fixed in a medium? According to Section 101:

A work is "fixed" in a tangible medium of expression when its embodiment in a copy or phonorecord, by or under authority of the author, is sufficiently permanent or stable to permit it to be perceived, reproduced, or otherwise communicated for a period of more than transitory duration. A work consisting of sounds, images, or both, that are being transmitted, is "fixed" for purposes of this title if a fixation of the work is being made simultaneously with its transmission.[10]

Suppose an enterprising skywriter composes a love poem in the sky to her fiancé during half time of the Super Bowl. A few miles away, another romantic scribbles in the ocean sand the opening of a modernized version of the great film epic, *Beach Blanket Bingo*. How can these two original works of authorship be copyrighted? Both face a major obstacle—they are not yet fixed in a tangible medium of expression. Almost as soon as the love poem is written in the sky, it evaporates into thin air. Thus, its transitory nature prevents it from being "fixed" for purposes of copyright. The same holds true for the film's opening sequence because it ends up blowing in the wind. How does one "fix" them? An easy way is to write them on a piece of paper or perhaps photograph or videotape them before they fade. But won't paper eventually deteriorate? (The yellowed and tattered newspaper clippings from our glory days in high school are testament to this.) Fixation does not require permanency, only, as indicated earlier, that the medium be sufficiently permanent or stable to allow it to be perceived, copied, or otherwise communicated for more than a transitory duration. (By the way, the film sequence has another problem—potential copyright infringement as an unauthorized derivative work, if published, which is returned to later.)

THE COPYRIGHT OWNER

There is a world of difference between the treatment of copyright ownership under the 1909 statute and coexisting common law versus the treatment under the Copyright Act of 1976. Prior to January 1, 1978 (the effective date of the new statute, as mentioned earlier), when an author, artist, or other creator sold his or her copyright, the presumption was that all rights had been transferred unless rights were specifically reserved, usually in writing. For instance, an artist who sold her original painting to someone effectively transferred copyright ownership as well because the common law recognized that the sale of certain types of creative works invoked transfer of the copyright to the purchaser. The presumption works in the opposite direction. None of the exclusive rights enumerated earlier nor any subdivision of those rights can be legally transferred by the copyright owner unless the transfer is in writing and signed by the copyright owner or the owner's legal representative.

Under the new statute, unless a work is a "work made for hire," the copyright is immediately vested in the creator. If there is more than one creator (i.e., there is joint authorship), the copyright belongs to all of them. The creator or creators can, of course, transfer their rights, but the transfer of any exclusive rights must be in writing. Oral agreements are sufficient for the transfer of nonexclusive rights. For example, a freelance artist could have a valid oral agreement with an advertising agency to create a series of drawings to be used in commercials for a life insurance company. At the same time, she could have an agreement with a magazine to do similar illustrations for a feature story. However, if the artist chose to transfer (a) an exclusive right, such as the sole right to reproduce the drawings; (b) a subdivided right, such as the right to reproduce the drawings in commercials; or (c) the right to produce a derivative work, such as a training film based on the drawings, she would need to make the transfer in writing for it to be binding. The sole exception to this rule is a work made for hire, which exists in two situations: (a) a work prepared by an employee within the scope of his or her employment; or (b) a work specially ordered or commissioned for use as a contribution to a collective work, as part of a motion picture or other audiovisual work, as a translation, as a supplementary work, as a compilation, as an instructional text, as a test, as answer material for a test, or as an atlas, if the parties expressly agree in a written instrument signed by them that the work shall be considered a work made for hire.

In the case of a work made for hire, the employer is considered the author for purposes of copyright, and automatically acquires all rights, exclusive and nonexclusive, unless the parties have signed an agreement to the contrary. Thus, the employer effectively attains the status of creator of the work. For instance, a full-time copywriter for an advertising agency would have no rights to the copy she created for the agency, which would instead own the copyright. In contrast, a photo sold by a freelance photographer for use in a press release normally would not be a work made for hire unless the photographer, who is contractually an independent contractor, and the public relations firm had signed a contract specifically stating that the photo would be a work made for hire. Suppose a public relations writer writes a novel about a fictional head of a public relations firm who solves major crime mysteries. The book is written at home on his own time, but much of his inspiration comes from his observations at work. Is the novel a work made for hire? Clearly not, because the writing was completed outside the scope of his employment, although he may have gotten some ideas from interactions with his colleagues. Serving as a source of inspiration alone is not enough for an employer of an individual to claim copyright. An employer–employee relationship must have existed in the context in which the work is created.

In 1996, NBC-TV "Tonight Show" host Jay Leno caught the wrath of shock-jock Howard Stern over the rights to show a tape of a show on which Stern was a guest. The shock-jock had appeared 3 months earlier on the show with two women in bikinis who kissed on the lips while the show was being taped. When the show was broadcast later, that scene was edited, and NBC refused to grant Stern the rights to show the unedited version on his E! cable program. Although Stern was on the show, NBC, not the shock-jock, owned the copyright.[11]

WORK MADE FOR HIRE: COMMUNITY FOR CREATIVE NON-VIOLENCE V. REID

Freelancers create much of the copyrighted material today, and work made for hire principles play a major role in the copyright status of their creative output. Unfortunately, the 1976 law left a gaping hole on this issue. Although the statute defines dozens of terms, from an *anonymous work* to a *work made for hire,* it does not define *employer, employee,* or *scope of his or her employment.* In 1989, however, the Supreme Court of the United States settled some perplexing questions regarding works made for hire by enunciating a clear principle for determining whether an individual is an "employee." In *Community for Creative Non-Violence v. Reid,* in an opinion written by Justice Thurgood Marshall, the Court unanimously held: "To determine whether a work is for hire under the Act [Copyright Act of 1976], a court must first ascertain, using principles of general common law of agency, whether the work was prepared by an employer or an independent contractor. After making this determination, the court can apply the appropriate subsection of § 101."[12]

The Court then indicated those factors under the general common law of agency to be applied in determining whether the hired party is an employee or an independent contractor, including:

> . . . the hiring party's right to control the manner and means by which the product is accomplished. Among the other factors relevant to this inquiry are the skill required; the source of the instrumentalities and tools; the location of the work; the duration of the relationship between the parties; whether the hiring party has the right to assign additional projects to the hired party; the extent of the hired party's discretion over when and how long to work; the method of payment; the hired party's role in hiring and paying assistants; whether the work is part of the regular business of the hiring party; whether the hiring party is in business; the provision of employee benefits; and the tax treatment of the hired party. . . . No one of these factors is determinative.[13]

Agency law deals with the relationship between two individuals or between an individual and a corporation or other entity in which the person performs a task for the other within the context of master–servant, employer–employee, employer–independent contractor, or other similar relationships. The factors mentioned by the Court are among those cited by other courts in determining the relationship. Note the Court's holding that no one of these is determinative; instead, the factors are considered as a whole in the analysis. The facts of *Community for Creative Non-Violence v. Reid* are rather interesting, and provide insight into the Court's reasoning and its conclusion that sculptor James Earl Reid was an independent contractor. They also reinforce the need for written agreements in such situations, as discussed shortly.

In 1985, the Community for Creative Non-Violence (CCNV), a Washington, DC-based nonprofit organization for eliminating homelessness in America, reached an oral agreement with Reid to produce a statue with life-size figures for display in the annual Christmas season Pageant of Peace in Washington, DC. The original idea for the display came from association members. After negotiations over price and the materials used to make the statue, Reid and CCNV agreed to limit the cost to no more than $15,000, excluding Reid's donated services. The sculpture was made from a synthetic material to keep costs to a minimum. Reid was given a $3,000 advance. At the suggestion of Mitch Snyder, a member and trustee of the organization, Reid observed homeless people (both at CCNV's Washington shelter and on the streets) for ideas on how to portray the figures in the statue, entitled "Third World America."

Throughout November and the first half of December, he worked exclusively on the statue in his Baltimore, Maryland, studio. He was visited by several members of the agency, who checked on his progress and coordinated construction of the statue's base, which CCNV built on its own. CCNV paid Reid in installments, and he used the funds to pay a dozen or so people over time who served as assistants during the process. During their visits, CCNV representatives made suggestions about the design and construction of the sculpture, and the artist accepted most of them, such as depicting the family (a man, woman, and infant) with its personal belongings in a shopping cart rather than in a suitcase, as Reid had wanted. When Reid delivered the completed work on December 24, 1985, he received the final installment of the agreed price of $15,000. CCNV then placed the statue on its base (a steam grate) and displayed it for a month near the pageant, after which it was returned to Reid for minor repairs.

Several weeks later, when CCNV's Snyder devised plans to take the work on a fundraising tour of several cities, the creator objected because he felt the statue would not withstand the tour. When Snyder asked that the sculpture be returned, Reid refused, registered the work in his name with the U.S. Copyright Office, and announced his intentions to take the sculpture on a less ambitious tour than CCNV had planned. Snyder immediately filed copyright registration in the agency's name. Snyder and CCNV then sued Reid and his photographer (who never appeared in court and claimed no interest in the work) for return of the sculpture and a decision on copyright ownership.

A district court judge granted a preliminary injunction, ordering that the piece be returned to CCNV. (Injunctions are among the remedies available to copyright owners against infringers, as discussed later in this chapter.) At the end of a 2-day bench trial, the court decided that CCNV exclusively owned the copyright to the sculpture because it was a work made for hire under Section 101 of the Copyright Act. According to the district court, the agency was "the motivating force" in "Third World America's creation and Reid was an employee for purposes of copyright." The U.S. Court of Appeals for the District of Columbia held that Reid owned the copyright because the sculpture was not a work made for hire, and thus reversed the trial court ruling and remanded the case. According to the appellate court, "Third World America" was not a work made for hire under any of the provisions of the Copyright Act, including Section 101. Applying agency law principles, the court thus held that Reid was an independent contractor, not an employee, although the court did remand the case back to the trial court to determine whether Reid and CCNV may have been joint authors. The U.S. Supreme Court affirmed the decision of the U.S. Court of Appeals, remanding the case back to the trial court to determine whether CCNV and Reid were joint authors of the work.

Community for Creative Non-Violence v. Reid, as expected, has already had a major impact on the issue of work made for hire. Although the decision did not settle all of the questions surrounding the concept of work made for hire, it gave clearer guidance for the lower federal courts, and remains one of the most important copyright cases decided by the Court since the new law took effect. At the time the case was decided, there were several conflicting lower appellate court holdings on the issue. Now it is clear that the presumption will be that a work is not a work made for hire unless there is a written agreement indicating the existence of the traditional employer–employee relationship. As the justices noted in their reasoning, the legislative history of the 1976 Act provides strong evidence that Congress meant to establish two mutually exclusive ways for a work to acquire work made for hire status, as indicated in Section 101. The Court also pointed out that, "only enumerated categories of commissioned works may be accorded work for hire status . . . [and that the] . . . hiring party's right to control the product simply is not determinative."[14] The Court specifically rejected an "actual control test" that CCNV argued should be determinative. Under such a test, the hiring party could claim the copyright if it closely monitored the production of the work, but the Supreme Court said this approach "would impede Congress' paramount goal in revising the 1976 Act of enhancing predictability and certainty of copyright ownership."[15] The Court went on to note: ". . . Because that test hinges on whether the hiring party has closely monitored the production process, the parties would not know until late in the process, if not until the work is completed, whether a work will ultimately fall within § 101(1)."[16] The idea, as the Court believed Congress intended in 1976, is that it must be clear at the time a work is created who owns the copyright.

JOINT OWNERSHIP—AN ALTERNATIVE TO WORK FOR HIRE?

Section 101 of the Copyright Act defines a *joint work* as "a work prepared by two or more authors with the intention that their contributions be merged into inseparable or independent parts of a unitary whole."[17] Unless there is a written agreement stating otherwise, joint authors are considered co-owners of the copyright in a work. Although the Supreme Court held that Reid was an independent contractor, not an employee, it agreed with the appellate court that he and the organization might be joint authors, with this matter to be determined by the U.S. District Court.[18] Joint authorship is certainly advantageous to the hiring party because a joint author has an undivided interest in the work, and can make use of the work without seeking permission from the other joint owner or owners unless the owners expressly agree in writing how the copyright ownership in the work is to be divided. Thus, although *Community for Creative Non-Violence v. Reid* was a major victory for freelancers, it created a problem that one First Amendment expert characterizes as "gratuitous joint-authorship claims of commissioning parties," which he believes could be remedied if Congress enacted a statute banning commissioning parties from asserting joint authorship based primarily on supervision of the production of the copyrighted work.[19] Under such a law, freelancers would not inadvertently become joint authors because the parties would have to agree in writing in advance if the work were to be considered jointly authored.[20]

WORKS NOT PROTECTED BY COPYRIGHT

People unfamiliar with the law wrongly assume that any creative work can be protected by copyright. Although the 1976 statute is broad, certain types of works do not fall under its wings. The most obvious example is a work that has not been fixed in a tangible medium; but the Act excludes "any idea, procedure, process, system, method of operation, concept, principle, or discovery."[21] Although such works have no protection in and of themselves, expressions of them can be copyrighted. For example, a university professor who writes a textbook based on his ideas about advertising and public relations law cannot protect his ideas per se, but the expression of those ideas—a book—is copyrighted the moment it is created and put in a tangible medium. Titles, names, short phrases, slogans, familiar symbols and designs, and mere listings of ingredients and contents have no copyright protection, although these may enjoy other forms of legal protection, such as trademarks, as indicated earlier in this chapter. Any attorney practicing copyright law can verify that one of the most common questions clients ask is: "What do I need to do to copyright this great idea I have?" The "shocking" answer is: "Sorry. You can't copyright an idea; you can only copyright the expression of that idea." After a discussion about original works of authorship, tangible media, and automatic copyright, the client usually recovers from the shock.

How this principle works is illustrated by the appearance in 1996 of two "three-ingredient" cookbooks by competing publishers. Writer Rozanne Gold had talked with two publishers about a cookbook of recipes using three basic ingredients to produce easy-to-fix but great-tasting meals. Both publishers made her offers, and she signed on with Viking to produce *Recipes 1-2-3*. The other publisher, HarperCollins, came out about the same time with its version of the idea: *Cooking With Three Ingredients* by Andrew Schloss.[22]

A 1980 Second Circuit U.S. Court of Appeals decision demonstrates how the courts, at least, divide the line between an idea and the expression of an idea. In *Hoehling v. Universal City Studios, Inc.*,[23] the federal appellate court ruled that Universal had not infringed on the copyright of A. A. Hoehling's book, *Who Destroyed the Hindenburg?*, in a movie about the explosion of the German dirigible at Lakehurst, New Jersey, in 1937. The film was based on a book by Michael Mooney published in 1972, 10 years after Hoehling's work. Both books theorized that Eric Spehl, a disgruntled crew member who was among the 36 people killed in the disaster, had planted a bomb in one of the gas cells. Although the 1975 movie, which was a fictionalized account of the event, used a pseudonym for Spehl, its thesis about the cause of the tragedy was similar to that in Hoehling's book. (Investigators concluded that the airship blew up after static electricity ignited the hydrogen fuel, but speculation has always abounded about the actual cause.)

A U.S. District Court judge issued a summary judgment in favor of Universal City Studios and the U.S. Circuit Court of Appeals upheld the decision. According to the court:

> A grant of copyright in a published work secures for its author a limited monopoly over the expression it contains. The copyright provides a financial incentive to those who would add to the corpus of existing knowledge by creating original works. Nevertheless, the protection afforded the copyright holder has never extended to history, be it documentary fact or explanatory hypothesis. The rationale for this doctrine is that the cause of knowledge is best served when history is the common property of all, and each generation remains free to draw upon the discoveries and insights of the past. Accordingly, the scope of copyright in historical accounts is narrow indeed, embracing no more than the author's original expression of particular facts and theories already in the public domain.[24]

Hoehling claimed there were other similarities, including random duplication of phrases and the chronology of the story, but the court saw no problem with such overlap:

> For example, all three works [Hoehling had sued the author of a second work with a similar thesis as well] contain a scene in a German beer hall, in which the airship's crew engages in revelry prior to the voyage. Other claimed similarities concern common German greetings of the period such as "Heil Hitler," or songs such as the German National anthem. These elements, however, are merely scenes a faire, that is, "incidents, characters or settings which are as a practical matter indispensable, or at least standard, in the treatment of a given topic." Because it is virtually impossible to write about a particular era or fictional theme without employing certain "stock" or standard literary devices, we have held that scenes a faire are not copyrightable as a matter of law [citing earlier decision].[25]

Four more categories of work also lack copyright protection:

1. Any work of the U.S. government, although the government can have copyrights transferred to it by assignment, bequest, or other means. State and local governments are not precluded from copyrighting works; only the federal government comes under this rule.

2. Works consisting wholly of common information having no original authorship, such as standard calendars, weight and measure charts, rulers, and so on. Works that contain such information can be copyrighted even though the information cannot be. For instance, a calendar with illustrations of herbs for each month could be copyrighted, but the copyright would extend only to the illustrations and any other original work on the calendar, not the standard calendar.

3. Public domain works (i.e., works that were never copyrighted or whose copyright duration has expired).

4. Facts.

The Copyright Act of 1976 prohibits the federal government from copyrighting works it creates, but the government can acquire copyright for works it did not create. U.S. postage stamp designs are copyrighted, as witnessed by the copyright notice in the margins of sheets and booklets, despite that the U.S. Postal Service is a semiautonomous federal agency. Typically, the Postal Service contracts with freelance artists who design the stamps and then transfer the copyrights to the agency.

Although most government works such as Federal Trade Commission (FTC) pamphlets on fraudulent telephone schemes and U.S. Public Health Service studies on AIDS are not copyrighted, until March 1, 1989 (when the United States joined the Berne Convention, as discussed later), publications incorporating noncopyrighted U.S. government works or portions of such works were required to carry a notice indicating that such use had been made, specifying either (a) the portion or portions of the work that are federal government material, or (b) the portion or portions of the work for which the author is asserting copyright. Such a notice is no longer mandatory, but the U.S. Copyright Office still strongly recommends that such a notice be posted to prevent innocent infringement,[26] a topic discussed later in the section on infringement.

Under the 1909 law, copyright protection lasted for a maximum of two terms of 28 years each, for a total of 56 years. As indicated in the next section, even works copyrighted before the new law took effect had the period of protection extended, but any work that was copyrighted prior to 1903 or any work whose copyright was not timely renewed no longer has protection. Thus, some works copyrighted as late as 1949 went into the public domain because no copyright renewal application was filed. This is the reason that one can find such great prices on some old movies and television shows, including classics, at the local Wal-Mart or K-Mart. Copyright owners simply did not bother at the time to renew the copyright. Once a work becomes public domain property, no royalties have to be paid and no permission needs to be sought from any owner. Usually the copyright owners felt there was no viable market for the works: No videocassette recorders were around, and television viewers had lost interest in old films and vintage television shows. But copyright owners who had foresight filed applications for renewal and were amply rewarded when the VCR and cable television created a new market for nostalgia.

Under the 1909 statute, facts alone could not be copyrighted. The expression of facts does enjoy protection, of course. Thus, although news cannot be copyrighted, newscasts can be. In *Miller v. Universal City Studios*,[27] the Second U.S. Circuit Court of Appeals overturned a U.S. District Court decision that Universal had infringed the copyright of Gene Miller, a Pulitzer Prize-winning reporter for the *Miami Herald*, in a book entitled *83 Hours Till Dawn* about Barbara Mackle. Mackle was rescued after being kidnapped and buried underground for 5 days in a box in which she could have survived for only a week. The trial court was impressed by the approximately 2,500 hours that Miller said he had spent researching and writing the book: "To this court it doesn't square with reason or common sense to believe that Gene Miller would have undertaken the research required . . . if the author thought that upon completion of the book a movie producer or television network could simply come along and take the profits of the books and his research from him."[28]

Although there were several similarities between Miller's book and the script for Universal's docudrama, *The Longest Night*, including some of the same factual errors, the appellate court ordered a new trial on the ground that "the case was presented and argued to the jury on a false premise: that the labor of research by an author is protected by copyright."[29] The court indicated that Miller had presented sufficient evidence that an infringement may have occurred, but on other theories of copyright law, not on the basis of research alone. According to the Court of Appeals, "The valuable distinction in copyright law between facts and expression of facts cannot be maintained if research is held to be copyrightable. There is no rational basis for distinguishing between facts and the research involved in obtaining the facts."[30]

In 1991, the Supreme Court of the United States attempted to clarify the concept of "originality," which is closely linked to the facts versus compilation of facts distinction. In *Feist Publications, Inc. v. Rural Telephone Service Co.*,[31] the Court unanimously held, in an opinion by Justice O'Connor, that the white pages of a telephone directory could not be copyrighted. The case involved a telephone book publisher that used the names and telephone numbers from a telephone company's directory to compile its own area-wide telephone directories. The Court noted that, although the telephone company could claim copyright ownership to the directory as a whole, it could not prevent a competitor from using its compilation of names, towns, and phone numbers to create its own directory. Facts are not copyrightable, the justices said, but compilations of facts can generally be copyrighted.

The decision stressed that hard work or "sweat of the brow" is not enough; there must be originality, which the Court characterized as the *sine qua non* of copyright. "To be sure, the requisite level of creativity is extremely low; even a slight amount will suffice,"[32] Justice O'Connor wrote. She went on to note that originality and novelty are not the same for purposes of copyright, and cited the example of two poets who independently create the same poem: "Neither work is novel, yet both are original and, hence, copyrightable."[33]

MISAPPROPRIATION AND UNFAIR COMPETITION

Misappropriation is a broad tort that covers a variety of situations, including the commercial use of a person's name, image, or likeness, as discussed in chapter 10. This common law creature, also known as *unfair competition*, has been incorporated into most state statutes and in the federal Lanham Act, the same statute that in 1947 revised trademark law. It is occasionally invoked in addition to or in lieu of a copyright infringement suit. The idea of the tort, as illustrated in the classic Supreme Court of the United States decision in *International News Service v. Associated Press* (*INS v. AP*),[34] is that one should not be permitted to compete unfairly through the misappropriation of the toils of another, especially by palming off another's work as one's own. Like copyright infringement, misappropriation is a form of intellectual theft, but it usually does not approach the standards for copyright infringement.

In *INS v. AP*, the International News Service (INS) owned by the infamous "yellow journalism" publisher, William Randolph Hearst, admitted pirating AP stories from early editions of AP member newspapers and from AP bulletin boards. AP claimed that INS also bribed AP employees to get stories before they were actually sent to AP newspapers. INS editors rewrote some of the stories and sent others verbatim to its own subscribers. In its defense, INS claimed that, because the AP did not copyright its stories, the information was in the public domain. INS also claimed that it could not get information about World War I because INS reporters had been denied access to the Allied countries, thanks to Hearst's pro-German stance.

In a 7–1 decision, the Supreme Court of the United States upheld a Second Circuit Court of Appeals decision granting AP an injunction against INS's use of AP stories. The Court reasoned that, although the Constitution does not grant a monopoly, even for a limited period, to the first person to communicate a news event, INS's methods were "an unauthorized interference with the normal operation [of AP's business] . . . precisely at the point where the profit is to be reaped."[35] The justices concluded that INS's misappropriation of AP's stories created unfair competition that could therefore be prohibited.

COPYRIGHT DURATION

The term of copyright was fairly simple prior to enactment of the Copyright Act of 1976. Under the 1909 statute, copyright protection began on the day the work was published, or on the date it was registered if unpublished, and continued for 28 years. If the copyright were renewed by filing the appropriate form and fee with the Copyright Office during the 28th year, the protection continued for another 28-year term and then went into the public domain. The new statute is much more generous, but the precise term of protection depends on a number of factors, including whether the work was created before, on, or after January 1, 1978; whether the work is a work made or hire; and the identifying status of the work. Table 14.1 is an attempt to simplify duration.

For works that had already secured federal copyright protection before January 1, 1978, an additional 19 years of protection was tacked on to the previous maximum of 56 years, assuming the copyright owner filed or files a renewal application during the last year of the first term of 28 years. In effect, this provision created a relatively easy way of equalizing duration of copyright under the 1909 law with duration under the 1976 statute. Congress could have chosen to make the periods precisely the same, but this would have made the calculations extremely difficult because the old law was not tied to an author's life and copyright protection did not begin until registration or publication. Beginning in 1962, while Congress was debating the provisions of a long-over-

TABLE 14.1
Copyright Duration in Years

| Date of Creation | Identifying Status | | | |
	Author Named	Pseudonym	Anonymous	Work for Hire
Created before 1/1/78	75*	75*	75*	75*
Created after 1/1/78	Life of author + 50**	75/100***	75/100****	75/100****

*If renewal is filed during last (28th) year of first term.

**If more than one author, life of last surviving author + 50 years.

***75 years from publication or 100 years from creation, whichever comes first, unless the author's real name is indicated on the copyright registration form, in which case the term is the same as an "author named" work.

****75 years from publication or 100 years from creation, whichever comes first.

due new statute to replace the 1909 one, a series of congressional enactments extended the second term of all renewed copyrights that would have expired between September 19, 1962, and December 31, 1976.[36] Then a provision of the 1976 Act extended the period further by granting an automatic maximum of 75 years protection for copyrighted works that had already been renewed and began their second term anytime during December 31, 1976, to December 31, 1977. The extension was automatic because no additional forms had to be filed for the extension (only the renewal form for the second term).

Taken as a whole, the prior extensions and the provisions of the new statute effectively granted a maximum of 75 years of protection for all copyrighted works that had not lost copyright protection before September 19, 1962. Protection was lost, of course, if the copyrighted work had fallen into the public domain prior to that date, either because of a lack of renewal or expiration of both copyright terms. Thus, the only way one can safely assume that a work is not copyrighted is to check the copyright notice on the work or the date on the registration form in the copyright office and determine that it was copyrighted more than 75 years ago. The present law contains no provision for reviving the copyright for any works that have gone into the public domain.

WORKS CREATED BUT NEITHER PUBLISHED NOR COPYRIGHTED BEFORE JANUARY 1, 1978

Under the present law, neither publication nor registration is required for copyright. However, as already noted, one of these conditions must have been met under the old statute. But what about those works that were never copyrighted, but instead were filed away in a drawer or framed on Aunt Sally's wall? Because there was no effective way to establish a date of creation for these works, Congress had to devise a different scheme for determining how long they were to be protected or if they could be copyrighted at all. The solution was simple, although the calculations are a bit complicated. The legislators opted to automatically protect these works, which had enjoyed common law protection in individual states, but were no longer shielded by the common law because the new law explicitly nixed common law copyright. The duration of protection for such works is computed the same way as works created on or after January 1, 1978—life of the author (or last surviving author if more than one) plus 50 years for works whose author is identified, or if pseudonymous and the author's actual name is indicated on the registration form. For anonymous works and works made for hire, the protection is 75 years from publication or 100 years from creation, whichever is shorter. However, Congress provided that the term for such a work would expire no earlier than December 31, 2002, or if the work is published on or before that date, the term will not expire until December 31, 2027. The key to extending protection is to publish a work by the end of 2002 so it can enjoy an additional 25 years of protection. (The criteria for publication are specified later in this chapter.) Even if an author has been dead for 50 years, the work is automatically copyrighted, and thus protected at least until the end of 2002, so long as it was not previously copyrighted and did not fall into the public domain. As you can see, by publishing a work on or before the end of 2002, the copyright owner has protection automatically extended another 25 years. This provision was designed to incorporate some of the protection previously afforded by common law copyright but without recognizing common law protection. The new law obviously makes common law protection unnecessary anyway for works created after January 1, 1978, because copyright automatically exists from the moment of creation.

Anyone or any entity, including advertisers and public relations firms, attempting to use works created prior to January 1, 1978, that were not previously copyrighted through registration or publication must be cautious because even old works may still have copyright protection. This provision in the law is not widely known, even among media professionals. The same defenses, such as fair use, apply to these works as to newer works, but communication practitioners are sometimes lulled into making extensive use of old, unpublished, and unregistered materials on the assumption that they are in the public domain when, in fact, they may still be copyrighted.

Sooner or later even the great classics fall into the public domain, as happened with the great writer Willa Cather's novel, *O Pioneers!*, published in 1913. When Cather died in 1947, her will provided that the novel could not be adapted for film. The copyright finally expired in 1988, and a movie version appeared in 1992 on CBS-TV starring Jessica Lange. No permission had to be sought from the former copyright owners of the novel.

COPYRIGHT RENEWAL

For works created on or after January 1, 1978, there is no renewal. When the author has been dead 50 years, or for some pseudonymous and all anonymous works and works made for hire, the copyright death bell tolls after 75 or 100 years, and anyone can make use of the work in any way he or she sees fit. From January 1, 1978, to June 25, 1992, the copyright also expired if the owner of a work copyrighted prior to January 1, 1978, failed to file a renewal application during the last year of the first 28-year copyright term. All of this changed, however, on June 26, 1992, when Public Law 102-307 took effect. This law, which amended Section 304(a) of the U.S. Copyright Act of 1976, automatically extended copyrights secured between January 1, 1964, and December 31, 1977, an additional 47 years, thus eliminating the need for filing a renewal application. The previous law specifically required that all renewals be filed between December 31 of the 27th year and December 31 of the 28th year of the first term. If renewal were not done during the 1-year time frame, the work permanently lost protection. With this automatic extension granted by the 1992 law, renewal has become a moot issue. (One final note: All copyright terms run to the end of the calendar year in which the copyright would otherwise expire, thus granting as much as a year of additional protection for some works. For example, a painting by an artist who died on January 1, 1997, would be copyrighted automatically until December 31, 2047.)

COPYRIGHT NOTICE

One of the most persistent myths about copyright, perhaps because the 1909 statutory requirements were so rigid, is that a copyright notice cannot be placed on a work unless it has been registered. Nothing could be further from the truth. The new law not only permits posting of the copyright notice on all works—registered and unregistered—but actually encourages this practice. Under the 1909 law, published works that did not bear a copyright notice were lost forever in the twilight zone of public domain. Unless they were registered, unpublished works had no federal protection anyway, and thus a copyright notice was irrelevant. Until March 1, 1989, when the United States joined the Berne Convention for the Protection of Literary and Artistic Works,[37] published works were required to post a correct copyright notice or risk losing protection. Even an incorrect notice subjected the work to possible loss of protection. Copyright notice is now optional for all works published on or after March 1, 1989, although it is still highly recommended that the notice be posted anyway, as discussed shortly.

Copyright notice is still mandatory for works published before March 1, 1989, although failure to include the notice or giving an incorrect notice does not automatically negate the copyright, as it did under the 1909 law. Instead, the copyright owner is permitted to take certain steps, as provided in Sections 405 and 406 of the statute, to preserve the copyright. These steps include: (a) registering the work before it is published, before the omission took place, or within 5 years after the error occurs; and (b) making a reasonable effort to post a correct notice on all subsequent copies.[38] If these steps are not followed, the work will automatically go into the public domain in the United States 5 years after publication. The work may continue to have protection in some other countries, depending on their copyright provisions. Some omissions are not considered serious enough to require correction, such as failing to place the notice on only a few copies, dating a notice more than a year later after the first publication, and leaving off the © symbol ("C" in a circle), the word *Copyright*, or the abbreviation *Copr.*

Although not mandatory for works first published on or after March 1, 1989, a copyright notice is highly recommended: It gives the world notice that the work is protected, and provides useful information, including the copyright owner and year of publication, to anyone who may wish to seek permission to use the work. Providing the notice also prevents an individual or organization from claiming innocent infringement as a defense to unauthorized use. Under Section 405(b) of the Copyright Act, a person who infringes on a copyrighted work by relying innocently on the omission of a copyright notice on a work published before March 1, 1989, cannot be held liable for actual or statutory damages before being notified by the owner of the infringement.[39] The "innocent infringer" must demonstrate that he or she was misled by the omission of notice, and can still be sued for any profits from the infringement if the court allows.

Similar provisions in the statute provide an innocent infringement defense for works first published without notice on or after March 1, 1989. Under Section 401(d) (dealing with "visually perceptible copies") and Section 402(d) ("phonorecords of sound recordings"), if the correct copyright notice appears on the copies of the work to which an infringer had access, the defendant cannot claim innocent infringement in mitigation of actual or statutory damages (except for employees of nonprofit educational institutions, libraries, and archives, and employees of public broadcasting entities under certain conditions). Thus, it is important that all published works carry a proper copyright notice although it is no longer required.

Under the 1976 statute, copyright notice has never been required for unpublished works, but unpublished works have always been permitted to carry the notice. An individual or organization cannot use the defense of innocent infringement for unauthorized use of an unpublished work. This defense is available for published works that omit the notice. Freelancers, in particular, are often hesitant about posting a notice on unpublished materials, especially those submitted for review, because they believe publishers will be offended. Unfortunately, this is a misconception. The 1976 Copyright Act was designed to offer strong protection to original works of authorship, and the creators of those works should not be reluctant to exercise their rights and notify others of their intentions. They have nothing to lose by posting a copyright notice on all works—published and unpublished.

PROPER NOTICE

For purposes of notice, the copyright law divides works into two categories: (a) visually perceptible copies ("copies from which the work can be visually perceived, either directly or with the aid of a machine or device"[40]), and (b) phonorecords of sound recordings.[41] The first category includes all copyrighted works except phonorecords of sound recordings. The distinction is important because the notices are different for the two. For visually perceptible copies, the key three elements of notice are:

1. The symbol © ("C" encircled), the word *Copyright*, or the abbreviation *Copr.*
2. The year of first publication.
3. The name of the copyright owner.

Examples of a proper notice are:

1. © 1997 Roy L. Moore
2. Copyright 1997 Ronald Farrar
3. Copr. 1997 Erik Collins

The first example is the one most recommended because it is the only form acceptable under the Universal Copyright Convention (UCC), of which the United States is a member. The UCC was founded in 1952 in Geneva, Switzerland, to bring international uniformity to copyright; it revised its rules at a meeting in Paris in 1971 (which the United States implemented on July 10, 1974). For phonorecords of sound recordings, the notice is the same, except the symbol ℗ (the letter *P* encircled) is used instead of ©, *copyright*, or *copr.* (e.g., ℗ 1997 Roy L. Moore). If a work is unpublished, there is no mandatory form for notice because notice is not required anyway, but a recommended form is: Unpublished work © 1997 Ronald Farrar. For works that incorporate U.S. government materials, the notice must include a statement distinguishing the author's work from the U.S. government work, if published before March 1, 1989. Two examples are:

1. © 1997 Erik Collins. Copyright claimed in all information, except information from U.S. government documents on pages 100–110.
2. © 1997 Roy L. Moore. Chapter 10 and photo on page 11 are U.S. government works.

Similar notices should be placed on works published after March 1, 1989, although no longer required. They are particularly useful for informing potential users which portions are copyrighted.

PLACEMENT OF NOTICE

The copyright statute is fairly vague about where a copyright notice should be placed, but the Copyright Office has issued regulations that are quite specific, although flexible.[42] The statute says simply that for visually perceptible copies,

"The notice shall be affixed to copies in such manner and location as to give reasonable notice of the claim of copyright."[43] Congress delegated authority to prescribe regulations regarding notice to the Copyright Office in the same provision.[44] A similar provision governs phonorecords: "The notice shall be placed on the surface of the phonorecord, or on the phonorecord label or container, in such a manner and location as to give reasonable notice of the claim of copyright."[45] Examples of conforming positions of notice in the Copyright Office regulations for books are: (a) title page, (b) page immediately following the title page, (c) either side of front or back cover, and (d) first or last page of the main body of the work.[46] For *collective works* (defined earlier in this chapter), only one copyright notice needs to be given (i.e., it is not necessary, although permissible, for each separate and independent work to carry its own notice). Collective works include magazines, journals, encyclopedias, newspapers, and anthologies. The exception to this rule is advertising. If an advertiser wishes to comply with notice requirements, it must include a separate notice such as to defeat a defense for innocent infringement or to comply with international regulations.

COPYRIGHT INFRINGEMENT

The Copyright Act of 1976 has considerable teeth for punishing infringers. Chapter 5 of the Act provides a wide variety of remedies, including civil and criminal penalties and injunctions. The 1989 revision implementing the Berne Convention treaty increased the penalties even more. The statute sends a clear message that copyright infringement does not pay. An *infringer* is defined as "[a]nyone who violates any of the exclusive rights of the copyright owner . . . or who imports copies or phonorecords into the United States in violation of section 602" ("Infringing importation of copies or phonorecords").[47]

The list of individuals and organizations who have been sued (many successfully) for copyright infringement reads like a *Who's Who*. In 1995, singer Billy Ray Cyrus settled out of court with a songwriter who claimed in a lawsuit that Cyrus used substantial portions of the songwriter's work in the hit, "She's Not Crying Anymore." In the same year, Starware Publishing Corporation and its president were ordered by a U.S. District Court judge to pay Playboy Enterprises $1.1 million in damages for downloading photographs from a computer bulletin board and then putting them on a CD-ROM for sale. Playboy was also awarded $50,000 for trademark infringement.[48] In 1984, the Roman Catholic Archdiocese of Chicago was found guilty of copyright infringement by a U.S. District Court jury and ordered to pay $3.2 million in damages for using copyrighted hymns without permission. The rights were owned by Dennis Fitzpatrick, a composer and president of F.E.L. Publications Ltd. of Los Angeles. The archdiocese unsuccessfully claimed that it had made an honest mistake and had not intentionally avoided paying royalties.[49] In 1988, reggae musician Patrick Alley of the Bronx sued rock artist Mick Jagger in U.S. District

Court in New York, claiming that Jagger's 1985 hit, "Just Another Night," contained the chorus of Alley's 1979 song by the same name. After hearing testimony from experts on both sides and from Jagger himself, which included singing of some of the lyrics, the federal jury ruled there was no infringement.[50] In 1989, Walt Disney Productions ordered the Very Important Babies Daycare Center in Hallandale, Florida, to remove paintings of Mickey and Minnie Mouse, Donald Duck, and Goofy from its walls because of copyright infringement.[51] (Although the characters are trademarks, their depictions, such as drawings, are copyrighted.) Even legal research firms have entered the fray. After 3 years of litigation, West Publishing Company and Mead Data Central, the two largest computerized legal research companies in the country, agreed to a settlement in 1988, under which Mead would pay license fees to use West's case reporting scheme known as "star pagination" from West's copyrighted National Reporter System.[52]

Mead, which, as indicated earlier, owned the Lexis computer research service, claimed that West's system could not be copyrighted because it lacked originality, and was therefore tantamount to public property. Garrison Keillor, the star of National Public Radio's (NPR) "A Prairie Home Companion," sued the noncommercial network in 1988 for copyright infringement after NPR included a Keillor speech in its catalog of cassettes offered for sale to the public. The tape contained Keillor's presentation to the National Press Club the year before, which was carried live on NPR. Keillor claimed he owned the rights to the recording, and that he had never granted NPR permission to tape and distribute it in its catalog. The two parties reached an out-of-court settlement, in which the radio network agreed to make available 400 cassettes of the speech free to anyone who requested one.[53]

Although infringement suits usually attract little, if any, attention in the mass media, except in cases involving major figures, the stakes can be quite high, especially with videotaped movies and computer software. Two motion picture industry executives, John D. Maatta of N.I.W.S. Productions (a subsidiary of Lorimar Telepictures) and Lorin Brennan of Carolco Pictures, indicate that video piracy takes two basic forms: (a) unauthorized duplication and sale, in which a pirate acquires a master, makes duplicates, and then sells them; and (b) "second generation" video piracy, in which a pirate forges copyright documents so it appears that he or she is the legitimate owner and then goes to another country and forces the rightful owner to prove its claim of title.[54] In June 1996, Westech College in California paid more than $220,000 to Autodesk, Inc. as part of a settlement after the school admitted that it had made 75 illegal copies of Autodesk's software, AutoCAD.[55]

According to the *Wall Street Journal*, the Business Software Alliance estimates that even with a year-long government crackdown in 1993 against copyright pirates, nearly all (99%) of the software in Thailand was illegal.[56] Meanwhile, the crackdown continues in this country against pirated videotapes. More videos are now being encoded with Macrovision, a special system that makes it difficult to copy prerecorded movies. *Video* magazine estimates that the average number of illegal copies in homes with videocassette recorders dropped from 5.6 in 1991 to 3.7 in 1994.[57] Other steps to combat piracy are being taken as well. For example, before Warner Brothers released the movie *Batman* in 1989, the studio marked each of the 4,000 prints distributed to theaters with a unique electronic code that appeared on any video copies so investigators could trace pirated copies to a specific source.[58] Warner Brothers, in coordination with the Motion Picture Association of America, announced a reward of $15,000 to anyone providing information that led to the arrest and conviction of anyone for pirating the movie and a $200 reward for the first 15 pirated copies turned in.[59]

When China and the United States signed a new trade agreement in the summer of 1996, China agreed to more vigorously enforce international copyright laws—a promise it had made a year earlier, but failed to carry out. According to the U.S. government, China had deprived U.S. software manufacturers, motion picture producers, and publishers of billions of dollars in lost revenue from the manufacture and sale of pirated copies. None of the trade agreements would be signed, according to U.S. negotiators, until China agreed to the crackdown, which the country eventually did.

INTERNATIONAL PROTECTION AGAINST COPYRIGHT INFRINGEMENT

U.S. companies are able to take criminal and civil action against infringers in other countries because of various international agreements the United States has signed and conventions treaties it has joined. However, there is no universal international copyright; instead, the treatment afforded works copyrighted in the United States differs considerably from country to country. One of the earliest international copyright agreements was the 1910 Buenos Aires Convention, which the United States joined in 1911 with several Latin American states, including Argentina, Bolivia, and Panama. But there are even earlier bilateral agreements, such as the one made with Cuba in 1903 that is still in effect. The two most important international copyright conventions are the Universal Copyright Convention (UCC) and the Berne Union for the Protection of Literary and Artistic Property (Berne Convention). Both have substantially simplified international copyright by bringing some consistency in international protection.

The United States joined the UCC in 1955, and revisions made at a subsequent UCC in 1971 became effective here in 1974. The most sweeping changes in international copyright were wrought by the Berne Convention, which met first in Berlin in 1908 and most recently in Paris in 1971. The United States, however, did not join the convention until March 1, 1989, after 78 other nations were already members. Some of the changes effected by the Act implementing Berne membership have been discussed previously, and others are mentioned later. Suffice it to point out that at least a few of the revisions were fairly substantial. The most important impact was that the United States must now treat the copyrighted works of nationals of other Berne Convention countries the same as it treats works of its own citizens, and member countries must offer at least the same protection for U.S. works as they do for those of their own citizens.[60] You can expect to see more moves by U.S. firms to haul more and more international pirates into courts in their own countries so they can be punished. For the first time, the United States can really hit the infringers where it hurts—the pocketbook. Finally, all works created on or after March 1, 1989, by citizens of Berne Convention countries, and all works first published in a Berne Convention country enjoy automatic protection in the United States. No registration or other formality is necessary.

On January 1, 1996, the International Agreement on Trade-Related Aspects on Intellectual Property Rights (TRIPS), which was part of the General Agreement on Tariffs and Trade (GATT), took effect. The agreement, which affects all members of the World Trade Organization, including the United States, allows copyright protection to be automatically restored under certain conditions to works from other countries that had gone in the public domain in the United States. For example, this restoration of copyright applies to works from countries that had no copyright agreements with the United States at the time the work was published, or works that did not have the requisite copyright notice before the Berne Implementation Act removed that formality.[61]

DEFENSES TO INFRINGEMENT

There are seven major defenses to copyright infringement, although the first one is technically not a defense, but a mitigation of damages: (a) innocent infringement, (b) consent, (c) compulsory license (for certain types of works), (d) public property, (e) statute of limitations, (f) expiration of copyright or public domain, and (g) fair use. Each of the first six is briefly explained, and then fair use is treated in detail.

Innocent Infringement

Innocent infringement, as indicated earlier, occurs when a person uses a copyrighted work without consent on the good faith assumption that the work is not copyrighted because the work has been publicly distributed without a copyright notice. The innocent infringer must prove that he or she was misled by the omission of such notice, and can still be liable, at the court's discretion, for profits made from the infringement, although the person would not have to pay actual or statutory damages. Thus, this claim, if proved, merely mitigates damages; the innocent infringer can still have to fork over any profits. There are two major limitations to this "defense." First, an individual cannot claim innocent infringement in the case of works published after March 1, 1989—the effective date of the Berne Convention Implementation Act of 1988. (The Berne Convention does not require a copyright notice on any works—published or unpublished—and thus effectively prohibits a claim of innocent infringement.)

Second, innocent infringement can only be claimed for published works, not for unpublished works, because a copyright notice was not required for unpublished works even before March 1, 1989.

Consent

As noted earlier, the transfer of any of the exclusive rights and any subdivision of those rights must be in writing to be effective. This means, quite simply, that consent in most cases must be written. The typical way in which a right is transferred is through a contract. The Copyright Office does not publish a model contract, but there are dozens of copyright and intellectual property handbooks—some geared to attorneys and others aimed at laypersons—that provide sample agreements. Section 205 of the 1976 Copyright Act allows, but does not require, parties to record transfer agreements in the Copyright Office.[62]

With such a recording, the individual to whom a right or rights have been transferred gains some important legal advantages, including serving as constructive notice[63] of the terms of the agreement to other parties if certain conditions have been met.[64] Recordation also provides a public record of the terms of the agreement, and—if certain conditions are met—establishes priorities between conflicting transfers.[65] It is extremely important that recordations of transfers comply completely with the provisions in Section 205 and rules of the Copyright Office. A $20 fee must also be paid for each document. All transfer documents are first checked by the Copyright Office to make sure they comply with the requirements, and then they are cataloged and microfilmed for the public record.[66] Anyone can gain access to copies of the documents through the Copyright Office's online computer file, known as COHD, or by using the microfilm readers/printers in the Copyright Card Catalog in the Library of Congress in Washington, DC.[67]

Another provision in the statute deals with terminations of transfers. Under Section 203, a copyright owner can terminate a grant of any exclusive or nonexclusive right after 35 years by notifying the individual or organization to whom the right was transferred.[68] This is an often overlooked provision that can certainly work to the advantage of a copyright owner. It applies to both works that were created on and after January 1, 1978, as well as those created before that date, so long as the transfer of rights was executed on or after the date. (Of course, the work must not have already lost copyright protection.) The owner can make the termination effective anytime during a 5-year period beginning at the end of 35 years from the date of execution of the transfer or from date of publication, if the transfer involves publication, to the end of 40 years from the day the transfer was effective, whichever term ends first.[69] This special termination of transfers provision does not apply to works made for hire, nor to a grant to prepare a specific derivative work.[70] Termination of transfers is another fringe benefit of the new copyright law that can be useful, especially when a work is slow in gaining popularity. The exception regarding derivative works simply provides that, where an author has granted someone the right to do a particular derivative work, that right cannot be terminated if the specific derivative work has been completed before the 5-year termination window. However, the author can terminate the right of the person to any other derivative works.

Compulsory License

One of the most controversial and complicated provisions of the Copyright Act of 1976 was Section 111, which provides a mechanism by which the "secondary transmission of a primary transmission embodying a performance or display of a work is not an infringement of copyright . . ."[71] if certain conditions are met. For example, the management of a hotel, apartment complex, or similar type of housing can retransmit the signals of local television and radio stations to the private lodgings of guests or residents if no direct charge is made, so long as the secondary transmission is not done by a cable system.[72] This is a rather complex area of copyright law, which has little impact on advertising and public relations, primarily because it deals with cable and satellite transmissions of television programs, phonorecords, jukeboxes, and noncommercial broadcasting. The idea is that, by paying a specified fee to the government, the record company or other entity (such as a cable company) can make use of certain copyrighted works, such as songs or television signals, without obtaining consent from the copyright holder. Until December 1993, the rates were set by a three-person Copyright Royalty Tribunal, which also distributed the fees (royalties) to the appropriate owners after deducting an amount for overhead. The Tribunal was eliminated in 1993, and its powers were transferred to ad hoc arbitration panels set up by the Librarian of Congress.

The primary beneficiaries of the royalties generated by compulsory licensing have been program syndicators, represented principally by the Motion Picture Association of America (MPAA). This group has typically gotten more than two thirds of the licensing revenue each year, but there are several other recipients, including the music industry (represented by the American Society of Composers, Authors, and Publishers [ASCAP], and Broadcast Music, Inc. [BMI]), professional and college sports associations, and even National Public Radio (NPR).

Other Types of Licensing

There is one other mechanism for licensing that enables a potential user of a copyrighted work to avoid having to negotiate with individual copyright owners—the blanket license. Blanket licenses, which are purchased for a fee based on a percentage of a radio or television station's revenue, allow a broadcaster to publicly perform any of the music for which the licensing agency has acquired a nonexclusive right. The two primary licensing agencies in the United States are ASCAP and BMI.[73] Both organizations serve similar functions. ASCAP, a membership association of approximately 30,000 composers, authors, and publishers founded in 1914, has nonexclusive rights to more than 3 million musical compositions.[74] BMI, a nonprofit corporation formed in 1939, has about 50,000 writer and publisher affiliates, and holds nonexclusive rights to the public performance of more than 1 million musical compositions.[75] Both agencies grant blanket licenses to broadcast stations so they can use any of the music licensed to the agency without having to obtain the permission of individual copyright owners. Unlike the old law, the 1976 statute makes it clear that playing a recorded copyrighted song without consent or a license is infringement.

Thus, although for many years radio stations paid no royalties when they played recorded music (which they usually obtained free from recording industry promoters anyway), they must now pay royalties even if they actually purchased the record. At one time, record companies and performers were happy to have airtime, and therefore did not object to the scheme under which they provided free copies in return for airplay. However, many copyright owners realized they were losing considerable sums in royalties with the arrangement, and successfully pushed Congress to include broadcast use under public performances protected by the new statute.

Blanket licensing is an efficient mechanism for collecting the millions of dollars in royalties because individual copyright owners are not faced with the onerous task of monitoring broadcast stations around the country to catch copyright violators and then prosecute them. Instead, the licensing agency can handle this. The income from the fees garnered by each agency is distributed, after a deduction for administrative expenses, to the copyright owners with whom the agency has an agreement. Typically, the composer of a licensed song gets the same share of royalties as the publisher. A blanket license normally grants a TV station two types of rights: synchronization and performance. A "sync" right allows the licensee to copy a musical recording onto the soundtrack of a film or videotape in synchronization with action so a single work is produced. A performance right allows the station to transmit the work to the public, either live or recorded. Both ASCAP and BMI also offer a program license that grants the broadcaster the right to as many of the compositions licensed by the agency that the stations wishes on a specific program. The fee for this license is a set percent of the advertising revenue from the program.[76]

Over the years, blanket licensing has survived a number of legal challenges, most recently in 1984 in *Buffalo Broadcasting Co. v. American Society of Composers, Authors and Publishers,*[77] in which the Second Circuit U.S. Court of Appeals overturned a U.S. District Court decision that blanket licensing constituted an unlawful restraint of trade. The district court's injunction against ASCAP and BMI to prevent them from licensing nondramatic music performance rights to local stations for syndicated programming was also lifted by the U.S. Court of Appeals. On further appeal, the Supreme Court of the United States denied certiorari.[78]

Broadcasters are not the only ones affected by licensing. In 1982, the Second Circuit U.S. Court of Appeals held that Gap clothing stores could be enjoined for copyright infringement for playing copyrighted music without a license.[79] The company retransmitted a radio station's signal over a speaker system to customers in its stores. There are dozens of music services, such as Muzak, Super Radio, and the Instore Satellite Network, that offer stores and other public facilities audio services. Most are delivered via satellite and are unscrambled, but they cannot be broadcast without consent, which involves paying a monthly fee with the proceeds shared with owners of the copyrighted music, including composers and publishers. An office, store, or other business (whether for-profit or non-profit) does not have the right to rebroadcast radio signals even if they are from a local commercial or noncommercial station because the station's blanket license covers only the original broadcast, not any other "public performance." A secretary who listens to his or her favorite country/western station at the office each day is not engaging in copyright infringement, but a metropolitan newspaper that retransmits the local top 40 station to its 50 individual offices in the building without consent is likely in violation.

Finally, it is no secret that ASCAP, BMI, and other licensing agencies routinely monitor radio and television stations and visit restaurants, bars, department stores, and other public facilities to spot potential copyright infringers. The latter are usually warned and threatened with a lawsuit if they do not halt infringement or obtain a blanket or other appropriate license. Millions of dollars are at stake, and the copyright law provides writers, artists, performers, composers, and publishers with powerful tools of enforcement, as indicated later. Licensing agencies are merely acting on behalf of their members or affiliates in aggressively pursuing infringers.

Public Property

Certain kinds of works are considered public property because they have no original authorship and, as such, cannot be copyrighted. These include "standard calendars, height and weight charts, tape measures and rulers, and lists or tables taken from public documents or other common sources."[80] Public property also includes works created by the federal government, as noted earlier, but bear in mind that the U.S. government can have copyrights transferred to it by individuals who are not regular government employees. Although not required because of the Berne Convention, a copyright notice will usually be posted on those works for which the government is claiming copyright under a transfer, but the government usually does not include a notice on noncopyrighted works to inform the reader that the work is in the public domain. Instead, the idea of the government appears to be that it is not necessary to inform the public that a particular government work can be used without consent. Specifically, U.S. government bookstores, such as the main office in Washington, DC, carry thousands of noncopyrighted government works for sale, ranging from congressional reports to wildlife posters that can be reproduced without consent. Most of the materials are printed by the U.S. Government Printing Office.

Statute of Limitations

The statute of limitations for both criminal and civil violations of copyright is 3 years. According to Section 507, "No criminal proceeding shall be maintained . . . unless it is commenced within three years after the cause of action arose,"[81] and "No civil action shall be maintained . . . unless it is commenced within three years after the claim accrued."[82] Thus, a plaintiff has a fairly lengthy period in which to file an infringement suit against an alleged offender, and the federal government (usually the Federal Bureau of Investigation [FBI]) must file any criminal charges against an alleged infringer within the 3 years. If such actions are not initiated within that time, the statute of limitations imposes a complete bar, no matter how serious or extensive the infringement. For example, an unscrupulous writer who uses another writer's chapter without consent in his or her book published in January 1996 could be sued anytime until January 1999 for the initial publication. However, if the writer continues to publish the book with the pirated chapter, he or she can still be held liable in February 2002 for a book he or she permitted to be sold in March 1991, although the initial infringement occurred more than 3 years prior. Thus, each publication, sale, and so on constitutes a separate and new infringement. Because the statute of limitations is relatively long, it is rarely used as a defense to either criminal or civil infringement.

Expiration of Copyright

In 1893, Patty Smith Hill and her sister, Mildred J. Hill, two kindergarten and Sunday school teachers from Louisville, Kentucky, composed a melody whose lyrics later become the famous song, "Happy Birthday to You."[83] The song was not published and copyrighted, however, until 1935. In 1988, the Sengstack family of Princeton, New Jersey, which for 50 years had owned Birchtree, Ltd., the company that owned the copyright to the song,[84] sold the company along with the rights to "Happy Birthday to You" to Warner Chappell (a division of Warner Communications, Inc., and the largest music publisher in the world) for a reported $25 million.[85] Why did Warner want the copyright to the song? According to the *Guinness Book of World Records*, it is one of the three most popular songs in the English language, along with "Auld Lang Syne" and "For He's a Jolly Good Fellow."[86] The good news is that the song garners royalties of about $1 million a year; the bad news is that it becomes a public domain work in 2010, when its 75-year-old copyright expires. The other two popular songs are already in the public domain because their copyrights have long expired. "Happy Birthday to You" lives on. Interestingly, the Sengstack family reportedly sold the copyright because Birchtree did not have the resources to aggressively protect the copyright and market the song.[87]

Until the song attracted attention with its sale in 1988, most people assumed that it was not copyrighted. The song is sung every day at thousands of birthday parties and no royalty is paid because it would be difficult to enforce the copyright in those situations. But when the song is sung on television or radio, or when its lyrics appear in an advertisement, a royalty is due and chances are very good that it is paid because Warner rightfully protects the songs for which it owns the copyright. It is essential that everyone, including public relations and advertising professionals, make absolutely sure that a work's copyright has expired before assuming that it is public domain and making use of the work without consent. As indicated previously, once the copyright expires, the work remains in the public domain forever, but copyright duration under the new law is quite extensive, both for works that were copyrighted before the statute took effect and for works that are created on or after January 1, 1978.

Fair Use

Fair use is the one defense to copyright infringement with which most people are familiar. Unfortunately, it is also the most misunderstood concept about copyright, as the various myths about fair use can attest. Myth 1: If less than 10% of a work is used, that is fair use. The truth: There is no specified amount, either in the statute or in case law. Myth 2: If one acknowledges (i.e., gives credit) when one includes excerpts from another's work, that is fair use, and no consent needs to be obtained. The truth: Fair use has nothing to do with whether one gives credit. In fact, as noted earlier, when one acknowledges using the other person's work, one is, in a sense, admitting possible infringement if one does not have a legitimate defense otherwise. Myth 3: If the use would seem fair to a reasonable person, then it is fair use. The truth: If one has a gut feeling that what one is doing is "unfair" or "wrong," one is probably treading on dangerous ground and committing infringement. However, if one feels comfortable, one's actions still may not be fair use. For example, many people see nothing wrong with dubbing a compact disc album onto an audiotape if they already own the disk. Under the statute, this is not permissible as fair use; although one's chances of being sued in such a case are virtually nil when it is for home use, the act is, nevertheless, infringement. A final myth: Fair use is a First Amendment right. The truth: Nothing could be further from the truth. Fair use has always been a common law creature that was given federal statutory life only in 1978, when the new law took effect. Interestingly, the courts, including the Supreme Court of the United States, in recent years have either ignored or dismissed claims of First Amendment or other constitutional protection by defendants in fair use cases. The moral: Throw up the statute as a "fair use" shield, but do not expect the First Amendment to be a savior when one has used copyrighted material without consent.

WHAT IS FAIR USE?

Congress included dozens of definitions in the Copyright Act of 1976, from *anonymous work* to *widow* and *widower*, but *fair use* is deliberately not among them because the legislators had difficulty defining the concept, as indicated in a 1976 report of the House of Representatives Judiciary Committee:

The judicial doctrine of fair use, one of the most important and well-established limitations on the exclusive right of copyright owners, would be given express statutory recognition for the first time in section 107. The claim that a defendant's acts constituted a fair use rather than an infringement has been raised as a defense in innumerable copyright actions over the years, and there is ample case law recognizing the existence of the doctrine and applying it. . . . Although the courts have considered and ruled upon the fair use doctrine over and over again, no real definition of the concept has ever emerged. Indeed, since the doctrine is an equitable rule of reason, no generally applicable definition is possible, and each case raising the question must be decided on its own facts.[88]

Thus, Congress chose instead to incorporate into Section 107 four criteria that had evolved from the courts in determining fair use. In determining whether the use made of a work in a particular case is fair use the factors to be considered shall include:

(1) the purpose and character of the use, including whether such use is of a commercial nature or is for nonprofit educational purposes;
(2) the nature of the copyrighted work;
(3) the amount and substantiality of the portion used in relation to the copyrighted work as a whole; and
(4) the effect of the use upon the potential market for or value of the copyrighted work.[89]

Section 107 mentions specific examples of purposes that can involve fair use, including "criticism, comment, news reporting, teaching (including multiple copies for classroom use), scholarship, or research."[90]

Although it is not part of the statute, and it cannot be used to definitively determine the intent of Congress in enacting the Copyright Act, the House Report gives an indication of the law's purpose:

> The statement of the fair use doctrine in Section 107 offers some guidance to users in determining when the principles of the doctrine apply. However, the endless variety of situations and combinations of circumstances that can rise in particular cases precludes the formulation of exact rules in the statute. The bill endorses the purpose and general scope of the judicial doctrine of fair use, but there is no disposition to freeze the doctrine in the statute, especially during a period of rapid technological change. Beyond a broad statutory explanation of what fair use is, and some of the criteria applicable to it, the courts must be free to adapt the doctrine to particular situations on a case-by-case basis. Section 107 is intended to restate the present judicial doctrine of fair use, not to change, narrow, or enlarge it in any way.[91]

Thus, Congress chose to establish broad guidelines and trust the courts to determine, on a case-by-case basis, what is and is not fair use, and that is exactly what the courts have done, occasionally even revealing gaps in the statute. There have been hundreds of court decisions dealing with fair use, under both the 1909 and 1976 statutes, but this section focuses on those that have had a major impact and/or illustrate important aspects of the concept. Each of the four factors is important, but none is, by itself, determinative. Instead, the courts evaluate each situation in light of all four and attempt to strike a balance among them, as illustrated in a 1968 decision by a U.S. District Court in New York. In *Time, Inc. v. Bernard Geis Associates*,[92] the federal trial court ruled that the author and publisher of a book containing charcoal sketches of frames from the famous Zapruder copyrighted film of President John F. Kennedy's assassination constituted fair use. When Kennedy was killed on November 22, 1963, amateur photographer Abraham Zapruder took color, 8-mm moving pictures of the shooting. Zapruder had three copies made; two were given to the U.S. Secret Service with the understanding that they would not be made public, but used only for the government's investigation. He then signed a contract with *Life*, under which the magazine acquired ownership of all three copies for $150,000. *Life* subsequently published individual frames of the film in various issues, but did not register its copyright until 1967, although the magazine issues in which the frames appeared had already been registered. Although the Zapruder family owns the copyright to the film, the original has been in the custody of the National Archives under an agreement with the family. In April 1997, a federal government Assassination Records Review Board ruled the film was public property, the first step toward allowing copies to be obtained under the Freedom of Information Act. The Zapruder family has for years been making copies available for noncommercial use for $50.

Bernard Geis Associates negotiated unsuccessfully with Time, Inc. (the publisher of *Life*) for the right to publish several frames from the Zapruder film in a book, *Six Seconds in Dallas*, by Josiah Thomas.[93] After being denied the right, Thomas and the publisher hired a professional artist to draw charcoal sketches of the frames, 22 of which appeared in the book when it was published in late 1967. Time, Inc. sued for copyright infringement, and Bernard Geis claimed fair use as a defense, arguing that *Life* had no valid copyright in the film. A U.S. District Court judge balanced each of the four factors (described earlier) and issued a summary judgment in favor of Bernard Geis Associates. Judge Wyatt determined that Time, Inc. had a valid copyright, but the book had made fair use of the film and therefore had not infringed:

> There is a public interest in having the fullest information available on the murder of President Kennedy. Thompson did serious work on the subject and has a theory entitled to public consideration. While doubtless the theory could be explained with sketches of the type used at page 87 of the Book and in *The Saturday Evening Post*, the explanation actually made in the Book with copies is easier to understand. The Book is not bought because it contained the Zapruder pictures; the Book is bought because of the theory of Thompson and its explanation, supported by Zapruder pictures. There seems little, if any, injury to plaintiff, the copyright owner. There is no competition between plaintiff and defendants. Plaintiff does not sell the Zapruder pictures as such and no market for the copyrighted work appears to be affected. defendants do not publish a magazine. There are

projects for use by plaintiff of the film in the future as a motion picture or in books, but the effect of the use of certain frames in the Book on such projects is speculative. It seems more reasonable to speculate that the Book would, if anything, enhance the value of the copyrighted work; it is difficult to see any decrease in its value.[94]

Although this case was decided prior to the 1976 statute, it illustrates well how courts balance the factors. Notice that the court was particularly concerned about Factor 4—the effect of the use on the potential market for or value of the copyrighted work. The judge made it clear that the two parties were not in competition; indeed, the book could even increase the value of the film. He also weighed the public interest served in line with Factor 1. In another part of the decision, the Court noted that, although Thompson had made "deliberate appropriation in the Book, in defiance of the copyright owner . . . it was not the nighttime activities of Thompson which enabled defendants to reproduce Zapruder frames in the Book. They could have secured such frames from the National Archives, or they could have used the reproductions in the Warren Report or in the issues of *Life* itself."[95]

In 1985, the Supreme Court of the United States issued one of the most important fair use decisions thus far. In *Harper & Row v. Nation Enterprises*,[96] the Court held in a 6–3 decision written by Justice Sandra Day O'Connor that *Nation* magazine had infringed the copyright jointly owned by Harper & Row and Reader's Digest Association to the unpublished memoirs of former President Gerald Ford. In early 1977, shortly after he stepped down as president, Gerald Ford signed a contract with Harper & Row and *Reader's Digest* to publish his then-unwritten autobiography. Ford granted the two publishers the right to publish the manuscript in book form and as a serial ("first serial rights"). In 1979, they sold *Time* magazine the exclusive right to excerpt 7,500 words from Ford's account of his pardon of former President Richard M. Nixon for any crimes connected with the 1972 attempted burglary by Nixon operatives of the Democratic campaign headquarters at the Watergate office building in Washington, DC. (Nixon was forced to resign from the presidency as a result of his involvement in the cover-up of the burglary.) The contract with *Time* included provisions that the magazine be allowed to publish the excerpt approximately 1 week before the book would be shipped to bookstores, and that *Time* retained the right to renegotiate part of its payment if the material in the book were published before the excerpt. In March 1979, an unidentified source furnished Victor Navasky, editor of the *Nation*, with a monthly political commentary magazine, with a copy of the unpublished manuscript, *A Time to Heal: The Autobiography of Gerald R. Ford*.

Before *Time* could publish its excerpt, in April *Nation* carried a 2,250-word feature that included verbatim quotes of 300–400 words from the original manuscript. According to the Court, these quotes composed about 13% of the *Nation* article, and the editor made no independent commentary nor did any independent research because, as he admitted at trial, he wanted to scoop *Time*.

Time thus decided not to publish its excerpt, and refused to pay Harper & Row and Reader's Digest Association the remaining $12,500 of the $25,000 it had agreed to pay for the prepublication rights. Harper & Row and Reader's Digest then filed suit against *Nation* for copyright infringement. The U.S. District Court for the Southern District of New York ruled against *Nation* in its defense of fair use, and awarded the plaintiffs $12,500 in actual damages for copyright infringement. However, the Second Circuit U.S. Court of Appeals reversed, holding that, although the memoirs were copyrighted, the *Nation*'s disclosure of the information was "politically significant" and newsworthy, and thus fair use. The Supreme Court of the United States disagreed with the lower appellate court. The Court analyzed the case in light of each of the four factors, but paid particular attention to the fourth factor:

> In evaluating character and purpose [factor one] we can not ignore the *Nation*'s stated purpose of scooping the forthcoming hardcover and *Time* abstracts. The *Nation*'s use had not merely the incidental effect but the intended purpose of supplanting the copyright holder's commercially valuable right of first publication. . . .
> The fact that a work is unpublished is a critical element of its "nature." Our prior discussion establishes that the scope of fair use is narrower with respect to unpublished works. While even substantial quotations might qualify as fair use in a review of a published work or a news account of a speech that had been delivered to the public or disseminated to the press, . . . the author's right to control the first public appearance of his expression weighs against such use of the work before its release. The right of first publication encompasses not only the choice whether to publish at all, but also the choices when, where and in what form first to publish a work.[97]

On the third factor (amount and substantiality), the Court noted that, although "the words actually quoted were an insubstantial portion" of the book, *Nation*, as the District Court said, "took what was essentially the heart of the book."[98] The Court cited the *Nation* editor's own testimony at trial as evidence that he selected the passages he ultimately published "precisely because they qualitatively embodied Ford's distinctive expression."[99]

On the last factor (effect of the use on the potential market), the Court was particularly critical of the *Nation*'s action and its impact. Noting that this factor "is undoubtedly the single most important element of fair use," the majority pointed to the trial court's finding of an actual effect on the market, not simply a potential effect: ". . . *Time*'s cancellation of its projected serialization and its refusal to pay the $12,500 were the direct result of the infringement. . . . Rarely will a case of copyright infringement present such clear cut evidence of actual damage. Petitioners [Harper & Row and Reader's Digest] assured *Time* that there would be no other authorized publication of any portion of the unpublished manuscript prior to April 23, 1979."[100]

The justices went on to contend: "Placed in a broader perspective, a fair use doctrine that permits extensive prepublication quotations from an unreleased manuscript without the copyright owner's consent poses substantial potential for damage to the marketability of first serialization rights in general."[101] Thus, *Harper & Row v. Nation Enterprises* has typically been classified as an "unpublished works" case, but at least one copyright expert views the decision differently. Kenneth M. Vittor, vice president and associate general counsel of McGraw-Hill, Inc., believes the holding "is more properly understood as an attempt by the Court to protect the right of authors to choose the timing of the first publication of their soon-to-be-published works."[102]

Three major points emerge from this decision. First, a defense of fair use is less likely to succeed in the case of an unpublished work than with a published work. Would *Nation* have won if all the circumstances had been the same except that the extensive excerpt from Ford's memoirs had already appeared in *Time*? What if both the book and the *Time* excerpt had already been published? The Court apparently assumed that the manuscript had been purloined, although the *Nation* magazine editor apparently had not been directly involved. This allegation hurt the magazine's claim that the information was in the public interest. As the Court iterated, the book took 2 years to produce, including hundreds of taped interviews that then had to be distilled into a single work. If one were allowed to profit from taking another's work under these circumstances, the Court felt authors would be discouraged from creating original works, thereby depriving the public of important historical information. In other words, if a researcher/author faces the risk that his or her work will garner no rewards, such as royalties, that person is unlikely to be interested in conducting the extensive research and making the other efforts necessary to produce the work that might ultimately add to public knowledge. The Court was also concerned that offering protection for *Nation* in this case would establish a precedent in which the defense of fair use would be broadened so much that it would "effectively destroy any expectation in the work of a public figure."[103]

The principles established in *Harper & Row v. Nation Enterprises* played a major role 2 years later in an important copyright decision by the Second Circuit U.S. Court of Appeals. In *Salinger v. Random House*,[104] the federal appellate court granted an injunction sought by reclusive writer J. D. Salinger (author of the classic and popular 1951 novel, *The Catcher in the Rye*) against publication of Ian Hamilton's unauthorized biography, *J.D. Salinger: A Writing Life*. Hamilton made extensive use of information, including direct quotes, he had obtained from some 70 copyrighted letters Salinger had sent to various individuals, who had, in turn, donated them to several university libraries. Although the biographer had substantially altered the book before it went to press after complaints from Salinger, the latter was not satisfied and filed suit for copyright infringement.

The U.S. District Court sided with Hamilton and refused to issue the injunction (one of the remedies available for infringement, as indicated shortly) because it felt most of the material used from the letters was protected by fair use because it consisted primarily of Salinger's ideas expressed in Hamilton's own words, rather than Salinger's specific expressions. The U.S. Court of

Appeals reversed, holding that Hamilton was not protected by fair use and that, under *Harper & Row v. Nation*, unpublished works "normally enjoy complete protection against copying any protected expression."[105] According to the appellate court, "Public awareness of the expressive content of the letters will have to await either Salinger's decision to publish or the expiration of his copyright."[106] Interestingly, Salinger indicated that he had no intentions of publishing the letters, but because he wrote them, the copyright belonged to him, not the recipients. Thus, in the eyes of the court, he had every right to halt publication of their content. The Supreme Court of the United States denied certiorari in the case. Two years later, the Second Circuit tackled the fair use issue once again in a case that has particularly troubled many First Amendment experts, not because of its outcome, but because of the court's opinion. In *New Era Publications International v. Henry Holt & Co.*,[107] the Court of Appeals affirmed a U.S. District Court decision not to grant an injunction against publication of a highly critical and unauthorized biography of the controversial L. Ron Hubbard, founder of the Church of Scientology. Applying the principles established in *Salinger v. Random House*, District Court Judge Pierre N. Leval had ruled that Russell Miller's *Bare-Faced Messiah: The True Story of L. Ron Hubbard* had infringed on the copyrights held by New Era Publications to Hubbard's writings because "there is a body of material of small, but more than negligible size, which, given the strong presumption against fair use of unpublished material, cannot be held to pass the fair use test."[108] However, Judge Leval ruled an injunction was not appropriate because of First Amendment concerns over prior restraint that outweighed the copyright owner's interests in the case, and because New Era could still seek damages (another remedy for infringement discussed shortly).

The Second Circuit Court upheld the trial court decision, but on the ground of laches, not fair use. Laches is the equitable doctrine that when a party unreasonably delays asserting a right or claim to the detriment of the other party, its request is dismissed. According to the court, New Era had failed to make any efforts to protect its copyrights until the biography was actually published, although it had clearly been aware for several years that Miller's work was underway: "The prejudice suffered by Holt as a result of New Era's unreasonable and inexcusable delay in bringing action invokes the bar of laches."[109] Miller had gathered most of his information about Hubbard from court documents, interviews with Hubbard acquaintances, news stories, and Hubbard's own writings, including letters and diaries.

The appellate court particularly noted its displeasure with U.S. District Court Judge Leval's analysis, especially his First Amendment concerns: "We are not persuaded ... that any First Amendment concerns not accommodated by the Copyright Act are implicated in this action."[110] The U.S. Court of Appeals felt that the biography was a much more serious infringement than the trial court had claimed. Henry Holt filed a request for rehearing on the issue of fair use in the case, although it had won on the laches ground, but the appellate court rejected the request in a sharply divided 7–5 opinion.[111]

One year later, the same appellate court in another fair use case involving another unauthorized biography of L. Ron Hubbard overturned a U.S. District Court injunction against publication of Jonathan Caven-Atack's *A Piece of Blue Sky: Scientology, Dianetics and L. Ron Hubbard Exposed*. In *New Era Publications International v. Carol Publishing Group*,[112] the Second Circuit U.S. Court of Appeals ruled in favor of Carol Publishing (which had published the biography) on all four fair use factors. The appellate court felt the materials used in the work were particularly protected because they had been taken from dozens of published works rather than Hubbard's unpublished writings. The court noted that the works were factual, and that the scope of fair use is greater for factual than nonfactual writings, and that the amount of the materials used in the biography were neither qualitatively nor quantitatively substantial. Finally, the court said that, although the book was intended to make profits, and that it might "discourage potential purchasers of the authorized biography [which New Era planned to publish], this is not necessarily actionable under the copyright laws. . . . Harm to the market for a copyrighted work or its derivatives caused by a 'devastating critique' that 'diminished sales by convincing the public that the original work was of poor quality' is not 'within the scope of copyright protection.'"[113] Although the last decision provided some comfort for biographers and other writers who use primarily published materials in their works, the earlier decisions continue to haunt those who want to use unpublished documents.

The aftermath of the *Salinger v. Random House* and *New Era Publications v. Holt* decisions, according to one news account, was self-censorship by book publishers with "the authors themselves try[ing] to figure our history in a straitjacket."[114] Although Second Circuit opinions are binding only on federal courts in Vermont, Connecticut, and New York, its opinions have traditionally been very influential on courts in other circuits. The Supreme Court of the United States denied certiorari in both cases, and there is no indication that the Court is likely to tackle this issue anytime soon. In the meantime, historians and other researchers can be expected to exercise extreme care in using unpublished materials, including those of public figures, even when the information is already readily accessible to the public in libraries and other depositories. *Harper & Row v. Nation* may have opened a can of worms that will haunt or at least chill the dissemination of information based on unpublished materials used without the consent of the author or other copyright owner. In 1992, President George Bush signed legislation that amended Section 107 of the Copyright Act to include: "The fact that such a work is unpublished shall not itself bar a finding of fair use if such finding is made upon consideration of the above factors."[115] Had this provision been in effect at the time the Copyright Act of 1976 took effect, *Salinger* and similar cases may well have been decided differently.

In a test case of fair use in 1992, *American Geophysical Union v. Texaco*,[116] U.S. District Court Judge Pierre N. Leval ruled that it was not fair use under Section 107 when a Texaco scientist made single copies of articles from the *Journal of Catalysis*. The parties in the case, Texaco (as defendant) and American Geophysical Union and 82 other publishers of scientific and technical journals (as plaintiffs), agreed in advance to a limited-issue bench (nonjury) trial. Both sides stipulated that the scope of the trial would be limited to the photocopying of eight articles by the one scientist from the one journal. According to the testimony at trial, Texaco scientists such as Dr. Donald Chickering II (whose name was drawn at random for the case among those who worked for Texaco) routinely have the company library make single copies of articles from journals to which the company subscribes. The advantages of this procedure include permitting the workers to keep easily referenced files in their desks or on their office shelves, eliminating the risks of errors when data are transcribed from articles and then taken back to lab for research, and making it possible from them to take articles home to read. The judge held this was not fair use, and thus an infringement because: (a) Texaco's use was for commercial gain, (b) substantial portions of the works were copied, and (c) Texaco's use deprived the copyright holder of potential royalties. One solution suggested by the judge was for the company to obtain clearance from the nonprofit Copyright Clearance Center, which grants blanket advanced permission for a specified fee to photocopy (usually noted on the copyrighted material).

In 1994, the Second Circuit U.S. Court of Appeals, in an interlocutory appeal[117] from the district court, upheld the trial court's decision, but with somewhat different reasoning.[118] The appellate court held that three of the four fair use factors, including the purpose and character of use (first factor) and the effect on potential market and value (fourth factor), favored the publisher. The majority opinion disagreed with a dissenting opinion filed by Circuit Judge Jacobs, who contended that the majority's ruling would require that an intellectual property lawyer be posted at each photocopy machine. As the majority saw it, all Texaco had to do in the specific circumstances of the case was to simply take advantage of existing licensing schemes or work out one on its own.

A year later, the Second Circuit amended its ruling to note that its decision was limited to the specific question of whether photocopying by the company's 400 or 500 scientists was fair use. According to the court, "We do not deal with the question of copying by an individual, for personal use in research or otherwise, recognizing that under fair use doctrine or the *de minimis* doctrine, such a practice by an individual might well not constitute an infringement."[119] The message the appellate court seemed to be sending was that photocopying on an individual basis, such as for research, would not ordinarily constitute copyright infringement. The problem in this case was that Texaco had a policy of encouraging the photocopying—at least of single copies—by its scientists as a group, which meant there was the potential for hundreds of copies of articles being made, thereby presumably depriving the publishers of potential royalties. Keep in mind that Texaco had legal subscriptions to the journals, but that it is a commercial enterprise.

Two major court decisions have had a particularly important impact on the use of copyrighted materials in higher education. On March 28, 1991, U.S.

District Court Judge Constance Baker Motley of the Southern District of New York issued a decision that has had a major effect on how colleges and universities use copyrighted materials in the classroom. In *Basic Books, Inc. v. Kinko's Graphics Corp.*,[120] the federal trial court judge soundly rejected Kinko's claim that the fair use doctrine permitted it to photocopy without consent anthologies of copyrighted materials as part of its "Professor Publishing" program. Under the program, the firm photocopied journal articles, book chapters, and other copyrighted materials selected by college and university instructors as readings for their classes. These anthologies were then sold for profit to students. The suit was filed in April 1989 by eight publishers who said two of the stores owned by the graphics company had engaged in copyright infringement by photocopying substantial portions of 12 books for use in anthologies used at New York University, Columbia University, and the New School for Social Research. Neither the schools nor the professors involved were named as defendants.[121]

In her 57-page opinion, Judge Motley held that Kinko's had intentionally violated the copyright statute, and ordered the chain to pay $510,000 in actual damages as well as the plaintiffs' court costs and attorneys' fees. She also issued an injunction barring the company from photocopying and selling copies of copyrighted materials without obtaining the consent of copyright owners and paying any royalties requested. As a result, Kinko's changed its Professor Publishing program policies to comply with the court order, including obtaining permission for the photocopying of any copyrighted material from the copyright owner or requiring the professor to obtain such permission even when he or she believes the photocopying would be protected under the fair use doctrine.[122] The company eventually phased out the program.

In 1986, a U.S. District Court judge in California granted summary judgment for the University of California–Los Angeles (UCLA) in a copyright infringement suit filed against the university by BV Engineering, a computer software company based in California. The company had asked for $70,000 in damages from UCLA for allegedly making unauthorized copies of seven computer programs and user manuals for which BV Engineering owned the copyright. The federal trial court judge ruled that the 11th Amendment to the U.S. Constitution barred state-supported institutions from being successfully sued under federal laws, including the Copyright Act of 1976, unless Congress specifically allows such litigation or the state has explicitly waived its immunity.[123] In *BV Engineering v. University of California at Los Angeles*,[124] the Ninth Circuit U.S. Court of Appeals upheld the lower court decision; in 1989, the U.S. Supreme Court denied certiorari. Because the case simply pointed to a gap in the 1976 statute, Congress quickly revised the federal copyright statute with little opposition. Colleges and universities generally supported the bill because they, too, own copyrights that they also prefer to protect from infringement by state agencies.

The impact of the case was rather minimal even before the new law because the court's holding did not exempt individual professors from being held liable, nor did it prevent a copyright owner from seeking an injunction against a state agency for infringement. The decision merely barred BV Engineering from obtaining damages, thanks to an oversight by Congress. Under the revision, effective November 15, 1990,[125] the definition of *anyone* for purposes of infringement now includes "any State, any instrumentality of a State, and any officer or employee of a State or instrumentality of a State acting in his or her official capacity."[126] The Act also makes it clear that any "State, any instrumentality of a State, and any officer or employee of a State acting in his or her official capacity, shall not be immune, under the Eleventh Amendment of the Constitution of the United States or under any other doctrine of sovereign immunity, from suit in Federal court" for copyright infringement.[127] The revised statute also preserves the same remedies, including actual damages, profits, statutory damages, and so on, for infringement that are available for nongovernmental entities.[128] The net effect of the new law is to put state governments in the same position as everyone else (except the federal government) for purposes of copyright infringement.

Section 107 of the 1976 statute specifically mentions criticism, comment, and news reporting as purposes that can be considered fair use. However, as the courts have made clear, these uses do not always enjoy protection in an infringement suit. In May 1991, a U.S. District Court Judge in Atlanta awarded WSB-TV $108,000 plus attorneys' fees and courts cost against TV News Clips for videotaping portions of the station's local newscasts and selling them to the public.[129] The court also issued a permanent injunction barring the company from making any further copies of newscasts or offering them for sale. TV News Clips charged clients $65 for the first program and $30 for each additional program. In October 1983, the same company was ordered to pay $35 in damages to another Atlanta station, WXIA-TV,[130] which eventually obtained an injunction prohibiting the service from making any copies of the station's newscasts.[131]

In 1991, several Los Angeles police were indicted for assault and other charges for allegedly beating or failing to stop the beating of Rodney King, an area motorist pulled over for speeding. George Holiday, an amateur photographer, videotaped the beating from his apartment window. The videotape was shown hundreds of times on television stations around the country and on the major networks after it was allegedly distributed by a Los Angeles TV station without consent of Holiday, who owned the copyright to the tape, which had also been registered with the Copyright Office. Holiday's attorney reportedly mailed a letter to more than 900 television stations around the country demanding payment for use of the film.

In 1992, Gordon Lish won a $2,000 judgment for copyright infringement against *Harper's*, which had published more than half of the fiction writer-editor-teacher's unpublished letter to his students. In *Lish v. Harper's Magazine Foundation*,[132] U.S. District Court Judge Morris E. Lasker's ruling rejected the magazine's claim of fair use because the evidence supported Lish on the first three factors associated with fair use, although the publication had little or no impact on the market for the letter (fourth factor).

On March 7, 1994, the Supreme Court of the United States handed down
its decision in the long-awaited case of *Luther R. Campbell a.k.a. Luke Skyywalker
v. Acuff-Rose Music, Inc.*[133] The original song, "Oh, Pretty Woman," was written
by Roy Orbison and William Dees in 1964. Twenty-five years later, Luther R.
Campbell wrote a song, "Pretty Woman," which was intended to satirize the
original work. Orbison–Dees' song is a rock ballad about a man's fantasies
concerning a woman he sees walking down the street. In contrast, Campbell's
tune is a rap song that includes lines such as "Big hairy woman you need to
shave that stuff" and "Two timin' woman girl you know you ain't right."

Campbell asked Acuff-Rose Music, Inc., the copyright owner of the original
song, for a license to use the song in a rap version by "2 Live Crew," but
Acuff-Rose refused. 2 Live Crew recorded its version anyway on the album,
"As Clean as They Wanna Be," which sold almost 250,000 copies within less
than a year. Acuff-Rose filed a copyright infringement suit in U.S. District
Court. The trial court granted a summary judgment for the defendants on the
ground that the 2 Live Crew song was a parody of the original, and thus fair
use under the Copyright Act of 1976.

On appeal, the Sixth Circuit U.S. Court of Appeals reversed the trial court
in a 2–1 decision, holding that the 2 Live Crew song's "blatantly commercial
purpose . . . prevents this parody from being fair use." The appellate court
analyzed the song on the four factors of fair use under Section 107 of the
Copyright Act, and found that: (a) every commercial use, as was the case here,
is presumptively unfair (Factor 1—purpose and character of use), (b) this work
fell within the categories of work the copyright intended to protect (Factor
2—nature of the copyrighted work), (c) by "taking the heart of the original and
making it the heart of a new work," 2 Live Crew had taken too much (Factor
3—amount and substantiality), and (d) because "the use of the work is wholly
commercial, . . . we presume a likelihood of future harm to Acuff-Rose exists"
(Factor 4—effect on the potential market).[134]

The Supreme Court of the United States also invoked the four factors, but
came to a different conclusion. The Court noted that, on the first factor, parodies
by definition must draw to some extent on the original work they are criticizing:
". . . For the purposes of Copyright law, the nub of the definitions, and the
heart of any parodist's claim to quote from existing material, is the use of some
elements of a prior author's composition to create a new one that, at least in
part, comments on the author's works."[135]

The Court went on to note, "The threshold question when fair use is raised
in defense of parody is whether a parodic character may reasonably be perceived."[136] The justices said the 2 Live Crew song "reasonably could be perceived as commenting on the original or criticizing it, to some degree. 2 Live
Crew juxtaposes the romantic musings of a man whose fantasy comes true,
with degrading taunts, a bawdy demand for sex, and a sigh of relief from
paternal responsibility."[137]

Factor 1 is only one factor in the fair use determination, according to the
Court, and commercial use should not be presumptively considered unfair.

The Supreme Court spent little time with Factor 2, noting that this criterion had never been much help "in separating the fair use sheep from the infringing goats in a parody case." The Court differed substantially with the Court of Appeals on Factor 3. The opinion noted that, although parodists cannot "skim the cream and get away scot free," the lower court "was insufficiently appreciative of parody's need for the recognizable sight or sound when it ruled 2 Live Crew's use unreasonable as a matter of law." The Supreme Court could not make a final determination from the record on the fourth factor. The opinion noted that the defendants put themselves at a disadvantage in moving for summary judgment "when they failed to address the effect on the market for rap derivatives, and confined themselves to uncontroverted submissions that there was likely no effect on the market for the original."[138] Nevertheless, the Court did not see this as a fatal flaw, and criticized the appellate court for applying the presumption that commercial use was unfair use on this factor, as it had done on the first factor. Parodies and the originals usually serve different markets, according to the justices. "We do not, of course, suggest that a parody may not harm the market at all, but when a lethal parody, like a scathing theater review, kills demand for the original, it does not produce a harm cognizable under the Copyright Act,"[139] the Court said. The key is whether the parody is acting as a substitute or as criticism.

In reversing the judgment and remanding it back to the trial court, the Supreme Court held:

> It was error for the Court of Appeals to conclude that the commercial nature of 2 Live Crew's parody of "Oh Pretty Woman" rendered it presumptively unfair. No such evidentiary presumption is available to address either the first factor, the character and purpose of the use, or the fourth, market harm, in determining whether a transformative use, such as parody, is a fair one. The court also erred in holding that 2 Live Crew had necessarily copied excessively from the Orbison original, considering the parodic purpose of the use.[140]

In July 1994, a Milwaukee songwriter, Jordon Sage, filed suit in U.S. District Court against the group Meat Loaf and songwriter Jim Steinman for copyright infringement. He sought $5 million in damages, contending that Meat Loaf's "Objects in the Rear View Mirror May Appear Closer Than They Are" is substantially similar to a song he wrote in 1989 and sent to publishers working with the rock group. In 1994, a group of freelance writers sued the *New York Times* and four other companies for reproducing their work in electronic form without authorization. The writers had been compensated for the use of their works in print, but argued they are entitled to additional royalties for electronic use.

REMEDIES FOR INFRINGEMENT

Under Section 501(a) of the current copyright statute, anyone (including state agencies and officials, as discussed) who violates any of the exclusive rights of the copyright owner is an infringer. The statute provides a wide range of remedies from injunctions to criminal penalties, although it does not codify common law infringement. To prove infringement, a plaintiff must demonstrate that (a) he or she owns the copyright to the infringed work, and (b) the defendant(s) copied the work. The latter involves proving the defendant(s) had access to the work and that the two works are substantially similar. Proving ownership is usually not difficult because the owner simply has to produce sufficient evidence that he or she created the work or that the rights to the work were transferred to him or her. Registration is one way to establish this because it constitutes *prima facie* evidence in court of the validity of the copyright if it is made prior to or within 5 years after publication. Sometimes ownership may be in dispute, however, as illustrated in a 1990 decision by the Supreme Court of the United States involving the 1954 Alfred Hitchcock movie, *Rear Window*. In *Stewart v. Abend*,[141] the Supreme court ruled 6–3 that actor James Stewart and the late film director Alfred Hitchcock had violated the copyright of Sheldon Abend to *Rear Window* when they released the film in 1981 for television and in 1983 put it on videocassette and videodisc.

The complicated story began in 1942, when a short story entitled "It Had to Be Murder" by Cornell Woolrich appeared in *Dime Detective* magazine. In 1945, Woolrich sold the movie rights only, not the copyright itself, to the story to B. G. De Sylva Productions for $9,250, with an agreement that De Sylva would have the same rights for the renewal period (which under the statute at that time was an additional 28 years). In 1953, De Sylva sold the movie rights to a production company owned by Stewart and Hitchcock, which made the story into the still highly popular classic film, *Rear Window*.[142] When Woolrich died in 1968, he left his estate, including copyrights to his works, to Columbia University. Chase Manhattan Bank, the executor for Woolrich's estate, renewed the copyright and, in 1971, sold the renewed movie rights to "It Had to Be Murder" to Sheldon Abend, a literary agent, for $650.[143] In that same year, the movie was made available for television, and Abend informed Stewart, Hitchcock's estate, and MCA, Inc. (which had released the film) that he would file suit for copyright infringement if the movie were distributed further. When MCA ignored the warning and allowed the ABC Television Network to broadcast *Rear Window*, Abend made good on his threat and sued, but the parties eventually settled out of court, with Abend getting $25,000. The saga continued, however.

In 1977, the Second Circuit U.S. Court of Appeals held that a company that had acquired derivative rights to a work still retained those rights even if the transfer of rights from the original work had expired.[144] MCA relied on that holding because *Rear Window* was a derivative work, and re-released the film in 1983 on videocassette and for cable television. Abend filed suit once again, and it was dismissed by a U.S. District Court judge. On appeal, the Ninth Circuit U.S. Court of Appeals reversed, and the Supreme Court of the United States upheld the decision 6–3. Abend stood to make millions of dollars in profits because the re-release had generated more than $12 million worldwide by the time of the Supreme Court decision, plus another $5 million in profits from release on home video.[145] Writing for the majority, Justice Sandra Day

O'Connor said the 1977 Second Circuit decision was wrong because the 1909 statute in effect at the time of the ruling provides that the original copyright to a work continues, if renewed, even if derivative rights have been granted. Thus, derivative rights expire when the original copyright expires, and the owner of the original rights can prevent the owner of the derivative rights from continuing to use the work. The Court was not sympathetic to the complaint by MCA, Stewart, and Hitchcock's heirs that "they will have to pay more for the use of works that they have employed in creating their own works. . . . [S]uch a result was contemplated by Congress and is consistent with the goals of the Copyright Act."[146] The decision affected hundreds of films and was estimated to cost the movie industry millions of dollars.[147]

Demonstrating access is usually a relatively simple matter, especially when a work has been widely distributed. But occasionally a defendant is able to prove lack of access. A typical example occurred in 1988, when rocker Mick Jagger successfully fought a copyright infringement suit against him for his hit song, "Just Another Night."[148] Reggae musician, Patrick Alley, claimed the chorus from Jagger's song had been lifted from his 1979 recording, "Just Another Night." Alley claimed that Jagger had access to his song through a drummer who had played on both records, and that Jagger probably heard Alley's song when it was played on several smaller New York radio stations. As noted earlier in this chapter, Jagger denied he had heard the song, and a U.S. District Court jury in New York ruled in his favor after hearing testimony from the defendant that included him singing some of his lyrics.[149]

Substantial similarity is typically the key in deciding an infringement case. Although it was rendered prior to enactment of the current copyright statute, a 1977 ruling by the Ninth Circuit U.S. Court of Appeals has become a leading case on the criteria for evaluating substantial similarity. In cases of direct copying, such as a chapter, extensive excerpts, and appropriation of exact wording, proof of copying is usually cut and dried, but indirect proof is typically all that can be shown, and this can be done with evidence of substantial similarity. In *Sid and Marty Krofft Television Productions, Inc. v. McDonald's Corp.*,[150] the creators of the show "H.R. Pufnstuf" successfully claimed that McDonald's television commercials infringed on their copyright because the McDonaldland setting in the hamburger chain's ads and the characters portrayed in them were substantially similar to those in "H.R. Pufnstuf." The U.S. Court of Appeals applied a two-prong test in reaching its conclusion. First, is there substantial similarity between the underlying general ideas of the two works? If the answer is "no," there is no infringement. If "yes," the second question is: Is there substantial similarity in the manner of expression of the two works? If "yes," there is infringement. If no, the lawsuit fails. Both of these are questions of fact for a jury to determine or for the judge in a bench trial. Substantial similarity is often difficult for a plaintiff to prove on the two questions, but as the Krofft case illustrates, this can be done. The court found that McDonaldland and H.R. Pufnstuf's Living Island had substantially similar characters, scenery, dialogue, and other features. Some of the most damning evidence presented at trial was that former Krofft employees had helped design and build McDonaldland.[151]

A classic case of substantial similarity involved the highly popular movie, *Jaws*. In 1982, a U.S. District Court in California found that the movie, *Great White*, was substantially similar to *Jaws*, and therefore an infringement.[152] The similarities were quite striking, as the court noted, including similar characters (an English sea captain and a shark hunter who together track down a vicious shark), a similar plot, and even opening and closing sequences that were virtually identical. The judge in the case felt that it was obvious that "the creators of *Great White* wished to be as closely connected with the plaintiff's motion picture *Jaws* as possible."[153] The producers of the infringing movie were ordered to pay damages, and an injunction was issued to further ban distribution of the film. *Great White* was dead with no sequels in sight.

The similarities were also striking in a 1989 Seventh Circuit U.S. Court of Appeals decision involving greeting cards.[154] For 2 years, Ruolo designed distinctive greeting cards for Russ Berrie & Company under a contract granting the latter the exclusive right to produce and sell them under the "Feeling Sensitive" line. When the contract expired and Ruolo notified the company that it would not be renewed, Russ Berrie marketed a similar line of cards, known as "Touching You." The appeals court upheld a jury decision that Russ Berrie had infringed because the cards were substantially similar, including being designed for similar occasions and identical in size and layout. Both cards featured two colored stripes on the left side, on which a foil butterfly is superimposed, and one colored stripe on the right side. Both series of cards were printed on cream-colored paper with handwritten messages in brown ink. The Court of Appeals characterized the action as trade dress infringement, in which the substantial similarities lie in the overall image or "look and feel" of the works, as evidenced in size, shape, color, graphics, packaging, and other visual aspects. The appellate court upheld the jury award of $4.3 million.

This same "look and feel test" is often applied in determining infringement in computer software cases, although a recent article on the issue concluded that, "while broad protection may be given by some courts to the structure, sequence and organization of a program, copyright law provides no general protection for the overall 'look and feel' of a computer program."[155] The author predicted that patent law will emerge to grant the necessary protection that copyright law does not provide for computer software.[156]

Remedies for Infringement: Injunctions, Impoundment, and Disposition

Under Section 502 of the Copyright Act, federal courts can grant both temporary and permanent ("final") injunctions to prevent infringement once infringement has been proved. The permanent injunction against *Great White*, as mentioned earlier, is an example of how this form of equitable relief can be effective. With the injunction, the movie could no longer be distributed, shown, or sold any-where in the United States. Although injunctions are clearly a form of prior restraint, the courts have indicated they are constitutionally permissible to prevent further infringement of intellectual property rights. A mere threatened infringement is usually not sufficient to warrant an injunction, but once in-fringement is proved, an injunction becomes a potent weapon available for the copyright owner. As with all injunctions, violations can subject a defendant to citation for contempt and fines as determined by the court.

Section 503 provides two other effective remedies—impoundment and dis-position. Impoundment involves the government seizing potentially infringing materials or forcing a defendant to turn them over to the custody of the court until the case is decided. In its final decision, the court can also "order the destruction or other reasonable disposition of all copies or phonorecords" determined to violate copyright.[157] The federal courts rarely have to resort to these remedies, but they clearly have the authority to use them.

Remedies for Infringement: Damages and Profits

The most common remedy for infringement is an award of damages. A copy-right owner who files suit against an alleged infringer can opt at any time before the court issues its decision (before "final judgment") for either actual damages along with any additional profits or statutory damages, but he or she cannot recover both. Under Section 504, an infringer can be liable for actual damages caused by the infringement, plus any profits attributable to the in-fringement. All the copyright owner needs to show at trial to establish the amount of profit is the infringer's gross revenue.[158] A defendant can offset the profits awarded the plaintiff by proving deductible expenses and any portion of the profits that did not come from the infringement. Otherwise, he or she may have to fork over all profits. There is no limit on the amount of actual damages the copyright owner can recover, so long as there is sufficient evidence to demonstrate the extent of the harm suffered. As with all civil suits in federal courts, judges have a responsibility to ensure that awards are not excessive in light of the evidence presented at trial. However, the judge and jury have considerable discretion in determining what is reasonable.

The 1988 revision of the Copyright Act[159] substantially increased the amount of statutory damages available. If the copyright owner of an infringed work chooses statutory damages instead of actual damages and profits, he or she can obtain an award from $500 (minimum) to $20,000 (maximum) for each work infringed, depending on what the court considers an appropriate amount. If the copyright owner can prove that the infringement was willful, he or she can recover, at the court's discretion, up to $100,000 for each work.[160] However, if the infringer can convince the court that he or she was not aware and had no reason to believe that he or she was infringing (i.e., innocent infringement), the court can reduce the statutory damages to as low as $200.[161]

There is a "fair use" provision tucked away in Section 504, under which "an employer or agent of a nonprofit educational institution, library, or archives acting within the scope of his or her employment . . ." cannot be held liable for statutory damages for infringement in reproducing a work if the person "believed and had reasonable grounds for believing that the use was a fair use."[162] A similar exception is made for public broadcasting employees who infringe by performing or reproducing a published nondramatic literary work.

Other Remedies for Infringement

Under Section 505, the court can award court costs (i.e., the full cost of litigation for that side) and reasonable attorney's fees to whichever side wins.[163] These remedies are at the discretion of the judge. Finally, under certain circumstances, anyone who willfully infringes for commercial or private financial gain can be fined up to $250,000 and/or imprisoned for a maximum of 5 years. These offenses include such actions as reproducing or distributing during any 180-day period at least 1,000 phonorecords or copies of one or more sound recordings,[164] or at least 65 copies of one or more motion pictures or other audiovisual works.[165] Most videotape recordings now carry the standard FBI warning, complete with seal, at the beginning of the tape. The FBI is indeed the primary police authority for enforcing the criminal provisions of the copyright statutes. The statutes also include a provision making it a federal crime to traffic in counterfeit labels for phonorecords and copies of motion pictures and other audiovisual works.[166]

Despite its best efforts, Congress left some gaps in the copyright law, many of which have been closed with various amendments enacted since the legislation originally passed in 1976. The most prominent gap, at least from the consumer perspective, was revealed in the one Supreme Court of the United States copyright decision with which the public is familiar—*Sony Corp. of America v. Universal City Studios, Inc.*[167] The "Sony decision," or "Betamax case" as it is popularly known, is probably the most misinterpreted and misunderstood case involving copyright since the new statute took effect. Some of the misunderstanding can be traced to inaccuracies in news stories about the decision, and to the apparent general attitude among the public that home videotaping is a fair use and should not be regulated.

The case developed when Universal Studios, Walt Disney Productions, and other television production companies sued the Sony Corporation, the largest manufacturer of videocassette recorders (VCRs)[168] sold in the United States at that time, for contributory copyright infringement. The production companies claimed the Japanese firm marketed to the public the technology to infringe on copyrighted works they owned. This infringement occurred, according to the plaintiffs, when consumers used Sony's Betamax VCRs[169] to record copyrighted programs broadcast on local stations, including "time-shifting," or recording for later use programs not viewed at the time they were broadcast. (The Court characterized this practice as the principal use of a VCR by the average owner.) A U.S. District Court judge for the Central District of California ruled that recording of broadcasts carried on the public airwaves was a fair use of copyrighted works, and thus Sony could not be held liable as a contributory infringer even if such home recording were infringement. The Ninth Circuit U.S. Court of Appeals reversed the trial court's decision, but the Supreme Court of the United States reversed the appellate court ruling. In a narrow decision that only dealt with Sony's liability for manufacturing and marketing the recorders, the Court agreed with the district court that the company was not guilty of contributory infringement. In a 5–4 opinion written by Justice John Paul Stevens, the Court concluded that home time-shifting was fair use:

> In summary, the record and findings of the District Court lead us to two conclusions. First, Sony demonstrated a significant likelihood that substantial numbers of copyright holders who license their works for broadcast on free television would not object to having their broadcasts time-shifted by private viewers. And second, respondents failed to demonstrate that time-shifting would cause any likelihood of nonminimal harm to the potential market for, or the value of, their copyrighted works. The Betamax is, therefore, capable of substantial noninfringing uses. Sony's sale of such equipment to the general public does not constitute contributory infringement of respondents' rights.[170]

The Court went on to note that there is no indication in the Copyright Act that Congress intended to make it unlawful for consumers to record programs for later viewing in the home or to prohibit the sale of recorders. "It may well be that Congress will take a fresh look at this new technology, just as it so often has examined other innovations in the past. But it is not our job to apply laws that have not yet been written."[171] After the decision, several bills were proposed in Congress to respond to the Court's holding, such as taxing recorders and blank tapes, but most legislators apparently felt the political fallout from such legislation would be too great.

The Sony decision, which barely attracted a majority of the justices, left many unanswered questions. Is videotaping at home an infringement? Although the Court said that the record supported the trial court's decision that home time-shifting was fair use, the fair use doctrine does not mention such use as permissible. In fact, a literal application of the four criteria for fair use would appear not to protect this practice. For example, home taping typically involves recording the entire program (more than a substantial portion under Factor 3); its purpose is entertainment, rather than nonprofit educational use (Factor 1). Contrary to the Court's musings, such taping likely negatively affects the potential market for the work (Factor 4). Is it fair use to record cable television programs, including pay channels? Is it fair use to edit programs as they are recorded, such as deleting commercials? Do recorded programs have to be erased as soon as they are viewed, or is it fair use to archive them for future multiple viewings?

REGISTRATION

Although registration is no longer required for copyright protection,[172] there are some major advantages and the process is relatively simple. The advantages include:

1. Public record of the copyright.
2. Standing in court to file suit for infringement.
3. If made within 5 years of publication, *prima facie* evidence in court of the copyright's validity.
4. If made within 3 months after publication or prior to infringement, the availability of statutory damages and attorney's fees.

Registration may be made anytime during the duration of the copyright by simply sending the following in the same envelope or package to the Copyright Office:

1. A completed application form (different types of works have different forms, as indicated below).
2. A $20 filing fee (for most works).
3. One copy or phonorecord if the work is unpublished or was first published outside the United States, or two copies or phonorecords if the work was first published in the United States.

There are 21 different registration forms, and it is essential that the correct form be filed. There is even a Form CA to correct or amplify information given on an earlier form. Form TX is used to register published and unpublished nondramatic literary works, including advertising copy if primarily text. Form TX is also used for reference works, directories, catalogs, and compilations of information. (See the appendices for a sample form.) Form VA is used for works of the visual arts, such as sculptures and architecture, and works used in the sale or advertising of goods and services if the copyrightable material is primarily pictorial or graphic. Motion pictures and other audiovisual works use Form PA. Form SR is for sound recordings, and there are forms for certain types of group registrations. Public relations agencies frequently use Form SE, which is for serials such as periodicals, newspapers, annuals, journals, and proceedings and transactions of societies. In late 1996, the Copyright Office introduced shorter versions ("short forms") for forms PA, TX, and VA. These are one-page forms that may be used only when the author is the sole owner of the work, the work is not a work made for hire, and it is completely new. Registration is effective the day the Copyright Office receives the properly completed application, fee, and materials. Certificates can take as long as 4 months, but most are mailed within 1–2 months. The certificates are simply copies of the form signed and dated by the Copyright Office.

COPYRIGHT PROTECTION FOR NEWER TECHNOLOGIES

Copyright protection exists for a wide range of technologies, including computer programs, automated databases, and semiconductor chips (also known as mask works). Computer programs have been the subject of considerable litigation even with the new statute, but the courts have made it clear that computer software enjoys copyright protection. In June 1988, the Copyright Office announced, after public hearings and a review of public comments, that it would "require that all copyrightable expression embodied in a computer program owned by the same claimant, including computer screen displays, be registered on a single application form" (Form TX or PA).[173] Until that time, conflicting court opinions had muddled the issue of whether a single form could be used. Now the question appears resolved, although other new technologies will undoubtedly raise other questions. The courts have also made it clear that copyright protection covers object codes, source codes, and microcodes in software, as well as the overall structure of the program, or the "look and feel" as it is commonly known.

The copyright statute does not specifically mention automated databases, but the Copyright Office and the courts interpret the legislative history of the Act to include automated databases as compilations of facts, and thus literary works.[174] Such databases, as with all copyrightable works, must involve originality and not simply be a mere mechanical collection of information.[175] Finally, semiconductor chips (sometimes called *integrated circuits*) were added to the list of copyrightable works with the Semiconductor Chip Protection Act of 1984.[176] The provisions regarding these mask works differ from those of other works.

MORAL RIGHTS

The most controversial issue in the debate over whether the United States should join the Berne Convention was Article 6bis, which requires Convention members to protect the moral rights or *droit moral* of authors.[177] These rights are entirely independent of copyright, but by agreeing to adhere to the Convention, the United States is obligated to abide by all of the provisions, including those involving moral rights. Moral rights fall into two categories under the Convention: paternity rights and integrity rights, both of which have been formally recognized in many other countries for some time. Paternity rights involve the right to be credited as the author of a work and to prevent others from attributing a work to you that is essentially not your work. For example, a publisher who, without consent, omitted the name of the primary author from a book or a magazine editor who, without consent, falsely attributed an article to a well-known author to sell more copies or lend credibility to the magazine would be violating paternity rights. (Even if the famous author contributed a small amount to the work, his or her name cannot be used without his or her consent.) Integrity rights basically involve "the right to object to distortion, other alteration of a work, or derogatory action prejudicial to the author's honor or reputation in relation to the work."[178] A classic example of the latter was the 1976 Second Circuit U.S. Court of Appeals decision to grant a preliminary injunction against the ABC Television Network on the ground that the copyright of the British comedy troupe known as Monty Python of "Monty Python's Flying Circus" fame was violated when the network extensively edited the programs primarily to make room for commercials.[179] The court held that the changes significantly impaired the integrity of the works, and that Monty Python had the right to prevent "distortion or truncation" of its creations. The court cited the common law, copyright law, and Section 43(a) of the Lanham Act dealing with unfair competition for its authority. Thus, although the comedy team had granted the British Broadcasting Corporation (BBC) the right to license the programs overseas, that right did not include allowing licensees to significantly distort them.

PLAGIARISM

Space precludes an extensive discussion of plagiarism, or the misappropriation of another's intellectual or creative works. However, it should be noted that this is a recurrent problem. It is often difficult to demonstrate plagiarism, but accusations crop up from time to time. During the 1988 presidential election, one of the primary candidates admitted to quoting a British statesman without attribution. A few years ago, a prominent syndicated advice columnist was accused of recycling some of her earlier columns without informing readers of the fact (a form of self-plagiarism, perhaps?). H. Joachim Maitre, dean of Boston University's College of Communications, resigned a week after he was accused of plagiarism for using several passages that were identical or nearly identical to those in an article by Public Broadcasting System film critic, Michael Medved.[180] His alleged plagiarism was uncovered by the *Boston Globe*. Most actions of this type do not result in a lawsuit for copyright infringement, but the resultant negative publicity is often punishing. Smart advertising and public relations professionals know that when there is any doubt about whether a reader, listener, or viewer would be misled into thinking that a work is entirely original when it is not, clear attribution is essential for both expressions and ideas. Attribution will not necessarily prevent a successful lawsuit for copyright infringement, but it can at least alleviate perceptions of plagiarism.

SUMMARY AND CONCLUSIONS

Trademarks have considerable protection under both state and federal laws, but trademark holders must take aggressive steps to ensure that their marks do not become diluted, and risk going into the public domain. Most advertisers and other commercial and noncommercial enterprises constantly monitor the use of their trademarks for possible infringement, while making sure that they treat the trademarks of others with appropriate respect.

Copyright is strictly a federal matter because the Copyright Act of 1976 eliminated state copyright laws and common law copyright. The Act made other substantial changes in copyright law, not the least of which was significantly increasing the amount and duration of copyright protection for original works of authorship. Public perceptions and even those of communication professionals still consist of myths and distortions that bear little relationship to the real world of copyright. Many writers and artists still find it difficult to believe that copyright protection exists automatically on creation of a work in a tangible form without benefit of registration, and that attribution alone does not protect one from a successful infringement suit. The concept of "fair use" is even more difficult to comprehend, and the courts and Congress have added to the confusion.

Nevertheless, the new federal copyright statute is a powerful arsenal for the creators of original works of authorship. The fact that copyrighted works, other than works made for hire and anonymous works, are protected for 50 years beyond the last surviving author's death reflects the tone of law. It is an author's law, plain and simple, and advertising and public relations practitioners must be cautious in using the expressions of others. The law is not very forgiving, as attested by its provisions granting remedies from injunctions and damages to criminal penalties.

15

Self-Regulation by the Industry

Some years ago, a television station executive, a friend of one of the authors, received a snippy letter from the Code Authority of the National Association of Broadcasters (NAB). The letter complained that his station had committed a violation of the NAB Code. In euphemistic language, the letter referred to "products and services of a personal nature" that must be advertised with "special emphasis on ethics and the canons of good taste." His station's specific offense? "Seems we've been running commercials for Preparation H during the dinner hour," he said, adding that any additional advertising for that particular "product of a personal nature" in the future would be telecast during a different time period. He considered it an honor that his station had earned the right to display the NAB Seal, a photo of which he proudly televised to viewers during sign-on and sign-off each day. He did not want to risk having his station's seal revoked in a dispute over the timing of an ad for a medication to treat hemorrhoids.

Not all problems with the NAB Code were so easily resolved. From the beginning—the NAB Radio Code was adopted in 1929 and the Television Code in 1952—the NAB urged its members to pledge themselves to adhere to this ambitious attempt by an industry to police itself. The Code Authority reviewed some 2,000 new commercials a year, including advertisers' documentation of claims made by commercials, and monitored how member stations handled advertising as well as programming. A monthly advisory, *Code News*, would admonish member stations and networks to beware of current policy. For example: "Presentation of marriage, the family, and similarly important human relationships, and material with sexual connotations, shall not be treated exploitatively or irresponsibly, but with sensitivity."

But enforcing such lofty objectives was not easy. First, NAB membership was purely voluntary (typically only about 40% of all U.S. radio stations and

60% of the TV stations). Second, the only punishment the NAB could mete out to a Code violator was to forbid that station to display the code seal—something less than a compelling penalty.[1]

Eventually, the NAB Code was challenged in the courts. The specific issue involved the Code's policy on "clutter"—in this case, a rule against advertising similar or related products in the same commercial message (e.g., two different models of Chevrolet). The NAB Code Authority felt this confused viewers. The U.S. Department of Justice felt it was a restraint of trade. The court agreed with the Justice Department.[2] Facing further court challenges to other parts of the Code, the NAB decided shortly thereafter to abandon the Code altogether.

The failure of the NAB Code illustrates the difficulty the mass communications industry has in policing itself. A vigorous self-regulatory code may punish some offenders, but it may face the far greater risk of being judged a monopolistic attempt to restrain trade. An attempt to limit freedom of expression, for advertisements as well as other communications messages, may infringe on the constitutional protections afforded by Article I and the First and Fourteenth Amendments of the U.S. Constitution. In short, the self-regulation highway can be a narrow one, its surface often mottled by potholes. Still, there are a number of self-regulatory principles and practices that can work throughout the advertising industry; this chapter examines some of them.

THE RIGHT TO REFUSE SERVICE

Central to self-regulation in mass communications is the right of the publisher or broadcaster to reject material offered for print or broadcast. The rejection can come if that information is thought to place the publisher or broadcaster on shaky ethical or legal ground, or for whatever reason the material might be objectionable. Refusal of service is a powerful weapon, liberally utilized.

The National Broadcasting Company (NBC) will not accept an advertisement that is a testimonial if, in NBC's judgment, the testimonial "does not fairly reflect what a substantial proportion of other consumers are likely to experience."[3] CBS, Inc., will not telecast a commercial for cereal or other breakfast products unless the message clearly establishes "in audio and video, for at least three seconds, the role of the product within the framework of a nutritionally balanced breakfast."[4] Capital Cities/ABC, Inc., will not sell advertisements for fireworks, handguns, and attendant ammunition, nor permit the use of firearms as props in nonfirearm advertising unless the ads are for legitimate security services, military recruiting, and the like.[5] These and numerous other stipulations are listed in the advertising guidelines and policies of these networks, enforced by their broadcast standards departments.

Although self-regulatory policies and enforcement levels vary widely throughout the media industry, most publications and broadcasters have adopted some form of acceptability guidelines for advertising messages. For example, the San Francisco *Chronicle*'s advertising policy has this to say about comparative price claims:

> An advertiser may offer a price reduction or savings by comparing his selling price with his own former selling price; the *current* price of *identical* merchandise sold by other merchants; or the current price of comparable items sold by others, providing the advertisement is clear as to which of these references the comparative price or savings claim relates.
>
> Ads containing price comparisons of comparable items from competitive stores or manufacturers must be accompanied with documentation of the price survey which include stores or manufacturers, date survey conducted, size, model number or other data necessary to make a fair comparison.

These and other restrictions are well supported by law and the courts. Mass media owners and managers are in control of the content of their publications or broadcasts. That territory was well staked out in a 1933 case, *Shuck v. The Carroll Daily Herald*. When an Iowa newspaper would not accept an advertisement for a local cleaning concern, the cleaner sued to compel the publisher to run the ad anyway. The Iowa federal court upheld the publisher's right to refuse service:

> The newspaper business is an ordinary business. It is a business essentially private in its nature—as private as that of the baker, grocer, or milkman, all of whom perform a service on which, to a greater or lesser extent, the communities depend, but which bears no relation to the public as to warrant its inclusion in the category of businesses charged with a public use. If a newspaper were required to accept an advertisement, it could be compelled to publish a news item. . . .
>
> Thus, as a newspaper is a strictly private enterprise, the publishers thereof have a right to publish whatever advertisements they desire and to refuse to publish whatever advertisements they do not desire to publish.[6]

That mandate would not prove absolute, as later court decisions would affirm, but a broad principle was laid down: The owner, and not the customer or anyone else, of a print or broadcast business decides what is published or broadcast. Forty years later, the Supreme Court reaffirmed that principle in *Miami Herald Publishing Co. v. Tornillo*. In this case, a political candidate, incensed by two editorial attacks on his record by the newspaper, insisted that the newspaper publish his reply to the attacks verbatim. Tornillo invoked an ancient Florida statute that provided the "right of reply" to one who had been damaged by the press. When the paper refused, Tornillo brought suit and lost. Calling Tornillo's demand an "intrusion into the function of editors," the Supreme Court of the United States struck down the Florida right-of-reply statute:

> A newspaper is more than a passive receptacle or conduit for news, comment, and advertising. The choice of material to go into a newspaper, and the decisions made as to limitations on the size and content of the paper, and treatment of public issues and public officials—whether fair or unfair—constitute the exercise of editorial control and judgment. It has yet to be demonstrated how governmental regulation of this crucial process can be exercised consistent with First Amendment guarantees of a free press as they have evolved to this time.[7]

Thus, a publisher or broadcast station owner generally has the right to refuse to accept an advertisement—even if that advertisement is for a product that can be lawfully sold. The publisher or station owner can insist that any advertisement deemed unsuitable be modified to conform to the publication's (or station's or network's) acceptability policies or else face rejection. Benjamin Franklin, the entrepreneurial genius who was the first American ever to make a fortune in the printing business, was also among the first to insist that he was in charge of his own publications. "My newspaper," he wrote tersely, "is not a stagecoach with seats on it for everyone."[8]

Another pioneer in the self-regulation of advertising was Clark W. Bryan, who, in the spring of 1885, brought out the first issue of a new magazine called *Good Housekeeping*. Clark envisioned "a family journal conducted in the highest interests of the household," and dedicated the magazine "to produce and perpetuate perfection, or as near perfection as may be obtained in the household." The assignment was not an easy one, especially at a time when national markets were being created for advertising messages. Clark's readers, he felt, might be confused and misled:

> Their mothers and grandmothers had bought from reputable local merchants whatever household necessities could not be produced at home. But now, food and other products were beginning to come from distant, untried suppliers, who were themselves struggling with the new problems of mass production. Many firms had grossly inadequate standards of quality control. Others were deliberately out to cheat the public.
> "Spanish olive oil" was often made from cottonseed. Canned vegetables proved to be decayed. Many patent medicines, guaranteed to cure anything that ailed you, contained as much as 40 percent alcohol, and unsuspecting mothers quieted their children with "soothing syrup" whose active ingredient was morphine.[9]

Clark regarded himself as a guardian of his readers' interests. By 1901 he had established the Good Housekeeping Institute, a laboratory for testing products to be advertised in the magazine. A product that was not what it claimed to be or did not perform as it should would not be advertised in the pages of *Good Housekeeping*. A product that did pass was awarded the magazine's famous "Seal of Approval."

Advertising testing and verification procedures throughout the media industry tend to be far less elaborate than *Good Housekeeping*'s, but many publications and broadcasters do have—and enforce—broad guidelines. For example, the *Chicago Tribune* has established nine basic principles for advertising acceptability. These principles are in accord with the advertising standards of the Better Business Bureau, and city, state, and federal agencies:

1. Every advertisement must constitute a clear statement, invitation, offer, proposition, or announcement made in good faith.
2. This newspaper encourages placement of positive advertising and recognizes the need for competitive statements in many situations. However,

we discourage disparaging or negative advertising, which, directly or indirectly, tends to mislead or reflect unfairly on competitive organizations, institutions, merchandise, or services.

3. Advertising is not acceptable that, in the opinion of this newspaper, is judged indecent, salacious, suggestive, or offensive, or that contains text or illustrations in poor taste.

4. Advertising is not acceptable that contains attacks of a personal, racial, or religious nature.

5. Advertising is not acceptable if submitted with the expectation of receiving publicity in news or feature columns.

6. Advertising is not acceptable that tends to destroy the confidence of readers or advertisers. This includes advertising that is misleading, deceptive, or fraudulent, or that grossly exaggerates or makes unwarranted claims.

7. Advertising is not acceptable that may cause injury to the health or morale of our readers.

8. Advertising is not acceptable that, in the opinion of this newspaper, evades or violates any law, regulation, or ordinance—municipal, state, or federal—or attempts to encourage such an evasion or violation.

9. The *Chicago Tribune* reserves the right to reject any advertising that, in its opinion, is unacceptable.

Publications or broadcasters that do not approve of certain products may elect to refuse, on principle, to advertise them. For example, *The Gamecock*, a student newspaper at the University of South Carolina, will not accept advertisements from persons or organizations selling ready-to-go term papers on a variety of topics. *The Reader's Digest* includes the following warning in its rate card: "The publisher reserves the right to reject any advertising or to limit the advertising content of any edition (National, Demographic, or Regional). Advertising for cigarettes, tobacco and alcoholic beverage products are not accepted."

Moreover, the publication or broadcaster can require advertisers to provide a great deal of information before deciding whether to accept an advertising message. At NBC, among others throughout the industry, the advertising guidelines state:

For each commercial, advertising agencies are asked to submit a shooting script or storyboard, a new product sample and label/package insert, substantiation for all material claims, authentication of all demonstrations and testimonial statements. When the pre-production discussions have concluded and the agency has produced the commercial, the finished version must be submitted for screening and final clearance.

The policies at CBS and Capital Cities/ABC are much the same. ABC's guidelines include this language:

In order to determine the acceptability of commercial material submitted for broadcast, Capital Cities/ABC has the right to investigate the advertiser and the accuracy of all statements and claims made in commercial copy. When affirmative claims are made for a product or service, the law requires the advertiser to have substantiation or documentation providing a reasonable basis for the claims. . . .

Capital Cities/ABC reserves the right at any time to revoke its approval of and to require the elimination or revision of any advertising matter which is inconsistent with Capital Cities/ABC standards and policies. Capital Cities/ABC also reserves the right to require revision of any advertising matter to meet emergency circumstances or situations of unusual significance.

In determining whether to accept or reject advertising messages, each publisher or broadcaster insists on making its own decision, regardless of how others might act. The San Francisco Newspaper Agency, publisher of that city's two major dailies, enforces this policy:

The San Francisco *Chronicle* and the San Francisco *Examiner* support the advertising codes of American Business and the Better Business Bureau.

The San Francisco *Chronicle* and the San Francisco *Examiner* will never knowingly publish advertising which in its judgment:

1. Is designed to mislead, deceive, or defraud.
2. Is in violation of local, state, or federal laws.
3. Is offensive or in poor taste.

Nothing in these standards, use of specific industry codes or other advisory resources will in any way limit the right of these newspapers to exercise independent judgment in accepting or rejecting advertising for publication.

The San Francisco *Chronicle* and the San Francisco *Examiner* reserve the right to decline any advertising which in their opinion is unacceptable.[10]

Note the phrases "in its [the newspaper's] judgment," "independent judgment," and "in their opinion." These mean that the newspapers, not some outside mediator or regulatory agency, decide what is acceptable. If a newspaper rejects a movie ad because the artwork in the ad is deemed too racy for a family audience, the movie people have two choices: (a) modify the ad to make it acceptable, or (b) try to get the ad published elsewhere.

But what if there is, for all practical purposes, no "elsewhere" available (i.e., no other newspaper of consequence in that particular market)? Some disgruntled advertisers have protested that a monopoly newspaper is, or should be, a common carrier, like the telephone company, water company, or only mass transit system in the area. Such reasoning has never found much support in the courts. Freedom of the press and broadcasting includes the freedom both to publish and *not* to publish, as the owner thinks is warranted. This has led to a cynical statement that "the only person who has freedom of the press is the owner." That assertion has some validity. But, in defense of the publishers and broadcasters, governments and the courts historically do not make good editors—at least they have not in countries where the media are not in private hands.

The courts have affirmed the owner's right to control content on solid constitutional grounds:

1. Article I, Section 10 of the U.S. Constitution says "No State shall enter into any law ... impairing the obligation of contracts." Advertising is sold on a contract basis. If a state is not permitted to impair a contract already made, presumably it cannot compel an unwilling publisher or broadcaster to enter into one.
2. An attempt to tell media owners they must accept an advertisement or an article flies in the face of the press freedom granted by the First Amendment.
3. Telling an owner that an advertisement or article must be printed in effect deprives that owner of property—space in a publication or precious broadcast time—without due process of law, a violation of the Fifth Amendment.[11]

Thus, the media's right to refuse service is powerful and ingrained. But like so much else connected to the First Amendment, that right is not absolute.

PROBLEMS WITH REFUSAL OF SERVICE:
I. RESTRAINT OF TRADE

If a newspaper or broadcaster's refusal to accept advertising is found to be an anticompetitive form of business practice, then the federal authorities may step in. This is precisely what happened in *Lorain Journal v. United States*, a 1951 case involving an aggressive newspaper in upstate Ohio. The Lorain *Journal* and its sister paper, the *Times Herald*, together enjoyed nearly saturation circulation coverage in this well-to-do market on the shores of Lake Erie. The newspaper company had also sought a license to operate a radio station, but the Federal Communications Commission (FCC) chose instead to award the license to a different company situated in Elyria, a nearby community. Furious at this threat to its advertising income (its only other competitor had been one weekly newspaper), the Lorain *Journal* decided to play hardball. If you advertise with the radio station, the newspaper warned its customers, we will refuse your advertising in our newspaper. It was a menacing announcement, coming from the most powerful ad medium in the market, and advertisers were intimidated by it. Some promptly canceled their radio ads, driving the new radio station toward financial ruin.

At this point, the Justice Department interceded with an antitrust suit against the *Journal*, alleging that the newspaper's heavy-handed action was an attempt to monopolize trade in violation of the Sherman Antitrust Act. A federal court granted an injunction against the paper, effectively preventing it from carrying out its threat to punish advertisers who did business with the radio station. The newspaper argued that the injunction violated the newspaper's First Amendment right to refuse service and to exercise its freedom of the press. On appeal, the Supreme Court of the United States, by a 7–0 vote, upheld the lower court, charging that the newspaper's "bold, relentless, and predatory commercial behavior" was in no way protected by the First Amendment. In a stinging rebuke to the newspaper, Justice Harold Burton wrote for the Court:

> A single newspaper, already enjoying a substantial monopoly in its area, violates the "attempt to monopolize" clause of the Sherman Act ... when it uses its monopoly to destroy threatened competition. ... The right claimed by the publisher is neither absolute nor exempt from regulation ... [Refusal to accept advertising] as a purposeful means of monopolizing interstate commerce is prohibited by the Sherman Act. The operator of the radio station, equal with the publisher of a newspaper, is entitled to the protection of the Act.[12]

Much the same kind of thing happened a few years later in a much larger market, Kansas City. Here the morning *Times* and the afternoon *Star* were published by the same large company, which also owned a local radio station and a television station. The issue here was a "forced combination," as it was called, in which advertisers who wanted to buy space in one paper were actually required to buy space in both, or be denied the right to buy advertising time on the powerful newspaper-owned radio and television stations.

Again, the Justice Department moved in, making a case that the *Star–Times* company wielded enough monopolistic clout to unfairly curtail competition—in effect forcing readers and advertisers to accept terms that would not be possible under reasonably competitive conditions. The newspaper defended by claiming that the *Star* and the *Times* were in fact separate newspapers, competing with each other. The trial court disagreed, finding that the newspaper company was indeed a monopoly, and that its forced combination advertising practices were in criminal violation of the Sherman Act. When the Eighth U.S. Circuit Court of Appeals upheld the ruling, the newspaper company chose to settle the case by signing a consent decree agreeing to tough terms dictated by the Justice Department: The newspaper would sell off its radio and TV stations and end its practice of requiring advertisers to buy space in both papers if they wanted to use only one.

Losses in cases such as this can prove quite expensive. The antitrust convictions became the basis for individual lawsuits filed by advertisers and others who had been hurt by anticompetitive practices. If an advertiser can prove the newspaper's monopolistic behavior hurt business, the advertiser can recover treble damages, or three times the amount it actually lost due to the newspaper's advertising policy. A number of such lawsuits were filed in both Lorain, Ohio, and in Kansas City in the wake of the Justice Department's victories. Legal defenses in such matters do not come cheap, and most of the suits were settled out of court.[13]

To reiterate, a publisher or broadcaster that refuses an advertisement on ethical grounds or as a matter of appropriateness and taste is on solid ground. But a publisher or broadcaster that refuses an advertisement in an attempt to control or stifle competition is not, and may be heading for trouble.

PROBLEMS WITH REFUSAL OF SERVICE:
II. PUBLICLY OWNED MEDIA

Although most of the commercial mass communications media are privately owned, some are not. Included in this latter group are mass transit systems, which carry "car cards," or poster advertising, and scholastic and collegiate newspapers. With these nonprivate media, the right to refuse certain advertising messages is less clear-cut.

To a great degree, the right of a publicly owned communications medium to refuse advertising is directly connected to the extent to which that medium has become a public forum for "cause" or "idea" advertising. For example, during the turbulent 1960s, a California-based group called "Women for Peace" sought to purchase car cards on buses owned by the Alameda–contra costa mass transit system. Calling for an end to the Vietnam war, the placards urged bus riders to express their concern for a permanent cease fire in letters to President Lyndon B. Johnson. The transit system refused to accept the advertising, claiming that political messages and advertising on controversial subjects were not allowed. The Women for Peace sued, arguing that other "cause" and "idea" advertising messages—although perhaps on less controversial matters than a politically negotiated settlement of the war in Vietnam—had been accepted by the transit system previously. The Women for Peace eventually won the case in the California Supreme Court. The opinion held:

> We conclude that defendants [the transit authority], having opened a forum for the expression of ideas by providing facilities for advertisements on its buses, cannot for reasons of administrative convenience decline to accept advertising expressing opinions and beliefs within the ambit of First Amendment protection.[14]

New York City's Metropolitan Transportation Authority and the Niagara Frontier Transit were likewise overruled by the courts after they had initially refused to accept a quasipolitical ad and an abortion rights group ad, respectively.[15]

However, the Supreme Court of the United States, in *Lehman v. City of Shaker Heights*, held that a public transit system could safely reject "cause" advertising if no public forum had been created. The Shaker Heights mass transit advertising policy was to accept commercial advertising messages only; a request to carry a car card bearing a political message was rejected. The Supreme Court ruled in favor of the Shaker Heights system, saying that the commercial-messages-only policy did not create a public forum, and thus the refusal to accept a political ad was justified.[16]

Student newspapers published in state-supported high schools and colleges are also regarded by the law as government-owned. Hence, the right to refuse advertising is likewise complicated. Among the factors to be considered is the degree to which the publication is an integral part of the curriculum or, conversely, an independent student voice. If it is the former (i.e., a laboratory publication published under faculty supervision), the courts may find the paper to be a nonpublic forum and school authorities can safely exercise control over content. The Supreme Court, in a 1988 case, *Hazelwood School District v. Kuhlmeier*, established that a school, through its principal in his capacity as publisher of a laboratory newspaper, "may disassociate itself from speech that is ungrammatical, poorly written, inadequately researched, biased or prejudiced, vulgar or profane, or suitable for immature audiences." In this case, Hazelwood's principal had censored considerable portions of a student-produced laboratory newspaper because, he said, the passages in question were offensive and possibly invaded the privacy of several members of the student body. One of the student editors sued, claiming her First Amendment rights had been infringed on by the principal's decision. Siding with the principal, the majority opinion, written by Justice White, held that educators: ". . . do not offend the First Amendment by exercising editorial control over the style and content of student speech in school-sponsored expressive activities so long as their actions are reasonably related to legitimate pedagogical concerns."[17]

An independent student newspaper, especially at the college level, generally has more freedom. The student editor, if permitted to exercise independent judgment, is granted First Amendment freedom as well. For example, in *Mississippi Gay Alliance v. Goudelock*, a student editor at Mississippi State University chose to refuse an advertisement offering legal aid and counseling to gay and lesbian students. The campus Gay Alliance sued, demanding that its ad be accepted and published. But the Fifth U.S. Court of Appeals sided with the editor, finding that the refusal was an editorial judgment on the part of the student, made without state interference, and safeguarded by the First Amendment.[18]

Another factor to be considered is the degree to which the student newspaper has become a public forum. A college newspaper, the *Royal Purple* at Wisconsin State University–Whitewater, had a policy of refusing "editorial advertisements" expressing political views, as well as other advertising that might "attack an institution, group, person, or product." Under this policy, the paper refused some political advertising. A lawsuit ensued, and the U.S. District Court overturned the *Royal Purple* decision to refuse to carry the advertising. Judge James Doyle held that:

> Defendant's acceptance of commercial advertisements and of those public service announcements that do not "attack an institution, group, person, or product" and their rejection of editorial advertisements constitutes an impermissible form of censorship.
>
> There can be no doubt that defendants' restrictive advertising policy—a policy enforced under color of state law—is a denial of free speech and expression.[19]

Some legal scholars have argued that there is, or should be, a First Amendment right of access to the media of mass communications. Prominent among those holding this view has been Professor Jerome A. Barron, who contended that the mass media are censors because they restrict the information and opinions they disseminate, and because they can deny new or unpopular ideas to be presented to the wider audience. The "marketplace of ideas," as envisioned by John Milton, John Stuart Mill, Oliver Wendell Holmes, and others, cannot work unless the media are truly open to all, Barron maintained. Those individuals who do not control the media, he added, should at least be able to express their views through them. "At the very minimum," Barron wrote, "the creation of two remedies is essential—(1) a nondiscriminating right to purchase editorial advertisements in daily newspapers, and (2) a right of reply for public figures and public officers defamed in newspapers."[20]

Barron's position has not found widespread acceptance in the courts. Indeed, the "right of reply," which he advocated and which is recognized in a number of other countries, was specifically shot down by the Supreme Court of the United States in *Tornillo*, cited earlier. In the process, the Court reaffirmed that private owners can exercise control over the content of the media they own. However, the courts have also held that there is, or can be, a right of access to publicly owned media, but the access is a limited one, narrowly defined: If a state-owned medium (e.g., a transit system advertising program, or a state-owned student newspaper) chooses to become a public forum by accepting "cause" (as opposed to purely commercial) advertising, then it cannot refuse to accept other types of "cause" advertising, even the far more controversial "cause" messages, so long as the decision is made by an agent of the state.[21] However, if the decision to refuse "cause" advertising is made by someone not acting as an agent of the state (e.g., the student editor of an independent campus newspaper), that refusal will likely be upheld, even in a state-owned media situation.

CONSUMERISM

Recent years have seen a striking growth in consumer protection organizations—groups with a mission to bring pressure to bear on businesses to explain and protect the power and rights of consumers. These groups include the Consumer Federation of America, the National Council of Senior Citizens, the national board of the Young Women's Christian Association, and the National Consumer League, as well as consumer advocacy groups across the country. Many environmental groups and their formidible numbers of members are also concerned with consumer issues.

Throughout much of this country's history, American consumers have been essentially passive, bound by their own pride in individual shrewdness as horsetraders, loath to go whining to the government if a product or a deal went sour. The operative phrase was *caveat emptor*—let the buyer beware— meaning that a purchaser should examine, judge, and test the product before making an offer to buy. Although the courts applied this maxim more to auctions, livestock sales, and the like than to consumer products and services (often accompanied by warranties), there was still widespread reluctance on the part of U.S. consumers to complain.

Like much else in our history, consumer passivity changed into highly charged political activism during the late 1960s and 1970s. Venting their frustrations to business and government, militant consumers demanded that they be given more information and better products and services. Although it could not precisely be characterized as a consumer revolt, the consumerism movement was highly vocal and politically astute, bringing about substantial reforms in the way many products were produced, labeled, and advertised. The frustration of the buying public has been attributed to these triggering causes:

1. Exposure in the mass media of the shortcomings of business, along with powerful muckraking books such as Ralph Nader's *Unsafe at Any Speed* and Donald A. Randall's *The Great American Auto Repair.*
2. Rising costs, especially for health care and interest charges, and oil and gas products.
3. Massive dissatisfaction with the quality of many U.S.-made products.
4. Corruption of officials and business leaders.
5. An increase in the educational level and sophistication of the consumer.[22]

Much of the consumers' anger has been directed at advertising. "Advertising," proclaimed one congressman during the early years of the consumerism movement, "causes people to buy things they don't need with money they don't have to impress neighbors they don't know." Although many would sharply question that assertion, on the grounds that it assumes advertising wields far more influence than it actually does, the fact remains that consumers were demanding more power and getting it. In the past, it could be argued, the consumer possessed essentially just one right, the right to refuse to buy a product, and one expectation, that the product would be safe and perform satisfactorily. Now, consumers contend, they have additional entitlements: (a) the right to be adequately informed about the more important aspects of the product, (b) the right to be protected against questionable products and marketing practices, and (c) the right to influence products and marketing practices in directions that will enhance the quality of life.[23]

Beyond that, many companies have been under pressure—real, or perhaps anticipated—to assure their customers that the products being advertised were manufactured under environmentally safe conditions, reflecting genuine adherence to water and air pollution control standards, the recycling of scarce resources whenever possible, and other ecological concerns.

Like many of the political and social reforms originating in the turbulent 1960s, the consumer movement has endured. Today, private consumer groups such as the Consumer Federation of America have formed powerful alliances with state and federal consumer protection agencies. The Consumers Union of the United States, a nonprofit agency, provides information and guidance to members throughout the country. *Consumer Reports,* a monthly magazine that will not accept commercial advertising, publishes research studies on products and services of all types, ranging from new cars to microwave ovens to nutritional content of canned fruit drinks to yields and performance records on mutual funds, for its audience of well over 2 million subscribers each month.

Shrewd advertisers have been impressed with the popular appeal of consumerism and have modified their advertising and marketing accordingly, providing more factual information, strengthening their warranties, and setting up "hot lines" and other response mechanisms to improve customer service.

INDUSTRY CODES

Despite the problems with enforceability of an industry-wide code, such as those encountered by the NAB, a number of mass communications organizations, associations, and industries have adopted broad sets of guidelines affecting their particular fields. Nine such codes are presented in their entirety in Appendix A.

BUSINESS EFFORTS TO MAINTAIN PUBLIC CONFIDENCE IN ADVERTISING

The Council of Better Business Bureaus, through an ambitious program of voluntary self-regulation, for more than 20 years has provided a mechanism for challenging advertising that may be deemed unethical, misleading, or deceptive. The Council's two principal bodies are the National Advertising Division (NAD), which offers an alternate, private dispute-resolution mechanism for national advertisers, and the National Advertising Review Board (NARB), which is, in effect, a court of appeals for NAD decisions. As with other alternate dispute-resolution services, neither the NAD nor the NARB has any official judicial standing. For instance, it cannot: (a) levy a fine on offenders, (b) order an advertiser to stop publishing or broadcasting an ad, (c) prevent anyone from advertising, or (d) boycott an advertiser, product, or service.

Indeed, the only real power this process has comes with publicity (the deliberations are kept confidential, but the findings are made public), and perhaps a certain amount of peer pressure it generates. The idea is to allow neutral arbitrators to recommend solutions to advertising disputes without going through the trauma and expense of formal litigation in the courts. The system seems to have worked well over time: More than 3,200 advertising disputes have been resolved through use of the NAD/NARB process.[24] Advertising leaders claim that this demonstrates a highly successful record of voluntary industry compliance.

NAD's mission is to look into complaints about truth and accuracy in national (but not purely local) advertising messages. Once the NAD launches an inquiry into an advertising claim, it gathers information from all sides about it, determines the key issues, and then issues an opinion as to whether the claims have been substantiated. If a claim is found to be unproved, the NAD does not administer penalties, but simply asks the advertiser to modify or discontinue making the claim. The advertiser may voluntarily abide by the NAD recommendation (most do), but may choose instead to appeal the NAD finding to the NARB.

The NARB is a peer review group composed of a five-member panel, chosen from among the 80 NARB members—advertising professionals and others representing the general public. Since it was established in 1971, NARB has considered 72 cases on appeal. In all but one case, there was total compliance by the parties involved. Although this is a voluntary process, with no real power in and of itself, the NAD/NARB can, and will, turn a file over to a government agency (usually the Federal Trade Commission [FTC]) if a truly deceptive advertising practice is found and not corrected.

Most NAD/NARB cases are initiated by business organizations objecting to the advertising practices of a competitor. But some inquiries are prompted by trade associations, Better Business Bureaus, or consumers. The process is far faster than the court system is apt to be: Each NAD/NARB complaint must be resolved, including a written decision, within 60 business days.

For example, in 1994, Borden, Inc., complained that the Dannon Company was misleading in its advertising for Dannon Premium Lowfat Plain Yogurt. Specifically, the NAD was asked to look into several specific claims appearing in Dannon print advertising:

1. "Taste The Plain Best."
2. "A national taste test proves it. Dannon Lowfat Plain Yogurt is the best tasting of all yogurts."
3. ". . . it's plainly the best."
4. "TOPS IN TASTE."

Borden charged that Dannon's claims were based on a sample of 150, all women, mostly located in markets not served by Mountain High, its entry in that industry, and that the survey did not test the full range of products available nationally. By leaving out male respondents and avoiding direct product-to-product comparisons, Borden argued, the Dannon survey was invalid.

The NAD found that the Dannon study was good as far as it went—"extensive, thorough, and analytical"—but that it did not go far enough to justify the conclusions Dannon drew from it. NAD concluded that, in the context of this particular advertising campaign, the taste superiority claims appear to be overly broad interpretations of the advertiser's survey findings: "The breadth and specificity of the distinct provable claims of taste superiority permeate and define all other statements in the advertising copy," the NAD opinion held, recommending that the Dannon claims be discontinued. Dannon disagreed with the NAD's conclusion and defended its survey methodology and interpretations. Nevertheless, Dannon agreed to discontinue advertising the claims that were challenged.[25]

This aspect of advertising self-regulation has drawn high praise from the FTC and other government agency leaders, and from the industry itself. In 1993, *Advertising Age* editorialized: "NAD has worked remarkably well over the years. Even grumbling losers accept NAD's decisions for the good of the self-regulatory process. It will continue to succeed only as marketers continue to cooperate."[26]

CONCLUSION

In a free society, no one is required to respond to an advertising message. Customers who purchase a product or service because of an advertisement do so, to a considerable degree, because they have faith in the ad or in the communications medium that carried the ad, or both. It is in the economic best interests of the advertiser and the communications industry to make sure this faith is continuously justified. That is why acceptability codes and other self-regulatory policies are so important to the advertising and communications media. The public relations field, early to grasp the significance of self-regulation, has long since had on the books carefully drawn codes of professional conduct.

There are laws and governmental agencies to enforce them, but the laws cannot resolve everything and the bureaucratic enforcement of them can be cumbersome. Self-regulation is designed to pick up where the laws leave off, head off problems before they develop, cover ethical and strictly legalistic concerns, and allow a complex and often vulnerable industry to help police itself.

16

Obscenity and Indecency

Indecency and obscenity are often intertwined in the public's eye, especially in discussions about whether the government should impose prior restraint. But from a First Amendment perspective, they are much different. Quite simply, indecency has constitutional protection, but obscenity cannot hide behind the shield of the First Amendment. The majority of cases concerning sexually oriented commercial speech involve indecency rather than obscenity. One reason for this may be that, except for those directly promoting sexually explicit movies, videos, magazines, and books, most ads and public relations materials avoid pornographic references out of fear of offending the targeted audience or drawing the wrath of law enforcement officials. A second reason may lie in the lesser protection accorded commercial speech under the U.S. Constitution, as dictated by the Supreme Court of the United States in a long line of commercial speech cases leading to *Central Hudson Gas & Electric Corporation v. Public Service Commission of New York*,[1] discussed at length in previous chapters in this book. Finally, the disparity may reflect the reality that, contrary to popular myth, sex—particularly hardcore sex—does not necessarily sell. This does not mean, however, that sex appeal and sexual innuendo are verboten. Indeed, it is difficult to escape the blatant appeals to sex in ads for products from autos to zippers that pervade the mass media. Nevertheless, most advertisers and public relations professionals meticulously eschew crossing the line from indecency to obscenity.

OBSCENITY VERSUS INDECENCY

Both obscenity and indecency often invite official condemnation, usually in the form of prior restraint or prosecution, but only indecency can actually claim First Amendment protection, according to the Supreme Court of the United

States, the final arbiter of such matters. The Court has made it clear in a series of cases, as discussed in the next section, that once a work has been officially declared obscene through the judicial process, it can be banned without fear of violating the U.S. Constitution. The terms *sexually explicit* and *obscene* are not synonymous, but the two often go hand in hand because one prerequisite of obscenity is that it appeal to prurient interests. *Prurient* is traditionally defined as expressing or exciting lust, lasciviousness, or lewdness. In other words, a work must be erotic to be obscene—it must sexually excite someone. The erotic appeal is only one dimension of obscenity, but it is, by far, the most important, as is seen shortly. For example, gory, graphic, and extremely violent films may be highly offensive and upset moviegoers. However, regardless of their level of gore and violence, they cannot be obscene because of the lack of appeal to prurient interests. The portrayal of violent sex, of course, could be considered obscene if the appropriate conditions are met.

In contrast, indecency need not appeal to prurient interests, although it may employ language or depictions that invoke sexual connotations. For example, uttering four-letter epithets on a television talk show may be indecent, but it is not obscene even though the expressions may represent acts that, if portrayed in the form of a motion picture or photograph, could meet the legal definition of obscenity. The concept of indecency is confused even more by the fact that obscenity involves the *depiction* of conduct, not conduct itself, while indecency can involve either depiction or actual conduct. Nude dancing, an issue that the Supreme Court tackled in a plurality opinion in *Barnes v. Glen Theatre, Inc.*,[2] concerns indecency, not obscenity, because it involves conduct, rather than the portrayal of conduct. Finally, the term *pornographic* is often used as a synonym for *obscene*, but there is a major distinction: *Pornography* and *pornographic* are not legal concepts; they are just lay terms for *obscenity* or *obscene*, designations recognized by the courts.

OBSCENITY: FROM *HICKLIN* TO *ROTH*

Obscenity has a long and colorful history. Some scholars say it can be traced back to ancient civilizations, which depicted not only nudity, but even specific sex acts in drawings, paintings, sculptures, and, of course, stories. Six centuries ago, William Chaucer (1340–1400), the great English poet, wrote of bawdy escapades such as those of the Wife of Bath in *The Canterbury Tales*, a classic today but a rather raunchy literary work in its day. Chaucer was by no means alone in his occasionally erotic portrayals, but it took the invention of wood-block printing by the Chinese and the movable-type printing press of Johann Gutenberg (1400–1468) to offer obscenity the big boost it needed—mass print-ing. Obscenity has been suppressed by the state throughout its history, whether in the form of erotic sculptures or explicit photos downloaded on the so-called "information superhighway." In July 1994, Carleen and Robert Thomas, both 38, were convicted in U.S. District Court in Memphis, Tennessee, of transmitting obscenity via interstate phone lines on a members-only electronic bulletin board known as the "Amateur Action Bulletin Board System." The couple were residents of Milpitas, California, at the time, and operated their service from there, but they were prosecuted in Tennessee after a complaint was filed by a state resident. They were convicted on 11 counts of obscenity for sending photos via e-mail that included bestiality and other sexual fetishes. The Thomases were acquitted of charges of child pornography.[3] Eight months later, according to one report, the service was still in business, advertising itself as "the nastiest place on Earth!"[4] Only one visible change had occurred in the interim—subscribers are immediately greeted with a notice that the bulletin board "is for the private use of citizens of the United States!" and that use "by law enforcement agents, postal inspectors, and informants is prohibited!"[5]

Such cases have led to the creation of a new term, *cyberporn*, to describe Internet pornography, as new technologies dramatically change the obscenity landscape. For example, there are strict federal and state statutes barring the dissemination of child pornography, but the courts have yet to determine whether such laws cover techniques such as *morphing*, in which a photo of a nude adult can be electronically altered to become an image of a child.[6] Only a relatively small percentage of information on the Internet deals with sexually oriented topics, but such materials have attracted disproportionate attention from the mass media and politicians.

The modern-day story of obscenity in the United States actually began in Great Britain about 130 years ago. In 1868, a British court handed down a decision known as *Regina v. Hicklin*,[7] which effectively set the standard for judging obscenity in England, as well as in many jurisdictions in the United States where the courts accepted this test. British trial court Judge Hicklin enforced a recently enacted obscenity law by ordering the confiscation and destruction of copies of a pamphlet entitled *The Confessional Unmasked*, which contained depictions of sex acts. On appeal to the Queen's Bench, Lord Chief Justice Cockburn upheld the lower court decision and formulated a test for obscenity that became appropriately known as the Hicklin test: "whether the tendency of the matter charged as obscene is to deprave and corrupt those whose minds are open to such immoral influences and into whose hands a publication of this sort might fall."[8]

A careful reading of this test reveals that the officials and judges can use its wording to effectively bar any and all sexually oriented works, given that (a) the whole publication can be considered obscene if any portion, no matter how small, tends "to deprave and corrupt," and (b) the material is obscene if it has a tendency to deprave and corrupt even the most sensitive and easily swayed individuals. Prosecution was made even easier because the crown did not have to demonstrate that a publication actually fell into the hands of those who could be affected by immoral influences. All the government had to do was merely show that the work might end up in the wrong hands—and, of course, there was no problem taking isolated passages out of context.

One American entrepreneur played a key role in the prosecution of obscenity in this country during the *Hicklin* era—Anthony Comstock (1844–1915). Founder and director of the New York Society for the Suppression of Vice, Comstock lobbied state legislatures and Congress to enact statutes that became popularly known as "Comstock laws." These laws enabled officials to prosecute the most mundane and innocuous sex-related works, and led to the destruction of probably thousands of tons of materials. Comstock's critics coined a new term to describe his actions—*Comstockery*, or the ruthless censorship of offensive literary and dramatic works.[9] Comstock got help from the U.S. Post Office, which took primary responsibility for enforcing federal obscenity statutes involving the mail. In fact, Comstock served during much of his life as a paid special agent for the Post Office; as a result, he got a share of the fines imposed on offenders by the courts.

Public concern about obscenity has wavered over the decades. A Time/CNN poll of 600 adult Americans in June 1995 found that more than 4 out of 10 (44%) were "very concerned" about "the amount of sex depicted in movies, television shows and popular music," and 26% were "fairly concerned."[10] More than 6 out of 10 of the respondents approved greater restrictions on what is shown on television (66%), the lyrics of popular music (62%), and the movies (61%) "as a way to improve the moral climate of this country."[11] There have been times in this country when obscenity flourished, and other periods when there was extensive suppression.

Wars often inflame censors to act, and the Civil War (1861–1865) was no exception. As stories leaked out about soldiers consuming pornographic works, Comstock and his compatriots rode to the moral rescue by pushing for the enforcement of existing laws and the passage of new laws to combat the feared tide of obscenity after the war. The Supreme Court of the United States shrewdly managed to avoid arbitrating the confrontation between the Comstock moralists on one side and the civil libertarians on the other side, who saw harm to free speech in the crusades of Comstock. In an 1896 case, the Court simply accepted a New York trial court's definition of obscenity that came straight from *Hicklin*. *Lew Rosen v. The United States*[12] focused on the question of whether the state had to demonstrate that a defendant knew materials he mailed were obscene to prove the defendant's guilt. The Court said "no." Inevitably, the Court would have to face the music and define obscenity so that speech deserving protection would not have to suffer the same suppression as that of less deserving speech, such as obscenity.

In the mid-1930s, the Supreme Court had its first chance to formulate a test for obscenity, only to see it slip away when the federal government backed down. In 1933, *Hicklin* began its slide toward obscurity when U.S. District Court Judge John M. Woolsey ruled that Irish writer James Joyce's controversial work, *Ulysses*, was not obscene, and thus could be imported into the United States.[13] The book had been published in 1922 in Paris, but it was banned for years in England and the United States. Customs officers had seized the controversial novel under the 1930 Tariff Act when a publisher's representative attempted to import a copy. Rejecting the *Hicklin* rule, Judge Woolsey constructed a new test that threw out the old standard that permitted a work to be judged on isolated passages. According to Judge Woolsey, a work is obscene if "it tends to stir the sex impulses or to lead to sexually impure or lustful thoughts. Whether a particular book would tend to excite such impulses must be the test by the court's opinion as to its effect [judged as a whole] on the person with average sex instincts."[14] Note that the *Hicklin* test has been replaced by the requirement that a work be judged as a whole, and the court is to evaluate the effect of the material on the average person, not the sensitive individuals of *Hicklin*. There was another significant change as well. A work must "lead to sexually impure and lustful thoughts" instead of "deprave and corrupt." In other words, the material must appeal to prurient or erotic interests. In 1934, the Second Circuit U.S. Court of Appeals upheld the district court decision.[15] The U.S. government decided not to appeal the appellate court decision, thus preventing the case from reaching the Supreme Court.

In 1931, in *Near v. Minnesota*,[16] the Supreme Court had indicated in a ruling on prior restraint that "the primary requirements of decency may be enforced against obscene publications." Thus, obscenity became one of the areas in which governmental prior restraint could be justified, along with "incitements to acts of violence and the overthrow by force of orderly government," as well as "actual obstruction to its [the government's] recruiting service or the publication of sailing dates of transports or the number and location of troops." (The latter is equivalent to "national security matters" in today's lexicon.) However, it would take 26 more years before the Court would actually say that obscenity had no constitutional protection, and attempt to actually define obscenity.

In 1957, in *Butler v. Michigan*,[17] the Supreme Court took the first step toward defining obscenity when it struck down as unconstitutional a provision in the Michigan Penal Code that banned any material "tending to incite minors to violent or depraved or immoral acts manifestly tending to the corruption of the morals of youth."[18] The unanimous opinion written by Justice Frankfurter compared the state's argument that it had to ban materials to adults to protect young people to burning "the house to roast the pig." The opinion went on to note, "We have before us legislation not reasonably restricted to the evil with which it is said to deal. The incidence of this enactment is to reduce the adult population of Michigan to reading only what is fit for children."[19]

Four months later, in *Roth v. United States and Alberts v. California*,[20] the Supreme Court of the United States for the first time enunciated a definition of obscenity that it struggled with for the next 16 years, until even its author, Justice Brennan, repudiated it in *Miller v. California*.[21] The majority opinion, written by Justice Brennan, made it clear that obscenity had no First Amendment protection: "The dispositive question is whether obscenity is utterance within the area of protected speech and press. [footnote omitted] Although this is the first time the question has been squarely presented to this court, either under the First Amendment or under the Fourteenth Amendment, expressions found in numerous opinions indicate that this Court has always assumed that obscenity is not protected by the freedoms of speech and press."[22]

The opinion went on to note, "All ideas having even the slightest redeeming social importance . . . have the full protection of the guarantees, unless excludable because they encroach upon the limited area of more important interests."[23] But, the Court held, "implicit in the history of the First Amendment is the rejection of obscenity as utterly without redeeming social importance," and thus "obscenity is not within the area of constitutionally protected speech or press."[24]

The majority opinion made it clear that sexually oriented materials are not automatically considered obscene, noting that "sex and obscenity are not synonymous." According to the Court:

> Obscene material is material which deals with sex in a manner appealing to prurient interest. [footnote omitted] The portrayal of sex, *e.g.* in art, literature and scientific works, [footnote omitted] is not itself sufficient reason to deny material the constitutional protection of freedom of speech and press. Sex, a great and mysterious force in human life, has indisputably been a subject of absorbing interest to mankind through the ages; it is one of the vital problems of human interest and public concern.[25]

The Court specifically rejected the *Hicklin* test, characterizing it as "unconstitutionally restrictive of the freedoms of speech and press." In affirming the convictions of the defendants, the Supreme Court said that the trial courts in both cases had properly defined obscenity. Both Roth and Alberts were convicted on charges of mailing obscene materials, including advertising. The Supreme Court favorably cited the judge's instructions to the jury in the *Roth* case. (Alberts was convicted in a bench trial.) The judge in *Roth* had said that the test of obscenity is "the effect of the book, picture or publication considered as a whole . . . upon the average person in the community."[26] He went on to say that the jurors should ask themselves whether the work "offend[s] the conscience of the community by present-day standards."[27]

The Court thus ended up with a four-prong "utterly without redeeming social value" test: (a) whether to the average person, (b) applying contemporary community standards, (c) the dominant theme of the material taken as a whole, (d) appeals to prurient interests. In the decades since this decision, the Court has spent considerable time attempting to define terms such as *average person, community standards* and *prurient interests.*

Chief Justice Earl Warren filed a brief separate concurring opinion, in which he said, "The conduct of the defendant is the central issue, not the obscenity of a book or picture." According to the Chief Justice, "The defendants in both these cases were engaged in the business of purveying textual or graphic matter openly advertised to appeal to the erotic interests of their customers. They were plainly engaged in the commercial exploitation of the morbid and shameful craving for materials with prurient effect."[28] Justice Harlan concurred with the decision regarding Alberts, but dissented from the decision in Roth. Justices Douglas and Black dissented from the entire opinion.

Note that the charges against both defendants included disseminating advertisements for obscene materials. It is not clear from the Court's decision whether the ads met the legal definition of obscenity. Presumably, however, this would make no difference because the statutes forbade advertising of obscene matters. The federal obscenity statute, under which Roth was prosecuted, specifically included advertising: "Every written or printed card, letter, circular, book, pamphlet, *advertisement*, or notice of any kind giving information, directly or indirectly, where, or how, or from whom, or by what means any of such mentioned matters, articles, or things may be obtained or made . . . [italics added]."[29] Alberts was convicted under a California statute that said, "Every person who wilfully and lewdly . . . [w]rites, composes, or publishes any notice or *advertisement* of any such writing, paper, book, picture, print or figure . . . [italics added]."[30]

What if an advertisement promotes a work as obscene, but the work does not necessarily meet the legal definition of obscenity? That was the central issue in the *Ginzburg v. United States*.[31] Justice Brennan, joined by four other justices including Chief Justice Warren, once again wrote the majority opinion in an obscenity case, this time upholding the conviction of Ralph Ginzburg on 28 counts of violating federal obscenity statutes. Ginzburg was fined $28,000 and sentenced to 5 years in prison for mailing *EROS*, an expensive hardcover magazine dealing with sex; *Liaison*, a biweekly sex-oriented newsletter; and a short book entitled *The Housewife's Handbook on Selective Promiscuity*. When Ginzburg tried to get permission from postmasters of Intercourse and Blue Ball, Pennsylvania, to mail *EROS*, they turned him down, but he did get approval to use Middlesex, New Jersey. The trial court saw these attempts as proof that Ginzburg was engaged in the "sordid business of pandering"—an attempt to sell the publications "on the basis of salacious appeal." In footnotes, the Court includes the specific promotions for the publications. For example, *EROS* was advertised as "a new quarterly devoted to the subject of Love and Sex" and "the rave of the American intellectual community," but "the rage of prudes everywhere!" The ads also said that the magazine "is frankly and avowedly concerned with erotica," and that it was a "genuine work of art." *Liaison* was advertised as "Cupid's Chronicle . . . not a scandal sheet . . . [but] . . . aimed at intelligent, educated adults who can accept love and sex as part of life."[32]

The prosecution and the Court conceded that the publications may not have been obscene, but countered that if works are pandered to meet the criteria for obscenity, "in close cases evidence of pandering may be probative with respect to the nature of the material in question and thus satisfy the *Roth* test."[33] The majority opinion went on to explain:

> It is important to stress that this analysis simply elaborates the test by which the obscenity vel non of the material must be judged. Where an exploitation of in-

terests in titillation by pornography is shown with respect to material lending itself to such exploitation through pervasive treatment or description of sexual matters, such evidence may support the determination that the material is obscene even though in other contexts the material would escape such condemnation.[34]

The lesson of *Ginzburg*, which still stands despite the fact that the Supreme Court enunciated a new test for obscenity 7 years later, is that advertising and promoting a work in a manner indicating that it is sexually provocative will trigger a legal presumption that it is obscene, even if the work taken by itself would not be considered obscene. Ginzburg touted his publications as having artistic and social value while treating sex with candor. For example, his ads made this claim about *EROS*: "The publication of this magazine—which is frankly and avowedly concerned with erotica—has been enabled by recent court decisions ruling that a literary piece or painting, though explicitly sexual in content, has a right to be published if it is a genuine work of art."[35] This led Justice Douglas to comment, in Footnote 3 of his dissenting opinion, "In effect, then, these advertisements represented that the publications are not obscene."[36] Ginzburg was probably referring to the Supreme Court's decision in 1964 in *Jacobellis v. Ohio*,[37] in which the Supreme Court reversed the conviction of a manager of a motion picture house of two counts of obscenity under Ohio law for showing *Les Amants* ("The Lovers"), in which a married woman has an affair with a younger man. The movie's conclusion includes a fairly explicit sex scene. Although six justices, including Justice Brennan, voted to reverse the conviction, there was no majority holding. Justice Brennan, joined by Justice Goldberg, reiterated the *Roth* test, including its determination that obscenity has no constitutional protection because it is "utterly without redeeming social importance." In his concurring opinion, Justice Stewart said that the First and Fourteenth Amendments require that only "hard-core" obscenity be banned, but he did not define *hard-core*. Instead, he made a statement that has become one of the most quoted regarding obscenity: "But I know it when I see it, and the motion picture involved in this case is not that."[38]

In his reference to "recent court cases," Ginzburg also may have been referring to *A Quantity of Copies of Books v. Kansas*,[39] handed down the same day as *Jacobellis*. In the former case, 7 of the justices ruled unconstitutional a state statute under which prosecutors could get search warrants to seize alleg-edly obscene materials before an adversary hearing in court to determine whether they were obscene. Once again, a majority of justices could not coalesce on the rationale for the decision. There had been a hearing in the case, in which 1,715 copies of 31 paperbacks were destroyed by the sheriff, but it simply involved the state's attorney general appearing before the district court judge, without benefit of arguments from the newsstand owner.

Prior to *Ginzburg*, the Supreme Court of the United States handed down three other important obscenity decisions. In *Smith v. California*,[40] the Court unanimously reversed the conviction of a Los Angeles bookstore owner for violating a municipal ordinance barring the possession of any obscene or indecent writings, including books, in any place of business. Justice Brennan wrote the majority opinion, joined by four other justices. The Court held that the ordinance was unconstitutional because it made booksellers liable even if they were unaware of a book's contents. To pass constitutional muster, the Court said, the law must require the government to prove scienter—that the seller had knowledge of the contents of the allegedly obscene materials.

In *Manual Enterprises v. Day*,[41] in a majority opinion written by Justice Harlan, the Court reversed a U.S. Post Office Department ban against the mailing of several gay magazines with titles such as *MANual, Grecian Pictorial*, and *Trim*, which the justices characterized as "dismally unpleasant, uncouth and tawdry." Nevertheless, the Court said they were protected because they merely featured male nudity, and were not patently offensive. Justice Harlan noted that the Post Office had not been permitted to ban female nudity, and male nudes were no more objectionable, even though the male nudity was directed to gay men. Obscene materials must affront community standards (i.e., be patently offensive) to justify banning them.

Three years later, the Court unanimously struck down a Maryland statute that mandated movie theaters to submit their films to a state board of censors before showing them to the public. In *Freedman v. Maryland*,[42] the Court, in an opinion written by Justice Brennan, said the law was a clear violation of the First Amendment because it placed the burden of proof on the exhibitor, and failed to provide a means for prompt judicial scrutiny of an adverse decision by the board, which granted licenses only to films it deemed not to be obscene. Ronald Freedman was convicted for showing the film, *Revenge at Daybreak*, prior to submitting it to the board. In its arguments against Freedman's appeal, the board conceded that the movie was not obscene, and thus would have been approved if it had been submitted. The majority saw the law as unconstitutional prior restraint because it "fails to provide adequate safeguards against undue inhibition of protected expression." The Court said that, to survive First Amendment scrutiny, such screening must have three procedural safeguards: (a) "the burden of proving that the film is unprotected expression must rest on the censor"; (b) the state may require advance submission of all films, but such a process "cannot be administered in a manner which would lend an effect of finality to the censor's determination whether a film constitutes protected expression"; and (c) "the procedure must also assure a prompt final judicial decision, to minimize the deterrent effect of an interim and possibly erroneous denial of a license."[43]

On the same day as *Ginzburg*, the Supreme Court handed down two other obscenity decisions. The first, popularly known as the "Fanny Hill" case,[44] involved a civil equity suit brought by the Massachusetts Attorney General against the book commonly known as *Fanny Hill* ("Memoirs of a Woman of Pleasure"); the attorney general wanted to have the work declared obscene. A trial court determined that the novel was obscene, and the state supreme court affirmed. Six justices voted to reverse the lower court decisions, but there was no majority opinion. Instead, Justice Brennan wrote a plurality opinion, joined by Chief Justice Warren and Justice Fortas, that strongly reaffirmed the *Roth* test. The opinion said that the state supreme court erred when it said the jury was not required to find the work was "utterly without redeeming social value" to declare it obscene.

The novel *Fanny Hill* was first published in England in 1750. It had been widely available in this country since the 19th century, but Massachusetts wanted to ban the book, which had been reissued by the publisher, G.P. Putnam's Sons, in 1963. According to Justice Douglas' concurring opinion, the publisher had "an unusually large number of orders" from universities and libraries, and the Library of Congress had requested the right to translate the novel into Braille. The equity suit was filed only against the book, not against the publisher or distributor. Justice Douglas included as an appendix to his opinion a copy of a speech by a Universalist minister favorably comparing the writings of widely known clergyman Dr. Norman Vincent Peale with *Fanny Hill*. According to the Reverend John R. Graham, "I firmly believe that *Fanny Hill* is a moral, rather than an immoral, piece of literature." He went on to assert, "I have a feeling that many people fear the book *Fanny Hill*, not because of its sexual scenes, but because the author raises serious question with the issue of what is moral and what is immoral."[45]

Fanny Hill is fairly mild eroticism by today's standards and, as the experts testified in court, is a literary classic. Nevertheless, as Justice Clark pointed out in his dissenting opinion, it includes scenes of: ". . . lesbianism, female masturbation, homosexuality between young boys, the destruction of a maidenhead with consequent gory descriptions, the seduction of a young virgin boy, the flagellation of male by female, and vice versa, followed by fervid sexual engagement, and other abhorrent acts, including over two dozen separate bizarre descriptions of different sexual intercourses between male and female characters."[46]

The third decision handed down by the Court on the same day as *Ginzburg* was *Mishkin v. New York*.[47] Edward Mishkin was sentenced to 3 years in prison and fined $12,500 for selling obscene books described by Justice Brennan in his majority opinion as depicting "such deviations as sado-masochism, fetishism and homosexuality." Titles included *Dance with the Dominant Whip* and *Mrs. Tyrant's Finishing School*. The materials, which featured explicit sexual acts, were clearly hard-core pornography, but Mishkin argued on appeal that they failed the *Roth* test for prurient interest because the average person would not find them sexually exciting. The Court rejected this unusual argument and voted 6–3 to uphold his conviction. According to the Court, "Where the material is designed for and primarily disseminated to a clearly defined sexual group, rather than the public at large, the prurient-appeal requirement of the *Roth* test is satisfied if the dominant theme of the material taken as a whole appeals to the prurient interest in sex of the members of that group."[48]

During the next 7 years, the Supreme Court of the United States continued to more or less cling to the *Roth* test without actually offering much light on what the test meant or how it was to be applied. In 1967, the Court issued a per curiam opinion, in which it reversed the convictions in three cases involving the dissemination of obscene works to willing adults.[49] One case involved the sale of two books entitled *Lust Pool* and *Shame Agent*. Another involved the magazines *High Heels* and *Spree*; the magazines in the third case were *Ace, Bachelor, Cavalcade, Gent, Gentleman, Modern Man, Sir* and *Swank*, several of which are still on the market.

One year later, the Court voted 8–1, in an opinion written by Justice Marshall, to strike down a Dallas, Texas, ordinance that required films to be restricted from persons under age 16 unless judged to be suitable for young audiences. Unsuitable films—those portraying sexual promiscuity or whose dominant effect on youths was to "arouse sexual desire"—were permitted under the ordinance to be shown to adults, but not to anyone under 16. On the same day, in *Ginsberg v. New York*,[50] the Court upheld a New York variable obscenity statute, which prohibited the knowing sale of "materials harmful to minors" to people under 17, regardless of whether the works would be considered obscene for adults. The general purpose of such laws, which other courts have consistently upheld, is to keep sexually oriented materials out of the hands of minors, even when such works are perfectly permissible for adults.

In 1969, in a unanimous decision written by Justice Marshall, the Court held that individuals could not be punished for merely possessing obscene materials in their own home. In *Stanley v. Georgia*,[51] the justices reversed the conviction of a suspected bookmaker for violating a state statute that prohibited the knowing possession of obscene works, even in one's home. During the execution of a search warrant for evidence of illegal gambling, police found three sexually explicit 8-mm films in a desk drawer in Robert E. Stanley's bedroom. They found no bookmaking evidence, but instead charged him with possession of obscene materials. According to the majority opinion, "Whatever may be the justifications for other statutes regarding obscenity, we do not think they reach into the privacy of one's own home. If the First Amendment means anything, it means that a State has no business telling a man, sitting alone in his own house, what books he may read or what films he may watch."[52]

During the next 3 years, the Supreme Court issued no major obscenity decisions. Thanks to the emergence of a new conservative majority, by 1973, the Court was ready to agree on a new test for obscenity. This new majority, consisting of Chief Justice Burger and Associate Justices White, Blackmun, Powell, and Rehnquist, issued no fewer than five decisions on the same day— June 21, 1973—dramatically changing the status of obscenity laws. All were 5–4 decisions, with each majority opinion written by Chief Justice Burger.

THE *MILLER* STANDARD FOR OBSCENITY

In the first of the five decisions, the Court established the test for obscenity that it still uses and probably will continue to apply into the next century. More than 25 years later, *Miller v. California*[53] is alive and well. Justice Burger made it clear from the outset in *Miller* that it and the other four cases were "being reviewed by the Court in a re-examination of standards enunciated in earlier cases involving what Mr. Justice Harlan called 'the intractable obscenity problem.' "[54] Marvin Miller was convicted in a jury trial of violating California's obscenity statutes after he made a mass mailing of brochures advertising the sale of four books entitled *Intercourse, Man-Woman, Sex Orgies Illustrated*, and *An Illustrated History of Pornography*, as well as a film entitled *Marital Intercourse*. He was prosecuted after a complaint from a restaurant owner and his mother, who opened an envelope with five unsolicited brochures that had been sent through the mail. According to the majority opinion, the issue in the case was "the application of a State's criminal obscenity statute to a situation in which sexually explicit materials have been thrust by aggressive sales action upon unwilling recipients who had in no way indicated any desire to receive such materials."[55]

The Court formulated a new three-prong conjunctive test for obscenity:

> The basic guidelines for the trier of fact must be: (a) whether "the average person, applying contemporary community standards" would find that the work taken as a whole appeals to the prurient interest; (b) whether the work depicts or describes, in a patently offensive way, sexual conduct specifically defined by the applicable state law; and (c) whether the work, taken as a whole, lacks serious literary, artistic, political, or scientific value.[56]

The opinion then noted that it was specifically rejecting the "*utterly* without redeeming social value" constitutional standard of *Memoirs v. Massachusetts*, and that "it is not our function to propose regulatory schemes for the States." But the Court went on to cite what it called "a few plain examples" of what a state could include under Part (b) as "patently offensive." These included representations or descriptions of (a) "ultimate sexual acts, normal or perverted, actual or simulated"; and (b) "masturbation, excretory functions, and lewd exhibition of the genitals." According to the Court, "Sex and nudity may not be exploited without limit by films or pictures exhibited or sold in places of public accommodation any more than live sex and nudity can be exhibited or sold without limit in such public places."[57]

The majority opinion went to great lengths to counter the dissents of Justices Brennan, Douglas, Stewart, and Marshall—particularly Justice Brennan, who had written the majority or plurality opinions in most of the previous obscenity cases, but who did an about-face in *Miller* and the other four cases. As the majority noted, Justice Brennan "abandoned his former position and now maintains that no formulation of this Court, the Congress, or the States can adequately distinguish obscene material unprotected by the First Amendment from protected expression."[58]

The Court reaffirmed its holding in *Roth* and subsequent cases that obscenity enjoys no First Amendment protection, but that only "hard-core" sexual conduct was to be punished under the new test. Finally, the justices held that "obscenity is to be determined by applying 'contemporary community standards' . . . not national standards."[59] As the Court indicated, "It is neither realistic nor constitutionally sound to read the First Amendment as requiring that the people of Maine or Mississippi accept public depiction of conduct found tolerable in Las Vegas or New York City."[60]

The Court appeared pleased that, for the first time since *Roth*, "a majority of this Court has agreed on concrete guidelines to isolate 'hard core' pornography from expression protected by the First Amendment."[61] In what turned out to be an accurate prophecy, the Court then recognized that the "attempt to provide positive guidance to federal and state courts alike" with this decision "may not be an easy road, free from difficulty." No truer words were ever spoken about defining obscenity, and the Court decisions in the decades since this decision have clouded more than clarified the picture.

In the second decision handed down that day, *Paris Adult Theatre I v. Slaton*,[62] two Atlanta adult theaters and their owners had civil complaints filed against them by a local prosecutor and the local state solicitor, asking that two films, *Magic Mirror* and *It All Comes Out in the End*, be declared obscene and therefore enjoined from further showings. The trial court dismissed the complaints, but the Georgia Supreme Court unanimously reversed, holding that the films were "hard core pornography" leaving "little to the imagination." The movies featured scenes of simulated fellatio, cunnilingus, and group sex. There were no explicit posters or other displays outside the theaters, and a sign posted at the entrance shared by the two theaters said, "Adult Theatre—You must be 21 and able to prove it. If viewing the nude body offends you, Please Do Not Enter." The 5–4 Supreme Court of the United States decision vacated the case and remanded it to the state supreme court for reconsideration in light of *Miller*.

The majority opinion agreed with the Georgia Supreme Court that the theaters did not have First Amendment protection, even though the movies were presumably shown only to consenting adults:

> In particular, we hold that there are legitimate state interests at stake in stemming the tide of commercialized obscenity, even assuming it is feasible to enforce effective safeguards against exposure to juveniles and to passersby. Rights and interests "other than those of the advocates are involved." These include the interest of the public in the quality of life and the total community environment, the tone of commerce in the great city centers, and, possibly, the public safety itself.[63]

Justice Brennan's dissent, to which the majority opinion frequently referred, included four options in dealing with obscenity: (a) take obscenity essentially out of federal control and give it back to the states by drawing a line between protected and unprotected speech and allowing the states to regulate unprotected information; (b) accept the *Miller* test; (c) leave enforcement of obscenity laws to juries, with the Supreme Court and other appellate courts intervening only "in cases of extreme departure from prevailing standards"; and (d) take an absolutist view, such as that of Justices Black and Douglas, that bars the suppression of any sexually oriented expression. Justice Brennan then offered his own proposal, which he favored: Allow sexually oriented materials to be restricted under the First and Fourteenth Amendments only in the manner in which they are distributed, and only when there are strong and legitimate state interests, such as protecting juveniles and nonconsenting adults.

The other three cases decided that same day were relatively minor in their significance. In one case, the Court ruled that an unillustrated book with explicit descriptive material could be persecuted; in the other two cases, the Court upheld federal statutes—one banning the importation of obscene matter, whether for personal or commercial use, and another prohibiting transportation of obscenity by common carrier.

ONWARD FROM *MILLER*

The road from *Miller* has been paved with relatively few decisions, although there have been a few interesting side paths. In the year following *Miller et al.*, the Court handed down two obscenity decisions on the same day near the end of its term. In *Hamling v. United States*,[64] the Court, in a 5–4 opinion written by Justice Rehnquist, affirmed the convictions of four individuals and two corporations for mailing 55,000 copies of a brochure advertising *The Illustrated Presidential Report of the Commission on Obscenity and Pornography*.[65] A jury could not decide whether the report was obscene, but did judge the brochure to be obscene. According to the Court, the single-sheet brochure included a series of pictures portraying various sex acts, such as male and female masturbation, fellatio, cunnilingus, lesbianism, group sex, and even bestiality. Neither the Ninth Circuit Court of Appeals nor the Supreme Court had any problem with affirming the convictions. The issue was simply which rules of law would apply. The majority held that: (a) jurors in federal obscenity cases could draw on their knowledge of the local community in determining contemporary community standards, (b) jurors can choose to ignore the testimony of expert witnesses because they are the experts ("average person"), and (c) the government is required to demonstrate that a defendant had actual knowledge of the contents of obscene works to prove *scienter*, not that the person knew the materials were obscene.

On the same day as *Hamling*, the Court made it clear in *Jenkins v. Georgia*[66] that it meant what it said in *Miller*—obscenity must be in the form of hard-core pornography. The Court, in a unanimous opinion written by Justice Rehnquist, overturned the conviction of Billy Jenkins, a drive-in theater owner, for violating Georgia obscenity statutes by showing the movie *Carnal Knowledge*, starring Candice Bergen (now on "Murphy Brown" on CBS-TV), Ann Margret, and Art Garfunkel of Simon and Garfunkel fame. This was a movie that was critically acclaimed and on several "Best 10" lists in 1971. A jury convicted Jenkins and fined him $750; the Georgia Supreme Court, in a split vote, upheld his conviction. The Supreme Court of the United States acknowledged that the broader subject matter of the film was sex, and that there are scenes in which sexual conduct is understood to take place, but "the camera does not focus on the bodies of the actors at such times." As the Court noted, "There is no exhibition of the actors' genitals, lewd or otherwise during these scenes. There are occasional scenes of nudity, but nudity alone is not enough to make material legally obscene under the *Miller* standards."[67]

CHILD PORNOGRAPHY

Children have been recognized for some time as a protected class by the courts, and thus worthy of State protection that might otherwise not be applicable to adults. However, only within the last few decades have Congress and the courts made a sustained and concerted effort to protect children from exploitation such as child labor and sexual abuse. For example, in 1918, the Supreme Court of the United States held that Congress did *not* have the authority under the U.S. Constitution's Commerce Clause to ban the transportation in interstate commerce of goods made by children under the age of 14.[68] Fortunately, the Court eventually reversed itself, albeit more than two decades later, noting that the earlier ruling "has not been followed" and that it "should be and is now overruled."[69] Interestingly, the latter case did not involve child labor, but instead dealt with the ability of Congress to enforce provisions of the Fair Labor Standards Act of 1938 regulating the hours and wages of employees even when involved in local manufacturing.

During the last few decades, the concern with protecting children has extended to keeping pornography out of the hands of children and preventing the creation and dissemination of child pornography, commonly known as "kiddie porn." As noted earlier, the Court upheld variable obscenity statutes in 1968 in *Ginsberg v. New York*, under the rationale that a state had the right to protect minors—in this case, anyone under the age of 17—from exposure to "girlie" magazines that did not necessarily meet the definition of obscenity for adults. With this ruling, the Court effectively created a lower standard for obscenity for minors.

However, the Court has taken a dim view of attempts to ban indecent speech to adults on the ground that children would gain access to such content. For example, in 1989, the Court struck down a ban on indecent telephone messages under Section 223(b) of the Communications Act of 1934, as amended. In *Sable Communications of California v. Federal Communications Commission*,[70] the Court held that, although the section's ban on obscene telephone speech was constitutional, the prohibition against indecent calls violated the First Amendment. The case involved so-called "dial-a-porn" services, which the Federal Communications Commission (FCC) required to take extensive steps to ensure that there were no underage callers. The FCC argued that only a total ban on such calls would prevent children from accessing the sexually explicit messages. According to the majority opinion, there was no evidence that less restrictive means were not available to protect minors. In other words, the government had failed to prove there were no other ways of banning access to children.

Nine years after *Ginsberg*, the New York legislature enacted a statute that made it a felony for anyone who knowingly promoted sexual performances by children under the age of 16 by distributing material depicting such performances.[71] *Sexual performance* was defined as "any performance or part thereof which includes sexual conduct by a child less than sixteen years of age," and *sexual conduct* was defined as "actual or simulated sexual intercourse, deviate sexual intercourse, sexual bestiality, masturbation, sado-masochistic abuse, or lewd exhibition of the genitals."[72] To *promote* meant "to procure, manufacture, issue, sell, give, provide, lend, mail, deliver, transfer, transmute, publish, distribute, circulate, disseminate, present, exhibit *or advertise*, or to offer or agree to the same" (italics added).[73] Five years after enactment of the New York statute, the Supreme Court agreed to hear the first major challenge to the constitutionality of the law, *New York v. Ferber*.[74] The case involved the owner of an adult bookstore who had been convicted of selling two films of young boys masturbating.

When the New York Court of Appeals reversed Ferber's conviction, the state appealed to the Supreme Court of the United States to decide the following question: To prevent the abuse of children who are made to engage in sexual conduct for commercial purposes, could the New York State Legislature, consistent with the First Amendment, prohibit the dissemination of material that shows children engaged in sexual conduct, regardless of whether such material is obscene? The Supreme Court of the United States answered in the affirmative, holding that the state statute, as applied to the defendant and others involved in the distribution of similar material, did not violate the First Amendment as applied to the states through the Fourteenth Amendment. The New York Court of Appeals had overturned the convictions on the grounds that the statute was underinclusive and overbroad because it punished the depiction of "nonobscene adolescent sex." The state appellate court noted that, unlike a companion statute involving adult obscenity, the child pornography statute contained no explicit reference to "knowing dissemination."

According to the Supreme Court of the United States, however, states have greater leeway in regulating sexual depictions of children than adults because (a) the use of children in such materials can be harmful to their physiological, emotional, and mental health; (b) *Miller* is not the appropriate test for child obscenity; (c) the advertising and sale of child pornography provides an economic motive for creating such materials; (d) there is little, if any, value in allowing live sexual performances and photos of children engaging in sex; and (e) rejecting First Amendment protection for child pornography is much in line with the Court's prior decisions regarding unprotected speech.

Note the Court's concern with the commercial nature of child pornography, as indicated in the third rationale. Justice White wrote the majority opinion in the case, joined by Justices Powell, Rehnquist, and O'Connor, as well as Chief Justice Burger. There were no dissenters, with the remaining four justices concurring with the result. For example, Justice Brennan, joined by Justice

Marshall, noted that he agreed "with much of what is said in the Court's opinion," and that, as he pointed out earlier in the Court's opinion in *Ginsburg*, "the State has a special interest in protecting the well-being of its youth." His concern with the majority opinion was that he believed it permitted a statute to outlaw works depicting children that had "serious literary, artistic, scientific or medical value."[75] The majority acknowledged that this could occur, but reasoned that this was "the paradigmatic case of a state statute whose legitimate reach dwarfs its arguably impermissible applications," and that the "tiny fraction of materials" involved could be dealt with on a case-by-case basis.

In 1977, Congress enacted a "Protection of Children Against Sexual Exploitation Act" that included severe penalties for the creation, distribution, and dissemination of child pornography.[76] The resulting statute was amended in 1984,[77] 1986,[78] 1988,[79] and 1990.[80] The current statute provides a fine of up to $100,000 and/or imprisonment of up to 10 years for anyone who "employs, uses, persuades, induces, entices or coerces any minor" to engage in or assist in the engagement of sexually explicit conduct for producing a visual depiction. The same penalties are provided for individuals who make, print, or publish any notice or advertisement for such visual depictions. A prior conviction increases the penalties to $200,000 and/or 5–15 years imprisonment. Organizations convicted of a violation can be assessed a fine of up to $250,000.[81]

There have been numerous convictions under the 1977 Act over the years, including several convictions for transmitting child pornography via the Internet. The most serious challenge to the Act came in November 1994 in *United States v. X-Citement Video, Inc.*[82] The owner and operator of an adult video store was convicted on three counts of violating the 1977 Act after he sold an undercover police officer 49 videotapes featuring Traci Lords before her 18th birthday and shipped eight tapes of the underage Lords to Hawaii. On a second appeal, the Ninth Circuit U.S. Court of Appeals, in a divided vote, found the statute facially unconstitutional because it lacked a scienter requirement in the section regarding the age of the minor. As noted earlier in the discussion of *Smith v. California*, obscenity laws must require the prosecution to prove *scienter* under the Constitution. Rubin Gottesman, the bookstore owner, argued that the law was phrased such that "knowingly" (the *scienter* requirement) did not modify the sections dealing with the age of the minor and the explicit nature of the material, but merely modified the section regarding the production and dissemination of such material. In its 7–2 decision, the Court had no problem construing the application of "knowingly" to all of the sections, including those involving the age of the minor and the explicitness of the materials. The Court did not discuss in detail the major social problems associated with child pornography, nor the overwhelming demand from the public for statutes banning the use and depiction of minors in sexually oriented materials. Instead, the Court took the direct approach of recognizing an implied scienter requirement based on the presumed intent of Congress to outlaw child pornography.

Kiddie porn continues to be a serious social problem, but tough federal and state statutes appear to have dealt a major blow to a business characterized by

Congress in 1984 as "a highly organized, multi-million-dollar industry which operates on a nationwide scale."[83] In 1990, the Supreme Court of the United States, citing *Ferber*, upheld an Ohio child pornography statute under which a man was convicted for possessing photos of a nude male adolescent in sexually explicit poses. In *Osborne v. Ohio*,[84] the Court distinguished the case from *Stanley v. Georgia*, discussed earlier, in which it struck down a state law barring the private possession of obscene materials on privacy grounds. The justification in this case, the Court contended, was Ohio's compelling interest in protecting the physical and psychological well-being of children, as well as in destroying the market for the materials by prosecuting individuals who own such works. The Court also held that the statute was not unconstitutionally overbroad because the state had limited its prosecutions to the viewing and possession of lewd exhibition of or graphic focus on the genitals of minors, even though the statute could conceivably be used to prosecute nonobscene photos of nude children.

In the fall of 1995, a Calvin Klein advertising campaign for jeans featuring young models in provocative poses came under fire from both public interest groups and the U.S. Justice Department. The ads, which included adolescents with their underwear exposed, were carried in newspapers and magazines, as well as on television and on the sides of New York City public transit buses. The company quickly dropped the ads after the Justice Department indicated it was investigating the possibility that the promotion violated federal child pornography statutes.

BEYOND *FERBER* AND *MILLER*

Neither *Ferber* nor *Miller* could settle all of the issues surrounding adult and child pornography, of course, but the precedents they established have stood the test of time. In *City of Renton v. Playtime Theatres, Inc.*,[85] the Supreme Court held that a city ordinance restricting adult theaters to certain zones did not violate the First Amendment even though the works involved were not necessarily obscene. The Court found it persuasive that the ordinance did not impose an outright ban on the theaters, and that the city was responding to "serious problems" created by the theaters. A few months later, the Court upheld the constitutionality of a New York state statute that allowed prosecutors to shut down an adult bookstore used for illicit sex activities, including prostitution.[86]

In the same year, 1986, the Court held that, contrary to the judgment of the New York Court of Appeals, there is no higher probable cause standard under the First Amendment for warrants to seize books and movies than for weapons and drugs.[87] The following year, the Court ruled in a 5–4 decision that community standards do *not* apply to the third prong of the *Miller* test ("whether the work, taken as a whole, lacks serious literary, artistic, political or scientific value"). The majority said that, instead, the "proper inquiry" for a jury in an obscenity case is "whether a reasonable person [rather than 'an ordinary member of any given community'] would find such value in the material, taken as a whole."[88] Although it is not clear what the Court meant by "reasonable person" versus "ordinary member," the Court appeared to imply that a national standard of some type was appropriate. The Court did indicate that a work does not have to garner majority approval in a community to warrant First Amendment protection. In other words, the value of a work does not vary from community to community based on acceptance in each community.

RICO STATUTES AND OBSCENITY

In 1986, a commission appointed the previous year by U.S. Attorney General Edwin Meese to look at obscenity in America issued the results of its study, which cost the government $500,000. The 1,960-page report, which has become known as *The Attorney General Commission on Pornography Report*,[89] made a series of recommendations, including strengthening state and federal obscenity statutes, banning obscenity on cable television, and creating a high-level U.S. Department of Justice task force on obscenity. The Commission also said federal and state agencies should make greater use of Racketeer Influenced and Corrupt Organizations (RICO) statutes, which allow prosecutors to seize the assets of illegal enterprises when the government can demonstrate a pattern of racketeering. In 1970, Congress had included a RICO provision in the Organized Crime Control Act[90]; in 1984, the Act was amended to include obscenity prosecutions.

The federal statute has been widely used to crack down on pornography, and most states now have RICO statutes that include obscenity. In 1989, the U.S. Supreme Court handed down a decision involving the first real test of a state RICO statute in obscenity convictions. The case, *Fort Wayne Books, Inc. v. Indiana*,[91] involved two separate bookstores and their operators. The Court upheld the Indiana RICO statute at issue as constitutional, although its provisions provided more severe punishments than those under the state's obscenity statutes. (The RICO statute included obscenity among other criminal activities, but the state had separate obscenity statutes as well.) According to the Court, the stiffer RICO provisions simply provided another deterrent to the sale of pornography, which the state had a legitimate right to create. One of the bookstore operators had the contents of his store seized without the benefit of an adversarial hearing. The Court held that such a pretrial seizure was improper because of the risk of prior restraint. As the majority opinion noted, there had been no determination made prior to the seizure that the items confiscated were obscene, nor even that a RICO violation had taken place. "While a single copy of a book or film may be seized and retained for evidentiary purposes based on a finding of probable cause, books or films may not be taken out of circulation completely until there has been a determination of obscenity after an adversary hearing,"[92] the justices said.

Four years after *Fort Wayne Books*, the Court upheld the use of the federal RICO statute in an obscenity case. In *Alexander v. United States*,[93] the Court upheld the convictions of the owner of numerous businesses selling sexually explicit materials for violating both the federal obscenity statutes and the RICO

Act by selling seven obscene items at several of his stores. The trial court handed down a prison term and fine for the defendant, and ordered him to forfeit his businesses and close to $9 million he had earned through racketeering. The Court had no problem with the forfeiture, pointing out that this case was different from that of *Fort Wayne Books* because Alexander's assets had been seized only after the appropriate procedures had been followed. The Court did remand the case back to the lower appellate court to consider his claims that the forfeiture, combined with his prison term and the fine, was excessive under the Eighth Amendment,[94] noting, however, that the defendant had been involved in extensive criminal activities over a long period.

NEWSPAPER AND MAGAZINE ADS
FOR ADULT MATERIALS

So far, the broadcast industry has generally avoided carrying advertising for sexually explicit works, such as X-rated movies and adult bookstores, perhaps out of fear of possible public criticism or even FCC reprisals. But general circulation newspapers and magazines have not been as conservative. Some major newspapers and magazines have formal or informal policies that bar advertising for adult-oriented materials and adult entertainment, but most print outlets routinely accept such advertising. Unless a publication includes explicit images in its ads, it is highly unlikely that it could be successfully prosecuted for promoting obscenity, so long as a particular work has not been legally determined to be obscene.

For example, a newspaper that carries ads for theaters that show X-rated films or for adult bookstores would be highly unlikely to face the ire of the local district attorney. Some newspapers, magazines, and broadcast stations refuse to carry ads for NC-17-rated movies. The major studios have released few movies under the NC-17 rating, which was created in 1990 by the Motion Picture Association of America (MPAA)—the industry group that rates movies voluntarily submitted to it. The MPAA had to come up with the rating, which indicates "No children under 17 admitted," because it needed to fill in the gap left after it did not apply for a trademark for the "X" rating when it created the ratings system in 1968. Just as with the parental advisory labels on recorded music, specific movie ratings have absolutely no legal standing in obscenity prosecutions. In other words, a court cannot automatically assume that an X-rated or NC-17-rated film is obscene. Ratings and warning labels are strictly advisory for consumers.

SPECIAL PROBLEMS WITH INDECENCY
AND OBSCENITY IN BROADCASTING

In November 1994, the FCC ruled that stations may not refuse to carry graphic antiabortion political advertisements, but that they can confine them to time slots when children are less likely to be in the audience.[95] (This action is commonly known as "channeling.") The ruling came after stations complained to the FCC about being forced under the "reasonable access" provisions of the FCC Act to carry the explicit ads of candidates such as Michael Bailey, a Republican candidate for Congress from Indiana during the 1992 election. After his television commercials appeared showing graphic images of aborted fetuses, stations were flooded with complaints from viewers. Other antiabortion candidates picked up on the trend, with more than a dozen of them getting permission from Bailey to use his ads. Some viewers even filed lawsuits seeking injunctions to stop the ads. The stations were in a "no win" situation because, in 1992, the FCC's Mass Media Bureau ruled, based on a complaint about similar ads for Republican Congressional candidate Daniel Becker of Georgia, that the political spots did not meet the FCC criteria for indecency. A 1984 informal FCC staff opinion said that programming that stations believe in good faith is indecent can be channeled to the so-called "safe harbor" hours of 8:00 p.m.–6:00 a.m. A few stations used the opinion to justify restricting the times when the ads were broadcast, but it took the 1994 FCC decision to make channeling official. The ruling did say that the time shifting must be done in good faith based on the graphic nature of the ad, and that it can not be done simply because the station disagrees with the message.[96]

Broadcasting has always been treated differently from the print media when it comes to indecency. Beginning with the so-called "seven dirty words" decision in 1978,[97] and continuing more recently with the D.C. Circuit Court of Appeals' decisions in two cases known as *ACT III*[98] and *Act IV*,[99] the courts have given Congress and the FCC considerable leeway in regulating obscenity, although not permitting an outright ban. In the "seven dirty words" case, which involved the broadcast of a George Carlin monologue including utterances such as *fuck* and *shit*, the U.S. Supreme Court in a plurality decision upheld the FCC's declaratory order that the broadcast was indecent. In *ACT III*, the D.C. appellate court held that the FCC was justified in creating a "safe harbor" period from 10 p.m. to 6 a.m., during which any indecent broadcasts would be confined. In *ACT IV*, the same court ruled that the FCC had the authority to impose fines on broadcasters that violate its "safe harbor" rules, including a $1.7 million fine against Infinity Broadcasting for carrying shock jock Howard Stern's show.

According to a story in *The Washington Post Magazine*, by May 1995, Stern's broadcasts had resulted in total FCC fines of $1.885 million against the stations that carry his show.[100] Stern has been cited seven times—five times more than his nearest competitor. The highest fine after Stern's is $40,000. When Stern's employer, Infinity Broadcasting, petitioned the FCC for permission to buy Los Angeles station KRTH-FM in 1994 for $100 million, a record sum for a radio station, the FCC balked until Infinity agreed to pay an additional fine of $400,000 for Stern's violations. According to the *Post*, Infinity did not pay the fine nor any of the other fines before the sale was consummated.[101] Four months after the *Post* article appeared, the FCC reached a settlement with Infinity Broadcasting, in which the company agreed to "voluntarily" pay the U.S. Treasury $1.715 million, and the FCC agreed to absolve Infinity of any wrongdoing and to halt all pending actions against the broadcaster. Neither side characterized the payment as a fine even though the amount was essentially the same as the total fines sought by the FCC. The rationale the courts accept is that broadcasting is such a pervasive medium that it is difficult to escape its reach.

INDECENCY ON CABLE TELEVISION

As with broadcasting, cable television outlets face severe criminal penalties under both federal and state statutes if they carry obscene programming. The Cable Television and Consumer Protection and Competition Act of 1992 contained several provisions regarding obscene and indecent programming.[102] These include a provision allowing cable operators to deny access to anyone seeking to lease a channel to carry programming that the operator "reasonably believes describes or depicts sexual or excretory activities or organs in a patently offensive manner as measured by contemporary community standards." This phrasing is much in line with the FCC's definition of indecency in broadcasting. The Act also provides for civil and criminal liability for cable operators who carry obscene programs on public, educational, and governmental (PEG), and leased access channels.

The FCC was also directed under the Act to establish rules (a) requiring cable operators who carry indecent programming on leased access channels to block the channels unless the consumer requests in writing that the channel not be blocked, and (b) allowing cable operators to ban "obscene material, sexually explicit conduct, or material soliciting or promoting unlawful conduct." The FCC began the appropriate rule-making proceedings shortly after the Act took effect; in June 1995, the U.S. Court of Appeals for the D.C. Circuit in a 6–4 decision upheld the indecency and obscenity provisions of the Act and the FCC's implementation of them.[103] The circuit court reasoned that there was no violation of the First Amendment because there was no absolute ban on indecent programs, and cable operators had a choice on whether to block such programming. On appeal, the Supreme Court of the United States granted certiorari in 1996.

INDECENCY ON THE INTERNET

In February 1996, President Clinton signed into law the Telecommunications Act of 1996. One of the provisions of the statute, the Communications Decency Act (CDA), was immediately challenged in the courts. Under the Act, anyone who uses a computer to transmit indecent material faces possible imprisonment of up to 2 years and fines up to $500,000. At a Freedom Forum seminar a month after the law took effect, U.S. Senator Patrick Leahy (D–Vt.), who had voted against the measure, characterized the CDA as "unconstitutional."[104]

Because Congress knew the provision was likely to be challenged, it included a provision in the CDA that the federal courts would grant expedited review. The U.S. District Court for the Eastern District of Pennsylvania quickly granted a temporary restraining order that barred enforcement of the CDA, pending appellate court review.

After hearing oral arguments and reviewing reams of documents filed in the case, a special three-judge panel, headed by Chief Judge Sloviter of the Third Circuit U.S. Court of Appeals, unanimously agreed with Leahy, granting a preliminary injunction requested by the American Civil Liberties Union, the American Library Association, several online services, the Society of Professional Journalists, and 50,000 Internet users.[105] Defendants in the case included U.S. Attorney General Janet Reno and the Department of Justice.

In its decision, the court viewed the Internet as more analogous to the telephone or print media than the broadcast media, and pointed to the fact that one person can literally speak instantaneously to millions of people around the world. According to the separate opinion of one member of the panel, District Judge Stewart Dalzell, "Any content-based regulation of the Internet, no matter how benign the purpose, could burn the global village to roast the pig."[106] Two provisions of the Act were being challenged—one dealing with *indecent* communication (which the Act did not define)[107] and the other dealing with *patently offensive* communication, which was defined in traditional terms similar to that in broadcasting as "measured by contemporary community standards . . . [the depiction or description of] . . . , sexual or excretory activities or organs."[108] To obtain a preliminary injunction, which would only be effective until it is overturned or upheld on appeal, a plaintiff must show there is "a reasonable probability of eventual success in the litigation," and that the person or entity would suffer irreparable harm if the law were enforced. According to the panel, the plaintiffs had demonstrated this. This case is now on appeal to the U.S. Supreme Court for a final decision in 1997. This case could prove to be one of the most important First Amendment cases ever decided about the new technologies. In all likelihood, the Supreme Court of the United States, which must hear the case, will side with the plaintiffs, holding that the Internet is more akin to the telephone or print media than to the broadcast media. If so, Internet users will enjoy greater freedom than that of professional broadcasters.

LIVE NUDITY AS COMMERCIAL SPEECH

Live performances that meet the *Miller* test of obscenity can obviously be punished, but what about nude entertainment that is not obscene? If such nude dancing is not obscene, could it nonetheless be regulated as commercial speech? The Supreme Court has handed down several decisions over the years involving nude performances, but the Court has granted First Amendment protection in only one case. The justices first confronted the issue of nude performances more than four decades ago, when they upheld an obscenity conviction of a stripper on the grounds that it was a valid exercise of the state's police power.[109] Subsequent cases involved liquor licenses for establishments that featured live, nude entertainment; in every instance, the Court basically held that states could ban such dancing where liquor was sold.[110] Only one exception emerged, and it appears to have been misinterpreted by many lower courts. In *Doran v. Salem Inn, Inc.*,[111] the Court unanimously overturned a preliminary injunction issued by a New York trial court judge against three bars that featured topless dancing. The Court said the state statute involved was too broad, and thus unconstitutional, because its ban on nudity applied to all live entertainment, including artistic works.

One way in which the Court could justify severe restrictions on nude entertainment would be to classify it as commercial speech, and thus subject to the *Central Hudson* test. So far, however, the Court has chosen not to do this, as illustrated in its 1991 decision in *Barnes v. Glen Theatre*.[112] The case began when two Indiana businesses, including the Kitty Kat Lounge, asked a U.S. District Court to enjoin the state from enforcing its public indecency statute against them because they featured totally nude dancing. The state law required dancers to wear pasties and a G-string. The district court held that such nude dancing was not expressive conduct, and therefore not worthy of First Amendment protection. The Seventh U.S. Circuit Court of Appeals reversed, holding that nonobscene dancing when done for entertainment was protected expression that conveyed eroticism and sexuality. The Supreme Court in a plurality decision said Indiana's enforcement of the public indecency statute to halt totally nude dancing did not violate the First Amendment. According to the plurality opinion written by Chief Justice Rehnquist, and joined by Justices O'Connor and Kennedy, "Nude dancing of the kind sought to be performed here is expressive conduct within the outer perimeters of the First Amendment's guarantee of freedom of expression."[113] The Court applied the intermediate scrutiny test of *United States v. O'Brien*, discussed earlier in this book. The opinion noted that the governmental interest in the case was to regulate public safety, health, and morals, and that the requirement that dancers wear a minimum amount of clothing did not prevent the dancers from still conveying an erotic message. In his concurring opinion, Justice Souter said the state was also justified in its actions by its concern with preventing prostitution, sexual assaults, and other criminal activities associated with such establishments.

CURRENT OBSCENITY AND INDECENCY CASES

When President Clinton first was elected in 1992, there was speculation that the new FCC with his appointees would take the same tough stance toward indecent broadcasts as the previous Commission. Time has proved the pundits correct, with the FCC consistently cracking down on broadcasts it considers indecent. For example, in February 1994, Evergreen Media Corporation, which owns radio station WLUP in Chicago, settled with the FCC in a suit filed by the agency. The FCC fined the station for broadcasts in 1987 and 1989 that included: (a) a caller parodying Neil Diamond's song "September Morn" with a version called "Kiddie Porn," (b) a joke from a caller about a gay bar with the punch line, "May I push your stool in for you?", and (c) an explicit dialogue criticizing an interview with dethroned Miss America, Vanessa Williams. After the company refused to pay a $6,000 fine levied against it in 1991, the FCC sued for collection. In 1993, the FCC once again fined the station for indecency for a 1991 broadcast referring to penis size and a later broadcast in which the hosts substituted "penis" for "Venus" in a parody of Frankie Avalon's song.

Under the settlement, which the court approved, the company agreed to pay the FCC $10,000 in fines and set up an internal policy under which employees must comply with FCC indecency regulations. The FCC agreed to drop its suit if WLUP received no notices of liability for indecency for 6 months.[114]

Sexually explicit programming may be disappearing from most of cable television, but it appears to be thriving on home satellite services. In 1990, the owners of the Home Dish Only (HDO) Satellite Network pleaded guilty to two misdemeanor charges of distributing obscene materials in Montgomery County, Alabama, and were fined $5,000 and ordered to pay two children's homes $75,000. HDO had operated a XXX-rated satellite service known as American Exxxtasy for 4 years. HDO also paid a $150,000 fine and signed a consent decree with the U.S. Attorney General's Office after federal obscenity charges were filed against it. Under the consent decree, the company agreed to erase all taped movies and not promote or distribute sexually explicit films. Interestingly, American Exxxtasy was a scrambled (encrypted) service available only by subscription. The service remained silent for 4 years, but reappeared in 1994 on satellite television under the name Exxxtasy. It is not available in at least six states, including Alabama, Mississippi, North Carolina, Tennessee, Oklahoma, and Utah. There are no injunctions in these states against Exxxtasy, but the network will not sell its service to satellite viewers in those states, which have a reputation for aggressively fighting obscenity. Another service has also joined the lineup of X-rated entertainment on satellite. "TV Erotica" claims to be "America's hottest adult movie channel," offering XXX movies on both a subscription and pay-per-view basis. Playboy, Adam & Eve, Spice, and Spice 2 are among the services that continue to offer adult-oriented movies, but not X- or XXX-rated ones.

In February 1995, the FBI arrested a 20-year-old University of Michigan student for posting a story on the Internet that included discussion about his fantasy of raping, torturing, and killing a classmate whom he named. The events discussed with a fellow Internet user in Canada never occurred, and the student never made any actual threats against his classmate. Jake Baker was charged with five counts of transmitting by e-mail a threat to kidnap or injure. However, U.S. District Court Judge Avern Cohn ruled that Baker's discussions had First Amendment protection and dismissed the charges. Baker was jailed for 29 days after he was charged.

Even when authorities do not consider expressions or images to be obscene or indecent, public pressure sometimes intervenes. For example, several ABC-TV Network affiliates refused to carry the police drama, "NYPD Blue," when it first appeared in 1993, but most of them signed back on after the show became one of the most critically acclaimed dramas in television history and won an Emmy for best drama. The program included partial nudity and explicit language. The next year, an exhibit at an art gallery run by Roman Catholic nuns in San Antonio, Texas, had to be moved to another art gallery after the nuns were severely criticized and received threats of violence. The exhibit that aroused public ire and criticism from the Roman Catholic Church featured the works of Houston artist Donell Hill, which included flesh-colored sculptures of genitalia and a painting of an angel having intercourse at an altar. It was Michael Jackson's genitals that created controversy when the singer released his new video, "You Are Not Alone," in 1995. When the video made its television debut, however, a computer process was used to "remove" his nudity. A persistent rumor, rather than public pressure, led University of Kentucky officials to redesign the official Wildcat logo after it had been in circulation for almost a decade. The rumor, which became so widespread that it garnered extensive media coverage, was that the wildcat's tongue resembled a penis. The only change in the new design was a softening of the "penis tongue," as the rumormongers called it.

ETHICAL DILEMMAS FACING THE MEDIA

Although the news media and, especially, press associations have generally given considerable attention to attempts by the government and the public to ban sexually oriented and indecent works, and have provided support to combat such censorship, advertisers and advertising agencies have generally not entered the fray so readily. This tendency is rather ironic because advertising and other forms of commercial speech have frequently been targets of government and public censorship efforts, as witnessed by Calvin Klein's aborted campaign, discussed earlier in this chapter. Public relations specialists share a similar reluctance to speak out, although they share the limelight when their clients come under fire and they have to explain their positions. When the Third Circuit U.S. Court of Appeals convicted a man in 1994 for buying mail-order videos showing underage girls' clothed genital areas, the Clinton administration initially chose to argue in its appellate brief before the Supreme Court of the United States that the lower appellate court had erred because it used "an impermissibly broad standard" to define child pornography. After a public uproar and criticism from some members of Congress, the administration reconsidered its position, arguing in a new brief that the Court should reject the man's appeal. The Court agreed with the government and denied certiorari.

The ethical dilemma is compounded by the increasing scientific evidence that pornography can have antisocial effects. In a comprehensive analysis of the existing research on the association of the acceptance of rape myths and exposure to pornography, Mike Allen and three other authors found almost no association in studies using nonexperimental methodologies, but found a positive association in experimental studies.[115] Rape myths are beliefs that individuals have "about rape as a sex crime for which the victim bears partial or even primary responsibility."[116] The authors make it clear that the results are mixed, and that the "implication of the findings for those advocating certain types of media content controls remains unanswered."[117] Their recommendation that more research be conducted is well taken, especially in light of the positive association (but no proof of causation yet) that emerges in experimental studies between exposure to erotic materials and acceptance of rape myths.

Professor Albert C. Gunther of the University of Wisconsin pointed to an interesting phenomenon associated with public perceptions about pornography.[118] According to Gunther's research, a substantial majority of U.S. adults believe other people are more negatively affected by pornography than themselves. His study also found that support for restrictions on pornography parallels this discrepancy between effect on self versus effect on others. Thus, he concluded, "People's attitudes or behaviors may be influenced, not by media content directly, but by their perception of the effects of such content on others. And people may be particularly influenced when, accurately or not, they see others as more negatively affected than they are themselves."[119]

SUMMARY AND CONCLUSIONS

The three-prong test of *Miller v. California*, which is nearing its 25th anniversary, is still *the* test for determining whether a work is obscene—whether it be in the form of a film, an advertisement, or even a press release. The Supreme Court has consistently held that obscenity enjoys no First Amendment protection. In contrast, indecency can claim some First Amendment protection, depending on the context in which it appears. For example, the FCC and the courts, including the Supreme Court of the United States, use the limited public resource or scarcity rationale to justify restrictions on indecent programming in broadcasting. Congress has taken a somewhat different approach to indecency on cable television. Because cable and satellite television are "invited" into the home as subscription services, Congress has simply given cable operators the option of refusing to carry indecent programming without incurring liability for prior restraint; further, it has left satellite services alone, except primarily for obscenity statutes and technical standards. Some forms of indecent expression, such as nude dancing, have such limited First Amendment protection, according to the Supreme Court in *Barnes v. Glen Theatre*, that a state's interest in protecting the health, safety, and morals of the community can easily override any constitutional limitations. Most of the cases on obscenity and indecency have been outside the realm of purely commercial speech, except for the advertising and promotion of sexually explicit materials. But these decisions and the various federal and state obscenity statutes nevertheless have serious implications for advertisers and public relations specialists, especially given the proliferation of sex appeal in commercial speech, especially advertising.

Journalistic Privilege, Free Press/ Fair Trial Issues, and Problems in Gaining Access to Information

While the principal focus of this text is on the laws and regulations affecting commercial speech, readers should also be aware of a number of legal issues related to the news-gathering and disseminating process facing the print and broadcast journalists with whom they share the marketplace of ideas.

Among these issues are the arguments for and against granting journalists a constitutional or statutory "privilege" to withhold information from legislative and judicial authorities. A second issue is the inevitable tensions involved in protecting the freedom of journalists to fully and accurately report on the criminal and civil law processes while at the same time ensuring that those parties actually involved in the legal process are afforded the right to a fair and unbiased judicial proceeding that the Constitution promises.

A third important issue is the balancing of the degree of First Amendment or statutory right of access to public records and public meetings versus the competing important governmental interests in protecting privacy and efficient policy making.

The reader should note that this chapter is purposely written from the perspective of the news journalist because the issues discussed most directly impact the news gathering process. However, these issues have implications for public relations practitioners and, to a lesser degree, advertising professionals as well. These are noted in the chapter where appropriate.

JOURNALISTIC PRIVILEGE: PRACTICAL ISSUES

Imagine that you recently asked one of your friends, a part-time reporter for a local daily newspaper in your area, to give you a ride to get your car at the repair shop. She agreed, but added "I hope you don't mind if we make just one brief stop while I meet with a man at a restaurant he owns that's on our way." The reporter hoped to obtain information from the source (local mobster Harry "The Horse" Smith) to be used as the basis for a story the reporter was working on for the next day's edition about illegal drug dealing. This was fine with you and, rather than waiting outside in her car, you accompanied the reporter to the interview, sitting quietly in a corner of the tavern's back room in which the reporter interviewed the source (the reporter told the source that you were "just another reporter").

During the course of the interview, the source unexpectedly described not only how illegal drugs are brought into the county but allowed the reporter to take pictures of a demonstration (with no faces shown) of how easy it is to divide a parcel of these drugs into small packages designed for sale to school children. Before doing so, however, the source asked for and received a promise from the reporter that everything connected with the interview was "off the record" and that the reporter would not reveal where, how, or from whom the information was obtained.

The reporter's subsequent story, published as a page-one exposé, caught the attention of a state grand jury investigating illegal drug dealing. The grand jury then asked that a subpoena be issued to the reporter, ordering her to appear to testify as to the source of the information about drug sales and to provide any other information that might assist the grand jury in its investigations. The reporter has so far refused to testify, and, as a result, risks being found in contempt of court, a position that could land the journalist in jail and/or require her to pay criminal or civil fines.

It is just this kind of scenario that has created a demand by many in the journalistic community for the recognition of a "journalistic privilege." Being granted a privilege in the law usually means that the person accorded the privilege is excused from following normal legal rules except under certain specific instances or, more rarely, is excused from complying with such requirements in all circumstances. Those in favor of extending such a privilege to journalists argue that such legal dispensation should be granted in cases in which the journalist has been ordered to satisfy otherwise legitimate requests for information made by a court, grand jury, or governmental commission or committee with which any other citizen would be compelled by law to comply.

The arguments for granting a journalist the privilege to withhold information from governmental authorities are based both on the practical difficulties faced by a reporter in gathering information without such legal protection and the possibility that, in the absence of such a journalistic privilege, information with important implications for public policy might never reach readers and viewers.

In an era of general public distrust of government and big business, it should come as no surprise that, for reasons ranging from the honorable to the most mean-spirited self-interest, many people with information about possible wrongdoing or malfeasance in office are reluctant to reveal that information to governmental authorities. Whether they fear retaliation on the job, physical harm to themselves or their families, prosecution for criminal activity, or involvement in an uncomfortable situation, people who are "in the know" often will not complain or publicly blow the whistle. They may confide in a journalist, however, with the idea that the journalist, in making the information public, can set the wheels of reform in motion. Often the price of that confidence is a promise by the reporter never to reveal anything that could lead to the source of the information.

The ability (and the right) of the reporter to make and keep such a pledge of confidentiality is an important weapon in the arsenal of journalists in ensuring that the news media can effectively fulfill their function as a community watchdog. That important societal role would be made much more difficult if journalists were forced to reveal the source of the information. Not only would journalists lose an important and reliable informant in current as well as subsequent investigations (and bear the moral responsibility of possibly placing that individual in jeopardy), but it is likely that other potential sources would be much more reluctant to divulge information to the news media if they believed their confidences also might be disclosed.

Additionally, reporters argue, the watchdog role of the news media would be subverted by turning reporters into de facto agents of the government through a process of routinely subpoenaing journalists to appear before legislative or judicial bodies and forcing them to reveal with whom they had spoken and the subject matter of such conversations, on pain of being held in contempt if they refuse to answer. As a reporter who refused to provide information to a grand jury in Ohio explained, "I believe reporters should not be used by our society as cops. If I cooperated [with the grand jury request], it would shatter the credibility of all reporters. If I cooperated, any sources looking at me—past, present or future—would wonder, 'Can I trust her?' "[1]

An issue of greater concern is the harm caused to the public by the failure of the reporter to acquire the information when confidences cannot be kept between reporter and source, at least according to many of those in favor of such a privilege. Although it is true that the reporter's job becomes more difficult if confidential sources are afraid or unwilling to provide information without a guarantee that their names will not become known, the fact remains that journalists still will be able to produce a product at the end of the day, albeit perhaps an inferior one. Thus, recognizing a journalistic privilege, although generally described as helping the news media, actually is meant to benefit the public.

These arguments are buttressed by the numerous instances of wrongdoing that have come to light only through the collaborative efforts between confidential sources and investigative reporters. Examples range from the Watergate investigations of the early 1970s that eventually resulted in the resignation of President Richard M. Nixon to revelations of illegal or unethical behavior in the 1990s by state legislators, other state and local officials, and private corporations in New York, South Carolina, Virginia, and elsewhere.

With so many arguments in its favor, the reader might assume that the acceptance of a journalistic privilege at the state and federal levels has become commonplace. Such an assumption would be in error. Although it is true that many states have provided some kind of privilege, either by statute or court decision, and that a number of federal appeals courts have interpreted the Supreme Court of the United States' rulings in this area as recognizing a qualified First Amendment-based privilege, strong countervailing arguments against a legal privilege for journalists have served to limit, and in some instances defeat efforts to recognize or create such a privilege.

One of these arguments is that a bedrock principle in the American legal system requires every person who possesses information that could assist in the quest for ascertaining truth in the administration of justice to come forward and provide that information if required by law to do so. Courts, grand juries, and other investigative governmental bodies could not function if people were free to flout this principle. For this reason, failure to provide such information, or to do so untruthfully, usually is considered a serious criminal offense.

Because acquiring the most accurate and comprehensive information possible is so vital to the orderly administration of justice, and because those who wish to exert a privilege not to comply with a request for such testimonial evidence often have information that would materially assist in the search for truth, it is no wonder that the maxim has developed that *"all privileges of exemption from this duty* [to testify] *are exceptional* and are therefore to be discountennanced." (emphasis in the original)[2]

Yet some privileges, either by tradition or by law, do exist. The privilege to be free from the requirement of self-incrimination is recognized as a fundamental liberty and enshrined in the provisions of the federal constitution. Reaching far back into our antecedents in the English legal system, the American common law today continues to recognize that privileged communications exist in the interactions between husband and wife; attorney and client; physician and patient; and priest (or other member of the clergy) and penitent. Although the extent and nature of each of these privileged situations varies, the general rule is that if the relationships satisfy the definitions specified by law, the confidences shared in these relationships are privileged and may not be subjected to judicial or investigative scrutiny.

Each of these privileged relationships is based on a societal view that says we consider that other values—for example, family harmony, the ablest legal representation, and the health of the body and the soul—are of more importance than the acquisition of information that could be obtained by revealing the confidences shared in each of these relationships. The reader should not lose sight, however, of the tremendous assistance obtaining such information would provide to those charged with ascertaining truth and administering justice (and the statement it makes of the kind of society we live in that we choose to forego acquiring such information, a decision not shared by many other societies).

The probative value of such information should also help explain why many in the legal system, while perhaps not seriously challenging the continuation of long-held privileges, are loath to create additional privileges in the law to protect the confidences shared in other relationships. Journalists are by no means alone in requesting that privilege be extended to them. Arguments have been advanced by psychologists, school counselors, social workers, and individuals in a wide variety of other occupations and professions claiming that their relationships with clients or patients or counselees should be recognized in the law as confidential. Faced with these demands, it should come as little surprise that courts and legislatures have shown such resistance to opening the door even slightly to the recognition of additional privileges beyond those already recognized by the constitution or in the history of the common law.

Journalists face other formidable obstacles as well in obtaining widespread acceptance within the legal community of a privilege to protect their sources of information. Although credentialing or accrediting procedures may serve to officially designate those who are allowed or recognized as eligible to practice in specific professions or occupations, no such procedures exist to certify who is and who is not a journalist. In fact, most journalists actively resist the notion of any such licensing scheme, arguing that such a system would be a violation of the First Amendment. Extending privilege to journalists, therefore, presents the possibility of difficult definitional problems. Such issues often arise when a journalistic privilege is asserted by a freelance writer, an academic preparing a manuscript for submission to a scholarly journal, a documentary filmmaker, or a novelist.

Another problem relates to the legal rationale usually advanced for protecting those relationships, such as attorney–client, that are recognized as privileged in existing law. The extension of privilege in such a situation generally is seen as a means to protect the nonprofessional party to the relationship. For example, the confidentiality of the relationship between an attorney and client is meant to ensure that clients may speak openly and candidly to their legal representatives regarding legal matters or in the preparation of a case without fear that an attorney subsequently will be forced to reveal these confidences. A privileged situation normally comes into existence the moment the professional nature of the relationship is established (as opposed to a casual conversation at a social gathering, for example). If, however, clients do not object to revealing the contents of a privileged conversation, attorneys normally will not be exempted from providing information to a court or other legal body by claiming their own privilege.

Those in favor of recognition of a journalistic privilege, however, suggest that unlike other relationships, the privilege should protect the journalist (e.g., the professional) and not the source. According to this argument, journalists should be able to make the decision as to whether a privileged situation exists, the nature and extent of the privilege, and decide to withhold information or reveal it, irrespective of the wishes of the source.

A third problem with the recognition of a journalistic privilege is the skepticism of many jurists and others in the legal community about the need for such a privilege. These critics argue that promises of confidentiality may be too easily given and that there is little hard evidence that the flow of important information to the public would be seriously lessened if a privilege were not recognized or that significant gains for the public are achieved if sources are encouraged to talk to journalists about wrongdoing rather than report it to the proper authorities.

Additionally, because the shielding of sources often prevents law enforcement officials from identifying individuals who themselves have committed an illegal or unethical act (for example, the drug dealer who provided information to the reporter in the hypothetical scenario that began this discussion of journalistic privilege), many in the legal community are also troubled by the notion of a privilege that permits journalists to rise above the law by ignoring their civic responsibility to immediately report criminal activity or malfeasance in office to the proper authorities. As Justice White noted in the seminal Supreme Court decision in this area, "we cannot seriously entertain the notion that [a privilege should exist] on the theory that it is better to write about crime than to do something about it,"[3] including providing timely information to investigators or courts.

Journalistic Privilege: Legal Issues

In part to counter the arguments against extending a privilege to journalists, and also because they understand that there must be a legal as well as practical rationale underlying the push to have such privilege recognized, many supporters of journalistic privilege ground their advocacy in the First Amendment. Although admitting that requiring journalists to name their sources or provide other information to legal authorities is not a direct, content-based "abridgment" of speech, these advocates argue that the inhibition of sources, the threat to journalistic integrity, and the resulting restriction on the free flow of information of importance to the public caused by requiring journalists to reveal information raise significant First Amendment issues.

By no means, however, is there unanimous support for a First Amendment rationale as the basis for a privilege, even by those who are strong supporters of the general concept of journalistic privilege. Those who object to a constitutionally based privilege do so because, they argue, such a position requires an interpretation of the First Amendment to provide one level of constitutional protection for "regular" individuals and a second, higher level for "journalists," a position they find untenable.

To understand this better, we need to return to our hypothetical example that began this discussion of journalistic privilege. Remember that you accompanied your friend the reporter while she interviewed a source. Her subsequent story was based on information provided only after the reporter promised the identity of the informant would remain confidential. A grand jury later subpoenaed the reporter and ordered her to reveal the source of her article. Assume, for the moment, that the reporter argued that she had a First Amendment privilege to withhold that information and further assume that a court upheld her argument, ruling that she did not have to testify.

As you may imagine, the court's action has upset the members of the grand jury who, after all, are charged with the duty of investigating drug trafficking in the area and now feel stymied in this search by the refusal of the journalist to provide relevant, material information. A quick-witted member of the grand jury, however, has an idea. "Does anyone else know to whom the reporter spoke and maybe what was said?" he asks. Suddenly, all eyes are looking directly at you!

Wondering how in the world you got involved in an investigation of illegal drugs, you call your friend, asking how she avoided testifying. She tells you that the court accepted the argument that she has a First Amendment-based journalistic privilege not to testify and suggests you try a similar tact.

See the problem? Unless you happen to have a press card or can convince the court that somehow you also should be treated as a journalist, it is extremely unlikely the court will grant you a similar privilege, despite the fact that you only saw and heard exactly what the reporter did. Those who are concerned by what, to them, seem contradictory outcomes in such a case usually argue that the constitution does not provide the basis for a journalistic privilege because the First Amendment should be interpreted as protecting every individual equally and therefore cannot be "twisted" into differentiating journalists from nonjournalists.

Those who are in favor of a journalistic privilege, but who reject a First Amendment-based rationale, generally instead opt for achieving their objective by statutory means on a state-by-state basis by urging legislatures to pass so-called "shield laws." Shield laws are seldom drafted in such a way as to create an absolute privilege for journalists to refuse to testify in all cases. Instead, most create a qualified privilege that provides protection for reporters under most circumstances but that can be overcome if the governmental body seeking information from the reporter can justify its request by meeting the requirements established in the statute.

Branzburg v. Hayes: The Supreme Court and Journalistic Privilege

The idea that journalists should be granted a legal privilege to withhold information gained widespread popular support within the news media community by the late 1960s. A number of states had passed shield laws, which were the subject of subsequent court challenges by judges and grand juries seeking information from reporters. In a number of these cases, as well as in cases in the federal system, the argument had also been made that the First Amendment should be construed as conferring a constitutional privilege. Thus the stage was set for the Supreme Court of the United States to hear a case focusing on the extent, if any, of a First Amendment-based journalistic privilege.

The opportunity presented itself in *Branzburg v. Hayes*,[4] a consolidated appeal of three cases involving reporter privilege, two from state supreme courts and one from the federal court of appeals for the ninth circuit. The facts of the case, involving Branzburg, a reporter for the *Louisville* (Kentucky) *Courier Journal*, in part parallel those in our opening scenario. The reporter, working on a story about drug dealing, promised confidentiality to his informants whom he had observed and photographed synthesizing hashish from marijuana. Subpoenaed by a county grand jury investigating illegal drug sales, Branzburg refused to reveal the names of the persons he had observed. A second story resulted in another subpoena, but this time the reporter refused to appear before the grand jury at all. In each instance, Branzburg's attorneys, in addition to the practical arguments in favor of recognizing a privilege for journalists, argued that there were three legal bases for their position: the First Amendment, Kentucky's state constitutional protections of speech, and the state's shield law.

Ultimately, the Kentucky Supreme Court rejected all of these arguments, holding that the First Amendment did not provide a federal constitutional shield and that nothing in the state constitution could be construed as creating a privilege for journalists. The Kentucky court further held that Kentucky's shield law provided "a newsman the privilege of refusing to divulge the identity of an informant"[5] but added that "the statute did not permit a reporter to refuse to testify about events [the reporter] had observed personally. . . ."[6] Branzburg then took his appeal to the Supreme Court.

The second case in the *Branzburg* trilogy, *In re Pappas*, involved a reporter working for a New Bedford, Massachusetts television station. Pappas was permitted to enter and report from inside the local headquarters of the radical Black Panthers group during a period of social unrest on the condition that he not "disclose anything he saw or heard inside . . . except an anticipated police raid. . . ."[7] The raid never materialized and Pappas never prepared a story. Nonetheless, a county grand jury subsequently summoned him to appear and to tell all he had learned by being inside the headquarters. Pappas refused, citing both the state and federal constitutional protections of speech (Massachusetts had no shield law). On appeal, the Supreme Judicial Court of Massachusetts upheld a lower court's order to provide the requested information, noting that a privilege to avoid testifying in Massachusetts was "limited" and that "[t]he principle that the public 'has a right to every man's evidence' " was the general rule recognized by the state.[8] The state high court also concluded that the federal constitution provided no privilege to avoid testifying in such circumstances. Pappas appealed this latter ruling to the Supreme Court of the United States.

U.S. v. Caldwell, the third case on appeal, involved a reporter for *The New York Times* who also was covering the activities of radical groups, including the Black Panthers. A federal grand jury in California investigating the causes of recent civil unrest in that state subpoenaed Caldwell, ordering him to bring with him "notes and tape recordings of interviews . . . reflecting statements made for publication by officers and spokesmen for the Black Panther Party. . . ."[9] Although the order to produce materials was eventually withdrawn, Caldwell was still subpoenaed to personally appear before the grand jury to testify about his knowledge of possible criminal activity. Caldwell refused, citing the First Amendment.

A federal district court then ordered the reporter to be jailed for contempt of court, but a federal appeals court for the ninth circuit reversed that decision, holding that the First Amendment provided a qualified constitutional privilege for news gathering. Faced with state court decisions denying the existence of a First Amendment-based journalistic privilege in Kentucky and Massachusetts and a federal appeals court holding to the contrary in the states covered by the ninth circuit, the Supreme Court of the United States granted the petitions for certiorari in all three cases and consolidated them for consideration of the privilege issue.

Those hoping that the Court's decision in *Branzburg* would provide a definitive answer as to whether the First Amendment provides a privilege for journalists, however, were to be disappointed. In a divided opinion, the Court upheld the orders directed against the three journalists but, at the same time, appeared to hold that there was at least some First Amendment-based protection for reporters to protect their sources from forced disclosure.

Justice White, in an opinion joined by Chief Justice Burger and Justices Blackmun and Rehnquist, strongly rejected the notion of constitutional privilege. "We do not question the significance of free speech ... [n]or is it suggested that news gathering does not qualify for First Amendment protection. ... But these cases involve no intrusions upon speech ... no prior restraint or restriction on what the press may publish, and no express or implied command that the press publish what it prefers to withhold."[10] In addition, wrote Justice White, there is "[n]o exaction or tax for the privilege of publishing, and no penalty, civil or criminal related to the content of published material is at issue here. The use of confidential sources by the press is not forbidden or restricted. ... The sole issue before us is the obligation of reporters to respond to grand jury subpoenas as other citizens do and to answer questions relevant to an investigation into the commission of crime."[11]

Noting that the First Amendment had been interpreted as permitting "incidental burdening" of the press in enforcing other laws and that the press was not free to invade privacy, defame, ignore laws applicable to others, or to gain special access to records, meetings, or places,[12] "[i]t is thus not surprising," said Justice White, "that the great weight of authority is that newsmen are not exempt from the normal duty of appearing before a grand jury and answering questions relevant to a criminal investigation."[13] While observing that a number of states had enacted statutes to provide a journalistic privilege, White added that "[u]ntil now, the only testimonial privilege for unofficial witnesses ... in the Federal Constitution is the Fifth Amendment privilege against compelled self-incrimination. We are asked to create another by interpreting the First Amendment to grant newsmen a testimonial privilege that other citizens do not enjoy. This we decline to do."[14]

The reasons for this disinclination, explained Justice White, included the law's historic dislike of privilege in general, a concern that extending a privilege to journalists could inhibit law enforcement officials and courts from investigating criminal activity, the possibility that informants themselves could escape criminal liability, and skepticism about the dire results predicted by reporters for the news-gathering process if such a privilege were not extended. The Court also envisioned problems in determining to whom such a constitutional privilege should be extended, "a questionable procedure in light of the traditional doctrine that liberty of the press is the right of the lonely pamphleteer who uses carbon paper or a mimeograph just as much as of the large metropolitan publisher who utilizes the latest photocomposition methods."[15] Justice White indicated as well that states (and the federal government) were free to establish journalistic privilege by statute or other means if they so chose.

In contrast to the opinion authored by Justice White, the four Justices in dissent found a First Amendment-based privilege for journalists that, in effect, mirrored the holding of the federal court of appeals in *Caldwell*. Justice Stewart, writing for two other Justices (Justice Douglas filed his own dissenting opinion), argued that the reasons for a constitutional privilege were compelling enough to warrant recognizing a privilege to protect journalists and their sources in most circumstances. Such a privilege was qualified, however, meaning that it could be overcome if the court or other governmental agency seeking to compel the reporter's testimony could demonstrate that the information sought was highly relevant, could be obtained from no other source, and was essential to a substantial governmental interest. Clearly, however, the constitution, according to Justice Stewart, places the burden of meeting this three-prong test on the government and, unless the government can show such evidence, a journalist has a First Amendment privilege to refuse to testify.

With four Justices in *Branzburg* firmly committed to the position that the First Amendment does not provide a privilege for journalists, and four others just as convinced that it does, all eyes turned to the swing vote of Justice Powell. Unfortunately for those seeking a decision that would settle this issue once and for all, Justice Powell contributed an opinion that seemed to come down squarely in the middle. He concurred with Justice White's opinion that a First Amendment-based privilege would be inapplicable in the three cases constituting this appeal because the journalists had actually witnessed criminal activity. On the other hand, Justice Powell seemed to find at least some constitutional basis for according journalists privilege in other (unspecified) situations, noting that "This Court does not hold that newsmen, subpoenaed to testify before a grand jury, are without constitutional rights with respect to the gathering of news or in safeguarding their sources."[16]

The upshot of Justice Powell's enigmatic opinion is that today, those who argue that the First Amendment provides no privilege for journalists cite *Branzburg* as authority for their position, and those who argue that indeed there is such constitutional protection also cite *Branzburg* as upholding their view. As the reader may imagine, lower federal and state courts have been confused when encountering such arguments and, predictably, many have recognized a First Amendment privilege whereas others have not. The majority of courts that have recognized some form of journalistic privilege usually have adopted the *Branzburg* minority's three-prong test although, according to a recent analysis, they "often have applied it in a manner resulting in a requirement that the journalist testify."[17]

At the time of this writing, 29 states had adopted some form of shield law, although they vary considerably in terms of who and what is protected and when such protection is provided. It appears that such shield laws will withstand challenge unless they interfere with the constitutional right of defendants accused of a crime to obtain evidence to defend themselves. Although attempts have been made for almost two decades, Congress has so far refused to act to enact a federal shield law.

Major issues of recent contention in claims-of-privilege cases have involved (a) subpoenas directed at broadcast "outtakes," (b) how thorough a court or other governmental entity must be in exhausting all other avenues to obtain information before establishing that the reporter is the sole source, and (c) the remedies legally available to a court if privilege is asserted by the journalist in a libel trial to protect the source of the allegedly libelous statements.

In a case promising potentially serious ramifications for journalists (and of interest to public relations practitioners as well), the Supreme Court of the United States upheld a breach of contract-like claim by a source against a newspaper in Minnesota that revealed his identity after promising him it would not do so. That case, *Cohen v. Cowles Media Co.*,[18] would appear to place journalists promising confidentiality in the unfortunate position of facing contempt of court citations, involving jail terms and/or fines, if they do not reveal information when called to testify and the possibility of payment of substantial money damages to the aggrieved source if they do. Public relations professionals dealing with the news media in situations where requests are made for confidentiality should be aware that courts in other situations may not wish or be able to follow the *Cohen* precedent because of differing state laws. Recognizing that despite a pledge of secrecy, a journalist may be placed under tremendous pressure to reveal the source of his or her information, the prudent public relations professional would be well advised not to provide confidential information to the news media if such provision is conditioned on a promise that the journalist will not reveal the source.

FREE PRESS/FAIR TRIAL ISSUES

Let's return to the hypothetical example that began this chapter. Your friend the reporter was writing a story about illegal drug dealing that got both her and you in hot water with a state grand jury investigating the same topic. Assume now that the grand jury gave up its attempts to get evidence from you and the reporter but obtained enough information from undercover police investigations to return an indictment of Harry "The Horse" Smith, the original source of the story. City police, armed with an arrest warrant, found Harry walking down the street, handcuffed him, threw him into a squad car, took him downtown, and booked him. Nobody read him his rights (the so-called *Miranda*[19] warning), nobody offered to allow a phone call to an attorney, in fact, nobody got to see Harry for three days because the police kept him locked in the basement of the jail, seated in a straight-backed chair with the light from a 500-watt bulb shining in his eyes while teams of burly police officers constantly interrogated him.

Harry finally cracked under the strain and confessed, not only to drug dealing but to the murder of two rival mobsters. He told police that they could find the evidence they needed, including a still-smoking revolver with bullets matching those found in one of the victims, a blood-stained knife with Harry's fingerprints on it, and a diary in Harry's handwriting revealing how he planned his foul deeds buried under the old oak tree in his backyard. The police rushed to Harry's house and, sure enough, dug up all the evidence Harry said would be there. Police Chief O'Malley then stepped forward at a specially called press conference and announced to the world that Harry had been caught, confessed to the crimes, the police had uncovered all of the evidence described, and that "obviously we have caught the bum that did it—he's guilty as sin."

By now, most if not all of you probably have wanted to raise objections about police conduct described in this hypothetical situation. You probably have seen enough television programs about law enforcement and the judicial process to feel that courts would never allow the police to operate in this high-handed fashion and hope to make the charges stick. Much of the evidence gathered by the police in this example likely would be non-admissible in court because the judge, in order to ensure a fair trial, would employ the so-called "exclusionary rule" to keep it out. This rule of evidence has been developed by courts (and approved by the Supreme Court of the United States) as a tool to ensure that police and prosecutors do not violate the rights of those charged with a crime in the process of enforcing the criminal law. This means that police and prosecutors know that evidence that could very well be useful, and perhaps decisive, in proving the guilt of the criminally accused may be excluded from consideration by the jury unless the law enforcement officials play by the rules.

The rules work because police and prosecutors measure their success in how many bad guys are apprehended, convicted, and removed as threats to society. It is doubtful that any modern-day law enforcement agency would operate the way the police did in our hypothetical scenario. But if it did or, in a more likely occurrence the police inadvertently made a mistake in the enforcement process, the courts have the responsibility and the power (the "exclusionary rule") to prevent the jury from being prejudiced by learning about the tainted evidence. Unfortunately from the perspective of the court, however, no such power exists to prevent *potential* jurors from learning about the tainted evidence by reading or hearing about it in their local and national media.

Remember the press conference conducted by the police chief in our scenario? He not only spoke in detail about the evidence, but conclusively stated the guilt of the accused. The newspapers and television stations serving the area would be sure to report this as news—it might even be the lead story. Assume that on returning to your residence at the end of the day you picked up your mail but put it aside long enough to get a snack before dinner and to watch an evening local television news show. The program leads with a full report of the details of the press conference. Now, having been exposed to news about Harry's confession, police discovery of murder weapons, the accused killer's diary, and the police chief's conclusions about Harry's guilt, you open your mail and discover that you have been chosen for jury duty.

See the problem? If you were selected for the jury pool in Harry's upcoming trial, you would have been exposed to pretrial publicity about evidence prejudicial to Harry's case that you would not have learned about as a juror in the courtroom because the evidence would not have been admitted. Because of your prior knowledge, you might ask to be excused from jury duty or be challenged by one of the parties to the case. But what if almost everyone in town has been exposed to the prejudicial information. How can Harry be assured of a fair and unbiased trial by his peers in these circumstances?

At the heart of the "free press/fair trial" issue is this conflict—the courts' responsibility to assure the criminally accused and, to a lesser degree, the people (represented by the prosecutor) the right to a fair and unbiased trial versus the responsibility of the mass media to accurately and comprehensively report the news and carry out this task free from unwarranted governmental interference.

For much of the nation's history, this conflict was only theoretical. The press was able to disseminate what it wanted and, if the rights of the criminally accused were diminished, it was just too bad. But as concerns about protection of civil liberties increased in the 1950s, courts became more and more worried about the prejudicial publicity problem. Things came to a head with the Supreme Court's decision in *Sheppard v. Maxwell*.[20] Dr. Sheppard, an osteopathic surgeon, was charged with murder in the slaying of his wife. Sheppard claimed an intruder had invaded their home, knocked him unconscious, and killed Mrs. Sheppard, but police soon made Sheppard their number one suspect. In what today would likely be called a "media circus," the newspapers covering the case employed sensational headlines suggesting his guilt, officials made public statements of a similar nature prior to trial, and the news media were given almost free reign inside and outside the courtroom during the trial. Found guilty and sent to prison, Sheppard pursued the appeal of his conviction all the way to the Supreme Court which, in a landmark decision, overturned the conviction and ordered a new trial on the basis that the trial judge failed to "fulfill his duty to protect [Sheppard] from the inherently prejudicial publicity which saturated the community and to control disruptive influences in the courtroom."[21]

Many of the Court's suggestions for trial courts to use as remedies for alleviating potential bias are familiar to most readers today. These include a delay of trial or other proceedings, change of venue, maintaining order inside the courtroom, intensive screening of potential jurors to root out bias, instructions to the jury to avoid reading or viewing the news media while the case proceeds and, in more extreme cases, sequestering the jury for the length of the trial. With these tools at a judge's disposal once the jury pool is chosen, there is little reason to worry about prejudicial publicity reaching the jury unless the judge fails to do his or her duty. Unfortunately, however, the remedies that are most effective in minimizing bias require the judge to have control over the jury members. These measures are largely ineffective in preventing pre-trial prejudicial publicity from reaching potential jurors.

This conundrum—trial court judges charged by the Court with eliminating prejudicial publicity or risk having their cases overturned on appeal yet being unable to effectively use the remedies for prevention suggested by the Court— led to the first great confrontation between the legal system and the press over the issue of free press/fair trial: the use of prior restraints or so-called "gag orders."

NEBRASKA PRESS ASSOCIATION v. STUART: USE OF PRIOR RESTRAINT TO ENSURE FAIR TRIALS

Charged by the Supreme Court of the United States with the responsibility for mitigating the effects of prejudicial pre-trial publicity but lacking effective means to carry out this responsibility, a few trial courts began to experiment with restraining orders directed at the press. These orders, placed on news media representatives in the early stages of a criminal case, usually allowed the press to be present at pre-trial hearings or other proceedings and to obtain information from law enforcement officials but mandated that the press not publicize certain kinds of potentially prejudicial information or, in some circumstances, not to disseminate information of any kind about an upcoming case. Those violating such orders ran the substantial risk of being found in contempt of court and made to pay fines and/or spend time in jail.

The effectiveness of these court orders, quickly dubbed "gag rules" by the news media, made their use attractive to other judges and the number of courts employing them in some form across the country quickly snowballed. Because these court orders also undeniably were examples of government agencies employing prior restraint (as discussed in chap. 1, the most constitutionally suspect method of governmental abridgement of speech), it was only a matter of time before a challenge to their use arrived at the door of the Court.

The case that presented the Court with the opportunity to speak out about the legitimacy of the use of such restraints was *Nebraska Press Association v. Stuart*,[22] an appeal of a decision by the Nebraska Supreme Court. The sensational facts of the case included the murder of all six members of a family living in the small town of Sutherland, Nebraska (population 850). Police almost immediately suspected Erwin Simants who turned himself in to authorities the next day. Because mass murder was not a common occurrence in Nebraska, the case garnered widespread attention from both regional and national print and broadcast media.

After 3 days of constant publicity, both Simants' attorney and the county prosecutor asked a county court judge to issue an order prohibiting the media from divulging "news which would make difficult, if not impossible, the impaneling of an impartial jury and tend to prevent a fair trial."[23] The judge granted the motion which "prohibited everyone in attendance from 'releasing or authorizing the release for public dissemination in any form or manner whatsoever any testimony given or evidence adduced. . . .' "[24] After a preliminary hearing, Simants was bound over for trial to the state district court presided over by Judge Stuart. Various journalistic organizations, including the Nebraska Press Association representing the state's newspapers, as well as individual newspapers and broadcast stations asked Judge Stuart to lift the restraining order issued by the county court.

Finding that there was "a clear and present danger that pre-trial publicity could impinge upon the defendant's right to a fair trial,"[25] the judge refused the request to lift the restraint on publication, but modified the county court's original order to reflect the voluntary Nebraska Bar-Press Guidelines for disseminating information that had been worked out by print and broadcast media associations in cooperation with various law enforcement personnel and judicial officers. The Nebraska Bar-Press Guidelines, like those that had been adopted by many other states, suggested that in criminal cases it would be inappropriate to report information about a suspect's confession or other admissions, the results of physical tests that might be inadmissible in court (such as a lie-detector test), opinions by officials about guilt and innocence, or other statements that might inflame or influence potential jurors to which the actual jury hearing the case might not be exposed.

Despite the fact that the Nebraska Press Association had participated in the drafting of these guidelines, it, along with other news media representatives, appealed to the Nebraska Supreme Court, asking that the restraining order be overturned, on the premise that making voluntary guidelines mandatory violated their free speech/press rights. When the Nebraska high court refused, the press association took its appeal to the Supreme Court of the United States.

Characterizing the "problems presented by this case [as] almost as old as the Republic,"[26] Chief Justice Burger, writing for the majority (all nine justices agreed on the outcome), traced problems of prejudicial publicity surrounding criminal proceedings back to the trial of Aaron Burr for treason in 1807. Commenting that even then Chief Justice Marshall had expressed concern about the problems in selecting an unbiased jury that had been exposed to public discussions and newspaper accounts about the case, and observing that the "speed of communication and the pervasiveness of the modern news media have exacerbated these problems,"[27] the Court nonetheless concluded that such sensational cases "are relatively rare, and we have held in other cases that trials have been fair in spite of widespread publicity."[28]

Noting that a trial judge had a number of measures at his or her disposal to minimize the effects of prejudicial publicity, including changing the location (venue) of the trial, delaying the proceedings, interrogation of potential jurors to determine bias, instructing jurors as to how they should view the evidence in a case, restraining participants in the case from discussing it with the news media, regulating the activities of the media in the courtroom, and sequestering the jury, the Court upheld the appeal by the Nebraska Press Association on First Amendment grounds. In so holding, however, the Court did not rule out the use of judicial restraining orders in future cases. Instead, the Court created a three-part test for determining the constitutionality of such restraints of the media.

First, said the Court, the judge issuing a restraining order directed against the press must be able to show a clear record of "intense and pervasive"[29] news coverage that demonstrates that prejudicial pretrial publicity has occurred, is likely to continue and that such "publicity might impair the defendant's right to a fair trial."[30] The second part of the test requires the judge to demonstrate on the record that he or she investigated the feasibility of employing one or more of the alternatives to prior restraint just discussed but found that no other method or methods would be sufficient to protect the defendant's right to a fair trial. Part three of the test relates to "the probable efficacy of prior restraint on publication as a workable method of protecting [the defendant's] right[s]."[31] Noting that, as a practical matter, a court must have jurisdiction over the parties involved in a case if its orders are not to be ignored, the Court pointed out that in a sensational case (like the O. J. Simpson murder trial, for example), it would be of little avail for a judge to issue a restraining order that could apply only to local or regional media but not control the coverage of the case by national media.

From the point of view of the news media, the results of the *Nebraska Press Association* case produced two important results, one good and one bad. The good news was that, while not prohibiting so-called gag rules completely, the Court's three-prong test signaled a clear message to lower courts seeking to enforce such rules that it was extremely unlikely the constitutionality of such prior-restraint orders directed against the news media would be sustained in future cases. This has proven to be the case. Note, however, that the Court explicitly suggested that such restraints would be justifiable if imposed on other participants in the case including public relations professionals representing clients involved in the litigation. You should not trifle with or make fun of a court order. The savvy public relations practitioner would be wise to both follow such orders to the letter in releasing information to the public (if in doubt, consult with the court before speaking) and counsel clients about their responsibilities to do likewise.

The bad news for the news media in *Nebraska Press Association* was contained in language in the Court's majority opinion that seemed to view with approval the Nebraska Supreme Court's suggestion to the trial court that closing the preliminary hearing and other pre-trial proceedings to the public (including the news media) was an acceptable alternative to prior restraint.[32] Soon, trial courts, faced with the continuing mandate to protect defendants from the effects of prejudicial pre-trial publicity but prohibited by the decision of the Court in *Nebraska Press Association* from using gag rules (except in rare circumstances), began to deny the press and public access to pre-trial judicial hearings and other proceedings in increasing numbers. It was only a matter of time before closing the courtroom doors, thus denying to the public the ability to scrutinize the workings of the judicial process, also was challenged in the courts as a violation of the constitution.

The case presenting this opportunity was *Gannett Co. v. DePasquale*.[33] One day, Wayne Clapp and two of his buddies went fishing on Seneca Lake in upstate New York. Only his buddies returned. Police, alerted to Clapp's disappearance by his family, found his bullet-ridden boat and surmised that Clapp had met a violent end. Newspapers in the area, including one owned by Gannett Co., reported the story of Clapp's apparent death and the apprehension of the two suspects in Michigan several days later. The stories included details about the case against the suspects including statements made by them to police and the discovery of a supposed murder weapon. As the case against them developed, both defendants moved to suppress various pieces of evidence, including much of the information they had given to police, on the grounds "that those statements had been given involuntarily. They also sought to suppress physical evidence seized as fruits of the allegedly involuntary confessions,"[34] specifically, the revolver said to have been involved in the killing.

At the pre-trial suppression-of-evidence hearing before Judge DePasquale, defendants' attorneys asked that the press be barred from the proceedings on the grounds that there already had been significant adverse publicity about the case and that there was a threat to the fair-trial rights of the accused if the press were allowed to report on evidence that might be excluded at trial. The prosecution did not oppose the motion and neither did representatives of the media, although a reporter for the Gannett newspaper was present in the courtroom. Judge DePasquale granted the defendants' request and closed the hearing to the public. When Gannett's attorneys later objected to the closure, Judge De-Pasquale, although noting that the press had a limited constitutional right of access, refused to lift the closure order on the basis that allowing the press to report on the outcome of a hearing to suppress evidence "would pose a 'reasonable probability of prejudice to these defendants' . . . [and] ruled that the interest of the press and the public was outweighed in this case by the defendants' right to a fair trial."[35] When the New York Court of Appeals upheld Judge DePasquale's ruling, Gannett took its case to the Supreme Court of the United States.

Interestingly, Gannett's major arguments in favor of opening the pre-trial procedure to public scrutiny rested in the Sixth Amendment's guarantee of a "public" trial rather than on a First Amendment analysis, although free speech and press issues were presented as alternative grounds for opening the proceedings. This strategy may have been chosen because of a series of rulings by the Court in prior cases that seemed to suggest that there was no general First Amendment right of access either to information or to gain entrance to meetings or governmental facilities. As the Court (in *Gannett*) noted, "In *Pell v. Procuiner*, *Saxbe v. Washington Post Co.* and *Houchins v. KQED, Inc.*, this Court upheld prison regulations that denied to members of the press access to prisons superior to that afforded to the public generally."[36]

The Court's majority opinion, in rejecting First Amendment arguments in favor of overturning Judge DePasquale's closure order, held that the pre-trial proceeding in *Gannett* should not be differentiated from this line of decisions, especially because media representatives had been present when the order was issued and had failed to object at that time, a hearing had been granted the newspaper company in which to argue for openness and because the closure order was "only temporary. Once the danger of prejudice had dissipated, a transcript of the suppression hearing was made available."[37] Chief Justice Burger, in a concurring opinion, specifically noted that a First Amendment-based claim of access was inapplicable in this case because *Gannett* involved a pre-trial proceeding unknown at the time the First Amendment was adopted.

Finding equally little merit in the news organization's arguments for a general right of access rooted in the Sixth Amendment[38] (the guarantee of a "speedy and public trial" is a guarantee "to a person charged with the commission of a criminal offense, and to him *alone*" [italics added]),[39] the Court upheld the trial judge's closure order as an acceptable measure for mitigating prejudicial pre-trial publicity.

Based on the precedent of *Gannett*, lower courts across the country increased their use of closure as a means of ensuring defendants a fair trial. This movement finally culminated in *Richmond Newspapers, Inc. v. Virginia*[40] in which a judge closed an actual criminal trial, thus setting the stage for a second chance for First Amendment-based arguments in favor of public access to judicial proceedings. The case involved the fourth trial of a defendant accused of murdering a hotel manager. His conviction in the first trial was reversed on appeal because a blood-stained shirt was improperly introduced as evidence. A second trial ended when a juror was forced to retire and no alternate was available. The third trial was aborted when it was discovered that a prospective juror had read about the earlier attempts to try the defendant (including the bloody-shirt evidence) and informed other jurors about these efforts.

At the beginning of trial four, defense counsel, citing the possibility of prejudicial publicity, asked the judge to close the proceedings to the press and public. When neither the prosecution nor the journalists present objected, the judge cleared the courtroom "of all parties except the witnesses when they testify."[41] At a subsequent hearing, requested by the Richmond Newspapers, Inc. to protest closure, the trial judge refused to vacate his order (finding the criminal defendant's arguments about the number of trials to date and the smallness of the community persuasive) and the trial continued with the press and public barred. The defendant was eventually found not guilty of murder. The Virginia Supreme Court upheld the validity of the trial court's closure order and Richmond Newspapers took their case to the Supreme Court of the United States.

While the Court was fragmented in deciding on an overall rationale for its decision (Chief Justice Burger's opinion was joined by only two other justices and no other opinion represented the views of more than two justices), seven justices agreed that the lower court's order should be overturned on First Amendment grounds. The Chief Justice's opinion began by observing that "this precise issue . . . has not previously been before this Court. . . . [H]ere for the first time the Court is asked to decide whether a criminal *trial* itself may be closed to the public upon the unopposed request of a defendant [absent] any demonstration that closure is required to protect the defendant's superior right to a fair trial . . ." (italics added).[42] Tracing the origins of a tradition of openness for such trials to before the Norman conquest of England in 1066 AD, Chief Justice Burger noted that this tradition had been brought over to the English colonies in America and had become part of the American legal system. Based on this evidence, the Chief Justice concluded that "From this unbroken, uncontradicted history, supported by reasons as valid today as in centuries past, . . . a presumption of openness inheres in the very nature of a criminal trial under our system of justice."[43]

Despite this presumption, however, Virginia officials argued that no explicit provision of the constitution guarantees that the press and public should be permitted access to all criminal trials. Although agreeing in principle, the Chief Justice found that "In guaranteeing freedoms such as those of speech and press, the First Amendment can be read as protecting the right of everyone to attend trials. . . . '[T]he First Amendment goes beyond protection of the press and the self-expression of individuals to prohibit government from limiting the stock of information from which members of the public may draw.' "[44] Although not providing a general right of access, Chief Justice Burger held that "The right of access to places traditionally open to the public, as criminal trials have long been, may be seen as assured by the amalgam of the First Amendment guarantees of speech and press; and their affinity to the right of assembly is not without relevance."[45] The Chief Justice concluded that despite the failure of the constitution to enumerate a guarantee of access, "the right to attend criminal trials is implicit in the guarantees of the First Amendment; without the freedom to attend such trials, which people have exercised for centuries, important aspects of freedom of speech and 'of the press could be eviscerated.' "[46]

Although the Chief Justice, in fashioning a limited First Amendment-based right of access, was careful to maintain the distinction between pretrial proceedings and actual criminal trials that he had articulated in *Gannett*, the limitation almost immediately began to suffer erosion. In *Globe Newspaper v. Norfolk County Superior Court*,[47] the Court struck down a state law mandating closing of trials involving victims of sexual offenses under the age of 18 on the basis that the law permitted no judicial discretion. Such a law, said the Court, could not be squared with the constitutional presumption of openness of criminal proceedings. In *Press Enterprise Co. v. Riverside County Superior Court*,[48] the Court held that jury selection was so integral to the criminal trial process and was so intimately related to the actual trial that it too was presumptively open to the press and public despite arguments that, in addition to prejudicial pre-trial publicity, potential jurors and witnesses might be intimidated or embarrassed by media reports.

In a later case with the same name, often referred to as *Press-Enterprise II*,[49] the Court was presented with the rather unusual situation of a pre-trial preliminary hearing that continued for 41 days in a case involving a nurse charged with multiple murders of patients under his care. Unlike a typical preliminary hearing, in which the prosecution's task is to convince a neutral magistrate that there is enough evidence to warrant going forward with a criminal case against the accused and which generally lasts no more than a day or two, the proceedings in *Press-Enterprise II* involved extensive medical and scientific evidence as well as testimonial evidence from the defendant's co-workers, most of which was subject to searching cross examination by the defendant's legal counsel.

At the beginning of the proceedings, the defendant asked that the preliminary hearing be closed. The trial judge granted the motion, which was unopposed, on the basis that "closure was necessary because the case had attracted national publicity and 'only one side may get reported in the media.' "[50] At the end of the preliminary hearing, *Press-Enterprise* asked that the transcript of the proceedings be made public but the judge denied the request. The appeal of the closure and sealing of the transcript was taken to the California Supreme Court, which upheld the lower court. The Supreme Court of the United States granted certiorari and overturned the lower court's decisions on First Amendment grounds.

The Court recognized the lower courts' concerns about ensuring the defendant's rights to a fair trial and that its own rulings in earlier cases might be construed as to deny First Amendment claims of access. However, said the Court, despite the fact that the closure order involved a pre-trial proceeding, "the First Amendment question cannot be resolved solely on the label we give the event, i.e., 'trial' or otherwise, particularly where the preliminary hearing functions much like a full-scale trial."[51] Instead, said the Court, a possible constitutional right of access must be based on "two complementary considerations. First, . . . we have considered whether the place and process have *historically* been open to the press and general public" (italics added).[52] Second, the Court added, "the Court has traditionally considered whether public access plays a significant *positive role* in the functioning of the particular process in question" (italics added).[53]

Finding that although in California, proceedings like grand jury deliberations have not been open to public scrutiny, "there has been a tradition of accessibility to preliminary hearings of the type conducted in [this case]."[54] In fact, noted the Court, "From [the case of Aaron] Burr until the present day, the near uniform practice of state and federal courts has been to conduct preliminary hearing in open court."[55] Although some states historically have allowed preliminary hearings to be closed on occasion, the Court noted that "even in these States the proceedings are presumptively open to the public and are closed only for cause shown."[56] Based on its decisions in *Richmond Newspapers* and *Press-Enterprise I* that public access "is essential to the proper functioning of the criminal justice system,"[57] the Court held that when conducted like those in California, "preliminary hearings are sufficiently like a trial to justify the same conclusion."[58]

After the series of cases ending in *Press-Enterprise II*, lower courts apparently got the message that closing criminal court proceedings to minimize prejudicial publicity should not be the method of choice except in unusual situations. Lower courts, therefore, have increasingly turned to delay, change of venue, and especially to the use of gag rules on police and trial participants to prevent them talking to the press to try to ensure that the rights of the criminally accused are not abridged. Although there has been no opportunity for the Court to expand on its rulings in this area, it seems a safe bet that there is little enthusiasm on the part of the current members of the Court for narrowing the trend to openness recognized for criminal proceedings. There remains the question, however, of whether this trend will be extended to provide a constitutional right of access to civil proceedings. Although most civil trials are routinely open to the public, lower courts, at least for the time being, still retain a greater ability to deny access if they so choose. Arguably, the benefits of public access to criminal proceedings articulated by the Court in cases ranging from *Richmond Newspapers* to *Press-Enterprise II* should equally adhere to civil proceedings with equal validity.

CAMERAS IN THE COURTROOM— A SPECIAL ACCESS PROBLEM

In 1927, Charles Lindbergh captured the imagination of the world when he flew his airplane, the *Spirit of St. Louis*, solo between New York and Paris. He returned to the United States a hero and his fame increased as he toured the country and then foreign countries as well with his bride, Anne Morrow Lindbergh. Tragically, their lives were shattered in 1934 when their infant son was kidnapped and later killed. The details of the kidnapping, the arrest of a suspect, Bruno Hauptmann, and his subsequent trial for murder created a news media frenzy, so much so that the American Bar Association was moved to adopt Canon 35 of its code of legal ethics which banned broadcast coverage as well as still photography in courtrooms.

The prohibition of cameras and microphones in the courtroom continued to be enforced for more than four decades until, recognizing that modern technology had reduced the intrusiveness of the broadcasting and photography, the courts began to slowly experiment with allowing their access to pre-trial and trial proceedings. In *Chandler v. Florida*[59] in 1981, the Supreme Court of the United States held that it was not an inherent abridgement of a defendant's rights to a fair trial to allow cameras and microphones in the courtroom. However, the Court did not find a blanket right of access for such mechanical devices, leaving it to the states and lower federal courts to establish rules and guidelines for allowing or prohibiting their presence. Today, with the advent of Court TV, which is carried on many cable systems, and the nationwide televising of high profile trials like those of William Kennedy Smith (acquitted of a charge of rape) and O. J. Simpson (found not guilty of killing his former wife and an acquaintance), the presence of cameras in the courtroom has become commonplace.

The O. J. Simpson case, however, illustrates not only the benefits but the downside of extensive coverage by the electronic media both inside and outside the courtroom. Although presenting an accurate portrayal of a major criminal trial (at least in California) with all its moments of great drama, as well as the much more common hours of routine legal procedure, the Simpson pre-trial and trial proceedings also were rife with public bickering and posturing of lawyers for both sides, innumerable problems with selecting and keeping jury members, extensive legal wranglings concerning the validity of DNA evidence, and the relevance of taped interviews indicating racial bias by one of the prosecution's star witnesses in a case involving a defendant many in the public believed from the start was guilty as charged.

The resulting dismay with the Simpson proceedings and the legal process in general voiced by members of the viewing public on call-in talk shows, letters-to-the-editor, and public opinion polls produced calls for renewed prohibitions on cameras in the courtroom by members of the legal profession concerned both with the image of the judical system and the effects of the telecasts on participants in other criminal proceedings.

Journalistic Privilege, Free Press/Fair Trial Issues, and the Trial of Susan Smith: A Case Study

Perhaps nowhere was the negative fallout from the coverage of the Simpson trial as well as the ongoing tensions between the courts and the mass media demonstrated more dramatically than in trial of Susan Smith, a 22-year-old South Carolina mother charged with the drowning deaths of her two young sons. Although the murder of children by a parent is not considered as newsworthy in America as it once was, the events surrounding the Smith case, including Smith's story that her children had been abducted by an African-American man, her tearful requests that her children be returned broadcast on network television, and then the startling revelation that all of this was a lie and that she herself had steered her automobile into a lake near her home with her two children strapped in their carseats inside, ensured that her subsequent trial would be a major media event.

Recognizing the high probability of possible pre-trial publicity (while Smith's hometown, Union, SC, has a population of about 10,000, a total of only 40,000 people live in all of Union County), police initially were extremely cautious about giving out information during their investigation, but eventually did release the news that Smith had confessed to the crime and permitted the news media to view the crime scene. The judge, fearing that it might be difficult to obtain an unbiased jury from among the residents of the county, did not attempt to gag the media but instead, following the options suggested in *Nebraska Press Association*, placed a restraining order prohibiting any public discussion of the case on the prosecution's staff, defense attorneys, all potential witnesses, police, and any others who might have access to or knowledge of evidence that might be at issue in the trial.

Despite these efforts, Twyla Decker, a reporter for the Columbia, SC *State* newspaper, obtained information for a story that was subsequently published in the newspaper about the defendant's psychiatric profile both during and after the commission of the crime. Believing that the individual revealing this information to the reporter might have been covered by his restraining order, the judge ordered the reporter to reveal the name of her source. Decker refused, citing South Carolina's recently enacted shield law and free speech protections guaranteed by the state and federal constitutions. The South Carolina shield law was modeled after the three-part test of *Branzburg* and was generally regarded as an example of a statute providing strong protection for the news media.

The trial judge ruled, however, that the shield law was inapplicable or, in the alternative, that the test for the governmental agency seeking to overcome the provisions of the shield law (information that is highly relevant, incapable of being provided by an alternative source, and needed by the government to establish its case) had been satisfied. Finding equally little merit in the reporter's arguments of constitutional protection, the judge ordered Decker to either turn over the information or face going to jail on charges of criminal contempt of court.

On appeal, the South Carolina Supreme Court upheld the lower court.[60] In a ruling hostile to the concept of journalistic privilege, the court made mincemeat of the state's shield law, ruling that it was only applicable to information provided to a reporter that is already in the public domain. This interpretation ruled out large categories of information, such as health records, sealed agreements, or grand jury discussions, that often form the bases for reporters' stories. The high court also held that the word "parties" in the language of the statute does not refer to governmental bodies or agencies but only to plaintiffs and defendants. Such an interpretation severely limits the scope of the South Carolina law because the exertion of a privilege most often occurs in situations like the hypothetical case that began this chapter involving a grand jury, court, or investigatory agency seeking information from the reporter. Finally, the South Carolina court found that even if the shield law had been applicable, the trial court judge's decision that the court's need for the information overcame the law's protection was correct. On receipt of the high court's ruling, however, the trial judge stayed his decision about the fate of the newspaper reporter until the Susan Smith trial was completed.

While all this was transpiring, the pre-trial proceedings, including suppression-of-evidence hearings and jury selection, were proceeding. And so were the preparations for covering the trial by the major television networks, syndicated tabloid news programs, and local and regional television stations from Charlotte, NC to Atlanta. As the trial date neared, the broadcast media commandeered much of the rental property in the town to house its personnel, built a fortress-like phalanx of make-shift broadcasting booths on risers stretching the length of one city block in front of the Union County courthouse, and incessantly interviewed Union residents brave enough to venture downtown about their opinions of the trial and the possible penalty Susan Smith should face if convicted of the crimes with which she was charged.

Perhaps this build-up of media presence caused a last-minute decision by the trial judge to grant the Susan Smith defense team's request to ban all electronic and photographic equipment from the courtroom, despite the fact that extensive modifications of the courtroom to facilitate the electronic media requested by the judge had already been completed. The judge cited the possible reluctance of witnesses to testify truthfully if their testimony were shown on television as the principal reason for his decision, but it is fair to speculate, given that everyone in the small town would almost immediately be aware of such testimony, that he was more concerned with losing control of the proceedings and risk becoming another Judge Ito (the trial judge in the O. J. Simpson case), criticized for his performance and satirized on widely viewed late-night television shows.

Because the admittance of electronic media and photographic cameras in the courtroom is by statute left to the discretion of the trial judge in South Carolina, the judge's exclusion of electronic media was not able to be appealed. As a result, the reporting of the trial was left entirely to print media and to the broadcasting of the renderings of courtroom artists. Susan Smith eventually was found guilty of the crimes as charged but the jury unanimously voted to send her to prison for life rather than impose the death penalty, which could have been implemented under South Carolina law. At the conclusion of the trial, the trial judge elected not to send *The State* newspaper reporter to jail for disobeying his pre-trial disclosure order.

Until the memory of the O. J. Simpson trial fades, courts and legal commentators may continue to regard requests to broadcast criminal proceedings and expansive interpretations of journalistic privilege with suspicion. The negative media-related results of the Susan Smith trial should serve as a sobering reminder of the fragile nature of the free-speech protections for journalists when they try to protect the identity of their sources, despite state shield laws or when they seek access to courtrooms to report on the criminal or civil law processes.

FREEDOM OF INFORMATION AND ACCESS
TO PLACES ISSUES

Although the Supreme Court of the United States has expanded a right of access to criminal proceedings, no similar trend has been noted in finding a general constitutionally based right to acquire information or to gain admittance to physical locations. In fact, it seems safe to say that, except for criminal proceedings, as a rule, the First Amendment provides no right of access. In

Pell v. Procunier[61] and *Saxbe v. The Washington Post*,[62] for example, the Court specifically rejected claims that journalists have a special right to gain access to prisons and other governmental facilities, holding that the mass media have no greater right of access than the general public.

Lower federal and state courts have followed the Court's lead, ruling in almost every instance that journalists have no superior access rights to enter private property, gain entrance to crime scenes, or be admitted to meetings than those afforded the general public (although in practice the public relations staffs of most governmental agencies will accommodate the requests of journalists to gain access if their presence does not interfere with the department's operations). What is true for access to physical places is also true for access to records and other information. With the exception of material related to criminal proceedings, the courts consistently have held that the mass media have no greater right of access to records and documents than do members of the general public.

Just because the First Amendment has been interpreted as not providing a special right of access for journalists and the public, however, does not mean that the reasons for allowing access to records and places are without merit. To accomplish by statute what could not be achieved by constitutional interpretation, Congress passed the Freedom of Information Act (FOIA) in 1966,[63] supplemented by the 1974 Privacy Act,[64] to provide a qualified right of access to information maintained in the files of federal agencies. Each of the 50 states has now followed suit with its own Freedom of Information (FOI) law to provide a right of access to state records.

As the person to whom a freedom of information inquiry often is made or referred, the public relations professional in a governmental organization should become intimately familiar with both federal and state FOI statutes. The federal FOIA mandates that all federal executive branch and regulatory agencies disclose how and from whom their records may be obtained by the public for viewing and/or photocopying. The statute specifies that all final court opinions and orders related to agency matters, policy statements, and interpretations of regulations, documents, and records about agency actions or proposed actions not excepted from disclosure by the nine specific exemptions in the Act be made available for public inspection. Even if some parts of a document might be exempted, however, the Act requires the governmental agency producing the document to make a reasonable effort to ensure that the non-exempted portions are provided to members of the public seeking the information.

The first exemption to the requirements of disclosure in the Act is material designated by an executive order to be kept secret in the interests of national defense or foreign policy. This has proven in practice to be a rather large exception because Congress and the courts have given great deference to the executive branch in determining what is classified. The current test is simply whether disclosure could reasonably be expected to endanger national security. Not only can the government maintain a document as classified under the national security/foreign policy exemption, but it can even reclassify a document formerly in the public domain as secret after an FOIA request has been made.

The second exemption is for information that is related solely to the internal personnel rules and practices of an agency and the third is for documents already exempted by other federal statutes. The fourth exemption to the federal FOIA is for trade secrets or commercial and financial information that is considered to be privileged or confidential. Interestingly, this exemption gave rise to a decision by the Supreme Court of the United States of significance to corporate public relations professionals that held that the federal FOIA permits but does not require an agency to withhold documents that arguably fall within one of the exemptions. The case, *Chrysler Corp. v. Brown*,[65] involved a request for information about Chrysler Corporation's affirmative action policies. This information had been provided to the U.S. Department of Labor by Chrysler under federal statutory provisions requiring such submissions from any company with multiple contracts with the federal government. Before the information could be made public, Chrysler sought an injunction in a federal district court in Delaware to block its release. The trial court granted the injunction but this decision was subsequently overturned by the Court on the basis that the FOIA does not provide for private action by a company to prevent disclosures. Today, acting under executive order, federal agencies routinely notify organizations if information they have supplied is to be released to the public and the organizations are permitted a 10-day period to protest such release and, if necessary, to seek injunctive relief in federal district courts to stop the information from being divulged.

Exemption five to the federal FOIA protects inter-agency and intra-agency memoranda or letters from public disclosure. This exemption has been interpreted as protecting working papers and other documents that are produced as part of an agency's ongoing decision-making process as well as the "work-product" of government attorneys normally protected as privileged communications under normal rules of legal civil procedure. Exemption six, which protects personnel, medical, and other similar government files containing information of a normally private nature about specific individuals, has produced much controversy and litigation. In two cases reaching the Supreme Court of the United States, the Court sided with agency decisions to deny FOIA disclosure in situations involving requests for information about the citizenship status of foreign nationals and to allow *The New York Times* access to the last seconds of recorded conversations among the seven crew members of the space shuttle *Challenger* before the space craft exploded, killing all aboard.

Exemption seven has also seen its share of litigation and controversy. With the continuing emphasis on the reporting of crime news by American news media, the exemption created by the federal FOIA for records or other documents compiled for law enforcement purposes frequently has been challenged when law enforcement officials have declined to provide journalists with information about criminals or criminal investigations. Government agencies wishing to classify information related to law enforcement must demonstrate either that disclosure could reasonably be expected to interfere with enforcement procedures or deprive a person of a right to a fair trial, constitute an unwarranted invasion of privacy, identify a confidential source, reveal law enforcement techniques, or endanger the life or physical safety of an individual. Cases contesting refusals by federal agencies to release crime-related information have involved requests for FBI criminal identification "rap sheets," statements by potential witnesses in investigations of labor disputes, and documentation related to the Watergate conspiracy during President Richard Nixon's tenure in office.

The eighth exemption, permitting classification of information related to the examination, operation, or condition of a financial institution, and exemption nine, concerning documentation of geological and geophysical investigations have produced little litigation.

State FOI laws normally parallel their federal counterpart, complete with exemptions for law enforcement documents, confidential business data, and individual privacy interests. In addition, all states have passed statutes mandating open meetings of public bodies such as city commissions, state regulatory agencies, school boards, and so forth. Most of these so-called "sunshine laws" also provide for closed-door sessions when officials are discussing such things as legal matters, property acquisition, and individual personnel issues, although no official business may be finalized or final votes taken behind closed doors. Access to federal government agency meetings is provided by the "Government in the Sunshine Act" of 1977[66] that provides rights and exemptions similar to state laws.

Although procedures for requesting information vary, most FOIA statutes require a written request for specific information, that the governmental agency must meet within a specified time period or explain why the information is being withheld. The government normally is permitted to charge a nominal fee for compiling and photocopying documents, although the fee may be waived. Notification of public meetings must be posted so as to give enough time for the public to attend. Although emergency meetings are allowed, the emergency must be genuine. "Informal" meetings, such as cocktail parties, backyard barbecues, or early-morning breakfasts, where lawmakers "just happen" to get together, normally are treated as public meetings by open-meeting statutes and are therefore subject to the same requirements as regular meetings.

CONCLUSION

Arguments for and against granting journalists a constitutional or statutory "privilege" to withhold information, protecting the freedom of journalists to fully and accurately report on the criminal and civil law processes, and balancing the degree of access to public records and public meetings versus the competing important governmental interests in protecting privacy and efficient policy making continue to comprise a major portion of mass media law involving journalists. Although public relations and advertising professionals may also be affected by decisions of courts and legislators in these areas, it perhaps is more important to understand the problems journalists face in doing their job and, where ethical and appropriate, join them in fighting attempts to restrict freedom of speech.

Endnotes

CHAPTER 1

[1]UNITED STATES CONSTITUTION, Amendment I.

[2]*New York v. Sullivan*, 376 U.S. 254, 270 (1964).

[3]R. Bork, *Neutral Principles and Some First Amendment Problems*, 47 INDIANA LAW JOURNAL 1, 20 (1971).

[4]D. M. Rabban, *The First Amendment in its Forgotten Years*, 90 YALE LAW JOURNAL 514 (1981).

[5]*Barron v. Mayor of Baltimore*, 32 U.S. (7 Pet.) 243 (1833).

[6]*See*, e.g., F. J. TURNER, FRONTIER IN AMERICAN HISTORY (1920).

[7]C. 30, Tit. 1, § 3, 40 Stat. 217, 219 (comp. new st. 1918, § 1012c).

[8]*Schenck v. U.S.*, 249 U.S. 47 (1919).

[9]*Abrams v. U.S.*, 250 U.S. 616 (1919).

[10]*Schenck v. U.S.* at 52.

[11]*Id.*

[12]*See*, e.g., Criminal Anarchy Statute, New York Penal Laws § 160,161 (1909), originally enacted 1902.

[13]268 U.S. 652 (1925).

[14]283 U.S. 697 (1931).

[15]*New York Times v. U.S.*, 403 U.S. 713 (1971).

[16]*Bantam Books v. Sullivan*, 372 U.S. 58,70 (1963).

[17]341 U.S. 494 (1951).

[18]354 U.S. 298 (1957).

[19]*Dennis v. U.S.* at 511.

[20]*Id.*

[21]395 U.S. 444 (1969).

[22]M. B. NIMMER, NIMMER ON FREEDOM OF SPEECH: A TREATISE ON THE FIRST AMENDMENT (1988), § 2.05 [B] 2–29.

[23]*Schenck v. U.S.* at 52.

[24]NIMMER at § 2.05 [B] 2–29. *See*, e.g., *Marsh v. Alabama*, 326 U.S. 501 (1946).

[25]*See*, e.g., *Greer v. Spock*, 424 U.S. 828 (1976).

[26]NIMMER at § 2.03, 2–15.

[27]UNITED STATES CONSTITUTION, Amendment XIV.
[28]*Gitlow v. New York*, 268 U.S. 652, 666 (1925).
[29]*Whitney v. California*, 274 U.S. 357, 377 (1927).
[30]*See*, e.g., *Shaw v. Hunt*, _ U.S. _ (1996).
[31]360 U.S. 109 (1959).
[32]*Id.* at 126.
[33]NIMMER at § 2.02 2–9.
[34]44 Stat. 1162 (1927).
[35]48 Stat. 1064 (1934) 47 U.S.C.A. § 151 Et. seq.
[36]319 U.S. 190 (1943).
[37]413 U.S. 15 (1973).
[38]*Id.*
[39]*Texas v. Johnson*, 491 U.S. 997 (1989).
[40]*Barnes v. Glen Theatre*,_ U.S. _ 111 S. Ct. 2456 (1991).
[41]NIMMER at § 1.02 [A], 1–7.
[42]*Id.*, quoting *Whitney v. California*, 274 U.S. 357, 375 (1927).
[43]NIMMER at § 1.02 [A], 1–7.
[44]*Id.* at 1–8.
[45]*Id.* at 1–9.
[46]*Abrams v. U.S.* at 630.
[47]NIMMER at § 1.02 [B], 1–12.
[48]*Id.*
[49]274 U.S. 357 (1927).
[50]NIMMER at § 1.02 [G], 1–42.
[51]*Id.* at 1.02[I], 1–47, quoting V. BLASI, *The Checking Value in First Amendment Theory*, A.B.F. RES. J. (1977) 521.
[52]NIMMER at § 1.02 [H], 1–44.
[53]*Id.* at 1–45.

CHAPTER 2

[1]FTC, A GUIDE TO THE FEDERAL TRADE COMMISSION, (1992) 3.
[2]308 U.S. 147 (1939).
[3]*Id.* at 165.
[4]*Valentine v. Chrestensen*, 316 U.S. 52 (1942).
[5]§ 318 of the New York City Sanitary Code.
[6]*Valentine v. Chrestensen* at 53 n. 1.
[7]*Id.*
[8]*Id.* at 54.
[9]*Id.*
[10]*See*, e.g., *Pittsburgh Press Co. v. Pittsburgh Commission on Human Relations et al.*, 413 U.S. 376 (1973).
[11]413 U.S. 376 (1973).
[12]*Bigelow v. Virginia*, 421 U.S. 809 (1975).
[13]*Pittsburgh Press Co. v. Pittsburgh Commission on Human Relations et al.* at 385.
[14]*Id.* at 387.
[15]*Id.* at 388.
[16]*Id.* at 389.
[17]421 U.S. 809 (1975).
[18]*Id.* 811 n. 1.
[19]*Id.* at 812.
[20]*Id.* at 812, quoting Va. Code Ann. § 18.1–63 (1960).
[21]*Id.* at 814, quoting 213 Va. 193–195, 191 S.E. 2d at 174–176.

[22]410 U.S. 113 (1973).
[23]*Bigelow v. Virginia* at 815.
[24]*Id.* at 818.
[25]*Id.* at 821.
[26]*Id.* at 822.
[27]*Id.* at 825.
[28]*Id.*
[29]*Id.* at 826.
[30]*Id.*
[31]*Id.* at 825.
[32]425 U.S. 748 (1976).
[33]*Id.* at 749.
[34]*Id.* at 761.
[35]*Id.* at 763.
[36]*Id.*
[37]*Id.* at 765.
[38]*Id.*
[39]*Id.* at 769.
[40]*Id.* at 770.
[41]*Id.* at 771–772 n. 24.
[42]*Id.* at 772 n. 24.
[43]*Id.* at 773.
[44]*Bates et al. v. State Bar of Arizona*, 433 U.S. 350 (1977).
[45]*Id.* at 380.
[46]*Id.* at 381.
[47]*Id.*
[48]*Id.* at 366–367.
[49]*Id.* at 384.
[50]*Bates et al. v. State Bar of Arizona* at 367.
[51]*Ohralik v. Ohio State Bar Association*, 436 U.S. 447 (1978).
[52]*In re Primus*, 436 U.S. 412 (1978).
[53]*Ohralik v. Ohio State Bar Association* at 456.
[54]*Id.*
[55]*Id.* at 459.
[56]*In re Primus* at 438.
[57]447 U.S. 557 (1980).
[58]*Id.* at 560.
[59]*Id.* at 563.
[60]*Id.* at 566.
[61]*Id.* at 564.
[62]*Id.* at 599.
[63]*Id.* at 569.
[64]*Id.*
[65]*Id.* at 570.
[66]*Id.*
[67]453 U.S. 490 (1981).
[68]*Id.* at 493.
[69]*Id.* at 543.
[70]471 U.S. 626 (1985).
[71]466 U.S. 789 (1984).
[72]467 U.S. 691 (1984).
[73]472 U.S. 181 (1985).
[74]478 U.S. 328 (1986).
[75]*Id.* at 332.

[76]*Id.*

[77]*Id.* at 340.

[78]*Id.* at 341.

[79]*Id.*

[80]*Id.*

[81]*Id.* at 342.

[82]*Id.* at 343.

[83]*Id.* at 344.

[84]*Id.* at 346.

[85]*Id.*

[86]486 U.S. 466 (1988).

[87]*Id.* at 488.

[88]492 U.S. 469 (1989).

[89]*Id.* at 480.

[90]*Id.*

[91]496 U.S. 91 (1990).

[92]*Id.* at 110–111.

[93]*Id.* at 117.

[94]*Cincinnati v. Discovery Network, Inc.* _ U.S. _, 113 S.Ct. 1505 (1993).

[95]*Id.* at 1508.

[96]*Discovery Network, Inc. v. Cincinnati*, 946 F.2d 464, 468 (1991).

[97]*Id.* at 471.

[98]*Id.* at 472–473.

[99]*Cincinnati v. Discovery Network, Inc.* _ U.S. _, 113 S. Ct. 1509 (1993).

[100]*Id.* at 1510.

[101]*Id.*

[102]*Id.*

[103]*Id.* at 1511.

[104]*Id.* at 1511. n. 16.

[105]*Id.* at 1513.

[106]*Id.*

[107]*Id.*

[108]*Id.* at 1517.

[109]*Id.* at 1522.

[110]*Id.* at 1510.

[111]*Id.* at 1523.

[112]*Id.* at 1524.

[113]61 U.S. S.L.W. 4759 (June 25, 1993), 21 MED. L. RPRTR. 1577.

[114]732 F. Supp. 633, 637 (E.D. Va. 1990).

[115]*Id.* at 638.

[116]*Id.*

[117]*Id.*

[118]*Id.* at 639.

[119]*Id.*

[120]*Id.* at 641.

[121]*Id.* at 642.

[122]61 U.S. S.L.W. 4759 (June 25, 1993), 21 MED. L. RRPTR. 1577, 1581.

[123]*Id.*

[124]*Id.*

[125]*Id.*

[126]*Id.*

[127]*Id.* at 1582.

[128]*Id.*

[129]*Id.*

[130]*Cincinnati v. Discovery Network, Inc.*, at 1511.

[131]61 U.S. S.L.W. 4759 (June 25, 1993), 21 MED. L. RRPTR. 1577, 1582.

[132]*Id.* at 1578.

[133]*Id.* at 1585.

[134]*Id.* at 1586.

[135]*Id.* at 1587.

[136]*44 Liquormart, Inc. v. Rhode Island*, _ U.S. _ (1996).

[137]A. KOZINSKI and S. BANNER, *Who's Afraid of Commercial Speech?*, 76 VIRGINIA LAW REVIEW 627 (1990).

[138]R. COLLINS and D. SKOVER, *Commerce and Communication*, 71 TEXAS LAW REVIEW 697 (1993).

[139]A. KOZINSKI and S. BANNER, *The Anti-History and Pre-History of Commercial Speech*, 71 TEXAS LAW REVIEW 747, 752 (1993).

[140]*Id.* at 757.

[141]*Id.* at 758.

[142]*Abrams v. U.S.*, 250 U.S. 616, 630 (1919).

CHAPTER 3

[1]316 U.S. 52 (1942).

[2]*Id.* at 53.

[3]*Id.* at 54.

[4]376 U.S. 254 (1964).

[5]*Id.* at 265.

[6]*Id.* at 266.

[7]*Id.*

[8]*Id.*

[9]*Id.*

[10]*First National Bank of Boston v. Bellotti*, 435 U.S. 765 (1978).

[11]*Id.* at 767.

[12]*Id.* at 768.

[13]*Id.*

[14]*Id.* at 767.

[15]*Id.* at 793.

[16]*Id.* at 776.

[17]447 U.S. 530 (1980).

[18]*Id.* at 533.

[19]*Bellotti* p. 777.

[20]*Id.* at 552.

[21]*Id.* at 535.

[22]*Id.* at 537.

[23]*Id.* at 542.

[24]494 U.S. 652 (1990).

[25]*Id.* at 655.

[26]*Id.*

[27]*Id.* at 660.

[28]*Id.* at 657; citing *Buckley v. Valeo*, 424 U.S. 39,96 (1976); quoting *Williams v. Rhodes*, 393 U.S. 23 (1968).

[29]*Id.* at 657.

[30]*Id.* at 660.

[31]*Id.* at 662–664.

[32]*Id.* at 664.

[33]*Id.* at 698.

[34]*Id.* at 700.

[35]*Id.* at 713.

[36]*Id.*

[37]447 U.S. 557, 571 (1980).

[38]132 U.S. App. D.C. 14, 405 F. 2d 1082 (1968).

[39]447 U.S. 557, 571 (1980); citing 132 U.S. App. D.C. 14, 405 F. 2d 1082 (1968).

[40]413 U.S. 376 (1973).

[41]*Id.* at 385.

[42]*Id.*

[43]425 U.S. 748 (1976).

[44]421 U.S. 809 (1974).

[45]425 U.S. 748, 762 (1976); citing *Pittsburgh Press Co. v. Pittsburgh Commission on Human Relations et al.*, 413 U.S. 376, 385; *Haplinsky v. New Hampshire*, 315 U.S. 568, 572 (1942); *Roth v. United States*, 354 U.S. 476, 84 (1957).

[46]492 U.S. 469 (1989).

[47]*Pittsburgh Press Co. v. Pittsburgh Commission on Human Relations et al.* at 385.

[48] U.S. ___,113 S. Ct. 1505 (1993).

[49]433 U.S. 350 (1977).

[50]440 U.S. 1 (1979).

[51]447 U.S. 557 (1980).

[52]472 U.S. 749 (1985).

[53]*Id.* at 762.

[54]*Id.* at 790, quoting *Pittsburgh Press Co. v. Pittsburgh Commission on Human Relations et al.*, 413 U.S. 376, 385.

[55]*Bolger v. Youngs Drug Products Corp.*, 463 U.S. 60 (1983).

[56]*Central Hudson Gas & Electric Corp. v. Public Service Commission*, 447 U.S. 557, 561 (1980).

[57]*Id.* at 563 n. 5.

[58]*Bolger v. Youngs Drug Products Corp.* at 68.

[59]*Id.* at 61.

[60]*Id.* at 62.

[61]*Ohralik v. Ohio State Bar Association*, 436 U.S. 447, 455–456 (1978).

[62]*Bolger v. Youngs Drug Products Corp.* at 65.

[63]*Id.* at 66.

[64]*Virginia State Board of Pharmacy et al. v. Virginia Citizens Consumer Council, Inc., et al., supra*, at 762; quoting *Pittsburgh Press Co. v. Pittsburgh Commission on Human Relations et al.*, 413 U.S. 376, 385 (1973).

[65]*Id.*

[66]*Id.* at 67.

[67]*Central Hudson Gas & Electric Corp. v. Public Service Commission of New York* at 563 n. 5.

[68]*Id.* at 67 n. 14

[69] F. Supp. __, 22 Media Law Rptr. 1118 (S.D.N.Y. 1993).

[70]*Id.* at 1120.

[71]*Id.*

[72]531 N.Y.S. 2d 1002 (1988).

[73]*Id.* at 1011.

[74]505 N.Y.S. 2d 599 (July 31, 1986).

[75]119 A.D. 2d 13 (A.D. 1 Dept. 1986).

[76]*Id.* N.Y.S. ed 599 at 603.

[77]141 F.R.D. 534 (1992).

[78]949 F. 2d 1567 (1992).

[79]*Id.* at 1574, quoting *Central Hudson Gas & Electric Corp. v. Public Service Commission of New York*, at 561.

[80]570 F. 2d 157 (7th Cir. 1977).

[81]*Id.* at 159.

[82]*Id.* at 163.

[83]*In re R. J. Reynolds Tobacco Co.*, [1983–1987] Trade Reg. Rep. (CCH) ¶ 22, 385 at 23, 467 (Aug. 6, 1986) rev'd Trade Reg. Rep. (CCH) ¶ 22, 522 at 22, 180 (April 11, 1988), *stay denied*, Trade Reg. Rep. (CCH) ¶22, 549 at 22, 231 (June 3, 1988).

[84]*Id.*

[85]*Id.*

[86]*Id.*

[87]*Id.*

[88]388 U.S. 130 (1967).

[89]*Id.*

[90]418 U.S. 323 (1974).

[91]*New York Times v. Sullivan*, 376 U.S. 254, 270 (1964).

[92]*Bates et al. v. State Bar of Arizona*, 433 U.S. 350, 381 (1977).

[93]898 F 2d 914 (3rd Cir. 1990).

[94]*Id.* at 918.

[95]*Id.*

[96]*Id.*

[97]*Id.* at 919.

[98]*Id.*

[99]United States District Court for the Eastern District of Pennsylvania.

[100]*Id.* at 920.

[101]*Id.* at 932.

[102]*Id.*

[103]*Id.* at 934.

[104]*Ohralik v. Ohio State Bar Association* at 456.

[105]*Id.* at 935.

[106]*Bolger et al. v. Youngs Drug Products Corp.*, at 68.

[107]*Bolger et al. v. Youngs Drug Products Corp.*, at 67 n. 14.

[108]*First National Bank of Boston et al. v. Bellotti*, at 791.

[109]583 F 2d 421 (9th Cir. 1978).

[110]621 F 2d 195 (5th Cir. 1980).

[111]Fifth Circuit Federal Court of Appeals.

[112]*Id.* at 197.

[113]2 U.S.C. § 441 (a) 1988.

[114]To date, some 27 states have done so.

[115]424 U.S. 1 (1976).

[116]470 U.S. 480 (1985).

CHAPTER 4

[1]Sherman Anti-Trust Act, 15 U.S.C. §§ 1–7.

[2]15 U.S.C. § 45 (a) (1988).

[3]*Id.*

[4]15 U.S.C. § 53 (1988).

[5]316 U.S. 52 (1942).

[6]413 U.S. 376 (1973).

[7]425 U.S. 748 (1976).

[8]*Id.* at 770.

[9]*Id.* at 771.

[10]*Id.*

[11]427 U.S. 50 (1976).

[12]*Id.* at 69 n. 31.

[13]15 U.S.C. § 45 (a)(6).

[14]*Id.* at § 52 (b).

[15]*Id.* at § 55 (a)(1).

[16]201 U.S.P.Q. (BNA) 164 (E.D.N.Y. 1978), aff'd 593 F. 2d 463 (2d Cir. 1979).

[17](2d Cir. 1979).

[18]242 F. Supp. 302 (N.D. Ill. 1965).

[19](N.D. Ill. 1965).

[20]561 F. 2d 357 (D.C. Cir. 1977).

[21]45 Antitrust and Trade Reg. Rep. (BNA) no 1137, at 684 (Oct. 14, 1983).

[22]103 F.T.C. 110 (1984).

[23]K. A. PLEVAN and M. L. SIROKY, ADVERTISING COMPLIANCE HANDBOOK 109 (2d ed. 1991), citing *In re International Harvester Co.*, 104 F.T.C. 949, 1056 (1984).

[24]*In re Southwest Sunsites, Inc.*, 105 F.T.C. 7, 149 (1985); *aff'd* 785 F. 2d 1431 (9th Cir.); *cert. denied*, 479 U.S. 828 (1986).

[25]*Id.*

[26]380 U.S. 374 (1965).

[27]*See, e.g., In re Colgate-Palmolive Co.*, 77 F.T.C. 150 (1970).

[28]104 F.T.C. 949 (1984).

[29]*Id.* at 1059.

[30]*Id.*

[31]*Id.*

[32]*In re Pfizer, Inc.*, 81 F.T.C. 23 (1972).

[33]*Id.* at 24.

[34]*Id.* at 24–25.

[35]*Id.* at 62.

[36]*Id.*

[37]88 F.T.C. 84 (1976); *modified*, 570 F. 2d 157 (7th Cir. 1977); *cert. denied*, 439 U.S. 821 (1978).

[38]*Id.* at 191 (citations omitted).

[39]*Id.* n. 14.

[40]47 Antitrust and Trade Reg. Rep. (BNA), n. 1176 at 234 (Aug. 2, 1984).

[41]PLEVAN at 114. *See, e.g., Firestone Tire and Rubber Co. v. F.T.C.*, 481 F. 2d 246 (6th Cir. 1973).

[42]*See, e.g., Leon A. Tashof v. FTC*, 14 F. 2d 707 (D.C. Cir. 1970).

[43]*Pfizer* at 66.

[44]*Id.*

[45]481 F. 2d 246 (6th Cir. 1973).

[46]*U-Haul International, Inc. v. Jartran, Inc.*, 522 F. Supp. 1238, 1245 (D. Ariz. 1981); *aff'd* p. 127.

[47]61 F.T.C. 840 (1962).

[48]54 F.T.C. 648 (1957); *aff'd* 259 F. 2d 271 (1958).

[49]*Id.* at 653.

[50]89 Civ. 3586 (S.D.N.Y. Jan. 9, 1991).

[51]*Id.* at 42–43.

[52]104 F.T.C. 648 (1984).

[53]*Id.* at 844.

[54]*Id.* at 723.

[55]16 C.F.R. § 419 (1989).

[56]16 C.F.R. § 225 (a)(1987).

[57]*Id.* at § 255 (b).

[58]103 F.T.C. 110 (1984).

[59]*Id.* at 169.

[60]*Id.* at 171–172.

[61]92 F.T.C. 310 (1978).

[62]16 C.F.R. § 255.3 (b)(1987).

[63]94 F.T.C. 674 (1979).

[64]*Id.* at 680.
[65]278 F. 2d 337 (7th Cir. 1960).
[66]16 C.F.R. § 233.1–5 (1990).
[67]*Id.* at § 238.
[68]15 U.S.C. §§ 160-1614 and 1661–1665 (a)(1990).
[69]15 U.S.C. § 45 (b)(1973).
[70]*Sears, Roebuck & Co. v. F.T.C.*, 676 F. 2d 385, 391 (9th Cir. 1982).
[71]Codified in the Federal Cigarette Labeling and Advertising Act, 1965.
[72]562 F. 2d 749 (D.C. Cir. 1977); *cert. denied*, 435 U.S. 950 (1988).
[73]*Id.* at 762.
[74]*F.T.C. v. Pharmtech Research, Inc.*, 576 F. Supp. 294 (D.D.C. 1983).
[75]15 U.S.C. § 45 (m).
[76]464 F. Supp. 1037 (D. Del. 1978); *aff'd*, 662 F. 2d 955 (3rd Cir. 1981).
[77]561 F. 2d 357 (D.C. Cir. 1977).
[78](D.C. Cir. 1977).
[79]*Id.* at 364.
[80]*Id.*
[81]352 F. 2d 207 (2d Cir. 1976).
[82]638 F. 2d 443 (2d Cir. 1980).
[83]*Id.* at 452.
[84]16 C.F.R. § 260 (1992).
[85]FTC Guidelines § b—ACH 1993 Cumulative Supplement, at 96.

CHAPTER 5

[1]15 U.S.C. § 77z.
[2]*Id.* at § 78gg.
[3]*Id.* at § 78c (a)(18).
[4]THE SECURITIES AND EXCHANGE COMMISSION, THE WORK OF THE SECURITIES AND EXCHANGE COMMISSION (1974) at 1.
[5]*Ernst and Ernst v. Hochfelder*, 425 U.S. 185 (1976).
[6]*Id.*
[7]15 U.S.C. § 77 (a)(8), at § 78 (c).
[8]17 C.F.R. § 230.134.
[9]*S.E.C. v. Arvida Corporation*, 169 F. Supp. 211 (1958).
[10]38 S.E.C. 843 (1959).
[11]*Id.* at 851.
[12]*Id.* at 853.
[13]*S.E.C. v. Arvida* at 215.
[14]17 C.F.R. Ch. 11 (4-1-94 Edition) § 240.10b–1.
[15]15 U.S.C. §§ 78 (m), 78 (n).
[16]693 F. Supp. 1266 (D. Mass. 1988).
[17]779 F. 2d 793 (2d Cir. 1985).
[18]*Id.* at 794.
[19]*Id.* at 797.
[20]625 F. Supp. 221 (E.D.N.Y. 1985).
[21]*Id.* at 226.
[22]*LILCO v. Barbash*, 779 F. 2d 793 (2d Cir. 1985).
[23]*Id.* at 796.
[24]*Id.*
[25]*Id.*, citing Rule 14a–6 (g), 17 C.F.R. § 240.14a–6 (g).
[26]*Id.*, citing *Medical Comm. for Human Rights v. S.E.C.*, 432 F. 2d 659 (D.C. Cir. 1970).

[27]401 F. 2d 833 (1968).

[28]*Id.* at 845.

[29]17 C.F.R. Ch. 11 (4-1-94 Edition) § 240.10b–5.

[30]401 F. 2d 833, 856 (1968).

[31]*Id.* at 852.

[32]*Id.* at 848.

[33]17 C.F.R. Ch. 11 (4-1-94 Edition) § 240.10b–5.

[34]484 U.S. 19 (1987).

[35]For further discussion, *see* I. B. BROMBERG, *Disclosure Programs for Publicly Held Companies—A Practical Guide*, DUKE LAW REVIEW (1970), 1139.

[36]21 U.S.C. § 352.

[37]*Id.* at § 353 (b)(1)(g).

[38]*Id.* at § 353 (b)(1)(c).

[39]*Id.* at § 321 (m).

[40]310 F. 2d 67 (1962).

[41]263 F. Supp. 212 (1967).

[42]410 F. 2d 157 (1969).

[43]269 F. Supp. 162 (1967).

[44]425 U.S. 748 (1976).

[45]*Id.* at 771.

[46]415 P. 2d 21 (1966).

[47]352 F. 2d 286 (1965).

[48]21 C.F.R. § 202.1 (e).

[49]*Id.* at § 202.1 (e)(3)(iii).

[50]*Id.* at § 202.1 (3)(i).

[51]*Id.*

[52]*Id.* at § 202.1 (3)(iii)(a).

[53]*Id.* at § 201.6 (i).

[54]21 C.F.R. § 202.1 (6)(xiv).

[55]*Id.* at Ch. 1 (4-1-94 Edition) § 202.1 (6)(xv).

[56]*Id.* at (7)(v).

[57]*Id.* at (6)(xiii).

[58]*Id.* at (6)(xvii).

[59]*Id.* at (6)(xix).

[60]21 U.S.C. § 352 (n).

[61]*Id.* at (7)(viii).

[62]21 U.S.C. § 352 (n).

[63]*Id.*

[64]923 F. 2d 995, 18 MEDIA LAW REPORTER 1666 (1991); *cert. denied*, 112 S. Ct. 81 (1991).

[65]42 U.S.C. 3603(b).

[66]923 F. 2d 995 (1991).

[67]Pub. L. No. 88-352, § 70 et. seq., 78 Stat. 241, Title 42 U.S.C. § 2000e et. seq.

[68]464 F. 2d 1006 (5th Cir. 1972).

[69]413 U.S. 376 (1973).

[70]Pub. L. 90-202, 80 Stat. 602 (29 U.S.C. § 621), as amended in Pub. L. 95-256 (A.D. in Employment Amendments of 1978), 92 Stat. 189.

[71]Americans with Disabilities Act of 1990.

[72]*Id.*

[73]*Id.*

[74]Pub. L. 96-240, 90 Stat. 257 (1976); codified at Table 15 U.S.C. §§ 1667–1667e (1982).

[75]Pub. L. 93-495, Title V, 88 Stat. 1521 (1974); codified at 15 U.S.C. §§ 1691–1691f (1982).

[76]15 U.S.C. § 1811 (1982).

[77]453 U.S. 490 (1981).

[78]943 F. 2d 644 (1991).

[79]*Id.* at 644 Citing Civil Rights Act of 1968, Title 42 U.S.C. § 3604(c) (1968).

[80]15 U.S.C. §§ 1601–1614 and 1661–1665a (April 1990).

[81]U.S. CONSTITUTION, Amendment 21.

[82]447 U.S. 557 (1980).

[83] _ U.S. _ (1995).

[84] _ F. Supp. _ (1994), 1994 W.L. 136298 (D. Md. 1994).

[85]*Id.*

[86] _ F. Supp. _ (D. Md. 1994).

[87]*See* G. E. ROSDEN and P. E. ROSDEN, THE LAW OF ADVERTISING (1991).

[88]*Id.* at vol. 2, § 13–14.

[89]405 U.S. 233 (1972).

[90]Rosden at vol. 2, § 13–29.

[91]*Id.* at vol. 3, § 26–47.

[92]*Id.*

[93]*Id.* at vol. 4, § 57–29.

[94]Uniform Securities Act §§ 101–102.

[95]Rosden at vol. 4, § 57–30.

[96]DISCUS 425 13th St., N.W., Washington, D.C. 20004.

CHAPTER 6

[1]*Another year of growth*, 18 PRESSTIME 8 (May 1996).

[2]*Magazines' ad revenue up in '94; Allure, Details among big winners*, Lexington (Ky.) Herald-Leader (Newsday), Jan. 24, 1995, at Today-4, col. 1.

[3]*Advertisers pay big bucks for Super Bowl*, Knight-Ridder News Service, Lexington (Ky.) Herald-Leader, Jan. 26, 1995, at You-11, col. 1.

[4]McCann Erickson Worldwide Insider's Report, December 1994.

[5]Federal Trade Commission File No. 912 3336 (11/7/96).

[6]Federal Trade Commission Press Advisory No. C-3582 (6/7/95).

[7]*See Get the scoop: Haagen-Dazs not low fat*, Lexington (Ky.) Herald-Leader (The Washington Post), Nov. 22, 1994, at A-5, col. 3.

[8]*Id.*

[9]*See Followup: Bogus Health Drink, Latecomer Air-conditioner*, 60 CONSUMER REP. 447 (1995).

[10]380 U.S. 374, 85 S.Ct. 1035, 13 L.Ed.2d 904 (1965).

[11]*Id.*

[12]*Id.*

[13]22 Med.L.Rptr. 1913 (5th Cir. 1994).

[14]*Barry v. Arrow Pontiac, Inc.*, 100 N.J. 57, 494 A.2d 804 (1985).

[15]*Joe Conte Toyota Inc. v. Louisiana Motor Vehicle Commission*, citing Brief for Appellee at 11.

[16]*Id.*

[17]455 U.S. 191, 102 S.Ct. 929, 71 L.Ed.2d 64 (1982).

[18]496 U.S. 91, 110 S.Ct. 2281 (1990).

[19]22 Med.L.Rptr. 2513 (9th Cir. 1994).

[20]Calif. Bus. and Prof. Code § 17508.5(e).

[21]15 U.S.C. § 55(a)(1) (1996).

[22]570 F.2d 157, 3 Med.L.Rptr. 2196 (7th Cir. 1977).

[23]*Id., cert. denied*, 439 U.S. 821.

[24]577 F.2d 653, 4 Med.L.Rptr. 1459 (9th Cir. 1978).

[25]15 U.S.C. § 45.

[26]*United States v. Reader's Digest*, 464 F.Supp. 1037, 4 Med.L.Rptr. 2258 (D. Del. 1978).

[27]*United States v. Reader's Digest*, 662 F.2d 955, 7 Med.L.Rptr. 1903 (3rd Cir. 1981); *cert. denied*, 455 U.S. 908 (1982).

[28]726 F.2d 993 (4th Cir.); *cert. denied*, 469 U.S. 820 (1984).

[29]562 F.2d 749, 2 Med.L.Rptr. 2303 (D.C. Cir. 1977); *cert denied*, 435 U.S. 950 (1978).

[30]*Id.*

[31]425 U.S. 748, 96 S.Ct. 1817, 48 L.Ed.2d 346, 1 Med.L.Rptr. 1930 (1976).

[32]433 U.S. 350, 97 S.Ct. 2691, 53 L.Ed.2d 810, 2 Med.L.Rptr. 2097 (1977).

[33]442 F.2d 686 (2nd Cir. 1950).

[34]*Id.*

[35]Pub. L. No. 100-667 (1988).

[36]Lanham Act § 43(a), 15 U.S.C. 1125(a).

[37]Pub. L. No. 102-542 (1992).

[38]*See Serbin v. Ziebart International Corp.*, 11 F.3d 1163 (3rd Cir. 1993).

[39]*Standards of Practice of the American Association of Advertising Agencies* (as revised Sept. 18, 1990).

[40]436 F.Supp. 785, 3 Med.L.Rptr. 1097 (S.D. N.Y.); *aff'd*, 577 F.2d 160 (2nd Cir. 1978).

[41]*Id.*

[42]*Id.*

[43]*American Home Products Corp. v. Johnson & Johnson*, 654 F. Supp. 568 (S.D. N.Y. 1987).

[44]*Id.*

[45]This was accomplished through the Federal Trade Commission Improvements Act of 1980, Pub. L. No. 96-252, 94 Stat. 374 (codified as amended at 15 U.S.C. § 45 *et. seq.*). *See* P. Cameron Devore & Robert Sack, *Advertising and Commercial Speech*, in JAMES GOODALE, chairman, COMMUNICATIONS LAW 1994 683–684 (New York: Practising Law Institute, 1994) for a discussion of the FTC's response to Congress.

[46]H.R. 2243.

[47]*See Hooked on Tobacco: The Teen Epidemic*, 60 CONSUMER REP. 142 (1995).

[48]*Can First Amendment Save Camel's 'Old Joe'?* Lexington (Ky.) Herald-Leader (Cox News Service), Aug. 14, 1993, at Today-3, col. 3.

[49]*See Hooked on Tobacco, supra* note 48.

[50]*Cigarette Ads Found to Affect Teen-agers Most*, Lexington (Ky.) Herald-Leader (Associated Press), Aug. 18, 1994, at A3, col. 4.

[51]*See Cigarette Maker To Pull Ads from Sports Arenas*, Lexington (Ky.) Herald-Leader (Associated Press), June 7, 1995, at A9, col. 5.

[52]*See Hooked on Tobacco, supra* note 48 at 144.

[53]*R.J. Reynolds Co. v. Mangini; cert. denied*, _ U.S. _, 115 S.Ct. 577, 130 L.Ed.2d 493 (1994).

[54]*Billboard Firm Decides To Reject Cigarette Ads*, Lexington (Ky.) Herald-Leader (Wire Services), May 3, 1996, at B8, col. 1.

[55]*Novelli Brings Campaign for Tobacco-Free Kids to ASC*, The Annenberg School for Communication Newslink, Spring 1996, at 1.

[56]84 F.3d 734 (1996).

[57]*See Tobacco Suit: Round II*, 82 A.B.A.J. 18 (July 1996).

[58]*See* Federal Alcohol Administration Act, 49 Stat. 977, 27 U.S.C. 201 § 5(e)(2).

[59]*Adolph Coors Co. v. Brady*, 944 F.2d 1543 (1991).

[60]*Adolph Coors Co. v. Bentsen*, 2 F.3d 355 (1993).

[61]*Rubin v. Coors Brewing Co.*, 514 U.S. _, 115 S.Ct. 1585, 131 L.Ed.2d 532 (1995).

[62]*Id.*

[63]*Id.*

[64]*44 Liquor Mart v. Racine*, 39 F.3d 5, 22 Med.L.Rptr. 2409 (1st Cir. 1994); *rev'g*, 829 F.Supp. 543, 553 (D.R.I. 1993); *44 Liquor Mart v. Rhode Island*, _ U.S. _, 116 S.Ct. 1495, 134 L.Ed.2d 64, 24 Med.L.Rptr. 1673 (1996).

[65]R.I. Gen. L. § 3-8-7 and 2-8-8.1. At dispute also was Regulation 32 of the Rhode Island Liquor Control Administration.

[66]*44 Liquormart Inc. v. Rhode Island*, 829 F.Supp. 543, 553 (D.R.I. 1993).

[67]*44 Liquor Mart v. Rhode Island*, 39 F.3d 5, 22 Med.L.Rptr. 2409 (1st Cir. 1994).

[68]*Id.*

[69]*Id.*

[70]*Id.*

[71]*Id.*

[72]*Id.*

[73]*Florida Bar Association v. Went for It*, 513 U.S. __, 115 S.Ct. 2371, 132 L.Ed.2d 541, 23 Med.L.Rptr. 1801 (1995).

[74]*See Liquor Industry Ends Ban on TV, Radio Ads*, Lexington (Ky.) Herald-Leader (Wire Services), Nov. 8, 1996, at A1, col. 4; *Distillers Indulge Anew in TV Ads*, USA Today, Nov. 8, 1996, at B1, col. 2.

[75]*Memo Shows How Seagram Pondered TV Ads*, Lexington (Ky.) Herald-Leader (The Wall Street Journal), June 23, 1996, at Business Sundy 5, col. 1.

[76]*See FCC: Keep Liquor Ads on Ban Wagon*, Lexington (Ky.) Herald-Leader (Wire Services), Nov. 9, 1996, at A11, col. 2.

[77]*Continental Breaks Rank: Will Run Hard-Liquor Ads*, Multichannel News Digest, Nov. 11, 1996, Vol. 3, No. 46.

[78]*Id.*

[79]*Liquor Industry Ends Ban on TV, Radio Ads.*

[80]*Continental Breaks Rank.*

[81]*Liquor Industry Ends Ban on TV, Radio Ads.*

[82]116 S.Ct. 1495 (1996).

[83]*Anheuser-Busch, Inc. v. Schmoke*, CA 4, Nos. 94-1431 and 94-1432 (1996). *See also, Federal Appeals Court Distinguishes U.S. Supreme Court Decision, Upholds Baltimore Ban Banning Billboard Advertising of Alcoholic Beverages*, Freedom Forum First Amendment Center First Amendment Legal Watch, Nov. 22, 1996.

[84]*See* KENNETH A. PLEVAN & MIRIAM L. SIROKY, ADVERTISING COMPLIANCE HANDBOOK 89–96 (1988).

[85]Pub. L. No. 101-535, 104 Stat. 2353 (1990). *See* Vida Foubuster, *Regulation of Health Claims in Advertising by the Federal Trade Commission: Has the Enactment of the Nutrition and Labeling and Education Act of 1990 Significantly Changed the Commission's Policies?* Paper presented to the Association for Education in Journalism and Mass Communication Southeast Colloquium, Gainesville, Fla., March 1995, for a discussion of how the Act has affected FTC policies.

[86]*Standard Oil v. FTC.*

[87]*See Have You Noticed Seinfeld's Blender?* Lexington (Ky.) Herald-Leader (Knight-Ridder News Service), March 23, 1995, YOU-11, at col. 1.

CHAPTER 7

[1]*Pittsburgh Press Company v. The Pittsburgh Commission on Human Relations*, 413 U.S. 376, 93 S.Ct. 2553, 37 L.Ed.2d 669, 1 Med.L.Rptr. 1908 (1973).

[2]*Jeffrey Cole Bigelow v. Virginia*, 421 U.S. 809, 95 S.Ct. 2222, 44 L.Ed.2d 600, 1 Med.L.Rptr. 1919 (1975).

[3]*City of Cincinnati v. Discovery Network, Inc.*, 507 U.S. 410, 113 S.Ct. 1505, 123 L.Ed.2d 99, 21 Med.L.Rptr. 1161 (1993).

[4]*New York Times v. Sullivan*, 376 U.S. 254, 84 S.Ct. 710, 11 L.Ed.2d 686, 1 Med.L.Rptr. 1527 (1964).

[5]*Pittsburgh Press Company.*

[6]*Id.*, citing § 8(e) of the ordinance.

[7]*Id.*

[8]*Id.*

[9]*Id.*

[10]*Id.*

[11]*Id.* (Burger dissent).

[12]*Id.* (Stewart dissent).

[13]*Roe v. Wade*, 410 U.S. 113, 93 S.Ct. 705, 35 L.Ed.2d 147 (1973).

[14]*Bigelow v. Virginia.*

[15]Va. Code Ann. § 18.1–63 (1960) (later amended after Bigelow was charged).

[16]*Bigelow v. Virginia.*

[17]*Id.*

[18]*Id.*

[19]*Pittsburgh Press Company.*

[20]492 U.S. 469, 109 S.Ct. 3028, 106 L.Ed.2d 388 (1989).

[21]*City of Cincinnati v. Discovery Network, Inc.*

[22]*Id.* (Rehnquist dissent).

[23]*Central Hudson Gas & Electric Corp. v. Public Service Commission of New York,* 447 U.S. 557, 100 S.Ct. 2343, 65 L.Ed.2d 341, 6 Med.L.Rptr. 1497 (1980).

[24]*Id.*

[25]*Central Hudson Gas & Electric* (Stevens concurrence).

[26]*Consolidated Edison Company of New York v. Public Service Commission of New York,* 447 U.S. 530, 100 S.Ct. 2326, 65 L.Ed.2d 319, 6 Med.L.Rptr. 1518 (1980).

[27]*Id.*

[28]*Id.*

[29]*Red Lion Broadcasting v. Federal Communications Commission,* 395 U.S. 367, 89 S.Ct. 1794, 23 L.Ed.2d 371, 1 Med.L.Rptr. 2053 (1969).

[30]*John R. Bates and Van O'Steen v. State Bar of Arizona,* 433 U.S. 350, 97 S.Ct. 2691, 53 L.Ed.2d 810, 2 Med.L.Rptr. 2097 (1977).

[31]*Linmark Associates Inc. and William Mellman v. Township of Willingboro,* 431 U.S. 85, 97 S.Ct. 1614, 52 L.Ed.2d 155 (1977).

[32]*Gerald Daly and Hugh Carey v. Population Services International,* 431 U.S. 678, 97 S.Ct. 2010, 52 L.Ed.2d 675, 2 Med 1935 (1977).

[33]*Linmark Associates v. Willingboro.*

[34]*Id.*

[35]*Griswold v. Connecticut,* 381 U.S. 497, 85 S.Ct. 1678, 14 L.Ed.2d 510 (1965).

[36]*First National Bank of Boston v. Francis X. Bellotti,* 435 U.S. 765, 98 S.Ct. 1407, 55 L.Ed.2d 707, 3 Med.L.Rptr. 2105 (1978).

[37]*Id.* (majority opinion).

[38]*Id.*

[39]*Id.*

[40]*Id.*

[41]*Id.* (Burger concurrence).

[42]*William F. Bolger v. Youngs Drug Products Corp.,* 463 U.S. 60, 103 S.Ct. 2875, 77 L.Ed.2d 469 (1983).

[43]39 U.S.C. § 3001(e)(2).

[44]*Bolger v. Youngs Drug Products Corp.*

[45]*Id.*

[46]*Id.*

[47]*Id.* (Stevens concurrence).

[48]*Posadas de Puerto Rico Associates v. Tourism Company of Puerto Rico,* 478 U.S. 328, 106 S.Ct. 2968, 92 L.Ed.2d 266, 13 Med.L.Rptr. 1033 (1986).

[49]*Florida Bar v. Went for It, Inc.,* 513 U.S. __, 115 S.Ct. 2371, 132 L.Ed.2d 541, 23 Med.L.Rptr. 1801 (1995).

[50]The Florida Bar: Petition to Amend the Rules Regulating the Bar-Advertising Issues, 571 So.2d 451 (Fla. 1990).

[51]Interestingly, the Court mentions that the attorney in the original suit was disbarred before the case reached the U.S. Supreme Court for reasons unrelated to the case. Another lawyer was then substituted for the appeal.

[52]Florida Bar Rules of Professional Conduct 4–7.4(b) and 4–7.8(a).

[53]*McHenry v. Florida Bar,* 808 F.Supp. 1543 (M.D. Fla. 1992).

[54]*McHenry v. Florida Bar,* 21 F.3d 1038 (11th Cir. 1994); *cert. denied,* 512 U.S. __ (1994). We characterize the appellate court as "reluctantly" affirming because the U.S. Supreme Court said in its decision,

"The panel [11th Circuit] noted, in its conclusion, that it was 'disturbed that Bates and its progeny require the decision' that it reached."

[55]*Florida Bar v. Went for It, Inc.*

[56]*Id.*

[57]Majority opinion in Florida Bar, quoting from *Virginia State Board of Pharmacy.*

[58]*Ohralik v. Ohio State Bar Association*, 436 U.S. 447, 98 S.Ct. 1912, 56 L.Ed.2d 444 (1978).

[59]*In re Primus*, 436 U.S. 412, 98 S.Ct. 1893, 56 L.Ed.2d 417 (1978).

[60]*Ohralik v. Ohio State Bar Association.*

[61]*Florida Bar v. Went for It, Inc.*

[62]*Id.* (Rehnquist dissent).

[63]Under U.S. Supreme Court tradition, if the Chief Justice is in the majority when the final vote is taken during the Court's deliberations, he or she has the option of writing the majority opinion or designating the justice who will write it. If the Chief Justice is in the minority, the most senior justice in the majority writes the opinion or selects the justice to write it.

[64]*In re R.M.J.*, 455 U.S. 191, 102 S.Ct. 929, 71 L.Ed.2d 64, 7 Med.L.Rptr. 2545 (1982).

[65]*Zauderer v. Office of Disciplinary Counsel*, 471 U.S. 626, 105 S.Ct. 2265, 85 L.Ed.2d 652 (1985).

[66]*Shapero v. Kentucky Bar Association*, 486 U.S. 466, 108 S.Ct. 1916, 100 L.Ed.2d 475 (1988).

[67]*Zauderer v. Office of Disciplinary Counsel.*

[68]*Shapero v. Kentucky Bar Association.*

[69]*Id.*

[70]*Id.* (Plurality by Brennan).

[71]*Edenfield v. Fane*, 507 U.S. 761, 113 S.Ct. 1792, 123 L.Ed.2d 543, 21 Med.L.Rptr. 1312 (1993).

[72]*Id.* (Majority, quoting Edenfield majority).

[73]Originally, the *Central Hudson* test was characterized as a four-prong test, just as we have presented it in our discussions in this book. However, the Court in *Florida Bar* calls *Central Hudson* a three-prong test because it uses what we call the first prong ("Does it concern lawful activities and is not misleading?") as a screen and then begins the actual test with the question of whether there is a substantial government interest.

[74]Florida Bar (majority opinion), quoting *Edenfield.*

[75]*Id.* (quoting appellate court).

[76]*Id.*

[77]*Id.*

[78]*Ibanez v. Florida Department of Business and Professional Regulation, Board of Accountancy*, 512 U.S. _, 114 S.Ct. 2084, 129 L.Ed.2d 118 (1994).

[79]*Peel v. Attorney Registration and Disciplinary Commission of Illinois*, 496 U.S. 91, 110 S.Ct. 2281, 110 L.Ed.2d 83 (1990).

[80]*Id.* (O'Connor dissent).

[81]*Ibanez* (majority, citing *Edenfield*).

[82]*See* J. Podgers, *Image Problem*, 80 A.B.A.J. 66 (February 1994).

[83]C. Laughlin, *Ads on Trial*, 6 LINK 18 (May 1994).

[84]Florida Bar Association (Kennedy dissent).

[85]*Id.* (Kennedy dissent, citing Edenfield).

[86]*Id.* (Kennedy dissent).

[87]*Id.* (Kennedy dissent).

[88]*Id.*

[89]*In re Anis*, 126 N.J. 448, 599 A.2d 1265 (1992).

[90]*McHenry v. Florida Bar*, 66 F.3d 270 (11th Cir. 1995).

[91]*Friedman v. Rogers*, 440 U.S. 1, 99 S.Ct. 887, 59 L.Ed.2d 100, 4 Med.L.Rptr. 2213 (1979).

[92]*Id.*

[93]See *American Medical Association v. Federal Trade Commission*, 638 F.2d 443 (2d Cir. 1980); *aff'd*, 455 U.S. 676, 102 S.Ct. 1744, 71 L.Ed.2d 546 (1982).

[94]*Maceluch v. Wysong*, 680 F.2d 1062 (5th Cir. 1982).

[95]*Parker v. Kentucky Board of Dentistry*, 818 F.2d 504 (6th Cir. 1987).

CHAPTER 8

[1]AMERICAN LAW INSTITUTE, *Restatement of Torts*, 2d, 402A (1965).

[2]EDWARD J. KIONKA, *Torts: Injuries to Persons and Property* (1988), at 258.

[3]*McLaurin v. Hamer*, 164 S.E. 2 (1932), quoted in Walter Steigleman, *The Newspaperman and the Law* (William C. Brown, 1950), 355.

[4]*Nebraska Seed Co. v. Harsh*, 152 N.W. 310 (1938).

[5]*Editor & Publisher*, November 12, 1949; quoted by Steigleman, *op. cit.*, 356.

[6]*Id.*

[7]*California Business and Professional Code*, Para 17502, quoted in John D. Zelezny, *Communications Law* (Wadsworth, 1993), 407.

[8]*Eimann v. Soldier of Fortune Magazine, Inc.*, 880 F.2d 839 (5th Cir. 1989).

[9]*Braun v. Soldier of Fortune Magazine, Inc.*, 749 F. Supp. 1083 (M.D. Ala. 1990).

[10]Zelezny, *op. cit.*, 97.

[11]*Dunagin v. City of Oxford*, 718 F.2d 738 (1983).

[12]MICHAEL J. HANNAN III, *The Effect of Cipollone: Has the Tobacco Industry Lost Its Impenetrable Shield?*, 23 GEORGIA LAW REVIEW 763 (1989).

[13]*Id.*

[14]*Cipollone v. Liggett Group, Inc.*, 789 F.2d 181 (3d Cir. 1986); *cert. denied*, 479 U.S. 1043 (1987); *on remand*, 649 F. Supp. 664 (D.N.J. 1986) and 683 F. Supp. 1487 (D.N.J. 1988); *aff'd in part, rev'd in part*, 893 F.2d 541 (3d Cir. 1990); *cert. granted*, 111 S. Ct. 1386 (1991).

[15]Very helpful on this point is NORMAL L. GREENE, *Away from Ideology: A Review of Products Liability Defenses in the Era of Tort Reform*, 13 PACE LAW REVIEW 43 (1993).

[16]*Id.*

[17]*Thomas v. Winchester*, 6 New York 397 (1852).

[18]*MacPherson v. Buick Motor Co.*, 217 N.Y. 382, 111 N.E. 1050 (1916).

[19]*Restatement, op. cit.*, 402A.

[20]*Id.* at 402B.

[21]Quoted in MICHAEL GREENFIELD, CONSUMER TRANSACTIONS (2d. ed. 1990), at 169.

[22]Especially helpful here were Kionka, *op. cit.*, 258 ff, and BLACK'S LAW DICTIONARY (6th ed. 1990).

[23]*Uniform Commercial Code*, Section 2-313 (2).

[24]FEDERAL TRADE COMMISSION, *A Guide to the Federal Trade Commission* (1984); quoted in DWIGHT L. TEETER, JR., AND DON R. LE DUC, LAW OF MASS COMMUNICATIONS (7th ed. 1992), at 436.

[25]*Daly v. General Motors Corporation*, 20 Cal. 3d 725 (1978).

[26]*Rahmig v. Mosely Machinery Co.*, 226 Neb. 423, 412 N.W. 2d (1987).

[27]*Seagrams v. McGuire*, 34 Tex. Sup. Ct. J564 (1991).

[28]Quoted in JANET R. PRITCHETT, *Texas Supreme Court Refuses to Impose a Duty to Warn of Alcoholism Upon Beverage Alcohol Manufacturers*, 22 TEXAS TECH LAW REVIEW 937 (1991).

[29]Kionka, *op. cit.*, 258 ff.

[30]Greenfield, *op. cit.*, 166.

[31]BRUCE P. KELLER AND TIFFANY D. TRUNKO, *Consumer Use of RICO to Challenge False Advertising Claims*, AMERICAN LAW INSTITUTE (1991).

[32]*Bauder v. Ralston Purina Co.*, 1989 WL 143283 (E.D.Pa.); interview with Elkan Katz, attorney for Bauder, December 30, 1994.

[33]Quoted in GREENFIELD, CONSUMER TRANSACTIONS, *op. cit.*, 203.

[34]*Id.*

[35]*Id.* at 5.

[36]Quoted in *Haines v. Liggett Group, Inc.*, 814 F. Supp. 414 (424 F. Supp. D.N.J. 1993); reprinted in RICHARD A. DAYNARD, *The Third Wave of Tobacco Products Liability Cases*, TRIAL, (November 1994) at 34.

[37]DAYNARD, *op. cit.*

CHAPTER 9

[1]*Near v. Minnesota*, 283 U.S. 697.

[2]*See* GREG LISBY, *et al.*, *A Public Relations Perspective for Mass Communications Law Courses*, 48 JOURNALISM EDUCATOR (Summer 1993) at 67.

[3]ALEX S. JONES, *Iowa Experiment Offers Arbitration for Settling Libel Disputes Out of Court*, New York *Times*, May 4, 1987.

[4]*Dun & Bradstreet v. Greenmoss*, 472 U.S. 749.

[5]*Nieman-Marcus v. Lait*, 13 F.R.D. 311.

[6]*New York Times v. Sullivan*, 376 U.S. 254.

[7]*Id.*

[8]*Id.*

[9]*Gertz v. Welch*, 94 S.Ct. 2997.

[10]*Martin Marietta Corp. v. Evening Star Newspaper Co.*, 417 F. Supp., 956; also, KENNETH A. PLEVAN AND MIRIAM L. SIROKY, *Advertising Compliance Handbook* (2d ed. 1991) at 513–546.

[11]*Golden Bear Distributing System v. Chase Revel, Inc.*, 708 F. 2d 952.

[12]*Steaks Unlimited v. Deaner*, 623 F.2d 274; PLEVAN AND SIROKY, *Advertising Compliance Handbook*, at 519.

[13]*Coronado Credit Union v. KOAT Television, Inc.*, 99 N.M. 233; PLEVAN AND SIROKY, *Advertising Compliance Handbook*, at 518.

[14]WILLIAM E. FRANCOIS, *Mass Media Law and Regulation* (4th ed. 1986) at 97.

[15]AMERICAN LAW INSTITUTE, *Restatement of the Law of Torts* (2d ed. 1975), Sec. 649.

[16]*Id.*, Sec. 650A.

[17]PLEVAN AND SIROKY, *Advertising Compliance Handbook*, at 533.

[18]*Cherry v. Des Moines Leader*, 86 N.W. 323.

[19]*Id.*

[20]Dicta in *Gertz v. Welch*, 94 S. Ct. 2997 (1974).

[21]*See* especially *Milkovich v. Lorain Journal*, 110 S.Ct. 2705.

[22]*See* especially *Miami Herald v. Tornillo*, 418 U.S. 241.

[23]*Edwards v. National Audubon Society*, 556 F.2d 113.

[24]*Crane v. Arizona Republic*, 729 F. Supp 698; *Ward v. News Group International, Ltd.*, 733 F. Supp. 83, *inter alia*.

[25]*Restatement*, Sec. 623A.

[26]*Id.*

[27]*Id.*; PLEVAN AND SIROKY, *Advertising Compliance Handbook*, at 513–546.

[28]*Restatement*, Sec. 626.

[29]RICHARD J. CONVISER, *BAR/BRI Bar Review: Constitutional Law* (1993) at 17.

CHAPTER 10

[1]As later scholarship has noted, however, Warren's daughter was only 7 years old at the time. In "Demystifying a Landmark Citation," 13 *Suffolk U.L. Rev.* 875, Professor Jerome Barron suggests that Warren was in fact angry at press criticism of his father-in-law, Thomas Bayard, Sr., who had been a U.S. Senator and a member of President Grover Cleveland's cabinet.

[2]SAMUEL WARREN AND LOUIS BRANDEIS, *The Right to Privacy*, 4 HARVARD LAW REVIEW 193.

[3]WILLIAM L. PROSSER, *Privacy*, 48 CALIFORNIA LAW REVIEW (1960) at 383. This article, an invaluable review of privacy law developments up to that time, has been drawn on for much of the background material in this passage.

[4]*Roberson v. Rochester Folding Box Co.* 171 N.Y. 538, 64 N.E. 442.

[5]*Pavesich v. New England Life Ins. Co.*, 122 Ga. 190. 50 S.E. 68.

[6]*State v. Hinkle*, 229 P. 317.

[7]*Restatement of Torts*, 2d, Sec. 652D.

[8]*Jones v. Herald Post Co.*, 18 S.W. 2d 972.

[9]*Restatement*, Sec. 652D.

[10]*Mendosa v. Time Inc.*, 678 F. Supp. 967, as mentioned in KENNETH A. PLEVAN AND MIRIAM L. SIROKY, *Advertising Compliance Handbook* (2d. ed. 1991) at 553.

[11]RALPH L. HOLSINGER, *Media Law* (2d ed. 1991) at 217.

[12]*Namath v. Sports Illustrated*, 1 *Med. L. Rptr.* 1843.

[13]Quoted in an excellent discussion of privacy by GEORGE C. CHRISTIE AND JAMES E. MEEKS, *Cases and Materials on the Law of Torts* (1990) at 1088 ff.

[14]*Shields v. Gross*, 7 *Med. L. Rptr.* 2349. The case is well discussed also in HOLSINGER, MEDIA LAW, at 228.

[15]*McAndrews v. Roy*, 131 So. 2d 256. The case is admirably discussed as well in DON R. PEMBER, MASS MEDIA LAW (5th ed. 1989) at 212.

[16]AMERICAN SOCIETY OF MAGAZINE PHOTOGRAPHERS, *Stock Photography Handbook* (2d ed. 1990), at 123–139.

[17]*Id.* at 127.

[18]*Haelan Laboratories v. Topps Chewing Gum*, 202 F.2d 866; *cert. denied*, 346 U.S. 816. Throughout this passage, the author also drew heavily on CHRISTOPHER PESCE, *The Likeness Monster: Should the Right of Publicity Protect Against Imitation?*, 65 NEW YORK UNIVERSITY L. R. 782, and PLEVAN AND SIROKY, ADVERTISING COMPLIANCE HANDBOOK, at 547–595.

[19]*Allen v. National Video, Inc.*, 610 F. Supp. 612.

[20]PESCE, *The Likeness Monster*, at 782.

[21]*Haelan Laboratories v. Topps Chewing Gum*, 202 F.2d 866; *cert. denied*, 346 U.S. 816.

[22]There is some dispute on this point. WILLIAM L. PROSSER, HANDBOOK OF THE LAW OF TORTS (4th ed. 1971), found slim evidence to suggest the possibility of descendability (a 1945 Arizona case, *Reed v. Real Detective Pub. Co.*, 63 Ariz. 294), but as he noted, "there is no common law right of action for a publication concerning one who is already dead." This point is discussed in DWIGHT L. TEETER, JR., AND DON R. LE DUC, LAW OF MASS COMMUNICATIONS (7th ed. 1992) at 303.

[23]*Cher v. Forum International*, 692 F.2d 634.

[24]*Hirsch v. S. C. Johnson & Son*, 90 Wis. 2d 379.

[25]*Ali v. Playgirl*, 447 F. Supp. 723.

[26]*Onassis v. Christian Dior-New York, Inc.*, 472 N.Y.S. 2d 254.

[27]*Motschenbacher v. R. J. Reynolds Tobacco Co.*, 498 F.2d 821.

[28]*Carson v. Here's Johnny Portable Toilets*, 698 F.2d 831.

[29]*Groucho Marx Prods., Inc. v. Day & Night Co.*, 523 F. Supp. at 491; *Lugosi v. Universal Pictures*, 25 Cal. 3rd 813, as reported by PLEVAN AND SIROKY, ADVERTISING COMPLIANCE HANDBOOK, at 557.

[30]*Lahr v. Adell Chemical Co.*, 300 F.2d 256.

[31]*Midler v. Ford Motor Co.*, 849 F.2d 460.

[32]UPI dispatch of May 8, 1990, quoted by PESCE, *The Likeness Monster*, at 822.

[33]"Midler Case Stirs Debate on 'Alikes,'" *New York Times*, November 1, 1989.

[34]PESCE, *Likeness Monster*, at 818.

[35]RICHARD KURNIT, *Right of Publicity*, THE ENTERTAINMENT AND SPORTS LAWYER, 4, 3 (Winter/Spring 1986), at 15.

[36]*Zacchini v. Scripps-Howard Broadcasting Co.*, 433 U.S. 562.

[37]*Id.*

[38]TAMAR LEWIN, *Whose Life Is It, Anyway? It's Hard to Tell*, New York Times, November 21, 1982; HOLSINGER, MEDIA LAW, at 231.

CHAPTER 11

[1]*Sipple v. Chronicle Publishing Co.*, 154 Cal. App. 3rd 1040 (1984).

[2]*Melvin v. Reid*, 112 Cal. App. 285, 297 Pac. 91 (1931).

[3]JAMES WRIGHT, *Defamation, Privacy, and the Public's Right to Know: A National Problem and a New Approach*, 46 TEXAS LAW REVIEW 630 (1968).

[4]4 *Harvard Law Review* 193 (1890).

[5]*Restatement of Torts*, 2d, Sec. 652D.

[6]*Howard v. Des Moines Register and Tribune Co.*, 283 N.W. 2d 289 (1979).

[7]*Diaz v. Oakland Tribune, Inc.*, 139 Cal.App.3d 118, 188 Cal.Rptr. 762 (1983), 9 *Med. L. Rptr.* 1121. DWIGHT L. TEETER, JR., AND DON R. LE DUC, LAW OF MASS COMMUNICATIONS (7th ed. 1992); ch. 7 is especially helpful on this point.

[8]*Howard v. Des Moines Register and Tribune Co.*, 283 N.W. 2d 289 (1979).

[9]*Cape Publications, Inc. v. Bridges*, 423 So.2d 426 (1984).

[10]*Hawkins v. Multimedia*, 344 S.E. 2d 145 (1986).

[11]*Deaton v. Delta Democrat Publishing Company*, 326 So.2d 471 (1976).

[12]*Daily Times Democrat v. Graham*, 162 So. 2d 474 (1964).

[13]*Id.*

[14]*Schmitt v. Dallas Times Herald*, No. 5781-582 (New Mexico District Court, Santa Fe, 1982). Quoted in RALPH HOLSINGER, MEDIA LAW (2d. ed. 1991) at 216.

[15]*Barber v. Time, Inc.*, 159 S.W.2d 291 (1942).

[16]*Bilney v. Evening Star Newspaper Co.*, 43 Md.App. 560, 406 A.2d 652 (1979).

[17]*Virgil v. Time, Inc.*, 527 F.2d 1122 (1975).

[18]*Neff v. Time, Inc.*, 406 F. Supp. 858 (1976).

[19]*Briscoe v. Reader's Digest Association*, 483 P.2d 484 (1971).

[20]*Briscoe v. Reader's Digest Association*, 1 *Med.L. Rptr.* 1852 (1972); also Teeter and Le Duc, *op. cit.*, 281.

[21]*Briscoe v. Reader's Digest Association*, 483 P.2d 484 (1971).

[22]Reported in *Time*, October 18, 1948, 64. Also, WALTER A. STEIGLEMAN, THE NEWSPAPERMAN AND THE LAW (1950) at 227.

[23]*Sidis v. F-R Publishing Corp.*, 113 F.2d 806 (1940).

[24]Quoted in GEORGE C. CHRISTIE AND JAMES E. MEEKS, CASES AND MATERIALS ON THE LAW OF TORTS (2d ed. 1990) at 1116.

[25]DON R. PEMBER, MASS MEDIA LAW (6th ed. 1993) at 233.

[26]*Restatement of Torts*, 2d, Section 652D.

[27]WILLIAM L. PROSSER, *Privacy*, 48 CALIFORNIA LAW REVIEW (1960) at 397.

[28]*Cox Broadcasting Co. v. Cohn*, 420 U.S. 469 (1975).

[29]*The Florida Star v. B.J.F.*, 491 U.S. 524 (1989).

[30]*Globe Newspapers v. Superior Court for Norfolk County*, 457 U.S. 596 (1982).

[31]*Smith v. Daily Mail Publishing Co.*, 443 U.S. 97 (1979).

[32]Holsinger, *op. cit.*, 213, is especially helpful on this point.

[33]*Cox Broadcasting Co. v. Cohn*, 420 U.S. 469 (1975).

[34]*Trammell v. Citizen News Co.*, 285 Ky. 529 (1941); *Thompson v. Adelberg & Berman, Inc.*, 181 Ky. 487 (1918); *Brents v. Morgan*, 321 Ky. 765, 299 S.W. 867 (1927); *Bennett v. Norban*, 396 Pa. 94, 151 A.2d 892 (1959), cited by PROSSER, *op cit.*

CHAPTER 12

[1]*Leverton et al. v. Curtis Publishing Co.*, 192 F.2d 974 (1951).

[2]WILLIAM L. PROSSER, *Privacy*, 48 CALIFORNIA LAW REVIEW 383 (1960).

[3]*Id.*

[4]*Restatement of Torts*, 2d, Sec. 652A.

[5]*Crump v. Beckley Newspapers, Inc.*, 320 S.E. 2d 70 (1984).

[6]*Braun v. Flynt*, 726 F.2d 245 (1984).

[7]*Wood v. Hustler Magazine, Inc.*, 736 F.2d 1084 (1984).

[8]*Peay v. Curtis Publishing Co.*, 78 F. Supp. 305 (1948).

[9]*Arrington v. New York Times*, 5 *Media Law Reporter* 2581 (1980).

[10]*Cibenko v. Worth Publishers*, 510 F. Supp 761 (1981).

[11]DON R. PEMBER, MASS MEDIA LAW (5th ed. 1990) at 245 is particularly helpful on this point.

[12]*Cantrell v. Forest City Publishing Co.*, 95 S.Ct. 465 (1974).

[13]*Spahn v. Julian Messner*, 221 N.E. 2d 543 (1966).

[14]See especially *Hicks v. Casablanca Records*, 646 F. Supp. 426 (1978).

[15]*Pring v. Penthouse International, Ltd.*, 695 F.2d 438 (1982); the case is discussed more fully in RODNEY A. SMOLLA, SUING THE PRESS (1986) at 163 ff.

[16]SMOLLA, *op. cit.*, 54 ff; and RALPH L. HOLSINGER, MEDIA LAW (2d. ed. 1991) at 225 ff. are especially useful on this point.

[17]*Time, Inc., v. Hill*, 385 U.S. 374 (1967).

[18]*Id.*

[19]*Gertz v. Robert Welch, Inc.*, 418 U.S. 323 (1974).

[20]*Cantrell v. Forest City Publishing Co.*, 419 U.S. 245 (1974).

[21]*See* especially PEMBER, *op. cit.*, at 245 ff.

[22]Section 46, Comment C.

[23]*See* especially *Bear v. Reformed Mennonite Church*, 462 Pa. 330, 342 A.2d 105 (1975).

[24]*See* especially *Ford Motor Credit Co. v. Sheehan*, 373 So.2d 956 Fla. App. (1979).

[25]*Harris v. Jones*, 281 Md. 560, 380 A.2d 611 (1977).

[26]*Samms v. Eccles*, 11 Utah 2d 289, 358 P.2d 344 (1961).

[27]*Meiter v. Cavanaugh*, 40 Colo.App. 454 (1978).

[28]*Hood v. Naeter Brothers Publishing Co.*, 562 S.W. 2d 770 (1978).

[29]*Hustler Magazine v. Falwell*, 485 U.S. 46 (1988).

[30]Quoted by DIANE LEENHEER ZIMMERMAN, *False Light Invasion of Privacy: The Light that Failed*, 64 NEW YORK UNIVERSITY LAW REVIEW 364 (1989).

[31]*Id.* at 453.

CHAPTER 13

[1]U.S. CONST. art. I, § 8.

[2]U.S. CONST. art. VI.

[3]U.S. CONST. art. I, § 8.

[4]Pub. L. No. 100-418 (1989).

[5]Pub. L. No. 98-417 (1984) and Pub. L. No. 100-670 (1988) had granted such an extension for drugs, but the 1989 Act broadened the extension to include patents for other inventions and discoveries.

[6]*See* 35 U.S.C. § 101.

[7]*See* 35 U.S.C. § 161.

[8]*See* 35 U.S.C. § 171.

[9]All patent infringement suits must be brought in the U.S. District Court. Other federal courts and state courts have no jurisdiction. Appeals from the U.S. District Court are then heard exclusively by the U.S. Court of Appeals for the Federal Circuit. Upon a *writ of certiorari*, a discretionary writ, the U.S. Supreme Court can, if it so chooses, hear any appeals from the federal Circuit.

[10]*In re Alappat*, 33 F.3d 1526, 13 U.S.P.Q. 2d 1545 (Fed. Cir. 1994).

[11]35 U.S.C. § 103.

[12]*Polaroid v. Eastman Kodak*, 789 F.2d 1556, 229 U.S.P.Q. 561 (Fed. Cir. 1986); *cert. denied*, 479 U.S. 850.

[13]*See* N.C. Gen. Stat. § 66-152 (1) (1995).

[14]*See* 764 ILCS 1065/3 (a).

[15]*Pepsico, Inc. v. Redmond and the Quaker Oats Co.*, 54 F.3d 1262, 35 U.S.P.Q. 2d (BNA) 1010 (7th Cir. 1995).

[16]5 U.S.C. § 552 (1994).

[17]18 U.S.C. § 1905 (1994).

[18]*See Chrysler Corp. v. Brown*, 441 U.S. 281 (1979) for an interesting case involving this issue.

[19]*Kewanee Oil Co. v. Bicron Corp.*, 416 U.S. 470 (1974).

[20]*Dow Chemical v. United States*, 476 U.S. 227 (1986).

[21]*Ruckelshaus v. Monsato Co.*, 467 U.S. 986 (1984).

[22]*See Java Can Get You In Hot Water*, Lexington (Ky.) Herald-Leader, June 15, 1996, at A11, col. 1.

[23]U.S. DEPT. OF COMMERCE, PATENT & TRADEMARK OFFICE, BASIC FACTS ABOUT TRADEMARKS (November 1996).

[24]Pub. L. No. 100-667 (1988).

[25]*Qualitex Company v. Jacobson Products, Inc.* _ U.S. _, 115 S.Ct. 1300, 131 L.Ed.2d 248 (1995).

[26]*In re General Electric Co.*, 199 U.S.P.Q. 560 (T.T.A.B. 1978).

[27]*St. Petersburg (Fla.) Times*, August 29, 1994, at 2.

[28]*Wall Street Journal*, August 30, 1994, at B5.

[29]15 U.S.C. § 1051.

[30]U.S. DEPT. OF COMMERCE, PATENT AND TRADEMARK OFFICE, BASIC FACTS ABOUT TRADEMARKS (November 1996).

[31]AMERICAN BAR ASSOCIATION, WHAT IS A TRADEMARK? (1995).

[32]Goldstein, THE ASSOCIATED PRESS STYLEBOOK AND LIBEL MANUAL 217 (Ed.) (1996).

[33]*Mead Data Central, Inc. v. Toyota Motor Sales, U.S.A., Inc.*, 875 F.2d 1026, 10 U.S.P.Q.2d 1961 (2nd Cir. 1989). Also see Prather, *How Toyota Got 'Lexus' for Name of New Car*, Lexington (Ky.) Herald-Leader, at A1, col. 1.

[34]*Toyota Has New Logo—But Does Anyone Get It?*, Lexington (Ky.) Herald-Leader, at A1, col. 1.

[35]*G. Heileman Brewing Co., Inc. v. Anheuser-Busch, Inc.*, Nos. 88-1223, 88-1309, 88-1310 (April 26, 1989); *see LA Law*, A.B.A.J., Aug. 1989, at 92.

[36]*L.L. Bean, Inc. v. Drake Publishers, Inc.*, 811 F.2d 26, 13 Med.L.Rptr. 2009 (1st Cir. 1987).

[37]*San Francisco Arts and Athletics, Inc. v. United States Olympic Committee*, 483 U.S. 522, 107 S.Ct. 925 (1987).

CHAPTER 14

[1]KITCH & PERLMAN, LEGAL REGULATION OF THE COMPETITIVE PROCESS 622 (1979).

[2]17 U.S.C. § 102 (1996).

[3]*Id.*

[4]17 U.S.C. § 101 (1996).

[5]17 U.S.C. § 101 (1996).

[6]17 U.S.C. § 101 (1996).

[7]17 U.S.C. § 106 (1996).

[8]17 U.S.C. § 102 (a) (1996).

[9]17 U.S.C. § 101 (1996).

[10]*Id.*

[11]Huff, *Leno Says Stern Should Blame NBC, Not Him*, Lexington (Ky.) Herald-Leader, February 16, 1996, at Weekender8, col. 1.

[12]*Community for Creative Non-Violence v. Reid*, 490 U.S. 730, 109 S.Ct. 2166, 104 L.Ed.2d 811, 16 Med.L.Rptr. 1769 (1989).

[13]*Id.*

[14]*Id.*

[15]*Id.*

[16]*Id.*

[17]17 U.S.C. § 101 (1996).

[18]Since neither party sought review of the appellate court's remand order, the Supreme Court did not determine whether joint authorship was applicable in this case.

[19]K. Middleton, *Freelance Photographers and Publishers: The Need for a Contract to Establish Joint Authorship in Commissioned Works.* Paper presented to the Association for Education in

Journalism and Mass Communication Southeast Regional Colloquium, Orlando, Florida, April 1991, at 23.

[20]*Id.*

[21]17 U.S.C. § 102 (1994).

[22]THOMPSON, *Triple Taste*, Lexington (Ky.) Herald-Leader, May 30, 1996, at You-6, col. 1.

[23]*Hoehling v. Universal City Studios, Inc.*, 618 F.2d 972, 6 Med.L.Rptr. 1053 (2d Cir. 1980); *cert. denied*, 449 U.S. 841 (1980).

[24]*Id.*

[25]*Id.*

[26]*See* U.S. COPYRIGHT OFFICE, COPYRIGHT BASICS (Circular 1) (1996), at 4.

[27]*Miller v. Universal City Studios, Inc.*, 650 F.2d 1365, 7 Med.L.Rptr. 1735 (5th Cir. 1981).

[28]*Miller v. Universal City Studios, Inc.*, 460 F.Supp. 984 (S.D. Fla. 1978).

[29]*Id.*

[30]*Id.*

[31]*Feist Publications, Inc. v. Rural Telephone Service Co.*, 499 U.S. 340, 111 S.Ct. 1282 (1991).

[32]*Id.*

[33]*Id.*

[34]*International News Service v. Associated Press*, 248 U.S. 215, 39 S.Ct. 68, 63 L.Ed. 211 (1918).

[35]*Id.*

[36]Public Laws 87-668, 89-142, 90-141, 90-416, 91-147, 91-555, 92-170, 92-566, and 93-573.

[37]Berne Convention Implementation Act of 1988, Pub. L. 100-568, 102 Stat. 2853.

[38]17 U.S.C. §§ 405 and 406 (1996).

[39]17 U.S.C. § 405(b) (1996).

[40]17 U.S.C. § 401(a) (1996).

[41]17 U.S.C. § 402(a) (1996).

[42]See 37 C.F.R. § 201.20 for the complete regulations. They are also reprinted in Circular 96-Section 201.20 ("Methods of Affixation and Positions of the Copyright Notice on Various Types of Works") (1996) of the Copyright Office and summarized in Circular 3 ("Copyright Notice") (1996) at 4-5 of the Copyright Office.

[43]17 U.S.C. § 401(c) (1996).

[44]*Id.*

[45]17 U.S.C. § 402(c) (1996).

[46]*See* 37 C.F.R. § 201.20(d) and U.S. COPYRIGHT OFFICE, COPYRIGHT NOTICE (Circular 3) (1996), at 4.

[47]17 U.S.C. § 501(a) (1996).

[48]*Playboy Enterprises, Inc. v. Starware Publishing Corp.*, 900 F.Supp. 438 (S.D. Fla. 1995).

[49]*Chicago Catholics Lose Copyright Case* ("National Digest" section), Atlanta Journal (wire reports), April 20, 1984, at A1, col. 1.

[50]*Jagger Gets Satisfaction in Lawsuit Over Song*, Lexington (Ky.) Herald-Leader (Associated Press), April 27, 1988, at A2, col. 3.

[51]*Before You Wish Upon A Star, Better Check the Copyright*, ("People" section), Lexington (Ky.) Herald-Leader (wire services), May 1, 1989, at A12, col. 1.

[52]Blodgett, *West, Mead Data Central Settle*, A.B.A. J., Sept. 1, 1988, at 36.

[53]*Garrison Keillor Settles Suit with National Public Radio* ("People" section), Cincinnati Post, June 24, 1988, at A2, col. 3.

[54]MAATTA & BRENNAN, 10 HASTINGS COMMENT L.J. 1081 (1988).

[55]*Investor's Business Daily*, June 18, 1996, at A8.

[56]*Wall Street Journal*, June 3, 1994, at A5C.

[57]*See Crackdown on Pirated Videotapes Continues*, Lexington (Ky.) Herald-Leader (Associated Press), March 2, 1994, at Community19, col. 4.

[58]JOSEPH, *'Batman' Takes on Those Villainous Video Purloiners*, Lexington (Ky.) Herald-Leader (Orlando Sentinel), Aug. 18, 1989, at B10, col. 1.

[59]*Id.*

[60]See U.S. COPYRIGHT OFFICE, INTERNATIONAL COPYRIGHT RELATIONS (Circular 38a) (1996) for a complete list of countries having copyright agreements with the United States.

[61]See U.S. COPYRIGHT OFFICE, COPYRIGHT AMENDMENTS CONTAINED IN THE URUGUAY ROUND AGREEMENTS ACT (URAA) (Circular 38a) (1995).

[62]17 U.S.C. § 205 (1996).

[63]*Constructive notice* is a legal term implying or imputing that the public has been notified in the eyes of the law by being provided a means for learning such information. In other words, by recording the agreement in the Copyright Office, the transferor and transferee have met any public notice requirements because anyone who examined the copies of the documents in the Copyright Office would know the terms of the agreement. This is in contrast to actual notice in which the parties have formally provided other parties with actual copies of the documents.

[64]*See* 17 U.S.C. § 205(c)(1)–(2) (1996).

[65]*See* 17 U.S.C. § 205(d) and (e) (1996).

[66]*See* U.S. COPYRIGHT OFFICE, RECORDATION OF TRANSFERS AND OTHER DOCUMENTS (Circular 12) (1996), at 4.

[67]*Id.*

[68]17 U.S.C. § 205 (1996).

[69]17 U.S.C. § 203(a)(3) (1996).

[70]17 U.S.C. § 203(b)(1) (1996).

[71]17 U.S.C. § 111 (1996).

[72]17 U.S.C. § 111(a)(1) (1996).

[73]Another licensing agency is SESAC, Inc. (which was once known as the Society of European State Authors and Composers), but ASCAP and BMI dominate the field.

[74]*See Buffalo Broadcasting Co., Inc. v. American Society of Composers, Authors and Publishers*, 744 F.2d 917 (2d Cir. 1984); *cert. denied*, 469 U.S. 1211, 105 S.Ct. 1181, 84 L.Ed.2d 329 (1985).

[75]*Id.*

[76]*Id.*

[77]*Id.*

[78]*Id.*

[79]*Sailor Music v. Gap Stores, Inc.*, 668 F.2d 84 (2nd Cir. 1981); *cert. denied*, 456 U.S. 945 (1982).

[80]U.S. COPYRIGHT OFFICE, COPYRIGHT BASICS (Circular 1) (1996), at 3.

[81]17 U.S.C. § 507(a) (1996).

[82]17 U.S.C. § 507(b) (1996).

[83]*$25 Million Deal Includes Ownership of Birthday Song*, Lexington (Ky.) Herald-Leader (New York Times News Service), Dec. 20, 1988, at A4, col. 4.

[84]*For A Song: "Happy Birthday to You" May Sell for $12 Million*, Lexington (Ky.) Herald-Leader (New York Times News Service), Oct. 20, 1988, at A2, col. 5.

[85]*$25 Million Deal Includes Ownership of Birthday Song, supra.*

[86]*Id.*

[87]*Id.*

[88]H.R. Rep. No. 94-1476, 94th Cong., 2nd Sess. 65 (1976). Excerpts are reproduced in U.S. COPYRIGHT OFFICE, REPRODUCTION OF COPYRIGHTED WORKS BY EDUCATORS AND LIBRARIANS (Circular 21) (1995), at 8-9.

[89]17 U.S.C. § 107 (1996).

[90]*Id.*

[91]H.R. Rep. No. 94-1476, *supra.*

[92]*Time, Inc. v. Bernard Geis Associates*, 293 F. Supp. 130 (S.D. N.Y. 1968).

[93]Bernard Geis Associates had offered all profits from the book to Time, Inc. in return for a license to use the copyrighted frames in the book, but the magazine publisher rejected the offer.

[94]*Time, Inc. v. Bernard Geis Associates.*

[95]*Id.*

[96]*Harper & Row Publishers, Inc. and The Reader's Digest Association, Inc. v. Nation Enterprises*, 471 U.S. 539, 105 S.Ct. 2218, 88 L.Ed.2d 588, 11 Med.L.Rptr. 1969 (1985).

[97]*Id.*

[98]*Id.*

[99]*Id.*

[100]*Id.*

[101]*Id.*

[102]VITTOR, *"Fair Use" of Unpublished Materials: 'Widow Censors,' Copyright and the First Amendment,* COM. LAW (Fall 1989) at 1.

[103]*Harper & Row v. Nation Enterprises.*

[104]*Salinger v. Random House,* 811 F.2d 90, 13 Med.L.Rptr. 1954 (2d Cir. 1987); *cert denied,* 108 S.Ct. 213 (1987).

[105]*Id.*

[106]*Id.*

[107]*New Era Publications International v. Henry Holt & Co.,* 873 F.2d 576, 16 Med.L.Rptr. 1559 (2d Cir. 1989).

[108]*Id.*

[109]*Id.*

[110]*Id.*

[111]*New Era Publications International v. Henry Holt & Co.; reh'g denied,* 884 F.2d 659, 16 Med.L.Rptr. 2224 (2d Cir. 1989).

[112]*New Era Publications International v. Carol Publishing Group,* 904 F.2d 152, 17 Med.L.Rptr. 1913 (2d Cir. 1990).

[113]*Id.*

[114]*See* KAPLAN, *The End of History? A Copyright Controversy Leads to Self-Censorship,* NEWSWEEK (Dec. 25, 1989) at 80.

[115]Pub. L. 102-492 (Oct. 24, 1992).

[116]*American Geophysical Union v. Texaco,* 85 Civ. 3446, 802 F.Supp. 1 (S.D. N.Y. 1992).

[117]Under the Federal Interlocutory Appeals Act, 28 U.S.C. § 1292 (b), a U.S. Court of Appeals can review any interlocutory order (an interim order pending final disposition of a controversy) in a civil case if the district court judge states in the decision that there is a controlling question of law on which there is apparent disagreement in the courts. The judge in this case had issued such an order so the appellate court could make the final determination.

[118]*American Geophysical Union v. Texaco,* 37 F.3d 881, 32 U.S.P.Q. 2d1545 (2d Cir. 1994).

[119]*American Geophysical Union v. Texaco,* 60 F.3d 913 (2d Cir. 1995).

[120]*Basic Books, Inc. v. Kinko's Graphics Corp.,* 758 F.Supp. 1522 (S.D. N.Y. 1991).

[121]*See* WATKINS, *Photocopying Chain Found in Violation of Copyright Law,* The Chronicle of Higher Education (April 3, 1991) at A1, col. 2, and at A19, col. 1.

[122]March 29, 1991, letter from Paul J. Orfalea, Chairperson of Kinko's, distributed to university and college professors.

[123]The 11th Amendment (adopted in 1798) says: "The Judicial power of the United States shall not be construed to extend to any suit in law or equity, commenced or prosecuted against one of the United States by Citizens of another State, or by Citizens or Subjects of any Foreign State."

[124]*BV Engineering v. University of California at Los Angeles,* 858 F.2d 1394 (9th Cir. 1988).

[125]Copyright Remedy Clarification Act of 1990, Pub. L. No. 101-553, 17 U.S.C. §§ 501(a) and 511 (1994).

[126]17 U.S.C. § 501(a) (1996).

[127]17 U.S.C. § 511(a) (1996).

[128]17 U.S.C. § 511(b) (1996).

[129]*Court Clips Wings of Atlanta Video Clipping Service,* BROADCASTING (June 10, 1991) at 63, 65.

[130]THOMPSON, *Ruling on Right to Copy TV News Clips Decides Little,* Atlanta Journal Oct. 14, 1983, at A16, col. 1.

[131]*Court Clips Wings of Atlanta Video Clipping Service, supra.*

[132]*Lish v. Harper's Magazine Foundation,* 807 F.Supp. 1090, 20 Med.L.Rptr. 2073 (S.D. N.Y. 1992). *See also* RESKE, *Gordon Lish's $2,000 Letter,* 79 A.B.A.J. 28 (February 1993).

[133]*Luther R. Campbell a.k.a. Luke Skyywalker v. Acuff-Rose Music, Inc.,* _ U.S. _, 114 S.Ct. 1164, 127 L.Ed.2d 500 (1994).

[134]*Id.*

[135]*Id.*

[136]*Id.*

[137]*Id.*

[138]*Id.*

[139]*Id.*

[140]*Id.*

[141]*Stewart v. Abend*, 495 U.S. 207, 110 S.Ct. 1750, 109 L.Ed.2d 184 (1990).

[142]*See* EPSTEIN, *Court Ruling Could Pull Classic Videos from Shelves*, Lexington (Ky.) Herald-Leader (Knight-Ridder News Service), April 25, 1990, at A1, col. 1. By 1990, the rerelease had generated more than $12 million worldwide.

[143]*Id.*

[144]*Rohauer v. Killiam Shows*, 551 F.2d 484 (2d Cir. 1977); *cert. denied*, 431 U.S. 949 (1977).

[145]Epstein, *supra.*

[146]*Steward v. Abend.*

[147]*See* Epstein, *supra.*

[148]*See Jagger Gets Satisfaction in Lawsuit Over Song*, Lexington (Ky.) Herald-Leader (Associated Press), April 27, 1988, at A2, col. 3.

[149]*Id.*

[150]*Sid and Marty Krofft Television Productions, Inc. v. McDonald's Corp.*, 562 F.2d 1157 (9th Cir. 1977).

[151]*Id.*

[152]*Universal City Studios, Inc. v. Film Ventures International, Inc.*, 543 F. Supp. 1134 (C.D. Calif. 1982).

[153]*Id.*

[154]*Ruolo v. Russ Berrie & Co.*, 886 F.2d 931 (7th Cir. 1989).

[155]ABRAMSON, *"Look and Feel" of Computer Software*, CASE AND COMMENT (Jan.–Feb. 1990) at 3.

[156]*Id.*

[157]17 U.S.C. § 503(b) (1996).

[158]17 U.S.C. § 504(b) (1996).

[159]Pub. L. No. 100-568, 102 Stat. 2853, 2860 (1988).

[160]The amounts prior to the October 31, 1988, enactment of the new law were $250 and $10,000, respectively.

[161]17 U.S.C. § 504(c)(2) (1996).

[162]*Id.*

[163]17 U.S.C. § 505 (1996).

[164]*See* 17 U.S.C. § 506 (1996) and 18 U.S.C. § 2319(b)(1)(A) (1996).

[165]18 U.S.C. § 2319(b)(1)(B) (1996).

[166]18 U.S.C. § 2318 (1996).

[167]*Sony Corp. of America v. Universal City Studios, Inc.*, 465 U.S. 1112, 104 S.Ct. 1619, 80 L.Ed.2d 1480 (1984).

[168]At the time of the Court's decision, these devices were called videotape recorders or VTRs, but the terminology has now changed to videocassette recorders (VCRs).

[169]Betamax VCRs used the Beta format, which since then has lost out to the VHS format; but at the time of the suit, Beta was the dominant format. Even Sony has now abandoned Beta for VHS in its VCRs for home use. Although some technical experts still argue that the Beta format was superior to VHS, VHS won the battle, primarily because manufacturers of VHS recorders outmaneuvered the Beta folks in the marketplace.

[170]*Sony Corp. of America v. Universal City Studios, Inc.*

[171]*Id.*

[172]Public Law 102-307, enacted on June 26, 1992, made even renewal registration optional by automatically extending the duration of copyright obtained between January 1, 1964, and December 31, 1977, to an additional 47-year period. No registration renewal needs to be filed for this extension. There are some advantages to renewal registration, however. *See* U.S. COPYRIGHT OFFICE, RENEWAL OF COPYRIGHT (Circular 15) (1993). One of the advantages

is that such registration serves as *prima facie* evidence of the validity of the copyright, just as it does with an original registration.

[173]*See* U.S. COPYRIGHT OFFICE, COPYRIGHT REGISTRATION FOR COMPUTER PROGRAMS (Circular 61) (1995), at 3.

[174]*See* U.S. COPYRIGHT OFFICE, COPYRIGHT REGISTRATION FOR AUTOMATED DATA DATABASES (Circular 65) (1992) at 2.

[175]The Copyright Act defines a *compilation* as "a work formed by the collection and assembling of preexisting materials or of data that are selected, coordinated, or arranged in such a way that the resulting work as a whole constitutes an original work of authorship." *See* 17 U.S.C. § 101 (1996).

[176]Pub. L. No. 98-62 (1984), effective Nov. 8, 1984.

[177]U.S. COPYRIGHT OFFICE, THE UNITED STATES JOINS THE BERNE UNION (Circular 93a) (1989) at 3.

[178]*Id.*

[179]*Gilliam v. American Broadcasting Cos., Inc.*, 538 F.2d 14 (2d Cir. 1976).

[180]*Boston U. Dean Resigns*, Lexington (Ky.) Herald-Leader (wire services), July 13, 1991, at A1, col. 1.

CHAPTER 15

[1]SYDNEY W. HEAD, *Broadcasting in America* (3rd ed. 1976) at 432–436.

[2]*U.S. v. National Association of Broadcasters*, 536 F. Supp. 149 (1982).

[3]NBC BROADCAST STANDARDS AND PRACTICES DEPARTMENT, ADVERTISING STAND-ARDS (1994) at 10.

[4]CBS, INC., TELEVISION NETWORK ADVERTISING GUIDELINES (1994), CTN 10.

[5]CAPITAL CITIES/ABC, INC., DEPARTMENT OF BROADCAST STANDARDS AND PRAC-TICES, ADVERTISING STANDARDS AND GUIDELINES (1992).

[6]*Shuck v. The Carroll Daily Herald*, 247 N.W. 813 (1933).

[7]*Miami Herald Publishing Co. v. Tornillo*, 418 U.S. 241 (1974).

[8]FRANK LUTHER MOTT, AMERICAN JOURNALISM (1961) at 54.

[9]*Good Housekeeping: The Magazine, Its Institute, and the Good Housekeeping Seal* (1994) at 2.

[10]*San Francisco Newspaper Agency, Advertising Standards and Rate* Policies (1990).

[11]RALPH HOLSINGER AND JON PAUL DILTS, MEDIA LAW (3rd ed. 1994) at 560 was helpful on this point.

[12]*Lorain Journal v. U.S.*, 342 U.S. 143 (1951).

[13]Especially helpful here was DWIGHT L. TEETER, JR., AND DON R. LE DUC, LAW OF MASS COMMUNICATIONS (7th ed. 1992) at 711.

[14]68 Cal.2d 51 (1967); quoted by TEETER AND LE DUC, *op. cit.*, 464.

[15]*Penthouse International Ltd. v. Koch*, 599 F. Supp. 1338 (S.D.N.Y. 1984); *Coalition for Abortion Rights and Against Sterilization Abuse v. Niagara Frontier Transportation Authority*, 584 F. Supp. 985 (W.D.N.Y. 1984).

[16]418 U.S. 298 (1974); HOLSINGER AND DILTS, *op. cit.*, at 560.

[17]*Hazelwood School District v. Kuhlmeier*, 484 U.S. 260 (1988).

[18]*Mississippi Gay Alliance v. Goudelock*, 536 F.2d 1073 (1976); *cert. denied*, 88 S.Ct. 855; HOLSINGER AND DILTS, *op. cit.*, at 560.

[19]*Lee v. Board of Regents of State Colleges*, 306 F. Supp. 1097 (W.D. Wis. 1969); TEETER AND LE DUC, *op. cit.*, at 464.

[20]JEROME A. BARRON, *Access to the Press—a New First Amendment Right*, 80 HARVARD LAW REVIEW 1641 (1967); see also MARC FRANKLIN, MASS MEDIA LAW (2d ed. 1982) at 20.

[21]See also HOLSINGER AND DILTS, *op. cit.*, 560ff, on this point.

[22]S. WATSON DUNN AND ARNOLD M. BARBAN, ADVERTISING: ITS ROLE IN MODERN MARKETING (6th ed. 1986) at 129.

²³PHILIP KOTLER, PRINCIPLES OF MARKETING (2d ed. 1983) at 620. Quoted in DUNN AND BARBAN, *op. cit.*, at 130.

²⁴Council of Better Business Bureaus, *1993 Annual Report*, 6.

²⁵*NAD Case Reports*, 24:5 (July, 1994), 81–84.

²⁶"The System Works," editorial in *Advertising Age*, April 19, 1993.

CHAPTER 16

¹447 U.S. 557, 100 S.Ct. 2343, 65 L.Ed.2d 319, 6 Med.L.Rptr. 1497 (1980).

²*Barnes v. Glen Theatre, Inc.*, 501 U.S. 560, 111 S.Ct. 2456, 115 L.Ed.2d 504 (1991).

³*See Couple Guilty in Computer Porn Case*, Lexington (Ky.) Herald-Leader, July 29, 1994, at A5, col. 1.

⁴*See Lawmakers Fighting Porn Billboards Along Information Superhighway*, Lexington (Ky.) Herald-Leader (New York Times News Service), March 26, 1995, at A15, col. 4.

⁵*Id.*

⁶*See* HENRY J. RESKE, *Computer Porn a Prosecutorial Challenge*, 80 A.B.A.J. 40 (December 1994).

⁷*Regina v. Hicklin*, L.R., 3 Q.B. 360 (1868).

⁸*Id.*

⁹*See* WEBSTER'S NEW WORLD DICTIONARY (3rd college edition) 286 (1988).

¹⁰*See* RICHARD LACAYO, *Violent Reaction*, TIME, June 12, 1995, at 26.

¹¹*Id.*

¹²*Lew Rosen v. The United States*, 161 U.S. 29, 16 S.Ct. 434, 40 L.Ed. 606 (1896).

¹³*United States v. One Book Called "Ulysses,"* 5 F. Supp. 182 (S.D.N.Y. 1933).

¹⁴*Id.*

¹⁵*United States v. One Book Called "Ulysses,"* 72 F.2d 705 (2nd Cir. 1934).

¹⁶*Near v. Minnesota*, 283 U.S. 697, 51 S.Ct. 625, 75 L.Ed. 1357, 1 Med.L.Rptr. 1001 (1931).

¹⁷*Butler v. Michigan*, 352 U.S. 380, 77 S.Ct. 524, 1 L.Ed.2d 412 (1957).

¹⁸*Id.*

¹⁹*Id.*

²⁰*Roth v. United States and Alberts v. California*, 354 U.S. 476, 77 S.Ct. 1304, 1 L.Ed.2d 412 (1957).

²¹*Miller v. California*, 413 U.S. 15, 93 S.Ct. 2607, 37 L.Ed.2d 419, 1 Med.L.Rptr. 1441 (1973).

²²*Roth and Alberts.*

²³*Id.*

²⁴*Id.*

²⁵*Id.*

²⁶*See Roth v. United States.*

²⁷*Id.*

²⁸*Roth and Alberts* (Warren concurring opinion).

²⁹*Id.* (majority opinion).

³⁰*Id.*

³¹*Ginzburg v. United States*, 383 U.S. 463, 86 S.Ct. 942, 1 Med.L.Rptr. 1409, 16 L.Ed.2d 31 (1966).

³²*Id.*

³³*Id.*

³⁴*Id.*

³⁵*Id.* at fn. 9.

³⁶*Id.* (Douglas dissent, fn. 3).

³⁷*Jacobellis v. Ohio*, 378 U.S. 184, 84 S.Ct. 1676, 12 L.Ed.2d 793 (1964).

³⁸*Ginzburg v. United States* (Stewart concurring opinion).

³⁹*A Quantity of Copies of Books v. Kansas*, 378 U.S. 205, 84 S.Ct. 1723, 12 L.Ed.2d 809 (1964).

⁴⁰*Smith v. California*, 361 U.S. 147, 80 S.Ct. 215, 4 L.Ed.2d 205 (1959).

⁴¹*Manual Enterprises v. Day*, 370 U.S. 478, 82 S.Ct. 1432 (1964).

⁴²*Freedman v. Maryland*, 380 U.S. 51, 85 S.Ct. 734, 13 L.Ed.2d 649 (1965).

⁴³*Id.*

[44]*A Book Named "John Cleland's Memories of a Woman of Pleasure" v. Attorney General of Massachusetts*, 383 U.S. 413, 86 S.Ct. 975, 16 L.Ed.2d 1, 1 Med.L.Rptr. 1390 (1966).

[45]*Id.* (Douglas concurring opinion, appendix).

[46]*Id.* (Clark dissent).

[47]*Mishkin v. New York*, 383 U.S. 502, 86 S.Ct. 958, 16 L.Ed.2d 56 (1966).

[48]*Id.*

[49]*Redrup v. New York, Austin v. Kentucky, and Gent v. Arkansas*, 386 U.S. 767, 87 S.Ct. 1414, 18 L.Ed.2d 515 (1967).

[50]*Ginsberg v. New York*, 390 U.S. 629, 88 S.Ct. 1274, 1 Med.L.Rptr. 1424 (1968).

[51]*Stanley v. Georgia*, 394 U.S. 557, 89 S.Ct. 1243, 22 L.Ed.2d 542 (1969).

[52]*Id.*

[53]*Miller v. California*, 413 U.S. 15, 93 S.Ct. 2607, 37 L.Ed.2d 419, 1 Med.L.Rptr. 1441 (1973).

[54]*Id.*

[55]*Id.*

[56]*Id.*

[57]*Id.*

[58]*Id.*

[59]*Id.*

[60]*Id.*

[61]*Id.*

[62]*Paris Adult Theatre I v. Slaton*, 413 U.S. 49, 93 S.Ct. 2628, 37 L.Ed.2d 445, 1 Med.L.Rptr. 1454 (1973).

[63]*Id.*

[64]*Hamling v. United States*, 418 U.S. 87, 94 S.Ct. 2887, 41 L.Ed.2d 590, 1 Med.L.Rptr. 1479.

[65]The book was an illustrated version of a report released in 1970 by a commission appointed by President Lyndon Johnson. The report, which came after thousands of hours and more than $2 million had been spent by the group, was rejected by President Richard Nixon. He rejected the majority's recommendations that all local, state, and federal censorship of sexually oriented materials directed to adults be ended, and that a comprehensive sex education program be launched in public schools. Only 12 of the 18 members of the commission signed the majority report. In its *Miller* decision, the Supreme Court of the United States referred only to the minority report.

[66]*Jenkins v. Georgia*, 418 U.S. 153, 153, 94 S.Ct. 2750, 1 Med.L.Rptr. 1479 (1974).

[67]*Id.*

[68]*Hammer v. Dagenhart*, 247 U.S. 251, 38 S.Ct. 529, 62 L.Ed.2d 1101 (1918).

[69]*United States v. Darby*, 312 U.S. 100, 61 S.Ct. 451, 85 L.Ed.2d 609 (1941).

[70]*Sable Communications of California v. Federal Communications Commission*, 492 U.S. 115, 109 S.Ct. 2829, 106 L.Ed.2d 93, 16 Med.L.Rptr. 1961 (1989).

[71]N.Y. Penal Law, Art. 263.

[72]§§ 263.00(1) and 263.00(3).

[73]§§ 263.00(5).

[74]*New York v. Ferber*, 458 U.S. 747, 102 S.Ct. 3348, 73 L.Ed.2d 1113, 8 Med.L.Rptr. 1809 (1982).

[75]*Id.* (Brennan concurring opinion).

[76]Pub. L. 95-225 (1977).

[77]Pub. L. 98-292 ("Child Protection Act of 1984").

[78]Pub. L. 99-628 ("Child Sexual Abuse and Pornography Act of 1986"); Pub. L. 99-500 and 99-591 ("Child Abuse Victims' Rights Act of 1986").

[79]Pub. L. 100-690 ("Child Protection and Obscenity Enforcement Act of 1988").

[80]Pub. L. 101-647 ("Child Protection Restoration and Penalties Enforcement Act of 1990").

[81]*See* 18 U.S.C. 2251 (1994).

[82]*United States v. X-Citement Video, Inc.*, 513 U.S. __, 115 S.Ct. 464, 130 L.Ed.2d 372 (1994).

[83]*See* Pub. L. 98-292 ("Child Protection Act of 1984").

[84]*Osborne v. Ohio*, 495 U.S. 103, 110 S.Ct. 1691, 109 L.Ed.2d 98 (1990).

[85]*City of Renton v. Playtime Theatres, Inc.*, 475 U.S. 41, 106 S.Ct. 925, 89 L.Ed.2d 29 (1986).

[86]*See Arcara v. Cloud Books, Inc.*, 478 U.S. 697, 106 S.Ct. 3172, 92 L.Ed. 568 (1986).

[87]*New York v. P.J. Video, Inc.*, 475 U.S. 868, 106 S.Ct. 1610, 89 L.Ed.2d 871 (1986).

[88]*Pope v. Illinois*, 481 U.S. 497, 107 S.Ct. 1918, 95 L.Ed.2d 439 (1987).

[89]Attorney General's Commission on Pornography: Final Report (July 1986).

[90]Racketeer Influenced and Corrupt Organizations (RICO) Act of 1970, 18 U.S.C. § 1961-68 (1994).

[91]*Fort Wayne Books, Inc. v. Indiana*, 489 U.S. 486, 109 S.Ct. 916, 103 L.Ed.2d 34, 16 Med.L.Rptr. 1337 (1989).

[92]*Id.*

[93]*Alexander v. United States*, 509 U.S. 544, 113 S.Ct. 2766, 125 L.Ed.2d 441, 21 Med.L.Rptr. 1609 (1993).

[94]The Eighth Amendment to the U.S. Constitution states, "Excessive bail shall not be required, nor excessive fines imposed, nor cruel and unusual punishments inflicted."

[95]*In the Matter of Petition for Declaratory Ruling Concerning Section 312 (a) (7) of the Communications Act.*

[96]*See Television Stations Must Run, But May Reschedule, Graphic Anti-Abortion Political Advertisements,* NEWS MEDIA & L. (Winter 1995), at 35–36.

[97]*FCC v. Pacifica Foundation*, 438 U.S. 726, 98 S.Ct. 3026, 57 L.Ed.2d 1073, 2 Med.L.Rptr. 1465 (1978).

[98]*Action for Children's Television v. FCC*, 58 F.3d 654 (D.C. Cir. 1995) (en banc) (ACT III).

[99]*Action for Children's Television v. FCC*, 59 F.3rd 1249 (D.C. Cir. 1995) (ACT IV).

[100]PAUL FARHI, *War of the Words, The Washington Post Magazine,* May 21, 1995, at 12.

[101]*Id.*

[102]47 U.S.C. §§ 532.

[103]*Alliance for Community Media v. FCC*, 56 F.3d 105 (D.C. Cir. 1995) (en banc).

[104]*Saving children or sacrificing rights?*, The Freedom Forum News, April 8, 1996, at 1.

[105]*American Civil Liberties Union et al. v. U.S. Attorney General Janet Reno*, Civil Action No. 96-963 and Civil Action No. 96-1458 (U.S.D.C. E.D. Pa. 1996). *See* O'Connor, *Judges Block 'Indecency' Law for the Internet,* Lexington (Ky.) Herald-Leader (Knight-Ridder News Service), June 13, 1996, at A1, col. 6.

[106]*ACLU v. Reno* (Dalzell separate opinion).

[107]Communications Decency Act of 1996 § 223(a).

[108]Communications Decency Act of 1996 § 223(d).

[109]*See Adams Newark Theatre Co. v. Newark*, 354 U.S. 931 (1956).

[110]*See, e.g., California v. LaRue*, 409 U.S. 109 (1972); *New York State Liquor Authority v. Bellanca*, 452 U.S. 714 (1981); and *City of Newport v. Iacobucci*, 479 U.S. 92 (1986).

[111]*Doran v. Salem Inn, Inc.*, 422 U.S. 922 (1975).

[112]*Barnes v. Glen Theatre*, 501 U.S. 560, 111 S.Ct. 2456, 115 L.Ed.2d 594 (1991).

[113]*Id.* (plurality opinion).

[114]*See Station Settles Indecency Case with FCC*, 24 NEWS MEDIA & L. (Spring 1994).

[115]*See* Allen, Emmers, Gebhardt and Giery, *Exposure to Pornography and Acceptance of Rape Myths,* 45 J. COMMUNICATION 5 (Winter 1995).

[116]*Id.*

[117]*Id.*

[118]GUNTHER, *Overrating the X-Rating: The Third Person Perception and Support for Censorship of Pornography,* 45 J. COMMUNICATION 27 (Winter 1995).

[119]*Id.* at 37.

CHAPTER 17

[1]Quoted in COMMUNICATIONS LAW (Vol. 3 1994) at 432.

[2]*Branzburg v. Hayes*, 408 U.S. 664, 690 n. 29 (1972); quoting B.J. Wigmore. Evidence, (McNaughton Rev. 1961) §2192, at 73.

[3]*Id.* at 692.

[4]The case consolidated *Branzburg* with *In re Pappas* and *U.S. v. Caldwell.*

[5]*Id.* at 669; quoting *Branzburg v. Pound*, 461 S.W. 2d 345 (1970).

[6]*Id.*

[7]*Id.* at 672.

[8]*Id.* at 674; quoting *In re Pappas*, 266 N.D. 2d 297, 299, 358 Mass. 604, 607 (1971).

[9]*Id.* at 675.

[10]*Id.* at 681.

[11]*Id.*

[12]*Id.* at 682.

[13]*Id.* at 685.

[14]*Id.* at 690.

[15]*Id.* at 704.

[16]*Id.* at 709.

[17]COMMUNICATIONS LAW (Vol. 3 1994) at 429.

[18] U.S. _, 111 S.Ct. 2513 (1991).

[19]*Miranda v. Arizona*, 384 U.S. 436 (1966).

[20]384 U.S. 333 (1966).

[21]*Nebraska Press Association v. Stuart*, 427 U.S. 539, 553 (1976); quoting *Sheppard v. Maxwell*, 384 U.S. 333, 363 (1966).

[22]427 U.S. 539 (1976).

[23]*Id.* at 542.

[24]*Id.*

[25]*Id.* at 543.

[26]*Id.* at 547.

[27]*Id.* at 548.

[28]*Id.* at 555.

[29]*Id.* at 561.

[30]*Id.*

[31]*Id.* at 565.

[32]*Id.* at 568.

[33]443 U.S. 368 (1979).

[34]*Id.* at 375.

[35]*Id.* at 376.

[36]*Id.* at 391; *Pell v. Procunier*, 417 U.S. 817 (1974); *Saxbe v. Washington Post Co.*, 417 U.S. 843 (1974); *Houchins v. KQED*, 438 U.S. 1 (1978).

[37]*Id.* at 393.

[38]UNITED STATES CONSTITUTION, Amendment VI.

[39]*Gannett Co. v. DePasquale*, at 379.

[40]448 U.S. 555 (1980).

[41]*Id.* at 560.

[42]*Id.* at 564.

[43]*Id.* at 573.

[44]*Id.* at 576; quoting *First National Bank of Boston v. Bellotti*, 435 U.S. 765, 783 (1978).

[45]*Id.* at 577.

[46]*Id.* at 580; quoting *Branzburg v. Hays*, 408 U.S. 664, 681 (1972).

[47]457 U.S. 596 (1982).

[48]464 U.S. 501 (1984).

[49]478 U.S. 1 (1986).

[50]*Id.* at 4.

[51]*Id.* at 7.

[52]*Id.* at 8.

[53]*Id.*

[54]*Id.* at 10.

[55]*Id.*

[56]*Id.* at 11.

[57]*Id.* at 12.

[58]*Id.*

[59]449 U.S. 560 (1981).

[60] S.C. __, #24272 Davis (slip opinion) (1995).

[61]417 U.S. 817 (1974).

[62]417 U.S. 843 (1974).

[63]5 U.S.C. § 552, as amended by Pub. L. No. 99-570, 1801-1804 (1986).

[64]5 U.S.C. § 552a, as amended by Pub. L. No. 97-365, 96 Stat. 1749 (1982).

[65]441 U.S. 281 (1979).

[66]5 U.S.C. § 552b.

Appendix A:
Professional Codes

CODE OF PROFESSIONAL STANDARDS
FOR THE PRACTICE OF PUBLIC RELATIONS

Declaration of Principles

Members of the Public Relations Society of America base their professional principles on the fundamental value and dignity of the individual, holding that the free exercise of human rights—especially freedom of speech, freedom of assembly, and freedom of the press—is essential to the practice of public relations.

In serving the interests of clients and employers, we dedicate ourselves to the goals of better communication, understanding, and cooperation among the diverse individuals, groups, and institutions of society, and of equal opportunity in the public relations profession.

We pledge:

To conduct ourselves professionally, with truth, accuracy, fairness, and responsibility to the public;

To improve our individual competence and advance the knowledge and proficiency of the professional through continuing research and education;

And to adhere to the articles of the Code of Professional Standards for the Practice of Public Relations as adopted by the governing Assembly of the Society.

Code of Professional Standards for the Practice
of Public Relations

1. A member shall conduct his or her professional life in accord with the public interest.

2. A member shall exemplify high standards of honesty and integrity while carrying out dual obligations to a client or employer and to the democratic process.

3. A member shall deal fairly with the public, with past or present clients or employers, and with fellow practitioners, giving due respect to the ideal of free inquiry and to the opinions of others.

4. A member shall adhere to the highest standards of accuracy and truth, avoiding extravagant claims or unfair comparisons and giving credit for ideas and words borrowed from others.

5. A member shall not knowingly disseminate false or misleading information and shall act promptly to correct erroneous communications for which he or she is responsible.

6. A member shall not engage in any practice which has the purpose of corrupting the integrity of channels of communications or the processes of government.

7. A member shall be prepared to identify publicly the name of the client or employer on whose behalf any public communication is made.

8. A member shall not use any individual or organization professing to serve or represent an announced cause, or professing to be independent or unbiased, but actually serving another or undisclosed interest.

9. A member shall not guarantee the achievement of specified results beyond the member's direct control.

10. A member shall not represent conflicting or competing interests without the express consent of those concerned, given after a full disclosure of the facts.

11. A member shall not place himself or herself in a position where the member's personal interest is or may be in conflict with an obligation to an employer or client, or others, without full disclosure of such interests to all involved.

12. A member shall not accept fees, commissions, gifts or any other consideration from anyone except clients or employers from whom services are performed without their express consent, given after full disclosure of the facts.

13. A member shall scrupulously safeguard the confidences and privacy rights of present, former, and prospective clients or employers.

14. A member shall not intentionally damage the professional reputation or practice of another practitioner.

15. If a member has evidence that another member has been guilty of unethical, illegal, or unfair practices, including those in violation of this Code, the member is obligated to present the information promptly to the proper authorities of the Society for action in accordance with the procedure set forth in Article XII of the Bylaws.

16. A member called as a witness in a proceeding for enforcement of this Code is obligated to appear, unless excused for sufficient reason by the judicial panel.

17. A member shall, as soon as possible, sever relations with any organization or individual if such relationship requires conduct contrary to the articles of this Code.

OFFICIAL INTERPRETATIONS OF THE CODE

Interpretation of Code Paragraph 1, which reads, "A member shall conduct his or her professional life in accord with the public interest."

The public interest is here defined primarily as comprising respect for and enforcement of the rights guaranteed by the Constitution of the United States of America.

Interpretation of Code Paragraph 6, which reads, "A member shall not engage in any practice which has the purpose of corrupting the integrity of channels or communications or the processes of government."

1. Among the practices prohibited by this paragraph are those that tend to place representatives of media or government under any obligation to the member, or the member's employer or client, which is in conflict with their obligations to media or government, such as:

a. the giving of gifts of more than nominal value;

b. any form of payment or compensation to a member of the media in order to obtain preferential or guaranteed news or editorial coverage in the medium;

c. any retainer or fee to a media employee or use of such employee if retained by a client or employer, where the circumstances are not fully disclosed to and accepted by the media employer;

d. providing trips, for media representatives, that are unrelated to legitimate news interest;

e. the use by a member of an investment or loan or advertising commitment made by the member, or the member's client or employer, to obtain preferential or guaranteed coverage in the medium.

2. This Code paragraph does not prohibit hosting media or government representatives at meals, cocktails, or news functions and special events that are occasions for the exchange of news information or views, or the furtherance

of understanding, which is part of the public relations function. Nor does it prohibit the *bona fide* press event or tour when media or government representatives are given the opportunity for an on-the-spot viewing of a newsworthy product, process, or event in which the media or government representatives have a legitimate interest. What is customary or reasonable hospitality has to be a matter of particular judgment in specific situations. In all of these cases, however, it is, or should be, understood that no preferential treatment or guarantees are expected or implied and that complete independence always is left to the media or government representative.

3. This paragraph does not prohibit the reasonable giving or lending of sample products or services to media representatives who have a legitimate interest in the products or services.

4. It is permissible, under Article 6 of the Code, to offer complimentary or discount rates to the media (travel writers, for example) if the rate is for business use and is made available to all writers. Considerable question exists as to the propriety of extending such rates for personal use.

Interpretation of Code Paragraph 9, which reads, "A member shall not guarantee the achievement of specified results beyond the member's direct control."

> This Code paragraph, in effect, prohibits misleading a client or employer as to what professional public relations can accomplish. It does not prohibit guarantees of quality or service. But it does prohibit guaranteeing specific results which, by their very nature, cannot be guaranteed because they are not subject to the member's control. As an example, a guarantee that a news release will appear specifically in a particular publication would be prohibited. This paragraph should not be interpreted as prohibiting contingent fees.

Interpretation of Code Paragraph 13, which reads, "A member shall scrupulously safeguard the confidences and privacy rights of present, former, and prospective clients or employers."

1. This article does not prohibit a member who has knowledge of client or employer activities that are illegal from making such disclosures to the proper authorities as he or she believes are legally required.
2. Communications between a practitioner and client/employer are deemed to be confidential under Article 13 of the Code of Professional Standards. However, although practitioner/client/employer communications are considered confidential between the parties, such communications are not privileged against disclosure in a court of law.
3. In the absence of any contractual arrangement, the client or employer legally owns the rights to papers or materials created for him.

Interpretation of Code Paragraph 14, which reads, "A member shall not intentionally damage the professional reputation or practice of another practitioner."

1. Blind solicitation, on its face, is not prohibited by the Code. However, if the customer list were improperly obtained, or if the solicitation contained references reflecting adversely on the quality of current services, a complaint might be justified.

2. This article applies to statements, true or false, or acts, made or undertaken with malice and with the specific purpose of harming the reputation or practice of another member. This article does not prohibit honest employee evaluations or similar reviews, made without malice and as part of ordinary business practice, even though this activity may have a harmful effect.

AN OFFICIAL INTERPRETATION OF THE CODE AS IT APPLIES TO POLITICAL PUBLIC RELATIONS

Preamble

In the practice of political public relations, a PRSA member must have professional capabilities to offer an employer or client quite apart from any political relationships of value, and members may serve their employer or client without necessarily having attributed to them the character, reputation, or beliefs of those they serve. It is understood that members may choose to serve only those interests with whose political philosophy they are personally comfortable.

Definition

"Political Public Relations" is defined as those areas of public relations that relate to:

a. the counseling of political organizations, committees, candidates, or potential candidates for public office; and groups constituted for the purpose of influencing the vote on any ballot issue;

b. the counseling of holders of public office;

c. the management, or direction, of a political campaign for or against a candidate for political office; or for or against a ballot issue to be determined by voter approval or rejection;

d. the practice of public relations on behalf of a client or an employer in connection with that client's or employer's relationships with any candidates or holders of public office, with the purpose of influencing legislation or government regulation or treatment of a client or employer, regardless of whether the PRSA member is a recognized lobbyist;

e. the counseling of government bodies, or segments thereof, either domestic or foreign.

Precepts

1. It is the responsibility of PRSA members practicing political public relations, as defined above, to be conversant with the various statutes, local, state, and federal, governing such activities and to adhere to them strictly. This includes, but is not limited to, the various local, state, and federal laws, court decisions, and official interpretations governing lobbying, political contributions, disclosure, elections, libel, slander, and the like. In carrying out this responsibility, members shall seek appropriate counseling whenever necessary.

2. It is also the responsibility of the members to abide by PRSA's Code of Professional Standards.

3. Members shall represent clients or employers in good faith, and while partisan advocacy on behalf of a candidate or public issue may be expected, members shall act in accord with the public interest and adhere to truth and accuracy and to generally accepted standards of good taste.

4. Members shall not issue descriptive material or any advertising or publicity information or participate in the preparation of use thereof that is not signed by responsible persons or is false, misleading, or unlabeled as to its source, and are obligated to use care to avoid dissemination of any such material.

5. Members have an obligation to clients to disclose what remuneration beyond their fees they expect to receive as a result of their relationship, such as commissions for media advertising, printing, and the like, and should not accept such extra payment without their client's consent.

6. Members shall not improperly use their positions to encourage additional future employment or compensation. It is understood that successful campaign directors or managers, because of the performance of their duties and the working relationship that develops, may well continue to assist and counsel, for pay, the successful candidate.

7. Members shall voluntarily disclose to employers or clients the identity of other employers or clients with whom they are currently associated, and whose interests might be affected favorably or unfavorably by their political representation.

8. Members shall respect the confidentiality of information pertaining to employers or clients past, present, and potential, even after the relationships cease, avoiding future associations wherein insider information is sought that would give a desired advantage over a member's previous clients.

9. In avoiding practices that might tend to corrupt the processes of government, members shall not make undisclosed gifts of cash or other valuable considerations that are designed to influence specific decisions of voters, legislators, or public officials on public matters. A business lunch or dinner, or other comparable expenditure made in the course of communicating a point of view or public position, would not constitute such a violation. Nor, for example, would a plant visit designed and financed to provide useful background information to an interested legislator or candidate.

10. Nothing herein should be construed as prohibiting members from making legal, properly disclosed contributions to the candidates, party, or referenda issues of their choice.

11. Members shall not, through use of information known to be false or misleading, conveyed directly or through a third party, intentionally injure the public reputation of an opposing interest.

AN OFFICIAL INTERPRETATION OF THE CODE
AS IT APPLIES TO FINANCIAL PUBLIC RELATIONS

"Financial public relations" is defined as "that area of public relations which relates to the dissemination of information that affects the understanding of stockholders and investors generally concerning the financial position and prospects of a company, and includes among its objectives the improvement of relations between corporations and their stockholders." The interpretation was prepared in 1963 [and has been amended several times since] by the Society's Financial Relations Committee, working with the Securities and Exchange Commission and with the advice of the Society's legal counsel. It is rooted directly in the Code with the full force of the Code behind it, and a violation of any of the following paragraphs is subject to the same procedures and penalties as violation of the Code.

1. It is the responsibility of PRSA members who practice financial public relations to be thoroughly familiar with and understand the rules and regulations of the SEC and the laws it administers, as well as other laws, rules, and regulations affecting financial public relations, and to act in accordance with their letter and spirit. In carrying out this responsibility, members shall also seek legal counsel, when appropriate, on matters concerning financial public relations.

2. Members shall adhere to the general policy of making full and timely disclosure of corporate information on behalf of clients or employers. The information disclosed shall be accurate, clear, and understandable. The purpose of such disclosure is to provide the investing public with all material information affecting security values or influencing investment decisions. In complying with the duty of full and timely disclosure, members shall present all material facts, including those adverse to the company. They shall exercise care to ascertain the facts and to disseminate only information they believe to be accurate. They shall not knowingly omit information, the omission of which might make a release false or misleading. Under no circumstance shall members participate in any activity designed to mislead or manipulate the price of a company's securities.

3. Members shall publicly disclose or release information promptly so as to avoid the possibility of any use of the information by any insider or third party. To that end, members shall make every effort to comply with the spirit and

intent of the timely-disclosure policies of the stock exchanges, NASD, and the SEC. Material information shall be made available on an equal basis.

4. Members shall not disclose confidential information the disclosure of which might be adverse to a valid corporate purpose or interest and whose disclosure is not required by the timely-disclosure provisions of the law. During any such period of nondisclosure members shall not directly or indirectly (a) communicate the confidential information to any other person, or (b) buy or sell or in any other way deal in the company's securities where the confidential information may materially affect the market for the security when disclosed. Material information shall be disclosed publicly as soon as its confidential status has terminated or the requirement of timely disclosure takes effect.

5. During the registration period, members shall not engage in practices designed to precondition the market for such securities. During registration, the issuance of forecasts, projections, predictions about sales and earnings, or opinions concerning security values or other aspects of the future performance of the company, shall be in accordance with current SEC regulations and statements of policy. In the case of companies whose securities are publicly held, the normal flow of factual information to shareholders and the investing public shall continue during the registration period.

6. Where members have any reason to doubt that projections have an adequate basis in fact, they shall satisfy themselves as to the adequacy of the projections prior to disseminating them.

7. Acting in concert with clients or employers, members shall act promptly to correct false or misleading information or rumors concerning clients' or employers' securities or business whenever they have reason to believe such information or rumors are materially affecting investor attitudes.

8. Members shall not issue descriptive materials designed or written in such a fashion as to appear to be, contrary to fact, an independent third-party endorsement or recommendation of a company or a security. Whenever members issue material for clients or employers, either in their own names or in the names of someone other than the clients or employers, they shall disclose in large type and in a prominent position on the face of the material the source of such material and the existence of the issuer's client or employer relationship.

9. Members shall not use inside information for personal gain. However, this is not intended to prohibit members from making *bona fide* investments in their company's or client's securities insofar as they can make such investments without the benefit of material inside information.

10. Members shall not accept compensation that would place them in a position of conflict with their duty to a client, employer, or the investing public. Members shall not accept stock options from clients or employers nor accept securities as compensation at a price below market price except as part of an overall plan for corporate employees.

11. Members shall act so as to maintain the integrity of channels of public communication. They shall not pay or permit to be paid to any publication or

other communications medium any consideration in exchange for publicizing a company, except through clearly recognizable paid advertising.

12. Members shall be in general be guided by the PRSA Declaration of Principles and the Code of Professional Standards for the Practice of Public Relations of which this is an official interpretation.

# # #

Discussion

1. What priorities of allegiance should public relations people give to the companies or clients that employ them, and to the public, which they also serve? Can all constituencies be served equally? 2. Though by definition they are concerned with the image of others, public relations practitioners often find they have an image problem of their own. Why does this problem exist? What, if anything, can be done about it?

# # #

STANDARDS OF PRACTICE OF THE AMERICAN ASSOCIATION OF ADVERTISING AGENCIES

We hold that a responsibility of advertising is to be a constructive force in business.

We hold that, to discharge this responsibility, advertising agencies must recognize an obligation, not only to their clients, but to the public, the media they employ, and to each other. As a business, the advertising agency must operate within the framework of competition. It is recognized that keen and vigorous competition, honestly conducted, is necessary to the growth and health of American business. However, unethical competitive practices in the advertising agency business lead to financial waste, dilution of service, diversion of manpower, loss of prestige, and tend to weaken public confidence both in advertisements and in the institutions of advertising.

We hold that the advertising agency should compete on merit and not by attempts at discrediting or disparaging a competitor agency, or its work, directly or by inference, or by circulating harmful rumors about another agency, or by making unwarranted claims of particular skill in judging or prejudging advertising copy.

To these ends, the American Association of Advertising Agencies has adopted the following *Creative Code* as being in the best interests of the public, the advertisers, the media, and the agencies themselves. The A. A. A. A. believes the Code's provisions serve as a guide to the kind of agency conduct that experience has shown to be wise, foresighted, and constructive. In accepting membership, an agency agrees to follow it.

Creative Code

We, the members of the American Association of Advertising Agencies, in addition to supporting and obeying the laws and legal regulations pertaining to advertising, undertake to extend and broaden the application of high ethical standards. Specifically, we will not knowingly create advertising that contains:

a. False or misleading statements or exaggerations, visual or verbal.
b. Testimonials which do not reflect the real opinion of the individual(s) involved.
c. Price claims which are misleading.
d. Claims insufficiently supported or that distort the true meaning of practicable application of statements made by professional or scientific authority.
e. Statements, suggestions, or pictures offensive to public decency or minority segments of the population.

We recognize that there are areas which are subject to honestly different interpretations and judgment. Nevertheless, we agree not to recommend to an advertiser, and to discourage the use of, advertising that is in poor or questionable taste or that is deliberately irritating through aural or visual content or presentation.

Comparative advertising shall be governed by the same standards of truthfulness, claim substantiation, tastefulness, etc., as apply to other types of advertising.

These Standards of Practice of the American Association of Advertising Agencies come from the belief that sound and ethical practice is good business. Confidence and respect are indispensable to success in a business embracing the many intangibles of agency service and involving relationships so dependent on good faith.

Clear and willful violations of this Code shall be referred to the Board of Directors of the American Association of Advertising Agencies for appropriate action, including possible annulment of membership as provided in Article IV, Section 5, of the Constitution and By-laws.

# # #

Discussion

In the 1950s the 4A's attempted to self-regulate the advertising business by setting up standards of competition for business that fixed agency compensation commission rates at 15 percent. However, the Justice Department interceded, holding that such enforcements constituted a restraint of trade. Do you see anything in the current version of the Creative Code, above, that might similarly be challenged in the courts?

# # #

OUTDOOR ADVERTISING ASSOCIATION OF AMERICA
CODE OF INDUSTRY PRINCIPLES

The Outdoor Advertising Association of America, Inc. (OAAA) endorses this Code and encourages its members to operate in conformance with the following principles:

1. We support billboards as a business use to be erected only in business areas.
2. We support the right to maintain lawfully erected billboards.
3. We support those laws which assure just compensation for the removal of legal conforming and nonconforming billboards.
4. We support the removal, without compensation, of illegally erected billboards and other signs.
5. We support new billboard locations in unzoned commercial and industrial areas only where there is bona fide business activity already in existence.
6. We support the exclusion of new billboards in areas of genuine scenic beauty outside of business areas.
7. We are committed to maintaining and improving the quality and appearance of billboard structures and locations.
8. We are committed to the use of new technologies to improve our ability to inform the traveling public.
9. We are committed to provide public service messages to promote worthy community causes.
10. We are committed to the use of billboards for political, editorial, and other noncommercial messages.
11. We are committed to a program which prohibits alcohol and tobacco advertisements that are intended to be read from, or within 500 feet of, established places of worship or primary and secondary schools.
12. We are committed to advertising a diversity of products and services.
13. We support the right to reject advertising that is misleading, in poor taste or otherwise incompatible with individual community standards.

# # #

Discussion

1. In #6 above, how would you define "genuine scenic beauty?" 2. A recent survey by the city of St. Louis found there were three times more billboards in predominantly black neighborhoods than in white neighborhoods, and that 76 percent of the billboards in the African-American neighborhoods promoted the sale of alcohol and tobacco products (compared to 42 percent in the white neighborhoods). Does this heavy targeting by tobacco and alcohol companies

of minority neighborhoods trouble you? If it does, would you propose a legislative solution? Is a self-regulatory remedy by the outdoor advertising industry—and/or by the advertisers themselves—likely to work?

# # #

BETTER BUSINESS BUREAU CODE

Fair Practice Code for Advertising and Selling of the Association of Better Business Bureau, Inc.

1. Serve the public with honest values.
2. Tell the truth about what is offered.
3. Tell the truth in a forthright manner so its significance may be understood by the trusting as well as the analytical.
4. Tell customers what they want to know, what they have the right to know and ought to know about what is offered, so that they may buy wisely and obtain the maximum satisfaction from their purchases.
5. Be prepared and willing to make good promises and without quibble on any guarantee offered.
6. Be sure that the normal use of merchandise or services offered will not be hazardous to public health or life.
7. Reveal material facts, the deceptive concealment of which might cause customers to be misled.
8. Advertise and sell merchandise or service on its merit and refrain from attacking your competitors or reflecting unfairly upon their products, services, or methods of doing business.
9. If testimonials are used, use only those competent witnesses who are sincere and honest in what they say about what you sell.
10. Avoid all tricky devices and schemes such as deceitful trade-in allowance, fictitious list prices, false and exaggerated comparative prices, "bait" advertising, misleading "free" offers, fake sales and similar practices which prey upon human ignorance and gullibility.

# # #

Discussion

The full, annotated text of the Better Business Bureau Code of Advertising, far too lengthy for reprinting here, insists that "the primary responsibility for truthful and nondeceptive advertising rests with the advertiser." How does this square with the traditional philosophy of shrewd horsetrading (*caveat emptor*) that has characterized so much of American business history?

# # #

SELF-REGULATORY GUIDELINES FOR CHILDREN'S
ADVERTISING COUNCIL OF BETTER BUSINESS
BUREAUS, INC.

[Note: The material that follows is excerpted from a far more detailed document prepared by the Children's Advertising Review Unit (CARU) of the National Advertising Division of the Council of Better Business Bureaus. The CARU defines children as being under twelve years of age.]

Principles

Six basic Principles underlie CARU's Guidelines for advertising directed to children:

1. Advertisers should always take into account the level of knowledge, sophistication and maturity of the audience to which their message is primarily directed. Younger children have a limited capacity for evaluating the credibility of information they receive. Advertisers, therefore, have a special responsibility to protect children from their own susceptibilities.

2. Realizing that children are imaginative and that make-believe play constitutes an important part of the growing up process, advertisers should exercise care not to exploit unfairly the imaginative quality of children. Unreasonable expectations of product quality or performance should not be stimulated either directly or indirectly by advertising.

3. Recognizing that advertising may play an important part in educating the child, advertisers should communicate information in a truthful and accurate manner with full recognition that the child may learn practices from advertising which can affect his or her health and well-being.

4. Advertisers are urged to capitalize on the potential of advertising to influence behavior by developing advertising that, wherever possible, addresses itself to positive and beneficial social behavior, such as friendship, kindness, honesty, justice, generosity, and respect for others.

5. Care should be taken to incorporate minority and other groups in advertisements in order to present positive and pro-social roles wherever possible. Social stereotyping and appeals to prejudice should be avoided.

6. Although many influences affect a child's personal and social development, it remains the prime responsibility of the parents to provide guidance for children. Advertisers should contribute to this parent–child relationship in a constructive manner.

[While these principles embody the CARU philosophy, there are in the code detailed guidelines dealing with Product Presentation and claims, disclosures and disclaimers, comparative claims, endorsements and promotion by program or editorial characters, premiums and promotions, kids' clubs, sweepstakes, safety, and children's use of 900/976 teleprograms. As an example—it is not possible here to publish all of the guidelines—here is what the Code has to say regarding sales pressure.]

Sales Pressure

Children are not as prepared as adults to make judicious, independent purchasing decisions. Therefore, advertisers should avoid using extreme sales pressure in advertising presentations to children.

1. Children should not be urged to ask parents or others to buy products. Advertisements should not suggest that a parent or adult who purchases a product or service is better, more intelligent or more generous than one who does not. Advertising directed toward children should not create a sense of urgency or exclusivity, for example, by using words like "now" and "only."

2. Benefits attributed to the product or service should be inherent in its use. Advertisements should not convey the impression that possession of a product will result in more acceptance of a child by his or her peers. Conversely, it should not be implied that lack of a product will cause a child to be less accepted by his or her peers. Advertisements should not imply that purchase and use of a product will confer upon the user the prestige, skills or other special qualities of characters appearing in the advertising.

3. All price representations should be clearly and concisely set forth. Price minimizations such as "only" or "just" should not be used.

# # #

Discussion

Under "Product Presentation and Claims," one Code guideline reads: "Portrayals of violence and presentations that could frighten or provoke anxiety in children should be avoided." Given that restriction, can certain products (such as some video games) be advertised at all? If so, how?

# # #

THE DIRECT MARKETING ASSOCIATION GUIDELINES FOR ETHICAL BUSINESS PRACTICE

The Direct Marketing Associations Guidelines for Ethical Business Practices are intended to provide individuals and organizations involved in direct mail and direct marketing with principles of conduct that are generally accepted nationally and internationally. These Guidelines reflect DMA's longstanding policy of high levels of ethics and the responsibility of the Association and direct marketers to maintain with the consumer and the community relationships that are based on fair and ethical principles.

What distinguishes these Guidelines, which are self-regulatory in nature, is that all are urged to support them in spirit and not treat their provisions as obstacles to be circumvented by legal ingenuity. The Guidelines are intended to be honored in light of their aims and principles.

These Guidelines represent DMA's general philosophy that self-regulatory measures are preferable to governmental mandates whenever possible. Self-regulatory actions are more readily adaptable to changing techniques, economic and social conditions, and they encourage widespread use of sound business practices.

Because it is believed that dishonest, misleading, immoral, salacious, or offensive communications make enemies for all advertising marketing, including direct response marketing, observance of these Guidelines by all concerned is recommended.

The Terms of the Offer

Honesty. Article #1.   All offers should be clear, honest, and complete so that the consumer may know the exact nature of what is being offered, the price, the terms of payment (including all extra charges), and the commitment involved in the placing of an order. Before publication of an offer, direct marketers should be prepared to substantiate any claims or offers made. Advertisements or specific claims which are untrue, misleading, deceptive, fraudulent, or unjustly disparaging or competitors should not be used.

Clarity. Article #2.   A simple statement of all the essential points of the offer should be clearly displayed in the promotional material. When an offer illustrates goods that are not included or that cost extra, these facts should be made clear.

Print Size. Article #3.   Print which by its small size, placement, or other visual characteristics is likely to substantially affect the legibility of the offer or exceptions to it should not be used.

Actual Conditions. Article #4.   All descriptions and promises should be in accordance with actual conditions, situations, and circumstances existing at the time of the promotion. Claims regarding any limitations (such as time or quantity) should be legitimate.

Disparagement. Article #5. Disparagement of any person or group on grounds of race, color, religion, national origin, sex, marital status, or age is unacceptable.

Standards. Article #6. Solicitations should not contain vulgar, immoral, profane, or offensive matter nor promote the sale of pornographic material or other matter not acceptable for advertising on moral grounds.

Advertising to Children. Article #7. Offers suitable for adults only should not be made to children.

Photographs and Art Work. Article #8. Photographs, illustrations, artwork, and the situations they represent should be accurate portrayals and current reproductions of the products, services, or other subjects in all particulars.

Sponsor and Intent. Article #9. All direct marketing contacts should disclose the name of the sponsor and each purpose of the contact. No one should make offers or solicitations in the guise of research or a survey when the real intent is to sell products or services or to raise funds.

Identity of Seller. Article #10. Every offer and shipment should sufficiently identify the name and street address of the direct marketer so that the consumer may contact the individual or company by mail or phone.

Solicitation in the Guise of an Invoice. Article #11. Offers that are likely to be mistaken for bills or invoices should not be used.

Postage and Handling Charges. Article #12. Postage or shipping charges, or handling charges, if any, should reflect as accurately as practicable actual costs incurred.

Special Offers

Use of the Word **Free** *and Other Similar Representations. Article #13.* A product or service which is offered without cost or obligation to the recipient may be unqualifiedly described as "free."

If a product or service is offered as "free," for a nominal cost, or at a greatly reduced price, and/or if the offer requires the recipient to purchase some other product or service, all terms and conditions should be clearly and conspicuously disclosed, in close conjunction with the use of the term "free" or other similar phrase.

When the term "free" is used or other similar representations are made (for example, 2-for-1, half-price or 1-cent offers), the product or service required to be purchased should not have been increased in price or decreased in quality or quantity.

Negative Opinion Selling. Article #14. All direct marketers should comply with the FTC regulation governing Negative Option Plans. Some of the major requirements of this regulation are as follows:

Offers which require the consumer to return a notice sent by the seller before each periodic shipment to avoid receiving merchandise should contain all important conditions of the plan including:

a. A full description of the obligation to purchase a minimum number of items and all the charges involved, and

b. the procedures by which the consumer will receive the announcements of selections, and a statement of their frequency, as well as how to reject unwanted items, and how to cancel after completing the obligation.

The consumer should be given advance notice of the periodic selection so that the consumer may have a minimum of ten days to exercise a timely choice.

Because of the nature of this kind of offer, special attention should be given to the clarity, completeness, and prominent placement of the terms of the initial offering.

Sweepstakes

Sweepstakes, as defined here, are promotion devices by which items of value (prizes) are awarded to participants by chance without the promoter's requiring them to render something of value to be eligible to participate (consideration). The co-existence of all three elements—prize, chance, and consideration—in the same promotion constitutes a lottery. It is illegal for any private enterprise to run a lottery.

When skill replaces chance, the promotion becomes a skill contest. When gifts (premiums or other items of value) are given to all participants independent of the elements of chance, the promotion is not a sweepstakes and should not be held out as such.

Use of the Term **Sweepstakes.** *Article #15.* Only those promotional devices which satisfy the definition stated above should be called or held out to be sweepstakes.

No-Purchase Option. Article #16. The no-purchase option as well as the method for entering without ordering should be clearly disclosed. Response devices used only for entering the sweepstakes should be as visible as those utilized for ordering the product or service.

Prizes. Article #17. Sweepstakes prizes should be advertised in a manner that is clear, honest, and complete so that the consumer may know the exact nature of what is being offered.

Photographs, illustrations, artwork, and the situations they represent should be accurate portrayals of the prizes listed in the promotion.

No award should be held forth directly or by implication as having substantial monetary value if it is of nominal worth. The value of a prize given should be stated at regular retail value, whether actual cost to the sponsor is greater or less.

Prizes should be delivered without cost to the participant. If there are certain conditions under which a prize or prizes will not be awarded, this fact should be disclosed in a manner that is easy to find and understand.

Premium. Article #18. If a premium, gift, or item of value is offered by virtue of a participant's merely entering the sweepstakes, without any selection process taking place, it should be clear that everyone will receive it.

Chances of Winning. Article #19. No sweepstakes promotion, or any of its parts, should state or imply that a recipient has won a prize when this is not the case. Winners should be selected in a manner that ensures fair application of the laws of chance.

Disclosure of Rules. Article #20. All terms and conditions of the sweepstakes, including entry procedures and rules, should be easy to find, read, and understand.

The following should be set forth clearly in the rules.

—No purchase of the advertised product or service is required in order to win a prize.

—Procedures for entry.

—If applicable, disclosure that a facsimile of the entry blank or promotional device may be used to enter the sweepstakes.

—The termination date for eligibility in the sweepstakes. The termination date should specify whether it is a date of mailing or receipt of entry deadline.

—The number, retail value, and complete description of all prizes offered, and whether cash may be awarded instead of merchandise. If a cash prize is to be awarded by installment payments, that fact should be clearly disclosed, along with the nature and timing of the payments.

—The approximate odds of winning a prize or a statement that such odds depend on number of entrants.

—The method by which winners will be selected.

—The geographic area covered by the sweepstakes and those areas in which the offer is void.

—All eligibility requirements, if any.

—Approximate dates when winners will be selected and notified.

—Publicity rights re: the use of the winner's name.

—Taxes are the responsibility of the winner.

—Provision of a mailing address to allow consumers to submit a self-addressed, stamped envelope to receive a list of winners of prizes over $25.00 in value.

Special Claims

Price Comparisons. Article #21. Price comparisons may be made two ways:

a. between one's price and a former, future, or suggested price.
b. between one's price and the price of a competitor's comparable product.

In all price comparisons, the compared price against which the comparison is made should be fair and accurate.

In each case of comparison to a former, suggested, or competitor's comparable product price, substantial sales should have been made at that price in the recent past.

For comparisons with a future price, there should be a reasonable expectation that the new price will be charged in the foreseeable future.

Guarantees. Article #22. If a product or service is offered with a "guarantee," or a "warranty," either the terms and conditions should be set forth in full in the promotion, or the promotion should state how the consumer may obtain a copy. The guarantee should clearly state the name and address of the guarantor and the duration of the guarantee.

Any requests for repair, replacement, or refund under the terms of a "guarantee" or "warranty" should be honored promptly. In an unqualified offer of refund, repair, or replacement, the customer's preference shall prevail.

Use of Test or Survey Data. Article #23. All test or survey data referred to in advertising should be competent and reliable as to source and methodology, and should support the specific claim for which it is cited. Advertising claims should not distort the test or survey results, nor take them out of context.

Testimonials and Endorsements. Article #24. Testimonials and endorsements should be used only if they are:

a. Authorized by the person quoted.
b. Genuine and related to the experience of the person giving them, and
c. Not taken out of context so as to distort the endorser's opinion or experience with the product.

The Product

Product Safety. Article #25. Products should be safe in normal use and free of defects likely to cause injury. To that end, they should meet or exceed the current, recognized health and safety norms, and should be adequately tested, when applicable. Information provided with the product should include proper directions for its use and full instructions covering assembly and safety warnings whenever necessary.

Product Distribution Safety. Article #26. Products should be distributed only in a manner that will provide reasonable safeguards against possibilities of injury.

Product Availability. Article #27. Direct marketers should offer merchandise only when it is on hand or when there is a reasonable expectation of its receipt.

Direct marketers should not engage in dry testing, unless that special nature of the offer is disclosed in the promotion.

Fulfillment

Unordered Merchandise. Article #28. Merchandise should not be shipped without having first received the customer's permission. The exceptions are samples or gifts clearly marked as such, and merchandise mailed by a charitable organization soliciting contributions, as long as all items are sent with a clear and conspicuous statement informing the recipient of an unqualified right to treat the product as a gift and to do with it as the recipient sees fit, at no cost or obligation to the recipient.

Shipments. Article #29. Direct marketers are reminded that they should abide by the FTC regulation regarding the prompt shipment of prepaid merchandise, the Mail Order Merchandise (Thirty-Day) Rule.

Beyond this regulation, direct marketers are urged to ship all orders as soon as possible.

Credit and Debt Collection

Equal Credit Opportunity. Article #30. A creditor should not discriminate on the basis of race, color, religion, national origin, sex, marital status, or age. If an individual is rejected for credit, the creditor should be prepared to give reasons why.

Debt Collection. Article #31. Unfair, misleading, deceptive or abusive methods should not be used for collecting money. The direct marketer should take reasonable steps to assure that those collecting on the direct marketer's behalf comply with this guideline.

Use of Mailing Lists

List Rental Practices. Article #32. Consumers who provide data that may be rented, sold, or exchanged for direct marketing purposes periodically should be informed of the potential for the rental, sale, or exchange of such data. Marketers should offer an opportunity to have a consumer's name deleted or suppressed upon request.

List compilers should suppress names from lists when requested by the individual.

For each list that is to be rented, sold, or exchanged, the DMA Mail Preference Service name-removal list and, when applicable, the DMA Telephone Preference Service name-removal list should be used. Names found on such suppression lists should not be rented, sold, or exchanged, except for suppression purposes.

All persons involved in the rental, sale, or exchange of lists and data should take reasonable steps to ensure that industry members follow these guidelines.

Personal Information. Article #33. Direct marketers should be sensitive to the issue of consumer privacy and should limit the combination, collection, rental, sale, exchange, and use of consumer data only to those data which are appropriate for direct marketing purposes.

Information and selection criteria that may be considered to be personal and intimate in nature by all reasonable standards should not provide the basis for lists made available for rental, sale, or exchange when there is a reasonable expectation by the consumer that the information will be kept confidential.

Any advertising or promotion for lists being offered for rental, sale, or exchange should reflect the fact that a list is an aggregate collection of marketing data. Such promotions should also reflect a sensitivity for the consumers on those lists.

List Usage Agreements. Article #34. List owners, brokers, compilers, and users should make every attempt to establish the exact nature of the list's intended usage prior to the sale or rental of the list. Owners, brokers, and compilers should not permit the sale of rental of their lists for an offer that is in violation of any of the Ethical Guidelines of DMA. Promotions should be directed to those segments of the public most likely to be interested in their causes or to have a use for their products and services.

List Abuse. Article #35. No list or list data should be used in violation of the lawful rights of the list owner nor the agreement between the parties; any such misuse should be brought to the attention of the lawful owner.

Telephone Marketing

Reasonable Hours. Article #36. All telephone contacts should be made during reasonable hours.

Taping of Conversations. Article #37. Taping of telephone conversations made for telephone marketing purposes should not be conducted without legal notice to or consent of all parties, or the use of a beeping device.

Telephone Name Removal/Restricted Contacts. Article #38. Telephone marketers should remove the name of any customer from their telephone lists when requested by the individual. Marketers should use the DMA Telephone Preference Service name-removal list and, when applicable, the Mail Preference Service name-removal list. Names found on such suppression lists should not be rented, sold, or exchanged, except for suppression purposes.

A telephone marketer should not knowingly call anyone who has an unlisted or unpublished telephone number, except in instances where the number was provided by the customer to that marketer.

Random dialing techniques, whether a manual or automated process, in which selection of those parties to be called is based on the location of their telephone numbers in a sequence of telephone numbers should not be used.

Disclosure and Tactics. Article #39. All telephone solicitations should disclose to the buyer, during the conversation, the cost of the merchandise, all terms, conditions, and the payment plan, and whether there will be postage and handling charges. At no time should "high pressure" tactics be utilized.

Use of Automatic Electronic Equipment. Article #40. No telephone marketer should solicit sales using automatic electronic dialing equipment unless the telephone immediately disconnects when the called person hangs up.

Fund-Raising

Commission Prohibition/Authenticity of Organization. Article #41. Fund-raisers should make no percentage or commission arrangements whereby any person or firm assisting or participating in a fund-raising activity is paid a fee proportionate to the funds raised, nor should they solicit for non-functioning organizations.

Laws, Codes, and Regulations

Article #42. Direct marketers should operate in accordance with the Better Business Bureau's Code of Advertising and be cognizant of and adhere to laws and regulations of the United States Postal Service, the Federal Trade Commission, the Federal Reserve Board, and other applicable federal, state, and local laws governing advertising, marketing practices, and the transaction of business by mail, telephone, and the print and broadcast media.

# # #

Discussion

The DMA code is the only one presented in this chapter that warns specifically in its opening passages that members are urged to honor the code in both letter and spirit and "not treat their provisions as obstacles to be circumvented by legal ingenuity." Are there any other codes in this chapter that would lend themselves to this advice? Which provisions of which codes?

In Article 39 (Disclosure and Tactics), the DMA code asserts that in telephone solicitations "at no time should 'high pressure' tactics be utilized." At what point does aggressive selling become "high pressure tactics?"

# # #

CODE OF ETHICS
Adopted by the Society of Professional Journalists
September 21, 1996

Preamble

Members of the Society of Professional Journalists believe that public enlightenment is the forerunner of justice and the foundation of democracy. The duty of the journalist is to further those ends by seeking truth and providing a fair and comprehensive account of events and issues. Conscientious journalists from all media and specialties strive to serve the public with thoroughness and honesty. Professional integrity is the cornerstone of a journalist's credibility.

Members of the Society share a dedication to ethical behavior and adopt this code to declare the Society's principles and standards of practice.

Seek Truth and Report It

Journalists should be honest, fair and courageous in gathering, reporting and interpreting information.

Journalists should:

- Test the accuracy of information from all sources and exercise care to avoid inadvertent error. Deliberate distortion is never permissible.
- Diligently seek out subjects of news stories to give them the opportunity to respond to allegations of wrongdoing.
- Identify sources whenever feasible. The public is entitled to as much information as possible on sources' reliability.
- Always question sources' motives before promising anonymity. Clarify conditions attached to any promise made in exchange for information. Keep promises.
- Make certain that headlines, news teases and promotional material, photos, video, audio, graphics, sound bites and quotations do not misrepresent. They should not oversimplify or highlight incidents out of context.
- Never distort the content of news photos or video. Image enhancement for technical clarity is always permissible. Label montages and photo illustrations.

- Avoid misleading re-enactments or staged news events. If re-enactment is necessary to tell a story, label it.
- Avoid undercover or other surreptitious methods of gathering information except when traditional open methods will not yield information vital to the public. Use of such methods should be explained as part of the story.
- Never plagiarize.
- Tell the story of the diversity and magnitude of the human experience boldly, even when it is unpopular to do so.
- Examine their own cultural values and avoid imposing those values on others.
- Avoid stereotyping by race, gender, age, religion, ethnicity, geography, sexual orientation, disability, physical appearance or social status.
- Support the open exchange of views, even views they find repugnant.
- Give voice to the voiceless; official and unofficial sources of information can be equally valid.
- Distinguish between advocacy and news reporting. Analysis and commentary should be labeled and not misrepresent fact or context.
- Distinguish news from advertising and shun hybrids that blur the lines between the two.
- Recognize a special obligation to ensure that the public's business is conducted in the open and that government records are open to inspection.

Minimize Harm

Ethical journalists treat sources, subjects and colleagues as human beings deserving of respect.
Journalists should:

- Show compassion for those who may be affected adversely by news coverage. Use special sensitivity when dealing with children and inexperienced sources or subjects.
- Be sensitive when seeking or using interviews or photographs of those affected by tragedy or grief.
- Recognize that gathering and reporting information may cause harm or discomfort. Pursuit of the news is not a license for arrogance.
- Recognize that private people have a greater right to control information about themselves than do public officials and others who seek power, influence or attention. Only an overriding public need can justify intrusion into anyone's privacy.
- Show good taste. Avoid pandering to lurid curiosity.
- Be cautious about identifying juvenile suspects or victims of sex crimes.
- Be judicious about naming criminal suspects before the formal filing of charges.

- Balance a criminal suspect's fair trial rights with the public's right to be informed.

Act Independently

Journalists should be free of obligation to any interest other than the public's right to know.
    Journalists should:

- Avoid conflicts of interest, real or perceived.
- Remain free of associations and activities that may compromise integrity or damage credibility.
- Refuse gifts, favors, fees, free travel and special treatment, and shun secondary employment, political involvement, public office and service in community organizations if they compromise journalistic integrity.
- Disclose unavoidable conflicts.
- Be vigilant and courageous about holding those with power accountable.
- Deny favored treatment to advertisers and special interests and resist their pressure to influence news coverage.
- Be wary of sources offering information for favors or money; avoid bidding for news.

Be Accountable

Journalists are accountable to their readers, listeners, viewers and each other.
    Journalists should:

- Clarify and explain news coverage and invite dialogue with the public over journalistic conduct.
- Encourage the public to voice grievances against the news media.
- Admit mistakes and correct them promptly.
- Expose unethical practices of journalists and the news media.
- Abide by the same high standards to which they hold others.

RADIO-TELEVISION NEWS DIRECTORS ASSOCIATION CODE OF BROADCAST NEWS ETHICS

The responsibility of radio and television journalists is to gather and report information of importance and interest to the public accurately, honestly, and impartially.
    The members of the Radio-Television News Directors Association accept these standards and will:

1. Strive to present the source or nature of broadcast news material in a way that is balanced, accurate, and fair.

A. They will evaluate information solely on its merits as news, rejecting sensationalism or misleading emphasis in any form.
B. They will guard against using audio or video material in a way that deceives the audience.
C. They will not mislead the public by presenting as spontaneous news any material which is staged or rehearsed.
D. They will identify people by race, creed, nationality, or prior status only when it is relevant.
E. They will clearly label opinion and commentary.
F. They will promptly acknowledge and correct errors.
2. Strive to conduct themselves in a manner that protects them from conflicts of interest, real or perceived. They will decline gifts or favors which would influence or appear to influence their judgments.
3. Respect the dignity, privacy, and well-being of people with whom they deal.
4. Recognize the need to protect confidential sources. They will promise confidentiality only with the intention of keeping that promise.
5. Respect everyone's right to a fair trial.
6. Broadcast the private transmissions of other broadcasters only with permission.
7. Actively encourage observance of this Code by all journalists, whether members of the Radio-Television News Directors Association or not.

# # #

Discussion

In item #3 above: How, while attempting to cover spectacular stories such as the murder trial of celebrity O. J. Simpson, can television news "respect the dignity, privacy, and well-being of people with whom they deal?"

THE LOUISVILLE *COURIER-JOURNAL* POLICY STATEMENT ON ETHICS

In its briefest form, our policy is that we insist on paying all expenses for any story we cover. We always expect to pay our own way.

Any travel for either a story or story-research is company travel. Even on chartered trips (such as accompanying a sports team) or hitchhiking on a state police plane, we insist on being billed for our pro-rata share of the expense.

If you cover a luncheon club meeting, you are expected to pay for your luncheon and turn in your expense account. We do not carry entertainment to the point of absurdity. There is nothing wrong with luncheon with a news source and having the tab picked up. However, we firmly believe in the *quid pro quo*—and staff people are expected to do their share (at company expense, of course) of reaching for the checks.

In sports, our staffers who cover accept press box tickets, but those who choose to go for their own pleasure are expected to pay like all other citizens. In two words: no passes. The same goes for field entertainment. Should any questions ever be raised about tickets for those we cover, we elect to pay.

No staff member may involve himself or herself in any outside writing activity without permission from the department head. Some "stringer" assignments have been approved for national publications, but there can be no outside involvement without review and consent.

Gifts are not accepted from any source. There are many which come to the various departments. These are turned in to the editor's office. They are contributed to charitable agencies (suitable toys to Children's Hospital; some foodstuffs to the Salvation Army; miscellaneous items to the Cabbage Patch Settlement) and letters sent to those sending the gifts, notifying them that the articles have gone to charity.

In the field of business news coverage, we have asked that our staffers never use for their own personal means any advance information that might come to them. There are bound to be occasions when men and women in this area of enterprise learn things which could be advantageous. All we ask is that no private action ever be taken until readers of our newspapers have the same opportunity.

You can see, therefore, that we have tried—and continue to try—to make this as honorable and ethical a newspaper operation as exists anywhere in the world. We do not stand over anyone's shoulder looking for violations. We have simply stated what we believe to be reasonable (although firm) guidelines and it has been our experience that staffers have welcomed these "rules of conduct" and abide by them with pride in themselves and their newspaper. We invite not only full collaboration but any suggestions for improvement.

# # #

Discussion

This statement, actually a memorandum written by Norman Isaacs, then editor of the *Courier-Journal*, to the staff in 1967, was one of the earlier "purity codes" of conduct for newspaper reporters and editors. In previous years, "freebies" and junkets were routinely accepted throughout the industry. Many newspapers have since adopted detailed ethical codes. Have tough professional codes and policy statements improved professionalism—or, perhaps more important, the appearance of professionalism—in the journalism field? Why or why not?

# # #

Appendix B:
The Constitution of the United States

PREAMBLE

WE THE PEOPLE of the United States, in Order to form a more perfect Union, establish Justice, insure domestic Tranquility, provide for the common defence, promote the general Welfare, and secure the Blessings of Liberty to ourselves and our Posterity, do ordain and establish this Constitution for the United States of America.

Articles

ARTICLE ONE

Section 1. All legislative powers herein granted shall be vested in a Congress of the United States, which shall consist of a Senate and House of Representatives.

Section 2. The House of Representatives shall be composed of members chosen every second year by the people of the several States, and the electors in each State shall have the qualifications requisite for electors of the most numerous branch of the State legislature.

No Person shall be a Representative who shall not have attained to the age of twenty five years, and been seven years a citizen of the United States, and who shall not, when elected, be an inhabitant of that State in which he shall be chosen.

Representatives and direct taxes shall be apportioned among the several States which may be included within this Union, according to their respective numbers, which shall be determined by adding to the whole number of free persons, including those bound to service for a term of years, and excluding Indians not taxed, three fifths of all other persons. The actual enumeration shall be made within three years after the first meeting of the Congress of the United States, and within every subsequent term of ten years, in such manner as they shall by law direct. The number of Representatives shall not exceed one for every thirty thousand, but each State shall have at least one Representative; and until such enumeration shall be made, the State of New Hampshire shall be entitled to choose three, Massachusetts eight, Rhode Island and Providence Plantations one, Connecticut five, New York six, New Jersey four, Pennsylvania eight, Delaware one, Maryland six, Virginia ten, North Carolina five, South Carolina five and Georgia three.

When vacancies happen in the Representation from any State, the executive authority thereof shall issue writs of election to fill such vacancies.

The House of Representatives shall choose their Speaker and other officers; and shall have the sole power of Impeachment.

Section 3. The Senate of the United States shall be composed of two Senators from each State, chosen by the legislature thereof, for six years; and each Senator shall have one Vote.

Immediately after they shall be assembled in consequence of the first election, they shall be divided as equally as may be into three classes. The seats of the Senators of the first class shall be vacated at the expiration of the second year, of the second class at the expiration of the fourth year, and of the third class at the expiration of the sixth year, so that one third may be chosen every second year; and if vacancies happen by resignation, or otherwise, during the recess of the legislature of any State, the executive thereof may make temporary appointments until the next meeting of the legislature, which shall then fill such vacancies.

No person shall be a Senator who shall not have attained to the age of thirty years, and been nine years a citizen of the United States, and who shall not, when elected, be an inhabitant of that State for which he shall be chosen.

The Vice-President of the United States shall be President of the Senate, but shall have no vote, unless they be equally divided.

The Senate shall choose their other officers, and also a President pro tempore, in the absence of the Vice-President, or when he shall exercise the office of President of the United States.

The Senate shall have the sole power to try all impeachments. When sitting for that purpose, they shall be on oath or affirmation. When the President of the United States is tried, the Chief Justice shall preside: And no Person shall be convicted without the concurrence of two thirds of the members present.

Judgment in cases of impeachment shall not extend further than to removal from office, and disqualification to hold and enjoy any office of honor, trust or profit under the United States: but the party convicted shall nevertheless be liable and subject to indictment, trial, judgment and punishment, according to law.

Section 4. The times, places and manner of holding elections for Senators and Representatives, shall be prescribed in each State by the legislature thereof; but the Congress may at any time by law make or alter such regulations, except as to the places of choosing Senators.

The Congress shall assemble at least once in every year, and such meeting shall be on the first Monday in December, unless they shall by law appoint a different day.

Section 5. Each house shall be the judge of the elections, returns and qualifications of its own members, and a majority of each shall constitute a quorum to do business; but a smaller number may adjourn from day to day, and may be authorized to compel the attendance of absent members, in such manner, and under such penalties as each house may provide.

Each house may determine the rules of its proceedings, punish its members for disorderly behavior, and, with the concurrence of two-thirds, expel a member.

Each house shall keep a journal of its proceedings, and from time to time publish the same, excepting such parts as may in their judgment require secrecy; and the yeas and nays of the members of either house on any question shall, at the desire of one fifth of those present, be entered on the journal.

Neither house, during the session of Congress, shall, without the consent of the other, adjourn for more than three days, nor to any other place than that in which the two Houses shall be sitting.

Section 6. The Senators and Representatives shall receive a compensation for their services, to be ascertained by law, and paid out of the Treasury of the United States. They shall in all cases, except treason, felony and breach of the peace, be privileged from arrest during their attendance at the session of their respective houses, and in going to and returning from the same; and for any speech or debate in either house, they shall not be questioned in any other place.

No Senator or Representative shall, during the time for which he was elected, be appointed to any civil office under the authority of the United States which shall have been created, or the emoluments whereof shall have been increased during such time; and no person holding any office under the United States, shall be a member of either house during his continuance in office.

Section 7. All bills for raising revenue shall originate in the House of Representatives; but the Senate may propose or concur with amendments as on other bills.

Every bill which shall have passed the House of Representatives and the Senate, shall, before it become a law, be presented to the President of the United

States; If he approve he shall sign it, but if not he shall return it, with his objections to that house in which it shall have originated, who shall enter the objections at large on their journal, and proceed to reconsider it. If after such reconsideration two thirds of that house shall agree to pass the bill, it shall be sent, together with the objections, to the other house, by which it shall likewise be reconsidered, and if approved by two thirds of that house, it shall become a law. But in all such cases the votes of both houses shall be determined by yeas and nays, and the names of the persons voting for and against the bill shall be entered on the journal of each house respectively. If any bill shall not be returned by the President within ten days (Sundays excepted) after it shall have been presented to him, the same shall be a law, in like manner as if he had signed it, unless the Congress by their adjournment prevent its return, in which case it shall not be a law.

Every order, resolution, or vote to which the concurrence of the Senate and House of Representatives may be necessary (except on a question of adjournment) shall be presented to the President of the United States; and before the same shall take effect, shall be approved by him, or being disapproved by him, shall be repassed by two thirds of the Senate and House of Representatives, according to the rules and limitations prescribed in the case of a bill.

Section 8. The Congress shall have power to lay and collect taxes, duties, imposts and excises, to pay the debts and provide for the common defence and general welfare of the United States; but all duties, imposts and excises shall be uniform throughout the United States;

To borrow money on the credit of the United States;

To regulate commerce with foreign nations, and among the several States, and with the Indian tribes;

To establish an uniform rule of naturalization, and uniform Laws on the subject of bankruptcies throughout the United States;

To coin money, regulate the value thereof, and of foreign coin, and fix the standard of weights and measures;

To provide for the punishment of counterfeiting the securities and current Coin of the United States;

To establish post-offices and post-roads;

To promote the progress of science and useful arts, by securing for limited times to authors and inventors the exclusive right to their respective writings and discoveries;

To constitute tribunals inferior to the Supreme Court;

To define and punish piracies and felonies committed on the high seas, and offenses against the law of nations;

To declare war, grant letters of marque and reprisal, and make rules concerning captures on land and water;

To raise and support armies, but no appropriation of money to that use shall be for a longer term than two years;

To provide and maintain a navy;

To make rules for the government and regulation of the land and naval forces;

To provide for calling forth the militia to execute the laws of the union, suppress insurrections and repel invasions;

To provide for organizing, arming, and disciplining, the militia, and for governing such part of them as may be employed in the service of the United States, reserving to the States respectively, the appointment of the officers, and the authority of training the militia according to the discipline prescribed by Congress;

To exercise exclusive legislation in all cases whatsoever, over such district (not exceeding ten miles square) as may, by cession of particular States, and the acceptance of Congress, become the seat of the Government of the United States, and to exercise like authority over all places purchased by the consent of the legislature of the State in which the same shall be, for the erection of forts, magazines, arsenals, dockyards, and other needful Buildings; and

To make all laws which shall be necessary and proper for carrying into execution the foregoing powers, and all other powers vested by this Constitution in the Government of the United States, or in any department or officer thereof.

Section 9. The migration or importation of such persons as any of the States now existing shall think proper to admit, shall not be prohibited by the Congress prior to the Year one thousand eight hundred and eight, but a tax or duty may be imposed on such importation, not exceeding ten dollars for each person.

The privilege of the writ of habeas corpus shall not be suspended, unless when in cases of rebellion or invasion the public safety may require it.

No bill of attainder or ex post facto law shall be passed.

No capitation, or other direct tax shall be laid, unless in proportion to the census or enumeration herein before directed to be taken.

No tax or duty shall be laid on articles exported from any State.

No preference shall be given by any regulation of commerce or revenue to the ports of one State over those of another: nor shall vessels bound to, or from, one State, be obliged to enter, clear, or pay duties in another.

No money shall be drawn from the Treasury, but in consequence of appropriations made by law; and a regular statement and account of the receipts and expenditures of all public money shall be published from time to time.

No title of nobility shall be granted by the United States; and no person holding any office of profit or trust under them, shall, without the consent of the Congress, accept of any present, emolument, office, or title, of any kind whatever, from any king, prince or foreign State.

Section 10. No State shall enter into any treaty, alliance, or confederation; grant letters of marque and reprisal; coin money; emit bills of credit; make anything but gold and silver coin a tender in payment of debts; pass any bill of attainder, ex post facto law, or law impairing the obligation of contracts, or grant any title of nobility.

No State shall, without the consent of the Congress, lay any imposts or duties on imports or exports, except what may be absolutely necessary for executing it's inspection laws: and the net produce of all duties and imposts, laid by any State on imports or exports, shall be for the use of the Treasury of the United States; and all such laws shall be subject to the revision and control of the Congress.

No State shall, without the consent of Congress, lay any duty of tonnage, keep troops, or ships of war in time of peace, enter into any agreement or compact with another State, or with a foreign power, or engage in war, unless actually invaded, or in such imminent danger as will not admit of delay.

ARTICLE TWO

Section 1. The executive power shall be vested in a President of the United States of America. He shall hold his office during the term of four years, and, together with the Vice-President chosen for the same term, be elected, as follows:

Each State shall appoint, in such manner as the legislature thereof may direct, a number of electors, equal to the whole number of Senators and Representatives to which the State may be entitled in the Congress: but no Senator or Representative, or person holding an office of trust or profit under the United States, shall be appointed an elector.

The electors shall meet in their respective States, and vote by ballot for two persons, of whom one at least shall not lie an inhabitant of the same State with themselves. And they shall make a list of all the persons voted for, and of the number of votes for each; which list they shall sign and certify, and transmit sealed to the seat of the government of the United States, directed to the President of the Senate. The President of the Senate shall, in the presence of the Senate and House of Representatives, open all the certificates, and the votes shall then be counted. The person having the greatest number of votes shall be the President, if such number be a majority of the whole number of electors appointed; and if there be more than one who have such majority, and have an equal number of votes, then the House of Representatives shall immediately choose by ballot one of them for President; and if no person have a majority, then from the five highest on the list the said House shall in like manner choose the President. But in choosing the President, the votes shall be taken by States, the representation from each State having one vote; a quorum for this purpose shall consist of a member or members from two thirds of the States, and a majority of all the States shall be necessary to a choice. In every case, after the choice of the President, the person having the greatest number of votes of the electors shall be the Vice-President. But if there should remain two or more who have equal votes, the Senate shall choose from them by ballot the Vice-President.

The Congress may determine the time of choosing the electors, and the day on which they shall give their votes; which day shall be the same throughout the United States.

No person except a natural born citizen, or a citizen of the United States, at the time of the adoption of this Constitution, shall be eligible to the office of President; neither shall any person be eligible to that office who shall not have attained to the age of thirty five years, and been fourteen years a resident within the United States.

In case of the removal of the President from office, or of his death, resignation, or inability to discharge the powers and duties of the said office, the same shall devolve on the Vice-President, and the Congress may by law provide for the case of removal, death, resignation or inability, both of the President and Vice-President, declaring what officer shall then act as President, and such officer shall act accordingly, until the disability be removed, or a President shall be elected.

The President shall, at stated times, receive for his services, a compensation, which shall neither be increased nor diminished during the period for which he shall have been elected, and he shall not receive within that period any other emolument from the United States, or any of them.

Before he enter on the execution of his office, he shall take the following oath or affirmation:

"I do solemnly swear (or affirm) that I will faithfully execute the office of President of the United States, and will to the best of my ability, preserve, protect and defend the Constitution of the United States."

Section 2. The President shall be Commander-in-Chief of the Army and Navy of the United States, and of the militia of the several States, when called into the actual service of the United States; he may require the opinion, in writing, of the principal officer in each of the executive departments, upon any subject relating to the duties of their respective offices, and he shall have power to grant reprieves and pardons for offenses against the United States, except in cases of impeachment.

He shall have power, by and with the advice and consent of the Senate, to make treaties, provided two thirds of the Senators present concur; and he shall nominate, and by and with the advice and consent of the Senate, shall appoint ambassadors, other public ministers and consuls, judges of the Supreme Court, and all other officers of the United States, whose appointments are not herein otherwise provided for, and which shall be established by law: but the Congress may by law vest the appointment of such inferior officers, as they think proper, in the President alone, in the courts of law, or in the heads of departments.

The President shall have power to fill up all vacancies that may happen during the recess of the Senate, by granting commissions which shall expire at the end of their next session.

Section 3. He shall from time to time give to the Congress information of the State of the Union, and recommend to their consideration such measures as he shall judge necessary and expedient; he may, on extraordinary occasions, convene both houses, or either of them, and in case of disagreement between them, with respect to the time of adjournment, he may adjourn them to such time as he shall think proper; he shall receive ambassadors and other public ministers; he shall take care that the laws be faithfully executed, and shall commission all the officers of the United States.

Section 4. The President, Vice-President and all civil officers of the United States, shall be removed from office on impeachment for, and conviction of, treason, bribery, or other high crimes and misdemeanors.

ARTICLE THREE

Section 1. The judicial power of the United States, shall be vested in one Supreme Court, and in such inferior courts as the Congress may from time to time ordain and establish. The judges, both of the supreme and inferior courts, shall hold their offices during good behavior, and shall, at stated times, receive for their services, a compensation, which shall not be diminished during their continuance in office.

Section 2. The judicial power shall extend to all cases, in law and equity, arising under this Constitution, the laws of the United States, and treaties made, or which shall be made, under their authority; to all cases affecting ambassadors, other public ministers and consuls; to all cases of admiralty and maritime jurisdiction; to controversies to which the United States shall be a party; to controversies between two or more States; between a State and citizens of another State; between citizens of different States; between citizens of the same State claiming lands under grants of different States, and between a State, or the citizens thereof, and foreign States, citizens or subjects.

In all cases affecting ambassadors, other public ministers and consuls, and those in which a State shall be party, the Supreme Court shall have original jurisdiction. In all the other cases before mentioned, the Supreme Court shall have appellate jurisdiction, both as to law and fact, with such exceptions, and under such regulations as the Congress shall make.

Trial of all crimes, except in cases of impeachment, shall be by jury; and such trial shall be held in the State where the said crimes shall have been committed; but when not committed within any State, the trial shall be at such place or places as the Congress may by law have directed.

Section 3. Treason against the United States, shall consist only in levying war against them, or in adhering to their enemies, giving them aid and comfort. No person shall be convicted of treason unless on the testimony of two witnesses to the same overt act, or on confession in open court.

The Congress shall have power to declare the punishment of treason, but no attainder of treason shall work corruption of blood, or forfeiture except during the life of the person attainted.

ARTICLE FOUR

Section 1. Full faith and credit shall be given in each State to the public acts, records, and judicial proceedings of every other State. And the Congress may by general laws prescribe the manner in which such acts, records and proceedings shall be proved, and the effect thereof.

Section 2. The citizens of each State shall be entitled to all privileges and immunities of citizens in the several States.

A person charged in any State with treason, felony, or other crime, who shall flee from justice, and be found in another State, shall on demand of the executive authority of the State from which he fled, be delivered up, to be removed to the State having jurisdiction of the crime.

No person held to service or labor in one State, under the laws thereof, escaping into another, shall, in consequence of any law or regulation therein, be discharged from such service or labor, But shall be delivered up on claim of the party to whom such service or labor may be due.

Section 3. New States may be admitted by the Congress into this Union; but no new States shall be formed or erected within the jurisdiction of any other State; nor any State be formed by the junction of two or more States, or parts of States, without the consent of the legislatures of the States concerned as well as of the Congress.

The Congress shall have power to dispose of and make all needful rules and regulations respecting the territory or other property belonging to the United States; and nothing in this Constitution shall be so construed as to prejudice any claims of the United States, or of any particular State.

Section 4. The United States shall guarantee to every State in this Union a republican form of government, and shall protect each of them against invasion; and on application of the legislature, or of the executive (when the legislature cannot be convened) against domestic violence.

ARTICLE FIVE

The Congress, whenever two thirds of both houses shall deem it necessary, shall propose amendments to this Constitution, or, on the application of the Legislatures of two thirds of the several States, shall call a convention for proposing amendments, which, in either case, shall be valid to all intents and purposes, as part of this Constitution, when ratified by the Legislatures of three fourths of the several States, or by conventions in three fourths thereof, as the one or the other mode of ratification may be proposed by the Congress; provided that no amendment which may be made prior to the Year One thousand eight hundred and eight shall in any manner affect the first and fourth Clauses in the Ninth Section of the first Article; and that no State, without its consent, shall be deprived of it's equal suffrage in the Senate.

ARTICLE SIX

All debts contracted and engagements entered into, before the adoption of this Constitution, shall be as valid against the United States under this Constitution, as under the Confederation.

This Constitution, and the laws of the United States which shall be made in pursuance thereof; and all treaties made, or which shall be made, under the authority of the United States, shall be the supreme law of the land; and the judges in every State shall be bound thereby, anything in the Constitution or laws of any State to the contrary notwithstanding.

The Senators and Representatives before mentioned, and the members of the several State Legislatures, and all executive and judicial officers, both of the United States and of the several States, shall be bound by oath or affirmation, to support this Constitution; but no religious test shall ever be required as a qualification to any office or public trust under the United States

ARTICLE SEVEN

The ratification of the Conventions of nine States, shall be sufficient for the establishment of this Constitution between the States so ratifying the same.

Done in Convention by the unanimous consent of the States present the seventeenth day of September in the year of our Lord one thousand seven hundred and eighty-seven and of the Independence of the United States of America the twelfth, in witness whereof we have hereunto subscribed our Names,

GEO. WASHINGTON—President and deputy from Virginia

New Hampshire
JOHN LANGDON
NICHOLAS GILMAN

Massachusetts
NATHANIEL GORHAM
RUFUS KING

Connecticut
WM SAML JOHNSON
ROGER SHERMAN

New York
ALEXANDER HAMILTON

New Jersey
WIL. LIVINGSTON
DAVID BREARLEY
WM PATERSON
JONA. DAYTON

Pennsylvania
B FRANKLIN
THOMAS MIFFLIN
ROBT MORRIS
GEO CLYMER
THOS FITZSIMONS
JARED INGERSOLL
JAMES WILSON
GOUV. MORRIS

Delaware
GEO READ
GUNNING BEDFORD JUN.
JOHN DICKINSON
RICHARD BASSETT
JACO. BROOM

Maryland
JAMES McHENRY
DAN of ST THO JENIFER
DANL CARROLL

Virginia
JOHN BLAIR
JAMES MADISON JR.

North Carolina
WM BLOUNT
RICHD DOBBS SPAIGHT
HU WILLIAMSON

South Carolina
J. RUTLEDGE
CHARLES COTESWORTH PINCKNEY
CHARLES PINCKNEY
PIERCE BUTLER

Georgia
WILLIAM FEW

ABR BALDWIN

<u>Attest</u>
William Jackson

Amendments

AMENDMENT ONE

Congress shall make no law respecting an establishment of religion, or prohibiting the free exercise thereof; or abridging the freedom of speech, or of the press; or the right of the people peaceably to assemble, and to petition the government for a redress of grievances.

AMENDMENT TWO

A well regulated militia, being necessary to the security of a free State, the right of the people to keep and bear arms, shall not be infringed.

AMENDMENT THREE

No soldier shall, in time of peace be quartered in any house, without the consent of the owner, nor in time of war, but in a manner to be prescribed by law.

AMENDMENT FOUR

The right of the people to be secure in their persons, houses, papers, and effects, against unreasonable searches and seizures, shall not be violated, and no warrants shall issue, but upon probable cause, supported by Oath or affirmation, and particularly describing the place to be searched, and the persons or things to be seized.

AMENDMENT FIVE

No person shall be held to answer for a capital, or otherwise infamous crime, unless on a presentment or indictment of a Grand Jury, except in cases arising in the land or naval forces, or in the militia, when in actual service in time of war or public danger; nor shall any person be subject for the same offence to be twice put in jeopardy of life or limb; nor shall be compelled in any criminal case to be a witness against himself, nor be deprived of life, liberty, or property, without due process of law; nor shall private property be taken for public use, without just compensation.

AMENDMENT SIX

In all criminal prosecutions, the accused shall enjoy the right to a speedy and public trial, by an impartial jury of the State and district wherein the crime shall have been committed, which district shall have been previously ascertained by law, and to be informed of the nature and cause of the accusation; to be confronted with the witnesses against him; to have compulsory process for obtaining witnesses in his favor, and to have the assistance of counsel for his defence.

AMENDMENT SEVEN

In suits at common law, where the value in controversy shall exceed twenty dollars, the right of trial by jury shall be preserved, and no fact tried by a jury, shall be otherwise re-examined in any court of the United States, than according to the rules of the common law.

AMENDMENT EIGHT

Excessive bail shall not lie required, nor excessive fines imposed, nor cruel and unusual punishments inflicted.

AMENDMENT NINE

The enumeration in the Constitution, of certain rights, shall not be construed to deny or disparage others retained by the people.

AMENDMENT TEN

The powers not delegated to the United States by the Constitution, nor prohibited by it to the States, are reserved to the States respectively, or to the people.

AMENDMENT ELEVEN

January 8, 1798

The judicial power of the United States shall not be construed to extend to any suit in law or equity, commenced or prosecuted against one of the United States by Citizens of another State, or by citizens or subjects of any foreign State.

AMENDMENT TWELVE

September 25, 1804

The electors shall meet in their respective States, and vote by ballot for President and Vice-President, one of whom, at least, shall not be an inhabitant of the same State with themselves; they shall name in their ballots the person voted for as President, and in distinct ballots the person voted for as Vice-President, and they shall make distinct lists of all persons voted for as President, and of all persons voted for as Vice-President and of the number of votes for each, which lists they shall sign and certify, and transmit sealed to the seat of the Government of the United States, directed to the President of the Senate; The President of the Senate shall, in the presence of the Senate and House of Representatives, open all the certificates and the votes shall then be counted; the person having the greatest number of votes for President, shall be the President, if such number be a majority of the whole number of Electors appointed; and if no person have such majority, then from the persons having the highest numbers not exceeding three on the list of those voted for as President, the House of Representatives shall choose immediately, by ballot, the President. But in choosing the President, the votes shall be taken by States, the representation from each State having one vote; a quorum for this purpose shall consist of a member or members from two-thirds of the States, and a majority of all the States shall be necessary to a choice. And if the House of Representatives shall not choose a President whenever the right of choice shall devolve upon them, before the fourth day of March next following, then the Vice-President shall act as President, as in the case of the death or other constitutional disability of the President. The person having the greatest number of votes as Vice-President, shall be the Vice-President, if such number be a majority of the whole number of Electors appointed, and if no person have a majority, then from the two highest numbers on the list, the Senate shall choose the Vice-Presiden; a quorum for the purpose shall consist of two-thirds of the whole number of Senators, and a majority of the whole number shall be necessary to a choice. But no person constitutionally ineligible to the office of President shall be eligible to that of Vice-President of the United States.

AMENDMENT THIRTEEN

December 18, 1865

Section 1. Neither slavery nor involuntary servitude, except as a punishment for crime whereof the party shall have been duly convicted, shall exist within the United States, or any place subject to their jurisdiction.

Section 2. Congress shall have power to enforce this AMENDMENT by appropriate legislation.

AMENDMENT FOURTEEN

July 28, 1868

Section 1. All persons born or naturalized in the United States, and subject to the jurisdiction thereof, are citizens of the United States and of the State wherein they reside. No State shall make or enforce any law which shall abridge the privileges or immunities of citizens of the United States; nor shall any State deprive any person of life, liberty, or property, without due process of law; nor deny to any person within its jurisdiction the equal protection of the laws.

Section 2. Representatives shall be apportioned among the several States according to their respective numbers, counting the whole number of persons in each State, excluding Indians not taxed. But when the right to vote at any election for the choice of Electors for President and Vice-President of the United States, Representatives in Congress, the executive and judicial officers of a State, or the members of the Legislature thereof, is denied to any of the male inhabitants of such State, being twenty-one years of age, and citizens of the United States, or in any way abridged, except for participation in rebellion, or other crime, the basis of representation therein shall be reduced in the proportion which the number of such male citizens shall bear to the whole number of male citizens twenty-one years of age in such State.

Section 3. No person shall be a Senator or Representative in Congress, or elector of President and Vice-President, or hold any office, civil or military, under the United States, or under any State, who, having previously taken an oath, as a member of Congress, or as an officer of the United States, or as a member of any State legislature, or as an executive or judicial officer of any State, to support the Constitution of the United States, shall have engaged in insurrection or rebellion against the same, or given aid or comfort to the enemies thereof. But Congress may by a vote of two-thirds of each House, remove such disability.

Section 4. The validity of the public debt of the United States, authorized by law, including debts incurred for payment of pensions and bounties for services in suppressing insurrection or rebellion, shall not be questioned. But neither the United States nor any State shall assume or pay any debt or obligation incurred in aid of insurrection or rebellion against the United States, or any claim for the loss or emancipation of any slave; but all such debts, obligations and claims shall be held illegal and void.

Section 5. The Congress shall have power to enforce, by appropriate legislation, the provisions of this AMENDMENT.

AMENDMENT FIFTEEN

March 30, 1870

Section 1. The right of citizens of the United States to vote shall not be denied or abridged by the United States or by any State on account of race, color, or previous condition of servitude.

Section 2. The Congress shall have power to enforce this AMENDMENT by appropriate legislation.

AMENDMENT SIXTEEN

February 25, 1913

The Congress shall have power to lay and collect taxes on incomes, from whatever source derived, without apportionment among the several States and without regard to any census or enumeration.

AMENDMENT SEVENTEEN

May 31, 1913

The Senate of the United States shall be composed of two senators from each State, elected by the people thereof, for six years; and each Senator shall have one vote. The electors in each State shall have the qualifications requisite for electors of the most numerous branch of the State legislature.

When vacancies happen in the representation of any State in the Senate, the executive authority of such State shall issue writs of election to fill such vacancies: Provided, That the legislature of any State may empower the executive thereof to make temporary appointments until the people fill the vacancies by election as the legislature may direct.

This amendment shall not be so construed as to affect the election or term of any senator chosen before it becomes valid as part of the Constitution.

AMENDMENT EIGHTEEN

January 29, 1919

Section 1. After one year from the ratification of this AMENDMENT, the manufacture, sale, or transportation of intoxicating liquors within, the importation thereof into, or the exportation thereof from the United States and all territory subject to the jurisdiction thereof for beverage purposes is hereby prohibited.

Section 2. The Congress and the several States shall have concurrent power to enforce this AMENDMENT by appropriate legislation.

Section 3. This AMENDMENT shall be inoperative unless it shall have been ratified as an amendment to the Constitution by the legislatures of the several States, as provided in the Constitution, within seven years from the date of the submission hereof to the States by Congress.

AMENDMENT NINETEEN

August 26, 1920

The right of citizens of the United States to vote shall not be denied or abridged by the United States or by any States on account of sex.

The Congress shall have power by appropriate legislation to enforce the provisions of this AMENDMENT.

AMENDMENT TWENTY

February 6, 1933

Section 1. The terms of the President and Vice-President shall end at noon on the twentieth day of January, and the terms of Senators and Representatives at noon on the third day of January, of the years in which such terms would have ended if this AMENDMENT had not been ratified; and the terms of their successors shall then begin.

Section 2. The Congress shall assemble at least once in every year, and such meeting shall begin at noon on the third day of January, unless they shall by law appoint a different day.

Section 3. If, at the time fixed for the beginning of the term of the President, the President-elect shall have died, the Vice-President-elect shall become President. If a President shall not have been chosen before the time fixed for the beginning of his term, or if the President-elect shall have failed to qualify, then the Vice-President-elect shall act as President until a President shall have qualified; and the Congress may by law provide for the case wherein neither a President-elect nor a Vice-President-elect shall have qualified, declaring who shall then act as President, or the manner in which one who is to act shall be selected, and such person shall act accordingly until a President or Vice-President shall have qualified.

Section 4. The Congress may by law provide for the case of the death of any of the persons from whom the House of Representatives may choose a President whenever the right of choice shall have devolved upon them, and for the case of the death of any of the persons from whom the Senate may choose a Vice-President whenever the right of choice shall have devolved upon them.

Section 5. Sections 1 and 2 shall take effect on the 15th day of October following the ratification of this AMENDMENT.

Section 6. This AMENDMENT shall be inoperative unless it shall have been ratified as an amendment to the Constitution by the legislatures of three-fourths of the several States within seven years from the date of its submission.

AMENDMENT TWENTY-ONE

December 5, 1933

Section 1. The eighteenth AMENDMENT of amendment to the Constitution of the United States is hereby repealed.

Section 2. The transportation or importation into any State, Territory, or possession of the United States for delivery or use therein of intoxicating liquors, in violation of the laws thereof, is hereby prohibited.

Section 3. The AMENDMENT shall be inoperative unless it shall have been ratified as an amendment to the Constitution by conventions in the several States, as provided in the Constitution, within seven years from the date of the submission hereof to the States by the Congress.

AMENDMENT TWENTY-TWO

February 26, 1951

Section 1. No person shall be elected to the office of the President more than twice, and no person who has held the office of President, or acted as President for more than two years of a term to which some other person was elected President shall be elected to the office of the President more than once. But this AMENDMENT shall not apply to any person holding the office of President when this AMENDMENT was proposed by the Congress, and shall not prevent any person who May be holding the office of President, or acting as President, during the term within which this AMENDMENT becomes operative from holding the office of President or acting as President during the remainder of such term.

Section 2. This AMENDMENT shall be inoperative unless it shall have been ratified as an amendment to the Constitution by the legislatures of three-fourths of the several States within seven years from the date of its submission to the States by the Congress.

AMENDMENT TWENTY-THREE

June 16, 1960

Section 1. The District constituting the seat of government of the United States shall appoint in such manner as the Congress may direct:
   A number of electors of President and Vice-President equal to the whole number of Senators and Representatives in Congress to which the District would be entitled if it were a State, but in no event more than the least populous State; they shall be in addition to those appointed by the States, but they shall be considered, for the purposes of the election of President and Vice-President, to be electors appointed by a State; and they shall meet in the district and perform such duties as provided by the twelfth AMENDMENT of amendment.

Section 2. The Congress shall have power to enforce this AMENDMENT by appropriate legislation.

AMENDMENT TWENTY-FOUR

February 4, 1964

Section 1. The right of citizens of the United States to vote in any primary or other election for President or Vice-President, for electors for President or Vice-President, or for Senator or Representative in Congress, shall not be denied or abridged by the United States or any State by reason of failure to pay any poll tax or other tax.

Section 2. The Congress shall have power to enforce this AMENDMENT by appropriate legislation.

AMENDMENT TWENTY-FIVE

February 10, 1967

Section 1. In case of the removal of the President from office or of his death or resignation, the Vice-President shall become President.

Section 2. Whenever there is a vacancy in the office of the Vice-President, the President shall nominate a Vice-President who shall take office upon confirmation by a majority vote of both Houses of Congress.

Section 3. Whenever the President transmits to the President pro tempore of the Senate and the Speaker of the House of Representatives his written declaration that he is unable to discharge the powers and duties of his office, and until he transmits to them a written declaration to the contrary, such powers and duties shall be discharged by the Vice-President as Acting President.

Section 4. Whenever the Vice-President and a majority of either the principal officers of the executive departments or of such other body as Congress may by law provide, transmit to the President pro tempore of the Senate and the Speaker of the House of Representatives their written declaration that the President is unable to discharge the powers and duties of his office, the Vice-President shall immediately assume the powers and duties of the office as Acting President.

Thereafter, when the President transmits to the President pro tempore of the Senate and the Speaker of the House of Representatives his written declaration that no inability exists, he shall resume the powers and duties of his office unless the Vice-President and a majority of either the principal officers of the executive department or of such other body as Congress may by law provide, transmit within four day to the President pro tempore of the Senate and the Speaker of the House of Representatives their written declaration that the President is unable to discharge the powers and duties of his office. Thereupon Congress shall decide the issue, assembling within forty-eight hours for that purpose if not in session. If the Congress, within twenty-one days after receipt of the latter written declaration, or, if Congress is not in session, within twenty-one days after Congress is required to assemble, determines by two-thirds vote of both Houses that the President is unable to discharge the powers and duties of his office, the Vice-President shall continue to discharge the same as Acting President; otherwise, the President shall resume the powers and duties of his office.

AMENDMENT TWENTY-SIX

July 1, 1971

Section 1. The right of citizens of the United States, who are eighteen years of age or older, to vote shall not be denied or abridged by the United States or by any State on account of age.

Section 2. The Congress shall have power to enforce this AMENDMENT by appropriate legislation.

AMENDMENT TWENTY-SEVEN

No law, varying the compensation for the services of the Senators and Representatives, shall take effect, until an election of Representatives shall have intervened.

Appendix C:
The United States Court System

The United States Court System

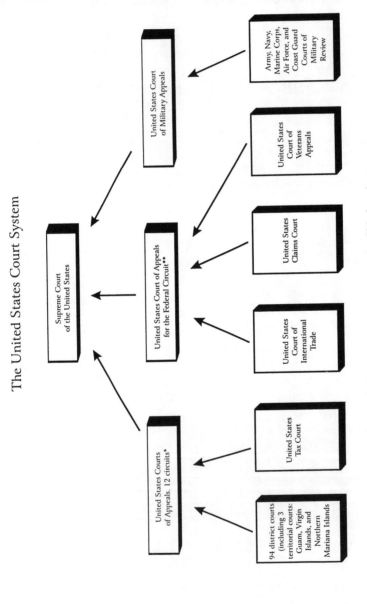

*The 12 regional courts of appeals also review cases from a number of federal agencies.

**The Court of Appeals for the Federal Circuit also receives cases from the International Trade Commission, the Merit Systems Protection Board, the Patent and Trademark Office, and the Board of Contract Appeals.

468

Appendix D:
Copyright Registration Forms

☑Filling Out Application Form VA

Detach and read these instructions before completing this form.
Make sure all applicable spaces have been filled in before you return this form.

BASIC INFORMATION

When to Use This Form: Use Form VA for copyright registration of published or unpublished works of the visual arts. This category consists of "pictorial, graphic, or sculptural works," including two-dimensional and three-dimensional works of fine, graphic, and applied art, photographs, prints and art reproductions, maps, globes, charts, technical drawings, diagrams, and models.

What Does Copyright Protect? Copyright in a work of the visual arts protects those pictorial, graphic, or sculptural elements that, either alone or in combination, represent an "original work of authorship." The statute declares: "In no case does copyright protection for an original work of authorship extend to any idea, procedure, process, system, method of operation, concept, principle, or discovery, regardless of the form in which it is described, explained, illustrated, or embodied in such work."

Works of Artistic Craftsmanship and Designs: "Works of artistic craftsmanship" are registrable on Form VA, but the statute makes clear that protection extends to "their form" and not to "their mechanical or utilitarian aspects." The "design of a useful article" is considered copyrightable "only if, and only to the extent that, such design incorporates pictorial, graphic, or sculptural features that can be identified separately from, and are capable of existing independently of, the utilitarian aspects of the article."

Labels and Advertisements: Works prepared for use in connection with the sale or advertisement of goods and services are registrable if they contain "original work of authorship." Use Form VA if the copyrightable material in the work you are registering is mainly pictorial or graphic; use Form TX if it consists mainly of text. NOTE: Words and short phrases such as names, titles, and slogans cannot be protected by copyright, and the same is true of standard symbols, emblems, and other commonly used graphic designs that are in the public domain. When used commercially, material of that sort can sometimes be protected under state laws of unfair competition or under the Federal trademark laws. For information about trademark registration, write to the Commissioner of Patents and Trademarks, Washington, D.C. 20231.

Architectural Works: Copyright protection extends to the design of buildings created for the use of human beings. Architectural works created on or after December 1, 1990, or that on December 1, 1990, were unconstructed and embodied only in unpublished plans or drawings are eligible. Request Circular 41 for more information.

Deposit to Accompany Application: An application for copyright registration must be accompanied by a deposit consisting of copies representing the entire work for which registration is to be made.

Unpublished Work: Deposit one complete copy.

Published Work: Deposit two complete copies of the best edition.

Work First Published Outside the United States: Deposit one complete copy of the first foreign edition.

Contribution to a Collective Work: Deposit one complete copy of the best edition of the collective work.

The Copyright Notice: For works first published on or after March 1, 1989, the law provides that a copyright notice in a specified form "may be placed on all publicly distributed copies from which the work can be visually perceived." Use of the copyright notice is the responsibility of the copyright owner and does not require advance permission from the Copyright Office. The required form of the notice for copies generally consists of three elements: (1) the symbol "©", or the word "Copyright," or the abbreviation "Copr."; (2) the year of first publication; and (3) the name of the owner of copyright. For example: "© 1995 Jane Cole." The notice is to be affixed to the copies "in such manner and location as to give reasonable notice of the claim of copyright." Works first published prior to March 1, 1989, must carry the notice or risk loss of copyright protection.

For information about notice requirements for works published before March 1, 1989, or other copyright information, write: Information Section, LM-401, Copyright Office, Library of Congress, Washington, D.C. 20559-6000.

LINE-BY-LINE INSTRUCTIONS

Please type or print using black ink.

1 SPACE 1: Title

Title of This Work: Every work submitted for copyright registration must be given a title to identify that particular work. If the copies of the work bear a title (or an identifying phrase that could serve as a title), transcribe that wording completely and exactly on the application. Indexing of the registration and future identification of the work will depend on the information you give here. For an architectural work that has been constructed, add the date of construction after the title; if unconstructed at this time, add "not yet constructed."

Previous or Alternative Titles: Complete this space if there are any additional titles for the work under which someone searching for the registration might be likely to look, or under which a document pertaining to the work might be recorded.

Publication as a Contribution: If the work being registered is a contribution to a periodical, serial, or collection, give the title of the contribution in the "Title of This Work" space. Then, in the line headed "Publication as a Contribution," give information about the collective work in which the contribution appeared.

Nature of This Work: Briefly describe the general nature or character of the pictorial, graphic, or sculptural work being registered for copyright. Examples: "Oil Painting"; "Charcoal Drawing"; "Etching"; "Sculpture"; "Map"; "Photograph"; "Scale Model"; "Lithographic Print"; "Jewelry Design"; "Fabric Design."

2 SPACE 2: Author(s)

General Instruction: After reading these instructions, decide who are the "authors" of this work for copyright purposes. Then, unless the work is a "collective work," give the requested information about every "author" who contributed any appreciable amount of copyrightable matter to this version of the work. If you need further space, request Continuation Sheets. In the case of a collective work, such as a catalog of paintings or collection of cartoons by various authors, give information about the author of the collective work as a whole.

Name of Author: The fullest form of the author's name should be given. Unless the work was "made for hire," the individual who actually created the work is its "author." In the case of a work made for hire, the statute provides that "the employer or other person for whom the work was prepared is considered the author."

What is a "Work Made for Hire"? A "work made for hire" is defined as: (1) "a work prepared by an employee within the scope of his or her employment"; or (2) "a work specially ordered or commissioned for use as a contribution to a collective work, as a part of a motion picture or other audiovisual work, as a translation, as a supplementary work, as a compilation, as an instructional text, as a test, as answer material for a test, or as an atlas, if the parties expressly agree in a written instrument signed by them that the work shall be considered a work made for hire." If you have checked "Yes" to indicate that the work was "made for hire," you must give the full legal name of the employer (or other person for whom the work was prepared). You may also include the name of the employee along with the name of the employer (for example: "Elster Publishing Co., employer for hire of John Ferguson").

"Anonymous" or "Pseudonymous" Work: An author's contribution to a work is "anonymous" if that author is not identified on the copies or phonorecords of the work. An author's contribution to a work is "pseudonymous" if that author is identified on the copies or phonorecords under a fictitious name. If the work is "anonymous" you may: (1) leave the line blank; or (2) state "anonymous" on the line; or (3) reveal the author's identity. If the work is "pseudonymous" you may: (1) leave the line blank; or (2) give the pseudonym and identify it as such (for example: "Huntley Haverstock, pseudonym"); or (3) reveal the author's name, making clear which is the real name and which is the pseudonym (for example: "Henry Leek, whose pseudonym is Priam Farrel"). However, the citizenship or domicile of the author must be given in all cases.

Dates of Birth and Death: If the author is dead, the statute requires that the year of death be included in the application unless the work is anonymous or pseudonymous. The author's birth date is optional but is useful as a form of identification. Leave this space blank if the author's contribution was a "work made for hire."

Author's Nationality or Domicile: Give the country of which the author is a citizen or the country in which the author is domiciled. Nationality or domicile must be given in all cases.

470

Nature of Authorship: Categories of pictorial, graphic, and sculptural authorship are listed below. Check the box(es) that best describe(s) each author's contribution to the work.

3-Dimensional sculptures: fine art sculptures, toys, dolls, scale models, and sculptural designs applied to useful articles.

2-Dimensional artwork: watercolor and oil paintings; pen and ink drawings; logo illustrations; greeting cards; collages; stencils; patterns; computer graphics; graphics appearing in screen displays; artwork appearing on posters, calendars, games, commercial prints and labels, and packaging, as well as 2-dimensional artwork applied to useful articles.

Reproductions of works of art: reproductions of preexisting artwork made by, for example, lithography, photoengraving, or etching.

Maps: cartographic representations of an area such as state and county maps, atlases, marine charts, relief maps, and globes.

Photographs: pictorial photographic prints and slides and holograms.

Jewelry designs: 3-dimensional designs applied to rings, pendants, earrings, necklaces, and the like.

Designs on sheetlike materials: designs reproduced on textiles, lace, and other fabrics; wallpaper; carpeting; floor tile; wrapping paper; and clothing.

Technical drawings: diagrams illustrating scientific or technical information in linear form such as architectural blueprints or mechanical drawings.

Text: textual material that accompanies pictorial, graphic, or sculptural works such as comic strips, greeting cards, games rules, commercial prints or labels, and maps.

Architectural works: designs of buildings, including the overall form as well as the arrangement and composition of spaces and elements of the design. NOTE: Any registration for the underlying architectural plans must be applied for on a separate Form VA, checking the box "Technical drawing."

3 SPACE 3: Creation and Publication

General Instructions: Do not confuse "creation" with "publication." Every application for copyright registration must state "the year in which creation of the work was completed." Give the date and nation of first publication only if the work has been published.

Creation: Under the statute, a work is "created" when it is fixed in a copy or phonorecord for the first time. Where a work has been prepared over a period of time, the part of the work existing in fixed form on a particular date constitutes the created work on that date. The date you give here should be the year in which the author completed the particular version for which registration is now being sought, even if other versions exist or if further changes or additions are planned.

Publication: The statute defines "publication" as "the distribution of copies or phonorecords of a work to the public by sale or other transfer of ownership, or by rental, lease, or lending"; a work is also "published" if there has been an "offering to distribute copies or phonorecords to a group of persons for purposes of further distribution, public performance, or public display." Give the full date (month, day, year) when, and the country where, publication first occurred. If first publication took place simultaneously in the United States and other countries, it is sufficient to state "U.S.A."

4 SPACE 4: Claimant(s)

Name(s) and Address(es) of Copyright Claimant(s): Give the name(s) and address(es) of the copyright claimant(s) in this work even if the claimant is the same as the author. Copyright in a work belongs initially to the author of the work (including, in the case of a work made for hire, the employer or other person for whom the work was prepared). The copyright claimant is either the author of the work or a person or organization to whom the copyright initially belonging to the author has been transferred.

Transfer: The statute provides that, if the copyright claimant is not the author, the application for registration must contain "a brief statement of how the claimant obtained ownership of the copyright." If any copyright claimant named in space 4 is not an author named in space 2, give a brief statement explaining how the claimant(s) obtained ownership of the copyright. Examples: "By written contract"; "Transfer of all rights by author"; "Assignment"; "By will." Do not attach transfer documents or other attachments or riders.

5 SPACE 5: Previous Registration

General Instructions: The questions in space 5 are intended to find out whether an earlier registration has been made for this work and, if so, whether there is any basis for a new registration. As a rule, only one basic copyright registration can be made for the same version of a particular work.

Same Version: If this version is substantially the same as the work covered by a previous registration, a second registration is not generally possible unless: (1) the work has been registered in unpublished form and a second registration is now being sought to cover this first published edition; or (2) someone other than the author is identified as a copyright claimant in the earlier registration, and the author is now seeking registration in his or her own name. If either of these two exceptions apply, check the appropriate box and give the earlier registration number and date. Otherwise, do not submit Form VA; instead, write the Copyright Office for information about supplementary registration or recordation of transfers of copyright ownership.

Changed Version: If the work has been changed and you are now seeking registration to cover the additions or revisions, check the last box in space 5, give the earlier registration number and date, and complete both parts of space 6 in accordance with the instruction below.

Previous Registration Number and Date: If more than one previous registration has been made for the work, give the number and date of the latest registration.

6 SPACE 6: Derivative Work or Compilation

General Instructions: Complete space 6 if this work is a "changed version," "compilation," or "derivative work," and if it incorporates one or more earlier works that have already been published or registered for copyright, or that have fallen into the public domain. A "compilation" is defined as "a work formed by the collection and assembling of preexisting materials or of data that are selected, coordinated, or arranged in such a way that the resulting work as a whole constitutes an original work of authorship." A "derivative work" is "a work based on one or more preexisting works." Examples of derivative works include reproductions of works of art, sculptures based on drawings, lithographs based on paintings, maps based on previously published sources, or "any other form in which a work may be recast, transformed, or adapted." Derivative works also include works "consisting of editorial revisions, annotations, or other modifications" if these changes, as a whole, represent an original work of authorship.

Preexisting Material (space 6a): Complete this space and space 6b for derivative works. In this space identify the preexisting work that has been recast, transformed, or adapted. Examples of preexisting material might be "Grunewald Altarpiece" or "19th century quilt design." Do not complete this space for compilations.

Material Added to This Work (space 6b): Give a brief, general statement of the additional new material covered by the copyright claim for which registration is sought. In the case of a derivative work, identify this new material. Examples: "Adaptation of design and additional artistic work"; "Reproduction of painting by photolithography"; "Additional cartographic material"; "Compilation of photographs." If the work is a compilation, give a brief, general statement describing both the material that has been compiled and the compilation itself. Example: "Compilation of 19th century political cartoons."

7,8,9 SPACE 7,8,9: Fee, Correspondence, Certification, Return Address

Deposit Account: If you maintain a Deposit Account in the Copyright Office, identify it in space 7. Otherwise leave the space blank and send the fee of $20 with your application and deposit.

Correspondence (space 7): This space should contain the name, address, area code, and telephone number of the person to be consulted if correspondence about this application becomes necessary.

Certification (space 8): The application cannot be accepted unless it bears the date and the **handwritten signature** of the author or other copyright claimant, or of the owner of exclusive right(s), or of the duly authorized agent of the author, claimant, or owner of exclusive right(s).

Address for Return of Certificate (space 9): The address box must be completed legibly since the certificate will be returned in a window envelope.

FORM VA

For a Work of the Visual Arts
UNITED STATES COPYRIGHT OFFICE

REGISTRATION NUMBER

_____

VA   VAU

EFFECTIVE DATE OF REGISTRATION

_____

Month   Day   Year

DO NOT WRITE ABOVE THIS LINE. IF YOU NEED MORE SPACE, USE A SEPARATE CONTINUATION SHEET.

1

TITLE OF THIS WORK ▼   **NATURE OF THIS WORK ▼** See instructions

PREVIOUS OR ALTERNATIVE TITLES ▼

PUBLICATION AS A CONTRIBUTION If this work was published as a contribution to a periodical, serial, or collection, give information about the collective work in which the contribution appeared.   **Title of Collective Work ▼**

If published in a periodical or serial give: Volume ▼   Number ▼   Issue Date ▼   On Pages ▼

2

a

NAME OF AUTHOR ▼   **DATES OF BIRTH AND DEATH**
Year Born ▼   Year Died ▼

Was this contribution to the work a "work made for hire"?
☐ Yes
☐ No

AUTHOR'S NATIONALITY OR DOMICILE
Name of Country
OR { Citizen of ▶ _____
Domiciled in▶ _____

WAS THIS AUTHOR'S CONTRIBUTION TO THE WORK
Anonymous?   ☐ Yes ☐ No
Pseudonymous? ☐ Yes ☐ No
If the answer to either of these questions is "Yes," see detailed instructions.

NATURE OF AUTHORSHIP Check appropriate box(es). **See instructions**
☐ 3-Dimensional sculpture   ☐ Map   ☐ Technical drawing
☐ 2-Dimensional artwork   ☐ Photograph   ☐ Text
☐ Reproduction of work of art   ☐ Jewelry design   ☐ Architectural work
☐ Design on sheetlike material

NOTE

Under the law, the "author" of a "work made for hire" is generally the employer, not the employee (see instructions). For any part of this work that was "made for hire" check "Yes" in the space provided, give the employer (or other person for whom the work was prepared) as "Author" of that part, and leave the space for dates of birth and death blank.

b

NAME OF AUTHOR ▼   **DATES OF BIRTH AND DEATH**
Year Born ▼   Year Died ▼

Was this contribution to the work a "work made for hire"?
☐ Yes
☐ No

AUTHOR'S NATIONALITY OR DOMICILE
Name of Country
OR { Citizen of ▶ _____
Domiciled in▶ _____

WAS THIS AUTHOR'S CONTRIBUTION TO THE WORK
Anonymous?   ☐ Yes ☐ No
Pseudonymous? ☐ Yes ☐ No
If the answer to either of these questions is "Yes," see detailed instructions.

NATURE OF AUTHORSHIP Check appropriate box(es). **See instructions**
☐ 3-Dimensional sculpture   ☐ Map   ☐ Technical drawing
☐ 2-Dimensional artwork   ☐ Photograph   ☐ Text
☐ Reproduction of work of art   ☐ Jewelry design   ☐ Architectural work
☐ Design on sheetlike material

3

a

YEAR IN WHICH CREATION OF THIS WORK WAS COMPLETED This information must be given ◀Year in all cases.

b

DATE AND NATION OF FIRST PUBLICATION OF THIS PARTICULAR WORK
Complete this information ONLY if this work has been published.   Month▶ _____ Day▶ _____ Year▶ _____   ◀ Nation

4

See instructions before completing this space.

COPYRIGHT CLAIMANT(S) Name and address must be given even if the claimant is the same as the author given in space 2. ▼

TRANSFER If the claimant(s) named here in space 4 is (are) different from the author(s) named in space 2, give a brief statement of how the claimant(s) obtained ownership of the copyright. ▼

DO NOT WRITE HERE OFFICE USE ONLY

APPLICATION RECEIVED
_____
ONE DEPOSIT RECEIVED
_____
TWO DEPOSITS RECEIVED
_____
FUNDS RECEIVED

MORE ON BACK ▶ • Complete all applicable spaces (numbers 5-9) on the reverse side of this page.
• See detailed instructions.   • Sign the form at line 8.

DO NOT WRITE HERE

Page 1 of _____ pages

472

DO NOT WRITE ABOVE THIS LINE. IF YOU NEED MORE SPACE, USE A SEPARATE CONTINUATION SHEET.

PREVIOUS REGISTRATION Has registration for this work, or for an earlier version of this work, already been made in the Copyright Office?
☐ Yes   ☐ No   If your answer is "Yes," why is another registration being sought? (Check appropriate box) ▼

a. ☐ This is the first published edition of a work previously registered in unpublished form.

b. ☐ This is the first application submitted by this author as copyright claimant.

c. ☐ This is a changed version of the work, as shown by space 6 on this application.

If your answer is "Yes," give: **Previous Registration Number ▼**   **Year of Registration ▼**

5

DERIVATIVE WORK OR COMPILATION Complete both space 6a and 6b for a derivative work; complete only 6b for a compilation.
a. **Preexisting Material** Identify any preexisting work or works that this work is based on or incorporates. ▼

b. **Material Added to This Work** Give a brief, general statement of the material that has been added to this work and in which copyright is claimed. ▼

6

See instructions
before completing
this space.

DEPOSIT ACCOUNT If the registration fee is to be charged to a Deposit Account established in the Copyright Office, give name and number of Account.
Name ▼   **Account Number ▼**

7

CORRESPONDENCE Give name and address to which correspondence about this application should be sent.   Name/Address/Apt/City/State/ZIP ▼

               Area Code and Telephone Number ▶

Be sure to
give your
daytime phone
◀ number

CERTIFICATION*   I, the undersigned, hereby certify that I am the
check only one ▼

☐ author

☐ other copyright claimant

☐ owner of exclusive right(s)

☐ authorized agent of _____
               Name of author or other copyright claimant, or owner of exclusive right(s) ▲

of the work identified in this application and that the statements made
by me in this application are correct to the best of my knowledge.

Typed or printed name and date ▼ If this application gives a date of publication in space 3, do not sign and submit it before that date.
               Date ▶

☞   **Handwritten signature (X) ▼**

8

9

Instructions for Short Form VA
For pictorial, graphic, and sculptural works

USE THIS FORM IF—

1. you are the **only** author and copyright owner of this work; *and*
2. the work was **not** made for hire, *and*
3. the work is completely new (does not contain a substantial amount of material that has been previously published or registered or is in the public domain).

If any of the above does not apply, you must use standard Form VA.
NOTE: Short Form VA is not appropriate for an anonymous author who does not wish to reveal his or her identity.

HOW TO COMPLETE SHORT FORM VA

- Type or print in black ink.
- Be clear and legible. (Your certificate of registration will be copied from your form.)
- Give only the information requested.

NOTE: You may use a continuation sheet (Form __/CON) to list individual titles in a collection. Complete Space A and list the individual titles under Space C on the back page. Space B is not applicable to short forms.

1 Title of This Work

You must give a title. If there is no title, state "UNTITLED." If you are registering an unpublished collection, give the collection title you want to appear in our records (for example: "Jewelry by Josephine, 1995 Volume"). Alternative title: If the work is known by two titles, you also may give the second title. If the work has been published as part of a larger work (including a periodical), give the title of that larger work instead of an alternative title, in addition to the title of the contribution.

2 Name and Address of Author/Owner of the Copyright

Give your name and mailing address. You may include your pseudonym followed by "pseud." Also, give the nation of which you are a citizen or where you have your domicile (i.e., permanent residence).
Please give daytime phone and fax numbers and email address, if available.

3 Year of Creation

Give the latest year in which you completed the work you are registering at this time. (A work is "created" when it is "fixed" in a tangible form. Examples: drawn on paper, molded in clay, stored in a computer.)

4 Publication

If the work has been published (i.e., if copies have been distributed to the public), give the complete date of publication (month, day, and year) and the nation where the publication first took place.

5 Type of Authorship in This Work

Check the box or boxes that describe your authorship in the material you are sending. For example, if you are registering illustrations but have not written the story yet, check only the box for "2-dimensional artwork."

6 Signature of Author

Sign the application in black ink and check the appropriate box. The person signing the application should be the author or his/her authorized agent.

7 Person to Contact for Rights and Permissions

This space is optional. You may give the name and address of the person or organization to contact for permission to use the work. You may also provide phone, fax, or email information.

8 Certificate Will Be Mailed

This space must be completed. Your certificate of registration will be mailed in a window envelope to this address. Also, if the Copyright Office needs to contact you, we will write to this address.

9 Deposit Account

Complete this space only if you currently maintain a deposit account in the Copyright Office.

MAIL WITH THE FORM—

- a $20.00 filing fee in the form of a check or money order (*no cash*) payable to "Register of Copyrights," **and**
- one or two copies of the work or identifying material consisting of photographs or drawings showing the work. See table (right) for the requirements for most works.
  Note: Request Circular 40a for more information about the requirements for other works. Copies submitted become the property of the U.S. Government.

Mail everything **(application form, copy or copies, and fee)** *in one package* to: Register of Copyrights
Library of Congress
Washington, D.C. 20559-6000

If you are registering:	And the work is *unpublished/published* send:
2-dimensional artwork in a book, map, poster, or print	a. And the work is *unpublished*, send one complete copy or identifying material
	b. And the work is *published*, send two copies of the best published edition
3-dimensional sculpture, 2-dimensional artwork applied to a T-shirt	a. And the work is *unpublished*, send identifying material
	b. And the work is *published*, send identifying material
a greeting card, pattern, commercial print or label, fabric, wallpaper	a. And the work is *unpublished*, send one complete copy or identifying material
	b. And the work is *published*, send one copy of the best published edition

QUESTIONS? Call (202) 707-3000 [TTY: (202) 707-6737] between 8:30 a.m. and 5:00 p.m. eastern time, Monday through Friday. For forms and informational circulars, call (202) 707-9100 24 hours a day, 7 days a week, or download them from the World Wide Web at http://www.loc.gov/copyright. Selected informational circulars are available from Fax-on-Demand at (202) 707-2600.

VA		VAU

Effective Date of Registration

Month	Day	Year

Application Received

Examined By	Deposit Received	
	One	Two

Correspondence	Fee Received
☐	

TYPE OR PRINT IN BLACK INK. DO NOT WRITE ABOVE THIS LINE.

Title of This Work: 1

Alternative title or title of larger work in which this work was published:

Name and Address of Author/Owner of the Copyright: 2

Nationality or domicile:
Phone, fax, and email:

Phone ( )   Fax ( )   Email

Year of Creation: 3

If work has been published, Date and Nation of Publication: 4

a. Date _____ _____ _____ *(Month, day, and year all required)*
                (Month)   (Day)   (Year)

b. Nation

Type of Authorship in This Work: 5
(Check all that this author created.)

☐ 3-Dimensional sculpture   ☐ Jewelry design
☐ 2-Dimensional artwork   ☐ Map
☐ Technical drawing   ☐ Text
☐ Photograph

Signature: 6

I certify that the statements made by me in this application are correct to the best of my knowledge.

Check one: ☐ Author   ☐ Authorized agent   ☜

Name and Address of Person to Contact for Rights and Permissions: 7

☐ Check here if same as #2 above.

Phone, fax, and email:

Phone ( )   Fax ( )   Email

8

Certificate will be mailed in window envelope to this address:

Name ▼

Number/Street/Apt ▼

City/State/ZIP ▼

9

Deposit Account # _____

Name _____

*17 U.S.C. § 506(e): Any person who knowingly makes a false representation of a material fact in the application for copyright registration provided for by section 409, or in any written statement filed in connection with the application, shall be fined not more than $2,500.

September 1996—100,000   ♻ PRINTED ON RECYCLED PAPER   ☆U.S. GOVERNMENT PRINTING OFFICE: 1996-405-104/40,015

✒Filling Out Application Form TX

Detach and read these instructions before completing this form.
Make sure all applicable spaces have been filled in before you return this form.

BASIC INFORMATION

When to Use This Form: Use Form TX for registration of published or unpublished nondramatic literary works, excluding periodicals or serial issues. This class includes a wide variety of works: fiction, nonfiction, poetry, textbooks, reference works, directories, catalogs, advertising copy, compilations of information, and computer programs. For periodicals and serials, use Form SE.

Deposit to Accompany Application: An application for copyright registration must be accompanied by a deposit consisting of copies or phonorecords representing the entire work for which registration is to be made. The following are the general deposit requirements as set forth in the statute:

Unpublished Work: Deposit one complete copy (or phonorecord).

Published Work: Deposit two complete copies (or one phonorecord) of the best edition.

Work First Published Outside the United States: Deposit one complete copy (or phonorecord) of the first foreign edition.

Contribution to a Collective Work: Deposit one complete copy (or phonorecord) of the best edition of the collective work.

The Copyright Notice: For works first published on or after March 1, 1989, the law provides that a copyright notice in a specified form "may be placed on all publicly distributed copies from which the work can be visually perceived." Use of the copyright notice is the responsibility of the copyright owner and does not require advance permission from the Copyright Office. The required form of the notice for copies generally consists of three elements: (1) the symbol "℗," or the word "Copyright," or the abbreviation "Copr."; (2) the year of first publication; and (3) the name of the owner of copyright. For example: "© 1995 Jane Cole." The notice is to be affixed to the copies "in such manner and location as to give reasonable notice of the claim of copyright." Works first published prior to March 1, 1989, **must** carry the notice or risk loss of copyright protection.

For information about notice requirements for works published before March 1, 1989, or other copyright information, write: Information Section, LM-401, Copyright Office, Library of Congress, Washington, D.C. 20559-6000.

LINE-BY-LINE INSTRUCTIONS
Please type or print using black ink.

1 SPACE 1: Title

Title of This Work: Every work submitted for copyright registration must be given a title to identify that particular work. If the copies or phonorecords of the work bear a title or an identifying phrase that could serve as a title, transcribe that wording *completely* and *exactly* on the application. Indexing of the registration and future identification of the work will depend on the information you give here.

Previous or Alternative Titles: Complete this space if there are any additional titles for the work under which someone searching for the registration might be likely to look or under which a document pertaining to the work might be recorded.

Publication as a Contribution: If the work being registered is a contribution to a periodical, serial, or collection, give the title of the contribution in the "Title of this Work" space. Then, in the line headed "Publication as a Contribution," give information about the collective work in which the contribution appeared.

2 SPACE 2: Author(s)

General Instructions: After reading these instructions, decide who are the "authors" of this work for copyright purposes. Then, unless the work is a "collective work," give the requested information about every "author" who contributed any appreciable amount of copyrightable matter to this version of the work. If you need further space, request Continuation sheets. In the case of a collective work such as an anthology, collection of essays, or encyclopedia, give information about the author of the collective work as a whole.

Name of Author: The fullest form of the author's name should be given. Unless the work was "made for hire," the individual who actually created the work is its "author." In the case of a work made for hire, the statute provides that "the employer or other person for whom the work was prepared is considered the author."

What is a "Work Made for Hire"? A "work made for hire" is defined as (1) "a work prepared by an employee within the scope of his or her employment"; or (2) "a work specially ordered or commissioned for use as a contribution to a collective work, as a part of a motion picture or other audiovisual work, as a translation, as a supplementary work, as a compilation, as an instructional text, as a test, as answer material for a test, or as an atlas, if the parties expressly agree in a written instrument signed by them that the works shall be considered a work made for hire." If you have checked "Yes" to indicate that the work was "made for hire," you must give the full legal name of the employer (or other person for whom the work was prepared). You may also include the name of the employee along with the name of the employer (for example: "Elster Publishing Co., employer for hire of John Ferguson").

"Anonymous" or "Pseudonymous" Work: An author's contribution to a work is "anonymous" if that author is not identified on the copies or phonorecords of the work. An author's contribution to a work is "pseudonymous" if that author is identified on the copies or phonorecords under a fictitious name. If the work is "anonymous" you may: (1) leave the line blank; or (2) state "anonymous" on the line; or (3) reveal the author's identity. If the work is "pseudonymous" you may: (1) leave the line blank; or (2) give the pseudonym and identify it as such (for example: "Huntley Haverstock, pseudonym"); or (3) reveal the author's name, making clear which is the real name and which is the pseudonym (for example, "Judith Barton, whose pseudonym is Madeline Elster"). However, the citizenship or domicile of the author **must** be given in all cases.

Dates of Birth and Death: If the author is dead, the statute requires that the year of death be included in the application unless the work is anonymous or pseudonymous. The author's birth date is optional but is useful as a form of identification. Leave this space blank if the author's contribution was a "work made for hire."

Author's Nationality or Domicile: Give the country of which the author is a citizen or the country in which the author is domiciled. Nationality or domicile **must** be given in all cases.

Nature of Authorship: After the words "Nature of Authorship," give a brief general statement of the nature of this particular author's contribution to the work. Examples: "Entire text"; "Coauthor of entire text"; "Computer program"; "Editorial revisions"; "Compilation and English translation"; "New text."

3 SPACE 3: Creation and Publication

General Instructions: Do not confuse "creation" with "publication." Every application for copyright registration must state "the year in which creation of the work was completed." Give the date and nation of first publication only if the work has been published.

Creation: Under the statute, a work is "created" when it is fixed in a copy or phonorecord for the first time. Where a work has been prepared over a period of time, the part of the work existing in fixed form on a particular date constitutes the created work on that date. The date you give here should be the year in which the author completed the particular version for which registration is now being sought, even if other versions exist or if further changes or additions are planned.

Publication: The statute defines "publication" as "the distribution of copies or phonorecords of a work to the public by sale or other transfer of ownership, or by rental, lease, or lending"; a work is also "published" if there has been an "offering to distribute copies or phonorecords to a group of persons for purposes of further distribution, public performance, or public display." Give the full date (month, day, year) when, and the country where, publication first occurred. If first publication took place simultaneously in the United States and other countries, it is sufficient to state "U.S.A."

4 SPACE 4: Claimant(s)

Name(s) and Address(es) of Copyright Claimant(s): Give the name(s) and address(es) of the copyright claimant(s) in this work even if the claimant is the same as the author. Copyright in a work belongs initially to the author of the work (including, in the case of a work made for hire, the employer or other person for whom the work was prepared). The copyright claimant is either the author of the work or a person or organization to whom the copyright initially belonging to the author has been transferred.

Transfer: The statute provides that, if the copyright claimant is not the author, the application for registration must contain "a brief statement of how the claimant obtained ownership of the copyright." If any copyright claimant named in space 4 is not an author named in space 2, give a brief statement explaining how the claimant(s) obtained ownership of the copyright. Examples: "By written contract"; "Transfer of all rights by author"; "Assignment"; "By will." Do not attach transfer documents or other attachments or riders.

5 SPACE 5: Previous Registration

General Instructions: The questions in space 5 are intended to show whether an earlier registration has been made for this work and, if so, whether there is any basis for a new registration. As a general rule, only one basic copyright registration can be made for the same version of a particular work.

Same Version: If this version is substantially the same as the work covered by a previous registration, a second registration is not generally possible unless: (1) the work has been registered in unpublished form and a second registration is now being sought to cover this first published edition; or (2) someone other than the author is identified as copyright claimant in the earlier registration, and the author is now seeking registration in his or her own name. If either of these two exceptions apply, check the appropriate box and give the earlier registration number and date. Otherwise, do not submit Form TX; instead, write the Copyright Office for information about supplementary registration or recordation of transfers of copyright ownership.

Changed Version: If the work has been changed and you are now seeking registration to cover the additions or revisions, check the last box in space 5, give the earlier registration number and date, and complete both parts of space 6 in accordance with the instructions below.

Previous Registration Number and Date: If more than one previous registration has been made for the work, give the number and date of the latest registration.

6 SPACE 6: Derivative Work or Compilation

General Instructions: Complete space 6 if this work is a "changed version," "compilation," or "derivative work" and if it incorporates one or more earlier works that have already been published or registered for copyright or that have fallen into the public domain. A "compilation" is defined as "a work formed by the collection and assembling of preexisting materials or of data that are selected, coordinated, or arranged in such a way that the resulting work as a whole constitutes an original work of authorship." A "derivative work" is "a work based on one or more preexisting works." Examples of derivative works include translations, fictionalizations, abridgments, condensations, or "any other form in which a work may be recast, transformed, or adapted." Derivative works also include works "consisting of editorial revisions, annotations, or other modifications" if these changes, as a whole, represent an original work of authorship.

Preexisting Material (space 6a): For derivative works, complete this space and space 6b. In space 6a identify the preexisting work that has been recast, transformed, or adapted. An example of preexisting material might be: "Russian version of Goncharov's 'Oblomov'." Do not complete space 6a for compilations.

Material Added to This Work (space 6b): Give a brief, general statement of the new material covered by the copyright claim for which registration is sought. Derivative work examples include: "Foreword, editing, critical annotations"; "Translation"; "Chapters 11-17." If the work is a compilation, describe both the compilation itself and the material that has been compiled. Example: "Compilation of certain 1917 Speeches by Woodrow Wilson." A work may be both a derivative work and compilation, in which case a sample statement might be: "Compilation and additional new material."

7 SPACE 7: Manufacturing Provisions

Due to the expiration of the Manufacturing Clause of the copyright law on June 30, 1986, this space has been deleted.

8 SPACE 8: Reproduction for Use of Blind or Physically Handicapped Individuals

General Instructions: One of the major programs of the Library of Congress is to provide Braille editions and special recordings of works for the exclusive use of the blind and physically handicapped. In an effort to simplify and speed up the copyright licensing procedures that are a necessary part of this program, section 710 of the copyright statute provides for the establishment of a voluntary licensing system to be tied in with copyright registration. Copyright Office regulations provide that you may grant a license for such reproduction and distribution solely for the use of persons who are certified by competent authority as unable to read normal printed material as a result of physical limitations. The license is entirely voluntary, nonexclusive, and may be terminated upon 90 days notice.

How to Grant the License: If you wish to grant it, check one of the three boxes in space 8. Your check in one of these boxes together with your signature in space 10 will mean that the Library of Congress can proceed to reproduce and distribute under the license without further paperwork. For further information, write for Circular 63.

9,10,11 SPACE 9,10,11: Fee, Correspondence, Certification, Return Address

Deposit Account: If you maintain a Deposit Account in the Copyright Office, identify it in space 9. Otherwise leave the space blank and send the fee of $20 with your application and deposit.

Correspondence (space 9) This space should contain the name, address, area code, and telephone number of the person to be consulted if correspondence about this application becomes necessary.

Certification (space 10): The application can not be accepted unless it bears the date and the **handwritten signature** of the author or other copyright claimant, or of the owner of exclusive right(s), or of the duly authorized agent of author, claimant, or owner of exclusive right(s).

Address for Return of Certificate (space 11): The address box must be completed legibly since the certificate will be returned in a window envelope.

FORM TX

For a Literary Work
UNITED STATES COPYRIGHT OFFICE

REGISTRATION NUMBER

_____

TX _____ TXU _____

EFFECTIVE DATE OF REGISTRATION

_____
Month   Day   Year

DO NOT WRITE ABOVE THIS LINE. IF YOU NEED MORE SPACE, USE A SEPARATE CONTINUATION SHEET.

1

TITLE OF THIS WORK ▼

PREVIOUS OR ALTERNATIVE TITLES ▼

PUBLICATION AS A CONTRIBUTION If this work was published as a contribution to a periodical, serial, or collection, give information about the collective work in which the contribution appeared. **Title of Collective Work ▼**

If published in a periodical or serial give: Volume ▼   Number ▼   Issue Date ▼   On Pages ▼

2

a

NAME OF AUTHOR ▼

DATES OF BIRTH AND DEATH
Year Born ▼   Year Died ▼

Was this contribution to the work a "work made for hire"?
☐ Yes
☐ No

AUTHOR'S NATIONALITY OR DOMICILE
Name of Country
OR { Citizen of ▶_____
Domiciled in▶_____

WAS THIS AUTHOR'S CONTRIBUTION TO THE WORK
Anonymous?   ☐ Yes ☐ No
Pseudonymous? ☐ Yes ☐ No
If the answer to either of these questions is "Yes," see detailed instructions.

NATURE OF AUTHORSHIP Briefly describe nature of material created by this author in which copyright is claimed. ▼

NOTE

Under the law, the "author" of a "work made for hire" is generally the employer, not the employee (see instructions). For any part of this work that was "made for hire" check "Yes" in the space provided, give the employer (or other person for whom the work was prepared) as "Author" of that part, and leave the space for dates of birth and death blank.

b

NAME OF AUTHOR ▼

DATES OF BIRTH AND DEATH
Year Born ▼   Year Died ▼

Was this contribution to the work a "work made for hire"?
☐ Yes
☐ No

AUTHOR'S NATIONALITY OR DOMICILE
Name of Country
OR { Citizen of ▶_____
Domiciled in▶_____

WAS THIS AUTHOR'S CONTRIBUTION TO THE WORK
Anonymous?   ☐ Yes ☐ No
Pseudonymous? ☐ Yes ☐ No
If the answer to either of these questions is "Yes," see detailed instructions.

NATURE OF AUTHORSHIP Briefly describe nature of material created by this author in which copyright is claimed. ▼

c

NAME OF AUTHOR ▼

DATES OF BIRTH AND DEATH
Year Born ▼   Year Died ▼

Was this contribution to the work a "work made for hire"?
☐ Yes
☐ No

AUTHOR'S NATIONALITY OR DOMICILE
Name of Country
OR { Citizen of ▶_____
Domiciled in▶_____

WAS THIS AUTHOR'S CONTRIBUTION TO THE WORK
Anonymous?   ☐ Yes ☐ No
Pseudonymous? ☐ Yes ☐ No
If the answer to either of these questions is "Yes," see detailed instructions.

NATURE OF AUTHORSHIP Briefly describe nature of material created by this author in which copyright is claimed. ▼

3

a **YEAR IN WHICH CREATION OF THIS WORK WAS COMPLETED** This information must be given ◀Year in all cases.

b **DATE AND NATION OF FIRST PUBLICATION OF THIS PARTICULAR WORK**
Complete this information ONLY if this work has been published.
Month ▶ _____ Day▶ _____ Year▶ _____
◀ Nation

4

See instructions before completing this space.

COPYRIGHT CLAIMANT(S) Name and address must be given even if the claimant is the same as the author given in space 2. ▼

TRANSFER If the claimant(s) named here in space 4 is (are) different from the author(s) named in space 2, give a brief statement of how the claimant(s) obtained ownership of the copyright. ▼

DO NOT WRITE HERE OFFICE USE ONLY

APPLICATION RECEIVED
_____
ONE DEPOSIT RECEIVED
_____
TWO DEPOSITS RECEIVED
_____
FUNDS RECEIVED

MORE ON BACK ▶ • Complete all applicable spaces (numbers 5-11) on the reverse side of this page.
• See detailed instructions. • Sign the form at line 10.

DO NOT WRITE HERE
Page 1 of _____ pages

DO NOT WRITE ABOVE THIS LINE. IF YOU NEED MORE SPACE, USE A SEPARATE CONTINUATION SHEET.

PREVIOUS REGISTRATION Has registration for this work, or for an earlier version of this work, already been made in the Copyright Office?

☐ Yes ☐ No If your answer is "Yes," why is another registration being sought? (Check appropriate box) ▼

a. ☐ This is the first published edition of a work previously registered in unpublished form.

b. ☐ This is the first application submitted by this author as copyright claimant.

c. ☐ This is a changed version of the work, as shown by space 6 on this application.

If your answer is "Yes," give: **Previous Registration Number ▼**   **Year of Registration ▼**

5

DERIVATIVE WORK OR COMPILATION Complete both space 6a and 6b for a derivative work; complete only 6b for a compilation.
a. Preexisting Material Identify any preexisting work or works that this work is based on or incorporates. ▼

b. Material Added to This Work Give a brief, general statement of the material that has been added to this work and in which copyright is claimed. ▼

See instructions
before completing
this space.

6

—space deleted—

7

REPRODUCTION FOR USE OF BLIND OR PHYSICALLY HANDICAPPED INDIVIDUALS A signature on this form at space 10 and a check in one of the boxes here in space 8 constitutes a non-exclusive grant of permission to the Library of Congress to reproduce and distribute solely for the blind and physically handicapped and under the conditions and limitations prescribed by the regulations of the Copyright Office: (1) copies of the work identified in space 1 of this application in Braille (or similar tactile symbols); or (2) phonorecords embodying a fixation of a reading of that work; or (3) both.

a ☐ Copies and Phonorecords   b ☐ Copies Only   c ☐ Phonorecords Only

See instructions.

8

DEPOSIT ACCOUNT If the registration fee is to be charged to a Deposit Account established in the Copyright Office, give name and number of Account.
Name ▼   Account Number ▼

9

CORRESPONDENCE Give name and address to which correspondence about this application should be sent.   Name/Address/Apt/City/State/ZIP ▼

Be sure to
give your
daytime phone
◄ number

Area Code and Telephone Number ►

CERTIFICATION* I, the undersigned, hereby certify that I am the

Check only one ►

☐ author
☐ other copyright claimant
☐ owner of exclusive right(s)
☐ authorized agent of _____

of the work identified in this application and that the statements made
by me in this application are correct to the best of my knowledge.

Name of author or other copyright claimant, or owner of exclusive right(s) ▲

10

Typed or printed name and date ▼ If this application gives a date of publication in space 3, do not sign and submit it before that date.

_____ Date ►_____

☞ Handwritten signature (X) ▼

**MAIL
CERTIFI-
CATE TO**

Name ▼

Number/Street/Apt ▼

City/State/ZIP ▼

Certificate
will be
mailed in
window
envelope

11

*17 U.S.C. § 506(e): Any person who knowingly makes a false representation of a material fact in the application for copyright registration provided for by section 409, or in any written statement filed in connection with the application, shall be fined not more than $2,500.

May 1995—300,000   ♻ PRINTED ON RECYCLED PAPER   ☼U.S. GOVERNMENT PRINTING OFFICE: 1995-387-237/47

479

✐Instructions for Short Form TX

For nondramatic literary works, including fiction and nonfiction, books, short stories, poems, collections of poetry, essays, articles in serials, and computer programs

USE THIS FORM IF—

1. you are the **only** author and copyright owner of this work; *and*
2. the work was **not** made for hire, *and*
3. the work is completely new (does not contain a substantial amount of material that has been previously published or registered or is in the public domain).

If any of the above does not apply, you must use standard Form TX.
NOTE: Short Form TX is not appropriate for an anonymous author who does not wish to reveal his or her identity.

HOW TO COMPLETE SHORT FORM TX

- Type or print in black ink.
- Be clear and legible. (Your certificate of registration will be copied from your form.)
- Give only the information requested.

NOTE: You may use a continuation sheet (Form __/CON) to list individual titles in a collection. Complete Space A and list the individual titles under Space C on the back page. Space B is not applicable to short forms.

1 Title of This Work

You must give a title. If there is no title, state "UNTITLED." If you are registering an unpublished collection, give the collection title you want to appear in our records (for example: "Joan's Poems, Volume 1"). Alternative title: If the work is known by two titles, you also may give the second title. If the work has been published as part of a larger work (including a periodical), give the title of that larger work in addition to the title of the contribution.

2 Name and Address of Author/Owner of the Copyright

Give your name and mailing address. You may include your pseudonym followed by "pseud." Also, give the nation of which you are a citizen or where you have your domicile (i.e., permanent residence).
Please give daytime phone and fax numbers and email address, if available.

3 Year of Creation

Give the latest year in which you completed the work you are registering at this time. (A work is "created" when it is written down, stored in a computer, or otherwise "fixed" in a tangible form.)

4 Publication

If the work has been published (i.e., if copies have been distributed to the public), give the complete date of publication (month, day, and year) and the nation where the publication first took place.

5 Type of Authorship in This Work

Check the box or boxes that describe your authorship in the copy you are sending with the application. For example, if you are registering a story and are planning to add illustrations later, check only the box for "text."
A "compilation" of terms or of data is a selection, coordination, or arrangement of such information into a chart, directory, or other form. A compilation of previously published or public domain material must be registered using a standard Form TX.

6 Signature of Author

Sign the application in black ink and check the appropriate box. The person signing the application should be the author or his/her authorized agent.

7 Person to Contact for Rights and Permissions

This space is optional. You may give the name and address of the person or organization to contact for permission to use the work. You may also provide phone, fax, or email information.

8 Certificate Will Be Mailed

This space must be completed. Your certificate of registration will be mailed in a window envelope to this address. Also, if the Copyright Office needs to contact you, we will write to this address.

9 Permission to Reproduce for Blind and Physically Handicapped Individuals

Public Law 104-197 eliminates the need for permission from the copyright holder before an authorized entity may reproduce or distribute copies or phonorecords of a previously published, nondramatic literary work if the copies or phonorecords are reproduced or distributed in specialized formats exclusively for use by blind or handicapped persons. P.L. 104-197 does not apply to standardized, secure, or norm-referenced tests and related material or to computer programs except those portions in conventional language.

10 Deposit Account

Complete this space only if you currently maintain a deposit account in the Copyright Office.

MAIL WITH THE FORM—

- a $20.00 filing fee in the form of a check or money order (*no cash*) payable to "Register of Copyrights," **and**
- one or two copies of the work. If the work is unpublished, send one copy. If published, send two copies of the best published edition. (If first published outside the U.S., send one copy either as first published or of the best edition.)
  Note: Inquire about special requirements for works first published before 1978. Copies submitted become the property of the U.S. Government.

Mail everything (**application form, copy or copies, and fee**) *in one package* to: Register of Copyrights
Library of Congress
Washington, D.C. 20559-6000

QUESTIONS? Call (202) 707-3000 [TTY: (202) 707-6737] between 8:30 a.m. and 5:00 p.m. eastern time, Monday through Friday. For forms and informational circulars, call (202) 707-9100 24 hours a day, 7 days a week, or download them from the World Wide Web at http://www.loc.gov/copyright. Selected informational circulars are available from Fax-on-Demand at (202) 707-2600.

SHORT FORM TX ■

For a Nondramatic Literary Work
UNITED STATES COPYRIGHT OFFICE

Registration Number

	TX	TXU

Effective Date of Registration

Month	Day	Year

Application Received

Examined By

Deposit Received

One	Two

Correspondence ☐

Fee Received

TYPE OR PRINT IN BLACK INK. DO NOT WRITE ABOVE THIS LINE.

Title of This Work:

Alternative title or title of larger work in which this work was published:

Name and Address of Author/Owner of the Copyright:

Nationality or domicile:
Phone, fax, and email:

Phone ( )   Fax ( )   Email

Year of Creation:

If work has been published, **Date and Nation of Publication:**

a. Date _____ (Month) _____ (Day) _____ (Year)   *(Month, day, and year all required)*

b. Nation

Type of Authorship in This Work:
(Check all that this author created.)

☐ Text (includes fiction, nonfiction, poetry, computer programs, etc.)
☐ Illustrations
☐ Photographs
☐ Compilation of terms or data

Signature:

*I certify that the statements made by me in this application are correct to the best of my knowledge.**
Check one: ☐ Author ☐ Authorized agent

Name and Address of Person to Contact for Rights and Permissions:

☐ Check here if same as #2 above.

Phone, fax, and email:

Phone ( )   Fax ( )   Email

—Space Deleted—

Certificate will be mailed in window envelope to this address:

| Name ▼ |
| Number/Street/Apt ▼ |
| City/State/ZIP ▼ |

Deposit Account # _____
Name _____

Appendix E:
Trademark Registration Forms

<table>
<tr><td rowspan="2">**TRADEMARK/SERVICE MARK
APPLICATION, PRINCIPAL
REGISTER, WITH DECLARATION**</td><td>MARK (Word(s) and/or Design)</td><td>CLASS NO.
(If known)</td></tr>
</table>

TO THE ASSISTANT COMMISSIONER FOR TRADEMARKS:

APPLICANT'S NAME:

APPLICANT'S MAILING ADDRESS:

(Display address exactly as it
should appear on registration)

APPLICANT'S ENTITY TYPE: (Check one and supply requested information)

Individual - Citizen of (Country):

Partnership - State where organized (Country, if appropriate): _____
Names and Citizenship (Country) of General Partners: _____

Corporation - State (Country, if appropriate) of Incorporation:

Other (Specify Nature of Entity and Domicile):

GOODS AND/OR SERVICES:

Applicant requests registration of the trademark/service mark shown in the accompanying drawing in the United States
Patent and Trademark Office on the Principal Register established by the Act of July 5, 1946 (15 U.S.C. 1051 et. seq., as
amended) for the following goods/services (**SPECIFIC GOODS AND/OR SERVICES MUST BE INSERTED HERE**):

_____
_____
_____
_____
_____

BASIS FOR APPLICATION: (Check boxes which apply, **but never both the first AND second boxes,** and supply requested information related to
each box checked.)

[ ] Applicant is using the mark in commerce on or in connection with the above identified goods/services. (15 U.S.C. 1051(a), as
amended.) Three specimens showing the mark as used in commerce are submitted with this application.
- Date of first use of the mark in commerce which the U.S. Congress may regulate (for example, interstate or
between the U.S. and a foreign country): _____
- Specify the type of commerce: _____
(for example, interstate or between the U.S. and a specified foreign country)
- Date of first use anywhere (the same as or before use in commerce date): _____
- Specify intended manner or mode of use of mark on or in connection with the goods/services: _____

(for example, trademark is applied to labels, service mark is used in advertisements)

[ ] Applicant has a bona fide intention to use the mark in commerce on or in connection with the above identified goods/services. (15
U.S.C. 1051(b), as amended.)
- Specify manner or mode of use of mark on or in connection with the goods/services: _____

(for example, trademark will be applied to labels, service mark will be used in advertisements)

[ ] Applicant has a bona fide intention to use the mark in commerce on or in connection with the above identified
goods/services, and asserts a claim of priority based upon a foreign application in accordance with 15 U.S.C.
1126(d), as amended.
- Country of foreign filing: _____   •Date of foreign filing: _____

[ ] Applicant has a bona fide intention to use the mark in commerce on or in connection with the above identified
goods/services and, accompanying this application, submits a certification or certified copy of a foreign
registration in accordance with 15 U.S.C 1126(e), as amended
- Country of registration: _____   • Registration number: _____

NOTE: Declaration, on Reverse Side, MUST be Signed

PTO Form 1478 (REV 6/96)
OMB No. 0651-0009 (Exp. 06/30/98)   U.S. DEPARTMENT OF COMMERCE/Patent and Trademark Office

DECLARATION

The undersigned being hereby warned that willful false statements and the like so made are punishable by fine or imprisonment, or both, under 18 U.S.C. 1001, and that such willful false statements may jeopardize the validity of the application or any resulting registration, declares that he/she is properly authorized to execute this application on behalf of the applicant; he/she believes the applicant to be the owner of the trademark/service mark sought to be registered, or if the application is being filed under 15 U.S.C. 1051(b), he/she believes the applicant to be entitled to use such mark in commerce; to the best of his/her knowledge and belief no other person, firm, corporation, or association has the right to use the above identified mark in commerce, either in the identical form thereof or in such near resemblance thereto as to be likely, when used on or in connection with the goods/services of such other person, to cause confusion, or to cause mistake, or to deceive; and that all statements made of his/her own knowledge are true and that all statements made on information and belief are believed to be true.

_____   _____
DATE   SIGNATURE

_____   _____
TELEPHONE NUMBER   PRINT OR TYPE NAME AND POSITION

INSTRUCTIONS AND INFORMATION FOR APPLICANT

TO RECEIVE A FILING DATE, THE APPLICATION <u>MUST</u> BE COMPLETED AND SIGNED BY THE APPLICANT AND SUBMITTED ALONG WITH:

1. The prescribed **FEE ($245.00)** for each class of goods/services listed in the application;
2. A **DRAWING PAGE** displaying the mark in conformance with 37 CFR 2.52;
3. If the application is based on use of the mark in commerce, **THREE (3) SPECIMENS** (evidence) of the mark as used in commerce for each class of goods/services listed in the application. All three specimens may be the same. Examples of good specimens include: (a) labels showing the mark which are placed on the goods; (b) photographs of the mark as it appears on the goods, (c) brochures or advertisements showing the mark as used in connection with the services.
4. An **APPLICATION WITH DECLARATION** (this form) - The application must be signed in order for the application to receive a filing date. Only the following persons may sign the declaration, depending on the applicant's legal entity: (a) the individual applicant; (b) an officer of the corporate applicant; (c) one general partner of a partnership applicant; (d) all joint applicants.

SEND APPLICATION FORM, DRAWING PAGE, FEE, AND SPECIMENS (IF APPROPRIATE) TO:

Assistant Commissioner for Trademarks
Box New App/Fee
2900 Crystal Drive
Arlington, VA 22202-3513

Additional information concerning the requirements for filing an application is available in a booklet entitled **Basic Facts About Registering a Trademark**, which may be obtained by writing to the above address or by calling: (703) 308-HELP.

484

<table>
<tr><td>ALLEGATION OF USE FOR INTENT-TO-USE
APPLICATION, WITH DECLARATION
(Amendment To Allege Use/Statement Use)</td><td>MARK (Identify the mark)</td></tr>
<tr><td></td><td>SERIAL NO.</td></tr>
</table>

TO THE ASSISTANT COMMISSIONER FOR TRADEMARKS:

APPLICANT NAME:

Applicant requests registration of the above-identified trademark/service mark in the United States Patent and Trademark Office on the Principal Register established by the Act of July 5, 1946 (15 U.S.C. §1051 *et seq.*, as amended). Three specimens per class showing the mark as used in commerce and the prescribed fees are submitted with this statement.

Applicant is using the mark in commerce on or in connection with the following goods/services (CHECK ONLY ONE):

☐ (a) those in the application or Notice of Allowance; **OR**

☐ (b) those in the application or Notice of Allowance **except** (if goods/services are to be deleted, list the goods/services to be **deleted**): _____
_____
_____

Date of first use in commerce which the U.S. Congress may regulate: _____
Specify type of commerce: _____
(for example, interstate and/or commerce between the U.S. and a foreign country)
Date of first use anywhere: _____

Specify manner or mode of use of mark on or in connection with the goods/services: (for example, trademark is applied to labels, service mark is used in advertisements): _____
_____
_____

The undersigned, being hereby warned that willful false statements and the like so made are punishable by fine or imprisonment, or both, under 18 U.S.C. §1001, and that such willful false statements may jeopardize the validity of the application or any resulting registration, declares that he/she is properly authorized to execute this Amendment to Allege Use or Statement of Use on behalf of the applicant; he/she believes the applicant to be the owner of the trademark/service mark sought to be registered; the trademark /service mark is now in use in commerce; and all statements made of his/her own knowledge are true and all statements made on information and belief are believed to be true.

_____   _____
Date   Signature

_____   _____
Telephone Number   Type or Print Name and Position

Check here if Request to Divide is being submitted with this statement (if Applicant wishes to proceed to publication or registration with certain goods/services on or in connection with which it has used the mark in commerce and retain an active application for any remaining goods/services, a divisional application and fee are required. 37 C.F.R. §2.87)

PLEASE SEE REVERSE FOR MORE INFORMATION

INSTRUCTIONS AND INFORMATION FOR APPLICANT

In an application based upon a bona fide intention to use a mark in commerce, **the Applicant must use its mark in commerce before a registration will be issued.** After use begins, the applicant must file the Allegation of Use. If the Allegation of Use is filed before the mark is approved for publication in the *Official Gazette* it is treated under the statute as **an Amendment to Allege Use (AAU).** If it is filed after the Notice of Allowance is issued, it is treated under the statute as a **Statement of Use (SOU).** The Allegation of Use cannot be filed during the time period between approval of the mark for publication in the *Official Gazette* and the issuance of the Notice of Allowance. The difference between the AAU and SOU is the time at which each is filed during the process.

Additional requirements for filing this Allegation of Use:

1) the fee of $100.00 per class of goods/services (**please note that fees are subject to change, usually on October 1 of each year**); and
2) three (3) specimens of the mark as used in commerce for each class of goods/services (for example, photographs of the mark as it appears on the goods, labels for affixation on goods, advertisements showing the mark as used in connection with services).

- The Applicant may list dates of use for one item in each class of goods/services identified in the Allegation of Use. The Applicant must have used the mark in commerce on all the goods/services in the class, however, it is only necessary to list the dates of use for one item in each class.

- Only the following persons may sign the verification on this form: (a) the individual applicant; (b) an officer of a corporate applicant; (c) one general partner of a partnership applicant; (d) all joint applicants.

- The goods/services in the Allegation of Use must be the same as those specified in the application or Notice of Allowance. The Applicant may limit or clarify the goods/services, but cannot add to or otherwise expand the identification specified in the application or Notice of Allowance. If goods/services are deleted, they may **not** be reinserted at a later time.

- Amendments to Allege Use are governed by Trademark Act §1(c), 15 U.S.C. §1051(c) and Trademark Rule 2.76, 37 C.F.R. §2.76. Statements of Use are governed by Trademark Act §1(d), 15 U.S.C. §1051(d) and Trademark Rule 2.88, 37 C.F.R. §2.88.

MAIL COMPLETED FORM TO:

ASSISTANT COMMISSIONER FOR TRADEMARKS
BOX AAU/SOU
2900 CRYSTAL DRIVE
ARLINGTON, VIRGINIA 22202-3513

Please note that the filing date of a document in the Patent and Trademarks Office is the date of receipt in the Office, not the date of deposit of the mail. 37 C.F.R. §1.6. To avoid lateness due to mail delay, use of the certificate of mailing set forth below, is encouraged.

COMBINED CERTIFICATE OF MAILING/CHECKLIST

Before filing this form, please make sure to complete the following:

- ☐ three specimens, per class have been enclosed;
- ☐ the filing fee of $100 (subject to change as noted above), per class has been enclosed; and
- ☐ the declaration has been signed by the appropriate party

CERTIFICATE OF MAILING

I do hereby certify that the foregoing are being **deposited** with the United States Postal Service as first class mail, postage prepaid, in an envelope addressed to the Assistant Commissioner for Trademarks, 2900 Crystal Drive, Arlington, VA 22202-3513, on _____ (date).

_____   _____
Signature   Date of Deposit

_____
Print or Type Name of Person Signing Certificate

This form is estimated to take 15 minutes to complete including time required for reading and understanding instructions, gathering necessary information, record keeping and actually providing the information. Any comments on the amount of time you require to complete this form should be sent to the Office of Management and Organization, U.S. Patent and Trademark Office, U.S. Department of Commerce, Washington, D.C. 20231. Do not send forms to this address.

<table>
<tr><td rowspan="2">REQUEST FOR EXTENSION OF TIME
TO FILE A STATEMENT
OF USE, WITH DECLARATION</td><td>MARK (Identify the mark)</td></tr>
<tr><td>SERIAL NO</td></tr>
</table>

TO THE ASSISTANT SECRETARY AND COMMISSIONER OF PATENTS AND TRADEMARKS:

APPLICANT NAME:

NOTICE OF ALLOWANCE MAILING DATE:

Applicant requests a six-month extension of time to file the Statement of Use under 37 CFR 2.89 in this application

Applicant has a continued bona fide intention to use the mark in commerce on or in connection with the following goods/ services: (Check One below)

⬜ Those goods/services identified in the Notice of Allowance.

⬜ Those goods/services identified in the Notice of Allowance except: (Identify goods services to be **deleted** from application)

_____

_____

_____

This is the _____ request for an Extension of Time following mailing of the Notice of Allowance.
(Specify: First - Fifth)

If this is not the first request for an Extension of Time, check one box below. If the first box is checked explain the circumstance(s) of the non-use in the space provided:

⬜   Applicant has not used the mark in commerce yet on all goods/services specified in the Notice of Allowance; however, applicant has made the following ongoing efforts to use the mark in commerce on or in connection with each of the goods/services specified above:

_____

_____

If additional space is needed, please attach a separate sheet to this form

⬜   Applicant believes that it has made valid use of the mark in commerce, as evidenced by the Statement of Use submitted with this request; however, if the Statement of Use does not meet minimum requirements under 37 CFR 2.88(e), applicant will need additional time in which to file a new statement.

The undersigned being hereby warned that willful false statements and the like so made are punishable by fine or imprisonment, or both, under 18 U.S.C. 1001, and that such willful false statements may jeopardize the validity of the application or any resulting registration, declares that he/she is properly authorized to execute this Request for an Extension of Time to File a Statement of Use on behalf of the applicant; and that all statements made of his/her own knowledge are true and all statements made on information and belief are believed to be true.

_____
Date

_____
Signature

_____
Telephone Number

_____
Type or Print Name and Position

    Check here if Request to Divide is being submitted with this statement (if Applicant wishes to proceed to publication or registration with certain goods/services on or in connection with which it has used the mark in commerce and retain an active application for any remaining goods/services, a divisional application and fee are required. 37 C.F.R. §2.87)

INSTRUCTIONS AND INFORMATION FOR APPLICANT

Applicant must file a Statement of Use within six months after the mailing of the Notice of Allowance based upon a bona fide intention to use a mark in commerce, UNLESS, within that same period, applicant submits a request for a six-month extension of time to file the Statement of Use. The written request **must**:

    (1)   be received in the PTO within six months after the issue date of the Notice of Allowance,

    (2)   include applicant's verified statement of continued bona fide intention to use the mark in commerce,

    (3)   specify the goods/services to which the request pertains as they are identified in the Notice of Allowance, and

    (4)   include a fee of $100 for each class of goods/services **(please note that fees are subject to change, usually on October 1 of each year).**

Applicant may request four further six-month extensions of time. No extensions may extend beyond 36 months from the issue date of the Notice of Allowance. Each further request must be received in the PTO within the previously granted six-month extension period and must include, in addition to the above requirements, a showing of GOOD CAUSE. This good cause showing must include:

    (1)   applicant's statement that the mark has not been used in commerce yet on all the goods or services specified in the Notice of Allowance with which applicant has a continued bona fide intention to use the mark in commerce, **and**

    (2)   applicant's statement of ongoing efforts to make such use, which may include the following: (a) product or service research or development, (b) market research, (c) promotional activities, (d) steps to acquire distributors, (e) steps to obtain required governmental approval, or (f) similar specified activity.

Applicant may submit one additional six-month extension request during the existing period in which applicant files the Statement of Use, unless the granting of this request would extend the period beyond 36 months from the issue date of the Notice of Allowance. As a showing of good cause for such a request, applicant should state its belief that applicant has made valid use of the mark in commerce, as evidenced by the submitted Statement of Use, but that if the Statement is found by the PTO to be defective, applicant will need additional time in which to file a new statement of use.

Only the following person may sign the declaration of the Request for Extension of Time: (a) the individual applicant; (b) an officer of corporate applicant; (c) one general partner of partnership applicant; (d) all joint applicants.

MAILING INSTRUCTIONS

MAIL COMPLETED FORM TO:

ASSISTANT COMMISSIONER FOR TRADEMARKS
BOX ITU
2900 CRYSTAL DRIVE
ARLINGTON, VIRGINIA 22202-3513

Please note that the filing date of a document in the Patent and Trademarks Office is the date of receipt in the Office, not the date of deposit of the mail. 37 C.F.R. §1.6. To avoid lateness due to mail delay, use of the certificate of mailing set forth below is encouraged.

CERTIFICATE OF MAILING

I do hereby certify that this correspondence is being **deposited** with the United States Postal Service as first class mail, postage prepaid, in an envelope addressed to the Assistant Commissioner for Trademarks, 2900 Crystal Drive, Arlington, VA 22202-3513, on _____ (date).

_____
Signature

Date of Deposit

_____
Print or Type Name of Person Signing Certificate

This form is estimated to take 15 minutes to complete including time required for reading and understanding instructions, gathering necessary information, record keeping and actually providing the information. Any comments on the amount of time you require to complete this form should be sent to the Office of Management and Organization, U.S. Patent and Trademark Office, U.S. Department of Commerce, Washington, D.C. 20231. Do not send forms to this address.

Appendix F:
Model Releases

SIMPLIFIED ADULT RELEASE

For valuable consideration received, I hereby grant to _____ ("Photographer") the absolute and irrevocable right and unrestricted permission, in respect of photographic portraits or pictures that he/she had taken of me or in which I may be included with others, to copyright the same, in his/her own name or otherwise; to use, re-use, publish, and re-publish the same in whole or in part, individually or in conjunction with other photographs, and in conjunction with any printed matter, in any and all media now or hereafter known, and for any purpose whatsoever, for illustration, promotion, art, editorial, advertising and trade, or any other purpose whatsoever without restriction as to alteration; and to use my name in connection therewith if he/she so chooses.

I hereby release and discharge Photographer from any and all claims and demands arising out of or in connection with the use of photographs, including without limitation any and all claims for libel or invasion of privacy.

This authorization and release shall also inure to the benefit of the heirs, legal representatives, licensees, and assigns of Photographer, as well as the person(s) for whom he/she took the photographs.

I am of full age and have the right to contract in my own name. I have read the foregoing and fully understand the contents thereof. This release shall be binding upon me and my heirs, legal representatives, and assigns.

Date: _____

_____
(Name)

_____

_____
(Witness)

_____
(Address)

MINOR RELEASE

In consideration of the engagement as a model of the minor named below, and for other good and valuable consideration herein acknowledged as received, upon the terms hereinafter stated, I hereby grant to _____ ("Photographer"), his/her legal representatives and assigns, those for whom Photographer is acting, and those acting with his/her authority and permission, the absolute right and permission to copyright and use, re-use, publish, and re-publish photographic portraits or pictures of the minor or in which the minor may be included, in whole or in part, or composite or distorted in character or form, without restriction as to changes or alterations from time to time, in conjunction with the minor's own or a fictitious name, or reproductions thereof in color or otherwise, made through any medium at his/her studios or elsewhere, and in any and all media now or hereafter known, for art, advertising, trade, or any other purpose whatsoever. I also consent to the use of any printed matter in conjunction therewith.

I hereby waive any right that I or the minor may have to inspect or approve the finished product or products or the advertising copy or printed matter that may be used in connection therewith or the use to which it may be applied.

I hereby release, discharge, and agree to save harmless Photographer, his/her legal representatives or assigns, and all persons acting under his/her permission or authority or those for whom he/she is acting, from any liability by virtue of any blurring, distortion, alteration, optical illusion, or use in composite form, whether intentional or otherwise, that may occur or be produced in the taking of said picture or in any subsequent processing thereof, as well as any publication thereof, including without limitation any claims for libel or invasion of privacy.

I hereby warrant that I am of full age and have every right to contract for the minor in the above regard. I state further that I have read the above authorization, release, and agreement, prior to its execution, and that I am fully familiar with the contents thereof. This release shall be binding upon me and my heirs, legal representatives, and assigns.

Date: _____

_____
(Minor's Name)

_____
(Father) (Mother) (Guardian)

_____
(Minor's Address)

_____
(Address)

_____
(Witness)

Table of Cases

Index